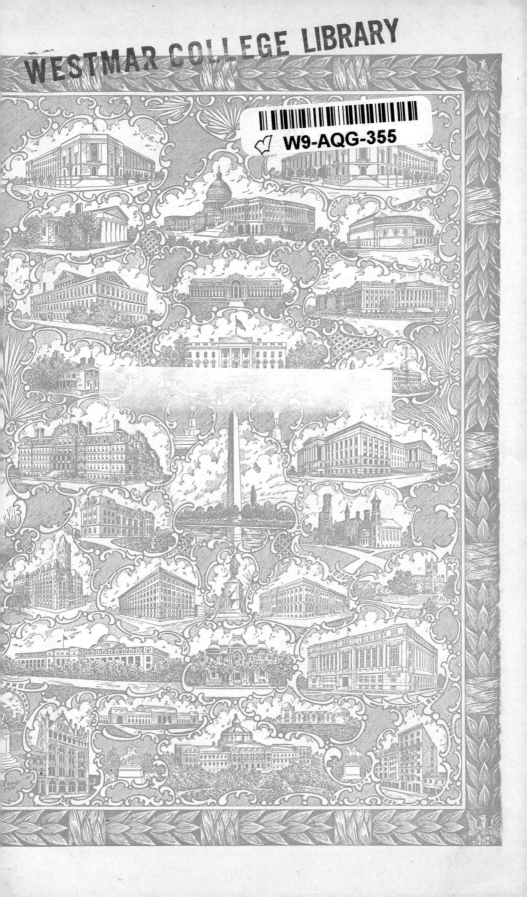

House of Representatives (Interior View)

HOUSE OF REPRESENTATIVES.—Situated in the left wing of the Capitol, as you approach from the east of it. Here Congress meets and at times it becomes quite a busy place.

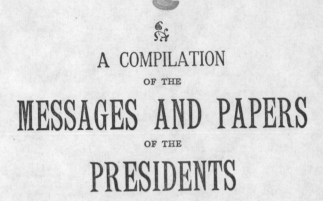

A COMPILATION

OF THE

MESSAGES AND PAPERS

OF THE

PRESIDENTS

Prepared Under the Direction of the Joint Committee
on Printing, of the House and Senate,
Pursuant to an Act of the Fifty-Second Congress
of the United States

(With Additions and Encyclopedic Index
by Private Enterprise)

VOLUME XIV

PUBLISHED BY

BUREAU OF NATIONAL LITERATURE, Inc.
NEW YORK

ILLUSTRATIONS IN VOLUME FOURTEEN

If in his judgment not incompatible with the public interest, to communicate to the Senate all communications which have been received by him or by any Department or officer, civil or military, from Aguinaldo or any other person undertaking to represent the people in arms against the United States in the Philippine Islands, or any alleged government or public authority of said people, and all replies to such communications;

Also, the proclamation sent by him to be issued to the people of the Philippine Islands, as actually directed by him to be issued, and the same as actually proclaimed by General Otis, if in any respect it was altered or any part of it was omitted;

Also, to inform the Senate whether any approval or disapproval was expressed by his authority, or that of the War Department, of such change, if any;

Also, all constitutions, forms of government, or proclamations issued by Aguinaldo, or any congress or legislative assembly or body claiming to be such, or convention of the people of the Philippine Islands, or any part thereof, or claiming to represent them or any part thereof, of which information may have come to him or to any Department of the Government;

Also, all instructions given by him to the commissioners of the Philippine Islands, or either of them;

Also, any information which may have come to him, or any Department of the Government, since January 1, 1898, in regard to any plans of the people in arms against the United States for the pillage of Manila, for risings in the city, or for the destruction of foreign property and the massacre of foreign residents;

Also, any information that may have come to him, or any Department of the Government, of the treatment of the other inhabitants of the Philippines by those in arms against the authority of the United States, and of the attitude and feeling of such other inhabitants or tribes toward the so-called government of Aguinaldo and his armed followers;

Also, any information that may have come to him, or any Department of the Government, of the treatment of prisoners, either Spanish or American, by the people in arms against the authority of the United States;

Also, any information that may have come to him, or any Department of the Government, as to any aid or encouragement received by Aguinaldo and his followers from persons in the United States; as to what pamphlets, speeches, or other documents emanating from the United States and adverse to its authority and to its policy were circulated in whole or in part among the Filipinos in arms against the United States, among the other inhabitants of the islands, or among the soldiers of the United States, and any information as to the effect, if any, of such pamphlets, speeches, and other documents, or of similar utterances in the United States upon the course of the rebellion against the United States;

Also, any further or other information which would tend to throw light upon the conduct and events of the insurrection against the authority of the United States in the Philippine Islands, and of the military movements for its suppression since January 1, 1898.

And that the President be further requested to communicate, without delay, so much of such information as is now in his possession or in that of any Department at Washington, without waiting to obtain so much of said information as may require considerable delay or communication with the Philippine Islands, and to communicate the remainder of the information as soon thereafter as it can be obtained,

I transmit herewith the following papers:

First. Copies of all communications which have been received by me, or by any Department or officer, civil or military, from Aguinaldo, or any other person undertaking to represent the people in arms against the United States in the Philippine Islands, or any alleged government or public authority of said people, and copies of all replies to such communications, so far as such communications and replies have been reported to me or to any Executive Department. Said copies of documents are appended hereto marked " I."

Second. Copy of instructions relating to a proclamation sent to General Otis and of the proclamation issued by General Otis pursuant thereto. Said copies of documents are appended hereto, marked " II." No disapproval of the said proclamation was expressed by my authority or that of the War Department. It was, in fact, approved by me, although no formal communication to that effect was sent to General Otis.

Also, among the papers marked " II," a letter of instructions to Maj.-Gen. Wesley Merritt, commanding the army in the Philippines, under date of May 28, 1898, and a proclamation issued by him to the people of the Philippines dated August 14, 1898.

Third. Copies of English translations of all constitutions, forms of government, or proclamations issued by Aguinaldo, or any congress or legislative assembly or body claiming to be such, or convention of the people of the Philippine Islands, or any part thereof, or claiming to represent them, or any part thereof, of which information has come to me or to any Department of the Government. Said copies of documents are appended hereto marked " III."

Fourth. Copies of all written instructions given by me to the commissioners to the Philippine Islands, or either of them. Said copies of documents are appended hereto marked " IV."

Fifth. Such information as has come to me, or any Department of the Government, since January 1, 1898, in regard to any plans of the people in arms against the United States for the pillage of Manila, for risings in the city, or for the destruction of foreign property and the massacre of foreign residents. Said copies of documents are appended hereto marked " V."

Sixth. The information which has come to me, or any Department of the Government, of the treatment of the other inhabitants of the Philippines by those in arms against the authority of the United States, and of the attitude and feeling of such other inhabitants or tribes toward the so-called government of Aguinaldo and his armed followers, is contained in the preliminary statement of the Philippine Commission, dated November 2, 1899, in the report of the Philippine Commission, dated January 31, 1900, and transmitted by me to Congress February 2, 1900, together with the preliminary statement, and the report of Maj.-Gen. E. S. Otis, United States Volunteers, commanding the Department of the Pacific and Eighth Army Corps, dated August 31, 1899, and transmitted to Congress with the report of the Secretary of War, dated November 29, 1899, with the accompanying documents.

Seventh. The information which has come to me, or any Department of the Government, of the treatment of prisoners, either Spanish or American, by the people in arms against the authority of the United States, is contained in the same documents.

Eighth. The information that has come to me, or any Department of the Government, as to any aid or encouragement received by Aguinaldo and his followers from persons in the United States, as to what pamphlets, speeches, or other documents emanating from the United States, and adverse to its authority and to its policy, were circulated, in whole or in part, among the Filipinos in arms against the United States, among the other inhabitants of the islands, or among the soldiers of the United States, and any information as to the effect, if any, of such pamphlets, speeches, and other documents, or of similar utterances in the United States upon the course of the rebellion against the United States is contained in the same documents, and the copies of documents appended hereto marked " VI." WILLIAM McKINLEY.

EXECUTIVE MANSION, *March 15, 1900.*
To the Senate of the United States:

In response to the resolution of the Senate of March 12, 1900, calling for the correspondence touching the request of the Government of the South African Republics for my intervention with a view to the cessation of hostilities, I transmit herewith a report of the Secretary of State furnishing the requested papers. WILLIAM McKINLEY.

EXECUTIVE MANSION, *March 21, 1900.*
To the Senate:

In response to the resolution of the Senate of January 23, 1900, requesting the President, " if in his opinion it is not incompatible with the public interest, to furnish the Senate with copies of the correspondence with the Republic of Colombia in relation to the Panama Canal and to the treaty between this Government and New Granada concluded December 12, 1846, not heretofore communicated," I transmit herewith a report from the Secretary of State, with accompanying papers.
WILLIAM McKINLEY.

EXECUTIVE MANSION,
Washington, March 27, 1900.
To the House of Representatives:

In response to the resolution of the House of Representatives of March 24, 1900, reading as follows:

WHEREAS the commercial community of the United States is deeply interested in ascertaining the conditions which are to govern trade in such parts of the Chinese

Empire as are claimed by various foreign powers to be within their "areas of interest"; and

WHEREAS bills are now pending before both Houses of Congress for the dispatch of a mission to China to study its economic condition: Therefore, be it

Resolved, That the President of the United States be requested to transmit to the House of Representatives, if not incompatible with the public service, such correspondence as may have passed between the Department of State and various foreign Governments concerning the maintenance of the "open door" policy in China,

I transmit herewith a report from the Secretary of State, with accompanying papers.　　　WILLIAM McKINLEY.

EXECUTIVE MANSION,
Washington, April 2, 1900.
To the Senate and House of Representatives:

I transmit herewith a copy of a letter from Mr. Ferdinand W. Peck, Commissioner-General of the United States to the Paris Exposition of 1900, dated November 17, 1899, submitting a detailed statement of the expenditures incurred under authority of law.

WILLIAM McKINLEY.

EXECUTIVE MANSION, *April 17, 1900.*
To the House of Representatives:

I transmit herewith a report from the Secretary of State in response to the resolution of the House of Representatives of March 23, 1900, calling for copies of any and all letters on file in the Department of State from citizens of the United States resident in the South African Republic from January 1, 1899, to the present time, making complaints of treatment by the South African Republic.

WILLIAM McKINLEY.

EXECUTIVE MANSION,
Washington, May 3, 1900.
To the House of Representatives:

I herewith return, without approval, House bill No. 4001, entitled "An act authorizing the rights of settlers on the Navajo Indian Reservation, Territory of Arizona." My objections to the bill are embodied in the following statement:

This tribe has a population of about 20,500 souls, of whom 1,000 dress in the manner of white men, 250 can read, and 500 use enough English for ordinary conversation. Last year they cultivated 8,000 acres, and possessed approximately 1,000,000 sheep, 250,000 goats, 100,500 cattle, 1,200 swine, and very considerable herds of horses and ponies.

Prior to January last the reservation, which is in the extreme north-eastern portion of the Territory of Arizona, consisted of lands set apart for the use of these Indians under the treaty of June 1, 1863 (15 Stat., 667), and subsequent executive orders. On account of the conditions naturally prevailing in that section, the reservation, as then constituted, was altogether inadequate for the purpose for which it was set apart. There was not a sufficient supply of grass or water within its borders for the flocks and herds of the tribe, and in consequence more than one-third of the Indians were habitually off the reservation with their flocks and herds, and were in frequent contention and strife with whites over pasturage and water.

After most careful inquiry and inspection of the reservation as it then existed, and of adjacent land by efficient officers in the Indian service, the Commission of Indian Affairs, with the concurrence of the Secretary of the Interior, recommended that the limits of the reservation be ex-tended westward so as to embrace the lands lying between the Navajo and Moqui Indian reservations on the east and the Colorado and Little Colorado Rivers and the Grand Canyon Forest Reserve on the west. This recommendation was supported by a very numerously signed petition from the white residents of that section, and also by a letter from the Governor of the Territory of Arizona, in which it was said:

I understand that a petition has been forwarded asking that the western limit be fixed at the Little Colorado River, as being better for all concerned and less liable to cause friction between the Indians and the whites. I earnestly hope that the prayer of the petitioners be granted, for the reason that the Little Colorado could be made a natural dividing line, distinct and well defined, and would extend the graz-ing territory of the Navajoes to a very considerable extent without seriously en-croaching upon the interests of white settlers who have their property in that neighborhood.

I think great care should be exercised in questions of this nature because of possible serious friction which may occur if the interests of all concerned are not carefully protected.

The investigation which preceded this recommendation, and upon which it was in part based, showed that with the boundaries of the res-ervation thus extended the Indians would be able to obtain within the limits of the reservation sufficient grass and water for their flocks and herds, and the Government would therefore be justified in confining them to the reservation, thus avoiding the prior contention and friction between them and the whites.

It appearing that but little aid had been extended to these Indians by the Government for many years, that they had taken on habits of in-dustry and husbandry, which entitled them to encouragement, and that it was neither just nor possible to confine them to the limits of a reser-vation which would not sustain their flocks and herds, an order was issued by me January 8 last, extending the reservation boundaries as recommended. The Indians have accepted this as an evidence of the good faith of the Government toward them, and it is now the belief of those charged with the administration of Indian affairs that further contention and friction between the Indians and whites will be avoided, if this arrangement is not disturbed.

The present bill proposes to open to miners and prospectors, and to the operation of the mining laws, a substantial portion of this reservation, including a part of the lands covered by the recent order. There has been no effort to obtain from the Indians a concession of this character, nor has any reason been presented why, if these lands are to be taken from them — for that will practically result from this bill, if it becomes a law, even though not so intended — it should not be done in pursuance of negotiations had with the Indians as in other instances.

The Indians could not understand how lands given to them in January as necessary for their use should be taken away without previous notice in May of the same year. While the Indians are the wards of the Government, and must submit to that which is deemed for their best interests by the sovereign guardian, they should, nevertheless, be dealt with in a manner calculated to give them confidence in the Government and to assist them in passing through the inevitable transition to a state of civilization and full citizenship. Believing that due consideration has not been given to the status and interests of the Indians, I withhold my approval from the bill.　　　　　　WILLIAM McKINLEY.

EXECUTIVE MANSION,
Washington, May 12, 1900.

To the Senate of the United States:

In reply to the resolution of the Senate, dated March 2, 1900, I send herewith copy of an order to the provost marshal general of Manila, dated March 8, 1900, and the various endorsements and reports thereon, whereby it appears that the traffic in wine, beer, and liquor in the city of Manila is now controlled under a rigidly enforced high-license system; that the number of places where the liquor is sold has greatly decreased; that all such places are required to be closed at 8:30 in the evening on week days and to be kept closed on Sundays, and that the orderly condition of the city compares favorably with cities of similar size in the United States.　　　　　　WILLIAM McKINLEY.

EXECUTIVE MANSION, *May 12, 1900.*

To the Senate of the United States:

In response to a resolution of the Senate of April 11, 1900, reading as follows:

Resolved, That the President be, and is hereby, requested, if not incompatible with public interest, to inform the Senate whether persons have been executed in Puerto

Rico by the Spanish method of garrote since he has been governing that country as Commander-in-Chief of the Army and Navy of the United States; and if so, the President is requested to inform the Senate why this mode of execution was adopted,

I transmit herewith copies of reports from Brig.-Gen. George W. Davis, United States Volunteers, military governor of Puerto Rico, which contain the information called for. WILLIAM McKINLEY.

EXECUTIVE MANSION,
Washington, May 19, 1900.

To the Senate:

In response to the following resolution of the Senate of April 28, 1900:

Resolved, That the President be, and he is hereby requested, if not incompatible with the public interest, to inform the Senate whether General Torres, one of the officers of the Philippine army, came to General Otis with a flag of truce on February 5, 1899, the day after the fighting commenced between our forces and those of the Filipinos, and stated to General Otis that General Aguinaldo declared that fighting had been begun accidentally, and was not authorized by him, and that Aguinaldo wished to have it stopped, and that to bring about a conclusion of hostilities he proposed the establishment of a neutral zone between the two armies of a width that would be agreeable to General Otis, so that during the peace negotiations there might be no further danger of conflict between the two armies, and whether General Otis replied that fighting having once begun, must go on to the grim end. Was General Otis directed by the Secretary of War to make such an answer? Did General Otis telegraph the Secretary of War on February 9, 1899, as follows: "Aguinaldo now applies for a cessation of hostilities and conference. Have declined to answer?" And did General Otis afterwards reply? Was he directed by the Secretary of War to reply, and what answer, if any, did he or the Secretary of War make to the application to cease fighting?

The President is also requested to inform the Senate whether the flag of the Philippine Republic was ever saluted by Admiral Dewey or any of the vessels of his fleet at any time since May 1, 1898. Did Admiral Dewey, at the request of Aguinaldo, or any officer under him, send the vessels *Concord* and *Raleigh* to Subig Bay to assist Aguinaldo's forces in the capture of the Spanish garrison at that place? Did said vessels assist in the capture of the Spanish garrison, and after the capture did they turn the prisoners thus taken over to the Philippine forces?"

I herewith transmit a copy of a cable dispatch to General Otis, dated April 30, 1900, and of his reply, dated May 1, 1900.

General Otis was not directed by the Secretary of War to make such an answer as is set forth in the resolution, nor were any answers to communications upon the subject of the cessation of hostilities prescribed by the Secretary of War to General Otis, but he was left to exercise in respect thereof his own judgment, based upon his superior knowledge of the conditions surrounding the troops under his command.

I also transmit a copy of a cable dispatch from General Otis, sent from Manila February 8, 1899, received in Washington February 9,

1899, being the same dispatch to which he refers in his reply of May 1, 1900 as misleading. So far as I am informed, General Otis did not afterwards reply, except as set forth in his dispatch of May 1, 1900. He was not directed by the Secretary of War to reply, and no answer was made by him or the Secretary of War to an application to cease fighting. There appears to have been no such application.

I further transmit a copy of a letter from the Secretary of the Navy to Admiral George Dewey, dated May 14, 1900, and a copy of the Admiral's reply, dated May 17, 1900.   WILLIAM McKINLEY.

EXECUTIVE MANSION, *May 22, 1900.*
To the Senate and House of Representatives:
I transmit herewith a report from the Secretary of State, with accompanying papers, relative to the status of Chinese persons in the Philippine Islands.   WILLIAM McKINLEY.

EXECUTIVE MANSION, *May 22, 1900.*
To the Senate and House of Representatives:
I transmit herewith, for the information of Congress, a communication from the Secretary of Agriculture, forwarding a report on the progress of the beet-sugar industry in the United States during the year 1899. It embraces the observations made by a special agent on the various phases of the beet-sugar industry of the Hawaiian Islands; also the results of analyses of sugar-beets received by the Department of Agriculture from the different States and Territories, together with much other information relating to the sugar industry.

Your attention is invited to the recommendation of the Secretary of Agriculture that 20,000 copies of the report be printed for the use of the Department, in addition to such number as may be desired for the use of the Senate and House of Representatives.

WILLIAM McKINLEY.

EXECUTIVE MANSION,
Washington, May 26, 1900.
To the Senate:
I transmit herewith, in answer to the resolution of the Senate of May 22, 1900, a report from the Secretary of State showing that the consul of the United States at Pretoria was directed on May 8, 1900, to forward copies of the constitutions of the South African Republic and the Orange Free State by return mail. Translations thereof will be communicated to the Senate at the earliest practicable date.

WILLIAM McKINLEY.

EXECUTIVE MANSION,
Washington, June 2, 1900.

To the Senate of the United States:

I transmit herewith, in further reply to the resolution of the Senate of April 10, 1900, having reference to Senate Document No. 336, Fifty-sixth Congress, first session, a further report from the Secretary of State, showing the places of residence of experts, clerks, officers, and employees of the Commission of the United States to the Paris Exposition of 1900, as well as the items of expenditures of the Commission for the months of January, February, and March, 1900, amounting to $211,583.25. WILLIAM McKINLEY.

EXECUTIVE MANSION,
Washington, June 6, 1900.

To the Senate of the United States:

In further response to the resolution of the Senate of January 17, 1900, requesting, among other things, information tending to throw light upon the conduct and events of the insurrection against the authority of the United States in the Philippine Islands, I transmit herewith a correspondence between the Secretary of War and the officers of the Second Division of the Eighth Army Corps.

WILLIAM McKINLEY.

EXECUTIVE MANSION, *December 3, 1900.*

To the Senate and House of Representatives:

At the outgoing of the old and the incoming of the new century you begin the last session of the Fifty-sixth Congress with evidences on every hand of individual and national prosperity and with proof of the growing strength and increasing power for good of Republican institutions. Your countrymen will join with you in felicitation that American liberty is more firmly established than ever before, and that love for it and the determination to preserve it are more universal than at any former period of our history.

The Republic was never so strong, because never so strongly intrenched in the hearts of the people as now. The Constitution, with few amendments, exists as it left the hands of its authors. The additions which have been made to it proclaim larger freedom and more extended citizenship. Popular government has demonstrated in its one hundred and twenty-four years of trial here its stability and security, and its efficiency as the best instrument of national development and the best safeguard to human rights.

When the Sixth Congress assembled in November, 1800, the population of the United States was 5,308,483. It is now 76,304,799.

Then we had sixteen States. Now we have forty-five. Then our territory consisted of 909,050 square miles. It is now 3,846,595 square miles. Education, religion, and morality have kept pace with our advancement in other directions, and while extending its power the Government has adhered to its foundation principles and abated none of them in dealing with our new peoples and possessions. A nation so preserved and blessed gives reverent thanks to God and invokes His guidance and the continuance of His care and favor.

In our foreign intercourse the dominant question has been the treatment of the Chinese problem. Apart from this our relations with the powers have been happy.

The recent troubles in China spring from the antiforeign agitation which for the past three years has gained strength in the northern provinces. Their origin lies deep in the character of the Chinese races and in the traditions of their Government. The Taiping rebellion and the opening of Chinese ports to foreign trade and settlement disturbed alike the homogeneity and the seclusion of China.

Meanwhile foreign activity made itself felt in all quarters, not alone on the coast, but along the great river arteries and in the remoter districts, carrying new ideas and introducing new associations among a primitive people which had pursued for centuries a national policy of isolation.

The telegraph and the railway spreading over their land, the steamers plying on their waterways, the merchant and the missionary penetrating year by year farther to the interior, became to the Chinese mind types of an alien invasion, changing the course of their national life and fraught with vague forebodings of disaster to their beliefs and their self-control.

For several years before the present troubles all the resources of foreign diplomacy, backed by moral demonstrations of the physical force of fleets and arms, have been needed to secure due respect for the treaty rights of foreigners and to obtain satisfaction from the responsible authorities for the sporadic outrages upon the persons and property of unoffending sojourners, which from time to time occurred at widely separated points in the northern provinces, as in the case of the outbreaks in Sze-chuen and Shan-tung.

Posting of antiforeign placards became a daily occurrence, which the repeated reprobation of the Imperial power failed to check or punish. These inflammatory appeals to the ignorance and superstition of the masses, mendacious and absurd in their accusations and deeply hostile in their spirit, could not but work cumulative harm. They aimed at no particular class of foreigners; they were impartial in attacking everything foreign.

An outbreak in Shan-tung, in which German missionaries were slain, was the too natural result of these malevolent teachings. The posting of seditious placards, exhorting to the utter destruction of foreigners and of every foreign thing, continued unrebuked. Hostile demonstrations toward the stranger gained strength by organization.

The sect, commonly styled the Boxers, developed greatly in the provinces north of the Yang-Tse, and with the collusion of many notable officials, including some in the immediate councils of the Throne itself, became alarmingly aggressive. No foreigner's life, outside of the protected treaty ports, was safe. No foreign interest was secure from spoliation.

The diplomatic representatives of the powers in Peking strove in vain to check this movement. Protest was followed by demand and demand by renewed protest, to be met with perfunctory edicts from the Palace and evasive and futile assurances from the Tsung-li Yamen. The circle of the Boxer influence narrowed about Peking, and while nominally stigmatized as seditious, it was felt that its spirit pervaded the capital itself, that the Imperial forces were imbued with its doctrines, and that the immediate counselors of the Empress Dowager were in full sympathy with the antiforeign movement.

The increasing gravity of the conditions in China and the imminence of peril to our own diversified interests in the Empire, as well as to those of all the other treaty governments, were soon appreciated by this Government, causing it profound solicitude. The United States from the earliest days of foreign intercourse with China had followed a policy of peace, omitting no occasions to testify good will, to further the extension of lawful trade, to respect the sovereignty of its Government, and to insure by all legitimate and kindly but earnest means the fullest measure of protection for the lives and property of our law-abiding citizens and for the exercise of their beneficent callings among the Chinese people.

Mindful of this, it was felt to be appropriate that our purposes should be pronounced in favor of such course as would hasten united action of the powers at Peking to promote the administrative reforms so greatly needed for strengthening the Imperial Government and maintaining the integrity of China, in which we believed the whole western world to be alike concerned. To these ends I caused to be addressed to the several powers occupying territory and maintaining spheres of influence in China the circular proposals of 1899, inviting from them declarations of their intentions and views as to the desirability of the adoption of measures insuring the benefits of equality of treatment of all foreign trade throughout China.

With gratifying unanimity the responses coincided in this common policy, enabling me to see in the successful termination of these negotiations proof of the friendly spirit which animates the various powers interested in the untrammeled development of commerce and industry in the Chinese Empire as a source of vast benefit to the whole commercial world.

In this conclusion, which I had the gratification to announce as a completed engagement to the interested powers on March 20, 1900, I hopefully discerned a potential factor for the abatement of the distrust of foreign purposes which for a year past had appeared to inspire the policy of the Imperial Government, and for the effective exertion by it of power and authority to quell the critical antiforeign movement in the northern provinces most immediately influenced by the Manchu sentiment.

Seeking to testify confidence in the willingness and ability of the Imperial administration to redress the wrongs and prevent the evils we suffered and feared, the marine guard, which had been sent to Peking in the autumn of 1899 for the protection of the legation, was withdrawn at the earliest practicable moment, and all pending questions were remitted, as far as we were concerned, to the ordinary resorts of diplomatic intercourse.

The Chinese Government proved, however, unable to check the rising strength of the Boxers and appeared to be a prey to internal dissensions. In the unequal contest the antiforeign influences soon gained the ascendancy under the leadership of Prince Tuan. Organized armies of Boxers, with which the Imperial forces affiliated, held the country between Peking and the coast, penetrated into Manchuria up to the Russian borders, and through their emissaries threatened a like rising throughout northern China.

Attacks upon foreigners, destruction of their property, and slaughter of native converts were reported from all sides. The Tsung-li Yamen, already permeated with hostile sympathies, could make no effective response to the appeals of the legations. At this critical juncture, in the early spring of this year, a proposal was made by the other powers that a combined fleet should be assembled in Chinese waters as a moral demonstration, under cover of which to exact of the Chinese Government respect for foreign treaty rights and the suppression of the Boxers.

The United States, while not participating in the joint demonstration, promptly sent from the Philippines all ships that could be spared for service on the Chinese coast. A small force of marines was landed at Taku and sent to Peking for the protection of the American legation. Other powers took similar action, until some four hundred men were assembled in the capital as legation guards.

Still the peril increased. The legations reported the development of the seditious movement in Peking and the need of increased provision for defense against it. While preparations were in progress for a larger expedition, to strengthen the legation guards and keep the railway open, an attempt of the foreign ships to make a landing at Taku was met by a fire from the Chinese forts. The forts were thereupon shelled by the foreign vessels, the American admiral taking no part in the attack, on the ground that we were not at war with China and that a hostile demonstration might consolidate the anti-foreign elements and strengthen the Boxers to oppose the relieving column.

Two days later the Taku forts were captured after a sanguinary conflict. Severance of communication with Peking followed, and a combined force of additional guards, which was advancing to Peking by the Pei-Ho, was checked at Langfang. The isolation of the legations was complete.

The siege and the relief of the legations has passed into undying history. In all the stirring chapter which records the heroism of the devoted band, clinging to hope in the face of despair, and the undaunted spirit that led their relievers through battle and suffering to the goal, it is a memory of which my countrymen may be justly proud that the honor of our flag was maintained alike in the siege and the rescue, and that stout American hearts have again set high, in fervent emulation with true men of other race and language, the indomitable courage that ever strives for the cause of right and justice.

By June 19 the legations were cut off. An identical note from the Yamen ordered each minister to leave Peking, under a promised escort, within twenty-four hours. To gain time they replied, asking prolongation of the time, which was afterwards granted, and requesting an interview with the Tsung-li Yamen on the following day. No reply being received, on the morning of the 20th the German minister, Baron von Ketteler, set out for the Yamen to obtain a response, and on the way was murdered.

An attempt by the legation guard to recover his body was foiled by the Chinese. Armed forces turned out against the legations. Their quarters were surrounded and attacked. The mission compounds were abandoned, their inmates taking refuge in the British legation, where all the other legations and guards gathered for more effective defense. Four hundred persons were crowded in its narrow compass. Two thousand native converts were assembled in a near-by palace under protection of the foreigners. Lines of defense were strengthened, trenches dug, barricades raised, and preparations made to stand a siege, which at once began.

From June 20 until July 17, writes Minister Conger, "there was scarcely an hour during which there was not firing upon some part of our lines and into some of the legations, varying from a single shot to a general and continuous attack along the whole line."

Artillery was placed around the legations and on the over-looking palace walls, and thousands of 3-inch shot and shell were fired, destroying some buildings and damaging all. So thickly did the balls rain, that, when the ammunition of the besieged ran low, five quarts of Chinese bullets were gathered in an hour in one compound and recast.

Attempts were made to burn the legations by setting neighboring houses on fire, but the flames were successfully fought off, although the Austrian, Belgian, Italian, and Dutch legations were then and subsequently burned. With the aid of the native converts, directed by the missionaries, to whose helpful co-operation Mr. Conger awards unstinted praise, the British legation was made a veritable fortress. The British minister, Sir Claude MacDonald, was chosen general commander of the defense, with the secretary of the American legation, Mr. E. G. Squiers, as chief of staff.

To save life and ammunition the besieged sparingly returned the incessant fire of the Chinese soldiery, fighting only to repel attack or make an occasional successful sortie for strategic advantage, such as that of fifty-five American, British, and Russian marines led by Captain Myers, of the United States Marine Corps, which resulted in the capture of a formidable barricade on the wall that gravely menaced the American position. It was held to the last, and proved an invaluable acquisition, because commanding the water gate through which the relief column entered.

During the siege the defenders lost 65 killed, 135 wounded, and 7 by disease—the last all children.

On July 14 the besieged had their first communication with the Tsung-li Yamen, from whom a message came inviting to a conference, which was declined. Correspondence, however, ensued and a sort of armistice was agreed upon, which stopped the bombardment and lessened the rifle fire for a time. Even then no protection whatever was afforded, nor any aid given, save to send to the legations a small supply of fruit and three sacks of flour.

Indeed, the only communication had with the Chinese Government related to the occasional delivery or dispatch of a telegram or to the demands of the Tsung-li Yamen for the withdrawal of the legations to the coast under escort. Not only are the protestations of the Chinese Government that it protected and succored the legations positively contradicted, but irresistible proof accumulates that the attacks upon them were made by Imperial troops, regularly uniformed, armed, and officered, belonging to the command of Jung Lu, the Imperial commander in chief. Decrees encouraging the Boxers, organizing them under prominent Imperial officers, provisioning them, and even granting them large sums in the name of the Empress Dowager, are known to exist. Members of the Tsung-li

Yamen who counseled protection of the foreigners were beheaded Even in the distant provinces men suspected of foreign sympathy were put to death, prominent among these being Chang Yen-hoon, formerly Chinese minister in Washington.

With the negotiation of the partial armistice of July 14, a proceeding which was doubtless promoted by the representations of the Chinese envoy in Washington, the way was opened for the conveyance to Mr. Conger of a test message sent by the Secretary of State through the kind offices of Minister Wu Ting-fang. Mr. Conger's reply, dispatched from Peking on July 18 through the same channel, afforded to the outside world the first tidings that the inmates of the legations were still alive and hoping for succor.

This news stimulated the preparations for a joint relief expedition in numbers sufficient to overcome the resistance which for a month had been organizing between Taku and the capital. Reinforcements sent by all the co-operating Governments were constantly arriving. The United States contingent, hastily assembled from the Philippines or dispatched from this country, amounted to some 5,000 men, under the able command first of the lamented Colonel Liscum and afterwards of General Chaffee.

Toward the end of July the movement began. A severe conflict followed at Tientsin, in which Colonel Liscum was killed. The city was stormed and partly destroyed. Its capture afforded the base of operations from which to make the final advance, which began in the first days of August, the expedition being made up of Japanese, Russian, British, and American troops at the outset.

Another battle was fought and won at Yangtsun. Thereafter the disheartened Chinese troops offered little show of resistance. A few days later the important position of Ho-si-woo was taken. A rapid march brought the united forces to the populous city of Tung Chow, which capitulated without a contest.

On August 14 the capital was reached. After a brief conflict beneath the walls the relief column entered and the legations were saved. The United States soldiers, sailors, and marines, officers and men alike, in those distant climes and unusual surroundings, showed the same valor, discipline, and good conduct and gave proof of the same high degree of intelligence and efficiency which have distinguished them in every emergency.

The Imperial family and the Government had fled a few days before. The city was without visible control. The remaining Imperial soldiery had made on the night of the 13th a last attempt to exterminate the besieged, which was gallantly repelled. It fell to the occupying forces to restore order and organize a provisional administration.

Happily the acute disturbances were confined to the northern provinces. It is a relief to recall and a pleasure to record the loyal conduct of the viceroys and local authorities of the southern and eastern provinces. Their efforts were continuously directed to the pacific control of the vast populations under their rule and to the scrupulous observance of foreign treaty rights. At critical moments they did not hesitate to memorialize the Throne, urging the protection of the legations, the restoration of communication, and the assertion of the Imperial authority against the subversive elements. They maintained excellent relations with the official representatives of foreign powers. To their kindly disposition is largely due the success of the consuls in removing many of the missionaries from the interior to places of safety. In this relation the action of the consuls should be highly commended. In Shan-tung and eastern Chi-li the task was difficult, but, thanks to their energy and the co-operation of American and foreign naval commanders, hundreds of foreigners, including those of other nationalities than ours, were rescued from imminent peril.

The policy of the United States through all this trying period was clearly announced and scrupulously carried out. A circular note to the powers dated July 3 proclaimed our attitude. Treating the condition in the north as one of virtual anarchy, in which the great provinces of the south and southeast had no share, we regarded the local authorities in the latter quarters as representing the Chinese people with whom we sought to remain in peace and friendship. Our declared aims involved no war against the Chinese nation. We adhered to the legitimate office of rescuing the imperiled legation, obtaining redress for wrongs already suffered, securing wherever possible the safety of American life and property in China, and preventing a spread of the disorders or their recurrence.

As was then said, "The policy of the Government of the United States is to seek a solution which may bring about permanent safety and peace to China, preserve Chinese territorial and administrative entity, protect all rights guaranteed to friendly powers by treaty and international law, and safeguard for the world the principle of equal and impartial trade with all parts of the Chinese Empire."

Faithful to those professions which, as it proved, reflected the views and purposes of the other co-operating Governments, all our efforts have been directed toward ending the anomalous situation in China by negotiations for a settlement at the earliest possible moment. As soon as the sacred duty of relieving our legation and its dependents was accomplished we withdrew from active hostilities, leaving our legation under an adequate guard in Peking as a channel of negotiation and settlement — a course adopted by others of the interested powers. Overtures of the empowered representatives of the Chinese Emperor have been considerately entertained.

The Russian proposition looking to the restoration of the Imperial power in Peking has been accepted as in full consonance with our own desires, for we have held and hold that effective reparation for wrongs suffered and an enduring settlement that will make their recurrence impossible can best be brought about under an authority which the Chinese nation reverences and obeys. While so doing we forego no jot of our undoubted right to exact exemplary and deterrent punishment of the responsible authors and abettors of the criminal acts whereby we and other nations have suffered grievous injury.

For the real culprits, the evil counselors who have misled the Imperial judgment and diverted the sovereign authority to their own guilty ends, full expiation becomes imperative within the rational limits of retributive justice. Regarding this as the initial condition of an acceptable settlement between China and the powers, I said in my message of October 18 to the Chinese Emperor:

I trust that negotiations may begin so soon as we and the other offended Governments shall be effectively satisfied of Your Majesty's ability and power to treat with just sternness the principal offenders, who are doubly culpable, not alone toward the foreigners, but toward Your Majesty, under whose rule the purpose of China to dwell in concord with the world had hitherto found expression in the welcome and protection assured to strangers.

Taking, as a point of departure, the Imperial edict appointing Earl Li Hung Chang and Prince Ching plenipotentiaries to arrange a settlement, and the edict of September 25, whereby certain high officials were designated for punishment, this Government has moved, in concert with the other powers, toward the opening of negotiations, which Mr. Conger, assisted by Mr. Rockhill, has been authorized to conduct on behalf of the United States.

General bases of negotiation formulated by the Government of the French Republic have been accepted with certain reservations as to details, made necessary by our own circumstances, but, like similar reservations by other powers, open to discussion in the progress of the negotiations. The disposition of the Emperor's Government to admit liability for wrongs done to foreign Governments and their nationals, and to act upon such additional designation of the guilty persons as the foreign ministers at Peking may be in a position to make, gives hope of a complete settlement of all questions involved, assuring foreign rights of residence and intercourse on terms of equality for all the world.

I regard as one of the essential factors of a durable adjustment the securement of adequate guarantees for liberty of faith, since insecurity of those natives who may embrace alien creeds is a scarcely less effectual assault upon the rights of foreign worship and teaching than would be the direct invasion thereof.

The matter of indemnity for our wronged citizens is a question of grave concern. Measured in money alone, a sufficient reparation may prove to be beyond the ability of China to meet. All the powers concur in emphatic disclaimers of any purpose of aggrandizement through the dismemberment of the Empire. I am disposed to think that due compensation may be made in part by increased guarantees of security for foreign rights and immunities, and, most important of all, by the opening of China to the equal commerce of all the world. These views have been and will be earnestly advocated by our representatives.

The Government of Russia has put forward a suggestion, that in the event of protracted divergence of views in regard to indemnities the matter may be relegated to the Court of Arbitration at The Hague. I favorably incline to this, believing that high tribunal could not fail to reach a solution no less conducive to the stability and enlarged prosperity of China itself than immediately beneficial to the powers.

Ratifications of a treaty of extradition with the Argentine Republic were exchanged on June 2 last.

While the Austro-Hungarian Government has in the many cases that have been reported of the arrest of our naturalized citizens for alleged evasion of military service faithfully observed the provisions of the treaty and released such persons from military obligations, it has in some instances expelled those whose presence in the community of their origin was asserted to have a pernicious influence. Representations have been made against this course whenever its adoption has appeared unduly onerous.

We have been urgently solicited by Belgium to ratify the International Convention of June, 1899, amendatory of the previous Convention of 1890 in respect to the regulation of the liquor trade in Africa. Compliance was necessarily withheld, in the absence of the advice and consent of the Senate thereto. The principle involved has the cordial sympathy of this Government, which in the revisionary negotiations advocated more drastic measures, and I would gladly see its extension, by international agreement, to the restriction of the liquor traffic with all uncivilized peoples, especially in the Western Pacific.

A conference will be held at Brussels December 11, 1900, under the Convention for the protection of industrial property, concluded at Paris March 20, 1883, to which delegates from this country have been appointed. Any lessening of the difficulties that our inventors encounter in obtaining patents abroad for their inventions and that our farmers, manufacturers, and merchants may have in the protection of their trade-marks is worthy of careful consideration, and your attention will be called to the results of the conference at the proper time.

In the interest of expanding trade between this country and South America, efforts have been made during the past year to conclude conventions with the southern republics for the enlargement of postal facilities. Two such agreements, signed with Bolivia on April 24, of which that establishing the money-order system is undergoing certain changes suggested by the Post-Office Department, have not yet been ratified by this Government. A treaty of extradition with that country, signed on the same day, is before the Senate.

A boundary dispute between Brazil and Bolivia over the territory of Acre is in a fair way of friendly adjustment, a protocol signed in December, 1899, having agreed on a definite frontier and provided for its demarcation by a joint commission.

Conditions in Brazil have weighed heavily on our export trade to that country in marked contrast to the favorable conditions upon which Brazilian products are admitted into our markets. Urgent representations have been made to that Government on the subject and some amelioration has been effected. We rely upon the reciprocal justice and good will of that Government to assure to us a further improvement in our commercial relations.

The Convention signed May 24, 1897, for the final settlement of claims left in abeyance upon the dissolution of the Commission of 1893, was at length ratified by the Chilean Congress and the supplemental Commission has been organized.

It remains for the Congress to appropriate for the necessary expenses of the Commission.

The insurrectionary movement which disturbed Colombia in the latter part of 1899 has been practically suppressed, although guerrillas still operate in some departments. The executive power of that Republic changed hands in August last by the act of Vice-President Marroquin in assuming the reins of government during the absence of President San Clemente from the capital. The change met with no serious opposition, and, following the precedents in such cases, the United States minister entered into relations with the new *de facto* Government on September 17.

It is gratifying to announce that the residual questions between Costa Rica and Nicaragua growing out of the Award of President

Cleveland in 1888 have been adjusted through the choice of an American engineer, General E. P. Alexander, as umpire to run the disputed line. His task has been accomplished to the satifaction of both contestants.

A revolution in the Dominican Republic toward the close of last year resulted in the installation of President Jimenez, whose Government was formally recognized in January. Since then final payment has been made of the American claim in regard to the Ozama bridge.

The year of the exposition has been fruitful in occasions for displaying the good will that exists between this country and France. This great competition brought together from every nation the best in natural productions, industry, science, and the arts, submitted in generous rivalry to a judgment made all the more searching because of that rivalry. The extraordinary increase of exportations from this country during the past three years and the activity with which our inventions and wares had invaded new markets caused much interest to center upon the American exhibit, and every encouragement was offered in the way of space and facilities to permit of its being comprehensive as a whole and complete in every part.

It was, however, not an easy task to assemble exhibits that could fitly illustrate our diversified resources and manufactures. Singularly enough, our national prosperity lessened the incentive to exhibit. The dealer in raw materials knew that the user must come to him; the great factories were contented with the phenomenal demand for their output, not alone at home, but also abroad, where merit had already won a profitable trade.

Appeals had to be made to the patriotism of exhibitors to induce them to incur outlays promising no immediate return. This was especially the case where it became needful to complete an industrial sequence or illustrate a class of processes. One manufacturer after another had to be visited and importuned, and at times, after a promise to exhibit in a particular section had been obtained, it would be withdrawn, owing to pressure of trade orders, and a new quest would have to be made.

The installation of exhibits, too, encountered many obstacles and involved unexpected cost. The exposition was far from ready at the date fixed for its opening. The French transportation lines were congested with offered freight. Belated goods had to be hastily installed in unfinished quarters with whatever labor could be obtained in the prevailing confusion. Nor was the task of the Commission lightened by the fact that, owing to the scheme of classification adopted, it was impossible to have the entire exhibit of any one country in the same building or more than one group of exhibits in the same part of any building. Our installations were scattered on both sides of the Seine and in widely remote suburbs of Paris, so that additional assistants were needed for the work of supervision and arrangement.

Despite all these drawbacks the contribution of the United States was not only the largest foreign display, but was among the earliest in place and the most orderly in arrangement. Our exhibits were shown in one hundred and one out of one hundred and twenty-one classes, and more completely covered the entire classification than those of any other nation. In total number they ranked next after those of France, and the attractive form in which they were presented secured general attention.

A criterion of the extent and success of our participation and of the thoroughness with which our exhibits were organized is seen in the awards granted to American exhibitors by the international jury, namely, grand prizes, 240; gold medals, 597; silver medals, 776; bronze medals, 541, and honorable mentions, 322 — 2,476 in all, being the greatest total number given to the exhibit of any exhibiting nation, as well as the largest number in each grade. This significant recognition of merit in competition with the chosen exhibits of all other nations and at the hands of juries almost wholly made up of representatives of France and other competing countries is not only most gratifying, but is especially valuable, since it sets us to the front in international questions of supply and demand, while the large proportion of awards in the classes of art and artistic manufactures afforded unexpected proof of the stimulation of national culture by the prosperity that flows from natural productiveness joined to industrial excellence.

Apart from the exposition several occasions for showing international good will occurred. The inauguration in Paris of the Lafayette Monument, presented by the school children of the United States, and the designing of a commemorative coin by our Mint and the presentation of the first piece struck to the President of the Republic, were marked by appropriate ceremonies, and the Fourth of July was especially observed in the French capital.

Good will prevails in our relations with the German Empire. An amicable adjustment of the long-pending question of the admission of our life-insurance companies to do business in Prussia has been reached. One of the principal companies has already been readmitted and the way is opened for the others to share the privilege.

The settlement of the Samoan problem, to which I adverted in my last message, has accomplished good results. Peace and contentment prevail in the islands, especially in Tutuila, where a convenient administration that has won the confidence and esteem of the kindly disposed natives has been organized under the direction of the commander of the United States naval station at Pago-Pago.

An Imperial meat-inspection law has been enacted for Germany. While it may simplify the inspections, it prohibits certain products heretofore admitted. There is still great uncertainty as to whether our well-nigh extinguished German trade in meat products can revive under its new burdens. Much will depend upon regulations not yet promulgated, which we confidently hope will be free from the discriminations which attended the enforcement of the old statutes.

The remaining link in the new lines of direct telegraphic communication between the United States and the German Empire has recently been completed, affording a gratifying occasion for exchange of friendly congratulations with the German Emperor.

Our friendly relations with Great Britain continue. The war in Southern Africa introduced important questions. A condition unusual in international wars was presented in that while one belligerent had control of the seas, the other had no ports, shipping, or direct trade, but was only accessible through the territory of a neutral. Vexatious questions arose through Great Britain's action in respect to neutral cargoes, not contraband in their own nature, shipped to Portuguese South Africa, on the score of probable or suspected ultimate destination to the Boer States.

Such consignments in British ships, by which alone direct trade is kept up between our ports and Southern Africa, were seized in application of a municipal law prohibiting British vessels from trading with the enemy without regard to any contraband character of the goods, while cargoes shipped to Delagoa Bay in neutral bottoms were arrested on the ground of alleged destination to enemy's country. Appropriate representations on our part resulted in the British Government agreeing to purchase outright all such goods shown to be the actual property of American citizens, thus closing the incident to the satisfaction of the immediately interested parties, although, unfortunately, without a broad settlement of the question of a neutral's right to send goods not contraband *per se* to a neutral port adjacent to a belligerent area.

The work of marking certain provisional boundary points, for convenience of administration, around the head of Lynn Canal, in accordance with the temporary arrangement of October, 1899, was completed by a joint survey in July last. The *modus vivendi* has so far worked without friction, and the Dominion Government has provided rules and regulations for securing to our citizens the benefit of the reciprocal stipulation that the citizens or subjects of either power found by that arrangement within the temporary jurisdiction of the other shall suffer no diminution of the rights and privileges they have hitherto enjoyed. But however necessary such an expedient may have been to tide over the grave emergencies of the situation. it is at best but an unsatisfactory makeshift, which should not be suffered to delay the speedy and complete establishment of the frontier line to which we are entitled under the Russo-American treaty for the cession of Alaska.

In this relation I may refer again to the need of definitely marking the Alaskan boundary where it follows the one hundred and forty-first meridian. A convention to that end has been before the Senate for some two years, but as no action has been taken I contemplate negotiating a new convention for a joint determination of the meridian by telegraphic observations. These, it is believed, will give more accurate and unquestionable results than the sidereal methods heretofore independently followed, which, as is known, proved discrepant at several points on the line, although not varying at any place more than 700 feet.

The pending claim of R. H. May against the Guatemalan Government has been settled by arbitration, Mr. George F. B. Jenner, British minister at Guatemala, who was chosen as sole arbitrator, having awarded $143,750.73 in gold to the claimant.

Various American claims against Haiti have been or are being advanced to the resort of arbitration.

As the result of negotiations with the Government of Honduras in regard to the indemnity demanded for the murder of Frank H. Pears in Honduras, that Government has paid $10,000 in settlement of the claim of the heirs

The assassination of King Humbert called forth sincere expressions of sorrow from this Government and people, and occasion was fitly taken to testify to the Italian nation the high regard here felt for the memory of the lamented ruler.

In my last message I referred at considerable length to the lynching of five Italians at Tallulah. Notwithstanding the efforts of the Federal Government, the production of evidence tending to inculpate the authors of this grievous offense against our civilization, and the repeated inquests set on foot by the authorities of the State of Louisiana, no punishments have followed. Successive grand juries have failed to indict. The representations of the Italian Government in the face of this miscarriage have been most temperate and just.

Setting the principle at issue high above all consideration of merely pecuniary indemnification, such as this Government made in the three previous cases, Italy has solemnly invoked the pledges of existing treaty and asked that the justice to which she is entitled shall be meted in regard to her unfortunate countrymen in our territory with the same full measure she herself would give to any American were his reciprocal treaty rights contemned.

I renew the urgent recommendations I made last year that the Congress appropriately confer upon the Federal courts jurisdiction in this class of international cases where the ultimate responsibility of the Federal Government may be involved, and I invite action upon the bills to accomplish this which were introduced in the Senate and House. It is incumbent upon us to remedy the statutory omission which has led, and may again lead, to such untoward results. I have pointed out the necessity and the precedent for legislation of this character. Its enactment is a simple measure of previsory justice toward the nations with which we as a sovereign equal make treaties requiring reciprocal observance.

While the Italian Government naturally regards such action as the primary and, indeed, the most essential element in the disposal of the Tallulah incident, I advise that, in accordance with precedent, and in view of the improbability of that particular case being reached by the bill now pending, Congress make gracious provision for indemnity to the Italian sufferers in the same form and proportion as heretofore.

In my inaugural address I referred to the general subject of lynching in these words:

Lynching must not be tolerated in a great and civilized country like the United States; courts, not mobs, must execute the penalties of the law. The preservation of public order, the right of discussion, the integrity of courts, and the orderly administration of justice must continue forever the rock of safety upon which our Government securely rests.

This I most urgently reiterate and again invite the attention of my countrymen to this reproach upon our civilization.

The closing year has witnessed a decided strengthening of Japan's relations to other States. The development of her independent judicial and administrative functions under the treaties which took effect July 17, 1899, has proceeded without international friction, showing the competence of the Japanese to hold a foremost place among modern peoples.

In the treatment of the difficult Chinese problems Japan has acted in harmonious concert with the other powers, and her generous cooperation materially aided in the joint relief of the beleaguered legations in Peking and in bringing about an understanding preliminary to a settlement of the issues between the powers and China. Japan's declarations in favor of the integrity of the Chinese Empire and the conservation of open world trade therewith have been frank and positive. As a factor for promoting the general interests of peace, order, and fair commerce in the Far East tne influence of Japan can hardly be overestimated.

The valuable aid and kindly courtesies extended by the Japanese Government and naval officers to the battle ship *Oregon* are gratefully appreciated.

Complaint was made last summer of the discriminatory enforcement of a bubonic quarantine against Japanese on the Pacific coast and of interference with their travel in California and Colorado under the health laws of those States. The latter restrictions have been adjudged by a Federal court to be unconstitutional. No recurrence of either cause of complaint is apprehended.

No noteworthy incident has occurred in our relations with our important southern neighbor. Commercial intercourse with Mexico continues to thrive, and the two Governments neglect no opportunity to foster their mutual interests in all practicable ways.

Pursuant to the declaration of the Supreme Court that the awards of the late Joint Commission in the La Abra and Weil claims were obtained through fraud, the sum awarded in the first case, $403,-030.08, has been returned to Mexico, and the amount of the Weil award will be returned in like manner.

A Convention indefinitely extending the time for the labors of the United States and Mexican International (Water) Boundary Commission has been signed.

It is with satisfaction that I am able to announce the formal notification at The Hague, on September 4, of the deposit of ratifications of the Convention for the Pacific Settlement of International Disputes by sixteen powers, namely, the United States, Austria, Belgium, Denmark, England, France, Germany, Italy, Persia, Portugal, Roumania, Russia, Siam, Spain, Sweden and Norway, and the Netherlands. Japan also has since ratified the Convention.

The Administrative Council of the Permanent Court of Arbitration has been organized and has adopted rules of order and a constitution for the International Arbitration Bureau. In accordance with Article XXIII of the Convention providing for the appointment by each signatory power of persons of known competency in questions of international law as arbitrators, I have appointed as members of this Court, Hon. Benjamin Harrison, of Indiana, ex-President of the United States; Hon. Melville W. Fuller, of Illinois, Chief Justice of the United States; Hon. John W. Griggs, of New Jersey, Attorney-General of the United States; and Hon. George Gray, of Delaware, a judge of the circuit court of the United States.

As an incident of the brief revolution in the Mosquito district of Nicaragua early in 1899 the insurgents forcibly collected from American merchants duties upon imports. On the restoration of order the Nicaraguan authorities demanded a second payment of such duties on the ground that they were due to the titular Government and that their diversion had aided the revolt.

This position was not accepted by us. After prolonged discussion a compromise was effected under which the amount of the second payments was deposited with the British consul at San Juan del Norte in trust until the two Governments should determine whether the first payments had been made under compulsion to a *de facto* authority. Agreement as to this was not reached, and the point was waived by the act of the Nicaraguan Government in requesting the British consul to return the deposits to the merchants.

Menacing differences between several of the Central American States have been accommodated, our ministers rendering good offices toward an understanding.

The all-important matter of an interoceanic canal has assumed a new phase. Adhering to its refusal to reopen the question of the forfeiture of the contract of the Maritime Canal Company, which was terminated for alleged nonexecution in October, 1899, the Government of Nicaragua has since supplemented that action by declaring the so-styled Eyre-Cragin option void for nonpayment of the stipulated advance. Protests in relation to these acts have been filed in the State Department and are under consideration. Deeming itself relieved from existing engagements, the Nicaraguan Government shows a disposition to deal freely with the canal question either in the way of negotiations with the United States or by taking measures to promote the waterway.

Overtures for a convention to effect the building of a canal under the auspices of the United States are under consideration. In the meantime, the views of the Congress upon the general subject, in the light of the report of the Commission appointed to examine the comparative merits of the various trans-Isthmian ship-canal projects, may be awaited.

I commend to the early attention of the Senate the Convention with Great Britain to facilitate the construction of such a canal and to remove any objection which might arise out of the Convention commonly called the Clayton-Bulwer Treaty.

The long-standing contention with Portugal, growing out of the seizure of the Delagoa Bay Railway, has been at last determined by a favorable award of the tribunal of arbitration at Berne, to which it was submitted. The amount of the award, which was deposited in London awaiting arrangements by the Governments of the United

States and Great Britain for its disposal, has recently been paid over to the two Governments.

A lately signed Convention of Extradition with Peru as amended by the Senate has been ratified by the Peruvian Congress.

Another illustration of the policy of this Government to refer international disputes to impartial arbitration is seen in the agreement reached with Russia to submit the claims on behalf of American sealing vessels seized in Bering Sea to determination by Mr. T. M. C. Asser, a distinguished statesman and jurist of the Netherlands.

Thanks are due to the Imperial Russian Government for the kindly aid rendered by its authorities in eastern Siberia to American missionaries fleeing from Manchuria.

Satisfactory progress has been made toward the conclusion of a general treaty of friendship and intercourse with Spain, in replacement of the old treaty, which passed into abeyance by reason of the late war. A new convention of extradition is approaching completion, and I should be much pleased were a commercial arrangement to follow. I feel that we should not suffer to pass any opportunity to reaffirm the cordial ties that existed between us and Spain from the time of our earliest independence, and to enhance the mutual benefits of that commercial intercourse which is natural between the two countries.

By the terms of the Treaty of Peace the line bounding the ceded Philippine group in the southwest failed to include several small islands lying westward of the Sulus, which have always been recognized as under Spanish control. The occupation of Sibutú and Cagayan Sulu by our naval forces elicited a claim on the part of Spain, the essential equity of which could not be gainsaid. In order to cure the defect of the treaty by removing all possible ground of future misunderstanding respecting the interpretation of its third article, I directed the negotiation of a supplementary treaty, which will be forthwith laid before the Senate, whereby Spain quits all title and claim of title to the islands named as well as to any and all islands belonging to the Philippine Archipelago lying outside the lines described in said third article, and agrees that all such islands shall be comprehended in the cession of the archipelago as fully as if they had been expressly included within those lines. In consideration of this cession the United States is to pay to Spain the sum of $100,000.

A bill is now pending to effect the recommendation made in my last annual message that appropriate legislation be had to carry into execution Article VII of the Treaty of Peace with Spain, by which the United States assumed the payment of certain claims for indemnity of its citizens against Spain. I ask that action be taken to fulfill this obligation.

The King of Sweden and Norway has accepted the joint invitation of the United States, Germany, and Great Britain to arbitrate claims growing out of losses sustained in the Samoan Islands in the course of military operations made necessary by the disturbances in 1899.

Our claims upon the Government of the Sultan for reparation for injuries suffered by American citizens in Armenia and elsewhere give promise of early and satisfactory settlement. His Majesty's good disposition in this regard has been evinced by the issuance of an irade for rebuilding the American college at Harpoot.

The failure of action by the Senate at its last session upon the commercial conventions then submitted for its consideration and approval, although caused by the great pressure of other legislative business, has caused much disappointment to the agricultural and industrial interests of the country, which hoped to profit by their provisions. The conventional periods for their ratification having expired, it became necessary to sign additional articles extending the time for that purpose. This was requested on our part, and the other Governments interested have concurred with the exception of one convention, in respect to which no formal reply has been received.

Since my last communication to the Congress on this subject special commercial agreements under the third section of the tariff act have been proclaimed with Portugal, with Italy, and with Germany. Commercial conventions under the general limitations of the fourth section of the same act have been concluded with Nicaragua, with Ecuador, with the Dominican Republic, with Great Britain on behalf of the island of Trinidad, and with Denmark on behalf of the island of St. Croix. These will be early communicated to the Senate. Negotiations with other Governments are in progress for the improvement and security of our commercial relations.

The policy of reciprocity so manifestly rests upon the principles of international equity and has been so repeatedly approved by the people of the United States that there ought to be no hesitation in either branch of the Congress in giving to it full effect.

This Government desires to preserve the most just and amicable commercial relations with all foreign countries, unmoved by the industrial rivalries necessarily developed in the expansion of international trade. It is believed that the foreign Governments generally entertain the same purpose, although in some instances there are clamorous demands upon them for legislation specifically hostile to American interests. Should these demands prevail I shall communicate with the Congress with the view of advising such legislation as may be necessary to meet the emergency.

The exposition of the resources and products of the Western Hemisphere to be held at Buffalo next year promises important results not only for the United States but for the other participating countries. It is gratifying that the Latin-American States have evinced the liveliest interest, and the fact that an International American Congress will be held in the City of Mexico while the exposition is in progress encourages the hope of a larger display at Buffalo than might otherwise be practicable. The work of preparing an exhibit of our national resources is making satisfactory progress under the direction of different officials of the Federal Government, and the various States of the Union have shown a disposition toward the most liberal participation in the enterprise.

The Bureau of the American Republics continues to discharge, with the happiest results, the important work of promoting cordial relations between the United States and the Latin-American countries, all of which are now active members of the International Union. The Bureau has been instrumental in bringing about the agreement for another International American Congress, which is to meet in the City of Mexico in October, 1901. The Bureau's future for another term of ten years is assured by the international compact, but the congress will doubtless have much to do with shaping new lines of work and a general policy. Its usefulness to the interests of Latin-American trade is widely appreciated and shows a gratifying development.

The practical utility of the consular service in obtaining a wide range of information as to the industries and commerce of other countries and the opportunities thereby afforded for introducing the sale of our goods have kept steadily in advance of the notable expansion of our foreign trade, and abundant evidence has been furnished, both at home and abroad, of the fact that the Consular Reports including many from our diplomatic representatives, have to a considerable extent pointed out ways and means of disposing of a great variety of manufactured goods which otherwise might not have found sale abroad.

Testimony of foreign observers to the commercial efficiency of the consular corps seems to be conclusive, and our own manufacturers and exporters highly appreciate the value of the services rendered not only in the printed reports but also in the individual efforts of consular officers to promote American trade. An increasing part of the work of the Bureau of Foreign Commerce, whose primary duty it is to compile and print the reports, is to answer inquiries from trade organizations, business houses, etc., as to conditions in various parts of the world, and, notwithstanding the smallness of the force employed, the work has been so systematized that responses are made with such promptitude and accuracy as to elicit flattering encomiums. The experiment of printing the Consular Reports daily for immediate use by trade bodies, exporters, and the press, which was begun in January, 1898, continues to give general satisfaction.

It is gratifying to be able to state that the surplus revenues for the fiscal year ended June 30, 1900, were $79,527,060.18. For the six preceding years we had only deficits, the aggregate of which from 1894 to 1899, inclusive, amounted to $283,022,991.14. The receipts for the year from all sources, exclusive of postal revenues, aggregated $567,240,851.89, and expenditures for all purposes, except for the administration of the postal department, aggregated $487,-713,791.71. The receipts from customs were $233,164,871.16, an increase over the preceding year of $27,036,389.41. The receipts from internal revenue were $295,327,926.76, an increase of $21,890,-765.25 over 1899. The receipts from miscellaneous sources were $38,748,053.97, as against $36,394,976.92 for the previous year.

It is gratifying also to note that during the year a considerable reduction is shown in the expenditures of the Government. The War Department expenditures for the fiscal year 1900 were $134,774,-767.78, a reduction of $95,066,486.69 over those of 1899. In the Navy Department the expenditures were $55,953,077.72 for the year 1900, as against $63,942,104.25 for the preceding year, a decrease of $7,989,026.53. In the expenditures on account of Indians there was a decrease in 1900 over 1899 of $2,630,604.38; and in the civil and miscellaneous expenses for 1900 there was a reduction of $13,418,-065.74.

Because of the excess of revenues over expenditures the Secretary of the Treasury was enabled to apply bonds and other securities to the sinking fund to the amount of $56,544,556.06. The details of the sinking fund are set forth in the report of the Secretary of the Treasury, to which I invite attention. The Secretary of the Treasury estimates that the receipts for the current fiscal year will aggregate $580,000,000 and the expenditures $500,000,000, leaving an excess of revenues over expenditures of $80,000,000. The present condition of the Treasury is one of undoubted strength. The available cash balance November 30 was $139,303,794.50. Under the form of statement prior to the financial law of March 14 last there would have been included in the statement of available cash gold coin and bullion held for the redemption of United States notes.

If this form were pursued, the cash balance including the present gold reserve of \$150,000,000, would be \$289,303,794.50. Such balance November 30, 1899, was \$296,495,301.55. In the general fund, which is wholly separate from the reserve and trust funds, there was on November 30, \$70,090,073.15 in gold coin and bullion, to which should be added \$22,957,300 in gold certificates subject to issue, against which there is held in the Division of Redemption gold coin and bullion, making a total holding of free gold amounting to \$93,047,373.15.

It will be the duty as I am sure it will be the disposition of the Congress to provide whatever further legislation is needed to insure the continued parity under all conditions between our two forms of metallic money, silver and gold.

Our surplus revenues have permitted the Secretary of the Treasury since the close of the fiscal year to call in the funded loan of 1891 continued at 2 per cent, in the sum of \$25,364,500. To and including November 30, \$23,458,100 of these bonds have been paid. This sum, together with the amount which may accrue from further redemptions under the call, will be applied to the sinking fund.

The law of March 14, 1900, provided for refunding into 2 per cent thirty-year bonds, payable, principal and interest, in gold coin of the present standard value, that portion of the public debt represented by the 3 per cent bonds of 1908, the 4 percents of 1907, and the 5 percents of 1904, of which there was outstanding at the date of said law \$839,149,930. The holders of the old bonds presented them for exchange between March 14 and November 30 to the amount of \$364,943,750. The net saving to the Government on these transactions aggregates \$9,106,166.

Another effect of the operation, as stated by the Secretary, is to reduce the charge upon the Treasury for the payment of interest from the dates of refunding to February 1, 1904, by the sum of more than seven million dollars annually. From February 1, 1904, to July 1, 1907, the annual interest charge will be reduced by the sum of more than five millions, and for the thirteen months ending August 1, 1908, by about one million. The full details of the refunding are given in the annual report of the Secretary of the Treasury.

The beneficial effect of the financial act of 1900, so far as it relates to a modification of the national banking act, is already apparent. The provision for the incorporation of national banks with a capital of not less than \$25,000 in places not exceeding three thousand inhabitants has resulted in the extension of banking facilities to many small communities hitherto unable to provide themselves with banks-ing institutions under the national system. There were organized from the enactment of the law up to and including November 30, 369 national banks, of which 266 were with capital less than $50,000, and 103 with capital of $50,000 or more.

It is worthy of mention that the greater number of banks being organized under the new law are in sections where the need of banking facilities has been most pronounced. Iowa stands first, with 30 banks of the smaller class, while Texas, Oklahoma, Indian Territory, and the middle and western sections of the country have also availed themselves largely of the privileges under the new law.

A large increase in national-bank-note circulation has resulted from the provision of the act which permits national banks to issue circulating notes to the par value of the United States bonds deposited as security instead of only 90 per cent thereof, as heretofore. The increase in circulating notes from March 14 to November 30 is $77,889,570.

The party in power is committed to such legislation as will better make the currency responsive to the varying needs of business at all seasons and in all sections.

Our foreign trade shows a remarkable record of commercial and industrial progress. The total of imports and exports for the first time in the history of the country exceeded two billions of dollars. The exports are greater than they have ever been before, the total for the fiscal year 1900 being $1,394,483,082, an increase over 1899 of $167,459,780, an increase over 1898 of $163,000,752, over 1897 of $343,489,526, and greater than 1896 by $511,876,144.

The growth of manufactures in the United States is evidenced by the fact that exports of manufactured products largely exceed those of any previous year, their value for 1900 being $433,851,756, against $339,592,146 in 1899, an increase of 28 per cent.

Agricultural products were also exported during 1900 in greater volume than in 1899, the total for the year being $835,858,123, against $784,776,142 in 1899.

The imports for the year amounted to $849,941,184, an increase over 1899 of $152,792,695. This increase is largely in materials for manufacture, and is in response to the rapid development of manufacturing in the United States. While there was imported for use in manufactures in 1900 material to the value of $79,768,972 in excess of 1899, it is reassuring to observe that there is a tendency toward decrease in the importation of articles manufactured ready for consumption, which in 1900 formed 15.17 per cent of the total imports, against 15.54 per cent in 1899 and 21.09 per cent in 1896.

I recommend that the Congress at its present session reduce the internal-revenue taxes imposed to meet the expenses of the war with

THE WHITE HOUSE

WHITE HOUSE.

The name of "White House" was given officially to the Executive Mansion during its occupancy by President Roosevelt, thus squaring official with unofficial nomenclature. The White House was begun in 1792, was occupied first by President Adams in 1800, was burned down by the British in 1814, and was restored in 1818. The building represents the English Renaissance style of architecture, and its name arises from the fact that its freestone is painted white. It is 170 feet long, 86 feet deep and two stories high. The first floor is used for public and official purposes, and the President's living quarters occupy the second floor. Among its famous rooms are the Blue Room, which is used for diplomatic functions, and the East Room, which is used for public receptions. (See article Executive Mansion in Encyclopedic Index.)

Spain in the sum of thirty millions of dollars. This reduction should be secured by the remission of those taxes which experience has shown to be the most burdensome to the industries of the people.

I specially urge that there be included in whatever reduction is made the legacy tax on bequests for public uses of a literary, educational, or charitable character.

American vessels during the past three years have carried about 9 per cent of our exports and imports. Foreign ships should carry the least, not the greatest, part of American trade. The remarkable growth of our steel industries, the progress of shipbuilding for the domestic trade, and our steadily maintained expenditures for the Navy have created an opportunity to place the United States in the first rank of commercial maritime powers.

Besides realizing a proper national aspiration this will mean the establishment and healthy growth along all our coasts of a distinctive national industry, expanding the field for the profitable employment of labor and capital. It will increase the transportation facilities and reduce freight charges on the vast volume of products brought from the interior to the seaboard for export, and will strengthen an arm of the national defense upon which the founders of the Government and their successors have relied. In again urging immediate action by the Congress on measures to promote American shipping and foreign trade, I direct attention to the recommendations on the subject in previous messages, and particularly to the opinion expressed in the message of 1899:

I am satisfied the judgment of the country favors the policy of aid to our merchant marine, which will broaden our commerce and markets and upbuild our sea-carrying capacity for the products of agriculture and manufacture, which, with the increase of our Navy, mean more work and wages to our countrymen, as well as a safeguard to American interests in every part of the world.

The attention of the Congress is invited to the recommendation of the Secretary of the Treasury in his annual report for legislation in behalf of the Revenue-Cutter Service, and favorable action is urged.

In my last annual message to the Congress I called attention to the necessity for early action to remedy such evils as might be found to exist in connection with combinations of capital organized into trusts, and again invite attention to my discussion of the subject at that time, which concluded with these words:

It is apparent that uniformity of legislation upon this subject in the several States is much to be desired. It is to be hoped that such uniformity, founded in a wise and just discrimination between what is injurious and what is useful and necessary in business operations, may be obtained, and that means may be found for the Congress, within the limitations of its constitutional power, so to supplement an effective code of State legislation as to make a complete system of laws throughout the United States adequate to compel a general observance of the salutary rules to which I have referred.

The whole question is so important and far-reaching that I am sure no part of it will be lightly considered, but every phase of it will have the studied deliberation of the Congress, resulting in wise and judicious action.

Restraint upon such combinations as are injurious, and which are within Federal jurisdiction, should be promptly applied by the Congress.

In my last annual message I dwelt at some length upon the condition of affairs in the Philippines. While seeking to impress upon you that the grave responsibility of the future government of those islands rests with the Congress of the United States, I abstained from recommending at that time a specific and final form of government for the territory actually held by the United States forces and in which as long as insurrection continues the military arm must necessarily be supreme. I stated my purpose, until the Congress shall have made the formal expression of its will, to use the authority vested in me by the Constitution and the statutes to uphold the sovereignty of the United States in those distant islands as in all other places where our flag rightfully floats, placing, to that end, at the disposal of the army and navy all the means which the liberality of the Congress and the people have provided. No contrary expression of the will of the Congress having been made, I have steadfastly pursued the purpose so declared, employing the civil arm as well toward the accomplishment of pacification and the institution of local governments within the lines of authority and law.

Progress in the hoped-for direction has been favorable. Our forces have successfully controlled the greater part of the islands, overcoming the organized forces of the insurgents and carrying order and administrative regularity to all quarters. What opposition remains is for the most part scattered, obeying no concerted plan of strategic action, operating only by the methods common to the traditions of guerrilla warfare, which, while ineffective to alter the general control now established, are still sufficient to beget insecurity among the populations that have felt the good results of our control and thus delay the conferment upon them of the fuller measures of local self-government, of education, and of industrial and agricultural development which we stand ready to give to them.

By the spring of this year the effective opposition of the dissatisfied Tagals to the authority of the United States was virtually ended, thus opening the door for the extension of a stable administration

over much of the territory of the Archipelago.   **Desiring to** bring
this about, I appointed in March last a civil Commission composed of
the Hon William H. Taft, of Ohio; Prof. Dean C. Worcester, of
Michigan; the Hon. Luke I. Wright, of Tennessee; the Hon. Henry
C. Ide, of Vermont, and Prof. Bernard Moses, of California.   The
aims of their mission and the scope of their authority are clearly set
forth in my instructions of April 7, 1900, addressed to the Secretary
of War to be transmitted to them:

In the message transmitted to the Congress on the 5th of December, 1899, I
said, speaking of the Philippine Islands: "As long as the insurrection continues
the military arm must necessarily be supreme.   But there is no reason why steps
should not be taken from time to time to inaugurate governments essentially popular in their form as fast as territory is held and controlled by our troops.   To this
end I am considering the advisability of the return of the Commission, or such of
the members thereof as can be secured, to aid the existing authorities and facilitate this work throughout the islands."

To give effect to the intention thus expressed, I have appointed Hon. William
H. Taft, of Ohio; Prof. Dean C. Worcester, of Michigan; Hon. Luke I. Wright,
of Tennessee; Hon. Henry C. Ide, of Vermont, and Prof. Bernard Moses, of California, Commissioners to the Philippine Islands to continue and perfect the work of
organizing and establishing civil government already commenced by the military
authorities, subject in all respects to any laws which Congress may hereafter enact.

The Commissioners named will meet and act as a board, and the Hon. William H.
Taft is designated as president of the board.   It is probable that the transfer of authority from military commanders to civil officers will be gradual and will occupy a
considerable period.   Its successful accomplishment and the maintenance of peace
and order in the meantime will require the most perfect co-operation between the
civil and military authorities in the islands, and both should be directed during the
transition period by the same Executive Department.   The Commission will therefore report to the Secretary of War, and all their action will be subject to your approval and control.

You will instruct the Commission to proceed to the city of Manila, where they
will make their principal office, and to communicate with the Military Governor of
the Philippine Islands, whom you will at the same time direct to render to them
every assistance within his power in the performance of their duties.   Without
hampering them by too specific instructions, they should in general be enjoined,
after making themselves familiar with the conditions and needs of the country, to
devote their attention in the first instance to the establishment of municipal governments, in which the natives of the islands, both in the cities and in the rural
communities, shall be afforded the opportunity to manage their own local affairs to
the fullest extent of which they are capable and subject to the least degree of
supervision and control which a careful study of their capacities and observation of
the workings of native control show to be consistent with the maintenance of law,
order, and loyalty.

The next subject in order of importance should be the organization of government in the larger administrative divisions corresponding to counties, departments,
or provinces, in which the common interests of many or several municipalities
falling within the same tribal lines, or the same natural geographical limits, may
best be subserved by a common administration.   Whenever the Commission is of
the opinion that the condition of affairs in the islands is such that the central
administration may safely be transferred from military to civil control they will

report that conclusion to you, with their recommendations as to the form of central government to be established for the purpose of taking over the control.

Beginning with the 1st day of September, 1900, the authority to exercise, subject to my approval, through the Secretary of War, that part of the power of government in the Philippine Islands which is of a legislative nature is to be transferred from the Military Governor of the islands to this Commission, to be thereafter exercised by them in the place and stead of the Military Governor, under such rules and regulations as you shall prescribe, until the establishment of the civil central government for the islands contemplated in the last foregoing paragraph, or until Congress shall otherwise provide. Exercise of this legislative authority will include the making of rules and orders, having the effect of law, for the raising of revenue by taxes, customs duties, and imposts; the appropriation and expenditure of public funds of the islands; the establishment of an educational system throughout the islands; the establishment of a system to secure an efficient civil service; the organization and establishment of courts; the organization and establishment of municipal and departmental governments, and all other matters of a civil nature for which the Military Governor is now competent to provide by rules or orders of a legislative character.

The Commission will also have power during the same period to appoint to office such officers under the judicial, educational, and civil-service systems and in the municipal and departmental governments as shall be provided for. Until the complete transfer of control the Military Governor will remain the chief executive head of the government of the islands, and will exercise the executive authority now possessed by him and not herein expressly assigned to the Commission, subject, however, to the rules and orders enacted by the Commission in the exercise of the legislative powers conferred upon them. In the meantime the municipal and departmental governments will continue to report to the Military Governor and be subject to his administrative supervision and control, under your direction, but that supervision and control will be confined within the narrowest limits consistent with the requirement that the powers of government in the municipalities and departments shall be honestly and effectively exercised and that law and order and individual freedom shall be maintained.

All legislative rules and orders, establishments of government, and appointments to office by the Commission will take effect immediately, or at such times as they shall designate, subject to your approval and action upon the coming in of the Commission's reports, which are to be made from time to time as their action is taken. Wherever civil governments are constituted under the direction of the Commission such military posts, garrisons, and forces will be continued for the suppression of insurrection and brigandage and the maintenance of law and order as the Military Commander shall deem requisite, and the military forces shall be at all times subject, under his orders, to the call of the civil authorities for the maintenance of law and order and the enforcement of their authority.

In the establishment of municipal governments the Commission will take as the basis of their work the governments established by the Military Governor under his order of August 8, 1899, and under the report of the board constituted by the Military Governor by his order of January 29, 1900, to formulate and report a plan of municipal government, of which His Honor Cayetano Arellano, President of the Audiencia, was chairman, and they will give to the conclusions of that board the weight and consideration which the high character and distinguished abilities of its members justify.

In the constitution of departmental or provincial governments they will give especial attention to the existing government of the island of Negros, constituted, with the approval of the people of that island, under the order of the Military Governor of July 22, 1899, and after verifying, so far as may be practicable, the reports of the successful working of that government they will be guided by the experience thus acquired so far as it may be applicable to the condition existing in other portions of the Philippines. They will avail themselves, to the fullest degree practicable, of the conclusions reached by the previous Commission to the Philippines.

In the distribution of powers among the governments organized by the Commission, the presumption is always to be in favor of the smaller subdivision, so that all the powers which can properly be exercised by the municipal government shall be vested in that government, and all the powers of a more general character which can be exercised by the departmental government shall be vested in that government, and so that in the governmental system, which is the result of the process, the central government of the islands, following the example of the distribution of the powers between the States and the National Government of the United States, shall have no direct administration except of matters of purely general concern, and shall have only such supervision and control over local governments as may be necessary to secure and enforce faithful and efficient administration by local officers.

The many different degrees of civilization and varieties of custom and capacity among the people of the different islands preclude very definite instruction as to the part which the people shall take in the selection of their own officers; but these general rules are to be observed: That in all cases the municipal officers, who administer the local affairs of the people, are to be selected by the people, and that wherever officers of more extended jurisdiction are to be selected in any way, natives of the islands are to be preferred, and if they can be found competent and willing to perform the duties, they are to receive the offices in preference to any others.

It will be necessary to fill some offices for the present with Americans which after a time may well be filled by natives of the islands. As soon as practicable a system for ascertaining the merit and fitness of candidates for civil office should be put in force. An indispensable qualification for all offices and positions of trust and authority in the islands must be absolute and unconditional loyalty to the United States, and absolute and unhampered authority and power to remove and punish any officer deviating from that standard must at all times be retained in the hands of the central authority of the islands.

In all the forms of government and administrative provisions which they are authorized to prescribe the Commission should bear in mind that the government which they are establishing is designed not for our satisfaction, or for the expression of our theoretical views, but for the happiness, peace, and prosperity of the people of the Philippine Islands, and the measures adopted should be made to conform to their customs, their habits, and even their prejudices, to the fullest extent consistent with the accomplishment of the indispensable requisites of just and effective government.

At the same time the Commission should bear in mind, and the people of the islands should be made plainly to understand, that there are certain great principles of government which have been made the basis of our governmental system which we deem essential to the rule of law and the maintenance of individual freedom, and of which they have, unfortunately, been denied the experience possessed by us; that there are also certain practical rules of government which we have found to be essential to the preservation of these great principles of liberty and law, and that these principles and these rules of government must be established and maintained in their islands for the sake of their liberty and happiness, however much they may conflict with the customs or laws of procedure with which they are familiar.

It is evident that the most enlightened thought of the Philippine Islands fully appreciates the importance of these principles and rules, and they will inevitably within a short time command universal assent. Upon every division and branch of the government of the Philippines, therefore, must be imposed these inviolable rules:

That no person shall be deprived of life, liberty, or property without due process of law; that private property shall not be taken for public use without just compensation; that in all criminal prosecutions the accused shall enjoy the right to a speedy and public trial, to be informed of the nature and cause of the accusation, to be confronted with the witnesses against him, to have compulsory process for obtaining witnesses in his favor, and to have the assistance of counsel for his defense; that excessive bail shall not be required, nor excessive fines imposed, nor cruel and unusual punishment inflicted; that no person shall be put twice in jeopardy for the same offense, or be compelled in any criminal case to be a witness against himself; that the right to be secure against unreasonable searches and seizures shall not be violated; that neither slavery nor involuntary servitude shall exist except as a punishment for crime; that no bill of attainder or *ex-post-facto* law shall be passed; that no law shall be passed abridging the freedom of speech or of the press, or the rights of the people to peaceably assemble and petition the Government for a redress of grievances; that no law shall be made respecting an establishment of religion, or prohibiting the free exercise thereof, and that the free exercise and enjoyment of religious profession and worship without discrimination or preference shall forever be allowed.

It will be the duty of the Commission to make a thorough investigation into the titles to the large tracts of land held or claimed by individuals or by religious orders; into the justice of the claims and complaints made against such landholders by the people of the island or any part of the people, and to seek by wise and peaceable measures a just settlement of the controversies and redress of wrongs which have caused strife and bloodshed in the past. In the performance of this duty the Commission is enjoined to see that no injustice is done; to have regard for substantial rights and equity, disregarding technicalities so far as substantial right permits, and to observe the following rules:

That the provision of the Treaty of Paris pledging the United States to the protection of all rights of property in the islands, and as well the principle of our own Government which prohibits the taking of private property without due process of law, shall not be violated; that the welfare of the people of the islands, which should be a paramount consideration, shall be attained consistently with this rule of property right; that if it becomes necessary for the public interest of the people of the islands to dispose of claims to property which the Commission finds to be not lawfully acquired and held disposition shall be made thereof by due legal procedure, in which there shall be full opportunity for fair and impartial hearing and judgment; that if the same public interests require the extinguishment of property rights lawfully acquired and held due compensation shall be made out of the public treasury therefor; that no form of religion and no minister of religion shall be forced upon any community or upon any citizen of the islands; that, upon the other hand, no minister of religion shall be interfered with or molested in following his calling, and that the separation between State and Church shall be real, entire, and absolute.

It will be the duty of the Commission to promote and extend, and, as they find occasion, to improve the system of education already inaugurated by the military authorities. In doing this they should regard as of first importance the extension of a system of primary education which shall be free to all, and which shall tend to fit the people for the duties of citizenship and for the ordinary avocations of a civilized community. This instruction should be given in the first instance in every part of the islands in the language of the people. In view of the great number of languages spoken by the different tribes, it is especially important to the prosperity of the islands that a common medium of communication may be established, and it is obviously desirable that this medium should be the English language. Especial attention should be at once given to affording full opportunity to all the people of the islands to acquire the use of the English language.

It may be well that the main changes which should be made in the system of taxation and in the body of the laws under which the people are governed, except such changes as have already been made by the military government, should be relegated to the civil government which is to be established under the auspices of the Commission. It will, however, be the duty of the Commission to inquire diligently as to whether there are any further changes which ought not to be delayed, and if so, they are authorized to make such changes subject to your approval. In doing so they are to bear in mind that taxes which tend to penalize or repress industry and enterprise are to be avoided; that provisions for taxation should be simple, so that they may be understood by the people; that they should affect the fewest practicable subjects of taxation which will serve for the general distribution of the burden.

The main body of the laws which regulate the rights and obligations of the people should be maintained with as little interference as possible. Changes made should be mainly in procedure, and in the criminal laws to secure speedy and impartial trials, and at the same time effective administration and respect for individual rights.

In dealing with the uncivilized tribes of the islands the Commission should adopt the same course followed by Congress in permitting the tribes of our North American Indians to maintain their tribal organization and government, and under which many of those tribes are now living in peace and contentment, surrounded by a civilization to which they are unable or unwilling to conform. Such tribal governments should, however, be subjected to wise and firm regulation, and, without undue or petty interference, constant and active effort should be exercised to prevent barbarous practices and introduce civilized customs.

Upon all officers and employees of the United States, both civil and military, should be impressed a sense of the duty to observe not merely the material but the personal and social rights of the people of the islands, and to treat them with the same courtesy and respect for their personal dignity which the people of the United States are accustomed to require from each other.

The articles of capitulation of the city of Manila on the 13th of August, 1898, concluded with these words:

"This city, its inhabitants, its churches and religious worship, its educational establishments, and its private property of all descriptions, are placed under the special safeguard of the faith and honor of the American Army."

I believe that this pledge has been faithfully kept. As high and sacred an obligation rests upon the Government of the United States to give protection for property and life, civil and religious freedom, and wise, firm, and unselfish guidance in the paths of peace and prosperity to all the people of the Philippine Islands. I charge this Commission to labor for the full performance of this obligation, which concerns the honor and conscience of their country, in the firm hope that through their labors all the inhabitants of the Philippine Islands may come to look back with gratitude to the day when God gave victory to American arms at Manila and set their land under the sovereignty and the protection of the people of the United States.

Coincidently with the entrance of the Commission upon its labors I caused to be issued by General MacArthur, the Military Governor of the Philippines, on June 21, 1900, a proclamation of amnesty in generous terms, of which many of the insurgents took advantage, among them a number of important leaders.

This Commission, composed of eminent citizens representing the diverse geographical and political interests of the country, and bringing to their task the ripe fruits of long and intelligent service in educational, administrative, and judicial careers, made great progress from the outset. As early as August 21, 1900, it submitted a preliminary report, which will be laid before the Congress, and from which it appears that already the good effects of returning order are felt; that business, interrupted by hostilities, is improving as peace extends; that a larger area is under sugar cultivation than ever before; that the customs revenues are greater than at any time during the Spanish rule; that economy and efficiency in the military administration have created a surplus fund of $6,000,000, available for needed public improvements; that a stringent civil-service law is in preparation; that railroad communications are expanding, opening up rich districts, and that a comprehensive scheme of education is being organized.

Later reports from the Commission show yet more encouraging advance toward insuring the benefits of liberty and good government to the Filipinos, in the interest of humanity and with the aim of building up an enduring, self-supporting, and self-administering community in those far eastern seas. I would impress upon the Congress that whatever legislation may be enacted in respect to the Philippine Islands should be along these generous lines. The fortune of war has thrown upon this nation an unsought trust which should be unselfishly discharged, and devolved upon this Government a moral as well as material responsibility toward these millions whom we have freed from an oppressive yoke.

I have on another occasion called the Filipinos "the wards of the nation." Our obligation as guardian was not lightly assumed; it must not be otherwise than honestly fulfilled, aiming first of all to benefit those who have come under our fostering care. It is our duty so to treat them that our flag may be no less beloved in the mountains of Luzon and the fertile zones of Mindanao and Negros than it is at home, that there as here it shall be the revered symbol of liberty, enlightenment, and progress in every avenue of development.

The Filipinos are a race quick to learn and to profit by knowledge. He would be rash who, with the teachings of contemporaneous history in view, would fix a limit to the degree of culture and advancement yet within the reach of these people if our duty toward them be faithfully performed.

The civil government of Puerto Rico provided for by the act of the Congress approved April 12, 1900, is in successful operation. The courts have been established. The Governor and his associates, working intelligently and harmoniously, are meeting with commendable success.

On the 6th of November a general election was held in the island for members of the Legislature, and the body elected has been called to convene on the first Monday of December.

I recommend that legislation be enacted by the Congress conferring upon the Secretary of the Interior supervision over the public lands in Puerto Rico, and that he be directed to ascertain the location and quantity of lands the title to which remained in the Crown of Spain at the date of cession of Puerto Rico to the United States, and that appropriations necessary for surveys be made, and that the methods of the disposition of such lands be prescribed by law.

On the 25th of July, 1900, I directed that a call be issued for an election in Cuba for members of a constitutional convention to frame a constitution as a basis for a stable and independent government in the island. In pursuance thereof the Military Governor issued the following instructions:

Whereas the Congress of the United States, by its joint resolution of April 20, 1898, declared—

"That the people of the island of Cuba are, and of right ought to be, free and independent.

"That the United States hereby disclaims any disposition or intention to exercise sovereignty, jurisdiction, or control over said island except for the pacification thereof, and asserts its determination, when that is accomplished, to leave the government and control of the island to its people;"

And whereas, the people of Cuba have established municipal governments, deriving their authority from the suffrages of the people given under just and equal laws, and are now ready, in like manner, to proceed to the establishment of a general government which shall assume and exercise sovereignty, jurisdiction, and control over the island:

Therefore, it is ordered that a general election be held in the island of Cuba on the third Saturday of September, in the year nineteen hundred, to elect delegates to a convention to meet in the city of Havana at twelve o'clock noon on the first Monday of November, in the year nineteen hundred, to frame and adopt a constitution for the people of Cuba, and as a part thereof to provide for and agree with the Government of the United States upon the relations to exist between that Government and the Government of Cuba, and to provide for the election by the people of officers under such constitution and the transfer of government to the officers so elected.

The election will be held in the several voting precincts of the island under, and pursuant to, the provisions of the electoral law of April 18, 1900, and the amendments thereof.

The election was held on the 15th of September, and the convention assembled on the 5th of November, 1900, and is now in session.

In calling the convention to order, the Military Governor of Cuba made the following statement:

As Military Governor of the island, representing the President of the United States, I call this convention to order.

It will be your duty, first, to frame and adopt a constitution for Cuba, and when that has been done to formulate what in your opinion ought to be the relations between Cuba and the United States.

The constitution must be adequate to secure a stable, orderly, and free government.

When you have formulated the relations which in your opinion ought to exist between Cuba and the United States the Government of the United States will doubtless take such action on its part as shall lead to a final and authoritative agreement between the people of the two countries to the promotion of their common interests.

All friends of Cuba will follow your deliberations with the deepest interest, earnestly desiring that you shall reach just conclusions, and that by the dignity, individual self-restraint, and wise conservatism which shall characterize your proceedings the capacity of the Cuban people for representative government may be signally illustrated.

The fundamental distinction between true representative government and dictatorship is that in the former every representative of the people, in whatever office, confines himself strictly within the limits of his defined powers. Without such restraint there can be no free constitutional government.

Under the order pursuant to which you have been elected and convened you have no duty and no authority to take part in the present government of the island. Your powers are strictly limited by the terms of that order.

When the convention concludes its labors I will transmit to the Congress the constitution as framed by the convention for its consideration and for such action as it may deem advisable.

I renew the recommendation made in my special message of February 10, 1899, as to the necessity for cable communication between the United States and Hawaii, with extension to Manila. Since then circumstances have strikingly emphasized this need. Surveys have shown the entire feasibility of a chain of cables which at each stopping place shall touch on American territory, so that the system shall be under our own complete control. Manila once within telegraphic reach, connection with the systems of the Asiatic coast would open increased and profitable opportunities for a more direct cable route from our shores to the Orient than is now afforded by the trans-Atlantic, continental, and trans-Asian lines. I urge attention to this important matter.

The present strength of the Army is 100,000 men — 65,000 regulars and 35,000 volunteers. Under the act of March 2, 1899, on the 30th of June next the present volunteer force will be discharged and the Regular Army will be reduced to 2,447 officers and 29,025 enlisted men.

In 1888 a Board of Officers convened by President Cleveland adopted a comprehensive scheme of coast-defense fortifications which involved the outlay of something over one hundred million dollars

This plan received the approval of the Congress, and since then regular appropriations have been made and the work of fortification has steadily progressed.

More than sixty millions of dollars have been invested in a great number of forts and guns, with all the complicated and scientific machinery and electrical appliances necessary for their use. The proper care of this defensive machinery requires men trained in its use. The number of men necessary to perform this duty alone is ascertained by the War Department, at a minimum allowance, to be 18,420.

There are fifty-eight or more military posts in the United States other than the coast-defense fortifications.

The number of these posts is being constantly increased by the Congress. More than $22,000,000 have been expended in building and equipment, and they can only be cared for by the Regular Army. The posts now in existence and others to be built provide for accommodations for, and if fully garrisoned require, 26,000 troops. Many of these posts are along our frontier or at important strategic points, the occupation of which is necessary.

We have in Cuba between 5,000 and 6,000 troops. For the present our troops in that island cannot be withdrawn or materially diminished, and certainly not until the conclusion of the labors of the constitutional convention now in session and a government provided by the new constitution shall have been established and its stability assured.

In Puerto Rico we have reduced the garrisons to 1,636, which includes 879 native troops. There is no room for further reduction here.

We will be required to keep a considerable force in the Philippine Islands for some time to come. From the best information obtainable we will need there for the immediate future from 45,000 to 60,000 men. I am sure the number may be reduced as the insurgents shall come to acknowledge the authority of the United States, of which there are assuring indications.

It must be apparent that we will require an army of about 60,000, and that during present conditions in Cuba and the Philippines the President should have authority to increase the force to the present number of 100,000. Included in this number authority should be given to raise native troops in the Philippines up to 15,000, which the Taft Commission believe will be more effective in detecting and suppressing guerrillas, assassins, and ladrones than our own soldiers.

The full discussion of this subject by the Secretary of War in his annual report is called to your earnest attention.

I renew the recommendation made in my last annual message that the Congress provide a special medal of honor for the volunteers

regulars, sailors, and marines on duty in the Philippines who voluntarily remained in the service after their terms of enlistment had
expired.

I favor the recommendation of the Secretary of War for the detail
of officers from the line of the Army when vacancies occur in the
Adjutant-General's Department, Inspector-General's Department,
Quartermaster's Department, Subsistence Department, Pay Department, Ordnance Department, and Signal Corps.

The Army cannot be too highly commended for its faithful and
effective service in active military operations in the field and the
difficult work of civil administration.

The continued and rapid growth of the postal service is a sure
index of the great and increasing business activity of the country.
Its most striking new development is the extension of rural free
delivery.   This has come almost wholly within the last year.   At
the beginning of the fiscal year 1899–1900 the number of routes in
operation was only 391, and most of these had been running less
than twelve months.   On the 15th of November, 1900, the number
had increased to 2,614, reaching into forty-four States and Territories, and serving a population of 1,801,524.   The number of applications now pending and awaiting action nearly equals all those
granted up to the present time, and by the close of the current
fiscal year about 4,000 routes will have been established, providing
for the daily delivery of mails at the scattered homes of about three
and a half millions of rural population.

This service ameliorates the isolation of farm life, conduces to
good roads, and quickens and extends the dissemination of general
information.   Experience thus far has tended to allay the apprehension that it would be so expensive as to forbid its general adoption or make it a serious burden.   Its actual application has shown
that it increases postal receipts, and can be accompanied by reductions in other branches of the service, so that the augmented revenues and the accomplished savings together materially reduce the
net cost.   The evidences which point to these conclusions are presented in detail in the annual report of the Postmaster-General,
which with its recommendations is commended to the consideration
of the Congress.   The full development of this special service, however, requires such a large outlay of money that it should be undertaken only after a careful study and thorough understanding of all
that it involves.

Very efficient service has been rendered by the Navy in connection
with the insurrection in the Philippines and the recent disturbance
in China.

A very satisfactory settlement has been made of the long-pending question of the manufacture of armor plate. A reasonable price has been secured and the necessity for a Government armor plant avoided.

I approve of the recommendations of the Secretary for new vessels and for additional officers and men which the required increase of the Navy makes necessary. I commend to the favorable action of the Congress the measure now pending for the erection of a statue to the memory of the late Admiral David D. Porter. I commend also the establishment of a national naval reserve and of the grade of vice-admiral. Provision should be made, as recommended by the Secretary, for suitable rewards for special merit. Many officers who rendered the most distinguished service during the recent war with Spain have received in return no recognition from the Congress.

The total area of public lands as given by the Secretary of the Interior is approximately 1,071,881,662 acres, of which 917,135,880 acres are undisposed of and 154,745,782 acres have been reserved for various purposes. The public lands disposed of during the year amount to 13,453,887.96 acres, including 62,423.09 acres of Indian lands, an increase of 4,271,474.80 over the preceding year. The total receipts from the sale of public lands during the fiscal year were $4,379,758.10, an increase of $1,309,620.76 over the preceding year.

The results obtained from our forest policy have demonstrated its wisdom and the necessity in the interest of the public for its continuance and increased appropriations by the Congress for the carrying on of the work. On June 30, 1900, there were thirty-seven forest reserves, created by Presidential proclamations under section 24 of the act of March 3, 1891, embracing an area of 46,425,529 acres.

During the past year the Olympic Reserve, in the State of Washington, was reduced 265,040 acres, leaving its present area at 1,923,840 acres. The Prescott Reserve, in Arizona, was increased from 10,240 acres to 423,680 acres, and the Big Horn Reserve, in Wyoming, was increased from 1,127,680 acres to 1,180,800 acres. A new reserve, the Santa Ynez, in California, embracing an area of 145,000 acres, was created during this year. On October 10, 1900, the Crow Creek Forest Reserve, in Wyoming, was created, with an area of 56,320 acres.

At the end of the fiscal year there were on the pension roll 993,529 names, a net increase of 2,010 over the fiscal year 1899. The number added to the rolls during the year was 45,344. The amount disbursed for Army pensions during the year was $134,700,597.24 and for Navy pensions $3,761,533.41, a total of $138,462,130.65, leaving an unexpended balance of $5,542,768.25 to be covered into the Treasury, which shows an increase over the previous year's expenditure of $107,077.70. There were 684 names added to the rolls during the year by special acts passed at the first session of the Fifty-sixth Congress.

The act of May 9, 1900, among other things provides for an extension of income to widows pensioned under said act to $250 per annum. The Secretary of the Interior believes that by the operations of this act the number of persons pensioned under it will increase and the increased annual payment for pensions will be between $3,000,000 and $4,000,000.

The Government justly appreciates the services of its soldiers and sailors by making pension payments liberal beyond precedent to them, their widows and orphans.

There were 26,540 letters patent granted, including reissues and designs, during the fiscal year ended June 30, 1900; 1,660 trademarks, 682 labels, and 93 prints registered. The number of patents which expired was 19,988. The total receipts for patents were $1,358,228.35. The expenditures were $1,247,827.58, showing a surplus of $110,400.77.

The attention of the Congress is called to the report of the Secretary of the Interior touching the necessity for the further establishment of schools in the Territory of Alaska, and favorable action is invited thereon.

Much interesting information is given in the report of the Governor of Hawaii as to the progress and development of the islands during the period from July 7, 1898, the date of the approval of the joint resolution of the Congress providing for their annexation, up to April 30, 1900, the date of the approval of the act providing a government for the Territory, and thereafter.

The last Hawaiian census, taken in the year 1896, gives a total population of 109,020, of which 31,019 were native Hawaiians. The number of Americans reported was 8,485. The results of the Federal census, taken this year, show the islands to have a total population of 154,001, showing an increase over that reported in 1896 of 44,981, or 41.2 per cent.

There has been marked progress in the educational, agricultural, and railroad development of the islands.

In the Territorial act of April 30, 1900, section 7 of said act repeals Chapter 34 of the Civil Laws of Hawaii whereby the Government was to assist in encouraging and developing the agricultural resources of the Republic, especially irrigation. The Governor of Hawaii recommends legislation looking to the development of such water supply as may exist on the public lands, with a view of promoting land settlement. The earnest consideration of the Congress is invited to this important recommendation and others, as embodied in the report of the Secretary of the Interior.

The Director of the Census states that the work in connection with the Twelfth Census is progressing favorably. This national undertaking, ordered by the Congress each decade, has finally resulted in the collection of an aggregation of statistical facts to determine the industrial growth of the country, its manufacturing and mechanical resources, its richness in mines and forests, the number of its agriculturists, their farms and products, its educational and religious opportunities, as well as questions pertaining to sociological conditions.

The labors of the officials in charge of the Bureau indicate that the four important and most-desired subjects, namely, population, agricultural, manufacturing, and vital statistics, will be completed within the limit prescribed by the law of March 3, 1899.

The field work incident to the above inquiries is now practically finished, and as a result the population of the States and Territories, including the Hawaiian Islands and Alaska, has been announced. The growth of population during the last decade amounts to over 13,000,000, a greater numerical increase than in any previous census in the history of the country.

Bulletins will be issued as rapidly as possible giving the population by States and Territories, by minor civil divisions. Several announcements of this kind have already been made, and it is hoped that the list will be completed by January 1. Other bulletins giving the results of the manufacturing and agricultural inquiries will be given to the public as rapidly as circumstances will admit.

The Director, while confident of his ability to complete the different branches of the undertaking in the allotted time, finds himself embarrassed by the lack of a trained force properly equipped for statistical work, thus raising the question whether in the interest of economy and a thorough execution of the census work there should not be retained in the Government employ a certain number of experts not only to aid in the preliminary organization prior to the taking of the decennial census, but in addition to have the advantage in the field and office work of the Bureau of trained assistants to facilitate the early completion of this enormous undertaking.

I recommend that the Congress at its present session apportion representation among the several States as provided by the Constitution.

The Department of Agriculture has been extending its work during the past year, reaching farther for new varieties of seeds and plants; co-operating more fully with the States and Territories in research along useful lines; making progress in meteorological work relating to lines of wireless telegraphy and forecasts for ocean-going vessels; continuing inquiry as to animal disease; looking into the extent and character of food adulteration; outlining plans for the care, preservation, and intelligent harvesting of our woodlands; studying soils that producers may cultivate with better knowledge of conditions, and helping to clothe desert places with grasses suitable to our arid regions. Our island possessions are being considered that their peoples may be helped to produce the tropical products now so extensively brought into the United States. Inquiry into methods of improving our roads has been active during the year; help has been given to many localities, and scientific investigation of material in the States and Territories has been inaugurated. Irrigation problems in our semiarid regions are receiving careful and increased consideration.

An extensive exhibit at Paris of the products of agriculture has made the peoples of many countries more familiar with the varied products of our fields and their comparative excellence.

The collection of statistics regarding our crops is being improved and sources of information are being enlarged, to the end that producers may have the earliest advices regarding crop conditions. There has never been a time when those for whom it was established have shown more appreciation of the services of the Department.

In my annual message of December 5, 1898, I called attention to the necessity for some amendment of the alien contract law. There still remain important features of the rightful application of the eight-hour law for the benefit of labor and of the principle of arbitration, and I again commend these subjects to the careful attention of the Congress.

That there may be secured the best service possible in the Philippine Islands, I have issued, under date of November 30, 1900, the following order:

The United States Civil Service Commission is directed to render such assistance as may be practicable to the Civil Service Board, created under the act of the United States Philippine Commission, for the establishment and maintenance of an honest and efficient civil service in the Philippine Islands, and for that purpose to conduct examinations for the civil service of the Philippine Islands, upon the request of the Civil Service Board of said islands, under such regulations as may be agreed upon by the said Board and the said United States Civil Service Commission.

The Civil Service Commission is greatly embarrassed in its work for want of an adequate permanent force for clerical and other assistance. Its needs are fully set forth in its report. I invite attention to the report, and especially urge upon the Congress that this important bureau of the public service, which passes upon the qualifications and character of so large a number of the officers and employees of the Government, should be supported by all needed appropriations to secure promptness and efficiency.

I am very much impressed with the statement made by the heads of all the Departments of the urgent necessity of a hall of public records. In every departmental building in Washington, so far as I am informed, the space for official records is not only exhausted, but the walls of rooms are lined with shelves, the middle floor space of many rooms is filled with file cases, and garrets and basements, which were never intended and are unfitted for their accommodation, are crowded with them. Aside from the inconvenience there is great danger, not only from fire, but from the weight of these records upon timbers not intended for their support. There should be a separate building especially designed for the purpose of receiving and preserving the annually accumulating archives of the several Executive Departments. Such a hall need not be a costly structure, but should be so arranged as to admit of enlargement from time to time. I urgently recommend that the Congress take early action in this matter.

I transmit to the Congress a resolution adopted at a recent meeting of the American Bar Association concerning the proposed celebration of John Marshall Day, February 4, 1901. Fitting exercises have been arranged, and it is earnestly desired by the committee that the Congress may participate in this movement to honor the memory of the great jurist.

The transfer of the Government to this city is a fact of great historical interest. Among the people there is a feeling of genuine pride in the Capital of the Republic.

It is a matter of interest in this connection that in 1800 the population of the District of Columbia was 14,093; to-day it is 278,718. The population of the city of Washington was then 3,210; to-day it is 218,196.

The Congress having provided for "an appropriate national celebration of the Centennial Anniversary of the Establishment of the Seat of the Government in the District of Columbia," the committees authorized by it have prepared a programme for the 12th of December, 1900, which date has been selected as the anniversary day.

Deep interest has been shown in the arrangements for the celebration by the members of the committees of the Senate and House of Representatives, the committee of Governors appointed by the President, and the committees appointed by the citizens and inhabitants of the District of Columbia generally. The programme, in addition to a reception and other exercises at the Executive Mansion, provides commemorative exercises to be held jointly by the Senate and House of Representatives in the Hall of the House of Representatives, and a reception in the evening at the Corcoran Gallery of Art in honor of the Governors of the States and Territories.

In our great prosperity we must guard against the danger it invites of extravagance in Government expenditures and appropriations; and the chosen representatives of the people will, I doubt not, furnish an example in their legislation of that wise economy which in a season of plenty husbands for the future. In this era of great business activity and opportunity caution is not untimely. It will not abate, but strengthen, confidence. It will not retard, but promote, legitimate industrial and commercial expansion. Our growing power brings with it temptations and perils requiring constant vigilance to avoid. It must not be used to invite conflicts, nor for oppression, but for the more effective maintenance of those principles of equality and justice upon which our institutions and happiness depend. Let us keep always in mind that the foundation of our Government is liberty; its superstructure peace. WILLIAM McKINLEY.

EXECUTIVE MANSION,
Washington, December 4, 1900.
To the Senate and House of Representatives:

I transmit herewith, for the information of Congress, copy of a letter from the Commissioner-General of the United States to the Paris Exposition of 1900, of November 17, 1900, giving a detailed statement of the expenditures of the commission for the year ended November 15, 1900. WILLIAM McKINLEY.

EXECUTIVE MANSION,
Washington, December 6, 1900.
To the Senate and House of Representatives:

I transmit herewith the report from the Secretary of State and accompanying papers relating to the claim against the United States of the Russian subject, Gustav Isak Dahlberg, master and principal owner of the Russian bark *Hans,* based on his wrongful and illegal arrest and imprisonment by officers of the United States District Court for the southern district of Mississippi, and, in view of the opinion expressed by the Department of Justice that the said arrest and detention of the complainant were wrongful and without the authority of law, I recommend the appropriation by Congress of the sum of $5,000 to reimburse the master and owners of the vessel for all losses and damages incurred by reason of his said wrongful and illegal arrest and detention. WILLIAM McKINLEY.

EXECUTIVE MANSION,
Washington, December 6, 1900.

To the Congress of the United States:

I transmit herewith a report from the Secretary of State, with accompanying papers, in relation to the lynching, in La Salle County, Tex., on October 5, 1895, of Florentino Suaste, a Mexican citizen.

Following the course pursued in the case of the lynching of three Italian subjects at Hahnville, La., on August 8, 1896, and in that of the lynching of the Mexican citizen, Luis Moreno, at Yreka, Cal., in August, 1895, I recommend the appropriation by Congress, out of humane consideration, and without reference to the question of liability of the Government of the United States, of the sum of $2,000, to be paid by the Secretary of State to the Government of Mexico, and by that Government distributed to the heirs of the above-mentioned Florentino Suaste. WILLIAM McKINLEY.

EXECUTIVE MANSION, *January 3, 1901.*

To the Senate of the United States:

In reply to a resolution of the Senate of December 19, 1900, directing the Secretary of War "to transmit to the Senate the report of Abraham L. Lawshe, giving in detail the result of his investigations, made under the direction of the War Department, into the receipts and expenditures of Cuban funds," the Senate is informed that for the reasons stated in the accompanying communication from the Secretary of War, dated December 28, 1900, it is not deemed compatible with the public interest to transmit the report to the Senate at this time.

WILLIAM McKINLEY.

EXECUTIVE MANSION,
Washington, January 16, 1901.

To the Senate and House of Representatives:

I transmit herewith for the information of the Congress a letter from the Secretary of Agriculture, in which he presents a preliminary report of investigations upon the forests of the southern Appalachian Mountain region. Upon the basis of the facts established by this investigation the Secretary of Agriculture recommends the purchase of land for a national forest reserve in western North Carolina, eastern Tennessee, and adjacent States. I commend to the favorable consideration of Congress the reasons upon which this recommendation rests.

WILLIAM McKINLEY.

EXECUTIVE MANSION, *January 25, 1901.*

To the Senate and House of Representatives:

For the information of the Congress and with a view to such action on its part as it may deem wise and appropriate I transmit a report of the Secretary of War, made to me under date of January 24, 1901, containing the reports of the Taft commission, its several acts of legislation, and other important information relating to the conditions and immediate wants of the Philippine Islands.

I earnestly recommend legislation under which the government of the islands may have authority to assist in their peaceful industrial development in the directions indicated by the Secretary of War.

WILLIAM McKINLEY.

EXECUTIVE MANSION,
Washington, January 29, 1901.

To the Congress:

I transmit herewith a report from the Secretary of State relating to the treaty between the United States and Spain, signed at Washington, November 7, 1900, providing for the cession of any and all islands of the Philippine Archipelago lying outside of the lines described in Article III of the treaty of peace of December 10, 1898.

I recommend the appropriation by Congress during the present session of the sum of one hundred thousand dollars for the purpose of carrying out the obligations of the United States under the treaty.

WILLIAM McKINLEY.

EXECUTIVE MANSION,
Washington, January 29, 1901.

To the Congress:

I transmit herewith a report from the Secretary of State relating to the lynching of two Italian subjects at Tallulah, La., on July 20, 1899.

I renew the recommendation made in my annual message to the Congress on December 3, 1900, that in accordance with precedent Congress make gracious provision for indemnity to the families of the victims in the same form as heretofore.

WILLIAM McKINLEY.

EXECUTIVE MANSION,
Washington, January 29, 1901.

To the Senate and House of Representatives:

I transmit herewith a communication from the Secretary of State accompanying the Commercial Relations of the United States for the year 1900, being the annual and other reports of consular and diplomatic officers upon the industries and commerce of foreign countries, with particular reference to the growing share of the United States in international trade. The advance in the general efficiency of our consular service in promoting trade, which was noted in my message of March 1, 1900, transmitting the reports for 1899, was even more marked than last year. The promptitude with which the reports of the consuls are printed and distributed, the generous recognition which is being increasingly accorded by our business interests to the practical value of their efforts for enlarging trade, and the continued testimony of competent foreign authorities to the general superiority of their commercial work, have naturally had a stimulating effect upon its consular corps as a whole, and experience in the discharge of their duties adds greatly to their efficiency. It is gratifying to be able to state that the improvement in the service, following closely upon the steady progress in expediting the publication of reports, has enabled the Department of State this year to submit the annual reports a month in advance of the usual time, and to make them as nearly as possible a contemporaneous picture of the trade of the world. In view of the great importance of these reports to our producers, manufacturers, exporters, and business interest generally, I cordially approve the recommendation of the Secretary of State that Congress shall authorize the printing as heretofore of an edition of 10,000 copies of the summary, entitled "Review of the World's Commerce," and of 5,000 copies of Commercial Relations (including this summary), to be distributed by the Department of State.

WILLIAM McKINLEY.

EXECUTIVE MANSION, *February 14, 1901.*

To the Senate and House of Representatives:

During our recent war with Spain the United States naval force on the North Atlantic Station was charged with varied and important duties, chief among which were the maintenance of the blockade of Cuba, aiding the army, and landing troops and in subsequent operations, and particularly in the pursuit, blockade, and destruction of the Spanish Squadron under Admiral Cervera.

This naval campaign, embracing objects of wide scope and grave responsibilities, was conducted with great ability on the part of the commander-in-chief, and of the officers and enlisted men under his command. It culminated in the annihilation of the Spanish fleet in the battle of July 3, 1898, one of the most memorable naval engagements in history.

The result of this battle was the freeing of our Atlantic coast from the possibilities to which it had been exposed from Admiral Cervera's fleet, and the termination of the war upon the seas.

I recommend that, following our national precedents, especially that in the case of Admiral Dewey and the Asiatic Squadron, the thanks of Congress be given to Rear-Admiral William T. Sampson, United States Navy, and to the officers and men under his command for highly distinguished conduct in conflict with the enemy, and in carrying on the blockade and naval campaign on the Cuban coast, resulting in the destruction of the Spanish fleet at Santiago de Cuba July 3, 1898.

WILLIAM McKINLEY.

EXECUTIVE MANSION, *February 21, 1901.*
To the Senate and House of Representatives:

I transmit herewith, for the information of the Congress and with a view to its publication in suitable form, if such action is deemed desirable, a special report of the United States Board on Geographic Names, relating to geographic names in the Philippine Islands, and invite attention to the recommendation of the Board:

"That in addition to the usual number, there be printed 15,000 copies: 2,000 copies for the use of the Senate, 3,000 copies for the use of the House of Representatives, and 10,000 copies for distribution by the Board to the Executive Departments and the public."

WILLIAM McKINLEY.

EXECUTIVE MANSION,
Washington, February 26, 1901.
To the Congress:

I transmit herewith, for the consideration of Congress, in connection with my message of January 29, 1901, relative to the lynching of certain Italian subjects at Tallulah, La., a report by the Secretary of State touching a claim for $5,000 presented by the Italian ambassador at Washington on behalf of Gaiseppe Defina, on account of his being obliged to abandon his home and business.

WILLIAM McKINLEY.

EXECUTIVE MANSION,
Washington, February 28, 1901.
To the Senate and House of Representatives:

I transmit herewith, in pursuance of the act of Congress approved July 1, 1898 (U. S. Stat. L., vol. 30, pp. 645, 646), the report of Mr

Ferdinand W. Peck, commissioner-general of the United States to the International Exposition held at Paris, France, during the year 1900.

WILLIAM McKINLEY.

EXECUTIVE MANSION,
Washington, March 1, 1901.

To the House of Representatives:

I return herewith, without approval, House bill No. 3204, entitled "An act to refer certain claims for Indian depredations to the Court of Claims."

General relief has been extended to citizens who have lost property by reason of Indian depredations by the act of March 3, 1891, conferring jurisdiction upon the Court of Claims to hear and determine such cases. That act provides for payment for damages growing out of depredations committed by any Indian or Indians belonging to a band, tribe, or nation in amity with the United States, excluding from consideration all claims which originated during the existence of actual hostilities between the United States and the Indian tribe.

In making this discrimination the act of 1891 follows the general principle which has been asserted in all general legislation which has ever been enacted for the payment of claims for property destroyed by Indians. The first act which promised such indemnity, that of May 19, 1796, contained the same restriction, and it was reported in every subsequent general act of Congress dealing with the subject. This policy, which has been clearly manifested from the beginning, is in accord with the recognized principle that the nation is not liable for damage to the private property of its citizens caused by the act of the public enemy. This statute has been thoroughly considered by the Court of Claims and by the Supreme Court and its interpretation fixed, and it has been declared to be in accord not only with the policy of Congress as expressed through the legislation of the century, but with the general principles of international law.

I am informed that the records of the Court of Claims show that the claims of four of the five beneficiaries named in the present bill have been presented to that court under the general law and decided adversely, the court having held that a state of war existed between the United States and the Sioux Indians in the year 1862 when the claims arose. The remaining claim, which originated under the same circumstances and at the same time, would, of course, be subject to the same defense if presented.

The bill provides that these claims shall be sent back to the Court of Claims for trial according to the principles and rules which governed the commission appointed under the act of February 16, 1863. That act which was a special act relating to losses occurring during the hostilities of the previous year, did not, of course, impose the requirement of amity, the claims allowed by the commission being paid out of the funds belonging to the hostile Indians sequestered by the statute. The effect of this bill, if it became a law, would be to provide for the payment out of the Treasury of the United States of these claims which were not presented for payment out of the Indian funds and which have been rejected by the courts under the general law. There are many hundreds of cases, aggregating a large amount claimed, which have been filed in the Court of Claims, but which are excluded from its jurisdiction for the same reason which necessitated the dismissal of the petitions filed by these claimants. There is no legal obligation on the part of the United States, and no promise, express or implied, for the payment of such claims.

The measure of governmental liability is fulfilled by the passage of the act of March 3, 1891, and the prompt payment of the judgments rendered thereunder. To single out for payment a few claims of this large class to the exclusion of all others would, in my judgment, be unjust; and such action would also with reason be cited as a precedent for extending governmental aid in all similar cases.

For the reasons given I am constrained to withhold my approval from the bill.   WILLIAM McKINLEY.

EXECUTIVE MANSION, *March 1, 1901.*
To the House of Representatives:

I transmit herewith a report from the Secretary of State in response to the resolution of the House of Representatives of February 19, 1901, requesting him to furnish that body "all the information in the possession of the State Department relating to the shipment of horses and mules from New Orleans in large numbers for the use of the British army in the war in South Africa."

WILLIAM McKINLEY.

EXECUTIVE MANSION,
Washington, March 2, 1901.
To the House of Representatives:

I return herewith, without approval, House bill No. 321, entitled "An act for the relief of the legal representative of Samuel Tewksbury, deceased."

This bill provides for the payment to the legal representative of Samuel Tewksbury, late of Scranton, Allegheny County, Pa., the sum of $5,697 in full compensation for the use and occupation by the United States Government of the brick building and premises owned by him in the city of Scranton, Pa., as a depot or barracks for United States

troops by the Provost Marshal of the United States from June, 1862, to June, 1865, inclusive.

The records of the War Department show that about April 26, 1865, Col. J. G. Johnson, Chief Quartermaster, forwarded to the office of the Quartermaster-General a claim of Samuel Tewksbury for use of a building at Scranton, Pa., from February 24, 1864, to February 3, 1865, stated at $1,133.33, and damage to said building at $1,400, total $2,533.33.

In forwarding these papers Colonel Johnson states as follows:

In the spring of 1864 Mr. Samuel Tewksbury presented to me through his agents a claim against the United States Government for use of the premises mentioned in the enclosed account accompanying the papers.

I learn from Mr. S. N. Bradford, Provost Marshal of the Twelfth District of Pennsylvania at Scranton, that lodgings were furnished to persons in military service at that place by Gardiner and Atkinson under a contract with the Provost Marshal, also that the contractors rented the building used for the above purpose from Mr. Tewksbury.

Considering it a matter entirely between that gentleman and his tenants, Messrs. Gardiner and Atkinson, I at that time refused to take any action in the matter whatever.

The claim was again submitted to the office of the Quartermaster-General on September 30, 1865, by Major W. B. Lane, and was returned on May 1, 1866, with the information that the United States had already paid for lodging of the troops under the control of the Provost Marshal at Scranton, Pa., during the time for which charge for rent is made.

The claimant was referred to the officer or person by whom the building was taken for compensation for its use. No other record of this case is found in the War Department, although it will be observed that the bill covers a period from June, 1862, to June, 1865, inclusive, while the claim as originally presented to the War Department was for occupancy of the building at Scranton, Pa., from February 24, 1864, to February 3, 1865.

It thus appears that when this claim was originally presented it was examined by the proper representative of the Government, and was rejected; that no such use and occupation as the United States Government had of claimant's building was under a contract between the Government and the tenants of claimant, and that payment therefor was duly made by the Government. Now after a lapse of some thirty-seven years the period of use and occupation covered by the claim has increased threefold, and the compensation asked therefor has more than doubled. Under the circumstances of this case I do not feel at liberty to approve the bill.   WILLIAM McKINLEY.

PRESIDENT McKINLEY'S SECOND INAUGURAL ADDRESS.

My Fellow-Citizens:

When we assembled here on the 4th of March, 1897, there was great anxiety with regard to our currency and credit. None exists now. Then our Treasury receipts were inadequate to meet the current obligations of the Government. Now they are sufficient for all public needs, and we have a surplus instead of a deficit. Then I felt constrained to convene the Congress in extraordinary session to devise revenues to pay the ordinary expenses of the Government. Now I have the satisfaction to announce that the Congress just closed has reduced taxation in the sum of $41,000,000. Then there was deep solicitude because of the long depression in our manufacturing, mining, agricultural, and mercantile industries and the consequent distress of our laboring population. Now every avenue of production is crowded with activity, labor is well employed, and American products find good markets at home and abroad.

Our diversified productions, however, are increasing in such unprecedented volume as to admonish us of the necessity of still further enlarging our foreign markets by broader commercial relations. For this purpose reciprocal trade arrangements with other nations should in liberal spirit be carefully cultivated and promoted.

The national verdict of 1896 has for the most part been executed. Whatever remains unfulfilled is a continuing obligation resting with undiminished force upon the Executive and the Congress. But fortunate as our condition is, its permanence can only be assured by sound business methods and strict economy in national administration and legislation. We should not permit our great prosperity to lead us to reckless ventures in business or profligacy in public expenditures. While the Congress determines the objects and the sum of appropriations, the officials of the executive departments are responsible for honest and faithful disbursement, and it should be their constant care to avoid waste and extravagance.

Honesty, capacity, and industry are nowhere more indispensable than in public employment. These should be fundamental requisites to original appointment and the surest guaranties against removal.

Four years ago we stood on the brink of war without the people knowing it and without any preparation or effort at preparation for the impending peril. I did all that in honor could be done to avert the war, but without avail. It became inevitable; and the Congress at its first regular session, without party division, provided money in anticipation of the crisis and in preparation to meet it. It came.

The result was signally favorable to American arms and in the highest degree honorable to the Government. It imposed upon us obligations from which we cannot escape and from which it would be dishonorable to seek escape. We are now at peace with the world, and it is my fervent prayer that if differences arise between us and other powers they may be settled by peaceful arbitration and that hereafter we may be spared the horrors of war.

Intrusted by the people for a second time with the office of President, I enter upon its administration appreciating the great responsibilities which attach to this renewed honor and commission, promising unreserved devotion on my part to their faithful discharge and reverently invoking for my guidance the direction and favor of Almighty God. I should shrink from the duties this day assumed if I did not feel that in their performance I should have the co-operation of the wise and patriotic men of all parties. It encourages me for the great task which I now undertake to believe that those who voluntarily committed to me the trust imposed upon the Chief Executive of the Republic will give to me generous support in my duties to "preserve, protect, and defend, the Constitution of the United States" and to "care that the laws be faithfully executed." The national purpose is indicated through a national election. It is the constitutional method of ascertaining the public will. When once it is registered it is a law to us all, and faithful observance should follow its decrees.

Strong hearts and helpful hands are needed, and, fortunately, we have them in every part of our beloved country. We are reunited. Sectionalism has disappeared. Division on public questions can no longer be traced by the war maps of 1861. These old differences less and less disturb the judgment. Existing problems demand the thought and quicken the conscience of the country, and the responsibility for their presence, as well as for their righteous settlement, rests upon us all — no more upon me than upon you. There are some national questions in the solution of which patriotism should exclude partisanship. Magnifying their difficulties will not take them off our hands nor facilitate their adjustment. Distrust of the capacity, integrity, and high purposes of the American people will not be an inspiring theme for future political contests. Dark pictures and gloomy forebodings are worse than useless. These only becloud, they do not help to point the way of safety and honor. "Hope maketh not ashamed." The prophets of evil were not the builders of the Republic, nor in its crises since have they saved or served it. The faith of the fathers was a mighty force in its creation, and the faith of their descendants has wrought its progress and furnished its defenders. They are obstructionists who despair, and who would destroy confidence in the ability of our people to solve wisely and for civilization the mighty problems resting upon them. The American people, intrenched in freedom at home, take their love for it with them wherever they go, and they reject as mistaken and unworthy the doctrine that we lose our own liberties by securing the enduring foundations of liberty to others. Our institutions will not deteriorate by extension, and our sense of justice will not abate under tropic suns in distant seas. As heretofore, so hereafter will the nation demonstrate its fitness to administer any new estate which events devolve upon it, and in the fear of God will "take occasion by the hand and make the bounds of freedom wider yet." If there are those among us who would make our way more difficult, we must not be disheartened, but the more earnestly dedicate ourselves to the task upon which we have rightly entered. The path of progress is seldom smooth. New things are often found hard to do. Our fathers found them so. We find them so. They are inconvenient. They cost us something. But are we not made better for the effort and sacrifice, and are not those we serve lifted up and blessed?

We will be consoled, too, with the fact that opposition has confronted every onward movement of the Republic from its opening hour until now, but without success. The Republic has marched on and on, and its step has exalted freedom and humanity. We are undergoing the same ordeal as did our predecessors nearly a century ago. We are following the course they blazed. They triumphed. Will their successors falter and plead organic impotency in the nation? Surely after 125 years of achievement for mankind we will not now surrender our equality with other powers on matters fundamental and essential to nationality. With no such purpose was the nation created. In no such spirit has it developed its full and independent sovereignty. We adhere to the principle of equality among ourselves, and by no act of ours will we assign to ourselves a subordinate rank in the family of nations.

My fellow-citizens, the public events of the past four years have gone into history. They are too near to justify recital. Some of them were unforeseen; many of them momentous and far-reaching in their consequences to ourselves and our relations with the rest of the world. The part which the United States bore so honorably in the thrilling scenes in China, while new to American life, has been in harmony with its true spirit and best traditions, and in dealing with the results its policy will be that of moderation and fairness.

We face at this moment a most important question—that of the future relations of the United States and Cuba. With our near neighbors we must remain close friends. The declaration of the purposes of this Government in the resolution of April 20, 1898, must be made good. Ever since the evacuation of the island by the army of Spain the Executive, with all practicable speed, has been assisting its people in the successive steps necessary to the establishment of a free and independent government prepared to assume and perform the obligations of international law which now rest upon the United States under the treaty of Paris. The convention elected by the people to frame a constitution is approaching the completion of its labors. The transfer of American control to the new government is of such great importance, involving an obligation resulting from our intervention and the treaty of peace, that I am glad to be advised by the recent act of Congress of the policy which the legislative branch of the Government deems essential to the best interests of Cuba and the United States. The principles which led to our intervention require that the fundamental law upon which the new government rests should be adapted to secure a government capable of performing the duties and discharging the functions of a separate nation, of observing its international obligations of protecting life and property, insuring order, safety, and liberty, and conforming to the established and historical policy of the United States in its relation to Cuba.

The peace which we are pledged to leave to the Cuban people must carry with it the guaranties of permanence. We became sponsors for the pacification of the island, and we remain accountable to the Cubans, no less than to our own country and people, for the reconstruction of Cuba as a free commonwealth on abiding foundations of right, justice, liberty, and assured order. Our enfranchisement of the people will not be completed until free Cuba shall "be a reality, not a name; a perfect entity, not a hasty experiment bearing within itself the elements of failure."

While the treaty of peace with Spain was ratified on the 6th of February, 1899, and ratifications were exchanged nearly two years ago, the Congress has indicated no form of government for the Philippine Islands. It has, however, provided an army to enable the Executive to suppress insurrection, restore peace, give security to the inhabitants, and establish the authority of the United States throughout the archipelago. It has authorized the organization of native troops as auxiliary to the regular force. It has been advised from time to time of the acts of the military and naval officers in the islands, of my action in appointing civil commissions, of the instructions with which they were charged, of their duties and powers, of their recommendations, and of their several acts under executive commission, together with the very complete general information they have submitted. These reports fully set forth the conditions, past and present, in the islands, and the instructions clearly show the principles which will guide the Executive until the Congress shall, as it is required to do by the treaty, determine "the civil rights and political status of the native inhabitants." The Congress having added the sanction of its authority to the powers already possessed and exercised by the Executive under the Constitution, thereby leaving with the Executive the responsibility for the government of the Philippines, I shall continue the efforts already begun until order shall be restored throughout the islands, and as fast as conditions permit will establish local governments, in the formation of which the full co-operation of the people has been already invited, and when established will encourage the people to administer them. The settled purpose, long ago proclaimed, to afford the inhabitants of the islands self-government as fast as they were ready for it will be pursued with earnestness and fidelity. Already something has been accomplished in this direction. The Government's representatives, civil and military, are doing faithful and noble work in their mission of emancipation and merit the approval and support of their countrymen. The most liberal terms of amnesty have already been communicated to the insurgents, and the way is still open for those who have raised their arms against the Government for honorable submission to its authority. Our countrymen should not be deceived. We are not waging war against the inhabitants of the Philippine Islands. A portion of them are making war against the United States. By far the greater part of the inhabitants recognize American sovereignty and welcome it as a guaranty of order and of security for life, property, liberty, freedom of conscience, and the pursuit of happiness. To them full protection will be given. They shall not be abandoned. We will not leave the destiny of the loyal millions in the islands to the disloyal thousands who are in rebellion against the United States. Order under civil institutions will come as soon as those who now break the peace shall keep it. Force will not be needed or used when those who make war against us shall make it no more. May it end without further bloodshed, and there be ushered in the reign of peace to be made permanent by a government of liberty under law!

MARCH 4, 1901.

PROCLAMATIONS.

___

BY THE PRESIDENT OF THE UNITED STATES OF AMERICA.

A PROCLAMATION.

Whereas public interests require that the Congress of the United States should be convened in extra session at twelve o'clock on the 15th day of March, 1897, to receive such communication as may be made by the Executive:

Now, therefore, I, William McKinley, President of the United States of America, do hereby proclaim and declare that an extraordinary occasion requires the Congress of the United States to convene in extra session at the Capitol in the city of Washington on the 15th day of March, 1897, at twelve o'clock, noon, of which all persons who shall at that time be entitled to act as members thereof, are hereby required to take notice.

Given under my hand and the seal of the United States at Washington the 6th day of March in the year of our Lord one thousand eight hundred and ninety-seven, and of the Independence of the United States the one hundred and twenty-first.

[SEAL.]

WILLIAM McKINLEY.

By the President:

JOHN SHERMAN,
Secretary of State.

BY THE PRESIDENT OF THE UNITED STATES.

THANKSGIVING PROCLAMATION.

In remembrance of God's goodness to us during the past year, which has been so abundant, "let us offer unto Him our thanksgiving and pay our vows unto the Most High." Under His watchful providence industry has prospered, the conditions of labor have been improved, the rewards of the husbandman have been increased, and the comforts of our homes multiplied. His mighty hand has preserved peace and protected the nation. Respect for law and order has been strengthened, love of free institutions cherished, and all sections of our beloved country brought into closer bonds of fraternal regard and generous co-operation.

For these great benefits it is our duty to praise the Lord in a spirit of humility and gratitude and to offer up to Him our most earnest supplications.   That we may acknowledge our obligation as a people to Him who has so graciously granted us the blessings of free government and material prosperity, I, William McKinley, President of the United States, do hereby designate and set apart Thursday, the twenty-fifth day of November, for national thanksgiving and prayer, which all of the people are invited to observe with appropriate religious services in their respective places of worship.   On this day of rejoicing and domestic reunion let our prayers ascend to the Giver of every good and perfect gift for the continuance of His love and favor to us, that our hearts may be filled with charity and good will, and we may be ever worthy of His beneficent concern.

In witness whereof I have hereunto set my hand and caused the seal of the United States to be affixed.

Done at the city of Washington this 29th day of October, in the year of our Lord one thousand eight hundred and ninety-[SEAL.]   seven, and of the Independence of the United States the one hundred and twenty-second.

WILLIAM McKINLEY.

By the President:
   JOHN SHERMAN,
         Secretary of State.

BY THE PRESIDENT OF THE UNITED STATES OF AMERICA.

A PROCLAMATION.

Whereas satisfactory proof has been given me that vessels of the United States in ballast which proceed to Mexico with the object of devoting themselves to pearl fishery and fishing on the Mexican coasts or for the purpose of receiving and carrying passengers and mail or of loading cattle, wood, or any other Mexican product and which shall go directly to ports open to general commerce so that thence they may be dispatched to their destination, and steam vessels of the United States are exempted from tonnage duties in Mexican ports;

Now, therefore, I, William McKinley, President of the United States of America, by virtue of the authority vested in me by the act of Congress approved July 24, 1897, entitled "An act to authorize the President to suspend discriminating duties imposed on foreign vessels and commerce," do hereby declare and proclaim that from and after the date of this, my proclamation, Mexican vessels in ballast which proceed to the United States with the object of fishing on the coast thereof or for the purpose of receiving and carrying passengers and mail or of loading cattle, wood, or any other product of the United States and which shall go directly to ports open to general commerce so that thence they may

PANAMA CANAL: THE CULEBRA CUT

THE PANAMA CANAL.

The commencement of the task of constructing the Panama Canal was the most important event of Roosevelt's Administration. The history of the undertaking is written by Roosevelt himself on pages 6662, 6758, 6881, 6901, 7401, 7480, 7611, 7648, 7667, 7685 and 7728. The message commencing on page 7685 describes his visit of inspection to the canal zone. President Taft continued the narrative, pages 7750, 7754, 7803, 7863 and 7898. The reader who desires a brief recital of the facts should refer to the article entitled "Panama Canal" in the encyclopedic index. The index references following this article will enable the reader to glean a complete and authentic knowledge of the subject from the messages of the Presidents, from Jackson to Taft, who have discussed the project.

The Culebra Cut, nine miles in strength, lies between Bas Obispo and the Pedro Miguel lock, and represents the greatest engineering difficulty in the construction of the Panama Canal. Five of its nine miles' length lie between a range of hills, much of whose soil is volcanic ash, which is unstable, and which hence has frequently caused slides, blocking the canal. The early French attempts at a canal had cut away the soil to a depth of 160 feet above sea level, but 120 more of those feet were removed before Uncle Sam was finished with the Cut.

be despatched to their destination, and Mexican steam vessels shall be exempted from the payment of the tonnage duties imposed by section 4219 of the Revised Statutes of the United States.

And this proclamation shall remain in force and effect until otherwise ordered by the President of the United States.

In witness whereof I have set my hand and caused the seal of the United States to be hereunto affixed.

Done at the city of Washington this 12th day of November, in the year of our Lord one thousand eight hundred and ninety-seven, and of the Independence of the United States the one hundred and twenty-second.

[SEAL.]

WILLIAM McKINLEY.

By the President:
    JOHN SHERMAN,
        Secretary of State.

BY THE PRESIDENT OF THE UNITED STATES OF AMERICA.

A PROCLAMATION.

Whereas by a joint resolution passed by the Congress and approved April 20, 1898,* and communicated to the Government of Spain, it was demanded that said Government at once relinquish its authority and government in the island of Cuba and withdraw its land and naval forces from Cuba and Cuban waters, and the President of the United States was directed and empowered to use the entire land and naval forces of the United States and to call into the actual service of the United States the militia of the several States to such extent as might be necessary to carry said resolution into effect; and

Whereas in carrying into effect said resolution the President of the United States deems it necessary to set on foot and maintain a blockade of the north coast of Cuba, including all ports on said coast between Cardenas and Bahia Honda, and the port of Cienfuegos. on the south coast of Cuba:

Now, therefore, I, William McKinley, President of the United States, in order to enforce the said resolution, do hereby declare and proclaim that the United States of America have instituted and will maintain a blockade of the north coast of Cuba, including ports on said coast between Cardenas and Bahia Honda, and the port of Cienfuegos, on the south coast of Cuba, aforesaid, in pursuance of the laws of the United States and the law of nations applicable to such cases. An efficient force will be posted so as to prevent the entrance and exit of vessels from the ports aforesaid. Any neutral vessel approaching any of said

* See pp. 6297-6298.

ports or attempting to leave the same without notice or knowledge of the establishment of such blockade will be duly warned by the commander of the blockading forces, who will indorse on her register the fact and the date of such warning, where such indorsement was made; and if the same vessel shall again attempt to enter any blockaded port she will be captured and sent to the nearest and convenient port for such proceedings against her and her cargo as prize as may be deemed advisable.

Neutral vessels lying in any of said ports at the time of the establishment of such blockade will be allowed thirty days to issue therefrom.

In witness whereof I have hereunto set my hand and caused the seal of the United States to be affixed.

Done at the city of Washington, this 22d day of April, [SEAL.] A. D., 1898, and of the Independence of the United States the one hundred and twenty-second.

WILLIAM McKINLEY.

By the President:
JOHN SHERMAN,
Secretary of State.

BY THE PRESIDENT OF THE UNITED STATES.

A PROCLAMATION.

Whereas a joint resolution of Congress was approved on the 20th day of April, 1898,* entitled "Joint resolution for the recognition of the independence of the people of Cuba, demanding that the Government of Spain relinquish its authority and government in the island of Cuba and to withdraw its land and naval forces from Cuba and Cuban waters, and directing the President of the United States to use the land and naval forces of the United States to carry these resolutions into effect;" and

Whereas by an act of Congress entitled "An act to provide for temporarily increasing the military establishment of the United States in time of war, and for other purposes," approved April 22, 1898, the President is authorized, in order to raise a volunteer army, to issue his proclamation calling for volunteers to serve in the Army of the United States:

Now, therefore, I, William McKinley, President of the United States, by virtue of the power vested in me by the Constitution and the laws, and deeming sufficient occasion to exist, have thought fit to call forth, and hereby do call forth, volunteers to the aggregate number of 125,000 in order to carry into effect the purpose of the said resolution, the same

* See pp. 6297–6298.

to be apportioned, as far as practicable, among the several States and Territories and the District of Columbia according to population and to serve for two years unless sooner discharged. The details for this object will be immediately communicated to the proper authorities through the War Department.

In witness whereof I have hereunto set my hand and caused the seal of the United States to be affixed.

Done at the city of Washington, this 23d day of April, [SEAL.] A. D. 1898, and of the Independence of the United States the one hundred and twenty-second.

WILLIAM McKINLEY.

By the President:
JOHN SHERMAN,
Secretary of State.

BY THE PRESIDENT OF THE UNITED STATES OF AMERICA.

A PROCLAMATION.

Whereas by an act of Congress approved April 25, 1898,* it is declared that war exists and that war has existed since the 21st day of April, A. D. 1898, including said day, between the United States of America and the Kingdom of Spain; and

Whereas, it being desirable that such war should be conducted upon principles in harmony with the present views of nations and sanctioned by their recent practice, it has already been announced that the policy of this Government will be not to resort to privateering, but to adhere to the rules of the Declaration of Paris:

Now, therefore, I, William McKinley, President of the United States of America, by virtue of the power vested in me by the Constitution and the laws, do hereby declare and proclaim:

1. The neutral flag covers enemy's goods with the exception of contraband of war.

2. Neutral goods not contraband of war are not liable to confiscation under the enemy's flag.

3. Blockades in order to be binding must be effective.

4. Spanish merchant vessels in any ports or places within the United States shall be allowed till May 21, 1898, inclusive, for loading their cargoes and departing from such ports or places; and such Spanish merchant vessels, if met at sea by any United States ship, shall be permitted to continue their voyage if on examination of their papers it shall appear that their cargoes were taken on board before the expiration of the above term: *Provided,* That nothing herein contained shall

* See p. 6348

apply to Spanish vessels having on board any officer in the military or naval service of the enemy, or any coal (except such as may be necessary for their voyage), or any other article prohibited or contraband of war, or any dispatch of or to the Spanish Government.

5. Any Spanish merchant vessel which prior to April 21, 1898, shall have sailed from any foreign port bound for any port or place in the United States shall be permitted to enter such port or place and to discharge her cargo, and afterwards forthwith to depart without molestation; and any such vessel, if met at sea by any United States ship, shall be permitted to continue her voyage to any port not blockaded.

6. The right of search is to be exercised with strict regard for the rights of neutrals, and the voyages of mail steamers are not to be interfered with except on the clearest grounds of suspicion of a violation of law in respect of contraband or blockade.

In witness whereof I have hereunto set my hand and caused the seal of the United States to be affixed.

Done at the city of Washington on the 26th day of April,
[SEAL.]   A. D. 1898, and of the Independence of the United States the one hundred and twenty-second.

WILLIAM McKINLEY.

By the President:
Alvey A. Adee,
Acting Secretary of State.

By the President of the United States of America.

A PROCLAMATION.

Whereas it is provided by section twenty-four of the act of Congress, approved March third, eighteen hundred and ninety-one, entitled, "An act to repeal timber-culture laws, and for other purposes." "That the President of the United States may, from time to time, set apart and reserve, in any State or Territory having public land bearing forests, in any part of the public lands wholly or in part covered with timber or undergrowth, whether of commercial value or not, as public reservations, and the President shall, by public proclamation, declare the establishment of such reservations and the limits thereof;"

And whereas, the public lands in the Territory of Arizona, within the limits hereinafter described, are in part covered with timber, and it appears that the public good would be promoted by setting apart and reserving said lands as a public reservation;

Now, therefore, I, William McKinley, President of the United States, by virtue of the power in me vested by section twenty-four of the aforesaid act of Congress. do hereby make known and proclaim that there is hereby reserved from entry or settlement and set apart as a Public Reservation all those certain tracts, pieces, or parcels of land lying and being situate in the Territory of Arizona, and within the boundaries particularly described as follows, to wit:

Beginning at the northeast corner of Section twelve (12), Township thirteen (13) North, Range three (3) West, Gila and Salt River Meridian, Arizona; thence southerly along the range line to the point for the southeast corner of Section twenty-five (25), said Township; thence westerly along the unsurveyed section line to the point for the southwest corner of Section twenty-eight (28), said Township; thence northerly alone the unsurveyed section line to the point for the northwest corner of Section nine (9), said Township; thence easterly along the unsurveyed and surveyed section line to the northeast corner of Section twelve (12), said Township, the place of beginning.

Excepting from the force and effect of this proclamation all lands which may have been, prior to the date hereof, embraced in any legal entry or covered by any lawful filing duly of record in the proper United States Land Office, or upon which any valid settlement has been made pursuant to law, and the statutory period within which to make entry or filing of record has not expired; and all mining claims duly located and held according to the laws of the United States and rules and regulations not in conflict therewith;

Provided, that this exception shall not continue to apply to any particular tract of land unless the entryman, settler, or claimant continues to comply with the law under which the entry, filing, settlement, or location was made.

Warning is hereby expressly given to all persons not to enter or make settlement upon the tract of land reserved by this proclamation.

In witness whereof I have hereunto set my hand and caused the seal of the United States to be affixed.

Done at the city of Washington, this 10th day of May, in the year of our Lord one thousand eight hundred and ninety-eight,
[SEAL.]   and of the Independence of the United States the one hundred and twenty-second.

WILLIAM McKINLEY.

By the President:
WILLIAM R. DAY,
Secretary of State.

By the President of the United States.

A PROCLAMATION.

Whereas an act of Congress was approved on the 25th day of April, 1898,* entitled "An act declaring that war exists between the United States of America and the Kingdom of Spain;" and

Whereas by an act of Congress entitled "An act to provide for temporarily increasing the military establishment of the United States in time of war and for other purposes," approved April 22, 1898, the President is authorized, in order to raise a volunteer army, to issue his proclamation calling for volunteers to serve in the Army of the United States:

Now, therefore, I, William McKinley, President of the United States, by virtue of the power vested in me by the Constitution and the laws, and deeming sufficient occasion to exist, have thought fit to call forth, and hereby do call forth, volunteers to the aggregate number of 75,000 in addition to the volunteers called forth by my proclamation of the 23d of April, in the present year,† the same to be apportioned, as far as practicable, among the several States and Territories and the District of Columbia according to population and to serve for two years unless sooner discharged. The proportion of each arm and the details of enlistment or organization will be made known through the War Department.

In witness whereof I have hereunto set my hand and caused the seal of the United States to be affixed.

Done at the city of Washington, this 25th day of May,
[SEAL.] A. D. 1898, and of the Independence of the United States
the one hundred and twenty-second.

WILLIAM McKINLEY.

By the President:
WILLIAM R. DAY,
Secretary of State.

By the President of the United States of America.

A PROCLAMATION.

Whereas it is provided by section twenty-four of the act of Congress approved March third, eighteen hundred and ninety-one, entitled, "An act to repeal timber-culture laws, and for other purposes," "That the President of the United States may, from time to time, set apart and reserve, in any State or Territory having public land bearing forests, in any part of the public lands wholly or in part covered with timber or undergrowth, whether of commercial value or not, as public reservations, and the President shall, by public proclamation, declare the establishment of such reservations and the limits thereof;''

And whereas it is further provided by the act of Congress, approved June fourth, eighteen hundred and ninety-seven, entitled, ''An act making appropriations for sundry civil expenses of the Government for the fiscal year ending June thirtieth, eighteen hundred and ninety-eight, and for other purposes,'' that '' The President is hereby authorized at any time to modify any executive order that has been or may hereafter be made establishing any forest reserve, and by such modification may reduce the area or change the boundary lines of such reserve, or may vacate altogether any order creating such reserve;''

And whereas the public lands in the Territory of New Mexico, within the limits hereinafter described, are in part covered with timber, and it appears that the public good would be promoted by setting apart and reserving said lands as a public reservation;

Now, therefore, I, William McKinley, President of the United States, by virtue of the power in me vested by the aforesaid acts of Congress, do hereby make known and proclaim that the boundary lines of the Forest Reservation in the Territory of New Mexico, known as ''The Pecos River Forest Reserve,'' created by proclamation of January eleventh, eighteen hundred and ninety-two, are hereby so changed and enlarged as to include all those certain tracts, pieces, or parcels of land lying and being situate in the Territory of New Mexico, and within the boundaries particularly described as follows, to wit:

Beginning at the southwest corner of Township seventeen (17) North, Range thirteen (13) East, New Mexico Principal Meridian, New Mexico; thence easterly along the Fourth (4th) Standard Parallel North, to its intersection with the west boundary line of the Las Vegas Grant; thence northerly along the west boundary lines of the Las Vegas and Mora Grants to the point of intersection with the southeast boundary line of the Rancho del Rio Grande Grant; thence along the boundary line of said grant in a southwesterly direction to the most southerly point thereof; thence southerly to the line of the Santa Barbary Grant; thence southeasterly and southerly to the southeast corner thereof; thence westerly along the south boundary line of said grant to the southwest corner thereof, and continuing westerly to the east boundary line of the Las Trampas Grant; thence in a general southwesterly direction following the boundary lines of the Las Trampas, Las Truchas, and San Fernando Santiago Grants to the point of intersection with the unsurveyed range line between Ranges ten (10) and eleven (11) East; thence southerly along the range line to the point for the southwest corner of Section eighteen (18), Fractional Township sixteen (16) North, Range eleven (11) East; thence easterly along the unsurveyed section line to the point for the southeast corner of Section thirteen (13), said town-ship; thence northerly along the range line to the northeast corner of Township seventeen (17) North, Range eleven (11) East; thence east-erly along the township line to the southeast corner of Township eighteen (18) North, Range twelve (12) East; thence southerly along the range line to the southwest corner of Township seventeen (17) North, Range thirteen (13) East, the place of beginning.

Excepting from the force and effect of this proclamation all lands which may have been, prior to the date hereof, embraced in any legal entry or covered by any lawful filing duly of record in the proper United States Land Office, or upon which any valid settlement has been made pursuant to law, and the statutory period within which to make entry or filing of record has not expired; and all mining claims duly located and held according to the laws of the United States and rules and regu-lations not in conflict therewith;

Provided, that this exception shall not continue to apply to any par-ticular tract of land unless the entryman, settler, or claimant continues to comply with the law under which the entry, filing, settlement, or loca-tion was made.

Warning is hereby expressly given to all persons not to enter or make settlement upon the tract of land reserved by this proclamation.

In witness whereof I have hereunto set my hand and caused the seal of the United States to be affixed.

Done at the city of Washington, this 27th day of May, in the year of our Lord one thousand eight hundred and ninety-eight, [SEAL.]   and of the Independence of the United States the one hun-dred and twenty-second.

WILLIAM McKINLEY.

By the President:
    J. B. MOORE,
        Acting Secretary of State.

BY THE PRESIDENT OF THE UNITED STATES OF AMERICA.

A PROCLAMATION.

Whereas pursuant to section 3 of the act of Congress approved July 24, 1897, entitled "An Act to provide revenue for the Government and to encourage the industries of the United States," the Governments of the United States and of the French Republic have in the spirit of amity, and with a desire to improve their commercial relations, entered into a Commercial Agreement in which reciprocal and equivalent con-cessions have been in the judgment of the President secured according to the provisions of said section, whereby the following articles of commerce, being the products and manufactures of the United States, are to be admitted into France on and after the 1st day of June, 1898, at the minimum rate of duty, not exceeding the rates respectively appearing in the following table, namely:

Canned meats	15	francs per 100 kilogs
Table fruits, fresh:		
Lemons, oranges, cedrats and their varieties not mentioned	5	" " " "
Mandarin oranges	10	" " " "
Common table grapes	8	" " " "
Apples and pears:		
For the table	2	" " " "
For cider and perry	1. 50	" " " "
Other fruits except hothouse grapes and fruits	3	" " " "
Fruits dried or pressed (excluding raisins):		
Apples and pears:		
For the table	10	" " " "
For cider and perry	4	" " " "
Prunes	10	" " " "
Other fruits	5	" " " "
Common woods, logs	0. 65	" " " "
Sawed or squared timber 80 mm. or more in thickness	1	" " " "
Squared or sawed lumber exceeding 35 mm. and less than 80 mm. in thickness	1. 25	" " " "
Wood sawed 35 mm. or less in thickness	1. 75	" " " "
Paving blocks	1. 75	" " " "
Staves	0. 75	" " " "
Hops	30	" " " "
Apples and pears crushed, or cut and dried	1. 50	" " " "
Manufactured and prepared Pork meats	5c	" " " "
Lard and its compounds	25	" " " "

Therefore, in further execution of the provisions of said section it is hereby declared that on and after the 1st day of June, 1898, and during the continuance in force of the Agreement aforesaid, and until otherwise declared, the imposition and collection of the duties heretofore imposed and collected upon the following named articles, the products of France, by virtue of said act are hereby suspended, and in place thereof the duties shall be imposed and collected thereon according to the provisions of said section 3 as follows:

On argols, or crude tartar, or wine lees, crude, five *per centum ad valorem.*

On brandies, or other spirits manufactured or distilled from grain or other materials, one dollar and seventy-five cents per proof gallon.

On paintings in oil or water colors, pastels, pen and ink drawings, and statuary, fifteen *per centum ad valorem.*

It is further declared that the rates of duty heretofore imposed and collected on still wines and vermuth, the product of France, under the provisions of the United States Tariff Act of 1897 are conditionally suspended, and in place thereof shall be imposed and collected on and after the 1st day of June next as follows, namely:

On still wines and vermuth, in casks, thirty-five cents per gallon; in bottles or jugs, per case of one dozen bottles or jugs containing each not more than one quart and more than one pint, or twenty-four bottles or jugs containing each not more than one pint, one dollar and twenty-five cents per case, and any excess beyond these quantities found in such bottles or jugs shall be subject to a duty of four cents per pint or fractional part thereof, but no separate or additional duty shall be assessed upon the bottles or jugs.

Now, therefore, be it known that I, William McKinley, President of the United States of America, have caused the above stated modifications of the customs duties of the respective countries to be made public for the information of the citizens of the United States of America.

In testimony whereof I have hereunto set my hand and caused the seal of the United States to be affixed.

Done at the city of Washington, this 30th day of May, one thousand eight hundred and ninety-eight, and of the Independence [SEAL.] of the United States of America the one hundred and twenty-second.

WILLIAM McKINLEY.

By the President:
WILLIAM R. DAY,
Secretary of State.

BY THE PRESIDENT OF THE UNITED STATES OF AMERICA.

A PROCLAMATION.

Whereas, for the reasons set forth in my proclamation of April 22, 1898,* a blockade of the ports on the northern coast of Cuba from Cardenas to Bahia Honda, inclusive, and of the port of Cienfuegos, on the south coast of Cuba, was declared to have been instituted; and

Whereas it has become desirable to extend the blockade to other Spanish ports:

Now, therefore, I, William McKinley, President of the United States, do hereby declare and proclaim that in addition to the blockade of the ports specified in my proclamation of April 22, 1898, the United States of America has instituted and will maintain an effective blockade of all the ports on the south coast of Cuba from Cape Frances to Cape Cruz, inclusive, and also of the port of San Juan, in the island of Puerto Rico.

* See pp. 6472-6473.

Neutral vessels lying in any of the ports to which the blockade is by the present proclamation extended will be allowed thirty days to issue therefrom with cargo.

In witness whereof I have hereunto set my hand and caused the seal of the United States to be affixed.

Done at the city of Washington, this 27th day of June, A. D., [SEAL.] 1898, and of the Independence of the United States the one hundred and twenty-second.

WILLIAM McKINLEY.

By the President:

J. B. MOORE,
Acting Secretary of State.

BY THE PRESIDENT OF THE UNITED STATES OF AMERICA.

A PROCLAMATION.

Whereas it is provided by section twenty-four of the act of Congress, approved March third, eighteen hundred and ninety-one, entitled "An act to repeal timber-culture laws, and for other purposes," "That the President of the United States may, from time to time, set apart and reserve, in any State or Territory having public land bearing forests, in any part of the public lands wholly or in part covered with timber or undergrowth, whether of commercial value or not, as public reservations, and the President shall, by public proclamation, declare the establishment of such reservations and the limits thereof;"

And whereas it is further provided by the act of Congress, approved June fourth, eighteen hundred and ninety-seven, entitled "An act making appropriations for sundry civil expenses of the Government for the fiscal year ending June thirtieth, eighteen hundred and ninety-eight, and for other purposes," that "The President is hereby authorized at any time to modify any executive order that has been or may hereafter be made establishing any forest reserve, and by such modification may reduce the area or change the boundary lines of such reserve, or may vacate altogether any order creating such reserve;"

And whereas the public lands in the State of California, within the limits hereinafter described, are in part covered with timber, and it appears that the public good would be promoted by setting apart and reserving said lands as a public reservation;

Now, therefore, I, William McKinley, President of the United States, by virtue of the power in me vested by the aforesaid acts of Congress, do hereby make known and proclaim that the boundary lines of the Forest Reservation in the State of California, known as "the Pine Mountain and Zaca Lake Forest Reserve," created by proclamation of

March second, eighteen hundred and ninety-eight, are hereby so changed and enlarged as to include all those certain tracts, pieces, or parcels of land lying and being situate in the State of California, and within the boundaries particularly described as follows, to wit:

Beginning at the northwest corner of fractional Township twelve (12) North, Range thirty (30) West, San Bernardino Base and Meridian, California; thence southerly along the range line to the southwest corner of said fractional township; thence westerly along the township line to the northwest corner of Section three (3), Township eleven (11) North, Range thirty-one (31) West; thence southerly along the section line to the southwest corner of Section twenty-two (22), said township; thence westerly along the section line to the northwest corner of Section thirty (30), said township; thence southerly along the range line between Ranges thirty-one (31) and thirty-two (32) West, to the northern boundary of the rancho Sisquoc; thence in a general southeasterly direction along the boundaries of the ranchos Sisquoc, La Laguna, Cañada de los Pinos or College Rancho, Tequepis, San Marcos, and Los Prietos y Najalayegua, to the range line between Ranges twenty-four (24) and twenty-five (25) West; thence southerly along said range line to the southeast corner of Township five (5) North, Range twenty-five (25) West; thence easterly along the township line between Townships four (4) and five (5) North, to the western boundary of the rancho Temascal; thence along the western, northern, and eastern boundary of said rancho to its intersection with the northern boundary of the rancho San Francisco; thence along the northern and eastern boundary of said rancho to its southeast corner and continuing southerly to the northern boundary of the Ex Mission de San Fernando Grant; thence along the northern boundary of said grant to its intersection with the range line between Ranges fourteen (14) and fifteen (15) West; thence northerly along said range line to the northeast corner of Section twenty-four (24), Township four (4) North, Range fifteen (15) West; thence easterly along the section line to the southeast corner of Section thirteen (13), Township four (4) North, Range thirteen (13) West; thence northerly along the range line to the southwest corner of Township five (5) North, Range twelve (12) West; thence easterly along the township line to the southeast corner of said township; thence northerly along the range line to the northeast corner of Section twelve (12) of said township; thence westerly along the section line to the northwest corner of Section seven (7), said township; thence northerly along the range line to the First (1st) Standard Parallel North; thence westerly along the First (1st) Standard Parallel North to the southeast corner of Township six (6) North, Range thirteen (13) West; thence northerly along the range line to the northeast corner of Section thirteen (13), said township; thence westerly along the section line to the northwest corner of Section thirteen (13), Township six (6) North.

Range fourteen (14) West; thence northerly along the section line to the northeast corner of Section two (2), said township; thence westerly along the township line to the northwest corner of Section four (4), said township; thence northerly along the section line to the northeast corner of Section five (5), Township seven (7) North, Range fourteen (14) West; thence westerly along the township line to the northwest corner of fractional Section one (1), Township seven (7) North, Range seventeen (17) West; thence northerly along the section line to the intersection with the southern boundary of the rancho La Liebre; thence northwesterly along the boundaries of the ranchos La Liebre and Los Alamos y Agua Caliente to the township line between Townships eight (8) and nine (9) North; thence westerly along said township line to the southeast corner of Township nine (9) North, Range twenty-two (22) West; thence northerly along the township line to the northeast corner of said township; thence westerly along the township line to the intersection with the southern boundary of the rancho Cuyama; thence westerly and northwesterly along the southern boundaries of the ranchos Cuyama to the Eighth (8th) Standard Parallel South; thence westerly along said parallel to the northwest corner of fractional Township twelve (12) North, Range thirty (30) West, the place of beginning.

Excepting from the force and effect of this proclamation all irrigation rights and lands lawfully acquired therefor and all lands which may have been, prior to the date hereof, embraced in any legal entry or covered by any lawful filing duly of record in the proper United States Land Office, or upon which any valid settlement has been made pursuant to law, and the statutory period within which to make entry or filing of record has not expired; and all mining claims duly located and held according to the laws of the United States and rules and regulations not in conflict therewith;

Provided, that this exception shall not continue to apply to any particular tract of land unless the entryman, settler, or claimant continues to comply with the law under which the entry, filing, settlement, or location was made.

Warning is hereby expressly given to all persons not to enter or make settlement upon the tract of land reserved by this proclamation.

In witness whereof I have hereunto set my hand and caused the seal of the United States to be affixed.

Done at the city of Washington, this 29th day of June, in the year of our Lord one thousand eight hundred and ninety-eight, and [SEAL.] of the Independence of the United States the one hundred and twenty-second.

WILLIAM McKINLEY

By the President:
J. B. MOORE,
Acting Secretary of State.

By the President of the United States of America.

A PROCLAMATION

Whereas satisfactory proof has been given to me that no tonnage or light-house dues or any equivalent tax or taxes whatever are imposed upon vessels of the United States in the port of Copenhagen, in the Kingdom of Denmark;

Now, therefore, I, William McKinley, President of the United States of America, by virtue of the authority vested in me by section eleven of the act of Congress, entitled "An Act to abolish certain fees for official services to American vessels, and to amend the laws relating to shipping commissioners, seamen, and owners of vessels, and for other purposes," approved June nineteenth, one thousand eight hundred and eighty-six, and in virtue of the further act amendatory thereof, entitled "An act to amend the laws relating to navigation and for other purposes," approved April four, one thousand eight hundred and eighty-eight, do hereby declare and proclaim that from and after the date of this, my Proclamation, shall be suspended the collection of the whole of the tonnage duty which is imposed by said section eleven of the act approved June nineteenth, one thousand eight hundred and eighty-six, upon vessels entered in the ports of the United States directly from the port of Copenhagen, in the Kingdom of Denmark.

Provided, that there shall be excluded from the benefits of the suspension hereby declared and proclaimed, the vessels of any foreign country in whose ports the fees or dues of any kind or nature imposed on vessels of the United States, or the import or export duties on their cargoes, are in excess of the fees, dues, or duties imposed on the vessels of such country or on the cargoes of such vessels; but this proviso shall not be held to be inconsistent with the special regulation by foreign countries of duties and other charges on their own vessels, and the cargoes thereof, engaged in their coasting trade, or with the existence between such countries and other States of reciprocal stipulations founded on special conditions and equivalents, and thus not within the treatment of American vessels under the most favored nation clause in treaties between the United States and such countries.

And the suspension hereby declared and proclaimed shall continue so long as the reciprocal exemption of vessels belonging to citizens of the United States and their cargoes, shall be continued in the said port of Copenhagen and no longer.

In witness whereof I have hereunto set my hand and caused the seal of the United States to be affixed.

Done at the city of Washington, this 19th day of July, in the year of our Lord one thousand eight hundred and ninety-eight, and [SEAL.] of the Independence of the United States the one hundred and twenty-third.

WILLIAM McKINLEY.

By the President:
WILLIAM R. DAY,
Secretary of State.

BY THE PRESIDENT OF THE UNITED STATES OF AMERICA.

A PROCLAMATION.

Whereas in the opening of the Cherokee Outlet, pursuant to section ten, of the act of Congress, approved March third, eighteen hundred and ninety-three, the lands known as the Eastern, Middle, and Western Saline Reserves, were excepted 'from settlement in view of three leases made by the Cherokee Nation prior to March third, eighteen hundred and ninety-three, under authority of the act of Congress, approved August seventh, eighteen hundred and eighty-two;

And whereas it appears that said leases were never approved as provided by law;

Now, therefore, I, William McKinley, President of the United States, by virtue of the power in me vested by section ten of said act of March third, eighteen hundred and ninety-three, do hereby declare and make known that all the lands in said saline reserves, as described in a proclamation dated August nineteenth, eighteen hundred and ninety-three, are hereby restored to the public domain and will be disposed of under the laws of the United States relating to public lands in said Cherokee Outlet, subject to the policy of the Government in disposing of saline lands.

In witness whereof, I have hereunto set my hand and caused the seal of the United States to be affixed.

Done at the city of Washington, this 27th day of July, in the year of our Lord, one thousand eight hundred and ninety- [SEAL.] eight, and of the Independence of the United States the one hundred and twenty-third.

WILLIAM McKINLEY.

By the President:
WILLIAM R. DAY,
Secretary of State.

By the President of the United States of America.

A PROCLAMATION.

Whereas by a protocol concluded and signed August 12, 1898,* by William R. Day, Secretary of State of the United States, and His Excellency Jules Cambon, ambassador extraordinary and plenipotentiary of the Republic of France at Washington, respectively representing for this purpose the Government of the United States and the Government of Spain, the United States and Spain have formally agreed upon the terms on which negotiations for the establishment of peace between the two countries shall be undertaken; and

Whereas it is in said protocol agreed that upon its conclusion and signature hostilities between the two countries shall be suspended and that notice to that effect shall be given as soon as possible by each Government to the commanders of its military and naval forces:

Now, therefore, I, William McKinley, President of the United States, do, in accordance with the stipulations of the protocol, declare and proclaim on the part of the United States a suspension of hostilities and do hereby command that orders be immediately given through the proper channels to the commanders of the military and naval forces of the United States to abstain from all acts inconsistent with this proclamation.

In witness whereof I have hereunto set my hand and caused the seal of the United States to be affixed.

Done at the city of Washington, this 12th day of August,
[SEAL.]   A. D. 1898, and of the Independence of the United States the one hundred and twenty-third.

WILLIAM McKINLEY.

By the President:
WILLIAM R. DAY,
Secretary of State.

By the President of the United States of America.

A PROCLAMATION.

Whereas it is provided by section twenty-four of the act of Congress, approved March third, eighteen hundred and ninety-one, entitled, "An act to repeal timber-culture laws, and for other purposes," "That the President of the United States may, from time to time, set apart and reserve, in any State or Territory having public land bearing

* See p. 6321.

forests, in any part of the public lands wholly or in part covered with timber or undergrowth, whether of commercial value or not, as public reservations, and the President shall, by public proclamation, declare the establishment of such reservations and the limits thereof;"

And whereas it is further provided by the act of Congress, approved June fourth, eighteen hundred and ninety-seven, entitled, "An act making appropriations for sundry civil expenses of the Government for the fiscal year ending June thirtieth, eighteen hundred and ninety-eight, and for other purposes," that "The President is hereby authorized at any time to modify any Executive order that has been or may hereafter be made establishing any forest reserve, and by such modification may reduce the area or change the boundary lines of such reserve, or may vacate altogether any order creating such reserve;"

And whereas, the public lands in the States of South Dakota and Wyoming, within the limits hereinafter described, are in part covered with timber, and it appears that the public good would be promoted by setting apart and reserving said lands as a public reservation ;

Now, therefore, I, William McKinley, President of the United States, by virtue of the power in me vested by the aforesaid acts of Congress, do hereby make known and proclaim that the boundary lines of the Forest Reservation in the State of South Dakota, known as "The Black Hills Forest Reserve," created by proclamation of February twenty-second, eighteen hundred and ninety-seven, are hereby so changed and enlarged as to include all those certain tracts, pieces or parcels of land lying and being situate in the States of South Dakota and Wyoming, and within the boundaries particularly described as follows, to wit :

Beginning at the southeast corner of Township five (5) South, Range five (5) East, Black Hills Meridian, South Dakota; thence northerly to the northeast corner of said township; thence easterly to the southeast corner of Section thirty-three (33), Township four (4) South, Range six (6) East; thence northerly to the southeast corner of Section nine (9), said township; thence easterly to the southeast corner of Section twelve (12), said township; thence northerly along the range line to the northeast corner of Section thirteen (13), Township one (1) North, Range six (6) East; thence westerly to the northwest corner of said section; thence northerly to the northeast corner of Section two (2), said township; thence westerly to the northwest corner of said section; thence northerly to the northeast corner of Section twenty-two (22), Township two (2) North, Range six (6) East; thence westerly to the southeast corner of Section seventeen (17), said township; thence northerly to the northeast corner of said section; thence westerly to the northwest corner of said section; thence northerly to the southeast corner of Section thirty (30), Township three (3) North, Range six (6) East; thence easterly to the southeast corner of Section twenty-seven (27), said township; thence northerly to the northeast corner of Section twenty-two (22), said township; thence westerly to the north-west corner of said section; thence northerly to the northeast corner of Section sixteen (16), said township; thence westerly to the northwest corner of said section; thence northerly to the northeast corner of Section eight (8), said township; thence westerly to the northwest corner of said section; thence northerly to the northeast corner of Section nineteen (19), Township four (4) North, Range six (6) East; thence westerly to the northwest corner of said section; thence northerly to the northeast corner of Section twelve (12), Township four (4) North, Range five (5) East; thence westerly to the northwest corner of said section; thence northerly to the northeast corner of Section thirty-five (35), Township five (5) North, Range five (5) East; thence westerly to the northwest corner of said section; thence northerly to the northeast corner of Section twenty-seven (27), said township; thence westerly to the northwest corner of said section; thence northerly to the northeast corner of Section twenty-one (21), said township; thence westerly to the southeast corner of Section thirteen (13), Township five (5) North, Range four (4) East; thence northerly to the northeast corner of said section; thence westerly to the northwest corner of said section; thence northerly to the northeast corner of Section two (2), said township; thence westerly to the northwest corner of Section four (4), said township; thence southerly to the southwest corner of said section; thence westerly to the southeast corner of Section two (2), Township five (5) North, Range three (3) East; thence northerly to the northeast corner of said section; thence westerly to the southeast corner of Section thirty-five (35), Township six (6) North, Range two (2) East; thence northerly to the northeast corner of Section twenty-six (26) said township; thence westerly to the southeast corner of Section twenty-four (24), Township six (6) North, Range one (1) East; thence northerly to the northeast corner of said section; thence westerly along the section line to its intersection with the boundary line between the States of South Dakota and Wyoming; thence southerly along said State boundary line to its intersection with the section line between Sections twenty-eight (28) and thirty-three (33), Township fifty-two (52) North, Range sixty (60) West, Sixth (6th) Principal Meridian, Wyoming; thence westerly to the northwest corner of Section thirty-six (36), Township fifty-two (52) North, Range sixty-one (61) West; thence southerly along the section line to its intersection with the Twelfth (12th) Standard Parallel North; thence easterly along said parallel to its intersection with the boundary line between the States of Wyoming and South Dakota; thence southerly along said State boundary line to its intersection with the section line between Sections eighteen (18) and nineteen (19), Township three (3) South,

Range one (1) East, Black Hills Meridian, South Dakota; thence easterly to the northwest corner of Section twenty-two (22), said township, thence southerly to the southwest corner of Section thirty-four (34), said township; thence easterly to the southeast corner of said township; thence southerly to the southwest corner of Section thirty (30), Township four (4) South, Range two (2) East; thence easterly to the southeast corner of Section twenty-seven (27), said township; thence southerly to the southwest corner of Section eleven (11), Township five (5) South, Range two (2) East; thence easterly to the northwest corner of Section eighteen (18), Township five (5) South, Range four (4) East; thence southerly to the southwest corner of said township; thence easterly to the southeast corner of Township five (5) South, Range five (5) East, the place of beginning; excepting and excluding from reservation all those certain tracts, pieces or parcels of land lying and being situate within the boundaries particularly described as follows, to wit:

Beginning at the northeast corner of Section twenty-four (24), Township five (5) North, Range three (3) East, Black Hills Meridian; thence westerly to the northwest corner of Section nineteen (19), said township; thence southerly to the northwest corner of Section thirty-one (31), said township; thence westerly to the northwest corner of Section thirty-six (36), Township five (5) North, Range two (2) East; thence southerly to the southwest corner of Section thirteen (13), Township four (4) North, Range two (2) East; thence easterly to the southeast corner of Section fifteen (15), Township four (4) North, Range three (3) East; thence northerly to the southwest corner of Section two (2), said township; thence easterly to the southeast corner of said section; thence northerly to the northeast corner of said section; thence easterly to the southeast corner of Township five (5) North, Range three (3) East; thence northerly to the northeast corner of Section twenty-four (24), said township, the place of beginning.

Excepting from the force and effect of this proclamation all lands which may have been, prior to the date hereof, embraced in any legal entry or covered by any lawful filing duly of record in the proper United States Land Office, or upon which any valid settlement has been made pursuant to law, and the statutory period within which to make entry or filing of record has not expired; and all mining claims duly located and held according to the laws of the United States and rules and regulations not in conflict therewith; *Provided*, That this exception shall not continue to apply to any particular tract of land unless the entryman, settler, or claimant continues to comply with the law under which the entry, filing, settlement, or location was made.

Warning is hereby expressly given to all persons not to enter or make settlement upon the tract of land reserved by this proclamation.

In witness whereof I have hereunto set my hand and caused the seal of the United States to be affixed.

Done at the city of Washington, this 19th day of September, in the year of our Lord, one thousand eight hundred and ninety-[SEAL.] eight, and of the Independence of the United States the one hundred and twenty-third.

WILLIAM McKINLEY.

By the President:

ALVEY A. ADEE,

Acting Secretary of State.

BY THE PRESIDENT OF THE UNITED STATES.

THANKSGIVING PROCLAMATION.

The approaching November brings to mind the custom of our ancestors, hallowed by time and rooted in our most sacred traditions, of giving thanks to Almighty God for all the blessings He has vouchsafed to us during the year.

Few years in our history have afforded such cause for thanksgiving as this. We have been blessed by abundant harvests; our trade and commerce have wonderfully increased; our public credit has been improved and strengthened; all sections of our common country have been brought together and knitted into closer bonds of national purpose and unity.

The skies have been for a time darkened by the cloud of war, but as we were compelled to take up the sword in the cause of humanity we are permitted to rejoice that the conflict has been of brief duration and the losses we have had to mourn, though grievous and important, have been so few, considering the great results accomplished, as to inspire us with gratitude and praise to the Lord of Hosts. We may laud and magnify His holy name that the cessation of hostilities came so soon as to spare both sides the countless sorrows and disasters that attend protracted war.

I do therefore invite all my fellow-citizens, as well those who may be at sea or sojourning in foreign lands as those at home, to set apart and observe Thursday, the 24th day of November, as a day of national thanksgiving, to come together in their several places of worship for a service of praise and thanks to Almighty God for all the blessings of the year, for the mildness of the seasons and the fruitfulness of the soil, for the continued prosperity of the people, for the devotion and valor of our countrymen, for the glory of our victory and the hope of a righteous peace, and to pray that the divine guidance which has brought us heretofore to safety and honor may be graciously continued in the years to come.

In witness whereof I have hereunto set my hand and caused the seal of the United States to be affixed.

Done at the city of Washington, this 28th day of October, [SEAL.] A. D. 1898, and of the Independence of the United States the one hundred and twenty-third.

WILLIAM McKINLEY.

By the President:
JOHN HAY,
Secretary of State.

BY THE PRESIDENT OF THE UNITED STATES.

A PROCLAMATION.

Whereas by joint resolution "to provide for annexing the Hawaiian Islands to the United States," approved July 7, 1898, the cession by the Government of the Republic of Hawaii to the United States of America, of all rights of sovereignty of whatsoever kind in and over the Hawaiian Islands and their dependencies, and the transfer to the United States of the absolute fee and ownership of all public, Government, or crown lands, public buildings, or edifices, ports, harbors, military equipment, and all other public property of every kind and description belonging to the Government of the Hawaiian Islands, was duly accepted, ratified, and confirmed, and the said Hawaiian Islands and their dependencies annexed as a part of the territory of the United States and made subject to the sovereign dominion thereof, and all and singular the property and rights hereinbefore mentioned vested in the United States of America; and

Whereas it was further provided in said resolution that the existing laws of the United States relative to public lands shall not apply to such lands in the Hawaiian Islands, but the Congress of the United States shall enact special laws for their management and disposition; and

Whereas it is deemed necessary in the public interests that certain lots and plats of land in the city of Honolulu be immediately reserved for naval purposes;

Now, therefore, I, William McKinley, President of the United States, by virtue of the authority in me vested, do hereby declare, proclaim, and make known that the following described lots or plats of land be and the same are hereby reserved for naval purposes until such time as the Congress of the United States shall otherwise direct, to wit:

1st. The water front lying between the Bishop Estate and the line of Richards Street including the site of prospective wharves, slips, and their approaches.

2d. The blocks of land embracing lots No. 86 to 91, 100 to 131, including Mililani Street to the intersection of Halekauwali Street; and the Government water lots lying between the Bishop Estate and Punchbowl and Allen Streets.

In witness whereof I have hereunto set my hand, and caused the seal of the United States to be affixed.

Done at the city of Washington, this 2d day of November, in the year one thousand eight hundred and ninety-eight, and of the [SEAL.]   Independence of the United States the one hundred and twenty-third.

WILLIAM McKINLEY.

By the President:

JOHN HAY,
Secretary of State.

HAWAIIAN CABLE CONCESSION.

To all to whom these presents shall come, Greeting:

Know ye, that: Whereas, by an Indenture made the 2d day of July, in the year of our Lord one thousand eight hundred and ninety-eight between Sanford B. Dole, President of the Republic of Hawaii for and in behalf of the Hawaiian Government of the one part and the Pacific Cable Company, a corporation organized and existing under the laws of the State of New York of the United States of America, of the other part, there was granted, conceded, and confirmed unto the party of the second part and its successors and assigns the right and privilege to lay, construct, land, maintain and operate telegraphic and magnetic lines or cables from a point or points on the Pacific Coast of the United States to a suitable landing place or places to be selected by the party of the second part in the Hawaiian Islands with terminus at Honolulu, Island of Oahu, and from and beyond the Hawaiian Islands to Japan and any islands or places necessary for stations for such cables between the Hawaiian Islands and Japan that lie north of the tenth degree or parallel of north latitude in the North Pacific Ocean, as an exclusive right and privilege together with an exemption from duties, charges, and taxes for and during the term of twenty years from the date expressed in said Indenture, to wit, the 21st day of June, A. D. 1898,—said right, privilege, and exemption being subject to the terms and conditions set forth in said Indenture;

And whereas among said terms and conditions it is declared and agreed by said Indenture that the party of the second part within two years from the approval (within eighteen months from the date of said contract) of an act by the Congress of the United States authorizing the party of the second part to construct and operate a submarine cable line between the United States and the Hawaiian Islands shall construct, lay in proper working order, and establish a submarine telegraph cable from a point or points on the Pacific coast of the United States to a landing place or places in the Hawaiian Islands with terminus at Honolulu, Island of Oahu, according to the specifications of said Indenture, and further, within three years from the approval of such act by the Congress of the United States, shall in like manner construct, lay in proper working order, and establish a submarine telegraph cable from a point or points at or near said Honolulu to Japan;

And whereas it is provided by said Indenture that the contract therein made and set forth shall not take effect, if at any time within six months from the date thereof, to wit, the 2d day of July, A. D., 1898, "the United States State Department" shall express its disapproval thereof;

And whereas, pursuant to a Joint Resolution of the Senate and House of Representatives of the United States of America in Congress assembled, approved July 7, 1898, to provide for annexing the Hawaiian Islands to the United States, the sovereignty of the said Hawaiian Islands was yielded up to the United States on the 12th day of August, A. D., 1898, becoming thenceforth vested in the United States of America.

And whereas, in view of the provisions of said Joint Resolution for the determination by the Congress of the United States of all matters of municipal legislation concerning the Hawaiian Islands, and because the subject matter and provisions of said Indenture are deemed to be proper subjects for the consideration and determination of the Congress of the United States, it is deemed expedient and necessary that the Congress of the United States consider and adopt such legislation, especially in regard to grants and contractual obligations to be controlled by and rest upon the United States of America as vested with sovereignty over said Hawaiian Islands, without let or hindrance by reason of any action of the Government of the Republic of Hawaii in respect to such grants and contractual obligations initiated by the said Government of the Republic of Hawaii prior to and incomplete at the time of the yielding up of the sovereignty of the Hawaiian Islands to the United States;

Now, therefore, I, John Hay, Secretary of State of the United States, do hereby express on the part of "the United States State Department" its disapproval of the contract stipulated in the said Indenture to the end that the same shall not take effect.

Given under my hand and the seal of the Department of State of the United States, in the city of Washington, D. C., this thirty-first day of December in the year of our Lord one thousand eight hundred and ninety-eight.

[SEAL.]

JOHN HAY.

BY THE PRESIDENT OF THE UNITED STATES OF AMERICA.

A PROCLAMATION.

Whereas it is provided by section twenty-four of the act of Congress, approved March third, eighteen hundred and ninety-one, entitled, "An act to repeal timber-culture laws, and for other purposes," "That the President of the United States may, from time to time, set apart and reserve in any State or Territory having public land bearing forests, in any part of the public lands wholly or in part covered with timber or undergrowth, whether of commercial value or not, as public reservations, and the President shall, by public proclamation, declare the establishment of such reservations and the limits thereof;"

And whereas it is further provided by the act of Congress, approved June fourth, eighteen hundred and ninety-seven, entitled, "An act making appropriations for sundry civil expenses of the Government for the fiscal year ending June thirtieth, eighteen hundred and ninety-eight, and for other purposes," that "The President is hereby authorized at any time to modify any executive order that has been or may hereafter be made establishing any forest reserve, and by such modification may reduce the area or change the boundary lines of such reserve, or may vacate altogether any order creating such reserve;"

And whereas the public lands in the State of California, within the limits hereinafter described, are in part covered with timber, and it appears that the public good would be promoted by setting apart and reserving said lands as a public reservation;

Now, therefore, I, William McKinley, President of the United States, by virtue of the power in me vested by the aforesaid acts of Congress, do hereby make known and proclaim that the boundary lines of the Forest Reservation in the State of California, known as "The Trabuco Cañon Forest Reserve," created by proclamation of February twenty-fifth, eighteen hundred and ninety-three, are hereby so changed and enlarged as to include all those certain tracts, pieces or parcels of land lying and being situate in the State of California, and within the boundaries particularly described as follows, to wit:

Beginning at the northeast corner of Section thirteen (13), Township five (5) South, Range six (6) West, San Bernardino Base and Meridian, California; thence westerly along the section line to the southeast corner of Section nine (9), said township; thence northerly along the section line to the northeast corner of Section four (4), said township; thence westerly along the township line to the northwest corner of Section three (3), Township five (5) South, Range seven (7) West; thence southerly along the section line to the southwest corner of Section thirty-four (34), said township; thence easterly along the township line to the southeast corner of said township; thence southerly along the range line between Ranges six (6) and seven (7) West, to its intersection with the northern boundary of the Rancho Mission Viejo or La Paz; thence along the northern and eastern boundary of said rancho to its intersection with the northern boundary of the Rancho Santa Margarita y Las Flores; thence along the northern boundary of said rancho to its intersection with the range line between Ranges four (4) and five (5) West; thence northerly along said range line to its intersection with the southern boundary of the Rancho Santa Rosa; thence in a northwesterly and northeasterly direction along the southern and western boundary of said rancho to its intersection with the township line between Townships six (6) and seven (7) South; thence westerly along said township line to the southeast corner of Township six (6) South, Range six (6) West; thence northerly along the range line to the northeast corner of Section thirteen (13), Township five (5) South, Range six (6) West, the place of beginning.

Excepting from the force and effect of this proclamation all lands which may have been, prior to the date hereof, embraced in any legal entry or covered by any lawful filing duly of record in the proper United States Land Office, or upon which any valid settlement has been made pursuant to law, and the statutory period within which to make entry or filing of record has not expired; *Provided*, that this exception shall not continue to apply to any particular tract of land unless the entryman, settler, or claimant continues to comply with the law under which the entry, filing, or settlement was made.

Warning is hereby expressly given to all persons not to make settlement upon the tract of land reserved by this proclamation.

In witness whereof, I have hereunto set my hand and caused the seal of the United States to be affixed.

Done at the city of Washington, this 30th day of January, in the year of our Lord one thousand eight hundred and ninety-nine, [SEAL.] and of the Independence of the United States the one hundred and twenty-third.

WILLIAM McKINLEY.

By the President:
JOHN HAY,
   Secretary of State.

BY THE PRESIDENT OF THE UNITED STATES OF AMERICA.

A PROCLAMATION.

Whereas satisfactory proof has been given to me by the Government of Mexico that no discriminating duties of tonnage or imposts are imposed or levied in the ports of Mexico upon vessels wholly belonging to citizens of the United States, or upon the produce, manufactures, or merchandise imported in the same from the United States, or from any foreign country:

Now, therefore, I, William McKinley, President of the United States of America, by virtue of the authority vested in me by section four thousand two hundred and twenty-eight of the Revised Statutes of the United States, do hereby declare and proclaim that, from and after the date of this, my proclamation, so long as vessels of the United States and their cargoes shall be exempt from discriminating duties as aforesaid, any such duties on Mexican vessels entering the ports of the United States, or on the produce, manufactures, or merchandise imported in such vessels, shall be suspended and discontinued, and no longer.

In testimony whereof I have hereunto set my hand and caused the seal of the United States to be affixed.

Done at the city of Washington, the 9th day of February, in the year of our Lord one thousand eight hundred and ninety-[SEAL.]   nine, and of the Independence of the United States the one hundred and twenty-third.

WILLIAM McKINLEY.

By the President:
    JOHN HAY,
        Secretary of State.

BY THE PRESIDENT OF THE UNITED STATES OF AMERICA.

A PROCLAMATION.

Whereas it is provided by section twenty-four of the act of Congress, approved March third, eighteen hundred and ninety-one, entitled "An act to repeal timber-culture laws, and for other purposes," "That the President of the United States may, from time to time, set apart and reserve, in any State or Territory having public land bearing forests, in any part of the public lands wholly or in part covered with timber or undergrowth, whether of commercial value or not, as public reservations, and the President shall, by public proclamation, declare the establishment of such reservations and the limits thereof;"

And whereas the public lands in the State of Montana, within the limits hereinafter described, are in part covered with timber, and it appears that the public good would be promoted by setting apart and reserving said lands as public reservations;

Now, therefore, I, William McKinley, President of the United States, by virtue of the power in me vested by section twenty-four of the aforesaid act of Congress, do hereby make known and proclaim that there are hereby reserved from entry or settlement and set apart as Public Reservations all those certain tracts, pieces, or parcels of land lying and being situate in the State of Montana and particularly described as follows, to wit:

Sections fourteen (14), twenty-four (24), twenty-six (26), and thirty-six (36), Township three (3) South, Range five (5) East; Sections two (2), twelve (12), fourteen (14), twenty-four (24), twenty-six (26), and thirty-six (36), Township four (4) South, Range five (5) East; Sections two (2), twelve (12), fourteen (14), and twenty-four (24), Township five (5) South, Range five (5) East; Sections fourteen (14), sixteen (16), eighteen (18), twenty (20), twenty-two (22), twenty-four (24), twenty-six (26), twenty-eight (28), thirty (30), thirty-two (32), thirty-four (34), and thirty-six (36), Township three (3) South, Range six (6) East; Sections two (2), four (4), six (6), eight (8), ten (10), twelve (12), fourteen (14), sixteen (16), eighteen (18), twenty (20), twenty-two (22), twenty-four (24), twenty-six (26), twenty-eight (28), thirty (30), thirty-two (32), thirty-four (34), and thirty-six (36), Township four (4) South, Range six (6) East; Sections two (2), four (4), six (6), eight (8), ten (10), twelve (12), fourteen (14), sixteen (16), eighteen (18), twenty (20), twenty-two (22), and twenty-four (24), Township five (5) South, Range six (6) East; Sections eighteen (18), and thirty (30), Township three (3) South, Range seven (7) East; Sections six (6), eighteen (18), and thirty (30), Township four (4) South, Range seven (7) East; and Sections six (6) and eighteen (18), Township five (5) South, Range seven (7) East, Principal Meridian, Montana.

Excepting from the force and effect of this proclamation all lands which may have been, prior to the date hereof, embraced in any legal entry or covered by any lawful filing duly of record in the proper United States Land Office, or upon which any valid settlement has been made pursuant to law, and the statutory period within which to make entry or filing of record has not expired; *Provided*, that this exception shall not continue to apply to any particular tract of land unless the entryman, settler, or claimant continues to comply with the law under which the entry, filing, or settlement was made.

Warning is hereby expressly given to all persons not to make settlement upon the tracts of land reserved by this proclamation.

In witness whereof, I have hereunto set my hand and caused the seal of the United States to be affixed.

Done at the city of Washington, this 10th day of February, in the year of our Lord one thousand eight hundred and ninety-[SEAL.] nine, and of the Independence of the United States the one hundred and twenty-third.

WILLIAM McKINLEY.

By the President:
JOHN HAY,
     Secretary of State.

62369

By the President of the United States of America.

A PROCLAMATION.

Whereas it is provided by section twenty-four of the act of Congress, approved March third, eighteen hundred and ninety-one, entitled, "An act to repeal timber-culture laws, and for other purposes," "That the President of the United States may, from time to time, set apart and reserve, in any State or Territory having public land bearing forests, in any part of the public lands wholly or in part covered with timber or undergrowth, whether of commercial value or not, as public reservations, and the President shall, by public proclamation, declare the establishment of such reservations and the limits thereof;"

And whereas the public lands in the State of Utah, within the limits hereinafter described, are in part covered with timber, and it appears that the public good would be promoted by setting apart and reserving said lands as a public reservation;

Now, therefore, I, William McKinley, President of the United States, by virtue of the power in me vested by section twenty-four of the aforesaid act of Congress, do hereby make known and proclaim that there is hereby reserved from entry or settlement and set apart as a Public Reservation all those certain tracts, pieces or parcels of land lying and being situate in the State of Utah and within the boundaries particularly described as follows, to wit:

Beginning at the northeast corner of Section twenty-four (24), Township twenty-four (24) South, Range two (2) East, Salt Lake Base and Meridian, Utah; thence southerly along the range line to the northeast corner of Section thirteen (13), Township twenty-five (25) South, Range two (2) East; thence easterly along the section line to the northeast corner of Section eighteen (18), Township twenty-five (25) South, Range three (3) East; thence southerly along the section line to the Fifth (5th) Standard Parallel South; thence westerly along said parallel to the northeast corner of Township twenty-six (26) South, Range two (2) East; thence southerly along the range line to the southeast corner of said township; thence westerly along the township line to the southwest corner of Section thirty-five (35), Township twenty-six (26) South, Range one (1) East; thence northerly along the section line to the Fifth (5th) Standard Parallel South; thence easterly along said parallel to the southwest corner of Township twenty-five (25) South, Range two (2) East; thence northerly along the range line to the northwest corner of Section nineteen (19), Township twenty-four (24) South, Range two (2) East; thence easterly along the section line to the northeast corner of Section twenty-four (24), said township, the place of beginning.

Excepting from the force and effect of this proclamation all lands which may have been, prior to the date hereof, embraced in any legal entry or covered by any lawful filing duly of record in the proper United

States Land Office, or upon which any valid settlement has been made pursuant to law, and the statutory period within which to make entry or filing of record has not expired; *Provided*, that this exception shall not continue to apply to any particular tract of land unless the entryman, settler or claimant continues to comply with the law under which the entry, filing, or settlement was made.

Warning is hereby expressly given to all persons not to make settlement upon the tract of land reserved by this proclamation.

In witness whereof, I have hereunto set my hand and caused the seal of the United States to be affixed.

Done at the city of Washington this 10th day of February, in the year of our Lord one thousand eight hundred and ninety-
[SEAL.] nine, and of the Independence of the United States the one hundred and twenty-third.

WILLIAM McKINLEY.

By the President:
JOHN HAY,
    Secretary of State.

BY THE PRESIDENT OF THE UNITED STATES OF AMERICA.

A PROCLAMATION.

Whereas, it is provided by section twenty-four of the act of Congress, approved March third, eighteen hundred and ninety-one, entitled, "An act to repeal timber-culture laws, and for other purposes," "That the President of the United States may, from time to time, set apart and reserve, in any State or Territory having public land bearing forests, in any part of the public lands wholly or in part covered with timber or undergrowth, whether of commercial value or not, as public reservations, and the President shall, by public proclamation, declare the establishment of such reservations and the limits thereof;"

And whereas, the public lands in the Territory of New Mexico, within the limits hereinafter described, are in part covered with timber, and it appears that the public good would be promoted by setting apart and reserving said lands as a public reservation;

Now, therefore, I, William McKinley, President of the United States, by virtue of the power in me vested by section twenty-four of the aforesaid act of Congress, do hereby make known and proclaim that there is hereby reserved from entry or settlement and set apart as a Public Reservation all those certain tracts, pieces or parcels of land lying and being situate in the Territory of New Mexico and within the boundaries particularly described as follows, to-wit:

Beginning at a point on the boundary line between New Mexico and Arizona where it is intersected by the north line of Township five (5)

South, Range twenty-one (21) West, New Mexico Principal Meridian, New Mexico; thence easterly along the township line to the northeast corner of Township five (5) South, Range sixteen (16) West; thence southerly along the range line between Ranges fifteen (15) and sixteen (16) West, to the southeast corner of Township eight (8) South, Range sixteen (16) West; thence easterly along the township line to the northeast corner of Township nine (9) South, Range fifteen (15) West; thence southerly along the range line to the southeast corner of said township; thence easterly along the township line to the northeast corner of Township ten (10) South, Range ten (10) West; thence southerly along the First Guide Meridian West, between Ranges nine (9) and ten (10) West, to its intersection with the Third (3rd) Standard Parallel South, between Townships fifteen (15) and sixteen (16) South; thence westerly along the said Third (3rd) Standard Parallel South to the southwest corner of Township fifteen (15) South, Range sixteen (16) West; thence northerly along the range line to the northwest corner of said township; thence westerly along the township line to the northeast corner of Township fifteen (15) South, Range nineteen (19) West; thence southerly along the range line to its intersection with the Third (3rd) Standard Parallel South; thence westerly along the Third (3rd) Standard Parallel South to its intersection with the boundary line between New Mexico and Arizona; thence northerly along said boundary line to the point where it intersects the north line of Township five (5) South, Range twenty-one (21) West, the place of beginning.

Excepting from the force and effect of this proclamation all lands which may have been, prior to the date hereof, embraced in any legal entry or covered by any lawful filing duly of record in the proper United States Land Office, or upon which any valid settlement has been made pursuant to law, and the statutory period within which to make entry or filing of record has not expired; *Provided*, that this exception shall not continue to apply to any particular tract of land unless the entryman, settler or claimant continues to comply with the law under which the entry, filing or settlement was made.

Warning is hereby expressly given to all persons not to make settlement upon the tract of land reserved by this proclamation.

In witness whereof, I have hereunto set my hand and caused the seal of the United States to be affixed.

Done at the city of Washington this second day of March, in the year of our Lord one thousand eight hundred and ninety-nine, and [SEAL.] of the Independence of the United States the one hundred and twenty-third.

WILLIAM McKINLEY.

By the President:
JOHN HAY,
Secretary of State.

BY THE PRESIDENT OF THE UNITED STATES.

A PROCLAMATION.

Whereas by a proclamation of the President of the United States, dated the second day of December, eighteen hundred and ninety-one, upon proof then appearing satisfactory that no tonnage or light-house dues or other equivalent tax or taxes were imposed upon American vessels entering the ports of the Island of Tobago, one of the British West India Islands, and that vessels belonging to the United States of America and their cargoes were not required in the ports of the said Island of Tobago to pay any fee or due of any kind or nature, or any import due higher than was payable by vessels from ports or places in the said Island of Tobago, or their cargoes, in the United States, the President did therefore declare and proclaim, from and after the date of his said proclamation of December second, eighteen hundred and ninety-one, the suspension of the collection of the whole of the duty of three cents per ton, not to exceed fifteen cents per ton per annum, imposed upon vessels entered in the ports of the United States from any of the ports of the Island of Tobago by section 11 of the act of Congress approved June nineteenth, eighteen hundred and eighty-six, entitled "An act to abolish certain fees for official services to American vessels and to amend the laws relating to shipping commissioners, seamen, and owners of vessels and for other purposes."

And whereas the President did further declare and proclaim in his proclamation of December second, eighteen hundred and ninety-one, that the said suspension should continue so long as the reciprocal exemption of vessels belonging to citizens of the United States and their cargoes should be continued in the said ports of the Island of Tobago and no longer;

And whereas it now appears upon satisfactory proof that tonnage or light-house dues, or a tax or taxes equivalent thereto, are in fact imposed upon American vessels and their cargoes entered in ports of the Island of Tobago higher and other than those imposed upon vessels and their cargoes entered in ports of the Island of Tobago, or their cargoes, entered in ports of the United States, so that said proclamation of December second, eighteen hundred and ninety-one, in its operation and effect contravenes the meaning and intent of said section 11 of the act of Congress approved June nineteenth, eighteen hundred and eighty-six;

Now, therefore, I, William McKinley, President of the United States of America, by virtue of the aforesaid section 11 of the act aforesaid, as well as in pursuance of the terms of said proclamation itself, do hereby revoke the said proclamation of December second, eighteen hundred and ninety-one suspending the collection of the whole of the duty of three cents per ton, not to exceed fifteen cents per ton per annum (which is imposed by the aforesaid section of said act) upon vessels entered in the ports of the United States from any of the ports of the Island of Tobago; this revocation of said proclamation to take effect on and after the date of this my proclamation.

In witness whereof, I have hereunto set my hand and caused the seal of the United States to be affixed.

Done at the city of Washington, this 13th day of March, in the year of our Lord one thousand eight hundred and ninety-nine,
[SEAL.]   and of the Independence of the United States the one hundred and twenty-third.

WILLIAM McKINLEY.

By the President:

JOHN HAY,
    Secretary of State.

BY THE PRESIDENT OF THE UNITED STATES.

A PROCLAMATION.

Whereas by a proclamation of the President of the United States, dated April seventh, eighteen hundred and eighty-five upon proof then appearing satisfactory that upon vessels of the United States arriving at the Island of Trinidad, British West Indies, no due was imposed by the ton as tonnage or as light money and that no other equivalent tax on vessels of the United States was imposed at said island by the British Government, the President did declare and proclaim from and after the date of his said proclamation of April seventh, eighteen hundred and eighty-five, the suspension of the collection of the tonnage duties of three cents per ton, not to exceed fifteen cents per ton per annum, imposed upon vessels entered in ports of the United States from any of the ports of the Island of Trinidad by section 14 of the act of Congress approved June twenty-six, eighteen hundred and eighty-four, entitled " An act to remove certain burdens on the American merchant marine and encourage the American foreign carrying trade and for other purposes; "

And whereas it now appears upon satisfactory proof that tonnage or light-house dues, or a tax or taxes equivalent thereto, are in fact imposed upon American vessels and their cargoes entered in ports of the Island of Trinidad higher and other than those imposed upon vessels from ports in the Island of Trinidad or their cargoes entered in ports of the United States, so that said proclamation of April seventh, eighteen hundred and eighty-five, in its operation and effect contravenes the

COLUMBUS STATUE AND UNION STATION, WASHINGTON

UNION STATION AND COLUMBUS STATUE.

The new Union station in Washington, D. C., built of Vermont gran-
ite, is one of the largest structures in America. It is 760 feet long, 343
feet wide, with a waiting-room 222 feet by 130 feet and 120 feet high.
The passenger concourse can accommodate 50,000 persons. In front is
the striking monument to Columbus, one of the many tributes to the Spanish navigator in the New World which he discovered.

meaning and intent of section 14 of the act of Congress approved June twenty-six, eighteen hundred and eighty-four, as amended by section 11 of the act of Congress approved June nineteenth, eighteen hundred and eighty-six, entitled " An act to abolish certain fees for official services to American vessels and to amend the laws relating to shipping commissioners, seamen, and owners of vessels and for other purposes; "

Now, therefore, I, William McKinley, President of the United States of America, by virtue of the aforesaid section 14 of the act of Congress approved June twenty-six, eighteen hundred and eighty-four as amended by the aforesaid section 11 of the act approved June nineteenth, eighteen hundred and eighty-six, do hereby revoke the said proclamation of April seventh, eighteen hundred and eighty-five, suspending the collection of the whole of the duty of three cents per ton, not to exceed fifteen cents per ton per annum (which is imposed by the aforesaid sections of said acts), upon vessels entered in the ports of the United States from any of the ports of the Island of Trinidad; this revocation of said proclamation to take effect on and after the date of this my proclamation.

In witness whereof, I have hereunto set my hand and caused the seal of the United States to be affixed.

Done at the city of Washington, this 13th day of March, in the year of our Lord one thousand eight hundred and ninety-nine,

[SEAL.]   and of the Independence of the United States the one hundred and twenty-third.

WILLIAM McKINLEY.

By the President:

JOHN HAY,

Secretary of State.

BY THE PRESIDENT OF THE UNITED STATES.

A PROCLAMATION.

Whereas, it is deemed necessary in the public interests that certain lands lying to the eastward of the city of San Juan, in Puerto Rico, be immediately reserved for naval purposes;

Now, therefore, I, William McKinley, President of the United States, by virtue of the authority in me vested, do hereby, declare, proclaim, and make known that the following-described lands be and the same are hereby reserved for naval purposes until such time as the Congress of the United States shall otherwise direct, to wit:

1st. The public land, natural, reclaimed, partly reclaimed, or which may be reclaimed, lying south of the Caguas Road, shown on the U. S. Hydrographic Map No. 1745 of July, 1898, and for 250 feet north of

207

said Caguas Road, to be bounded on the west by a true north and south line passing through the eastern corner of the railway station shown on said map, on the south by the shore of the harbor, and to extend east 2,400 feet, more or less, to include 80 acres.

2nd. The entire island lying to the southward of the above-described land, and described on the U. S. Hydrographic Map No. 1745, of July, 1898, as Isla Grande, or Manglar.

The Military Governor of the Island of Puerto Rico will make this transfer through the representative of the Navy, the Commandant of the United States Naval Station, San Juan, Puerto Rico, who will present this proclamation.

March 29, 1899.   WILLIAM McKINLEY.
By the President:
    JOHN HAY,
        Secretary of State.

BY THE PRESIDENT OF THE UNITED STATES OF AMERICA.

A PROCLAMATION.

Whereas, it is provided by section twenty-four of the act of Congress, approved March third, eighteen hundred and ninety-one, entitled, "An act to repeal timber-culture laws, and for other purposes," "That the President of the United States may, from time to time, set apart and reserve, in any State or Territory having public land bearing forests, in any part of the public lands wholly or in part covered with timber or undergrowth, whether of commercial value or not, as public reservations, and the President shall, by public proclamation, declare the establishment of such reservations and the limits thereof;"

And whereas, the public lands in the State of California, within the limits hereinafter described, are in part covered with timber, and it appears that the public good would be promoted by setting apart and reserving said lands as a public reservation;

Now, therefore, I, William McKinley, President of the United States, by virtue of the power in me vested by section twenty-four of the aforesaid act of Congress, do hereby make known and proclaim that there is hereby reserved from entry or settlement and set apart as a Public Reservation all those certain tracts, pieces or parcels of land lying and being situate in the State of California and particularly described as follows, to wit:

Townships eleven (11), twelve (12) and thirteen (13) North, Range sixteen (16) East, Mount Diablo Base and Meridian, California; Townships eleven (11), twelve (12) and thirteen (13) North, Range seventeen (17) East; and so much of Township eleven (11) North, Range eighteen (18) East, as lies west of the summit of the Sierra Nevada Range of mountains in El Dorado County, California.

Excepting from the force and effect of this proclamation all lands which may have been, prior to the date hereof, embraced in any legal entry or covered by any lawful filing duly of record in the proper United States Land Office, or upon which any valid settlement has been made pursuant to law, and the statutory period within which to make entry or filing of record has not expired; *Provided*, that this exception shall not continue to apply to any particular tract of land unless the entryman, settler or claimant continues to comply with the law under which the entry, filing or settlement was made.

Warning is hereby expressly given to all persons not to make settlement upon the tract of land reserved by this proclamation.

The reservation hereby established shall be known as The Lake Tahoe Forest Reserve.

In witness whereof, I have hereunto set my hand and caused the seal of the United States to be affixed.

Done at the city of Washington this 13th day of April, in the year of our Lord one thousand eight hundred and ninety-nine,
[SEAL.]   and of the Independence of the United States the one hundred and twenty-third.

WILLIAM McKINLEY.

By the President:
JOHN HAY,
    Secretary of State.

BY THE PRESIDENT OF THE UNITED STATES.

A PROCLAMATION.

Whereas, by the provisions of an act approved February 20, 1895, entitled "An act to disapprove the treaty heretofore made with the Southern Ute Indians to be removed to the Territory of Utah, and providing for settling them down in severalty where they may so elect and are qualified and to settle all those not electing to take lands in severalty, on the west forty miles of present reservation and in portions of New Mexico, and for other purposes, and to carry out the provisions of the treaty with said Indians June fifteenth, eighteen hundred and eighty," the agreement made by the commissioners on the part of the United States with the Southern Ute Indians of Colorado bearing date November thirteenth, eighteen hundred and eighty-eight, was annulled and the treaty made with said Indians June fifteenth, eighteen hundred and eighty, was directed to be carried out as therein provided and as further provided by general law for settling Indians in severalty; and

Whereas it was further provided by said act that within six months after the passage thereof, the Secretary of the Interior should cause allotment of land, in severalty, to be made to such of the Southern Ute Indians in Colorado, as might elect and be considered by him qualified to take the same out of the agricultural lands embraced in their present reservation in Colorado, such allotments to be made in accordance with the provisions of the act of Congress approved June fifteenth, eighteen hundred and eighty, entitled "An act to accept and ratify the agreement submitted by the confederated bands of Ute Indians in Colorado for the sale of their reservation in said State and for other purposes, and to make the necessary appropriations for carrying out the same," and the amendments thereto, as far as applicable, and the treaties theretofore made with said Indians; and

Whereas it was further provided that for the sole and exclusive use of such of said Indians as might not elect or be deemed qualified to take allotments in severalty as provided, there should be set apart and reserved all that portion of their reservation lying west of the range line between ranges thirteen and fourteen west of the New Mexico Principal Meridian, and also all of townships thirty-one and thirty-two of range fourteen, fifteen, and sixteen west of the New Mexico Principal Meridian and lying in the Territory of New Mexico, subject to the right of the Government to erect and maintain agency buildings thereon, and to grant rights of way through the same for railroads, irrigation ditches, highways and other necessary purposes; and

Whereas under the provisions of section four of said act it was made the duty of the President of the United States to issue his proclamation declaring the lands within the reservation of said Indians except such portions as might have been allotted or reserved under the provisions of the preceding sections of said act, open to occupancy and settlement, said unallotted and unreserved lands to be and become a part of the public domain of the United States and to become subject to entry, under the desert, homestead, and townsite law and the laws governing the disposal of coal, mineral stone and timber lands, but providing that no homestead settler should receive a title to any portion of such lands at less than one dollar and twenty-five cents per acre, and such settlers should be required to make a cash payment of fifty cents per acre at the time filing is made upon any of said lands; and providing that before said lands should be open to public settlement the Secretary of the Interior should cause the improvement belonging to the Indians on the lands then occupied by them to be appraised and sold at public sale to the highest bidder, except improvements on lands allotted to the Indians in accordance with this act; and providing that no sale of such improvements should be made for less than the appraised value and that the several purchasers of said improvements should, for thirty days after the issuance of the President's proclamation have the preference right of entry of the lands upon which the improvements purchased by them should be situated, but that the said purchase should not exceed one hundred and sixty acres and that the proceeds of such improvements should be paid to the Indians owning the same; and

Whereas it is further provided that the provisions of said act should take effect only upon the acceptance thereof and consent thereto by a majority of all the male adult Indians then located or residing upon the reservation, which acceptance should be at once obtained under such regulations as the Secretary of the Interior might prescribe; and

Whereas allotments have been made as provided for in said act, and all the other terms and considerations as required therein have been complied with, preceding to opening the unallotted and unreserved lands in said reservation to settlement and entry, except the sale of improvements on the NE ¼ NW ¼, S ½ NW ¼ and NW ¼ SW ¼ Sec. 1, T. 33 N., R. 9 W., belonging to Ignacio, an Indian, but said sale will be immediately ordered and the rights of the purchaser thereof will be protected for thirty days from date of this proclamation, as provided by the act, by instructions to the register and receiver of the local land office having jurisdiction over the same, and as this exception is not considered a bar to the opening of the unallotted and unreserved lands to settlement; and

Whereas I issued a proclamation on the 29th day of March, last, intended to open the lands to settlement and entry as authorized in said act, but as some question has arisen as to the boundaries proclaimed being sufficiently definite to cover the lands intended to be opened.

Now, therefore, I, William McKinley, President of the United States, for the purposes of removing any doubt and making the boundaries of said lands more definite, by virtue of the power in me vested by said act, do hereby issue this, my second proclamation, and do hereby declare and make known that all of the lands embraced in said reservation, saving and excepting the lands reserved for and allotted to said Indians, and the lands reserved for other purposes in pursuance of the provisions of said act, will, at and after the hour of twelve o'clock noon (mountain standard time) on the 4th day of May, A. D., eighteen hundred and ninety-nine, and not before, be open to settlement and entry under the terms of and subject to all the conditions, limitations, reservations and restrictions contained in said act, and the laws of the United States applicable thereto.

The lands to be opened to settlement and entry are described as lying within the following boundaries: Beginning at the point established by S. S. Gannett, Special Indian Agent, in June, 1897, at the intersection of the 107th meridian and the 37th parallel of latitude; thence north 15 miles along the eastern boundary of the reservation; thence westerly along the north boundary of the Southern Ute Indian Reservation to its intersection with the range line between ranges thirteen and fourteen west of the New Mexico Principal Meridian; thence south fifteen miles on said range line to the south boundary of the State of Colorado; thence easterly along the south boundary of the State of Colorado to the place of beginning.

The survey of the east boundary of the above tract through townships 32, 33, and 34 N., R. 1 W., and of that part of the north boundary in Tps. 34 N., Rs. 1 and 2 W., being in process of correction owing to errors found in said survey, notice is hereby given to all parties who may elect to make entries of lands adjoining the boundary lines subject to correction, that their entries will be at their own risk, and subject to such changes as to the boundaries of the several tracts so entered as may be found necessary in the progress of the correction of the erroneous survey, and that without recourse to the United States for any damage that may arise as the result of the correction survey.

The lands allotted to the Indians are for greater convenience particularly described in the accompanying schedule entitled "Schedule of lands within the Southern Ute Indian Reservation allotted to the Indians and withheld from settlement and entry by proclamation of the President dated April 13, 1899," and which schedule is made a part thereof.

An error having been made in 1873 in the survey and location of the eastern boundary of the reservation hereby opened to settlement and entry whereby certain lands constituting a part of the reservation were erroneously identified as being outside of the reservation, by reason of which several persons in good faith settled upon said lands under the belief that the same were unappropriated public lands open to settlement, and have since improved and cultivated, and are now residing upon the same with a view to the entry thereof under the public land laws, notice is hereby given that in so far as said persons possess the qualifications required by law, and maintain their said settlement and residence up to the time of the opening herein provided for, they will be considered and treated as having initiated and established a lawful settlement at the very instant at which the lands become open, and as having the superior right and claim to enter said lands, which right must be exercised within three months from the time of said opening.

In witness whereof, I have hereunto set my hand and caused the seal of the United States to be affixed.

Done at the city of Washington, this 13th day of April, in the year of our Lord one thousand eight hundred and ninety-nine, and [SEAL.] of the Independence of the United States the one hundred and twenty-third

WILLIAM McKINLEY.

By the President:
  JOHN HAY,
    Secretary of State.

SCHEDULE OF LANDS WITHIN THE SOUTHERN UTE INDIAN RESERVATION ALLOT-
TED TO THE INDIANS AND WITHHELD FROM SETTLEMENT AND ENTRY
BY PROCLAMATION OF THE PRESIDENT DATED APRIL 13, 1899.

In Township 32 North, Range 3 West.

Southwest quarter of southwest quarter of section 4; south half of southeast quarter and southeast quarter of southwest quarter of section 5; north half of northeast quarter, east half of northwest quarter, east half of southwest quarter and southwest quarter of southwest quarter of section 8; north half of northwest quarter and southeast quarter of northwest quarter of section 9; southeast quarter of southwest quarter and south half of southeast quarter of section 10; southwest quarter of southwest quarter of section 11; northwest quarter of northwest quarter of section 13; north half of northeast quarter and north half of northwest quarter of section 14; northeast quarter of northeast quarter of section 15; northwest quarter of northwest quarter of section 17; and northeast quarter of northeast quarter of section 18.

In Township 33 North, Range 3 West.

East half of section 3; northeast quarter, south half of northwest quarter and west half of southwest quarter of section 10; south half of southeast quarter and south half of southwest quarter of section 19; east half of northeast quarter, southeast quarter, east half of southwest quarter and southwest quarter of southwest quarter of section 20; northwest quarter and north half of southwest quarter of section 21; west half of northwest quarter of section 28; east half, east half of northwest quarter and northwest quarter of northwest quarter of section 29; north half of northeast quarter and north half of northwest quarter of section 30; and northeast quarter of section 32.

In Township 34 North, Range 3 West.

Southwest quarter of southwest quarter of section 22; northwest quarter of northwest quarter, south half of northwest quarter and southwest quarter of section 27; and north half of northwest quarter, southeast quarter of northwest quarter, south west quarter of northeast quarter and southeast quarter of section 34.

In Township 32 North, Range 4 West.

Southwest quarter of southeast quarter of section 10; southwest quarter of southwest quarter of section 13; south half of southeast quarter, south half of southwest quarter and northwest quarter of southwest quarter of section 14; west half of northeast quarter, south half of northwest quarter, west half of southeast quarter and southwest quarter of section 15; south half of section 16; south half of northeast quarter, south half of northwest quarter, north half of southeast quarter and north half of southwest quarter of section 17; south half of northeast quarter, north half of southeast quarter, southeast quarter of northwest quarter and northeast quarter of southwest quarter of section 18; north half and north half of southeast quarter of section 21; north half, north half of southeast quarter and north half of southwest quarter of section 22; north half, north half of southeast quarter and north half of southwest quarter of section 23; and west half of northwest quarter and northwest quarter of southwest quarter of section 24.

In Township 33 North, Range 4 West.

South half of northeast quarter, northwest quarter, north half of southeast quarter, southeast quarter of southeast quarter and northeast quarter of southwest quarter of section 23; south half of section 24; and north half of northeast quarter of section 25.

In Township 34 North, Range 4 West.

All of section 7; all of section 8; north half of section 9; all of section 10; north half, southwest quarter, north half of southeast quarter and southwest quarter of southeast quarter of section 11; northwest quarter and northwest quarter of southwest quarter of section 12; west half of northwest quarter and northwest quarter of southwest quarter of section 13; all of section 14; east half, east half of northwest quarter, and southwest quarter of section 15; south half of southeast quarter of section 16; north half of northeast quarter, north half of northwest quarter, southwest quarter of northwest quarter, and southwest quarter of section 18; west half of section 19; east half of southeast quarter of section 20; east half, east half of northwest quarter, and southwest quarter of section 21; north half of northeast quarter, north half of northwest quarter, southwest quarter of northwest quarter and northwest quarter of southwest quarter of section 22; north half of the northwest quarter of section 28; and northeast quarter of northeast quarter of section 29.

In Township 32 North, Range 5 West.

South half, south half of northeast quarter and south half of northwest quarter of section 9; south half of northwest quarter, and southwest quarter of section 10; west half of northwest quarter and west half of southwest quarter of section 14; all of section 15; east half, northwest quarter and north half of southwest quarter of section 16; northeast quarter of southeast quarter of section 19; north half of southeast quarter and north half of southwest quarter of section 20; and northeast quarter, south half of northwest quarter, northwest quarter of southeast quarter and north half of southwest quarter of section 21.

In Township 33 North, Range 5 West.

West half of northeast quarter, northwest quarter and northwest quarter of southwest quarter of section 1; east half, east half of northwest quarter, and southwest quarter of section 2; east half of southeast quarter and southwest quarter of southeast quarter of section 3; east half of southeast quarter and southwest quarter of southeast quarter of section 9; northeast quarter, east half of northwest quarter, southwest quarter of northwest quarter, northwest quarter of southeast quarter, and southwest quarter of section 10; northwest quarter of northeast quarter, and northwest quarter of section 11; west half of northwest quarter and west half of southwest quarter of section 15; east half, east half of northwest quarter and east half of southwest quarter of section 16; north half, north half of southeast quarter and north half of southwest quarter of section 21; west half of section 28; east half of section 29; north half of northeast quarter of section 32; and north half of northwest quarter of section 33.

In Township 34 North, Range 5 West.

East half, east half of northwest quarter and south half of southwest quarter of section 12; east half of northeast quarter, northwest quarter of northeast quarter and west half of northwest quarter of section 13; east half of northeast quarter of section 14; west half of section 25; south half of northeast quarter, southeast quarter and east half of southwest quarter of section 26; and east half of section 35.

In Township 32 North, Range 7 West.

West half of northwest quarter, west half of southeast quarter, and southwest quarter of section 3; all of section 4; east half of northeast quarter and east half of southeast quarter of section 5; east half of northeast quarter and east half of southeast quarter of section 8; all of section 9; west half, west half of northeast quarter and southeast quarter of section 10 ; west half, west half of northeast quarter and west half of southeast quarter of section 15 ; east half, east half of northwest quarter, northwest quarter of northwest quarter and east half of southwest quarter of section 16 ; northeast quarter of northeast quarter of section 17 ; northeast quarter of section 21 ; and northwest quarter of section 22.

In Township 33 North, Range 7 West.

South half of northeast quarter, south half of northwest quarter, and south half of section 1 ; south half of northeast quarter, and southeast quarter of section 2 ; northwest quarter of northeast quarter, and northwest quarter of section 4 ; all of section 5 ; all of section 6 ; north half and northeast quarter of southeast quarter of section 7 ; all of section 8 ; west half of northeast quarter, west half of southeast quarter, and west half of section 9 ; east half of section 11 ; all of section 12 ; all of section 13 ; east half of section 14 ; southwest quarter of southwest quarter of section 15 ; southeast quarter of northeast quarter, west half of northeast quarter, northwest quarter and south half of section 16 ; north half, southeast quarter, north half of southwest quarter and southeast quarter of southwest quarter of section 17 ; east half of northeast quarter, southwest quarter of northeast quarter and north half of southeast quarter of section 18 ; northeast quarter, and east half of northwest quarter of section 20 ; north half, southeast quarter, east half of southwest quarter and northwest quarter of southwest quarter of section 21 ; west half of northwest quarter, and southwest quarter of section 22 ; east half of section 23 ; all of section 24 ; all of section 25 ; northeast quarter of section 26 ; west half of section 27 ; east half, east half of northwest quarter, southwest quarter of northwest quarter, and southwest quarter of section 28 ; south half of northeast quarter, and southeast quarter of section 29 ; east half of northeast quarter and east half of southeast quarter of section 32 ; west half of northeast quarter, west half of southeast quarter, and west half of section 33 ; south half of northeast quarter, and southeast quarter of section 35 ; and all of section 36.

In Township 34 North, Range 7 West.

All of section 10 ; all of section 11 ; west half of northeast quarter, west half of southeast quarter, and west half of section 12 ; north half and southwest quarter of section 13 ; all of section 14 ; all of section 15 ; north half, southeast quarter, and east half of southwest quarter of section 21 ; all of section 22 ; all of section 23 ; north half and southwest quarter of section 24 ; northwest quarter of section 25 ; north half, west half of southeast quarter, and southwest quarter of section 26 ; all of section 27 ; northeast quarter, east half of northwest quarter, east half of southeast quarter, northwest quarter of southeast quarter and northeast quarter of southwest quarter of section 28 ; east half, and south half of southwest quarter of section 32 ; all of section 33 ; north half of northeast quarter, southwest quarter of northeast quarter, northwest quarter and south half of section 34 ; and west half of northeast quarter, northwest quarter, and west half of southwest quarter of section 35.

In Township 34 North, Range 8 West.

East half, east half of northwest quarter and east half of southwest quarter of section 7 ; west half and southeast quarter of section 8 ; west half of section 17 ; east half of section 18 ; east half and southwest quarter of section 19 ; west half of section 20 ; northwest quarter and south half of section 25 ; south half of section 26 ; west half of section 29 ; east half, east half of northwest quarter and east half of southwest quarter of section 30 ; all of section 31 ; west half of northwest quarter and west half of southwest quarter of section 32 ; north half and southeast quarter of section 35 ; and all of section 36

In Township 33 North, Range 9 West.

Southwest quarter of northeast quarter, south half of northwest quarter, southeast quarter, east half of southwest quarter and northwest quarter of southwest quarter of section 2; south half of northeast quarter, southeast quarter of northwest quarter, north half of southeast quarter, southwest quarter of southeast quarter, and southwest quarter of section 3; southeast quarter and south half of southwest quarter of section 4; east half and southwest quarter of section 8; north half of northwest quarter of section 9; west half of southeast quarter, and west half of section 17; east half of southeast quarter, and southwest quarter of section 18; east half of northeast quarter, northwest quarter, and southwest quarter of southwest quarter of section 19; northwest quarter, and east half of southwest quarter of section 20; west half of section 29; east half, south half of northwest quarter, northwest quarter of northwest quarter, and southwest quarter of section 30; east half, east half of northwest quarter, and southwest quarter of section 31; and west half of northwest quarter of section 32.

In Township 34 North, Range 9 West.

All of sections 12, 13, 24, 25 and 36.

In Township 33 North, Range 10 West.

All of section 1; west half of section 12; west half and southeast quarter of section 13; east half of section 24; and east half of section 25.

In Township 34 North, Range 10 West.

South half of section 13, and all of sections 24, 25 and 36.

In Township 34 North, Range 11 West.

East half of northeast quarter, and southeast quarter of section 7; north half, southeast quarter and east half of southwest quarter of section 8; west half of northwest quarter and west half of southwest quarter of section 9; west half of northeast quarter and east half of northwest quarter of section 17; and west half of section 18.

In Township 33 North, Range 12 West.

West half of northwest quarter, south half of southwest quarter and northwest quarter of southwest quarter of section 4; east half, east half of southwest quarter and southwest quarter of southwest quarter of section 5; northeast quarter, south half of northwest quarter and north half of southwest quarter of section 7; north half of northeast quarter and north half of northwest quarter of section 8; south half of northwest quarter and west half of southwest quarter of section 18; east half and northwest quarter of section 19; east half of section 30; and east half of section 31.

In Township 34 North, Range 12 West.

Southeast quarter and east half of southwest quarter of section 13; southeast quarter of southeast quarter of section 22; east half of northeast quarter, southwest quarter of northeast quarter, southeast quarter of northwest quarter, and south half of section 23; north half, west half of southeast quarter, and southwest quarter of section 24; northwest quarter of northeast quarter and north half of northwest quarter of section 25; north half of northeast quarter, north half of northwest quarter and southwest quarter of northwest quarter of section 26; east half, south half of northwest quarter, and southwest quarter of section 27; southeast quarter of section

28; all of section 33; and north half of northeast quarter, southwest quarter of northeast quarter, northwest quarter, and north half of southwest quarter of section 34.

In Township 33 North, Range 13 West.

Southeast quarter of northeast quarter and east half of southeast quarter of section 12; and east half of northeast quarter, southwest quarter of northeast quarter and east half of southeast quarter of section 13.

BY THE PRESIDENT OF THE UNITED STATES OF AMERICA.

A PROCLAMATION.

Whereas it is provided by section twenty-four of the Act of Congress, approved March third, eighteen hundred and ninety-one, entitled, " An act to repeal timber-culture laws, and for other purposes," "That the President of the United States may, from time to time, set apart and reserve, in any State or Territory having public land bearing forests, in any part of the public lands wholly or in part covered with timber or undergrowth, whether of commercial value or not, as public reservations, and the President shall, by public proclamation, declare the establishment of such reservations and the limits thereof;"

And whereas the public lands in the State of California, within the limits hereinafter described, are in part covered with timber, and it appears that the public good would be promoted by setting apart and reserving said lands as a public reservation;

Now, therefore, I, William McKinley, President of the United States, by virtue of the power in me vested by section twenty-four of the aforesaid Act of Congress, do hereby make known and proclaim that there is hereby reserved from entry or settlement and set apart as a Public Reservation all those certain tracts, pieces or parcels of land lying and being situate in the State of California and particularly described as follows, to wit:

Beginning at a point where the northwestern boundary of the rancho Santa Ana intersects the township line between Townships four (4) and five (5) North, Range twenty-three (23) West, San Bernardino Base and Meridian, California; thence westerly along the township line to the southwest corner of Township five (5) North, Range twenty-four (24) West; thence northerly along the range line to the southeast corner of the rancho Los Prietos y Najalayegua; thence in a general northwesterly direction along the southern boundaries of the ranchos Los Prietos y Najalayegua, San Marcos, Tequepis, Lomas de la Purificacion and Nojoqui to the eastern boundary of the rancho Las Cruces; thence in a general southerly direction along the eastern boundary of the said rancho Las Cruces to the northern boundary of the rancho Nuestra Señora del Refugio; thence in a general southeasterly direction along the northern boundaries of the ranchos Nuestra Señora del Refugio, Cañada del Corral, Los Dos Pueblos, La Goleta, Pueblo and Mission Lands of Santa Barbara and the rancho El Rincon (Arellanes) to its most eastern point; thence in a southwesterly direction along the southern boundary of said rancho to the point where it intersects the township line between Townships three (3) and four (4) North, Range twenty-five (25) West; thence easterly along the township line to the western boundary of the rancho Santa Ana; thence northeasterly along the western boundary of said rancho to its intersection with the township line between Townships four (4) and five (5) North, Range twenty-three (23) West, the place of beginning.

Excepting from the force and effect of this Proclamation all lands which may have been, prior to the date hereof, embraced in any legal entry or covered by any lawful filing duly of record in the proper United States Land Office, or upon which any valid settlement has been made pursuant to law, and the statutory period within which to make entry or filing of record has not expired: *Provided*, that this exception shall not continue to apply to any particular tract of land unless the entryman, settler or claimant continues to comply with the law under which the entry, filing or settlement was made.

Warning is hereby expressly given to all persons not to make settlement upon the tract of land reserved by this proclamation.

The reservation hereby established shall be known as The Santa Ynez Forest Reserve.

In witness whereof I have hereunto set my hand and caused the seal of the United States to be affixed.

Done at the city of Washington this 2d day of October, in the year of our Lord one thousand eight hundred and ninety-nine, and [SEAL.] of the Independence of the United States the one hundred and twenty-fourth.

WILLIAM McKINLEY.

By the President:
    DAVID J. HILL,
        Acting Secretary of State.

BY THE PRESIDENT OF THE UNITED STATES OF AMERICA.

A PROCLAMATION.

Whereas it is provided by section 13 of the act of Congress of March 3, 1891, entitled "An Act to amend title sixty, chapter three, of the Revised Statutes of the United States, relating to copyrights," that said act "shall only apply to a citizen or subject of a foreign state or nation when such foreign state or nation permits to citizens of the United

States of America the benefit of copyright on substantially the same basis as its own citizens; or when such foreign state or nation is a party to an international agreement which provides for reciprocity in the granting of copyright, by the terms of which agreement the United States of America may, at its pleasure, become a party to such agreement;"

And whereas it is also provided by said section that "the existence of either of the conditions aforesaid shall be determined by the President of the United States by proclamation made from time to time as the purposes of this act may require;"

And whereas satisfactory official assurances have been given that in the Republic of Costa Rica the law permits to citizens of the United States of America the benefit of copyright on substantially the same basis as to the citizens of that Republic:

Now, therefore, I, William McKinley, President of the United States of America, do declare and proclaim that the first of the conditions specified in section 13 of the act of March 3, 1891, now exists and is fulfilled in respect to the citizens of the Republic of Costa Rica.

In testimony whereof, I have hereunto set my hand and caused the seal of the United States to be affixed.

Done at the city of Washington, this 19th day of October, one thousand eight hundred and ninety-nine and of the Independence of the United States the one hundred and twenty-fourth.

[SEAL.]

WILLIAM McKINLEY.

By the President:
JOHN HAY,
    Secretary of State.

BY THE PRESIDENT OF THE UNITED STATES OF AMERICA.

A PROCLAMATION.

Whereas it is provided by section twenty-four of the act of Congress, approved March third, eighteen hundred and ninety-one, entitled "An act to repeal timber-culture laws, and for other purposes," "That the President of the United States may, from time to time, set apart and reserve, in any State or Territory having public land bearing forests, in any part of the public lands wholly or in part covered with timber or undergrowth, whether of commercial value or not, as public reservations, and the President shall, by public proclamation, declare the establishment of such reservations and the limits thereof;"

And whereas it is further provided by the act of Congress, approved June fourth, eighteen hundred and ninety-seven, entitled "An act making appropriations for sundry civil expenses of the Government for the fiscal year ending June thirtieth, eighteen hundred and ninety-eight, and for other purposes," that "The President is hereby authorized at any time to modify any executive order that has been or may hereafter be made establishing any forest reserve, and by such modification may reduce the area or change the boundary lines of such reserve, or may vacate altogether any order creating such reserve;"

And whereas the public lands in the Territory of Arizona, within the limits hereinafter described, are in part covered with timber, and it appears that the public good would be promoted by setting apart and reserving said lands as a public reservation;

Now, therefore, I, William McKinley, President of the United States, by virtue of the power in me vested by the aforesaid acts of Congress, do hereby make known and proclaim that the boundary lines of the Forest Reservation in the Territory of Arizona, known as "The Prescott Forest Reserve," created by proclamation of May tenth, eighteen hundred and ninety-eight, are hereby so changed and enlarged as to include all those certain tracts, pieces, or parcels of land lying and being situate in the Territory of Arizona, and within the boundaries particularly described as follows, to wit:

Beginning at the northeast corner of township thirteen (13) north, range one (1) west, Gila and Salt River Meridian, Arizona; thence southerly along the Gila and Salt River Meridian to the southeast corner of said township; thence easterly along the Third (3d) Standard Parallel north to the northeast corner of township twelve (12) north, range one (1) east; thence southerly along the range line to the southeast corner of township nine (9) north, range one (1) east; thence westerly along the township line to the southwest corner of township nine (9) north, range one (1) west; thence northerly along the range line to the northwest corner of said township; thence westerly along the township line to the southwest corner of township ten (10) north, range two (2) west; thence northerly along the range line to the southeast corner of township twelve (12) north, range three (3) west; thence westerly along the township line to the southwest corner of said township; thence northerly along the range line to the northwest corner of said township; thence westerly along the township line to the southwest corner of section thirty-five (35), township thirteen (13) north, range four (4) west; thence northerly along the section line to a point due west of the northwest corner of township fourteen (14) north, range three (3) west; thence easterly to the northeast corner of said township; thence southerly along the range line to the northwest corner of section nineteen (19), township thirteen (13) north, range two (2) west; thence easterly to the northeast corner of section twenty-four (24), said township; thence northerly to the northwest corner of township thirteen (13) north, range one (1) west; thence easterly to the northeast corner of said township, the place of beginning.

Excepting from the force and effect of this proclamation all lands which may have been, prior to the date hereof, embraced in any legal entry or covered by any lawful filing duly of record in the proper United States Land Office, or upon which any valid settlement has been made pursuant to law, and the statutory period within which to make entry or filing of record has not expired; *Provided*, that this exception shall not continue to apply to any particular tract of land unless the entry-man, settler, or claimant continues to comply with the law under which the entry, filing, or settlement was made.

Warning is hereby expressly given to all persons not to make settlement upon the tract of land reserved by this proclamation.

In witness whereof, I have hereunto set my hand and caused the seal of the United States to be affixed.

Done at the city of Washington, this 21st day of October,
[SEAL.] A. D. 1899, and of the Independence of the United States the one hundred and twenty-fourth.

WILLIAM McKINLEY.

By the President:
JOHN HAY,
Secretary of State.

BY THE PRESIDENT OF THE UNITED STATES.

THANKSGIVING PROCLAMATION.

A national custom dear to the hearts of the people calls for the setting apart of one day in each year as an occasion of special thanksgiving to Almighty God for the blessings of the preceding year. This honored observance acquires with time a tenderer significance. It enriches domestic life. It summons under the family roof the absent children to glad reunion with those they love.

Seldom has this nation had greater cause for profound thanksgiving. No great pestilence has invaded our shores. Liberal employment waits upon labor. Abundant crops have rewarded the efforts of the husband-men. Increased comforts have come to the home. The national finances have been strengthened, and public credit has been sustained and made firmer. In all branches of industry and trade there has been an un-equaled degree of prosperity, while there has been a steady gain in the moral and educational growth of our national character. Churches and schools have flourished. American patriotism has been exalted. Those engaged in maintaining the honor of the flag with such signal success have been in a large degree spared from disaster and disease. An honorable peace has been ratified with a foreign nation with which we were at war, and we are now on friendly relations with every power of earth.

The trust which we have assumed for the benefit of the people of

Cuba has been faithfully advanced. There is marked progress toward the restoration of healthy industrial conditions, and under wise sanitary regulations the island has enjoyed unusual exemption from the scourge of fever. The hurricane which swept over our new possession of Puerto Rico, destroying the homes and property of the inhabitants, called forth the instant sympathy of the people of the United States, who were swift to respond with generous aid to the sufferers. While the insurrection still continues in the island of Luzon, business is resuming its activity, and confidence in the good purposes of the United States is being rapidly established throughout the archipelago.

For these reasons and countless others, I, William McKinley, President of the United States, do hereby name Thursday, the thirtieth day of November next, as a day of general thanksgiving and prayer, to be observed as such by all our people on this continent and in our newly acquired islands, as well as those who may be at sea or sojourning in foreign lands; and I advise that on this day religious exercises shall be conducted in the churches or meeting-places of all denominations, in order that in the social features of the day its real significance may not be lost sight of, but fervent prayers may be offered to the Most High for a continuance of the Divine Guidance without which man's efforts are vain, and for Divine consolation to those whose kindred and friends have sacrificed their lives for country.

I recommend also that on this day so far as may be found practicable labor shall cease from its accustomed toil and charity abound toward the sick, the needy and the poor.

In witness whereof I have set my hand and caused the seal of the United States to be affixed.

Done at the city of Washington this 25th day of October, [SEAL.]   A. D. 1899, and of the Independence of the United States the one hundred and twenty-fourth.

WILLIAM McKINLEY.

By the President:
    JOHN HAY,
        Secretary of State.

BY THE PRESIDENT OF THE UNITED STATES.

A PROCLAMATION.

Whereas by joint resolution " to provide for annexing the Hawaiian Islands to the United States," approved July 7, 1898, the cession by the Government of the Republic of Hawaii to the United States of America, of all rights of sovereignty of whatsoever kind in and over the Hawaiian Islands and their dependencies, and the transfer to the United States of the absolute fee and ownership of all public, Government, or crown lands, public buildings, or edifices, ports, harbors, military equipment, and all other public property of every kind and description belonging to the Government of the Hawaiian Islands, was duly accepted, ratified, and confirmed, and the said Hawaiian Islands and their dependencies annexed as a part of the territory of the United States and made subject to the sovereign dominion thereof, and all and singular the property and rights hereinbefore mentioned vested in the United States of America; and

Whereas it was further provided in said resolution that the existing laws of the United States relative to public lands shall not apply to such lands in the Hawaiian Islands, but the Congress of the United States shall enact special laws for their management and disposition; and

Whereas it is deemed necessary in the public interests that certain lots and plats of land in the city of Honolulu be immediately reserved for naval purposes;

Now, therefore, I, William McKinley, President of the United States, by virtue of the authority in me vested, do hereby declare, proclaim, and make known that the following described lots or plats of land be and the same are hereby, subject to such legislative action as the Congress of the United States may take with respect thereto, reserved for naval purposes, to wit:

1st. Esplanade lots Nos. 94, 95, 96, 97, 98, and 99. Beginning at the south corner of Richards street and Halekauwila street, which point is S. 30° 25′ E., 343.6 feet from the east corner of the Hawaiian Electric Company building and run by the true Meridian:

S. 30° 25′ E. 304.50 feet along Halekauwila street.

S. 56° 49′ W. 100.12 feet along Mililani street.

N. 30° 25′ W. 300.60 feet along Government Lots Nos. 112–100.

N. 54° 34′ E. 100.38 feet along Richards street to the initial point. Area, 30,255 square feet.

2d. Esplanade lots Nos. 63, 64, 65, 66, 67, and 68. Beginning at the north corner of Alakea street and Allen street, as shown on Government Survey's Registered Map No. 1867, and running by true bearings:

N. 30° 25′ W. 200 feet along the northeast side of Allen street.

N. 59° 35′ E. 150 feet along the southeast side of Kilauea street.

S. 30° 25′ E. 200 feet along lots 62 and 69.

S. 59° 35′ W. 150 feet along the northwest side of Alakea street to the initial point. Area, 30,000 square feet.

3d. Lot at east corner of Mililani and Halekauwila streets. Beginning at the east corner of Halekauwila and Mililani streets, as shown on Government Survey Registered Map No. 1955, and running by true bearings:

N. 56° 49′ E. 110.5 feet along Mililani street.

S. 3° 52′ E. 69.5 feet along inner line of Waikahalulu water lots.

S. 56° 49′ W. 79.5 feet along Bishop Estate land.

N. 30° 25′ W. 60.5 feet along Halekauwila street to the initial point. Area, 5,72? square feet.

4th. A plat of land in Kewalo-uka. Beginning at a point on the upper side of Punchbowl Drive, which is 863 feet south and 2,817 feet east of Puowaina Trig. Station, as shown on Government Survey's Registered Map 1749, and running:

N. 00° 10' W. true 630 feet along Punchbowl Drive.

S. 57° 00' W. true 694 feet along Punchbowl Drive.

Thence along Punchbowl Drive in a northeasterly direction 900 feet; thence due east 840 feet (more or less) to the boundary of the land of Kalawahine; thence along boundary of the land of Kalawahine 1040 feet (more or less) to south angle of said land; thence S. 78° 30' W. true 397 feet (more or less) to Punchbowl Drive:

N. 84° 50' W. true 245 feet along Punchbowl Drive to initial point. Area 20 acres (more or less).

5th. Lots on Punchbowl Slope, Nos. 608, 609, and 610. Beginning at a point on the east side of Magazine street, 351.5 feet above the concrete post marking the east corner of Spencer and Magazine streets, as shown on Government Survey's Registered Map No. 1749, and runs:

N. 18° 10' E. true 150.0 feet along Magazine street.

N. 49° 12' E. true 226.7 feet along Government land.

S. 24° 11' E. true 91.0 feet along Government Road Reserve.

S. 77° 21' E. true 179.5 feet along same.

S. 13° 45' E. true 109.8 feet along Government land to north angle of Gr. 3813 to Dr. Wood.

S. 73° 30' W. true 121.3 feet along Gr. 3814 to H. M. Dow.

S. 76° 15' W. true 250.0 feet along Grs. 3999 and 4000.

N. 71° 50' W. true 102.5 feet along Gr. 4000 to initial point

Area, 83,588 square feet.

6th. Portion of reef of Kaakaukukui. Beginning at the Government Survey Station known as the "Battery" ∆ from which, Punchbowl ∆ bears N. 48° 18' 30'' E. true and the lighthouse vane

N. 56° 14' W. distant 1608.1 feet and running as follows:

N. 37° 40' W. true 760 feet along on the reef of Kaakaukukui.

S. 39° 00' W. true 3100 feet along the southeast side of main channel to a depth of 20 feet of water (more or less).

S. 9° 25' W. true 987 feet along the reef in about 20 feet of water.

N. 52° 23' E. true 3585 feet along on the reef to a point on the seashore at high water mark.

N. 35° 00' W. true 182 feet along the shore at high-water mark.

N. 5° 35' W. true 446 feet along Allen street extension to the southeast corner of the Battery wall.

S. 87° 20' W. true 120 feet to the initial point.

Area, $76\frac{25}{100}$ acres.

7th. Punchbowl street from Halekauwila street to Allen street. Beginning at the southwest corner of Halekauwila and Punchbowl streets, as shown on the Government blue print, and running in a westerly direction along the U. S. Naval Reservation 572 feet to Allen street, thence along Allen street 50 feet, thence in an easterly direction along the United States Naval Reservation 480 feet to land belonging to the Bishop Estate, thence 110 feet to the initial point.

In witness whereof I have hereunto set my hand and caused the seal of the United States to be affixed.

Done at the city of Washington, this 10th day of November, A. D. 1899, and of the Independence of the United States the one hundred and twenty-fourth.

[SEAL.]

WILLIAM McKINLEY.

By the President:

JOHN HAY,

Secretary of State.

BY THE PRESIDENT OF THE UNITED STATES OF AMERICA.

A PROCLAMATION.

Whereas it is provided by section 13 of the act of Congress of March 3, 1891, entitled "An act to amend title sixty, chapter three, of the Revised Statutes of the United States, relating to copyrights," that said act "shall only apply to a citizen or subject of a foreign state or nation when such foreign state or nation permits to citizens of the United States of America the benefit of copyright on substantially the same basis as its own citizens; or when such foreign state or nation is a party to an international agreement which provides for reciprocity in the granting of copyright, by the terms of which agreement the United States of America may, at its pleasure, become a party to such agreement;" and

Whereas it is also provided by said section that "the existence of either of the conditions aforesaid shall be determined by the President of the United States by proclamation made from time to time as the purposes of this act may require;" and

Whereas satisfactory official assurances have been given that in the Kingdom of the Netherlands and in the Netherlands' possessions the law permits to citizens of the United States of America the benefit of copyright on substantially the same basis as to subjects of the Netherlands:

Now, therefore, I, William McKinley, President of the United States of America, do declare and proclaim that the first of the conditions specified in section 13 of the act of March 3, 1891, now exists and is fulfilled in respect to the subjects of the Netherlands.

In testimony whereof, I have hereunto set my hand and caused the seal of the United States to be affixed.

[SEAL.] Done at the city of Washington, this 20th day of November, A. D. 1899, and of the Independence of the United States the one hundred and twenty-fourth.

WILLIAM McKINLEY.

By the President:
JOHN HAY,
        Secretary of State.

BY THE PRESIDENT OF THE UNITED STATES.

A PROCLAMATION.

To the People of the United States:

Garret Augustus Hobart, Vice-President of the United States, died at his home in Paterson, New Jersey, at 8:30 o'clock this morning. In him the Nation has lost one of its most illustrious citizens and one of its most faithful servants. His participation in the business life, and the law-making body of his native State was marked by unswerving fidelity and by a high order of talents and attainments; and his too brief career as Vice-President of the United States and President of the Senate exhibited the loftiest qualities of upright and sagacious statesmanship. In the world of affairs he had few equals among his contemporaries. His private character was gentle and noble. He will long be mourned by his friends as a man of singular purity and attractiveness whose sweetness of disposition won all hearts, while his elevated purposes, his unbending integrity and whole-hearted devotion to the public good deserved and acquired universal respect and esteem.

In sorrowing testimony of the loss which has fallen upon the country, I direct that on the day of the funeral the Executive Offices of the United States shall be closed and all posts and stations of the Army and Navy shall display the national flag at half-mast, and that the representatives of the United States in foreign countries shall pay appropriate tribute to the illustrious dead for a period of thirty days.

In witness whereof I have set my hand and caused the seal of the United States to be affixed.

[SEAL.] Done at the city of Washington, this 21st day of November, A. D. 1899, and of the Independence of the United States the one hundred and twenty-fourth.

WILLIAM McKINLEY

By the President:
JOHN HAY,
   Secretary of State.

BY THE PRESIDENT OF THE UNITED STATES OF AMERICA.

A PROCLAMATION.

Whereas The Olympic Forest Reserve, in the State of Washington, was established by proclamation dated February 22d, 1897, under and by virtue of section twenty-four of the act of Congress, approved March 3rd, 1891, entitled, "An act to repeal timber-culture laws, and for other purposes," which provides, "That the President of the United States may, from time to time, set apart and reserve, in any State or Territory having public lands wholly or in part covered with timber or undergrowth, whether of commercial value or not, as public reservations, and the President shall, by public proclamation, declare the establishment of such reservations and the limits thereof;"

And whereas it is further provided by the act of Congress, approved June 4th, 1897, entitled, "An act making appropriations for sundry civil expenses of the Government for the fiscal year ending June 30th,

1898, and for other purposes," that " The President is hereby authorized at any time to modify any executive order that has been or may hereafter be made establishing any forest reserve, and by such modification may reduce the area or change the boundary lines of such reserve, or may vacate altogether any order creating such reserve;"

Now, therefore, I, William McKinley, President of the United States, by virtue of the power vested in me by the aforesaid act of Congress, approved June 4th, 1897, do hereby make known and proclaim that there are hereby withdrawn and excluded from the aforesaid Olympic Forest Reserve and restored to the public domain all those certain tracts, pieces or parcels of land particularly described as follows, to wit:

Townships twenty-eight (28) north, ranges thirteen (13) and fourteen (14) west, Willamette Base and Meridian, Washington; fractional township twenty-eight (28) north, range fifteen (15) west; sections one (1) to eighteen (18), both inclusive, townships twenty-nine (29) north, ranges three (3), four (4) and five (5) west; sections four (4), five (5), six (6), seven (7) and the north half of section eight (8), township twenty-nine (29) north, range twelve (12) west; all of township twenty-nine (29) north, range thirteen (13) west, except sections thirteen (13), twenty-three (23), twenty-four (24), twenty-five (25) and twenty-six (26); township twenty-nine (29) north, range fourteen (14) west; fractional township twenty-nine (29) north, range fifteen (15) west; sections one (1) to twelve (12), both inclusive, township thirty (30) north, range nine (9) west; sections twenty-seven (27) to thirty-four (34), both inclusive, township thirty (30) north, range ten (10) west; sections twenty-five (25) to thirty-six (36), both inclusive, township thirty (30) north, range eleven (11) west; sections seventeen (17) to thirty-six (36), both inclusive, township thirty (30) north, range twelve (12) west; townships thirty (30) north, ranges thirteen (13) and fourteen (14) west; and township thirty (30) north, range fifteen (15) west.

That the lands hereby restored to the public domain shall be open to settlement from date hereof, but shall not be subject to entry, filing or selection until after ninety days notice by such publication as the Secretary of the Interior may prescribe.

In witness whereof, I have hereunto set my hand and caused the seal of the United States to be affixed.

Done at the city of Washington, this 7th day of April, A. D. [SEAL.] 1900, and of the Independence of the United States the one hundred and twenty-fourth.

WILLIAM McKINLEY

By the President:
JOHN HAY,
Secretary of State.

Whereas by section one of the act of July 1, 1892 (27 Stat., 62), entitled "An act to provide for the opening of a part of the Colville Reservation, in the State of Washington, and for other purposes" it is provided:

"That subject to the reservations and allotment of lands in severalty to the individual members of the Indians of the Colville Reservation in the State of Washington herein provided for, all the following described tract or portion of said Colville Reservation, namely: Beginning at a point on the eastern boundary line of the Colville Indian Reservation where the township line between townships thirty-four and thirty-five north, of range thirty-seven east, of the Willamette meridian, if extended west, would intersect the same, said point being in the middle of the channel of the Columbia river, and running thence west parallel with the forty-ninth parallel of latitude to the western boundary line of the said Colville Indian Reservation in the Okanagon river, thence north following the said western boundary line to the said forty-ninth parallel of latitude, thence east along the said forty-ninth parallel of latitude to the northeast corner of the said Colville Indian Reservation, thence south following the eastern boundary of said reservation to the place of beginning, containing by estimation one million five hundred thousand acres, the same being a portion of the Colville Indian Reservation, created by executive order dated July second, eighteen hundred and seventy-two, be, and is hereby, vacated and restored to the public domain, notwithstanding any executive order or other proceeding whereby the same was set apart as a reservation for any Indians or bands of Indians, and the same shall be open to settlement and entry by the proclamation of the President of the United States and shall be disposed of under the general laws applicable to the disposition of public lands in the State of Washington,"

and

Whereas it is provided by section three of said act,

"That each entryman under the homestead laws shall, within five years from the date of his original entry and before receiving a final certificate for the land covered by his entry, pay to the United States for the land so taken by him in addition to fees provided by law the sum of one dollar and fifty cents per acre, one third of which shall be paid within two years after the date of the original entry; but the rights or honorably discharged Union soldiers and sailors, as defined and described in sections twenty-three hundred and four and twenty-three hundred and five of the Revised Statutes of the United States, shall not be abridged, except as to the sum to be paid as aforesaid,"

and

Whereas by section six of said act it is provided:

"That the land used and occupied for school purposes at what is known as Tonasket school, on Bonaparte creek, and the site of the sawmill, gristmill, and other mill property on said reservation, is hereby reserved from the operation of this act, unless other lands are selected in lieu thereof: *Provided*, That such reserve lands shall not exceed in the aggregate two sections, and must be selected in legal subdivisions conformably to the public surveys, such selection to be made by the Indian Agent of the Colville Agency, under the direction of the Secretary of the Interior and subject to his approval: *Provided, however*, That said Indians may, in lieu of said sites, or either of them, select other lands of equal quantity, for such purposes, either on the vacated or unvacated portions of said reservation, the same to be designated in legal subdivisions by said Indian Agent, under the direction of and subject to the approval of the Secretary of the Interior, in which case said first-designated tracts shall not be exempt from the operation of this act; such selection to be made and approved within six months after the survey of said lands and the proclamation of the President,"

and

Whereas in a clause in the Indian Appropriation Act of July 1, 1898 (30 Stat., 571), it is provided:

"That the mineral lands only in the Colville Indian Reservation, in the State of Washington, shall be subject to entry under the laws of the United States in relation to the entry of minerals lands: *Provided*, That lands allotted to the Indians or used by the Government for any purpos or by any school shall not be subject to entry under this provision,"

and in another clause that,

"The Indian allotments in severalty provided for in said act shall be selected and completed at the earliest practicable time and not later than six months after the proclamation of the President opening the vacated portion of said reservation to settlement and entry, which proclamation may be issued without awaiting the survey of the unsurveyed lands therein. Said allotments shall be made from lands which shall at the time of the selection thereof be surveyed, excepting that any Indian entitled to allotment under said act who has improvements upon unsurveyed land may select the same for his allotment, whereupon the Secretary of the Interior shall cause the same to be surveyed and allotted to him. At the expiration of six months from the date of the proclamation by the President, and not before, the non-mineral lands within the vacated portion of said reservation which shall not have been allotted to Indians as aforesaid, shall be subject to settlement, entry and disposition under said act of July first, eighteen hundred and ninety-two: *Provided*, That the land used and occupied for school purposes at what is known as Tonasket school, on Bonaparte creek, and the site of the sawmill, gristmill and other mill property on said reservation, are hereby reserved from the operation of this act, unless other lands are selected in lieu thereof as provided in section six of the aforesaid act of July first, eighteen hundred and ninety-two,''

and

Whereas, all the terms, conditions and considerations required by said acts of July 1, 1892, and July 1, 1898, precedent to the issuance of the Proclamation provided for therein, have been, as I hereby declare, complied with:

Now, therefore, I, William McKinley, President of the United States, by virtue of the power in me vested by the statutes hereinbefore mentioned, do hereby declare and make known that all of said lands hereinbefore described, restored by the said act of July 1, 1892, will, at and after the hour of twelve o'clock noon (Pacific standard time) six months from date hereof, to wit: the 10th day of October, nineteen hundred, and not before, be open to settlement and entry under the terms of and subject to all the conditions, limitations, reservations and restrictions contained in the statutes above specified, and the laws of the United States, applicable thereto, saving and excepting such tracts as have been or may be allotted to or reserved or selected for, the Indians, or other purposes, under the laws herein referred to.

Sections sixteen and thirty-six in each township will be subject to such right of the State of Washington thereto as may be ascertained and determined by the land department in the administration of the grant of lands in place to that State for the support of common schools.

The lands which have been allotted to the Indians are for greater convenience particularly described in the accompanying schedule, entitled ''Schedule of lands allotted to the Indians in restored portion of Colville Reservation, Washington, and withheld from settlement and entry by proclamation of the President, dated April 10, 1900,'' and which schedule is made a part hereof.

Notice, moreover, is hereby given that it is by law enacted that at the expiration of six months from the date of the proclamation by the President, and not before, the non-mineral lands within the vacated portion of said reservation which shall not have been allotted to or reserved or selected for the Indians, or for other purposes, shall be subject to settlement, entry and disposition under said act of July 1, 1892; and all persons are hereby warned from attempting to make settlement on any of said lands prior to the date fixed for the opening hereof.

In witness whereof, I have hereunto set my hand and caused the seal of the United States to be affixed.

Done at the city of Washington, this 10th day of April, [SEAL.] A. D. 1900, and of the Independence of the United States the one hundred and twenty-fourth.

WILLIAM McKINLEY.

By the President:
JOHN HAY,
Secretary of State.

SCHEDULE OF LANDS ALLOTTED TO THE INDIANS IN RESTORED PORTION OF COLVILLE RESERVATION, WASHINGTON, AND WITHHELD FROM SETTLEMENT AND ENTRY BY PROCLAMATION OF THE PRESIDENT, DATED APRIL 10, 1900.

Township 35 North, Range 31 East.

A tract of land described as follows: Beginning at a large fir tree blazed on N. side being S. E. Cor. thence due N. 20 chains set post and made a mound thence due west 40 chains set post and made mound thence S. 20 chains set post being S. W. Cor. thence due E. 40 chains to point of beginning, in section 11 or 12.

A tract of land described as follows: Beginning at N. W. Cor. of 198 due W. 40 chains set post being S. E. Cor. thence due N. 20 chains set post thence due W. 40 chains set post thence due S. 20 chains set post thence due E. 40 chains to point of beginning, in section 10 or 11.

A tract of land described as follows: Beginning at a post and mound at N. W. Cor. thence due S. 20 chains set post thence due E. 40 chains set post S. E. Cor. thence due N. 20 chains set post thence due W. 40 chains to point of beginning, in section 6 or 7.

A tract of land described as follows: Beginning at S. W. Cor. of 200 thence due S. 20 chains set post thence due E. 40 chains set post thence due N. 20 chains, being N. E. Cor. thence due W. 40 chains to point of beginning, in section 6 or 7.

A tract of land described as follows: Beginning at S. E. Cor. of 201 thence due S. 40 chains being S. W. Cor. thence due E. 40 chains set post thence due N. 20 chains thence due W. 40 chains set post thence due S. 20 chains to point of beginning, in section 7 or 8.

Township 35 North, Range 32 East.

A tract of land described as follows: Set post and made mound for N. E. Cor. thence due S. 20 chains set post thence due W. 40 chains set post and made mound thence due N. 20 chains set post made a mound thence due E. 40 chains to point of beginning, in section 7 or 8.

Township 35 North, Range 36 East.

SE ¼, Sec. 24; NE ¼ NW ¼, NW ¼ NE ¼, Sec. 25.

Township 35 North, Range 37 East.

E ½ SE¼, Sec 9; lots 3, 4 and 5 of Sec. 10; lots 1 and 2 of Sec. 15; NE ¼ SW ¼ and lots 1, 2, 3, 4, 5 and 6 of Sec. 16; E ½ NE ¼, SE¼ of Sec. 19; W ½ NW ¼, W ½ SW ¼, SE¼ SW ¼ and lots 2, 3 and 4 of Sec. 20; NW ¼, W ½ SW¼ and lots 1, 2 and 4 of Sec. 29; E. NE¼, NW ¼ and S. ½ Sec. 30; NE ¼ and lots 1 and 2 of Sec. 31; NE ¼ NW ¼, lots 1, 2, 3 and 4 of Sec. 32.

Township 36 North, Range 28 East.

A tract of land described as follows: Beginning at a mound and stake run due north 20 chains thence due west 40 chains set post thence due S. 20 chains set post thence due E. 40 chains to point of beginning.

A tract of land described as follows: Beginning at NE Cor. of 188 run due N. 20 chains set post thence due W. 40 chains set post thence due S. 20 chains to N. W. Cor. 188 thence due E. 40 chains to point of beginning.

A tract of land described as follows: Beginning at N. W. Cor. of 188 thence due W. 40 chains set post thence due N. 20 chains set post thence due E. 40 chains to N. W. Cor. of 189 thence due S. 20 chains to the point of beginning.

A tract of land described as follows: Beginning at N. W. Cor. of 190 thence due N. 20 chains set post thence due E. 40 chains set post thence due S. 20 chains to N. E. Cor. of 190 thence due W. 20 chains to point of beginning.

A tract of land described as follows: Beginning at N. W. Cor. of 191 thence due N. 20 chains set post thence due E. 40 chains set post thence due S. 20 chains to N. E. Cor. of 191 thence due W. 40 chains to point of beginning.

A tract of land described as follows: Beginning at N. W. Cor. 190 thence due W. 20 chains set post thence due N. 40 chains set post thence due E. 20 chains to N. W. Cor. 192 thence due S. 40 chains to point of beginning.

A tract of land described as follows: Beginning at S. E. Cor. Sec. 32, Tp. 37, R. 28 run due S. 20 chains set post thence due E. 40 chains made rock mound thence due N. 20 chains to quarter Sec. Cor. of Sec. 33 on Tp. line, thence due W. 40 chains on Tp. line to point of beginning.

Township 36 North, Range 29 East.

A tract of land described as follows: Set post and made mound thence due N. 20 chains set post thence due E. 40 chains set post thence due S. 20 chains set post thence due W. 40 chains to point of beginning, in section 9.

A tract of land described as follows: Beginning on ninth standard parallel at quarter Cor. of Sec. 33 thence due S. 40 chains set post thence due W. 20 chains set post thence due N. 40 chains set post thence due E. on the 9th standard parallel 20 chains to point of beginning.

A tract of land described as follows: Beginning at S. W. Cor. of 215 on ninth standard parallel thence due E. 40 chains set post thence due S. 20 chains set post thence due W. 40 chains set post thence due N. 20 chains to place of beginning, in section 4 or 5.

Township 36 North, Range 30 East.

E ½ of NW ¼, W ½ NE ¼, SE ¼ NE ¼, NE ¼ SE ¼ of Sec. 33; SW ¼ NW ¼, N ½ SW ¼, W ½ SE ¼, SE ¼ SE ¼ of Sec. 34.

Township 36 North, Range 32 East.

NE ¼, W ½ SE ¼, E ½ SW ¼ of Sec. 1; NE ¼ NE ¼ and N ½ of SE ¼ of NE ¼ of Sec. 2; E ½ SE ¼ of Sec. 11; NW ¼ and W ½ SW ¼ of Sec. 12; W ½ NW ¼ and W ½ SW ¼ of Sec. 13; E. ½ NE¼ and E ½ SE ¼ of Sec. 14; NE ¼ and W ½ SE ¼ of Sec. 23; W½ SE ¼ of Sec. 26; E ½ NW ¼ and W ½ SW ¼ of Sec. 35.

Township 36 North, Range 33 East.

W ½ of E ½ of NW ¼ and W ½ of NW ¼ of Sec. 1; E ½ of E ½ of NE ¼ of Sec. 2; NE ¼, N ½ SE ¼, E ½ NW ¼ of Sec. 4; N ½ NE ¼ and NW ¼ NW ¼ of Sec. 5; N ½ NE ¼, SW ¼ NE ¼ and NW ¼ of Sec. 6.

Township 36 North, Range 37 East.

SW ¼ SE ¼ and lot 4 of Sec. 22; lot 1 of Sec. 26; W ½ NE ¼, W ½ SE ¼ and lots 1, 2, 3 and 4 of Sec. 27; SE ¼ NE ¼, NE ¼ SE ¼ of Sec. 33; NW ¼ NE ¼, S ½ NW ¼, SW ¼ and lots 1, 2, 3, 4 and 5 of Sec. 34; and lot 1 of Sec. 35.

Township 37 North, Range 27 East.

E ½ NE ¼, E ½ SE ¼ of Sec. 1; SE ¼ NW ¼ and lots 2, 3 and 4 of Sec. 3, the E ½ NW ¼ and NE ¼ of Sec. 12, The W ½ of E ½ of SW ¼ and lots 1, 2, 3, 4, and 5 of Sec. 16; Lots 1 and 2 of Sec. 20, W ½ NW ¼ of Sec. 21.

Township 37 North, Range 28 East.

W ½ NE ¼, E ½ NW ¼, E½ SW ¼, lots 4, 5, 6 and 7 of Sec. 6; N ½ NW ¼ Sec. 7; NW ¼ NE ¼, NE ¼ NW ¼, Sec. 9; S ½ SE ¼, SE ¼ SW ¼, Sec. 25; S ½ of Sec. 32; S ½ SW ¼ of Sec. 33, N ½ NE ¼ and NE ¼ NW ¼ of Sec. 36.

Township 37 North, Range 29 East.

N ½ SW ¼ of Sec. 27, lot 4 of Sec. 30, E ½ NE ¼, NW ¼ NE ¼, NE ¼ NW ¼ and lot 1 of Sec. 31; S ½ NW ¼, N ½ SW ¼ and SE ¼ of Sec. 32, W ½ SW ¼ of Sec. 33.

Township 37 North, Range 30 East.

W ½ NW ¼ of Sec. 1, E ½ NE ¼ of Sec. 2; SE ¼ of Sec. 3; S ½ NE ¼ of Sec. 8; S ½ NE ¼ and S ½ NW ¼ of Sec. 9; N ½ NE ¼ and N ½ NW ¼ Sec. 10.

Township 37 North, Range 33 East.

Lots 8 and 9, Sec. 5; Lots 3, 5, 12 and 13 of Sec. 8; E ½ NE ¼, SE ¼ SE ¼ and lots 1, 4, 7 and 8 of Sec. 17; NE ¼ NW ¼ and E ½ of Sec. 20; SW ¼ NW ¼ and NW ¼ SW ¼ of Sec. 21; NE¼, SE ¼ NW ¼, N ½ SE ¼, SW ¼ SE ¼, E ½ SW ¼ and SW ¼ SW ¼ of Sec. 29; SE ¼ SE ¼ of Sec. 30; NE ¼ NE ¼ of Sec. 31; NW ¼ NE ¼, N ½ NW ¼ and E ½ SE ¼ of Sec. 32; SE ¼ and S ½ SW ¼ of Sec. 33; E ½ SE ¼ and W ½ SW ¼ of Sec. 34; W ½ SW ¼ of Sec. 35.

Township 37 North, Range 37 East.

Lots 1, 2, 3 and 4, Sec. 1; SE ¼ NE ¼ and lot 1 of Sec. 2; S ½ SE ¼ SW ¼ of Sec. 3; NW¼ SE ¼ and lots 5, 6, 7, 8, 9, 10, 11 and 12 of Sec. 4; SE ¼ NE ¼ and lot 1 of Sec. 5; W ½ SW ¼ and lots 1, 2, 3, 4, 5, 6, 7, 8, 9 and 10 of Sec. 9; N ½ NE, Sec. 10; SW ¼ of Sec. 13; S ½ NE ¼, SE ¼ and SE ¼ of SW ¼ of Sec. 14; SW ¼ NW ¼, W ½ SW ¼, SE ¼ SW ¼ of Sec. 15; SE ¼ NE ¼ and NE ¼ SE ¼ of Sec. 16. S ½ NE ¼, E ½ NW ¼, NW ¼ NW ¼, NE ¼ of SW ¼ and N ½ SE ¼ of Sec. 22; E ½ NW ¼, SW ¼ NW ¼, E ½ SW ¼, NW ¼ SW ¼ and lots 1 and

2 and E ½ of Sec. 23; S ½ SE ¼ and S ½ SW ¼ Sec. 24; N ½ NE ¼ of Sec. 25; N ½ SW ¼ and lots 9, 10, 11 and 12 of Sec. 26; S ½ NE ¼, N ½ SE ¼, NE ¼ SW ¼ and lots 9, 10, 12, 13 and 14 of Sec. 27; Lots 1, 5, 7, 8, and 12 of Sec. 28, W ½ NE ¼, W ½ SE ¼ and lots 2, 3, 4 and 5 of Sec. 33.

Township 37 North, Range 38 East.

Lots 1, 2, 3, 4, 5, and 6 of Sec. 18; Lots 1, 3 and 4 of Sec. 19.

Township 38 North, Range 27 East.

SW ¼ NW ¼ and lot 6 of Sec. 2; Lots 6, 7, 8, and 9 of Sec. 3; Lots 4, 5, and 6 of Sec. 11; SE ¼ of NW ¼ and lots 7 and 8 of Sec. 14; Lot 3 of Sec. 22; W ½ NE ¼ of NW ¼ and lots 3, 4, 5, and 6 of Sec. 23; SE ¼ SE ¼ and lot 7 of Sec. 27; E ½ NE ¼, E ½ SE ¼ and lots 5, 6, 7, and 8 of Sec. 34.

Township 38 North, Range 28 East.

S ½ SE ¼ and SE ¼ SW ¼ of Sec. 10; SW ¼ of Sec. 11; N ½ NW ¼ Sec. 14; N ½ NE ¼ and N ½ NW ¼, Sec. 15; NE ¼ NE ¼ of Sec. 16; SW ¼ of Sec. 26; W ½ NE ¼, E ½ SW ¼ and lots 3 and 4 of Sec. 31.

Township 38 North, Range 29 East.

S ½ NW ¼ and lots 2, 3, and 4 of Sec. 4; NE ¼, S ½ NW ¼, N ½ SE ¼ and lots 3 and 4 of Sec. 5; E ½ NE ¼ of Sec. 6.

Township 38 North, Range 30 East.

E ½ SW¼ and SW ¼ SW¼ of Sec. 25; SE ¼ SE ¼ of Sec. 26; E ½ NE ¼ and E ½ SE ¼ of Sec. 35; W ½ NW ¼ of Sec. 36.

Township 38 North, Range 32 East.

E½ SE ¼ and SW ¼ SE ¼ of Sec. 25; W ½ NE ¼ and SE ¼ NE ¼ of Sec. 36.

Township 38 North, Range 33 East.

W ½ NW ¼ of Sec. 1; S ½ NE ¼ and lots 1 and 2 of Sec. 2; lot 4 of Sec. 3; lot 1 of Sec. 4; S ½ SE ¼ of Sec. 9; S ½ NE ¼, S ½ NW ¼, SE ¼ and E ½ SW ¼ of Sec. 15; NE ¼ of Sec. 16; S ½ NE ¼, SE ¼ and E ½ SW ¼ of Sec. 21; N ½ NE ¼ of Sec. 22; S ½ SE ¼, Sec. 26; N ½ NW ¼ of Sec. 27; N ½ NE ¼, NE ¼ NW ¼, SE ¼ and Lot 1 of Sec. 28; SW ¼ SE ¼ of Sec. 30; NW ¼ NE ¼ of Sec. 31; and N ½ NE ¼ of Sec. 35.

Township 38 North, Range 37 East.

S ½ SE ¼ of Sec. 4; SE ¼ SE ¼ of Sec. 5; NE ¼ NE ¼, E ½ SE ¼, SW ¼ SE ¼ of Sec. 8; Sec. 9; SE ¼ NE ¼, W ½ NW ¼, E ½ SE ¼, SW ¼ SE ¼ and SW ¼ of Sec. 10; SE ¼ NE ¼ and E ½ SE ¼ of Sec. 11; S ½ SW ¼ of Sec. 12; E ½ NE ¼, N ½ NW ¼ and lots 1 and 2 of Sec. 13; E ½ NE ¼, SW ¼ NE ¼, W ½ NW ¼, SE ¼, E ½ SW ¼ and NW ¼ SW ¼ of Sec. 14; Sec. 15; E ½, NW ¼ and N ½ SW ¼ of Sec. 16; N ½ NE ¼ of Sec. 17; E ½ NE ¼, N ½ SE ¼, SW ¼ SE ¼, SE ¼ SW ¼ and lot 5 of Sec. 21; NE ¼, S ½ NW ¼, NW ¼ NW ¼, N ½ SE ¼, N ½ SW ¼, and SW ¼ SW ¼ of Sec. 22; N ½ NE ¼, NW ¼ and S ½ SE ¼ of Sec. 23; NW ¼, NW ¼ SW ¼ and lot 5 of Sec. 25; SW ¼ SW ¼ and E ½ of Sec. 26; SE ¼ SE ¼ and SW ¼ of Sec. 27; NW ¼ NE ¼, E ½ SE ¼, SW ¼ SE ¼, SE ¼ SW ¼ and lots 2, 3, 4, and 5 of Sec. 28; SW ¼ NE ¼ and lots 3, 4, and 5 of Sec. 29; W ½ NE ¼, N ½ SE ¼, SW ¼ SE ¼, SE ¼ SW ¼ and lots 1, 2, 5. 6, and 8 of Sec. 33; N. E. ¼ NE ¼, and E ½ SE ¼ of Sec 35; lots 1, 2, and 3 of Sec. 36.

Township 38 North, Range 38 East.

Lots 1, 2, 3, 4, and 5 of Sec. 8; lot 5 of Sec. 19; and lots 1 and 2 of Sec. 30

Township 39 North, Range 27 East.

Lots 3 and 4 of Sec. 10; N ½ SW ¼ and lots 2, 3, 5, and 6 of Sec. 15; lots 5 and 6 of Sec. 16; E ½ NW ¼, NE ¼ SE ¼ and lots 6, 8, 9, 10, and 11 of Sec. 22; SE ¼ and lots 6, 7, 8, 9, 10, 11, and 12 of Sec. 27; lots 5, 6, 7, 8, and 9 of Sec. 34.

Township 39 North, Range 28 East.

NE ¼ NE ¼, S ½ NE ¼, SE ¼ NW ¼ and SE ¼ of Sec. 1; E ½ of Sec. 12; and SE ¼ of Sec. 36.

Township 39 North, Range 29 East.

W ½ SW ¼ of Sec. 3; SE ¼ and NW ¼ of Sec. 4; N ½ NW ¼ of Sec. 5; W ½ NW ¼ and SW ¼ of Sec. 6; W ½ NW ¼ of Sec. 7; N ½, SE ¼ and SE ¼ SW ¼ of Sec. 9; S ½ NW ¼, and SW ¼ of Sec 10; W ½ SE ¼ and E ½ SW ¼ of Sec 15; S ½ SW ¼ of Sec. 33.

Township 39 North, Range 30 East.

S ½ SE ¼ and SW ¼ of Sec. 4; E ½ NE ¼ and E ½ SE ¼ of Sec. 8; N ½ NE ¼ and N ½ NW ¼ of Sec. 9.

Township 39 North, Range 31 East.

A tract of land described as follows: Commencing at a stake marked "I. A." ran north at variation of 22° 30′ E. forty chains and set post at N.W. corner of claim thence east 20 chains and set N.E. corner thence south 40 chains setting S.E. corner thence west 20 chains to point of beginning.

A tract of land described as follows: Commencing at N.W corner of No. 12 thence east 10 chains to S.W. corner of allotment No. 13 thence due north 20 chains and set post thence due east 10 chains and set post thence due north 20 chains and set post thence due east 20 chains and set post thence due south 20 chains and set post thence due west 10 chains and set post thence due south 20 chains and set post thence due west 20 chains to S.W. corner of allotment No. 13.

A tract of land described as follows: Commencing at N.W. Cor. of No. 13, thence due east 10 chains and set post; thence due N. 20 chains and set post; thence due E. 10 chains and set post; thence due N. 20 chains and set post, thence due E. 20 chains and set post; thence due S. 20 chains and set post thence due W 10 chains and set post thence due S. 20 chains and set post thence due W. 20 chains to the S.W. corner of allotment No. 14.

A tract of land described as follows: Commencing at N.W. corner of No. 14 thence due north 40 chains and set post thence due east 20 chains and set post thence due S. 40 chains and set post thence due west 20 chains on line between Nos. 14 & 15 to place of beginning.

A tract of land described as follows: Commencing at the N.W. corner of No. 15, thence due east 10 chains and set post thence due north 40 chains and set post, thence due east 20 chains and set post, thence due south 40 chains set post for S.E. corner thence due west 20 chains to S.W. corner of No. 16.

Township 39 North, Range 32 East.

SW ¼ NE ¼, N ½ NW ¼ and SE ¼ NW ¼ of Sec. 2.

Township 39 North, Range 33 East.

SW ¼ NE ¼, SE ¼ NW ¼, NW ¼ SE ¼ and NE ¼ SW ¼ of Sec. 2; lots 1 and 2 of Sec. 9; Lot 1 of Sec. 10; lots 1, 2, 3, and 4 of Sec. 11; N ½ of S ½ of NE ¼ and lots 1, 2, 3, 4, 5, 6, 7, 8, and 9 of Sec. 12; N ½ SE ¼ and SW ¼ of Sec. 13; S ½ NE ¼, S ½ NW ¼, SW ¼ and lots 2, 3, 4, 5, and 6 of Sec. 14; SE ¼ SE ¼ and lots 1, 2, and 4 of Sec. 15; NE ¼ NE ¼ and lots 1, 5, and 6 of Sec. 16; NW ¼ NE ¼, NE ¼ NW ¼ and lots 6, 7, 8, and 9 of Sec. 17; W ½ Sec. 23; W ½ Sec. 24; W ½ NE ¼, E ½ NW ¼ and W ½ SE ¼ of Sec. 26; SW ¼ NW ¼ and NW ¼ SW ¼ of Sec. 29; SE ¼ SE ¼ of Sec. 33; SW ¼ SW ¼ of Sec. 34; E ½ of Sec. 35.

Township 39 North, Range 36 East.

SW ¼ NE ¼, W ½ SE ¼ and SE ¼ SW ¼ of Sec. 11, N. ½ SW ¼ of Sec. 13; S ½ NE ¼, SE ¼ NW ¼ and NE ¼ SE ¼ of Sec. 14.

Township 39 North, Range 37 East.

SE ¼ of Sec 8; S ½ NE ¼, W ½ SE ¼ and SE ¼ SW ¼ of Sec. 16; SE ¼ NE ¼ and SE ¼ of Sec. 17; N ½ NE ¼, NE ¼ NW ¼, S ½ NW ¼ and SW ¼ of Sec. 20; NE ¼, NE ¼ NW ¼ and E ½ SE ¼ of Sec 21; NW ¼ and E ½ SW ¼ of Sec. 29.

Township 39 North, Range 38 East.

SW ¼ SW ¼ of Sec. 12; W ½ NW ¼ and NW ¼ SW ¼ of Sec. 13; S ½ SW ¼ of Sec. 14; NW ¼ of Sec. 23.

Township 39 North, Range 39 East.

Lots 5, 6, and 7 of Sec. 2; SE ¼ NE ¼ and E ½ SE ¼ of Sec. 7; SW ¼ NW ¼ and W ½ SW ¼ of Sec 8; SW ¼ SE ¼ and SE ¼ SW ¼ of Sec. 9; W ½ NE ¼, E½ NW ¼, SW ¼ NW ¼ and lot 3 of Sec. 16; E ½ NE ¼, NW ¼ and NW ¼ SW ¼ of Sec. 17; NE ¼ NE ¼, SE ¼, and E ½ SW ¼ of Sec. 18.

Township 40 North, Range 27 East.

E ½ SE ¼ of Sec. 11; SW ¼ NE ¼, SE ¼ NW ¼, W ½ SE ¼ and SW ¼ of Sec. 12; NW ¼ of Sec. 13; E ½ NE ¼ of Sec. 14; W ½ of SW ¼ of NE ¼, NW ¼, W ½ of W ½ of SE ¼, E ½ SW ¼, and NW ¼ SW ¼ of Sec. 15; lot 5 of Sec. 21; NE ¼, N ½ SE ¼, SW ¼ SE ¼, S ½ SW ¼ and lots 2, 3, and 4 of Sec. 22; W ½ SE ¼ of Sec. 27.

Township 40 North, Range 28 East.

S ½ SE ¼ and lots 3 and 4 of Sec. 19; SW ¼ of Sec. 35.

A tract of land described as follows: Beginning at a stone monument on the international line, being the N.W. Cor. of allotment 116, thence running due east on boundary line 40 chains set post at N.E. Cor. thence due S. 20 chains set post marked "I. A." being S.E. Cor. thence due W. 40 chains set post at S.W. Cor. thence due N. 20 chains to the point of beginning, in section 2 or 3.

A tract of land described as follows: Beginning at S. W. Cor. of 116 thence due E. 40 chains to S. E. Cor. of 116 thence due S. 20 chains and set post being S. E. Cor. of 117 thence due W. 40 chains and set post at S. W. Cor. of allotment 117 thence due N. 20 chains to place of beginning being N. W. Cor. of No. 117.

A tract of land described as follows: Beginning at S. W. Cor. of 117 thence due E. 40 chains to S. E. Cor. of No. 117 thence due S. 20 chains to S. E. Cor. No. 118

and set post "I. A." thence due W. 40 chains to S. W. Cor. of No. 118 and set post "I. A." thence due N. 20 chains to point of beginning being N. W. Cor. of 118.

A tract of land described as follows: Beginning at S. W. Cor. 118 thence due E. 40 chains to S. E. Cor. of 118 thence due S. 20 chains to S. E. Cor. 119 and set post "I. A." thence due W. 40 chains to S. W. Cor. of 119 and set post thence due N. 20 chains to N. W. Cor. or point of beginning.

A tract of land described as follows: Beginning at S. E. Cor. of 116 thence due E. 40 chains to N. E. Cor. of 122 and set post "I. A." thence S. 20 chains to S. E. Cor. and set post thence due W. 40 chains to S. E. Cor. of No. 117 being S. W. Cor. of No. 122 thence due N. 20 chains to point of beginning, in Sec. 2 or 3.

A tract of land described as follows: Beginning at S. E. Cor. of 117 thence due E. 40 chains to S. E. Cor. of 122 thence due south 20 chains to S. E. Cor. of 123 set post "I. A." thence due W. 40 chains to S. E. Cor. of 118 thence due N. 20 chains to point of beginning, in section 2 or 3.

A tract of land described as follows: Beginning at boundary line N. E. Cor. of No. 116 thence due E. on boundary line 40 chains set post thence due S. 20 chains to N. E. Cor. of 122 thence due W. on line between 122 & 222 to N. W. Cor. of 122 thence N. 20 chains to place of beginning, in section 1 or 2.

A tract of land described as follows: Beginning at N. E. Cor. of 222 on boundary line thence due E. 40 chains set post thence due S. 20 chains set post thence due W. 40 chains to S. E. Cor. of 222 thence due N. 20 chains to place of beginning, in section 1 or 2.

A tract of land described as follows: Beginning at S. E. Cor. of 223 thence due S. 20 chains set post thence due W. 40 chains to N. E. Cor. of 123 thence due N. 20 chains to N. E. of 122 thence due E. 40 chains between line of 223 and 224 to place of beginning, in section 1 or 2.

A tract of land described as follows: Beginning at S. E. Cor. of 224 thence due S. 20 chains set post thence due W. 40 chains to S. E. Cor. of 123 thence due N. 20 chains to S. W. Cor. of 224 thence due E. 40 chains between line 224 & 225 to place of beginning, in section 1 or 2.

A tract of land described as follows: Beginning at S. E. Cor. of 225 thence due S. 20 chains set post thence due W. 40 chains set post thence due N. 20 chains to S. W. Cor. 225 thence due E. 40 chains on line between 225 & 226 to point of beginning, in section 1 or 2.

A tract of land described as follows: Beginning on boundary line at N. E. Cor. of 223 thence on boundary line due E. 20 chains set post thence due S. 40 chains set post thence due W. 20 chains to S. E. Cor. of 224 thence due N. 40 chains to place of beginning, in section 1 or 2.

Township 40 North, Range 29 East.

A tract of land described as follows: Set post on International boundary line being N. E. Cor. of 120 thence due S. 20 chains to S. E. Cor. and set post "I. A." thence due W. 40 chains and set post being S. W. Cor. of 120 thence due N. 20 chains to boundary line set post "I. A." being N. W. Cor. thence on boundary line 40 chains to point of beginning, in section 5 or 6.

A tract of land described as follows: Beginning at SE ¼ of 120 thence due S. 20 chains to S. E. Cor. and set post "I. A." thence W. 40 chains to S. W. Cor. and set post thence due N. 20 chains to N. W. Cor. thence due East 40 chains to point of beginning, Sec. 5 or 6.

NE ¼ and S ½ of Sec. 32; S. ½ SE ¼ and S ½ SW ¼ of Sec. 33.

Township 40 North, Range 30 East.

E ½ NW ¼ SW ¼ of Sec. 3; W ½ W ½ SW ¼ of Sec. 15; NE ¼ SE ¼ and all that part of the S ½ of S ½ of N ½ of NE ¼ lying south and east of Myers creek all that part of S ½ NE ¼ lying east of Myers creek, and all that part of the NW ¼ SE ¼ lying east of Myers creek and all that part of the S ½ SE ¼ lying east of Myers creek in Sec. 16; W ½ of SW ¼ of NE ¼, W ½ of NW ¼ of SE ¼, E ½ SW ¼, and all that part of W ½ SW ¼ lying east of Myers creek except one acre in Reno Quartz claim of Sec. 21; S ½ SE ¼ of Sec. 25; S¾ of W ½ of NE ¼ of NW ¼, S ¾ of E ½ of NW ¼ of NW ¼; S ¾ of E ½ of W ½ of NW ¼ of NW ¼; E ¾ of N ½ of SW ¼ of NW ¼, SE ¼ of SW ¼ of NW ¼ and N ½ of NW ¼ of SE ¼ of NW ¼ of Sec. 28; W ½ SE ¼ SE ¼ of Sec. 29; S ½ NW ¼ and SW ¼ of Sec. 30; E ½ NE ¼ and W ½ NE ¼ of SE ¼ of Sec. 32; S ½ NE ¼ of NW ¼, SE ¼ NW ¼, W ½ of W ½ of W ½ of NW ¼ and NE ¼ SW ¼ of Sec. 33.

Township 40 North, Range 31 East.

S ½ NE ¼, W ½ SE ¼ and NE ¼ SW ¼ of Sec. 25.

Township 40 North, Range 32 East.

E ½ SE ¼ NE ¼ and E ½ of E ½ of SE ¼ of Sec. 9; SW ¼ NE ¼, S ½ NW ¼, W ½ SE ¼ and SW ¼ of Sec. 10; W ½ of W ½ of NE ¼, W ½ of NE ¼ of NW ¼, SE ¼ NW ¼, NE ¼ SW ¼ and SW ¼ SW¼ and all that part of W ½ NW ¼ lying east of Kettle river, and all that part of NE ¼ NW ¼ lying east of Kettle river of Sec. 15; the E ½ NE ¼ NE ¼ and all that part of SE ¼ SE ¼ lying east of Kettle river in Sec. 16; lot 5 and all that part of the NW ¼ SW ¼, W ½ of NW ¼ of NE ¼ of SW ¼, SW ¼ of NE ¼ of SW ¼, NE ¼ of SW ¼ of SW ¼, and SE ¼ SW ¼ lying east of Kettle river in Sec. 22; lot 1, W ½ of SE ¼ of NW ¼ of SW ¼, all of NE ¼ of NW ¼ of NW ¼, SW ¼ SW ¼, and SW ¼ NW ¼ of SW ¼ lying east of Kettle river in Sec. 26; E ½ of NW ¼, E ½ SW ¼, W½ SE ¼, SE ¼ SE ¼ and lots 2, 3, 4, and 5 of Sec. 27; lot 3 of Sec. 30; E ½ NE ¼, NW ¼ NE ¼, E ½ of SW ¼ of NE ¼, E ½ of NW ¼ of SE ¼ and E ½ SE¼ of Sec. 34; W ½ of NW ¼ of NE ¼ of NW ¼, W ½ of SE ¼ of SW ¼, lots 1, 2, 3 and 4 and all that part of SW ¼ SW ¼ lying east of Kettle river.

Township 40 North, Range 33 East.

SE ¼ SE ¼ of Sec. 12; NE ¼ NE ¼, W ½ NE ¼, NE ¼ NW ¼, N ½ SE ¼ and SE ¼ SE ¼ of Sec. 13.

Township 40 North, Range 34 East.

S ½ NE ¼, SE ¼ NW ¼ and lots 1, 2 and 3 of Sec. 1; E ½ SW ¼ and lots 3, 6, 7, 8 and 11 of Sec. 3; SW ¼ NE ¼, S ½ NW ¼, N ½ SW ¼ and lots 1, 2, 3, 4 5 and 6 of Sec. 4; SE ¼ NE ¼ and NE ¼ SE ¼ of Sec. 5; SW ¼ SW ¼ of Sec. 7; E ½ SE ¼ of Sec. 8; E ½ NE ¼, N ½ SE ¼ and lots 1, 4 and 6 of Sec. 9; N ½ NW ¼, SW ¼ NW ¼ and NW ¼ SW ¼ of Sec. 10; SW ¼ SW ¼ of Sec. 13; S ½ NE ¼, SE ¼ and SE ¼ SW ¼ of Sec. 14; NW ¼ NE ¼ and NE ¼ NW ¼ of Sec. 15; E ½ NE ¼ of Sec. 17; NW ¼ NW ¼ of Sec. 18; SW ¼ NE¼, SE ¼ NW ¼, NW ¼ SE ¼ and NE ¼ SW ¼ of Sec. 19; N½ NE ¼, Sec. 23 NW ¼ NE ¼ and lots 1 and 2 of Sec. 30.

Township 40 North, Range 35 East.

N ½ of SE ¼ of NW ¼ and lots 3, 4 and N ½ of lot 5 of Sec. 6.

Township 40 North, Range 39 East.

SW ¼ SE ¼, SE¼ SW ¼ of Sec. 25; SE ¼ NE ¼ and lot 1 of Sec. 35; NE ¼ NE ¼, SW ¼ NE ¼, NW ¼ and lots 1. 2, 3 and 4 of Sec. 36.

STREET AND HARBOR SCENES IN SAN DOMINGO

SAN DOMINGO

"San Domingo is a Republic occupying the eastern portion of the Island of Haiti. The inhabitants are of mixed Spanish, Indian, and negro blood, with some pure Africans. The language is principally Spanish, though French and English are spoken. It claims an area of 18,045 square miles, and the population is estimated at 610,000.

In 1904, in consequence of intimations from Germany and Great Britain that they would be compelled to take action unless the just claims of their subjects received some recognition, the United States was compelled to interfere and it was arranged that the customs should be collected by the United States, one-third of the receipts being returned to carry on the Dominican Government and the other two-thirds being devoted to paying off the various creditors of Santo Domingo. This arrangement has worked very satisfactorily, the share received by the Dominican Government amounting to more than was received when the entire customs were collected by native officials."

Quoted from the article entitled "Santo Domingo" in the Encyclopedic Index, which carries the narrative down to date.

Township 40 North, Range 40 East.

SW ¼ SE ¼ of Sec. 11; NW ¼ NE ¼ of, E ½ SE ¼ of Sec. 19; S ½ NE ¼, S ½ NW ¼ and S ½ of Sec. 20; S ½ NE ¼, SE ¼ NW ¼, NW ¼ SE ¼, N ½ SW ¼, SW ¼ SW ¼ and lot 1 of Sec. 21; lots 2 and 3 of Sec. 22, lot 2 of Sec. 28; NE ¼ NW ¼ and lots 1 and 2 of Sec. 29; E ½ NE ¼, SW ¼ NE ¼, E ½ NW ¼ and lot 1 of Sec. 30; lots 3 and 4 of Sec. 31.

BY THE PRESIDENT OF THE UNITED STATES OF AMERICA.

A PROCLAMATION.

Whereas it is provided by section twenty-four of the act of Congress, approved March 3, 1891, entitled, "An act to repeal timber-culture laws, and for other purposes," "That the President of the United States may, from time to time, set apart and reserve, in any State or Territory having public land bearing forests, in any part of the public lands wholly or in part covered with timber or undergrowth, whether of commercial value or not, as public reservations, and the President shall, by public proclamation, declare the establishment of such reservations and the limits thereof;"

And whereas it is further provided by the act of Congress, approved June 4, 1897 entitled, "An act making appropriations for sundry civil expenses of the Government for the fiscal year ending June 30, 1898, and for other purposes," that "The President is hereby authorized at any time to modify any executive order that has been or may hereafter be made establishing any forest reserve, and by such modification may reduce the area or change the boundary lines of such reserve, or may vacate altogether any order creating such reserve;"

And whereas the public lands in the State of Wyoming, within the limits hereinafter described, are in part covered with timber, and it appears that the public good would be promoted by setting apart and reserving said lands as a public reservation;

Now, therefore, I, William McKinley, President of the United States, by virtue of the power in me vested by the aforesaid acts of Congress, do hereby make known and proclaim that the boundary lines of the Forest Reservation in the State of Wyoming, known as "The Big Horn Forest Reserve," created by proclamation of February 22, 1897, are hereby so changed and enlarged as to include all those certain tracts, pieces or parcels of land lying and being situate in the State of Wyoming, and within the boundaries particularly described as follows, to wit:

Beginning at the southeast corner of township forty-eight (48) north, range eighty-four (84) west, sixth (6th) principal meridian, Wyoming; thence northerly to the northeast corner of said township; thence easterly along the twelfth (12th) standard parallel north to the southeast corner of section thirty-three (33), township forty-nine (49) north, range eighty-three (83) west; thence northerly along the section line to the northeast corner of section four (4), township fifty (50) north, range eighty-three (83) west; thence westerly to the northeast corner of section two (2), township fifty (50) north, range eighty-four (84) west, thence northerly along the section line, allowing for the proper offset on the thirteenth (13th) standard parallel north, to the northeast corner of section fourteen (14), township fifty-three (53) north, range eighty-four (84) west, thence westerly to the northeast corner of section fourteen (14), township fifty-three (53) north, range eighty-five (85) west; thence northerly to the northeast corner of section two (2), said township; thence westerly to the northeast corner of section two (2), township fifty-three (53) north, range eighty-six (86) west; thence northerly to the northeast corner of section two (2), township fifty-four (54) north, range eighty-six (86) west; thence westerly to the southeast corner of township fifty-five (55) north, range eighty-seven (87) west; thence northerly to the northeast corner of said township; thence westerly to the northwest corner of said township; thence southerly to the southwest corner of said township; thence westerly to the northwest corner of township fifty-four (54) north, range eighty-eight (88) west; thence northerly along the range line, allowing for the proper offset on the fourteenth (14th) standard parallel north, to the point of intersection with the boundary line between the States of Wyoming and Montana; thence westerly along said state boundary line to its intersection with the range line between ranges ninety-two (92) west, and ninety-three (93) west; thence southerly along said range line, allowing for the proper offset on the fourteenth (14th) standard parallel north, to the northwest corner of township fifty-four (54) north, range ninety-two (92) west; thence easterly to the northeast corner of said township; thence southerly to the southeast corner of said township; thence easterly to the northeast corner of township fifty-three (53) north, range ninety-one (91) west; thence southerly to the southeast corner of said township; thence easterly along the thirteenth (13th) standard parallel north to the northwest corner of township fifty-two (52) north, range eighty-eight (88) west; thence southerly along the range line to the northwest corner of township fifty (50) north, range eighty-eight (88) west; thence easterly to the northwest corner of section three (3), said township; thence southerly along the section line to the southwest corner of section thirty-four (34), township forty-nine (49) north, range eighty-eight (88) west; thence easterly along the twelfth (12th) standard parallel north to the northwest corner of township forty-eight (48) north, range eighty-seven (87) west; thence southerly to the southwest corner of said township; thence easterly along the township line to the southeast corner of township forty-eight (48) north, range eighty-four (84) west, the place of beginning.

Excepting from the force and effect of this proclamation all lands which may have been, prior to the date hereof, embraced in any legal entry or covered by any lawful filing duly of record in the proper United States Land Office, or upon which any valid settlement has been made pursuant to law, and the statutory period within which to make entry or filing of record has not expired; *Provided*, that this exception shall not continue to apply to any particular tract of land unless the entryman, settler or claimant continues to comply with the law under which the entry, filing or settlement was made.

Warning is hereby expressly given to all persons not to make settlement upon the tract of land reserved by this proclamation.

In witness whereof, I have hereunto set my hand and caused the seal of the United States to be affixed.

[SEAL.]   Done at the city of Washington, this 29th day of June, A. D. 1900, and of the Independence of the United States the one hundred and twenty-fourth.

WILLIAM McKINLEY.

By the President:
  JOHN HAY,
    Secretary of State.

BY THE PRESIDENT OF THE UNITED STATES OF AMERICA.

A PROCLAMATION.

Whereas the German Government has entered into a Commercial Agreement with the United States in conformity with the provisions of the third section of the Tariff Act of the United States approved July 24, 1897, by which agreement in the judgment of the President reciprocal and equivalent concessions are secured in favor of the products of the United States:

Therefore, be it known that I, William McKinley, President of the United States of America, acting under the authority conferred by said act of Congress, do hereby suspend during the continuance in force of said agreement the imposition and collection of the duties imposed by the first section of said act upon the articles hereinafter specified, being the products of the soil and industry of Germany; and do declare in place thereof the rates of duty provided in the third section of said act to be in force and effect from and after the date of this proclamation, as follows, namely:

" Upon argols, or crude tartar, or wine lees, crude, five *per centum ad valorem*.

"Upon brandies, or other spirits manufactured or distilled from grain or other materials, one dollar and seventy-five cents per proof gallon.

"Upon still wines, and vermuth, in casks, thirty-five cents per gallon; in bottles or jugs, per case of one dozen bottles or jugs containing each not more than one quart and more than one pint, or twenty-four bottles or jugs containing each not more than one pint, one dollar and twenty-five cents per case, and any excess beyond these quantities found in such bottles or jugs shall be subject to a duty of four cents per pint or fractional part thereof, but no separate or additional duty shall be assessed upon the bottles or jugs.

"Upon paintings in oil or water colors, pastels, pen and ink drawings, and statuary, fifteen *per centum ad valorem*," of which the officers and citizens of the United States will take due notice.

In testimony whereof I have hereunto set my hand and caused the seal of the United States to be affixed.

Done at the city of Washington this 13th day of July, A.D. [SEAL.]   1900, and of the Independence of the United States of America the one hundred and twenty-fifth.

WILLIAM McKINLEY.

By the President:
JOHN HAY,
  Secretary of State.

BY THE PRESIDENT OF THE UNITED STATES OF AMERICA.

A PROCLAMATION.

Whereas His Majesty the King of Italy has entered into a reciprocal Commercial Agreement with the United States of America pursuant to and in accordance with the provisions of section 3 of the Tariff Act of the United States approved July 24, 1897, which agreement is in the English text in the words and figures following, to wit:

The President of the United States of America and His Majesty the King of Italy, mutually desirous to improve the commercial relations between the two countries by a Special Agreement relative thereto, have appointed as their Plenipotentiaries for that purpose, namely:

The President of the United States of America, the Honorable John A. Kasson, Special Commissioner Plenipotentiary, etc., and

His Majesty the King of Italy, His Excellency the Baron S. Fava, Senator of the Kingdom, his Ambassador at Washington, etc.,

Who being duly empowered thereunto have agreed upon the following articles:

ARTICLE I.

It is agreed on the part of the United States, pursuant to and in accordance with the provisions of the third section of the Tariff Act of the United States approved July 24, 1897, and in consideration of the concessions hereinafter made on the part of Italy in favor of the products and manufactures of the United States, that the existing duties imposed upon the following articles, being the product of the soil or industry of Italy, imported into the United States shall be suspended during the continuance in force of this agreement, and in place thereof the duties to be assessed and collected thereon shall be as follows, namely:

On argols, or crude tartar, or wine lees, crude, five *per centum ad valorem*.

On brandies, or other spirits manufactured or distilled from grain or other materials, one dollar and seventy-five cents per proof gallon.

On still wines, and vermuth, in casks, thirty-five cents per gallon; in bottles or jugs, per case of one dozen bottles or jugs containing each not more than one quart and more than one pint, or twenty-four bottles or jugs containing each not more than one pint, one dollar and twenty-five cents per case, and any excess beyond these quantities found in such bottles or jugs shall be subject to a duty of four cents per pint or fractional part thereof, but no separate or additional duty shall be assessed upon the bottles or jugs.

On paintings in oil or water colors, pastels, pen and ink drawings, and statuary, fifteen *per centum ad valorem*.

ARTICLE II.

It is reciprocally agreed on the part of Italy, in consideration of the provisions of the foregoing article, that so long as this convention shall remain in force the duties to be assessed and collected on the following described merchandise, being the product of the soil or industry of the United States, imported into Italy shall not exceed the rates hereinafter specified, namely:

Upon cotton seed oil	lire 21.50 per quintal.
" fish, pickled or in oil, excluding the tunny, preserved in boxes or barrels, sardines and anchovies	" 15.00 " "
" other fish, preserved	" 25.00 " "
" agricultural machinery	" 9.00 " "
" detached parts of agricultural machinery:	
(1) of cast iron	" 10.00 " "
(2) of other iron or steel	" 11.00 " "
" scientific instruments:	
(a) of copper, bronze, brass, or steel:	
(1) with spy-glasses or microscopes, or graduated scales or circles, spy-glasses for use on land, monocles, binocles, lenses, detached and mounted	" 30.00 " "
(2) not provided with any optical instrument, nor with graduated scales or circles	" 30.00 " "
(b) of all kinds, in the construction of which iron is evidently predominant	" 30.00 " "
" dynamo-electrical machines:	
(1) the weight of which exceeds 1000 kilograms	" 16.00 " "
(2) weighing 1000 kilograms or less	" 25.00 " "
" detached parts of dynamo-electrical machines	" 25.00 " "
" sewing machines:	
(1) with stands	" 25.00 " "
(2) without stands	" 30.00 " "
" varnishes, not containing spirits nor mineral oils	" 20.00 " "

The following articles shall be admitted free of duty:

Turpentine oil.

Natural fertilizers of all kinds.

Skins, crude, fresh, or dried, not suitable for fur; and fur skins.

ARTICLE III.

This agreement is subject to the approval of the Italian Parliament. When such approval shall have been given, and official notification shall have been given to the United States Government of His Majesty's ratification, the President shall publish his proclamation, giving full effect to the provisions contained in Article I of this agreement. From and after the date of such proclamation this agreement shall be in full force and effect, and shall continue in force until the expiration of the year 1903, and if not denounced by either party one year in advance of the expiration of said term shall continue in force until one year from the time when one of the high contracting parties shall have given notice to the other of its intention to arrest the operation thereof.

In witness whereof we, the respective Plenipotentiaries, have signed this agreement, in duplicate, in the English and Italian texts, and have affixed thereunto our respective seals.

Done at Washington, this 8th day of February, A. D. 1900.

JOHN A. KASSON. [SEAL.]
FAVA. [SEAL.]

And whereas said convention has been duly ratified on the part of His Majesty the King of Italy, official notice whereof has been received by the President,

Now, therefore, be it known that I, William McKinley, President of the United States of America, acting under the authority conferred by said act of Congress, do hereby suspend during the continuance in force of said agreement the imposition and collection of the duties mentioned in the first section of said act and heretofore collected upon the specified articles of Italian origin as described in said agreement, and do declare in place thereof the rates of duty provided in the third section of said act as recited in said agreement to be in full force and effect from and after the date of this Proclamation, of which the officers and citizens of the United States will take due notice.

In testimony whereof I have hereunto set my hand and caused the seal of the United States to be affixed.

Done at the city of Washington, this 18th day of July, [SEAL.] A. D. 1900, and of the Independence of the United States of America the one hundred and twenty-fifth.

WILLIAM McKINLEY.

By the President:
JOHN HAY,
Secretary of State.

BY THE PRESIDENT OF THE UNITED STATES OF AMERICA.

A PROCLAMATION.

Whereas it is provided by section twenty-four of the act of Congress, approved March 3rd, 1891, entitled, "An act to repeal timber-culture laws, and for other purposes," "That the President of the United

States may, from time to time, set apart and reserve, in any State or Territory having public land bearing forests, in any part of the public lands wholly or in part covered with timber or undergrowth, whether of commercial value or not, as public reservations, and the President shall, by public proclamation, declare the establishment of such reservations and the limits thereof;"

And whereas the public lands in the State of Wyoming, within the limits hereinafter described, are in part covered with timber, and it appears that the public good would be promoted by setting apart and reserving said lands as a public reservation;

Now, therefore, I, William McKinley, President of the United States, by virtue of the power in me vested by section twenty-four of the aforesaid act of Congress, do hereby make known and proclaim that there is hereby reserved from entry or settlement and set apart as a Public Reservation all those certain tracts, pieces or parcels of land lying and being situate in the State of Wyoming and particularly described as follows, to wit:

Beginning at the northeast corner of township fifteen (15) north, range seventy-one (71) west, sixth (6th) principal meridian, Wyoming; thence westerly along the township line to the northwest corner of section three (3), township fifteen (15) north, range seventy-two (72) west; thence southerly to the southwest corner section thirty-four (34), said township; thence easterly to the southeast corner of said section; thence southerly to the southwest corner of section eleven (11), township fourteen (14) north, range seventy-two (72) west; thence easterly to the southeast corner of section twelve (12), said township; thence southerly to the southwest corner of section thirty (30), township fourteen (14) north, range seventy-one (71) west; thence easterly to the southeast corner of section twenty-five (25), said township; thence northerly along the range line to the northeast corner of township fifteen (15) north, range seventy-one (71) west, the place of beginning.

Excepting from the force and effect of this proclamation all lands which may have been, prior to the date hereof, embraced in any legal entry or covered by any lawful filing duly of record in the proper United States Land Office, or upon which any valid settlement has been made pursuant to law, and the statutory period within which to make entry or filing of record has not expired: *Provided*, that this exception shall not continue to apply to any particular tract of land unless the entryman, settler or claimant continues to comply with the law under which the entry, filing or settlement was made.

Warning is hereby expressly given to all persons not to make settlement upon the tract of land reserved by this proclamation.

The reservation hereby established shall be known as The Crow Creek Forest Reserve.

In witness whereof I have hereunto set my hand and caused the seal of the United States to be affixed.

               Done at the city of Washington this 10th day of October,
[SEAL.]   A. D. 1900, and of the Independence of the United States the one hundred and twenty-fifth.

                                  WILLIAM McKINLEY.

By the President:
    JOHN HAY,
        Secretary of State.

BY THE PRESIDENT OF THE UNITED STATES OF AMERICA.

A PROCLAMATION.

To the People of the United States:

In the fullness of years and honors, John Sherman, lately Secretary of State, has passed away.

Few among our citizens have risen to greater or more deserved eminence in the national councils than he. The story of his public life and services is as it were the history of the country for half a century. In the Congress of the United States he ranked among the foremost in the House, and later in the Senate. He was twice a member of the Executive Cabinet, first as Secretary of the Treasury, and afterwards as Secretary of State. Whether in debate during the dark hours of our civil war, or as the director of the country's finances during the period of rehabilitation, or as a trusted councilor in framing the nation's laws for over forty years, or as the exponent of its foreign policy, his course was ever marked by devotion to the best interests of his beloved land, and by able and conscientious effort to uphold its dignity and honor. His countrymen will long revere his memory and see in him a type of the patriotism, the uprightness and the zeal that go to molding and strengthening a nation.

In fitting expression of the sense of bereavement that afflicts the Republic, I direct that on the day of the funeral the Executive Offices of the United States display the national flag at half mast and that the Representatives of the United States in foreign countries shall pay in like manner appropriate tribute to the illustrious dead for a period of ten days.

               Done at the city of Washington, this 22d day of October,
[SEAL.]   A. D. 1900, and of the Independence of the United States of America the one hundred and twenty-fifth.

                                  WILLIAM McKINLEY

By the President:
    JOHN HAY,
        Secretary of State.

By the President of the United States of America.

A PROCLAMATION.

It has pleased Almighty God to bring our nation in safety and honor through another year. The works of religion and charity have everywhere been manifest. Our country through all its extent has been blessed with abundant harvests. Labor and the great industries of the people have prospered beyond all precedent. Our commerce has spread over the world. Our power and influence in the cause of freedom and enlightenment have extended over distant seas and lands. The lives of our official representatives and many of our people in China have been marvelously preserved. We have been generally exempt from pestilence and other great calamities; and even the tragic visitation which overwhelmed the city of Galveston made evident the sentiments of sympathy and Christian charity by virtue of which we are one united people.

Now, therefore, I, William McKinley, President of the United States, do hereby appoint and set apart Thursday, the 29th of November next, to be observed by all the people of the United States, at home or abroad, as a day of thanksgiving and praise to Him who holds the nations in the hollow of His hand. I recommend that they gather in their several places of worship and devoutly give Him thanks for the prosperity wherewith He has endowed us, for seed-time and harvest, for the valor, devotion and humanity of our armies and navies, and for all His benefits to us as individuals and as a nation; and that they humbly pray for the continuance of His Divine favor, for concord and amity with other nations, and for righteousness and peace in all our ways.

In witness whereof I have hereunto set my hand and caused the seal of the United States to be affixed.

Done at the city of Washington this 29th day of October, [SEAL.] A. D. 1900, and of the Independence of the United States the one hundred and twenty-fifth.

WILLIAM McKINLEY.

By the President:
JOHN HAY,
Secretary of State.

By the President of the United States of America.

A PROCLAMATION.

Whereas public interests require that the Senate of the United States be convened at 12 o'clock on the 4th day of March next, to receive such communications as may be made by the Executive:

Now, therefore, I, William McKinley, President of the United States of America, do hereby proclaim and declare that an extraordinary occasion requires the Senate of the United States to convene at the Capitol in the city of Washington on the 4th day of March next, at 12 o'clock noon, of which all persons who shall at that time be entitled to act as members of that body are hereby required to take notice.

Given under my hand and the seal of the United States, at Washington, the 23d day of February, A. D. 1901, and of the Independence of the United States the one hundred and twenty-fifth.

[SEAL.]

WILLIAM McKINLEY.

By the President:

JOHN HAY,
Secretary of State.

BY THE PRESIDENT OF THE UNITED STATES.

A PROCLAMATION.

EXECUTIVE MANSION.
Washington, March 14, 1901.

To the People of the United States:

Benjamin Harrison, President of the United States from 1889 to 1893, died yesterday at 4:45 P. M., at his home in Indianapolis. In his death the country has been deprived of one of its greatest citizens. A brilliant soldier in his young manhood, he gained fame and rapid advancement by his energy and valor. As a lawyer he rose to be a leader of the bar. In the Senate he at once took and retained high rank as an orator and legislator; and in the high office of President he displayed extraordinary gifts as administrator and statesman. In public and in private life he set a shining example for his countrymen.

In testimony of the respect in which his memory is held by the Government and people of the United States, I do hereby direct that the flags on the Executive Mansion and the several Departmental buildings be displayed at half staff for a period of thirty days; and that suitable military and naval honors, under the orders of the Secretaries of War and of the Navy, be rendered on the day of the funeral.

Done at the city of Washington this 14th day of March, A. D. 1901, and of the Independence of the United States of America the one hundred and twenty-fifth.

[SEAL.]

WILLIAM McKINLEY.

By the President:

JOHN HAY,
Secretary of State.

By the President of the United States of America.

A PROCLAMATION.

Whereas The Washington Forest Reserve, in the State of Washington, was established by proclamation dated February 22d, 1897, under and by virtue of section twenty-four of the act of Congress, approved March 3d, 1891, entitled, " An act to repeal timber-culture laws, and for other purposes," which provides, " That the President of the United States may, from time to time, set apart and reserve, in any State or Territory having public lands wholly or in part covered with timber or undergrowth, whether of commercial value or not, as public reservations, and the President shall, by public proclamation, declare the establishment of such reservations and the limits thereof; "

And whereas it is further provided by the act of Congress, approved June 4th, 1897, entitled, " An act making appropriations for sundry civil expenses of the Government for the fiscal year ending June 30th, 1898, and for other purposes," that " The President is hereby authorized at any time to modify any executive order that has been or may hereafter be made establishing any forest reserve, and by such modification may reduce the area or change the boundary lines of such reserve, or may vacate altogether any order creating such reserve; "

Now, therefore, I, William McKinley, President of the United States, by virtue of the power vested in me by the aforesaid act of Congress, approved June 4th, 1897, do hereby make known and proclaim that there are hereby withdrawn and excluded from the aforesaid Washington Forest Reserve and restored to the public domain all those certain tracts, pieces or parcels of land particularly described as follows to wit:

The southwest quarter of section three (3), sections four (4) and five (5), the east half of section nine (9), the west half of section ten (10), the south half of section thirteen (13), the south half of section fourteen (14), section fifteen (15), the north half and southeast quarter of section twenty-three (23), sections twenty-four (24), twenty-five (25) and thirty-six (36), all in township thirty-five (35) north, range twenty (20) east, Willamette Meridian; what will be when surveyed the south half of township thirty-two (32) north, range twenty-one (21) east; what will be when surveyed the north half of township thirty-three (33) north, range twenty-one (21) east; townships thirty-four (34) and thirty-five (35) north, range twenty-one (21) east; townships thirty-one (31) to thirty-four (34), both inclusive, range twenty-two (22) east; what will be when surveyed sections thirty (30), thirty-one (31) and thirty-two (32) of township thirty-five (35) north, range twenty-two (22) east.

That the lands hereby restored to the public domain shall be open to settlement from date hereof, but shall not be subject to entry, filing or selection until after ninety days' notice by such publication as the Secretary of the Interior may prescribe.

In witness whereof, I have hereunto set my hand and caused the seal of the United States to be affixed.

[SEAL.] Done at the city of Washington this 3rd day of April, A. D. 1901, and of the Independence of the United States the one hundred and twenty-fifth.

WILLIAM McKINLEY.

By the President:
 JOHN HAY,
  Secretary of State.

BY THE PRESIDENT OF THE UNITED STATES OF AMERICA

A PROCLAMATION.

Whereas, by Executive Order dated December 27, 1875, sections 8 and 9, township 15 south, range 2 east, San Bernardino meridian, California, were with certain other tracts of land withdrawn from the public domain and reserved for the use of the Capitan Grande band or village of Mission Indians; and

Whereas the Commission appointed under the provisions of the act of Congress approved January 12, 1891, entitled "An act for the relief of the Mission Indians in the State of California" (U. S. Statutes at Large, vol. 26, page 712), selected for the said Capitan Grande band or village of Indians certain tracts of land intentionally omitted and excluded from such selection the said sections 8 and 9, township 15 south, range 2 east, and reported that the tracts thus omitted included the lands upon which were found the claims of Arthur F. Head and others; and

Whereas, the report and recommendations of the said Commission were approved by Executive Order dated December 29, 1891, which order also directed that "All of the lands mentioned in said report are hereby withdrawn from settlement and entry until patents shall have issued for said selected reservations and until the recommendations of said Commission shall be fully executed, and, by the proclamation of the President of the United States, the lands or any part thereof shall be restored to the public domain;" and

Whereas a patent was issued March 10, 1894, to the said Indians for the lands selected by the Commission as aforesaid and which patent also excluded the said sections 8 and 9, township 15 south, range 2 east; and

Whereas it appears that the said Arthur F. Head cannot make the requisite filings on the land occupied by him until it shall have been formally restored to the public domain, and that no good reason appears to exist for the further reservation of the said sections for the said band of Indians;

Now, therefore, I, William McKinley, President of the United States, by virtue of the power in me vested, do hereby declare and make known that the Executive Orders dated December 27, 1875, and December 29, 1891, are so far modified as to except from their provisions sections 8 and 9 of township 15 south, range 2 east, San Bernardino meridian, and the said sections are hereby restored to the public domain.

In witness whereof, I have hereunto set my hand and caused the seal of the United States to be affixed.

Done at the city of Washington this 16th day of April, [SEAL.] A. D. 1901, and of the Independence of the United States the one hundred and twenty-fifth.

WILLIAM McKINLEY.

By the President:
   JOHN HAY,
        Secretary of State.

PROCLAMATION.

Whereas the act of Congress entitled "An act to ratify and confirm an agreement with the Muscogee or Creek tribe of Indians and for other purposes," approved on the 1st day of March, 1901, contains a provision as follows:

That the agreement negotiated between the Commission to the Five Civilized Tribes and the Muscogee or Creek tribe of Indians, at the city of Washington on the 8th day of March, nineteen hundred, as herein amended, is hereby accepted, ratified, and confirmed, and the same shall be of full force and effect when ratified by the Creek national council. The principal chief, as soon as practicable after the ratification of this agreement by Congress, shall call an extra session of the Creek national council and lay before it this agreement and the act of Congress ratifying it, and if the agreement be ratified by said council, as provided in the constitution of said nation, he shall transmit to the President of the United States the act of council ratifying the agreement, and the President of the United States shall thereupon issue his proclamation declaring the same duly ratified, and that all the provisions of this agreement have become law according to the terms thereof: *Provided*, That such ratification by the Creek national council shall be made within ninety days from the approval of this act by the President of the United States,

And whereas the principal chief of the said tribe has transmitted to me an act of the Creek national council entitled "An act to ratify and confirm an agreement between the United States and the Muscogee Nation of Indians of the Indian Territory" approved the 25th day of May, 1901, which contains a provision as follows:

That said agreement, amended, ratified and confirmed by the Congress of the United States, as set forth in said act of Congress approved March 1, 1901, is hereby accepted, ratified and confirmed on the part of the Muscogee Nation and on the part of the Muscogee or Creek tribe of Indians constituting said Nation, as provided in said act of Congress and as provided in the Constitution of said Nation, and the Principal Chief is hereby authorized to transmit this act of the National Council ratifying said agreement to the President of the United States as provided in said act of Congress.

And whereas paragraph thirty-six of said agreement contains a provision as follows:

This provision shall not take effect until after it shall have been separately and specifically approved by the Creek national council and by the Seminole general council; and if not approved by either, it shall fail altogether, and be eliminated from this agreement without impairing any other of its provisions.

And whereas there has been presented to me an act of the Creek national council entitled "An act to disapprove certain provisions, relating to Seminole citizens, in the agreement between the Muscogee Nation and the United States, ratified by Congress March 1, 1901," approved the 25th day of May, 1901, by which the provisions of said paragraph thirty-six are specifically disapproved:

Now, therefore, I, William McKinley, President of the United States, do hereby declare said agreement, except paragraph thirty-six thereof, duly ratified and that all the provisions thereof, except said paragraph thirty-six which failed of ratification by the Creek national council, became law according to the terms thereof upon the 25th day of May, 1901.

In witness whereof, I have hereunto set my hand and caused the seal of the United States to be affixed.

Done at the city of Washington, this 25th day of June, [SEAL.] A. D. 1901, and of the Independence of the United States the one hundred and twenty-fifth.

WILLIAM McKINLEY.

By the President:
DAVID J. HILL,
Acting Secretary of State.

BY THE PRESIDENT OF THE UNITED STATES OF AMERICA.

A PROCLAMATION.

Whereas the Cascade Range Forest Reserve, in the State of Oregon, was established by proclamation dated September 28, 1893, under and by virtue of section twenty-four of the act of Congress, approved March 3, 1891, entitled, "An act to repeal timber-culture laws, and for other purposes," which provides, "That the President of the United States may, from time to time, set apart and reserve, in any State or

Territory having public lands wholly or in part covered with timber or undergrowth, whether of commercial value or not, as public reservations, and the President shall, by public proclamation, declare the establishment of such reservations and the limits thereof;"

And whereas it is further provided by the act of Congress, approved June 4, 1897, entitled, "An act making appropriations for sundry civil expenses of the Government for the fiscal year ending June 30, 1898, and for other purposes," that "The President is hereby authorized at any time to modify any executive order that has been or may hereafter be made establishing any forest reserve, and by such modification may reduce the area or change the boundary lines of such reserve, or may vacate altogether any order creating such reserve;"

Now, therefore, I, William McKinley, President of the United States, by virtue of the power vested in me by the aforesaid act of Congress, approved June 4, 1897, do hereby make known and proclaim that there is hereby reserved from entry or settlement, and added to and made a part of the aforesaid Cascade Range Forest Reserve, all those certain tracts, pieces or parcels of land lying and being situate in the State of Oregon and particularly described as follows, to wit:

The south half (S. ½) of township one (1) south, townships two (2) south, three (3) south, and four (4) south, range eleven (11) east, Willamette Meridian; township five (5) south, ranges nine (9) and ten (10) east; and so much of township six (6) south, ranges nine (9) and ten (10) east, as lies north of the Warm Springs Indian Reservation.

Excepting from the force and effect of this proclamation all lands which may have been, prior to the date hereof, embraced in any legal entry or covered by any lawful filing duly of record in the proper United States Land Office, or upon which any valid settlement has been made pursuant to law, and the statutory period within which to make entry or filing of record has not expired: *Provided*, that this exception shall not continue to apply to any particular tract of land unless the entryman, settler or claimant continues to comply with the law under which the entry, filing or settlement was made.

Warning is hereby expressly given to all persons not to make settlement upon the tract of land reserved by this proclamation.

In witness whereof, I have hereunto set my hand and caused the seal of the United States to be affixed.

Done at the city of Washington this 1st day of July, A. D. [SEAL.] 1901, and of the Independence of the United States the one hundred and twenty-fifth.

WILLIAM McKINLEY.

By the President:
DAVID J. HILL,
Acting Secretary of State.

BY THE PRESIDENT OF THE UNITED STATES OF AMERICA.

A PROCLAMATION.

Whereas it is provided by section twenty-four of the act of Congress, approved March 3rd, 1891, entitled "An act to repeal timber-culture laws, and for other purposes," "That the President of the United States may, from time to time, set apart and reserve, in any State or Territory having public land bearing forests, in any part of the public lands wholly or in part covered with timber or undergrowth, whether of commercial value or not, as public reservations, and the President shall, by public proclamation, declare the establishment of such reservations and the limits thereof."

And wheras the public lands in the Territory of Oklahoma, within the limits hereinafter described, are in part covered with timber, and it appears that the public good would be promoted by setting apart and reserving said lands as a public reservation;

Now, therefore, I, William McKinley, President of the United States, by virtue of the power in me vested by section twenty-four of the aforesaid act of Congress, do hereby make known and proclaim that there is hereby reserved from entry or settlement and set apart as a public reservation all those certain tracts, pieces or parcels of land lying and being situate in the Territory of Oklahoma and particularly described as follows, to wit:

Beginning at the southeast corner of township three (3) north, range fourteen (14) west, Indian Meridian, Territory of Oklahoma; thence north along the township line to the northeast corner of section twenty-four (24), township three (3) north, range fourteen (14) west; thence east on the section line to the southeast corner of section thirteen (13), township three (3) north, range thirteen (13) west; thence north along the range line between ranges twelve (12) and thirteen (13) west, to the northeast corner of the southeast quarter of section twelve (12), township three (3) north, range thirteen (13) west; thence west to the southwest corner of the northwest quarter of section twelve (12), township three (3) north, range thirteen (13) west; thence north to the southwest corner of section one (1), township three (3) north, range thirteen (13) west; thence west along the section line between sections two (2) and eleven (11), to the southwest corner of section two (2), township three (3) north, range thirteen (13) west; thence north along the section line between sections two (2) and three (3) to the southeast corner of the northeast quarter of section three (3), township three (3) north, range thirteen (13) west; thence west along the center line of sections three (3), four (4), five (5), and six (6), to the southwest corner of the northwest quarter of section six (6), township three (3) north, range thirteen (13) west; thence north along the range line between ranges thirteen (13) and fourteen (14) west to the northeast corner of section one (1), township three (3) north, range fourteen

(14) west; thence west along the township line between townships three (3) and four (4) north to the northwest corner of section two (2), township three (3) north, range fourteen (14) west; thence north to the northeast corner of section thirty-four (34), township four (4) north, range fourteen (14) west; thence west to the northwest corner of section thirty-four (34), township four (4) north, range fourteen (14) west; thence north to the northeast corner of the southeast quarter of section twenty-one (21), township four (4) north, range fourteen (14) west; thence west to the southwest corner of the northwest quarter of section twenty (20), township four (4) north, range fourteen (14) west; thence north to the northeast corner of section eighteen (18), township four (4) north, range fourteen (14) west; thence west to the northwest corner of section seventeen (17), township four (4) north, range fifteen (15) west; thence south to the southwest corner of section twenty-nine (29), township four (4) north, range fifteen (15) west; thence east to the southeast corner of section twenty-nine (29), township four (4) north, range fifteen (15) west; thence south to the southwest corner of section thirty-three (33), township four (4) north, range fifteen (15) west; thence east to the southeast corner of said section thirty-three (33), township four (4) north, range fifteen (15) west; thence south to the southwest corner of the northwest quarter of section ten (10), township three (3) north, range fifteen (15) west; thence east to the southeast corner of the northeast quarter of said section ten; thence south to the southwest corner of section twenty-six (26), township three (3) north, range fifteen (15) west; thence east to the southeast corner of said section twenty-six (26); thence south to the southwest corner of the northwest quarter of section thirty-six (36), township three (3) north, range fifteen (15) west; thence east to the center of section thirty-three (33), township three (3) north, range fourteen (14) west; thence south to the southwest corner of the southeast quarter of said section thirty-three (33); thence east along the township line between townships two (2) and three (3) north to the southeast corner of township three (3) north, range fourteen (14) west, the place of beginning.

Warning is hereby expressly given to all persons not to make settlement upon the tract of land reserved by this proclamation.

The reservation hereby established shall be known as the Wichita Forest Reserve.

In witness whereof I have hereunto set my hand and caused the seal of the United States to be affixed.

Done at the city of Washington this 4th day of July, A. D. [SEAL.] 1901, and of the Independence of the United States the one hundred and twenty-sixth. WILLIAM McKINLEY
By the President.
DAVID J. HILL,
Acting Secretary of State.

BY THE PRESIDENT OF THE UNITED STATES OF AMERICA.

A PROCLAMATION.

Whereas by an agreement between the Wichita and affiliated bands of Indians on the one part, and certain commissioners of the United States on the other part, ratified by act of Congress approved March 2, 1895 (28 Stat., 876, 894), the said Indians ceded, conveyed, transferred and relinquished, forever and absolutely, without any reservation whatever, unto the United States of America, all their claim, title and interest of every kind and character in and to the lands embraced in the following described tract of country now in the Territory of Oklahoma, to wit:

Commencing at a point in the middle of the main channel of the Washita River, where the ninety-eighth meridian of west longitude crosses the same, thence up the middle of the main channel of said river to the line of 98° 40′ west longitude, thence on said line of 98° 40′ due north to the middle of the channel of the main Canadian River, thence down the middle of the said main Canadian River to where it crosses the ninety-eighth meridian, thence due south to the place of beginning.

And whereas, in pursuance of said act of Congress ratifying said agreement, allotments of land in severalty have been regularly made to each and every member of said Wichita and affiliated bands of Indians, native and adopted, and the lands occupied by religious societies or other organizations for religious or educational work among the Indians have been regularly allotted and confirmed to such societies and organizations, respectively;

And whereas, by an agreement between the Comanche, Kiowa and Apache tribes of Indians on the one part, and certain commissioners of the United States on the other part, amended and ratified by act of Congress, approved June 6, 1900 (31 Stat., 672, 676), the said Indian tribes, subject to certain conditions which have been duly performed, ceded, conveyed, transferred, relinquished and surrendered forever and absolutely, without any reservation whatsoever, expressed or implied, unto the United States of America, all their claim, title and interest of every kind and character in and to the lands embraced in the following described tract of country now in the Territory of Oklahoma, to wit:

Commencing at a point where the Washita River crosses the ninety-eighth meridian west from Greenwich; thence up the Washita River, in the middle of the main channel thereof, to a point thirty miles, by river, west of Fort Cobb, as now established; thence due west to the north fork of Red River, provided said line strikes said river east of the one-hundredth meridian of west longitude; if not, then only to said meridian line, and thence due south, on said meridian line, to the said north Fork of Red River; thence down said north fork, in the middle of the main channel thereof, from the point where it may be first intersected by the lines above described, to the main Red River; thence down said Red River, in the middle of the main channel thereof, to its intersection with the ninety-eighth meridian of longitude west from Greenwich ; thence north, on said meridian line, to the place of beginning.

And whereas, in pursuance of said act of Congress ratifying the agreement last named, allotments of land in severalty have been regularly made to each member of said Comanche, Kiowa and Apache tribes of Indians; the lands occupied by religious societies or other organizations for religious or educational work among the Indians have been regularly allotted and confirmed to such societies and organizations, respectively; and the Secretary of the Interior, out of the lands ceded by the agreement last named, has regularly selected and set aside for the use in common for said Comanche, Kiowa and Apache tribes of Indians, four hundred and eighty thousand acres of grazing lands;

And whereas, in the act of Congress ratifying the said Wichita agreement, it is provided —

That whenever any of the lands acquired by this agreement shall, by operation of law or proclamation of the President of the United States, be open to settlement, they shall be disposed of under the general provisions of the homestead and townsite laws of the United States: *Provided*, That in addition to the land-office fees prescribed by statute for such entries the entryman shall pay one dollar and twenty-five cents per acre for the land entered at the time of submitting his final proof: *And provided further*, That in all homestead entries where the entryman has resided upon and improved the land entered in good faith for the period of fourteen months he may commute his entry to cash upon the payment of one dollar and twenty-five cents per acre. *And provided further*, That the rights of honorably discharged Union soldiers and sailors of the late civil war, as defined and described in sections twenty-three hundred and four and twenty-three hundred and five of the Revised Statutes, shall not be abridged: *And provided further*, That any qualified entryman having lands adjoining the lands herein ceded, whose original entry embraced less than one hundred and sixty acres, may take sufficient land from said reservation to make his homestead entry not to exceed one hundred and sixty acres in all said land to be taken upon the same conditions as are required of other entrymen: *Provided*, That said lands shall be opened to settlement within one year after said allotments are made to the Indians.

*   *   *   *   *   *   *

That the laws relating to the mineral lands of the United States are hereby extended over the lands ceded by the foregoing agreement.

And whereas in the act of Congress ratifying the said Comanche, Kiowa and Apache agreement, it is provided —

That the lands acquired by this agreement shall be opened to settlement by proclamation of the President within six months after allotments are made and be disposed of under the general provisions of the homestead and townsite laws of the United States: *Provided*, That in addition to the land-office fees prescribed by statute for such entries the entryman shall pay one dollar and twenty-five cents per acre for the land entered at the time of submitting his final proof: *And provided further*, That in all homestead entries where the entryman has resided upon and improved the land entered in good faith for the period of fourteen months he may commute his entry to cash upon the payment of one dollar and twenty-five cents per acre: *And provided further*, That the rights of honorably discharged Union soldiers and sailors of the late civil war, as defined and described in sections twenty-three hundred and four and twenty-three hundred and five of the Revised Statutes shall not be abridged: *And provided further*, That any person who, having attempted to but for any cause failed to secure a title in fee to a homestead under existing laws, or who made entry under what is known as the commuted provision of the homestead law, shall be qualified to make a homestead entry upon said lands: *And provided further*, That any qualified entryman having lands adjoining the lands herein ceded, whose original entry embraced less than one hundred and sixty acres in all, shall have the right to enter so much of the lands by this agreement ceded lying contiguous to his said entry as shall, with the land already entered, make in the aggregate one hundred and sixty acres, said land to be taken upon the same conditions as are required of other entrymen: *And provided further*, That the settlers who located on that part of said lands called and known as the "neutral strip" shall have preference right for thirty days on the lands upon which they have located and improved.

*　　　*　　　*　　　*　　　*　　　*　　　*

That should any of said lands allotted to said Indians, or opened to settlement under this act, contain valuable mineral deposits, such mineral deposits shall be open to location and entry, under the existing mining laws of the United States, upon the passage of this act, and the mineral laws of the United States are hereby extended over said lands.

And whereas, by the act of Congress approved January 4, 1901 (31 Stat., 727), the Secretary of the Interior was authorized to extend, for a period not exceeding eight months from December 6, 1900, the time for making allotments to the Comanche, Kiowa, and Apache Indians and opening to settlement the lands so ceded by them;

And whereas, in pursuance of the act of Congress approved March 3, 1901 (31 Stat., 1093), the Secretary of the Interior has regularly subdivided the lands so as aforesaid respectively ceded to the United States by the Wichita and affiliated bands of Indians and the Comanche, Kiowa, and Apache tribes of Indians into counties, attaching portions thereof to adjoining counties in the Territory of Oklahoma, has regularly designated the place for the county seat of each new county, has regularly set aside and reserved at such county seat land for a townsite to be disposed of in the manner provided by the act of Congress last named, and has regularly caused to be surveyed, subdivided, and platted the lands so set aside and reserved for disposition as such townsites;

And whereas, by the act of Congress last named, it is provided:

The lands to be opened to settlement and entry under the acts of Congress ratifying said agreements respectively shall be so opened by proclamation of the President, and to avoid the contests and conflicting claims which have heretofore resulted from opening similar public lands to settlement and entry, the President's proclamation shall prescribe the manner in which these lands may be settled upon, occupied, and entered by persons entitled thereto under the acts ratifying said agreements, respectively; and no person shall be permitted to settle upon, occupy, or enter any of said lands except as prescribed in such proclamation until after the expiration of sixty days from the time when the same are opened to settlement and entry.

And whereas, by the act of Congress last named the President was authorized to establish two additional United States land districts and land offices in the Territory of Oklahoma to include the lands so ceded as aforesaid, which land districts and land offices have been established by an order of even date herewith;

And whereas all of the conditions required by law to be performed prior to the opening of said tracts of land to settlement and entry have been, as I hereby declare, duly performed;

Now, therefore, I, William McKinley, President of the United States of America, by virtue of the power vested in me by law, do hereby declare and make known that all of the lands so as aforesaid ceded by the Wichita and affiliated bands of Indians, and the Comanche, Kiowa, and Apache tribes of Indians, respectively, saving and excepting sections sixteen, thirty-six, thirteen, and thirty-three in each township, and all lands located or selected by the Territory of Oklahoma as indemnity school or educational lands, and saving and excepting all lands allotted in severalty to individual Indians, and saving and excepting all lands allotted and confirmed to religious societies and other organizations, and saving and excepting the lands selected and set aside as grazing lands for the use in common for said Comanche, Kiowa, and Apache tribes of Indians, and saving and excepting the lands set aside and reserved at each of said county seats for disposition as townsites, and saving and excepting the lands now used, occupied, or set apart for military, agency, school, school farm, religious, Indian cemetery, wood reserve, forest reserve, or other public uses, will, on the 6th day of August, 1901, at 9 o'clock A. M., in the manner herein prescribed and not otherwise, be opened to entry and settlement and to disposition under the general provisions of the homestead and townsite laws of the United States.

Commencing at 9 o'clock A. M., Wednesday, July 10, 1901, and ending at 6 o'clock P. M., Friday, July 26, 1901, a registration will be had at the United States land offices at El Reno and Lawton, in the Territory of Oklahoma (the office at Lawton to occupy provisional quarters in the immediate vicinity of Fort Sill, Oklahoma Territory, until suitable quarters can be provided at Lawton), for the purpose of ascertaining what persons desire to enter, settle upon, and acquire title to any of said lands under the homestead law and of ascertaining their qualifications so to do. The registration at each office will be for both land districts, but at the time of registration each applicant will be required to elect and state in which district he desires to make entry. To obtain registration each applicant will be required to show himself duly qualified to make homestead entry of these lands under existing laws and to give the registering officer such appropriate matters of description and identity as will protect the applicant and the government against any attempted impersonation. Registration cannot be effected through the use of the mails or the employment of an agent, excepting that honorably discharged soldiers and sailors entitled to the benefits of section 2304 of the Revised Statutes of the United States, as amended by the act of Congress approved March 1, 1901 (31 Stat., 847), may present their applications for registration and due proofs of their qualifications through an agent of their own selection, but no person will be permitted to act as agent for more than one such soldier or sailor. No person will be permitted to register more than once or in any other than his true name. Each applicant who shows himself duly qualified will be registered and given a non-transferable certificate to that effect, which will entitle him to go upon and examine the lands to be opened hereunder in the land district in which he elects to make his entry; but the only purpose for which he may go upon and examine said lands is that of enabling him later on, as herein provided, to understandingly select the lands for which he will make entry. No one will be permitted to make settlement upon any of said lands in advance of the opening herein provided for, and during the first sixty days following said opening no one but registered applicants will be permitted to make homestead settlement upon any of said lands, and then only in pursuance of a homestead entry duly allowed by the local land officers or of a soldier's declaratory statement duly accepted by such officers.

The order in which, during the first sixty days following the opening, the registered applicants will be permitted to make homestead entry of the lands opened hereunder, will be determined by drawings for both the El Reno and Lawton districts publicly held at the United States land office at El Reno, Oklahoma, commencing at 9 o'clock A. M., Monday, July 29, 1901, and continuing for such period as may be necessary to complete the same. The drawings will be had under the supervision and immediate observation of a committee of three persons whose integrity is such as to make their control of the drawing a guaranty of its fairness. The members of this committee will be appointed by the Secretary of the Interior, who will prescribe suitable compensation for their services. Preparatory to these drawings the registration officers will, at the time of registering each applicant who shows himself duly qualified, make out a card, which must be signed by the applicant, stating the land district in which he desires to make homestead entry, and giving such a description of the applicant as will enable the local land officers to thereafter identify him. This card will be at once sealed in a separate envelope, which will bear no other distinguishing label or mark than such as may be necessary to show that it is to go into the drawing for the land district in which the applicant desires to make entry. These envelopes will be separated according to land districts and will be carefully preserved and remain sealed until opened in the course of the drawing as herein provided. When the registration is completed all of these sealed envelopes will be brought together at the place of drawing and turned over to the committee in charge of the drawing, who, in such manner as in their judgment will be attended with entire fairness and equality of opportunity, shall proceed to draw out and open the separate envelopes and to give to each enclosed card a number in the order in which the envelope containing the same is drawn. While the drawings for the two districts will be separately conducted they will occur as nearly at the same time as is practicable. The result of the drawing for each district will be certified by the committee to the officers of the district and will determine the order in which the applicants may make homestead entry of said lands and settlement thereon.

Notice of the drawings stating the name of each applicant and number assigned to him by the drawing will be posted each day at the place of drawing, and each applicant will be notified of his number by a postal-card mailed to him at the address, if any, given by him at the time of registration. Each applicant should, however, in his own behalf employ such measures as will insure his obtaining prompt and accurate information of the order in which his application for homestead entry can be presented as fixed by the drawing. Applications for homestead entry of said lands during the first sixty days following the opening can be made only by registered applicants and in the order established by the drawing. At each land office, commencing Tuesday, August 6, 1901, at 9 o'clock A. M., the applications of those drawing numbers 1 to 125, inclusive, for that district must be presented and will be considered in their numerical order during the first day, and the applications of those drawing numbers 126 to 250, inclusive, must be presented and will be considered in their numerical order during the second day, and so on at that rate until all of said lands subject to entry under the homestead law, and desired thereunder, have been entered. If any applicant fails to appear and present his application for entry when the number assigned to him by the drawing is reached, his right to enter will be passed until after the other applications assigned for that day have been disposed of, when he will be given another opportunity to make entry, failing in which he will be deemed to have abandoned his right to make entry under such drawing. To obtain the allowance of a homestead entry each applicant must personally present the certificate of registration theretofore issued to him, together with a regular homestead application and the necessary accompanying proofs, and with the regular land office fees, but an honorably discharged soldier or sailor may file his declaratory statement through the agent representing him at the registration. The production of the certificate of registration will be dispensed with only upon satisfactory proof of its loss or destruction. If at the time of considering his regular application for entry it appears that any applicant is disqualified from making homestead entry of these lands his application will be rejected, notwithstanding his prior registration. If any applicant shall register more than once hereunder, or in any other than his true name, or shall transfer his registration certificate he will thereby lose all the benefits of the registration and drawing herein provided for, and will be precluded from entering or settling upon any of said lands during the first sixty days following said opening.

Because of the provision in the said act of Congress approved June 6, 1900: "That the settlers who located on that part of said lands called and known as the 'neutral strip' shall have preference right for thirty days on the lands upon which they have located and improved," the said lands in the "neutral strip" shall for the period of thirty days after said opening be subject to homestead entry and townsite entry only by those who have heretofore located upon and improved the same, and who are accorded a preference right of entry for thirty days as aforesaid. Persons entitled to make entry under this preference right will be permitted to do so at any time during said period of thirty days following the opening without previous registration, and without regard to the drawing herein provided for, and at the expiration of that period the lands in said "neutral strip" for which no entry shall have been made will come under the general provisions of this proclamation.

The intended beneficiaries of the provision in the said acts of Congress, approved, respectively, March 2, 1895, and June 6, 1900, which authorizes a qualified entryman having lands adjoining the ceded lands, whose original entry embraced less than 160 acres, to enter so much of the ceded lands as will make his homestead entry contain in the aggregate not exceeding 160 acres, may obtain such an extension of his existing entry, without previous registration and without regard to the drawing herein provided for, only by making appropriate application, accompanied by the necessary proofs, at the proper new land office at some time prior to the opening herein provided for.

Any person or persons desiring to found, or to suggest establishing a townsite upon any of said ceded lands at any point not in the near vicinity of either of the county seats therein heretofore selected and designated as aforesaid, may, at any time before the opening herein provided for, file in the proper local land office a written application to that effect describing by legal subdivisions the lands intended to be affected, and stating fully and under oath the necessity or propriety of founding or establishing a town at that place. The local officers will forthwith transmit said petition to the Commissioner of the General Land Office with their recommendation in the premises. Such Commissioner, if he believes the public interests will be subserved thereby, will, if the Secretary of the Interior approve thereof, issue an order withdrawing the lands described in such petition, or any portion thereof, from homestead entry and settlement and directing that the same be held for the time being for townsite settlement, entry, and disposition only. In such event the lands so withheld from homestead entry and settlement will, at the time of said opening and not before, become subject to settlement, entry, and disposition under the general townsite laws of the United States. None of said ceded lands will be subject to settlement, entry, or disposition under such general townsite laws except in the manner herein prescribed until afte. the expiration of sixty days from the time of said opening.

Attention is hereby especially called to the fact that under the special provisions of the said act of Congress approved March 3, 1901, the townsites selected and designated at the county seats of the new counties into which said lands have been formed cannot be disposed of under the general townsite laws of the United States, and can only be disposed of in the special manner provided in said act of Congress, which declares:

The lands so set apart and designated shall, in advance of the opening, be surveyed, subdivided, and platted, under the direction of the Secretary of the Interior, into appropriate lots, blocks, streets, alleys, and sites for parks or public buildings, so as to make a townsite thereof: *Provided*, That no person shall purchase more than one business and one residence lot. Such town lots shall be offered and sold at public auction to the highest bidder, under the direction of the Secretary of the Interior, at sales to be had at the opening and subsequent thereto.

All persons are especially admonished that under the said act of Congress approved March 3, 1901, it is provided that no person shall be permitted to settle upon, occupy, or enter any of said ceded lands except in the manner prescribed in this proclamation until after the expiration of sixty days from the time when the same are opened to settlement and entry. After the expiration of the said period of sixty days, but not before, any of said lands remaining undisposed of may be settled upon, occupied and entered under the general provisions of the homestead and townsite laws of the United States in like manner as if the manner of effecting such settlement, occupancy and entry had not been prescribed herein in obedience to law.

It appearing that there are fences around the pastures into which, for convenience, portions of the ceded lands have heretofore been divided, and that these fences are of considerable value and are still the property of the Indian tribes ceding said lands to the United States, all persons going upon, examining, entering or settling upon any of said lands are cautioned to respect such fences as the property of the Indians and not to destroy, appropriate, or carry away the same, but to leave them undisturbed so that they may be seasonably removed and preserved for the benefit of the Indians.

The Secretary of the Interior shall prescribe all needful rules and regulations necessary to carry into full effect the opening herein provided for.

In witness whereof I have hereunto set my hand and caused the seal of the United States to be affixed.

                    Done at the city of Washington this 4th day of July, A. D.
[SEAL.]   1901, and of the Independence of the United States the one
          hundred and twenty-sixth.

                                        WILLIAM McKINLEY.
By the President:
    DAVID J. HILL,
        Acting Secretary of State.

BY THE PRESIDENT OF THE UNITED STATES OF AMERICA.

A PROCLAMATION.

Whereas the Olympic Forest Reserve, in the State of Washington, was established by proclamation dated February 22, 1897, under and by virtue of section twenty-four of the act of Congress, approved March 3, 1891, entitled "An act to repeal timber-culture laws, and for other purposes," which provides, "That the President of the United States may, from time to time, set apart and reserve, in any State or Territory having public lands bearing forests, in any part of the public lands wholly or in part covered with timber or undergrowth, whether of commercial value or not, as public reservations, and the President shall, by public proclamation, declare the establishment of such reservations and the limits thereof;"

And whereas it is further provided by the act of Congress, approved June 4, 1897, entitled, "An act making appropriations for sundry civil expenses of the Government for the fiscal year ending June 30, 1898, and for other purposes," that "The President is hereby authorized at any time to modify any executive order that has been or may hereafter be made establishing any forest reserve, and by such modification may reduce the area or change the boundary lines of such reserve, or may vacate altogether any order creating such reserve;" under which provision, certain lands were withdrawn and excluded from the said forest reserve by proclamation dated April 7, 1900;

Now, therefore, I, William McKinley, President of the United States, by virtue of the power vested in me by the aforesaid act of Congress, approved June 4, 1897, do hereby make known and proclaim that the boundary lines of the aforesaid Olympic Forest Reserve are hereby further changed so as to read as follows:

Beginning at the northeast corner of township twenty-one (21) north, range five (5) west, Willamette Meridian, Washington; thence northerly to the southeast corner of section twenty-five (25), township twenty-three (23) north, range five (5) west, thence westerly to the southwest corner of said section; thence northerly to the northwest corner of said section; thence westerly to the southwest corner of section twenty-three (23), said township; thence northerly to the northwest corner of said section; thence westerly to the southwest corner of section fifteen (15), said township; thence northerly to the northwest corner of section ten (10), said township; thence easterly to the northeast corner of section twelve (12), said township; thence northerly to the northwest corner of township twenty-three (23) north, range four (4) west; thence easterly to the northeast corner of said township; thence northerly to the northwest corner of township twenty-four (24) north, range three (3) west; thence easterly to the northeast corner of said township; thence northerly to the southwest corner of township twenty-eight (28) north, range two (2) west; thence easterly to the southeast corner of the southwest quarter of section thirty-three (33), said township; thence northerly along the quarter-section lines to the northeast corner of the northwest quarter of section twenty-one (21), township twenty-nine (29) north, range two (2) west; thence westerly along the section lines to the point for the southwest corner of section eighteen (18), township twenty-nine (29) north, range five (5) west; thence northerly to the northwest corner of said township; thence westerly to the southeast corner of township thirty (30) north, range eight (8) west; thence northerly to the northeast corner of section twenty-five (25), said township; thence westerly to the southwest corner of section twenty (20), said township; thence northerly to the northeast corner of section eighteen (18), said township; thence westerly to the point for the northeast corner of section thirteen (13), township thirty (30) north, range ten (10) west; thence northerly to the northeast corner of said township; thence westerly to the northwest corner of township thirty (30) north, range eleven (11) west; thence southerly to the southwest corner of section nineteen (19), said township; thence easterly to the southwest corner of section twenty-three (23), township thirty (30) north, range ten (10) west; thence southerly to the southwest corner of section thirty-five (35), said township; thence westerly to the northeast corner of section three (3), township twenty-nine (29), range eleven (11) west; thence southerly to the point for the northeast corner of section twenty-seven (27), said township; thence westerly to the point for the northwest corner of section thirty (30), said township; thence southerly to the southwest corner of said township; thence westerly to the northwest corner of township twenty-eight (28), range twelve (12) west; thence southerly to the southwest corner of said township; thence easterly to the northeast corner of township twenty-seven (27) north, range eleven (11) west; thence southerly to the southeast corner of section one (1), said township; thence westerly to the northwest corner of section ten (10), township twenty-seven (27) north, range twelve (12) west; thence southerly to the southwest corner of section fifteen (15), said township; thence easterly to the southwest corner of section thirteen (13), said township; thence southerly to the southwest corner of section twenty-four (24), said township; thence easterly to the northeast corner of section twenty-five (25), township twenty-seven (27) north, range eleven (11) west; thence southerly to the southeast corner of said township; thence westerly to the southwest corner of said township; thence southerly to the southwest corner of township twenty-five (25) north, range eleven (11) west; thence easterly to the northeast corner of township twenty-four (24) north, range eleven (11) west; thence southerly to the southeast corner of said township; thence westerly along the township line to its point of intersection with the north boundary of the Quinaielt Indian Reservation; thence southeasterly along the north boundary of said Indian Reservation to the eastern point of said reservation and southwesterly along the east boundary thereof to the point of intersection with the township line between townships twenty-one (21) and twenty-two (22) north; thence easterly to the northeast corner of township twenty-one (21) north, range ten (10) west; thence southerly to the southeast corner of section one (1), said township; thence easterly to the southwest corner of section six (6), township twenty-one (21) north, range eight (8) west; thence southerly to the southwest corner of section eighteen (18), said township; thence easterly to the southeast corner of section sixteen (16), said township; thence northerly to the northeast corner of section four (4), said township; thence easterly to the northeast corner of section six (6), township twenty-one (21) north, range seven (7) west; thence southerly to the southeast corner of said section; thence easterly to the northeast corner of section twelve (12), said township; thence southerly to the southeast corner of said section; thence easterly to the northeast corner of section sixteen (16), township twenty-one (21) north, range six (6) west; thence northerly to the point for the northeast corner of section nine (9), said township; thence easterly to the southwest corner of section six (6), township twenty-one (21) north, range five (5) west; thence northerly to the northwest corner of said township; thence easterly to the northeast corner of said township, the place of beginning.

Excepting from the force and effect of this proclamation all lands which may have been, prior to the date hereof, embraced in any legal entry or covered by any lawful filing duly of record in the proper United States Land Office, or upon which any valid settlement has been made pursuant to law, and the statutory period within which to make entry or filing of record has not expired: *Provided*, that this exception shall not continue to apply to any particular tract of land unless the entryman, settler, or claimant continues to comply with the law under which the entry, filing, or settlement was made.

Warning is hereby expressly given to all persons not to make settlement upon the lands reserved by this proclamation.

That the lands hereby restored to the public domain shall be open to settlement from date hereof, but shall not be subject to entry, filing, or selection until after ninety days' notice by such publication as the Secretary of the Interior may prescribe.

In witness whereof, I have hereunto set my hand and caused the seal of the United States to be affixed.

Done at the city of Washington, this 15th day of July, A. D. [SEAL.] 1901, and of the Independence of the United States the one hundred and twenty-sixth.

WILLIAM McKINLEY.

By the President:
JOHN HAY,
Secretary of State.

[CESSATION OF TARIFF—PORTO RICO.]

Whereas, by an act of Congress, approved April 12, 1900, entitled "an Act Temporarily to Provide Revenues and a Civil Government for Porto Rico and for other Purposes," it was provided that, "whenever the legislative assembly of Porto Rico shall have enacted and put into operation a system of local taxation to meet the necessities of the government of Porto Rico, by this act established, and shall by resolution duly passed so notify the President, he shall make proclamation thereof, and thereupon all tariff duties on merchandise and articles going into Porto Rico from the United States or coming into the United States from Porto Rico shall cease, and from and after such date all such merchandise and articles shall be entered at the several ports of entry free of duty;" and

Whereas by the same act it was provided, " that as soon as a civil government for Porto Rico shall have been organized in accordance with the provisions of this act, and notice thereof shall have been given to the President, he shall make proclamation thereof, and thereafter all collections of duties and taxes in Porto Rico under the provisions of this act shall be paid into the treasury of Porto Rico, to be expended as required by law for the government and benefit thereof, instead of being paid into the Treasury of the United States;" and

Whereas the legislative assembly of Porto Rico has enacted and put into operation a system of local taxation to meet the necessities of the government of Porto Rico as aforesaid, and has passed and caused to be communicated to me the following resolution:

A Joint Resolution of the Legislative Assembly of Porto Rico, notifying the President of the United States that the Legislative Assembly of Porto Rico has enacted and put into operation a system of local taxation to meet the necessities of the Government of Porto Rico, established by act of Congress, entitled "An act temporarily to provide revenues and a Civil Government for Porto Rico, and for other purposes," duly approved April 12th, 1900:

Be it Resolved by the Legislative Assembly of Porto Rico:

Whereas: A civil government for Porto Rico has been fully and completely organized in accordance with the provisions of an act of Congress entitled "An act temporarily to provide revenues and a civil government for Porto Rico, and for other purposes," duly approved April 12th, 1900, and:

Whereas: It was provided by the terms of said act of Congress, that whenever the Legislative Assembly of Porto Rico shall have enacted and put into operation a system of local taxation to meet the necessities of the Government of Porto Rico, by the aforesaid act established, and shall by resolution duly passed so notify the President, he shall make proclamation thereof, and thereupon all tariff duties on merchandise and articles going into Porto Rico from the United States, or coming into the United States from Porto Rico shall cease, and from and after such date all such merchandise and articles shall be entered at the several ports of entry free of duty:

Now therefore: The Legislative Assembly of Porto Rico in extraordinary session duly called by the Governor and held at San Juan, the Capital, on July 4th, A. D. 1901, acting pursuant to the authority and power in it vested by the provisions of the said act of Congress above referred to, does hereby notify the President of the United States that by virtue of an act of the Legislative Assembly of Porto Rico, entitled, "An act to provide revenue for the people of Porto Rico, and for other purposes," duly approved January 31st, A. D. 1901, and of other acts of the Legislative Assembly duly enacted at the first session of the Legislative Assembly of Porto Rico, duly held at San Juan, Porto Rico, commencing December 3rd, 1900, and ending January 31st, A. D. 1901, it has enacted and put into operation a system of local taxation to meet the necessities of the Government of Porto Rico, by the aforesaid act of Congress established.

The Legislative Assembly of Porto Rico hereby directs that a copy of this joint resolution be presented to the President of the United States, and hereby requests the Governor of Porto Rico to deliver the same to the President, to the end that proclamation may be made by him according to the provisions of the said act of Congress, and if it shall seem wise and proper to the President, that such proclamation may issue on the 25th day of July, the said day being a legally established holiday in Porto Rico commemorating the anniversary of the coming of the American flag to the Island.

WILLIAM H. HUNT,
President of the Executive Council.
MAN. F. ROSSY,
Speaker of the House of Delegates.
Approved, July 4th, A. D. 1901.

CHAS. H. ALLEN,
Governor.

Now, therefore, I, William McKinley, President of the United States, in pursuance of the provisions of law above quoted, and upon the foregoing due notification, do hereby issue this my proclamation, and do declare and make known that a civil government for Porto Rico has been organized in accordance with the provisions of the said act of Congress;

And I do further declare and make known that the Legislative Assembly of Porto Rico has enacted and put into operation a system of local taxation to meet the necessities of the government of Porto Rico.

In witness whereof I have hereunto set my hand and caused the seal of the United States to be affixed.

Done at the city of Washington this 25th day of July, [SEAL.] A. D. 1901, and of the Independence of the United States the one hundred and twenty-sixth.

WILLIAM McKINLEY.

By the President:

DAVID J. HILL,
Acting Secretary of State.

BY THE PRESIDENT OF THE UNITED STATES OF AMERICA.

A PROCLAMATION.

Whereas, it is provided by section twenty-four of the act of Congress, approved March third, eighteen hundred and ninety-one, entitled "An act to repeal the timber-culture laws, and for other purposes," "That the President of the United States may, from time to time, set apart and reserve, in any State or Territory having public land bearing forests, in any part of the public lands wholly or in part covered with timber or undergrowth, whether of commercial value or not, as public reservations, and the President shall, by public proclamation, declare the establishment of such reservations and the limits thereof;"

And whereas, the public lands in the State of Utah, within the limits hereinafter described, are in part covered with timber, and it appears that the public good would be promoted by setting apart and reserving said lands as a public reservation;

Now, therefore, I, William McKinley, President of the United States, by virtue of the power in me vested by section twenty-four of the aforesaid act of Congress, do hereby make known and proclaim that there is hereby reserved from entry or settlement and set apart as a Public Reservation all those certain tracts, pieces or parcels of land lying and being situate in the State of Utah and particularly described as follows, to wit:

Beginning at the northeast corner of section four (4), township ten (10) south, range three (3) east, Salt Lake base and Meridian, Utah; thence westerly along the township line to the northwest corner of section five (5), township ten (10) south, range two (2) east; thence southerly to the northeast corner of section nineteen (19), said township; thence westerly to the northwest corner of said section; thence southerly along the range line to the southwest corner of township twelve (12) south, range two (2) east; thence easterly to the southeast corner of said township; thence northerly to the northwest corner of section thirty (30), township eleven (11) south, range three (3) east; thence easterly to the southeast corner of section twenty-one (21), said township; thence northerly along the section line to the northeast corner of section four (4), township ten (10) south, range three (3) east, to the place of beginning.

Excepting from the force and effect of this proclamation all lands which may have been, prior to the date hereof, embraced in any legal entry or covered by any lawful filing duly of record in the proper United States Land Office, or upon which any valid settlement has been made pursuant to law, and the statutory period within which to make entry or filing of record has not expired: *Provided*, that this exception shall not continue to apply to any particular tract of land unless the entryman, settler or claimant continues to comply with the law under which the entry, filing or settlement was made.

Warning is hereby expressly given to all persons not to make settlement upon the tract of land reserved by this proclamation.

The reservation hereby established shall be known as The Payson Forest Reserve.

In witness whereof, I have hereunto set my hand and caused the seal of the United States to be affixed.

Done at the city of Washington this 3d day of August, [SEAL.] A. D. 1901, and of the Independence of the United States the one hundred and twenty-sixth.

WILLIAM McKINLEY.

By the President:

ALVEY A. ADEE,
Acting Secretary of State.

BY THE PRESIDENT OF THE UNITED STATES OF AMERICA.

A PROCLAMATION.

Whereas notice has been given me by the Louisiana Purchase Exposition Commission, in accordance with the provisions of section 9 of the act of Congress, approved March 3, 1901, entitled "An act to provide for celebrating the one hundredth anniversary of the purchase of the Louisiana territory by the United States by holding an international exhibition of arts, industries, manufactures, and the products of the soil, mine, forest and sea, in the city of St. Louis, in the State of Missouri," that provision has been made for grounds and buildings for the uses provided for in the said act of Congress:

Now, therefore, I, William McKinley, President of the United States, by virtue of the authority vested in me by said act, do hereby declare and proclaim that such International Exhibition will be opened in the city of St. Louis, in the State of Missouri, not later than the first day of May, 1903, and will be closed not later than the first day of December thereafter. And in the name of the Government and of the people of the United States, I do hereby invite all the nations of the earth to take part in the commemoration of the Purchase of the Louisiana Territory, an event of great interest to the United States and of abiding effect on their development, by appointing representatives and sending such exhibits to the Louisiana Purchase Exposition as will most fitly and fully illustrate their resources, their industries and their progress in civilization.

In testimony whereof, I have hereunto set my hand and caused the seal of the United States to be affixed.

Done at the city of Washington, this 20th day of August, [SEAL.] A. D. 1901, and of the Independence of the United States, the one hundred and twenty-sixth.

WILLIAM McKINLEY.

By the President:
JOHN HAY,
Secretary of State.

EXECUTIVE ORDERS.

EXECUTIVE MANSION, *March 28, 1898.*

It is hereby ordered that the following described tract of land situate on Kadiak Island, District of Alaska, be temporarily reserved and set apart as an experiment station for the use of the Department of Agriculture:

Beginning at a point in the easterly boundary line of the property now occupied by the Russian Greek Church in the village of Kadiak on Kadiak Island, Alaska; thence southeasterly to the water front on the Bay of Chiniak; thence following said water front one-half mile northeasterly to a point; thence northwesterly one-half mile to a point; thence southwesterly one-half mile to a point; thence southeasterly to a point of beginning, embracing 160 acres of land, more or less.

Provided that the temporary reservation above described shall not interfere with any prior rights of the natives or others to land within said reservation. WILLIAM McKINLEY.

EXECUTIVE MANSION,
Washington, May 7, 1898.

DEWEY,
Care American Consul, Hongkong:

The President, in the name of the American people, thanks you and your officers and men for your splendid achievement and overwhelming victory.

209

In recognition he has appointed you acting rear-admiral and will recommend a vote of thanks to you by Congress as a foundation for further promotion.

LONG.

EXECUTIVE MANSION,
Washington, May 19, 1898.

The SECRETARY OF WAR.

SIR: The destruction of the Spanish fleet at Manila, followed by the taking of the naval station at Cavite, the paroling of the garrisons, and the acquisition of the control of the bay, has rendered it necessary, in the further prosecution of the measures adopted by this Government for the purpose of bringing about an honorable and durable peace with Spain, to send an army of occupation to the Philippines for the twofold purpose of completing the reduction of the Spanish power in that quarter and of giving order and security to the islands while in the possession of the United States. For the command of this expedition I have designated Major-General Wesley Merritt, and it now becomes my duty to give instructions as to the manner in which the movement shall be conducted.

The first effect of the military occupation of the enemy's territory is the severance of the former political relations of the inhabitants and the establishment of a new political power. Under this changed condition of things the inhabitants, so long as they perform their duties, are entitled to security in their persons and property and in all their private rights and relations. It is my desire that the people of the Philippines should be acquainted with the purpose of the United States to discharge to the fullest extent its obligations in this regard. It will therefore be the duty of the commander of the expedition, immediately upon his arrival in the islands, to publish a proclamation declaring that we come not to make war upon the people of the Philippines, nor upon any party or faction among them, but to protect them in their homes, in their employments, and in their personal and religious rights. All persons who, either by active aid or by honest submission, co-operate with the United States in its efforts to give effect to this beneficent purpose will receive the reward of its support and protection. Our occupation should be as free from severity as possible.

Though the powers of the military occupant are absolute and supreme and immediately operate upon the political condition of the inhabitants, the municipal laws of the conquered territory, such as affect private rights of person and property and provide for the punishment of crime, are considered as continuing in force, so far as they are compatible with the new order of things, until they are suspended or superseded by the occupying belligerent; and in prac tice they are not usually abrogated, but are allowed to remain in force and to be administered by the ordinary tribunals substantially as they were before the occupation. This enlightened practice is, so far as possible, to be adhered to on the present occasion. The judges and the other officials connected with the administration of justice may, if they accept the authority of the United States, continue to administer the ordinary law of the land as between man and man under the supervision of the American commander-in-chief. The native constabulary will, so far as may be practicable, be preserved. The freedom of the people to pursue their accustomed occupations will be abridged only when it may be necessary to do so.

While the rule of conduct of the American commander-in-chief will be such as has just been defined, it will be his duty to adopt measures of a different kind if, unfortunately, the course of the people should render such measures indispensable to the maintenance of law and order. He will then possess the power to replace or expel the native officials in part or altogether, to substitute new courts of his own constitution for those that now exist, or to create such new or supplementary tribunals as may be necessary. In the exercise of these high powers the commander must be guided by his judgment and his experience and a high sense of justice.

One of the most important and most practical problems with which the commander of the expedition will have to deal is that of the treatment of property and the collection and administration of the revenues. It is conceded that all public funds and securities belonging to the government of the country in its own right and all arms and supplies and other movable property of such government may be seized by the military occupant and converted to the use of this Government. The real property of the state he may hold and administer, at the same time enjoying the revenues thereof; but he is not to destroy it save in the case of military necessity. All public means of transportation, such as telegraph lines, cables, railways, and boats belonging to the state may be appropriated to his use, but unless in case of military necessity they are not to be destroyed. All churches and buildings devoted to religious worship and to the arts and sciences, all schoolhouses, are, so far as possible, to be protected, and all destruction or intentional defacement of such places, of historical monuments or archives, or of works of science or art is prohibited save when required by urgent military necessity.

Private property, whether belonging to individuals or corporations, is to be respected, and can be confiscated only as hereafter indicated. Means of transportation, such as telegraph lines and cables, railways, and boats, may, although they belong to private individuals or corporations, be seized by the military occupant, but unless destroyed under military necessity, are not to be retained.

While it is held to be the right of a conqueror to levy contribu tions upon the enemy in their seaports, towns, or provinces which may be in his military possession by conquest, and to apply the proceeds to defray the expenses of the war, this right is to be exercised within such limitations that it may not savor of confiscation. As the result of military occupation the taxes and duties payable by the inhabitants to the former government become payable to the military occupant, unless he sees fit to substitute for them other rates or modes of contribution to the expenses of the government. The moneys so collected are to be used for the purpose of paying expenses of government under the military occupation, such as the salaries of the judges and the police, and for the payment of the expenses of the army.

Private property taken for the use of the army is to be paid for when possible in cash at a fair valuation, and when payment in cash is not possible receipts are to be given.

In order that there may be no conflict of authority between the army and the navy in the administration of affairs in the Philippines you are instructed to confer with the Secretary of the Navy so far as necessary for the purpose of devising measures to secure the harmonious action of those two branches of the public service.

I will give instructions to the Secretary of the Treasury to make a report to me upon the subject of the revenues of the Philippines, with a view to the formulation of such revenue measures as may seem expedient. All ports and places in the Philippines which may be in the actual possession of our land and naval forces will be opened, while our military occupation may continue, to the commerce of all neutral nations, as well as our own, in articles not contrabrand of war, and upon payment of the prescribed rates of duty which may be in force at the time of the importation.

WILLIAM McKINLEY.

EXECUTIVE MANSION,
Washington, May 19, 1898.

The SECRETARY OF THE TREASURY.

SIR: The destruction of the Spanish fleet at Manila, followed by the taking of the naval station at Cavite, the paroling of the garrisons, and the acquisition of the control of the bay, has rendered it necessary, in the further prosecution of the members adopted by this Government for the purpose of bringing about an honorable and durable peace with Spain, to send an army of occupation to the Philippines for the twofold purpose of completing the reduction of the Spanish power in that quarter and of giving to the islands order and security while in the possession of the United States. For the command of this expedition I have designated Major-General Wesley Merritt, and it now becomes my duty to give instructions as to the manner in which the movement shall be conducted.

It is held to be the right to levy contributions upon the enemy in all places which may be in military possession by conquest, and to apply the proceeds to defray the cost of the war, including the expenses of government during the military occupation. It is desirable, however, and in accordance with the views of modern civilization, to confine the exercise of this power, so far as possible, to the collection of such contributions as are equivalent to the duties and taxes already established in the territory. I have determined to order that all ports or places in the Philippines which may be in the actual possession of our land and naval forces by conquest shall be opened, while our military occupation may continue, to the commerce of all neutral nations, as well as our own, in articles not contraband of war, upon payment of the rates of duty which may be in force at the time when the goods are imported. In the execution of this policy it may be advisable to substitute new rates of duty and new taxes for those now levied in the Philippines. You are therefore instructed to examine the existing Spanish laws in relation to duties and taxes, and to report to me such recommendations as you may deem it proper to make with respect either to the rates of duties and taxes or to the regulations which should be adopted for their imposition and collection.

As the levy of all contributions in territory occupied by a belligerent is a military right derived from the law of nations, the collection and distribution of duties and taxes in the Philippines during the military occupation of the United States will be made, under the orders of the Secretary of War and the Secretary of the Navy, by the military or naval commanders, as the case may be, of the ports or places which may be in the possession of our forces. Your report is desired in order that I may be able to give the proper directions to the Department of War and of the Navy.

WILLIAM McKINLEY.

EXECUTIVE MANSION,
Washington, May, 19, 1898.
The SECRETARY OF THE NAVY.

SIR: The destruction of the Spanish fleet at Manila, followed by the taking of the naval station at Cavite, the paroling of the garrisons, and the acquisition of the control of the bay, has rendered it necessary, in the further prosecution of the measures adopted by this Government for the purpose of bringing about an honorable and durable peace with Spain, to send an army of occupation to the Philppines for the twofold purpose of completing the reduction of the Spanish power in that quarter and of giving to the islands order and security while in the possession of the United States. For the command of this expedition I have designated Major-General Wesley Merritt, and it now becomes my duty to give instructions as to the manner in which the movement shall be conducted.

I inclose herewith a copy of an order which I have this day addressed to the Secretary of War, setting forth the principles on which the occupation of the Philippines is to be carried out.* You are instructed to confer with the Secretary of War in order that measures may be devised by which any conflict of authority between the officers of our army and navy in the Philippines may be avoided.

I have given instructions to the Secretary of the Treasury to examine the subject of the duties and taxes imposed by Spain in the Philippines and to report to me any recommendations which he may deem it proper to make in regard to the revenues of the islands.† I have informed him, however, that the collection and disbursement of the duties and taxes collected there will, as a measure of military right derived from the law of nations, be made, under the orders of the Secretary of War and the Secretary of the Navy, by our military or naval commanders, as the case may be, at the ports or places which may be in possession of our forces.   WILLIAM McKINLEY.

EXECUTIVE MANSION,
Washington, July 4, 1898.

Admiral SAMPSON,
  Playa del Este, Cuba:

You have the gratitude and congratulations of the whole American people. Convey to your noble officers and crews, through whose valor new honors have been added to the American navy, the grateful thanks and appreciation of the nation.

WILLIAM McKINLEY.

THE PRESIDENT'S ADDRESS TO THE PEOPLE FOR THANKSGIVING AND PRAYER.

EXECUTIVE MANSION,
Washington, July 6, 1898.

To the People of the United States of America:

At this time, when to the yet fresh remembrance of the unprecedented success which attended the operations of the United States fleet in the bay of Manila on the 1st day of May last are added the

*See pp. 6569–6571.   †See pp. 6571–6572.

tidings of the no less glorious achievements of the naval and military arms of our beloved country at Santiago de Cuba, it is fitting that we should pause and, staying the feeling of exultation that too naturally attends great deeds wrought by our countrymen in our country's cause, should reverently bow before the throne of divine grace and give devout praise to God, who holdeth the nations in the hollow of His hands and worketh upon them the marvels of His high will, and who has thus far vouchsafed to us the light of His face and led our brave soldiers and seamen to victory.

I therefore ask the people of the United States, upon next assembling for divine worship in their respective places of meeting, to offer thanksgiving to Almighty God, who in His inscrutable ways, now leading our hosts upon the waters to unscathed triumph; now guiding them in a strange land, through the dread shadows of death, to success, even though at a fearful cost; now bearing them, without accident or loss, to far distant climes, has watched over our cause and brought nearer the success of the right and the attainment of just and honorable peace.

With the nation's thanks let there be mingled the nation's prayers that our gallant sons may be shielded from harm alike on the battle-field and in the clash of fleets, and be spared the scourge of suffering and disease while they are striving to uphold their country's honor; and withal let the nation's heart be stilled with holy awe at the thought of the noble men who have perished as heroes die, and be filled with compassionate sympathy for all those who suffer bereavement or endure sickness, wounds, and bonds by reason of the awful struggle. And above all, let us pray with earnest fervor that He, the Dispenser of All Good, may speedily remove from us the untold afflictions of war and bring to our dear land the blessings of restored peace and to all the domain now ravaged by the cruel strife the priceless boon of security and tranquillity.

WILLIAM McKINLEY.

WASHINGTON, D. C *July 8, 1898.*

General SHAFTER,
Playa, Cuba:

Telegram which it appears you did not receive read as follows:

The President directs me to say you have the gratitude and thanks of the nation for the brilliant and effective work of your noble army in the fight of July 1. The sturdy valor and heroism of officers and men fill the American people with pride. The country mourns the brave men who fell in battle. They have added new names to our roll of heroes. R. A. ALGER,
Secretary of War.

EXECUTIVE MANSION,
Washington, July 13, 1898.

The SECRETARY OF WAR.

SIR: The capitulation of the Spanish forces in Santiago de Cuba and in the eastern part of the Province of Santiago, and the occupation of the territory by the forces of the United States, render it necessary to instruct the military commander of the United States as to the conduct which he is to observe during the military occupation.

The first effect of the military occupation of the enemy's territory is the severance of the former political relations of the inhabitants and the establishment of a new political power. Under this changed condition of things the inhabitants, so long as they perform their duties, are entitled to security in their persons and property and in all their private rights and relations. It is my desire that the inhabitants of Cuba should be acquainted with the purpose of the United States to discharge to the fullest extent its obligations in this regard. It will therefore be the duty of the commander of the army of occupation to announce and proclaim in the most public manner that we come not to make war upon the inhabitants of Cuba, nor upon any party or faction among them, but to protect them in their homes, in their employments, and in their personal and religious rights. All persons who, either by active aid or by honest submission, co-operates with the United States in its efforts to give effect to this beneficent purpose will receive the reward of its support and protection. Our occupation should be as free from severity as possible.

Though the powers of the military occupant are absolute and supreme and immediately operate upon the political condition of the inhabitants, the municipal laws of the conquered territory, such as affect private rights of person and property and provide for the punishment of crime, are considered as continuing in force, so far as they are compatible with the new order of things, until they are suspended or superseded by the occupying belligerent; and in practice they are not usually abrogated, but are allowed to remain in force and to be administered by the ordinary tribunals substantially as they were before the occupation. This enlightened practice is, so far as possible, to be adhered to on the present occasion. The judges and the other officials connected with the administration of justice may, if they accept the supremacy of the United States, continue to administer the ordinary law of the land as between man and man under the supervision of the American commander-in-chief. The native constabulary will, so far as may be practicable, be preserved. The freedom of the people to pursue their accustomed occupations will be abridged only when it may be necessary to do so.

While the rule of conduct of the American commander-in-chief will be such as has just been defined, it will be his duty to adopt measures of a different kind if, unfortunately, the course of the people should render such measures indispensable to the maintenance of law and order. He will then possess the power to replace or expel the native officials in part or altogether, to substitute new courts of his own constitution for those that now exist, or to create such new or supplementary tribunals as may be necessary. In the exercise of these high powers the commander must be guided by his judgment and his experience and a high sense of justice.

One of the most important and most practical problems with which it will be necessary to deal is that of the treatment of property and the collection and administration of the revenues. It is conceded that all public funds and securities belonging to the government of the country in its own right and all arms and supplies and other movable property of such government may be seized by the military occupant and converted to his own use. The real property of the state he may hold and administer, at the same time enjoying the revenues thereof; but he is not to destroy it save in the case of military necessity. All public means of transportation, such as telegraph lines, cables, railways, and boats, belonging to the state may be appropriated to his use, but unless in case of military necessity they are not to be destroyed. All churches and buildings devoted to religious worship and to the arts and sciences, all schoolhouses, are, so far as possible, to be protected, and all destruction or intentional defacement of such places, of historical monuments or archives, or of works of science or art is prohibited save when required by urgent military necessity.

Private property, whether belonging to individuals or corporations, is to be respected, and can be confiscated only for cause. Means of transportation, such as telegraph lines and cables, railways, and boats, may, although they belong to private individuals or corporations, be seized by the military occupant, but unless destroyed under military necessity are not to be retained.

While it is held to be the right of the conqueror to levy contributions upon the enemy in their seaports, towns, or provinces which may be in his military possession by conquest, and to apply the proceeds to defray the expenses of the war, this right is to be exercised within such limitations that it may not savor of confiscation. As the result of military occupation the taxes and duties payable by the inhabitants to the former government become payable to the military occupant, unless he sees fit to substitute for them other rates or modes of contribution to the expenses of the government. The moneys so collected are to be used for the purpose of paying the expenses of government under the military occupation, such as the

salaries of the judges and the police, and for the payment of the expenses of the army.

Private property taken for the use of the army is to be paid for
when possible in cash at a fair valuation, and when payment in cash
is not possible receipts are to be given.

All ports and places in Cuba which may be in the actual possession of our land and naval forces will be opened to the commerce of
all neutral nations, as well as our own, in articles not contraband of
war, upon payment of the prescribed rates of duty which may be in
force at the time of the importation.

WILLIAM McKINLEY.

Washington, D. C., July 16, 1898.
General SHAFTER,
　　Commanding United States Forces, Santiago, Playa:

The President of the United States sends to you and your brave
army the profound thanks of the American people for the brilliant
achievements at Santiago, resulting in the surrender of the city and
all of the Spanish troops and territory under General Toral. Your
splendid command has endured not only the hardships and sacrifices
incident to campaign and battle, but in stress of heat and weather
has triumphed over obstacles which would have overcome men less
brave and determined. One and all have displayed the most conspicuous gallantry and earned the gratitude of the nation. The
hearts of the people turn with tender sympathy to the sick and
wounded. May the Father of Mercies protect and comfort them.

WILLIAM McKINLEY.

EXECUTIVE MANSION,
Washington, July 21, 1898.

In view of the occupation of Santiago de Cuba by the forces of the
United States, it is ordered that postal communication between the
United States and that port, which has been suspended since the
opening of hostilities with Spain, may be resumed, subject to such
military regulations as may be deemed necessary.

As other portions of the enemy's territory come into the possession of the land and naval forces of the United States, postal communication may be opened under the same conditions.

The domestic postal service within the territory thus occupied may
be continued on the same principles already indicated for the continuance of the local municipal and judicial administration, and it may
be extended as the local requirements may justify, under the supervision of the military commander.

The revenues derived from such service are to be applied to the expenses of conducting it, and the United States postage stamps are therefore to be used.

The Postmaster-General is charged with the execution of this order in co-operation with the military commander, to whom the Secretary of War will issue the necessary directions.

WILLIAM McKINLEY.

EXECUTIVE MANSION, *July 27, 1898.*

It is hereby ordered that the following described land situated on the Yukon River in the District of Alaska, be and here is reserved and set apart for the uses and purposes of a townsite, said land to be held subject to the townsite law or laws that are or may become applicable to the public lands in the District of Alaska, and so long as this reservation remains in force to be subject to disposition in no other manner whatever, to wit:

A tract of land commencing at a post on the right or north bank of the Yukon River, about one-half mile below Mayos Landing, marked U. S. M. R.; thence north from said post one mile; thence east two miles; thence south to the bank of the Yukon River; thence southwesterly along the bank of said river to the place of beginning, containing two square miles, more or less.

WILLIAM McKINLEY.

EXECUTIVE MANSION,
Washington, August 6, 1898.

Ordered, That the graves of our soldiers at Santiago shall be permanently marked. The present marking will last but a short time, and before its effacement occurs suitable and permanent markers should be put up.

The Secretary of War is charged with the execution of this order.

WILLIAM McKINLEY.

EXECUTIVE MANSION, *August 6, 1898.*

Paragraph 576 of the Consular Regulations is hereby amended so as to read as follows:

576. Consular Agents will be governed by the foregoing requirements in relation to official services and will render their quarterly reports in accordance with the prescribed forms to the principal Consular Officer who will transmit the same to the Auditor for the State and other Departments.

The amounts which may be found due at the Treasury on account of services rendered to American vessels and seamen will in all cases be sent by Treasury Warrant to the address of and payable to the order of the officer entitled thereto.

Forms Nos. 190 and 191 are established in full force and authority as parts of the Consular Regulations of September 30, 1898.

WILLIAM McKINLEY.

ADJUTANT-GENERAL'S OFFICE,
Washington, August 17, 1898.

Major-General MERRITT,
    Manila, Philippines:

The President directs that there must be no joint occupation with the insurgents. The United States, in the possession of Manila City, Manila Bay and Harbor, must preserve the peace and protect persons and property within the territory occupied by their military and naval forces. The insurgents and all others must recognize the military occupation and authority of the United States and the cessation of hostilities proclaimed by the President. Use whatever means in your judgment are necessary to this end. All law-abiding people must be treated alike.

By order Secretary War:

H. C. CORBIN,
Adjutant-General.

EXECUTIVE MANSION,
Washington, August 21, 1898.

Major-General MERRITT,
    United States Army, Manila:

In my own behalf and for the nation I extend to you and the officers and men of your command sincere thanks and congratulations for the conspicuously gallant conduct displayed in your campaign

WILLIAM McKINLEY.

EXECUTIVE MANSION,
Washington, August 21, 1898.

Admiral DEWEY,
    Manila:

Receive for yourself and for the officers, sailors, and marines of your command my thanks and congratulations and those of the nation for the gallant conduct all have again so conspicuously displayed.

WILLIAM McKINLEY.

ADJUTANT-GENERAL'S OFFICE,
Washington, December 4, 1898.

General OTIS,
  Manila, Philippine Islands:

By direction of the Secretary of War, following from the President is sent you for your early consideration.   CORBIN.

The President desires that Admiral Dewey and General Otis shall have an early conference and advise him what force and equipment will be necessary in the Philippine Islands. The President would be glad to have suggestions from these commanders as to the government of the islands, which of necessity must be by the Army and the Navy for some time to come. When these islands shall be ceded to us, it is his desire that peace and tranquillity shall be restored and as kind and beneficent a government as possible given to the people, that they may be encouraged in their industries and made secure in life and property. The fullest suggestions are invited.

                    WILLIAM McKINLEY.

EXECUTIVE MANSION, *December 9, 1898.*

By virtue of the authority vested in me as Commander-in-Chief of the Army and Navy of the United States, I hereby order and direct that during the occupancy by the military authorities of the United States of the island of Cuba and all islands in the West Indies west of the seventy-fourth degree, west longitude, evacuated by Spain, said islands shall constitute a collection district for customs purposes. Havana shall be the chief port of entry. An officer of the Army shall be assigned to such port, who shall be the collector of customs of the islands and of the chief port and shall have general jurisdiction over the collection of customs in the islands.

The ports of Matanzas, Cardenas, Cienfuegos, Sagua, Caibarien, Santiago, Manzanillo, Nuevitas, Guantanamo, Gibara, and Baracoa, in said islands, are hereby declared to be subports of entry, and an officer of the Army will be assigned to each of the subports, who will be the collector of customs of a subport and shall have general jurisdiction of the collection of customs at such port. He shall make weekly reports to the collector of customs of the islands at the chief port of all transactions at the subport over which he has jurisdiction, with copies of all entries of merchandise, duly certified.

The Secretary of War shall appoint such civilian deputy collectors, inspectors, and other employees as may be found necessary.

The collectors of the subports shall deposit all moneys collected by them with the collector of the islands, and a receipt from the collector of the islands must be taken in duplicate for all such deposits.

There shall be appointed an auditor, who shall be stationed at the chief port, whose duty it shall be to examine all entries of merchandise and if found correct to certify to them. Such auditor shall on the first of each month make a full and complete report, duly certified, to the Secretary of War of all duties collected at each port, with an itemized report of all expenditures made therefrom, which shall be referred to the Auditor for the War Department for audit.

All questions arising in the administration of customs in the islands shall be referred to the collector of the islands at the chief port for decision, from which there shall be no appeal, except in such cases as may be referred by the collector of the islands to the Secretary of War for his decision.

WILLIAM McKINLEY.

EXECUTIVE MANSION,
Washington, December 21, 1898.

The SECRETARY OF WAR.

SIR: The destruction of the Spanish fleet in the harbor of Manila by the United States naval squadron commanded by Rear-Admiral Dewey, followed by the reduction of the city and the surrender of the Spanish forces, practically effected the conquest of the Philippine Islands and the suspension of Spanish sovereignty therein.

With the signature of the treaty of peace between the United States and Spain by their respective plenipotentiaries at Paris, on the 10th instant, and as the result of the victories of American arms, the future control, disposition, and government of the Philippine Islands are ceded to the United States. In fulfillment of the rights of sovereignty thus acquired and the responsible obligations of government thus assumed, the actual occupation and administration of the entire group of the Philippine Islands become immediately necessary, and the military government heretofore maintained by the United States in the city, harbor, and bay of Manila is to be extended with all possible dispatch to the whole of the ceded territory.

In performing this duty the military commander of the United States is enjoined to make known to the inhabitants of the Philippine Islands that in succeeding to the sovereignty of Spain, in severing the former political relations of the inhabitants, and in establishing a new political power the authority of the United States is to be exerted for the security of the persons and property of the people of the islands and for the confirmation of all their private rights and relations.

It will be the duty of the commander of the forces of occupation to announce and proclaim in the most public manner that we come, not as invaders or conquerors, but as friends, to protect the natives in their homes, in their employments, and in their personal and religious rights. All persons who, either by active aid or by honest submission, co-operate with the Government of the United States to give effect to these beneficent purposes will receive the reward of its support and protection. All others will be brought within the lawful rule we have assumed, with firmness if need be, but without severity so far as may be possible.

Within the absolute domain of military authority, which necessarily is and must remain supreme in the ceded territory until the legislation of the United States shall otherwise provide, the municipal laws of the territory in respect to private rights and property and the repression of crime are to be considered as continuing in force and to be administered by the ordinary tribunals so far as practicable. The operations of civil and municipal government are to be performed by such officers as may accept the supremacy of the United States by taking the oath of allegiance, or by officers chosen as far as may be practicable from the inhabitants of the islands.

While the control of all the public property and the revenues of the state passes with the cession, and while the use and management of all public means of transportation are necessarily reserved to the authority of the United States, private property, whether belonging to individuals or corporations, is to be respected, except for cause duly established. The taxes and duties heretofore payable by the inhabitants to the late government become payable to the authorities of the United States, unless it be seen fit to substitute for them other reasonable rates or modes of contribution to the expenses of government, whether general or local. If private property be taken for military use, it shall be paid for when possible in cash at a fair valuation, and when payment in cash is not practicable receipts are to be given.

All ports and places in the Philippine Islands in the actual possession of the land and naval forces of the United States will be opened to the commerce of all friendly nations. All goods and wares not prohibited for military reasons, by due announcement of the military authority, will be admitted upon payment of such duties and other charges as shall be in force at the time of their importation.

Finally, it should be the earnest and paramount aim of the military administration to win the confidence, respect, and affection of the inhabitants of the Philippines by assuring to them in every possible way that full measure of individual rights and liberties which is the heritage of free peoples, and by proving to them that the mission of the United States is one of benevolent assimilation, substituting the mild sway of justice and right for arbitrary rule. In the fulfillment of this high mission, supporting the temperate administration of affairs for the greatest good of the governed, there must be sed ulously maintained the strong arm of authority to repress disturbance and to overcome all obstacles to the bestowal of the blessings of good and stable government upon the people of the Philippine Islands under the free flag of the United States.

WILLIAM McKINLEY.

ADJUTANT-GENERAL'S OFFICE,
Washington, December 21, 1898.

General OTIS,
Manila:

Answering your message of December 14, the President directs that you send necessary troops to Iloilo to preserve the peace and protect life and property. It is most important that there should be no conflict with the insurgents. Be conciliatory, but firm.

By order of the Secretary War: CORBIN.

EXECUTIVE MANSION,
Washington, December 22, 1898.

Until otherwise ordered no grants or concessions of public or corporate rights or franchises for the construction of public or *quasi* public works, such as railroads, tramways, telegraph and telephone lines, water works, gas works, electric-light lines, etc., shall be made by any municipal or other local governmental authority or body in Cuba, except, upon the approval of the major-general commanding the military forces of the United States in Cuba, who shall before approving any such grant or concession be so especially authorized by the Secretary of War. WILLIAM McKINLEY.

[Similar orders applying to Puerto Rico and to the Philippines were issued.]

EXECUTIVE MANSION,
Washington, December 22, 1898.

The SECRETARY OF WAR:

*   *   *   *   *   *   *

The major-general commanding the United States forces in Cuba and the senior naval officer of the American fleet in the port of Havana are directed to observe such arrangements and ceremonies for the evacuation of Havana, to take place on January 1, 1899, as may be communicated to them by the United States commissioners on evacuation. They will aid in carrying out such arrangements.

WILLIAM McKINLEY.

ADJUTANT-GENERAL'S OFFICE,
Washington, January 1, 1899 — 4:30 P. M.

General OTIS,
Manila:

The President considers it of first importance that a conflict brought on by you be avoided at this time, if possible. Cannot Miller get into communication with insurgents, giving them President's proclamation and informing them of the purposes of the Government, assuring them that while it will assert its sovereignty its purpose is to give them a good government and security in their personal rights.

By order Secretary War: CORBIN.

EXECUTIVE MANSION,
Washington, January 20, 1899.

The SECRETARY OF STATE:

My communication to the Secretary of War dated December 21, 1898,* declares the necessity of extending the actual occupation and administration of the city, harbor, and bay of Manila to the whole of the territory which by the treaty of Paris, signed on December 10, 1898, passed from the sovereignty of Spain to the sovereignty of the United States and the consequent establishment of military government throughout the entire group of the Philippine Islands.

While the treaty has not yet been ratified, it is believed that it will be by the time of the arrival at Manila of the commissioners named below. In order to facilitate the most humane, specific, and effective extension of authority throughout these islands and to secure with the least possible delay the benefits of a wise and generous protection of life and property to the inhabitants, I have named Jacob G. Schurman, Rear-Admiral George Dewey, Major-General Elwell S. Otis, Charles Denby, and Dean C. Worcester to constitute a commission to aid in the accomplishment of these results.

In the performance of this duty the commissioners are enjoined to meet at the earliest possible day in the city of Manila and to announce by a public proclamation their presence and the mission intrusted to them, carefully setting forth that while the military government already proclaimed is to be maintained and continued so long as necessity may require, efforts will be made to alleviate the burdens of taxation, to establish industrial and commercial prosperity, and to provide for the safety of persons and of property by such means as may be found conducive to these ends.

The commissioners will endeavor, without interference with the military authorities of the United States now in control of the Philip-

* See pp. 6581–6583.

pines, to ascertain what amelioration in the condition of the inhabitants and what improvements in public order may be practicable, and for this purpose they will study attentively the existing social and political state of the various populations, particularly as regards the forms of local government, the administration of justice, the collection of customs and other taxes, the means of transportation, and the need of public improvements.

They will report through the State Department, according to the forms customary or hereafter prescribed for transmitting and preserving such communications, the results of their observations and reflections, and will recommend such executive action as may from time to time seem to them wise and useful.

The commissioners are hereby authorized to confer authoritatively with any persons resident in the islands from whom they may believe themselves able to derive information or suggestions valuable for the purposes of their commission, or whom they may choose to employ as agents, as may be necessary for this purpose.

The temporary government of the islands is intrusted to the military authorities, as already provided for by my instructions to the Secretary of War of December 21, 1898,* and will continue until Congress shall determine otherwise. The commission may render valuable services by examining with special care the legislative needs of the various groups of inhabitants and by reporting, with recommendations, the measures which should be instituted for the maintenance of order, peace, and public welfare, either as temporary steps to be taken immediately for the perfection of present administration or as suggestions for future legislation.

In so far as immediate personal changes in the civil administration may seem to be advisable, the commissioners are empowered to recommend suitable persons for appointment to these offices from among the inhabitants of the islands who have previously acknowledged their allegiance to this Government.

It is my desire that in all their relations with the inhabitants of the islands the commissioners exercise due respect for all the ideals, customs, and institutions of the tribes and races which compose the population, emphasizing upon all occasions the just and beneficent intentions of the Government of the United States.

It is also my wish and expectation that the commissioners may be received in a manner due to the honored and authorized representatives of the American Republic, duly commissioned, on account of their knowledge, skill, and integrity, as bearers of the good will, the protection, and the richest blessings of a liberating rather than a conquering nation.

WILLIAM McKINLEY.

*See pp. 6581–6583.

EXECUTIVE MANSION, *January 31, 1899.*

It is hereby ordered that the following described tract of land situate near the north bank of Cook Inlet, adjoining the town of Kenai on the north, District of Alaska, be and it is hereby set apart as an agricultural experiment station, subject to any existing legal rights thereto, it being more particularly described in the field notes of the survey thereof, executed by C. C. Georgeson, Special Agent in charge of investigations, in August, 1898, under the direction of the Secretary of Agriculture, and shown on his plat of survey, all bearings being magnetic, to wit:

Beginning at a point located near the Russian Parsonage and Church, from which the nearest log barn belonging to the parsonage bears S. 68° 50′ E. 65 ft.; the spire of the church bearing S. 8° E. to the southeast corner of the cemetery fence, bearing north 13° W. 361 ft.; thence N. 9° W., 5,808 ft. to a point for the northeast corner of the tract; thence S. 9° E. 5,808 feet to a point for the southeast corner of the tract; thence S. 81° W. 2,400 feet to the place of beginning, containing 320 acres of land, more or less.

WILLIAM McKINLEY.

EXECUTIVE MANSION, *February 3, 1899.*

I, William McKinley, President of the United States, by virtue of the authority vested in me by Sections 3141 and 3142 of the Revised Statutes of the United States, hereby order:

That the counties of Alger, Baraga, Chippewa, Delta, Dickinson, Gogebic, Houghton, Iron, Keweenaw, Luce, Mackinac, Marquette, Menominee, Ontonagon and Schoolcroft, now a part of the First Internal Revenue Collection District of Michigan be transferred to and made a part of the Fourth Internal Revenue Collection District of Michigan.

WILLIAM McKINLEY.

EXECUTIVE MANSION,
Washington, D. C., April 1, 1899.

Under the Provisions of Section 2060, Revised Statutes, the Headquarters of the new Neech Lake Indian Agency in Minnesota are hereby ordered to be established on the tracts of land to be reserved for that purpose and which are known as parts of township 142, range 31 west, 5th Meridian, as described in the recommendation of the Commission of Indian Affairs, approved by the Secretary of the Interior.

WILLIAM McKINLEY.

EXECUTIVE MANSION,
Washington, D. C., April 1, 1899

It is hereby ordered that the Fort Stanton abandoned military reservation, New Mexico, containing ten thousand two hundred and forty (10,240) acres, more or less, with the buildings thereon be, and it is hereby reserved and set apart for the use of the Marine Hospital Service.

Except that the force and effect of this order shall not apply to any lands to which, prior to the date hereof, valid claims may have been attached under the Homestead or Mineral Land Laws.

WILLIAM McKINLEY.

EXECUTIVE MANSION,
Washington, D. C., April 1, 1899.

The change in location of the Office of the Humboldt Land District in California from Humboldt to Eureka is hereby ordered, under the provision of Section 2251 in the Revised Statutes of the United States.   WILLIAM McKINLEY.

EXECUTIVE MANSION,
Washington, D. C., April 3, 1899.

It is fitting that in behalf of the Nation, tribute of honor be paid to the memories of the noble men who lost their lives in their country's service during the late war with Spain.

It is more fitting, inasmuch as in consonance with a spirit of our free institutions, and in obedience to the most exalted prompting of patriotism, those who were sent to other shores to do battle for their country's honor, under their country's flag, went freely from every quarter of our beloved clime; each soldier, each sailor parting from home ties and putting behind him private interest in the presence of the stern emergency of unsought war with an alien foe, was an individual type of that devotion of the citizen to the State which makes our Nation strong in unity and action.

Those who died in other lands left in many homes the undying memories that attend the honored dead of all ages. It was fitting with the advent of peace, won by their sacrifice, their bodies should be gathered with tender care and restored to home and country. This has been done with the dead of Cuba and Puerto Rico. Those of the Philippines still rest where they fell, watched over by their surviving comrades and mourned with the love of a grateful nation.

The remains of many brought to our shores have been delivered to their families for private burial, but for others of the brave officers and men who perished, there has been reserved interment in the ground sacred to the soldiers and sailors, and amid tributes of national memories they have so well deserved.

I therefore order:

That upon the arrival of the cortege at the National Cemetery at Arlington, all proper military and naval honors be paid to the dead heroes; that suitable ceremonies shall attend their interment; that the customary salute of mourning be fired at the cemetery, and that on the same day at two o'clock P. M., Thursday, the sixth day of April, the National ensign be displayed at half staff on all public buildings, forts, camps and public vessels of the United States, and that at twelve o'clock noon of said day all the Departments of the Government at Washington shall be closed.

WILLIAM McKINLEY.

EXECUTIVE MANSION,
Washington, D. C., April 6, 1899.

In accordance with the provision of the Act of Congress approved June 4, 1897 (30 stat., 36), and by virtue of the authority thereby given and on the recommendation of the Secretary of the Interior, it is hereby ordered that the east half of the northwest quarter and the west half of the northeast corner of section twenty (20), township ten (10) south, range five (5) east, Willamette Meridian, Oregon, with the limits of the Cascade Range Forest Reservation, be restored to the Public Domain after sixty days' notice hereof by publication, as required by law, these tracts having been found better adapted to agricultural than forest purposes.

WILLIAM McKINLEY.

EXECUTIVE MANSION,
Washington, D. C., May 6, 1899.

By virtue of the authority vested in me as Commander-in-Chief of the Army and Navy of the United States, I hereby order and direct that during the maintenance of the Military Government of the United States in the Island of Puerto Rico and all Islands in the West Indies, east of the 74th degree west longitude, evacuated by Spain, there are hereby created and shall be maintained the offices of Auditor of the Islands, one Assistant Auditor for auditing the accounts of the Department of Customs and one Assistant Auditor for auditing the accounts of the Department of Postoffices who shall be appointed by the Secretary of War and whose duty shall be to audit all accounts of the Islands.

There is hereby created and shall be maintained the office of Treasurer of the Islands, which shall be filled by the appointment thereto of an officer of the regular army of the United States. The Treasurer of the Islands shall receive and keep all moneys arising from the revenues of the Islands and shall disburse or transfer the same only upon warrants issued by the Auditor of the Islands and countersigned by the Governor-General.

All rules and instructions necessary to carry into effect the provisions of Executive Orders relating to said Islands shall be issued by the Secretary of War. WILLIAM McKINLEY.

EXECUTIVE MANSION,
Washington, D. C., May 6, 1899.

By virtue of the authority vested in me as Commander-in-Chief of the Army and Navy of the United States, I hereby order and direct that during the maintenance of Military Government of the United States in the Island of Cuba and all Islands in the West Indies, west of the 74th degree west longitude, evacuated by Spain, there are hereby created and shall be maintained the offices of the Auditor of the Islands, one Assistant Auditor for auditing the accounts for the Department of Customs, and one Assistant Auditor for auditing the accounts of the Department of Postoffices who shall be appointed by the Secretary of War and whose duties shall be to audit all accounts of the Islands.

There is hereby created and shall be maintained the office of Treasurer of the Islands which shall be filled by the appointment thereto of an officer of the regular army of the United States. The Treasurer of the Islands shall receive and keep all moneys arising from the revenues of the Islands and shall disburse or transfer the same only upon warrants issued by the Auditor of the Islands and countersigned by the Governor-General.

All rules and instructions necessary to carry into effect the provisions of Executive Orders relating to said Islands shall be issued by the Secretary of War. WILLIAM McKINLEY.

EXECUTIVE MANSION,
Washington, D. C., May 10, 1899.

In accordance with the provisions of Act of Congress approved June 4th, 1897 (30 Stat. 36), and by virtue of the authority thereby given and on recommendation of the Secretary of the Interior, it is hereby ordered that Baker Lake and the surrounding lands within half mile of the shore thereof within the limits of the Washington Forest Reserve, State of Washington, be and they are hereby withdrawn from the operation of the proclamation dated February 22nd, 1897, creating such reserve are hereby reserved and set apart for the use of the United States Commission of Fish and Fisheries for the purpose of a Fish Cultural station.

Provided, That the Lake and surrounding land above described shall again become subject to the operation of the proclamation creating the Washington Forest Reserve whenever the use thereof for fish cultural purposes shall be abandoned by the United States Commission of Fish and Fisheries.

WILLIAM McKINLEY.

EXECUTIVE MANSION, *May 13, 1899.*

In the exercise of the power conferred upon me by the joint resolution of Congress, approved by the President on July 7, 1898, entitled "Joint Resolution to provide for annexing the Hawaiian Islands to the United States" the President of the United States hereby directs that the General Election provided for by the constitution of the Republic of Hawaii to be held on the last Wednesday in September next shall not be held. All elective officers whose terms of office shall expire before appropriate legislation shall have been enacted by the Congress of the United States shall be continued in their offices at the pleasure of the President of the United States.

[SEAL.] In witness whereof I have caused the seal of the United States to be hereunto affixed.

WILLIAM McKINLEY.

EXECUTIVE MANSION,
Washington, D. C., May 23, 1899.
To the Heads of the Executive Departments and the Public Printer:

It is hereby ordered that upon Wednesday, the 24th instant, the employees of the executive departments and the government printing office shall be excused from duty at 12:00 o'clock noon to enable them to participate in the Civic parade and other exercises of the Peace Jubilee on that day.

WILLIAM McKINLEY.

EXECUTIVE MANSION, *June 10, 1899.*

Consular court fees and fines imposed and collected by consular courts are hereby declared to be official. They are to be used to defer the expenses of consular courts, and detailed accounts of receipts and expenditures are to be rendered to the Secretary of State on the 30th of June of each year. Any surplus remaining at the end of the year after the expenses of the courts have been paid is to be turned into the Treasury.

The portions of the Executive Order of July 29, 1897, and the consular regulations in conflict with this order are hereby amended.

WILLIAM McKINLEY.

EXECUTIVE MANSION,
Washington, D. C., June 16, 1899.

Officers of the Customs in the Islands of Cuba may authorize the clearance under a permit for foreign ports, ports of the United States of vessels owned prior to June 1st, 1899 by residents of Cuba and owned at the time of clearance by citizens of Cuba under the signal and coast permit of Cuba. Such vessels may carry the American flag above the distinctive signal for the purpose of indicating that the Government of the United States pursuant to treaty has assumed and will discharge the obligations that may under International law result from the fact of the occupation of Cuba for the protection of life and property.

In granting such clearance under a permit vessels of the customs will advise masters or owners that clearance under permit and the use of the flag of the United States hereby authorized do not confer upon such vessels any rights and privileges which are conferred upon vessels of the United States by the status of treaties of the United States. The rights and privileges of such a vessel as to enter clearance dues, charges, etc., in foreign ports and in ports of the United States will be determined by the laws of the country in which the port may be situated.

Such vessel upon entering into a port of the United States would be subject to the provisions of Sections 2497, 4219 and 4225 of the Revised Statutes and such other laws as may be applicable.

The form and manner of the issuance of permits provided for in this paragraph shall be prescribed by the Secretary of War.

Tariff Circular No. 71, dated Washington, May 25th, 1899, is hereby rescinded.

WILLIAM McKINLEY.

EXECUTIVE MANSION,
Washington, D. C., June 27, 1899.

By virtue of the authority vested in me as Commander-in-Chief of the Army and Navy, I hereby order and direct that during the maintenance of the Military Government of the United States in the Island of Cuba and all islands of the West Indies west of the 74th degree. west longitude, evacuated by Spain, there are hereby created and shall be maintained, in addition to the office created by executive order of May 8, 1899, the office of Assistant Auditor for auditing the accounts of the departments of Internal Revenue and one Assistant Treasurer in the office of the Treasurer of the islands, who shall be appointed by the Secretary of War.

WILLIAM McKINLEY.

EXECUTIVE MANSION,
Washington, D. C., July 3, 1899.

1. Officers of the Customs in the Island of Puerto Rico, ceded to the United States by Spain, may issue a certificate of protection, entitling a vessel to which it is issued to the protection and flag of the United States on the high seas and in all ports, if the vessel is owned by:

  a. A citizen of the United States residing in Puerto Rico.

  b. A native inhabitant of Puerto Rico upon taking oath of allegiance to the United States.

  c. Resident of Puerto Rico before April 11, 1899, hitherto a subject of Spain, upon abjuring his allegiance to the crown of Spain and taking the oath of allegiance to the United States.

2. The master and the watch officers of a vessel to which a certificate of protection is issued shall be citizens of the United States or shall take the oath of allegiance to the United States, providing that the general commanding the forces of the United States in Puerto Rico may in his discretion in special cases waive these requirements in whole or in part.

3. Such certificate of protection shall entitle vessel to the same privileges and subject it to the same disabilities as are prescribed in Article XX of the Consular Regulations of 1896 for American or foreign built vessels transferred abroad to citizens of the United States.

4. The form and manner of the issue of certificates of protection provided for in this order shall be prescribed by the Secretary of War.

WILLIAM McKINLEY.

EXECUTIVE MANSION.
Washington, D. C., July 3, 1899.

1. Officers of the Customs in the Philippine Islands, ceded to the United States by Spain, may issue a certificate of protection entitling the vessel to which it is issued to the protection and flag of the United States on the High Seas and in all ports, if the vessel is owned by:

  a. A citizen of the United States residing in the Philippine Islands.

b. A native inhabitant of the Philippine Islands upon taking the oath of allegiance to the United States.

c. Residents of the Philippine Islands before April 11th, 1899 hitherto a subject of Spain, upon abjuring his allegiance to the Crown of Spain and taking the oath of allegiance to the United States.

2. The master and watch officer of a vessel to which a certificate of Protection is issued shall be citizens of the United States or shall take the oath of allegiance to the United States, providing that the General commanding the forces of the United States in Philippine Islands may, in his discretion in special cases, waive this requirement in whole or in part.

3. Such certificate of protection shall entitle the vessel to the same privileges and subject it to the same disabilities as are prescribed in Article XX of the Consular Regulations of 1896 for American or foreign vessels transferred abroad to citizens of the United States.

4. The form and manner of the issue of certificates of protection provided for in this order shall be prescribed by the Secretary of War.   WILLIAM McKINLEY.

EXECUTIVE MANSION,
Washington, D. C., July 24, 1899.

To the Secretary of the Treasury.

SIR:—It is provided in the "Act making appropriation for sundry civil expenses of the Government for the fiscal year ending June 30th, 1900, and for other purposes" that "The President of the United States is hereby authorized in case of threatened or actual epidemic of cholera, yellow fever, smallpox, bubonic plague or Chinese plague or black death to use the unexpended balance of the sums appropriated and reappropriated by the Sundry Civil Appropriation Act, approved July 1st, 1898, and the act making appropriation to supply discrepancies in the appropriations approved July 7th, 1898, and one hundred thousand dollars ($100,000.00) in addition thereto or so much thereof as may be necessary in the aid of State and local boards or otherwise in his discretion in preventing and suppressing the spread of the same and in such emergencies in the execution of any quarantine laws which may be then in force.

You are hereby directed to take charge of this expenditure for the purpose of enforcing the above provisions, and you are directed to employ for that purpose the Marine Hospital Service and to provide such other means as are necessary for the purpose aforesaid and to carry out such rules and regulations as may have been or shall be made by you in conformity therewith.

You will carefully supervise and examine all expenditures made in executing the aforesaid law and submit to me from time to time reports of such expenditures and statements of the work done.

WILLIAM McKINLEY.

EXECUTIVE MANSION,
Washington, D. C., August 17, 1899.

To the People of Cuba:

The disorganized condition of your island, resulting from the war and the absence of any generally recognized authority aside from the temporary Military Control of the United States, has made it necessary that the United States should follow the restoration of order and peaceful industry by giving its assistance and supervision to the successive steps by which you will proceed to the establishment of an effective system of self-government.

As a preliminary step in the performance of this duty I have directed that a census of the people of Cuba be taken, and have appointed competent and disinterested citizens of Cuba as Enumerators and Supervisors.

It is important for the proper arrangement of your new Government that the information sought shall be fully and accurately given and I request that by every means in your power you aid the officers appointed in the performance of their duties.

WILLIAM McKINLEY.

EXECUTIVE MANSION,
Washington, D. C., September 2, 1899.

To the Secretary of the Treasury:

SIR:—You are directed to transfer an additional sum of five thousand dollars ($5,000.00) from the appropriation made by the Joint Resolution approved July 7, 1898, entitled, "Joint Resolution to provide for the annexation of the Hawaiian Islands to the United States," to be expended at the discretion of the Executive and for the purpose of carrying that Joint Resolution into effect for the expenditure and enforcement of the Chinese Exclusion Laws in the Hawaiian Islands under the clause in said Resolution restricting the emigration of the Chinese to the Islands.

WILLIAM McKINLEY.

EXECUTIVE MANSION,
Washington, D. C., September 11, 1899.

Hon. JOHN HAY,
Secretary of State

You will notify the President of Hawaii that the Government of Hawaii has no power to make any sale or dispose of the public lands in the Islands.   That all proceedings taken or pending for such sale or disposition should be discontinued and that if any sales or agreements for sale have been made since the adoption of the Resolution of Annexation the purchasers should be notified that the same are null and void and any consideration paid to the legal authorities on account thereof should be refunded.   WILLIAM McKINLEY.

EXECUTIVE MANSION,
Washington, D. C., September 18, 1899.

In the exercise of the power conferred upon me by the Joint Resolution of Congress, approved by the President on July 7th, 1898, entitled "Joint Resolution to provide for annexing the Hawaiian Islands to the United States," the President of the United States hereby directs that the issue of Registers to vessels by the Authorities of Hawaii entitling such vessels to all the rights and privileges of Hawaiian vessels in the ports of Nations or upon the High Seas, shall hereafter cease.

[SEAL.]   In witness whereof I have caused the seal of the United States to be hereunto affixed.

WILLIAM McKINLEY.

EXECUTIVE MANSION,
Washington, D. C., September 29, 1899.

It is hereby ordered that the several Executive Departments, the Government Printing Office and the Navy Yard and Station at Washington be closed on Tuesday, October 3rd, to enable the employees to participate in the ceremonies attending the Reception of Admiral Dewey, United States Navy, and the presentation of the Sword of Honor to him, as authorized by a Joint Resolution of Congress, approved June 3rd, 1899.

WILLIAM McKINLEY.

EXECUTIVE MANSION,
Washington, D. C., November 4, 1899.

In furtherance of interchange between those absent in the service of their country and their families at home, it is hereby ordered that packages and parcels of mailable matter and containing only articles desired as gifts and souvenirs, and so marked, and with no commercial purpose, and not for sale, from Officers, Soldiers and Sailors serving in the Army and Navy and other persons employed in the Civil Service of the United States, in Hawaii, Puerto Rico, Guam, Philippine Islands and Cuba addressed to members of their families in the United States, or packages of the same personal character addressed from the United States to Officers, Soldiers, Sailors and others in the Public Service in said Islands may be sent through the mails, subject only to the domestic postal regulations of the United States.

The details of the execution of this order with all necessary safeguards will devolve on the Secretary of War and Postmaster-General.

WILLIAM McKINLEY.

EXECUTIVE MANSION,
Washington, D. C., November 10, 1899.

In accordance with the law that prescribes that the Army and Navy General Hospital at Hot Springs, Ark., "shall be subject to such rules, regulations, and restrictions as shall be provided by the President of the United States," the following amendment of the rules and regulations provided for its government in Executive Order of August 25, 1892, is authorized:

Enlisted men on the active list while under treatment or on duty in the hospital shall have the usual allowance of rations commuted at the rate of not to exceed forty cents (40c) per day for enlisted men in the army and thirty cents (30c) per day for enlisted men in the navy, to be paid to the Senior Medical Officer by the proper officers of the War and Navy Departments upon the receipt of monthly statements of accounts duly certified by the Surgeon-General of the Army. WILLIAM McKINLEY.

EXECUTIVE MANSION, *December 1, 1899.*
To all to whom these presents shall come; greeting:

Know ye, that reposing special trust and confidence in the integrity, prudence, and ability of John Hay, Secretary of State of the United States, I have invested him with full and all manner of power and authority, for me and in the name of the United States, to meet and confer with any person or persons duly authorized by the Government of his Imperial Majesty the German Emperor, King of Prussia, and the Government of her Britannic Majesty being entrusted with like power and authority, and with them to negotiate, conclude, and sign a convention to adjust amicably the questions which have arisen between the three Governments in respect to the Samoan group of islands, the same to be transmitted to the President of the United States for his ratification by and with the advice and consent of the Cabinet thereof.

In testimony whereof I have caused the seal of the United States to be hereunto affixed.

Given under my hand at the city of Washington, the 1st day of December, in the year of our Lord 1899, and of the Independence of the United States the one hundred and twenty-third.

[SEAL.]

WILLIAM McKINLEY.

By the President:
    JOHN HAY,
        Secretary of State.

EXECUTIVE MANSION,
Washington, D. C., January 3, 1900.

To prevent the introduction of epidemic diseases, it is ordered that provisions of the act of Congress, approved February 15, 1893, entitled, "An act granting additional quarantine powers and imposing additional duties upon the Marine Hospital Service," and all rules and regulations heretofore or hereafter prescribed by the Secretary of the Treasury under that act are to be given full force and effect in the Philippine Islands in so far as they are applicable, and the following additional rules and regulations are hereby promulgated:

The examination in ports of the Philippine Islands of incoming and outgoing vessels, and the necessary surveillance over their sanitary condition as well as of cargo, officers, crew and all personal effects is vested in and will be conducted by the Marine Hospital Service, and Medical Officers of that service will be detailed by the Secretary of the Treasury as Quarantine Officers at Ports of Manila and Iloilo immediately and at other ports in the Philippine Islands as soon as practicable or necessary.

Quarantine Officers shall have authority over incoming vessels, their wharfage and anchorage in so far as it is necessary for the proper enforcement of the quarantine regulations, including vessels of the Army Transport Service and non-combatant vessels of the Navy.

Collectors of Customs at ports of entry will not permit entry without quarantine certificates.

Any vessel leaving any port in the Philippine Islands for any port in the United States or its Dependencies shall obtain a bill of health from the quarantine officer when such officer is on duty, said bill of health to correspond to the Consular Bill of Health now required by Treasury Regulations, and the bill of health shall not be given to the outgoing vessel unless all quarantine regulations have been complied with. At ports where no medical officer is detailed, bills of health will be signed by the Collector of Customs or other officers to whom such duty has been regularly delegated. Special regulations relating to the bills of health to be obtained by vessels of the United States Navy will be promulgated by the Secretary of the Treasury.

The Medical Officer detailed under **this order** as Quarantine Officer at the Port of Manila shall be the **Chief** Quarantine Officer for the Philippine Islands. It shall be his duty to make appointments and removals from the service in the Philippines (subject to the approval of the Secretary of the Treasury), and shall authorize necessary expenditures under such regulations as the Secretary of the Treasury may prescribe.

The regulations for the government of the Marine Hospital Service shall, so far as practicable, have force and effect in the management of the Quarantine service in the Philippine Islands.

The expenses of the Quarantine service will be charged against the revenues of the islands, and a sum not to exceed three hundred thousand dollars ($300,000.00) in each fiscal year is hereby set aside from the revenues collected in said islands for this purpose. The expenses shall be paid therefrom upon a certificate of a detailed quarantine officer and upon the approval of the Chief Officer for the Philippine Islands.

The Chief Quarantine Officer shall render a report on the last day of each month to the supervising Surgeon General in the Marine Hospital Service, who will issue to him necessary instructions.

The Epidemic Fund will be reimbursed from the revenues of the islands for the cost of this undertaking, plans and materials ordered to be forwarded to the islands prior to the date of this order.

WILLIAM McKINLEY.

EXECUTIVE MANSION,
Washington, D. C., January 5, 1900.

By virtue of the authority vested in me by joint resolution of the Senate and House of Representatives of the United States accepting and confirming the cession of the Hawaiian Islands to the United States, it is hereby ordered and directed that out of the Government Reservation lying to the eastward of the Puowaina or Ruralhouse Hill in the Island of Ouhu, Hawaiian Islands, seven acres, more or less as hereinafter described and located, shall be set apart for the use of the United States Treasury Department as a site for a United States Marine Hospital for the port of Honolulu. This site shall consist of the seven acres situated north of the Makiki cemetery and bounded on the north and east by the sinuosities of the Punch Bowl road; on the south by a line projecting eastward from the powder magazine to intersect Punch Bowl road, this line being the southern boundary of the Government Reservation at that point; and on the west by an arbitrary north and south line drawn so as to leave seven (7) acres within this designated tract.

WILLIAM McKINLEY.

EXECUTIVE MANSION,
Washington, D. C., January 8, 1900.

It is hereby ordered that the tract of country lying west of the Navajo and Moqui Reservations, in the Territory of Arizona, embraced within the following described boundaries, viz: Beginning at the southwest corner of the Moqui Reservation and running due west to the Little Colorado River, thence down that stream to the Grand Canyon Forest Reservation, thence north on the line of that reserve to the northeast corner thereof, thence west to the Colorado River, thence up that stream to the Navajo Indian Reservation, be and the same is hereby withdrawn from sale and settlement until further order

WILLIAM McKINLEY.

EXECUTIVE MANSION,
Washington, D. C., January 19, 1900.

In accordance with the law that prescribes that the Army and Navy General Hospital at Hot Springs, Ark., shall be subject to such rules, regulations and restrictions as shall be provided by the President of the United States the following amendment of the rules and regulations providing for its Government and Executive Order of August 25th, 1892 is authorized: Enlisted men of the Army and Navy and Marine Corps on the retired list and honorably discharged soldiers and sailors of the Regular and Volunteer Army and Navy of the United States, shall pay for substance at the rate of 40 cents per day.

WILLIAM McKINLEY.

EXECUTIVE MANSION,
Washington, D. C., February 12, 1900.

Authority is hereby granted for the transfer of the sum of four hundred thousand, seven hundred and seventy-six dollars and sixty-five cents ($400,776.65) from the appropriation "Emergency Fund, War Department" act of March 13th, 1899, to the appropriation "Substance of the Army 1900" in accordance with the request of the Acting Commissary General of Subsistence which is approved by the Secretary of War.

WILLIAM McKINLEY.

PANAMA CANAL: THE PEDRO MIGUEL LOCKS

THE PANAMA CANAL.

The commencement of the task of constructing the Panama Canal was the most important event of Roosevelt's Administration. The history of the undertaking is written by Roosevelt himself on pages 6662, 6758, 6881, 6901, 7401, 7480, 7611, 7648, 7667, 7685 and 7728. The message commencing on page 7685 describes his visit of inspection to the canal zone. President Taft continued the narrative, pages 7750, 7754, 7803, 7863 and 7898. The reader who desires a brief recital of the facts should refer to the article entitled "Panama Canal" in the encyclopedic index. The index references following this article will enable the reader to glean a complete and authentic knowledge of the subject from the messages of the Presidents, from Jackson to Taft, who have discussed the project.

The Pedro Miguel lock is at the Pacific end of the summit level of the Canal, which is maintained by the Gatun spillway. The lock, about 5½ miles from the Pacific end of the Canal, represents a descent from a level of 85 feet to a level of 55 feet. The Spanish name was too much for many of the American engineers who worked on the Canal, and during its construction it was generally called the "Peter McGill Lock."

EXECUTIVE MANSION, *March 7, 1900.*

It is hereby ordered that the Executive Order of June 8, 1866, re-serving for light-house purposes among other lands a tract described as "twenty (20) acres at a cape about midway between Destruction Island and Flattery Rocks, falling within unsurveyed lands as laid down in blue shade upon diagram number 3 herewith," in the Terri-tory of Washington, be, and the same is, hereby canceled so far as it relates to the above described tract, and it is hereby ordered that in lieu thereof, lot one (1) section six (6), township twenty-eight (28) north, range fifteen (15) west, Willamette Meridian, Washing-ton, containing, according to the official plat on file in the General Land Office, approved May 29, 1882, 3.25 acres, be, and it is, hereby reserved for light-house purposes.

WILLIAM McKINLEY.

EXECUTIVE MANSION, *March 20, 1900.*

It is hereby ordered that the Executive Order of September 11, 1854, reserving for light-house purposes among other lands the tract at Cape Shoalwater, Territory of Washington, shaded blue on the diagram accompanying the order, be, and it is, hereby canceled so far as it relates to the tract above described.

WILLIAM McKINLEY.

EXECUTIVE MANSION, *March 21, 1900.*

The Secretary of the Navy is hereby directed to transfer to the Secretary of War for use in the transport service of the War Depart-ment the vessels *Badger* and *Resolute*, purchased by the Navy De-partment from the funds allotted from the emergency appropriation, national defense, act of March 8, 1898, at a cost of $842,000, these vessels being no longer required in the service of the navy.

WILLIAM McKINLEY.

EXECUTIVE MANSION, *May 1, 1900.* ·

The Collector of Customs of Puerto Rico will pay over to the Treasurer of Puerto Rico the net proceeds of the collections made by him under the provisions of the act of Congress approved April 12, 1900, entitled "An act temporarily to provide revenues and a Civil Government for Puerto Rico, and for other purposes," under such regulations as the Secretary of the Treasury may prescribe.

WILLIAM McKINLEY

EXECUTIVE MANSION, *May 14, 1900.*

It is hereby ordered that the NW ¼ of section 15, in township 23 north, of range 13 west, Gila and Salt River Base, and principal meridian in Arizona, conveyed to the United States by quit claim deed of [the Santa Fe Pacific Railroad Company, dated September 12, 1899, be and the same is hereby set apart, subject to certain exceptions, reservations, and conditions made by said company, as set forth in the deed aforesaid, for Indian school purposes, the Hualapai Indians as an addition to section 10 of the township and range above mentioned, set aside by executive order dated December 22, 1898, and designated therein as the "Hualapai Indian School Reserve."

WILLIAM McKINLEY.

EXECUTIVE MANSION, *May 26, 1900*

It is hereby ordered that Section 29, Section 30; the N¼, the SW¼, the N½ of the SE¼, and the SE¼ of the SE¼ of Section 31, and Section 32, Township 13, south, Range one (1) east, Montana, be and they are hereby reserved and set apart for the use of the United States Fish Commission of Fish and Fisheries for the purposes of a fish cultural station. WILLIAM McKINLEY.

EXECUTIVE MANSION, *May 26, 1900.*

Under authority of Section 3648 of the Revised Statutes of the United States, permission is hereby given that needful advances of money be made of moneys appropriated for the light-house establishment to the officers of the Army and Navy acting as Engineers or Inspectors, as Assistants to Engineers or Inspectors of the third light-house district for disbursement in carrying on the Puerto Rican light-house service. WILLIAM McKINLEY.

EXECUTIVE MANSION, *June 12, 1900.*

It is hereby ordered that fractional section 11, township 5 south, range 14 west, Florida, be and it is hereby reserved and set apart for light-house purposes. WILLIAM McKINLEY.

EXECUTIVE MANSION, *June 22, 1900.*

Whereas by the seventy-third section of an act entitled "An act to provide a government for the Territory of Hawaii," approved April 30, 1900, it was, among other things provided as follows: "That, subject to the approval of the President, all sales, grants, leases, and other dispositions of the public domain and agreements concerning the same, and all franchises granted by the Hawaiian government in conformity with the laws of Hawaii between the 7th day of July, 1898, and the 28th day of September, 1899, are hereby ratified and confirmed;" and

Whereas it appears by the certificate of Sanford B. Dole, President of the Republic of Hawaii, which bears date the 23d day of May, A. D., 1900, that the Hilo Railroad Company organized for the purpose of building and operating a Railroad or Railroads between and through the districts of Hilo Puna Hamakua, Kohala, Kona, and Kau, on the Island of Hawaii, Hawaiian Islands, was incorporated on the 28th day of March, A. D., 1899, under a charter of incorporation, a copy whereof is attached to said certificate; and that said incorporating and granting of said charter of incorporation were made in conformity with the general incorporating acts of the Republic of Hawaii, and that the granting of the franchise conferred thereby and all acts and proceedings contained in the premises were done and taken in conformity with the laws of the Republic of Hawaii;

Now, therefore, in conformity with the provision of the act aforesaid, the said franchise granted by the Hawaiian government to the Hilo Railroad Company is hereby approved.

WILLIAM McKINLEY.

EXECUTIVE MANSION, *June 27, 1900.*

On and after the first day of July, 1900, the classification and pay of the rating of electrician shall be as follows, but this order shall not reduce the pay of any enlisted man during his present enlistment below the pay at which he was enlisted, or which he is now receiving:

	per month.
Electrician, third class	$30.00
" 2d "	40.00
" 1st "	50.00
Chief Electrician	60.00

WILLIAM McKINLEY.

EXECUTIVE MANSION, *June 29, 1900.*

On and after July 15, 1900, there shall be detailed on the staff of the Military Governor of the Island of Cuba as Chief of the Quarantine Service established by Executive Order January 17, 1899, a commissioned officer of the Marine Hospital service, who shall on the first day of each month, or at such other periods as may be directed by the Military Governor, submit to the Military Governor a detailed estimate of the quarantine expenses of the Island of Cuba. After the approval of such estimate by the Military Governor the chief quarantine officer shall make requisition for the funds required in favor of the disbursing officer or agent, who shall pay the bills and vouchers on account of the quarantine service upon the certificate of an officer detailed under the Executive Order of January 17, 1899, and after approval by the chief quarantine officer. The disbursing officer or agent shall render his accounts of such disbursments in accordance with the rules and instructions to carry into effect the Executive Order of May 8, 1899, relative to the military government of the United States in the Island of Cuba, during the maintenance of such government.   WILLIAM McKINLEY.

EXECUTIVE MANSION, *August 2, 1900.*

The Island of Guimaras in the Philippine group is assigned to naval jurisdiction and control with a view to establishing thereon a naval base and station upon the strait of Iloilo, opposite the town of that name.   WILLIAM McKINLEY.

EXECUTIVE MANSION, *August 2, 1900.*

The sum of ten thousand dollars ($10,000) or so much thereof as may be necessary, is hereby allotted from the Emergency Fund, Navy Department, 1901, for the purpose of meeting the expenses of a survey of the Island of Guimaras in sufficient detail to fix the place of the coal wharf and shed, of the dry dock, and of the fleet anchorages, and to appraise the land of private ownership, which need to be condemned for the use of the government for its uses and for the land defense required.   WILLIAM McKINLEY.

EXECUTIVE MANSION, *August 23, 1900.*

It is hereby ordered that the following lands situate in California, viz: The north half of the southeast quarter, and the north half of the southwest quarter, section fourteen (14), in township three (3), south of range one (1), east of the San Bernardino meridian, being lands withdrawn from the public domain for the Mission Indians by Executive Order of August 25, 1877, be and the same are hereby restored to the public domain.   WILLIAM McKINLEY.

EXECUTIVE MANSION, *September 3, 1900.*

It is hereby ordered that the following described lands in the State of Mississippi be and they are hereby reserved for light-house purposes; viz:

Round Island, Mississippi. All of fractional sections three and four of township nine (9) south, range six (6) west, east of Pearl River, containing respectively about 16.50 acres and 33.34 acres.

Horn Island, Mississippi. All of fractional sections 31 of township nine (9) south, range five (5) west, and thirty-six (36) of township nine (9) south, range six (6) west, east of Pearl River, containing, respectively, about 51.69 and 286.20 acres.

Petite Bois Blanc Island, Mississippi. All of fractional section three (3) of township ten (10) south, range five (5) west, east of Pearl River, containing approximately 81.27 acres.

WILLIAM McKINLEY.

EXECUTIVE MANSION, *September 19, 1900.*

In accordance with the provisions of Section 179 of the Revised Statutes, as amended by an act making appropriations for the legislative, executive and judicial expenses of the government, approved August 5, 1882 (22 Stat., 238) Lieutenant-General Nelson A. Miles, commanding the Army of the United States is authorized and directed to perform the duties of Secretary of War during the illness or temporary absence from the seat of government of the Secretary of War whenever during such illness or absence the Assistant Secretary of War is also absent; in accordance with the same provisions, Major-General Henry C. Corbin, Assistant Adjutant-General of the Army is authorized and directed to perform the duties of Secretary of War whenever during such illness or absence the Assistant Secretary of War and the lieutenant-general commanding the Army are also absent. WILLIAM McKINLEY.

EXECUTIVE MANSION, *September 20, 1900.*
The Honorable Secretary of the Treasury.

SIR:— It is provided in the "Act making appropriations for sundry civil expenses of the Government for the fiscal year ending June 30, 1901, and for other purposes," approved June 6, 1900, that "The President of the United States is hereby authorized in case of threatened or actual epidemic of cholera, yellow fever, smallpox, bubonic plague, or Chinese plague or black death to use the unexpended balance of the sums appropriated and reappropriated by the sundry civil appropriation act approved June 4, 1897, and $500,000 in addition thereto or so much thereof as may be necessary in aid of constituting local boards or otherwise in his discretion in preventing and suppressing the spread of same; and in such emergency in the execution of any quarantine laws which may be then in force, the same to be immediately available."

You are hereby directed to take charge of this expenditure for the purpose of enforcing the above provisions, and you are directed to employ for that purpose the Marine Hospital Service and to provide such other means as are necessary for the purpose aforesaid, and to carry out such rules and regulations as have been or shall be made by you in conformity therewith.

You will carefully supervise and examine all expenditures made in executing the aforesaid law and submit to me from time to time reports of such expenditures and statements of work done.

WILLIAM McKINLEY.

EXECUTIVE MANSION, *October 10, 1900.*

On and after October 15, 1900, there shall be detailed on the staff of the Military Governor of the Islands of the Philippine Archipelago as chief of the quarantine service established by Executive Order of January 3, 1900, a commissioned officer of the Marine Hospital Service who shall on the first day of the month, and at such other periods as may be directed by the Military Governor submit to the Military Governor a detailed estimate of the quarantine expenses of the said Islands of the Philippine Archipelago. After the approval of such estimate by the Military Governor the Chief Quarantine officer shall make requisition for the funds required in favor of the disbursing officer or agent of the Treasury Department who shall pay the bills and vouchers on account of the quarantine service upon the certificate of an officer detailed under Executive Order of January 3, 1900 (said order being still in force except as herein mentioned), and after approval by the Chief Quarantine officer. The disbursing officer or agent shall be appointed by the Secretary of the Treasury as soon as practicable, and shall render his accounts of such disbursements in accordance with the rules and instructions to carry into effect the Executive Order of May 8, 1899, relative to the military government of the United States in the Islands of the Philippine Archipelago during the maintenance of such government.

WILLIAM McKINLEY.

EXECUTIVE MANSION, *October 10, 1900.*

It is hereby ordered that Sections 26, 27, 34 and 35 township 14 south, range 14 east, Gila and Salt River meridian Territory of Arizona, be and they are hereby reserved and set apart for the use of the United States Department of Agriculture for the purposes of an agricultural experiment station. WILLIAM McKINLEY.

EXECUTIVE MANSION, *October 13, 1900.*

By virtue of the authority vested in the President of the United States by Section 3141, Revised Statutes of the United States, I hereby order

That the county of Greer, which was formerly a part of the **State** of Texas, and as such was specifically declared a part of the 4th Internal Revenue District of Texas by Executive Order of June 29, 1881, be transferred to and made a part of the Internal Revenue District of Kansas, said county having been declared by the United States Supreme Court in decision rendered at the October term of 1895 to be a part of the Territory of Oklahoma, which Territory was added to the District of Kansas by Executive Order of March 30, 1886, prior to the date of the judicial decision above cited.

This order to take effect on the first day of November, 1900.

WILLIAM McKINLEY.

EXECUTIVE MANSION, *October 29, 1900.*

It is hereby ordered that lot 5 of the SW ¼ of the NE ¼, section 31, township 6 south, range 11 west, Florida, be, and it is, hereby reserved for light-house purposes.   WILLIAM McKINLEY.

EXECUTIVE MANSION, *November 30, 1900.*

The United States Civil Service Commission is directed to render such assistance as may be practicable to the Civil Service Board created under the act of the United States Philippine Commission, for the establishment and maintenance of a necessary and efficient civil service in the Philippine Island, and for that purpose to conduct examinations for the Civil Service of the Philippine Islands upon the request of the Civil Service Board of said Islands, under such regulations as may be agreed upon by the said Board and the said United States Civil Service Commission.   WILLIAM McKINLEY.

EXECUTIVE MANSION, *December 7, 1900.*

Whenever upon marches, guards, or in quarters, different corps of the army happen to join or do duty together and an official of the Marine Corps or the militia shall command the whole pursuant to the 122d article of war, such officer shall report his action and the operations of the force under his command through military channels to the Secretary of War as well as to his superiors in his own branch of the service.   WILLIAM McKINLEY.

EXECUTIVE MANSION, *December 13, 1900.*

To the Secretary of the Treasury:

The sum of $200,000 is hereby allotted and set apart from the appropriation made for the benefit and government of Puerto Rico by the Act of March 24, 1900 (31 Stat., p. 51), to be used for the extension of public education in Puerto Rico, including building and equipping of school houses in said Island.　　　WILLIAM McKINLEY.

EXECUTIVE MANSION, *December 14, 1900.*

By virtue of the authority vested in me as Commander-in-Chief of the Army and Navy of the United States of America, I hereby empower the Naval officer in command at the Island of Guam to act as Collector of Customs for said Island, with authority to appoint a deputy if necessary.

I further direct that any authority heretofore exercised under the direction of the commandant at said Naval Station in respect to the collection of customs be approved as if direct mention of such authority had been included in the Executive Order of February 1, 1900.

In case the commandant shall make such appointment from civil life he shall require of the appointee good and sufficient security for the due performance of the duties of the office.

Any authority heretofore exercised in the premises by the Naval Officer in command is hereby ratified as if said power to appoint had been conferred in said Executive Order of February 1, 1900.

　　　WILLIAM McKINLEY.

EXECUTIVE MANSION, *December 19, 1900.*

It is hereby ordered that the President's Order of January 9, 1884, transferring the Fort Yuma Military Reservation to the control of the Department of the Interior to be used for Indian purposes in connection with the Indian reservations established by the same order, be, and the same is, hereby revoked as to that part of said military reservation lying south of the Colorado River.

Inasmuch as said land has been abandoned for military purposes, as shown by executive orders of January 9, 1884, and July 22, 1884, it is further ordered and directed that the portion of said military reservation lying south of the Colorado River and being in the Territory of Arizona be, and the same is, hereby placed under the control of the Secretary of the Interior for disposition under the provisions of the Acts of Congress approved July 5, 1884 (23 Stat., p. 103), and August 22, 1894 (28 Stat., p. 491).

　　　WILLIAM McKINLEY.

EXECUTIVE MANSION, *February 2, 1901.*

By virtue of the authority vested in me as Commander-in-Chief of the Army and Navy of the United States, I hereby order and direct that that part of Executive Order dated May 8, 1899, relating to the appointment and creation of the office of Treasurer of the Island of Cuba, be amended as follows:

The office of Treasurer of the Island of Cuba shall on and after April 1, 1901, be placed under the jurisdiction of the Department of Finance of said Island, and shall be filled by the appointment thereto of a citizen of Cuba. The said appointment to be made by the Military Governor thereof, subject to the approval of the Secretary of War.   WILLIAM McKINLEY.

EXECUTIVE MANSION,
Washington, D. C., March 8, 1901.

On recommendation of the Military Governor of Cuba, approved by the Secretary of War, I hereby order and direct that the export rates of duty on tobacco, provided on page 50 of the "Customs Tariff for Ports in the Island of Cuba" promulgated by Executive Order dated March 31, 1900, shall be abolished on the 1st day of April, 1901.
WILLIAM McKINLEY.

EXECUTIVE MANSION,
Washington, D. C., March 9, 1901.

I, William McKinley, President of the United States, by virtue of the authority vested in me by Section 3141, Revised Statutes of the United States, hereby order that the States of North Dakota and South Dakota, now part of the Internal Revenue District of Nebraska, shall be detached from said District of Nebraska and constitute one District, to be known as the Internal Revenue District of Newark, South Dakota.

The Internal Revenue District of Nebraska shall comprise the State of Nebraska.

This order to take effect on the first day of May, 1901.
WILLIAM McKINLEY.

(ENDORSEMENTS.)

WAR DEPARTMENT,
Washington, D. C., March 9, 1901.

Secretary of War:

Recommends modification of executive order of June 4, 1892, setting apart a wood reservation for the post of Fort Fill, Oklahoma Territory, so as to make the eastern boundary coincident with the new 98 meridian (the boundary line between the Kiowa and Comanche Reservation and the Chickasaw Nation) as serving a mark pursuant to act of Congress of June 28, 1898 (30 Stats., 495).

EXECUTIVE MANSION,
Washington, D. C., March 11, 1901.

The within recommendation is approved. The Secretary of the Interior will cause this action to be noted on the records of the General Land Office.   WILLIAM McKINLEY.

EXECUTIVE MANSION,
Washington, D. C., March 12, 1901.

The executive order of May 8, 1899, relating to the Island of Cuba, as promulgated by the Assistant Secretary of War, May 11, 1899, is hereby amended by substituting the following:

By virtue of the authority vested in me as the Commander-in-Chief of the Army and Navy of the United States, I hereby order and direct that during the maintenance of Military Government by the United States in the Island of Cuba there is hereby created and shall be maintained the office of the Auditor for Cuba, to be filled by appointment of the Secretary of War, whose duties shall be to receive and audit all accounts of the island.

There is hereby created and shall be maintained the office of Deputy Auditor for Cuba, to be filled by appointment of the Secretary of War, whose duties shall be to sign, in the name of the Auditor, such official papers as the Auditor may designate, and perform such other duties as the Auditor may prescribe. He shall have authority of his superior as Acting Auditor in case of the death, resignation, sickness, or other absence of the Auditor.

There is hereby created and shall be maintained in the office of the Auditor the office of Chief Clerk, to be filled by appointment of the Auditor, and the Chief Clerk shall perform such duties as may be prescribed by the Auditor.

All rules and instructions necessary to carry into effect the provisions of executive orders relating to Cuba shall be issued by the Secretary of War, and such rules and instructions shall be enforced until the same are amended or revoked by the Secretary of War.

          WILLIAM McKINLEY.

EXECUTIVE MANSION,
Washington, D. C., March 14, 1901.

To the Secretary of the Treasury.

SIR:— The sum of two hundred thousand dollars is hereby allotted and set apart from the appropriation made for the benefit and Government of Puerto Rico by the Act of March 24, 1900 (31 Stat., p. 51) to be expended in improving and grading of various roads throughout the island of Puerto Rico such as "Neighboring Roads" between small municipalities.

          WILLIAM McKINLEY.

EXECUTIVE MANSION,
Washington, D. C., March 22, 1901.

To the Secretary of the Treasury.

SIR:— The sum of six thousand dollars is hereby allotted and set apart from the appropriation made for the benefit and Government of Puerto Rico by the Act of March 24, 1900 (131 Stat., p. 51) to be expended by the Treasurer of Puerto Rico upon accounts certified by the Auditor of the Island for refunding customs duties paid by certain contractors on materials intended for use under their con-tracts brought into Puerto Rico since May 1, 1900.

WILLIAM McKINLEY.

EXECUTIVE MANSION,
Washington, D. C., March 25, 1901.

Counsular officers will hereafter collect any fees for bills of health and supplemental bills of health issued foreign war vessels. The tariff of Consular fees is amended accordingly.

WILLIAM McKINLEY.

EXECUTIVE MANSION,
Washington, D. C., March 26, 1901.

It is hereby ordered that the unsurveyed portion of Eliza Island and Billingham Bay in section five (5), township thirty-six (36) north, range two (2) East Willamette meridian, Washington be, and it is hereby reserved for light-house purposes.

WILLIAM McKINLEY.

EXECUTIVE MANSION,
Washington, D. C., March 30, 1901.

It is hereby ordered that the hereinafter described tracts of land in the District of Alaska be, and they are hereby reserved and set apart for Reindeer stations, subject to any legal existing rights to any land in the limits of the reservation hereby established, to wit:

1. The entire peninsula of which Cape Denbigh forms the south-western extremity, situated in latitude 64 degrees, 30 minutes north, longitude 161 degrees, 30 minutes west from Greenwich, approxi-mately fifteen (15) miles in length and five (5) miles in width.

A tract of land bounded as follows: Beginning at a point about six miles above the mouth of the Unalaklik river and extending along the north bank of the Unalaklik river in a generally north-easterly direction ten miles; thence in a generally northwesterly direction ten miles; thence in a generally southwesterly direction ten miles; thence in a generally southeasterly direction to the point of beginning. WILLIAM McKINLEY.

EXECUTIVE MANSION,
Washington, D. C., April 2, 1901.

It is hereby ordered that all of Amaknam Island, District of Alaska, except the tract of land reserved for light-house purposes by executive order of Jan. 13th, 1899, and the tract of land embraced in amended survey M 58 of the North American Commercial Co. be, and it is hereby reserved for public purposes.

WILLIAM McKINLEY.

EXECUTIVE MANSION,
Washington, D. C., April 5, 1901.

The Secretary of the Navy is authorized to enlist in the Insular Force United States Navy, which is hereby established, not to exceed five hundred (500) Filipinos in the following ratings at the rates of pay indicated:

RATES	MONTHLY PAY
Navy Coxswains	$ 15.00
Navy Seamen	12.00
Navy Ordinary Seamen	10.00
Navy Machinists; First-class	28.00
Navy Machinists; Second-class	20.00
Navy Firemen; First-class	18.00
Navy Firemen; Second-class	15.00
Navy Coal Passers	11.00
Navy Sutlers	15.00
Navy Cooks	13.00
Navy Mess-Attendants	8.00

WILLIAM McKINLEY.

EXECUTIVE MANSION,
Washington, D. C., April 6, 1901.

It is hereby ordered that upon Tuesday the ninth (9th) instant such employees of the Executive Departments; the Government Printing Office and the Navy Yard and Station at Washington, as served in the Military or Naval services of the United States in the late Civil War of Spanish-American War, shall be excused from duty at one o'clock P. M. for the remainder of that day to enable them to participate in the exercises of the unveiling of the statue erected to the memory of the late General John A. Logan.

WILLIAM McKINLEY

EXECUTIVE MANSION,
Washington, D. C., April 15, 1901.

In accordance with provisions of act of Congress approved January 4th, 1897 (30 Stat., 34 and 36), and by virtue of the authority thereby given, and on the recommendation of the Secretary of the Interior, it is hereby ordered that the tracts hereinafter described and situated in township fifty-eight (58) north, range eighty-nine (89) west, within the limits of the Big Horn Forest reserve, in the State of Wyoming, be restored to the public domain after sixty days' notice hereof by publication, as required by law; these tracts having been found better adapted to agricultural than forest purposes, to wit:

What will be, when surveyed, all that portion of sections thirteen (13), fourteen (14), fifteen (15), sixteen (16), seventeen (17), in said township and range lying south of the said line between Montana and Wyoming, and all of sections twenty (20), twenty-one (21), twenty-two (22), twenty-three (23) twenty-four (24), twenty-five (25), twenty-six (26), and twenty-seven (27), all of said lands being in the State of Wyoming.

WILLIAM McKINLEY.

EXECUTIVE MANSION,
Washington, D. C., April 23, 1901.
To the Secretary of the Treasury.

SIR:—The sum of five hundred thousand dollars is hereby allotted and set aside from the appropriation made for the benefit and Government of Puerto Rico by the act of March 24th, 1900 (31 Stat., p. 51), to be expended for public and permanent improvements in Puerto Rico, under the supervision and subject to the approval of the Governor and Executive Council of the Island.

WILLIAM McKINLEY

EXECUTIVE MANSION,
Washington, D. C., April 29, 1901.

In case of the death, resignation, absence or sickness of the Secretary of the Navy, the Assistant Secretary of the Navy and the Chief of the Bureau of Navigation, Rear Admiral Charles O'Neil, U. S. Navy and Chief of the Bureau of Ordnance is, in pursuance of the provisions of Sections 177 and 179 of the Revised Statutes, hereby authorized and directed to perform the duties of Secretary of the Navy until a successor is appointed or until such absence or sickness shall cease.

WILLIAM McKINLEY

EXECUTIVE MANSION,
Washington, D. C., June 7, 1901.

The following " Classification of Vessels" and "Assignments to man afloat" are hereby established for the Navy in accordance with an act of Congress, approved March 3:

CLASSIFICATION OF VESSELS.

Torpedo Boat Destroyers: Torpedo boats, tugs, sailing ships and receiving ships shall not be rated. Other vessels shall be rated by tons of displacement as follows:

First Rates: Men of War when of eight thousand tons and above.

Second Rates: Men of War of four thousand tons and under eight thousand tons, and Converted and Auxiliary vessels of six thousand tons and above, except Colliers, Refrigerating ships, Distilling ships, Tank-steamers, Reporting ships, Hospital ships and other vessels constructed or equipped for special purposes.

Third Rates: Men of War from one thousand to four thousand tons and Converted and Auxiliary Vessels from one thousand to six thousand tons and Colliers, Refrigerating ships, Supply ships, Distilling ships, Tank-steamers, Report ships, Hospital ships and other vessels constructed or equipped for special purposes of four thousand tons and above.

Fourth Rates: All other vessels.

WILLIAM McKINLEY.

EXECUTIVE MANSION,
Washington, D. C., June 7, 1901.

Commandants to man the following:

An Admiral to man a fleet.

Rear-Admiral to man a fleet or squadron.

A Captain to man a division, or ship of the first or second rating or a ship not rated.

Commander to man a division or a ship of the second or third rating or ship not rated.

Lieutenant-Commander to man a ship of the third or fourth rating or a ship not rated.

A Lieutenant to man a ship of the fourth rating; a torpedo boat destroyer, torpedo boat, tug, tender or a ship not rated.

A Lieutenant, junior grade, to command a torpedo boat, tug, tender or ship not rated.

An Ensign to man a torpedo boat, tug or ship not rated.

WILLIAM McKINLEY.

EXECUTIVE MANSION,
Washington, D. C., June 10, 1901.

To the Secretary of the Treasury.

SIR:— The sum of five hundred thousand dollars, or so much thereof as remains unexpended, allotted and set aside by order of

April 23, 1901, from the appropriation made for the benefit and Government of Puerto Rico by the act of March 24, 1900 (31 Stat., p. 51), is to be devoted to public and permanent improvements in Puerto Rico and other governmental and public purposes therein, as provided in the said act, and it is to be expended under the supervision and subject to the approval of the Government and administrative authorities of the Island. WILLIAM McKINLEY.

EXECUTIVE MANSION,
Washington, D. C., June 21, 1901.

I hereby order and direct that Executive Order dated May 3, 1899, be amended so as to authorize the appointment of civilians as Collectors of Customs in the Philippine Archipelago.
WILLIAM McKINLEY.

EXECUTIVE MANSION,
Washington, D. C., June 21, 1901.

To the Secretary of War.

SIR: — Pending the cessation of conditions requiring a continuance of Military Government in the Philippine Islands, you are authorized to make the following order:

On and after the 4th day of July, 1901, until it shall otherwise be ordered, the President of the Philippine Commission will exercise the Executive Authority in all civil affairs of the Government in the Philippine Islands, heretofore exercised in such affairs by the Military Governor of the Philippines, and to that end, the Hon. W. H. Taft, President of the said Commission is hereby appointed Civil Governor of the Philippine Islands. Such executive authority will be exercised under and in conformity to the instructions to the Philippine Commissioners dated April 7th, 1900, and subject to the approval and control of the Secretary of War of the United States. The municipal and Provincial Civil Governments will then, or shall hereafter be established in said Islands and all persons performing duties pertaining to the offices of Civil Government in said Islands will, in respect of such duties report to the said Civil Government. The power to appoint Civil Officers, heretofore vested in the Philippine Commission or in the Military Government will be exercised by the Civil Governor with the advice and consent of the Commissioners.

The Military Governor of the Philippines is hereby relieved from the performance on and after the said fourth day of July of the civil duties hereinbefore described, but his authority will continue to be exercised as heretofore in those districts in which insurrection against the authority of the United States continues to exist or in which public order is not sufficiently restored to enable the Provincial Civil Government to be established under the instructions to the Commission dated April 7th, 1900.
WILLIAM McKINLEY.

EXECUTIVE MANSION.
Washington, D. C., June 21, 1901.

In accordance with the provision in Section 2253 of the Revised Statutes of the United States, and by virtue of the authority thereby given, it is hereby ordered that the existing boundary line between Coeur d'Alene and Lewiston Land Districts, State of Idaho, be and it is hereby changed and re-established as follows: Beginning on the boundary line between the States of Idaho and Washington at the northwest corner of directional township forty-two (42) north, range six (6) west, Boise meridian, thence east along the boundary line between townships forty-two (42) and forty-three (43) north, to the crest of the Bitter Root Mountains.

WILLIAM McKINLEY.

EXECUTIVE MANSION,
Washington, D. C., June 25, 1901.

The executive order of April 5, 1901, is hereby amended by striking out the word "Filipinos" and inserting in its stead "natives of the Islands of the Philippines and of the Island of Guam."

WILLIAM McKINLEY.

EXECUTIVE MANSION,
Washington, D. C., June 25, 1901.

In accordance with the provisions of the act of Congress approved June 4, 1897 (30 Stat., pp. 34–36), and by virtue of the authority thereby given, and on the recommendation of the Secretary of the Interior, it is hereby ordered that the tracts hereinafter described and situated within the limits of the Big Horn Forest Reservation in the State of Wyoming be restored to the public domain after sixty days' notice hereof by publication as required by law, these tracts having been found better adapted to agriculture than forest purposes, to wit: What will be, when surveyed, sections twenty-four (24) to thirty-six (36), both inclusive, in township fifty-five (55) north, range ninety-two (92) west; what will be, when surveyed, sections twenty-eight (28) to thirty-three (33), both inclusive, in township fifty-five (55) north, range ninety-one (91) west; sections thirty (30), thirty-one (31), thirty-two (32), and what will be, when surveyed, sections four (4), five (5), six (6), seven (7), eight (8), nine (9), sixteen (16), seventeen (17), eighteen (18), nineteen (19), twenty (20), twenty-one (21), twenty-eight (28), twenty-nine (29), and thirty-three (33), all in township fifty-four (54) north, range ninety-one (91) west; the southwest quarter remaining unsurveyed portion of section eighteen (18), all of sections nineteen (19), thirty (30), thirty-one

(31), and what will be, when surveyed, sections six (6) and seven (7), all in township fifty-three (53) north, range ninety (90) west.

WILLIAM McKINLEY.

EXECUTIVE MANSION,
Washington, D. C., June 29, 1901.

In accordance with provision of the act of Congress approved June 4, 1897 (30 Stat. 34, 36), and by virtue of authority thereby given, and on the recommendation of the Secretary of the Interior, it is hereby ordered that township twenty-two (22) south, range nine (9) east, and township twenty-three (23) south, range nine (9) east, Willamette meridian, Oregon, within the limits of the Cascade Range Forest Reservation be restored to the public Domain after sixty days' notice hereof by publication as required by law, these tracts having been found better adapted to agriculture than forest purposes.

WILLIAM McKINLEY.

EXECUTIVE MANSION,
Washington, D. C., July 24, 1901.
To the Secretary of the Treasury.

SIR:—I herewith allot and set apart the funds now remaining in the Treasury of the United States as a separate fund raised from duties and taxes collected in the United States under the provisions of the act of Congress entitled "An act temporarily to provide revenues and a Civil Government for Puerto Rico and for other purposes" approved April 12th, 1900, for public purposes in Puerto Rico; and these funds hereby allotted shall be devoted to public and permanent improvements in Puerto Rico and other Governmental and public purposes therein as set forth in the act of Congress approved March 24th, 1900 (31 Stat., p. 51), and shall be expended under the sole supervision and subject to the approval of the Governor and Administrative heads of the Island. WILLIAM McKINLEY.

EXECUTIVE MANSION,
Washington, D. C., August 19, 1901.

It is hereby ordered that so much of the Executive Order of December 28, 1898 as fixes the rates at which the Spanish Alphonsino (*centem*) and the French Louis shall be accepted in payment of customs, taxes, public and postal dues in the Island of Cuba is modified to read as follows:

Alphonsino (25 Peseta Piece) $4.78
Louis (20 Frank Piece) 3.83

WILLIAM McKINLEY

EXECUTIVE MANSION,
Washington, D. C., August 20, 1901.

It is hereby ordered that all tracts and parcels of land belonging to the United States situated on the Peninsula extending into the harbor on the south side of the city of San Juan, Puerto Rico, known as Barrio de la Puntilla, or Puntilla Point, bounded on the north by the south boundary of the Paseo de la Princesa and on the east, south and west by the navigable waters of the harbor at such part Warden's line as may be established by competent authority, be and the same are hereby reserved for naval purposes.

WILLIAM McKINLEY.

EXECUTIVE MANSION,
Washington, D. C., August 27, 1901.

It is hereby ordered that the Executive Order of Jan. 4th, 1901, reserve for light house purposes among other tracts of land or cites in the District of Alaska a tract described as follows : "Scotch Cap beginning at a point at low water mark, said point being three miles easterly of point at low water mark opposite Scotch Cap Pinnacle six (6) due north one mile, thence north seventy-one (71) degrees east true four (4) miles, thence south thirty-eight (38) degrees true to low water mark; thence follow the windings of the low water mark to place of beginning," be and the same is hereby canceled so far as it relates to the above described tract, and it is hereby ordered that in lieu thereof a tract described as follows : Scotch Cap beginning at point at low water mark on Unimak Island, said point being three miles easterly of a point at low water mark opposite Scotch Cap Pinnacle; thence due north one mile; thence north seventy-one (71) degrees west true to four miles; thence south thirty-eight degrees west true to low water mark, thence follow the windings of the low water mark to place of beginning, be and it is hereby reserved and set apart for light house purposes, subject to any legal existing rights thereto.   WILLIAM McKINLEY.

EXECUTIVE MANSION,
Washington, D. C., August 29, 1901.

In accordance with provisions of Section 179 Revised Statutes as amended by act approved August 5th, 1882 (22 Stats. at large 238), Brigadier-General G. S. Gillespie, Corps of Engineers, United States Army, is authorized and directed to perform the duties of Secretary of War during the temporary absence from the seat of Government of the Secretary of War and the Assistant Secretary of War.

WILLIAM McKINLEY.

PRESIDENT McKINLEY'S LAST PUBLIC UTTER-ANCE TO THE PEOPLE, BUFFALO, N. Y., SEPTEMBER 5TH, 1901.

President Milburn, Director General Buchanan, Commissioners, Ladies and Gentlemen:

I am glad to be again in the city of Buffalo and exchange greetings with her people, to whose generous hospitality I am not a stranger and with whose good will I have been repeatedly and signally honored. To-day I have additional satisfaction in meeting and giving welcome to the foreign representatives assembled here, whose presence and participation in this exposition have contributed in so marked a degree to its interest and success. To the Commissioners of the Dominion of Canada and the British colonies, the French colonies, the republics of Mexico and Central and South America and the commissioners of Cuba and Puerto Rico, who share with us in this undertaking, we give the hand of fellowship and felicitate with them upon the triumphs of art, science, education and manufacture which the old has bequeathed to the new century. Expositions are the timekeepers of progress. They record the world's advancement. They stimulate the energy, enterprise and intellect of the people and quicken human genius. They go into the home. They broaden and brighten the daily life of the people. They open mighty storehouses of information to the student. Every exposition, great or small, has helped to some onward step. Comparison of ideas is always educational, and as such instruct the brain and hand of man. Friendly rivalry follows, which is the spur to industrial improvement, the inspiration to useful invention and to high endeavor in all departments of human activity. It exacts a study of the wants, comforts and even the whims of the people and recognizes the efficiency of high quality and new pieces to win their favor. The quest for trade is an incentive to men of business to devise, invent, improve and economize in the cost of production.

Business life, whether among ourselves or with other people, is ever a sharp struggle for success. It will be none the less so in the future. Without competition we would be clinging to the clumsy antiquated processes of farming and manufacture and the methods of business of long ago, and the twentieth would be no further advanced than the eighteenth century. But though commercial competitors we are, commercial enemies we must not be.

The Pan-American exposition has done its work thoroughly, presenting in its exhibits evidences of the highest skill and illustrating the progress of the human family in the western hemisphere. This portion of the earth has no cause for humiliation for the part it has performed in the march of civilization. It has not accomplished everything from it. It has simply done its best, and without vanity or boastfulness, and recognizing the manifold achievements of others, it invites the friendly rivalry of all the powers in the peaceful pursuits of trade and commerce, and will co-operate with all in advancing the highest and best interests of humanity.

The wisdom and energy of all the nations are none too great for the world's work. The success of art, science, industry and invention is an international asset and a common glory.

After all, how near one to the other is every part of the world. Modern inventions have brought into close relation widely separated peoples and made them better acquainted. Geographic and political divisions will continue to exist, but distances have been effaced. Swift ships and swift trains are becoming cosmopolitan. They invade fields which a few years ago were impenetrable. The world's products are exchanged as never before, and with increasing transportation facilities come increasing knowledge and larger trade. Prices are fixed with mathematical precision by supply and demand. The world's selling prices are regulated by market and crop reports.

We travel greater distances in a shorter space of time and with more ease than was ever dreamed of by the fathers. Isolation is no longer possible or desirable. The same important news is read, though in different languages, the same day in all christendom. The telegraph keeps us advised of what is occurring everywhere, and the press fore-shadows, with more or less accuracy, the plans and purposes of the nations.

Market prices of products and of securities are hourly known in every commercial mart, and the investments of the people extend beyond their own national boundaries into the remotest parts of the earth. Vast transactions are conducted and international exchanges are made by the tick of the cable. Every event of interest is immediately bulletined. The quick gathering and transmission of news, like rapid transit, are of recent origin and are only made possible by the genius of the inventor and the courage of the investor. It took a special messenger of the Government, with every facility known at the time for rapid travel, nineteen days to go from the city of Washington to New Orleans with a message to General Jackson that the war with England had ceased and a treaty of peace had been signed. How different now!

We reached General Miles in Puerto Rico by cable, and he was able, through the military telegraph, to stop his army on the firing line with the message that the United States and Spain had signed a protocol suspending hostilities. We knew almost instantly of the first shots fired at Santiago, and the subsequent surrender of the Spanish forces was known at Washington within less than an hour of its consummation. The first ship of Cervera's fleet had hardly emerged from that historic harbor when the fact was flashed to our capital, and the swift destruction that followed was announced immediately through the wonderful medium of telegraphy.

So accustomed are we to safe and easy communication with distant lands that its temporary interruption, even in ordinary times, results in loss and inconvenience. We shall never forget the days of anxious waiting and awful suspense when no information was permitted to be sent from Pekin, and the diplomatic representatives of the nations in China, cut off from all communication, inside and outside of the walled capital, were surrounded by an angry and misguided mob that threatened their lives; nor the joy that filled the world when a single message from the Government of the United States brought through our minister the first news of the safety of the besieged diplomats.

At the beginning of the nineteenth century there was not a mile of steam railroad on the globe. Now there are enough miles to make its circuit many times. Then there was not a line of electric telegraph; now we have a vast mileage traversing all lands and seas. God and man have linked the nations together. No nation can longer be indifferent to any other. And as we are brought more and more in touch with each other the less occasion there is for misunderstandings and the stronger the disposition, when we have differences, to adjust them in the court of arbitration, which is the noblest forum for the settlement of international disputes.

My fellow citizens, trade statistics indicate that this country is in a state of unexampled prosperity. The figures are almost appalling. They show that we are utilizing our fields and forests and mines and that we are furnishing profitable employment to the millions of workingmen throughout the United States, bringing comfort and happiness to their homes and making it possible to lay by savings for old age and disability. That all the people are participating in this great prosperity is seen in every American community, and shown by the enormous and unprecedented deposits in our savings banks. Our duty is the care and security of these deposits, and their safe investment demands the highest integrity and the best business capacity of those in charge of these depositories of the people's earnings.

We have a vast and intricate business, built up through years of toil and struggle, in which every part of the country has its stake, and will not permit of either neglect or of undue selfishness. No narrow, sordid policy will subserve it. The greatest skill and wisdom on the part of the manufacturers and producers will be required to hold and increase it. Our industrial enterprises which have grown to such great proportions affect the homes and occupations of the people and the welfare of the country. Our capacity to produce has developed so enormously and our products have so multiplied that the problem of more markets requires our urgent and immediate attention. Only a broad and enlightened policy will keep what we have. No other policy will get more. In these times of marvelous business energy and gain we ought to be looking to the future, strengthening the weak places in our industrial and commercial system, that we may be ready for any storm or. strain.

By sensible trade arrangements which will not interrupt our home production we shall extend the outlets for our increasing surplus. A system which provides a mutual exchange of commodities, a mutual exchange is manifestly essential to the continued and healthful growth of our export trade. We must not repose in fancied security that we can forever sell everything and buy little or nothing. If such a thing were possible, it would not be best for us or for those with whom we deal. We should take from our customers such of their products as we can use without harm to our industries and labor. Reciprocity is the natural outgrowth of our wonderful industrial development under the domestic policy now firmly established. What we produce beyond our domestic consumption must have a vent abroad. The excess must be relieved through a foreign outlet and we should sell everywhere we can, and buy wherever the buying will enlarge our sales and productions, and thereby make a greater demand for home labor.

The period of exclusiveness is past. The expansion of our trade and commerce is the pressing problem. Commercial wars are unprofitable. A policy of good will and friendly trade relations will prevent reprisals. Reciprocity treaties are in harmony with the spirit of the times, measures of retaliation are not. If perchance some of our tariffs are no longer needed, for revenue or to encourage and protect our industries at home, why should they not be employed to extend and promote our markets abroad? Then, too, we have inadequate steamship service. New lines of steamers have already been put in commission between the Pacific coast ports of the United States and those on the western coasts of Mexico and Central and South America. These should be followed up with direct steamship lines between the eastern coast of the United States and South American ports. One of the needs of the times is to direct commercial lines from our vast fields of production to the fields of consumption that we have but barely touched. Next in advantage to having the thing to sell is to have the convenience to carry it to the buyer. We must encourage our merchant marine. We must have more ships. They must be under the American flag, built and manned and owned by Americans. These will not only be profitable in a commercial sense; they will be messengers of peace and amity wherever they go. We must build the Isthmian canal, which will unite the two oceans and give a straight line of water communication with the western coasts of Central and South America and Mexico. The construction of a Pacific cable cannot be longer postponed.

In the furthering of these objects of national interest and concern you are performing an important part. This exposition would have touched the heart of that American statesman whose mind was ever alert and thought ever constant for a larger commerce and a truer fraternity of the republics of the new world. His broad American spirit is felt and manifested here. He needs no identification to an assemblage of Americans anywhere, for the name of Blaine is inseparably associated with the Pan-American movement, which finds this practical and substantial expression, and which we all hope will be firmly advanced by the Pan-American congress that assembles this autumn in the capital of Mexico. The good work will go on. It cannot be stopped. These buildings will disappear; this creation of art and beauty and industry will perish from sight, but their influence will remain to

> Make it live beyond its too short living
> With praises and thanksgiving.

Who can tell the new thoughts that have been awakened, the ambitions fired and the high achievements that will be wrought through this exposition? Gentlemen, let us ever remember that our interest is in concord, not conflict, and that our real eminence rests in the victories of peace, not those of war. We hope that all who are represented here may be moved to higher and nobler effort for their own and the world's good, and that out of this city may come, not only greater commerce and trade, but more essential than these, relations of mutual respect, confidence and friendship which will deepen and endure.

Our earnest prayer is that God will graciously vouchsafe prosperity, happiness and peace to all our neighbors, and like blessings to all the peoples and powers of earth.

DEATH OF PRESIDENT McKINLEY.

ANNOUNCEMENT OF THE ASSASSINATION.

Buffalo, N. Y., Sept. 6—7 P. M.

The President was shot about 4 o'clock. One bullet struck him on the upper portion of the breastbone, glancing and not penetrating; the second bullet penetrated the abdomen five inches below the left nipple and one and a half inches to the left of the median line. The abdomen was opened through the line of the bullet wound. It was found that the bullet had penetrated the stomach. The opening in the front wall of the stomach was carefully closed with silk stitches, after which a search was made for a hole in the back wall of the stomach. This was found and also closed in the same way. The further course of the bullet could not be discovered, although careful search was made. The abdominal wound was closed without drainage. No injury to the intestines or other abdominal organ was discovered. The patient stood the operation well, pulse of good quality, rate of 130. Condition at the conclusion of operation was gratifying. The result cannot be foretold. His condition at present justifies hope of recovery.

GEORGE B. CORTELYOU,
Secretary to the President.

News at the White House.

The official announcement of the President's death was received at the White House at 2:35 o'clock, September 14, 1901, as follows:

Buffalo, September 14.

Col. B. F. Montgomery, Executive·Mansion, Washington:
The President died at 2:15 this morning.

GEORGE B. CORTELYOU.

Immediately upon receipt of the official dispatch the following was sent to Secretary Cortelyou:

Members of the executive staff in Washington are deeply affected, and beg to tender their profound sympathy to Mrs. McKinley.

O. F. PRUDEN,
Assistant Secretary.

Public Announcement of Death by the Physicians.

MILBURN HOUSE,
Buffalo, N. Y., Sept. 14.

The following report of the autopsy upon the remains of President McKinley was issued at 5 o'clock:

The bullet which struck over the breastbone did not pass through the skin, and did little harm. The other bullet passed through both walls of the stomach near its lower border. Both holes were found to be perfectly closed by the stitches, but the tissue around each hole had become gangrenous. After passing through the stomach the bullet passed into the back walls of the abdomen, hitting and tearing the upper end of the kidney. This portion of the bullet track was also gangrenous, the gangrene involving the pancreas. The bullet has not yet been found. There was no sign of peritonitis or disease of other organs. The heart walls were very thin. There was no evidence of any attempt at repair on the part of nature, and death resulted from the gangrene, which affected the stomach around the bullet wounds as well as the tissues around the further course of the bullet. Death was unavoidable by any surgical or medical treatment, and was the direct result of the bullet wound.

HARVEY D. GAYLORD, M. D.
HERMAN G. MATZINGER, M. D.
P. M. RIXEY, M. D.
MATTHEW D. MANN, M. D.
HERMAN MYNTER, M. D.
ROSWELL PARK, M. D.
EUGENE WASDIN, M. D.
CHARLES G. STOCKTON, M. D.

EDWARD G. JANEWAY, M. D.
W. D. JOHNSON, M. D.
W. P. KENDALL,
   Surgeon, U. S. A.
CHARLES CARY, M. D.
EDWARD L. MUNSON,
   Assistant Surgeon, U. S. A.
HERMANUS L. BAER, M. D.

ANNOUNCEMENT TO THE VICE-PRESIDENT.

At the residence of Mr. Ansley Wilcox, 641 Delaware Avenue, Buffalo, N. Y., Mr. Root stepped forward and said, with deep emotion: "Mr. Vice-President, I have been requested on behalf of the Cabinet of the late President — at least those who are present in Buffalo, all except two — to request that for reasons of weight affecting the affairs of Government you should proceed to take the constitutional oath of President of the United States."

THE VICE-PRESIDENT'S REPLY.

"I shall take the oath at once in accordance with your request, and in this hour of deep and terrible national bereavement I wish to state that it shall be my aim to continue absolutely unbroken the policy of President McKinley for the peace and prosperity and honor of our beloved country."

ANNOUNCEMENT OF THE ASSASSINATION TO REPRESENTATIVES OF THE UNITED STATES ABROAD.

(From the Washington Post, Sept. 15, 1901.)

DEPARTMENT OF STATE,
Washington, Sept. 14.

Sir: It is my painful duty to announce to you the death of William McKinley, President of the United States, in the city of Buffalo, at fifteen minutes past 2 in the morning of to-day, September 14.

Laid low by the act of an assassin, the week-long struggle to save his life has been watched with keen solicitude, not alone by the people of this country, who raised him from their own ranks to the high office he filled, but by the people of all friendly nations, whose messages of sympathy and hope, while hope was possible, have been most consolatory in this time of sore trial.

Now that the end has come, I request you to be the medium of communicating the sad tidings to the Government of the honored nation you so worthily represent, and to announce that in obedience to the prescriptions of the Constitution, the office of President has devolved upon Theodore Roosevelt, Vice-President of the United States.

Accept, sir, the renewed assurance of my highest consideration.

JOHN HAY.

ANNOUNCEMENT TO THE ARMY.

[GENERAL ORDER NO. 13.]

HEADQUARTERS OF THE ARMY,
ADJUTANT GENERAL'S OFFICE,
Washington, D. C. Sept. 16, 1901.

With great sorrow, the commanding general announces the death of William McKinley, President of the United States and, by statute, Commander-in-Chief of the District of Columbia Militia, which occurred at Buffalo, N. Y., at 2:15 o'clock A. M. on September 14, 1901.

Throughout his tragically terminated administration President McKinley was actively interested in the welfare of this organization and frequently gave it evidence of his sincere friendship. His distinguished services as soldier and civilian must incite to emulation and will result in purer patriotism and better citizenship wherever his career is studied.

The national flag will be displayed at half-staff on all armories from sunrise to sunset of each day until sunset of Thursday, the 19th instant, on which day the remains of the late Commander-in-Chief will be interred at Canton, Ohio.

The officers of the National Guard will wear the usual badge of mourning upon their swords, and the regimental and battalion colors will be draped in mourning for a period of thirty days.

By command of BRIG.-GEN. HARRIES.

CHARLES H. OURAND,
Major and Inspector General, Acting Adjutant-General.

By DIRECTION of the Acting Secretary of War, the National Guard of the District of Columbia will assemble for escort and parade duty on Tuesday, September 17, 1901, to participate in the funeral of William McKinley, late President of the United States and Commander-in-Chief of the District of Columbia Militia.

The brigade will assemble at 8:30 o'clock A. M., in column of companies, on Pennsylvania avenue facing east, its right resting on Nineteenth street northwest.

The order of formation, from right to left, will be as follows:

General staff and general non-commissioned staff.
Brigade Band.
Engineer Corps.
Second Regiment of Infantry.
First Regiment of Infantry.
Corps of field music.
First Separate Battalion.
Signal Corps.
Naval Battalion.
Ambulance Corps.

Undress uniform, forage caps, leggings, white standing collars, and white gloves will be worn; the Naval Battalion to be in its prescribed uniform.

All members of the general staff and general non-commissioned staff, and the field officers and adjutants of regiments will be mounted, and will wear the prescribed undress mounted uniform.

All commanding officers will assemble at the adjutant-general's office at 9:30 o'clock on the evening of September 16, to receive any special orders that may be issued.

Commanding officers of companies will furnish their battalion adjutants with "morning reports" immediately after the parade is dismissed, noting thereon the names of all officers and men absent from the parade without leave. Commanding officers of regiments, separate battalions, and separate companies will furnish these headquarters with consolidated morning reports before 10 o'clock A. M. of the 19th instant; will see that all enlisted men absent without leave are properly dealt with, and will report to these headquarters the names of all commissioned officers so absent.

By command of BRIG.-GEN. HARRIES.

CHARLES H. OURAND,
Major and Inspector General, Acting Adjutant-General.

OFFICIAL ORDERS SENT OUT.

SALUTES TO BE FIRED AND FLAGS LOWERED AFLOAT AND ASHORE.

Secretary of State Hay and Secretary of the Treasury Gage, the only Cabinet officers in town, held a consultation on the morning of the 13th as a result of which the following order was issued:

DEPARTMENT OF STATE,
Washington, Sept. 14.

To the Secretary of the Navy:

Out of respect to the memory of the President, the executive departments will be closed to-day and on the day of the funeral. JOHN HAY.

A similar order was communicated to all the heads and acting heads of the executive departments in Washington by government telegraph. They in turn issued the necessary orders for the closing of their respective departments, not only in Washington, but throughout the country. In a short time the large buildings were deserted, except by a few clerks detailed to aid their chiefs in the promulgation of necessary orders.

In addition to issuing the order closing the Navy Department, Acting Secretary Hackett dispatched the following order to every commander-in-chief, to every navy yard, and to every United States ship, stating simply:

It is with profound sorrow that the department announces to you the death of President McKinley at 2:15, September 14.

The Acting Secretary also issued the following order to the naval branch of the United States:

[SPECIAL ORDER NO. 12.]

NAVY DEPARTMENT,
Washington, Sept. 14, 1901.

The President of the United States died this morning at 2:15, in the city of Buffalo, N. Y. Officers and men of the navy and Marine Corps need not to be reminded of the public and private virtues of their late Commander-in-Chief. The whole people loved William McKinley, for he loved and trusted them.

As soldier, statesman, husband, and as a pure-minded, great-hearted American, his fame now belongs to his country.

Under the Constitution, Theodore Roosevelt, previously Vice-President, has become President and Commander-in-Chief of the navy and Marine Corps of the United States.   F. W. HACKETT,
Acting Secretary.

The ceremonies to be observed are provided for in the naval regulations as follows:

Upon the receipt of official intelligence of the death of the President of the United States, the senior officer shall direct that on the following day the ensign and union jack be displayed at half-mast from sunrise to sunset, and guns fired every half hour from all ships present. Similar orders shall be given at naval stations.

A naval regulation provides that salutes shall not be fired on Sunday except in cases wherein international courtesy would suffer from the breach. Therefore the firing of the guns will take place on Monday at those points where the department's announcement was received yesterday.

ORDER TO THE ARMY.

A dispatch was received at the War Department on the afternoon of the 13th from Secretary Root approving the draft of the order to the army, announcing the death of President McKinley. It was sent to all officers in command. The order follows:

HEADQUARTERS OF THE ARMY,
ADJUTANT GENERAL'S OFFICE,
Washington, September 14.

General orders:

1. The following order of the Secretary of War announces to the army the death of William McKinley, President of the United States:

WAR DEPARTMENT, *Washington, September 14.*

The distressing duty devolves upon the Secretary of War of announcing to the army the death of William McKinley, President of the United States, which occurred at Buffalo, N. Y., at 2:15 o'clock A. M., on the 14th day of September, 1901.

The grief into which the nation has been plunged at the untimely death of its Chief Magistrate will be keenly felt by the army of the United States, in which, in his early manhood, he rendered distinguished and patriotic services, and in whose welfare he manifested at all times a profound and abiding solicitude.

Appropriate funeral honors will be paid to the memory of the late President and Commander-in-Chief at the headquarters of every military division and department, at every military port, at the United States Military Academy, West Point, and at every camp of troops of the United States in the field.

The Lieutenant-General of the army will give the necessary instructions for carrying this order into effect.

ELIHU ROOT,
Secretary of War.

2. On the day after the receipt of this order at the headquarters of military commands in the field and at each military station and at the Military Academy, at West Point, the troops and cadets will be paraded at 10 o'clock, A. M., and the order read to them, after which all labor for the day will cease.

THIRTEEN GUNS AT DAWN.

3. At dawn thirteen guns will be fired at each military post, and afterward at intervals of thirty minutes between the rising and setting sun a single gun, and at the close of the day the salute of the Union of forty-five guns.

The national flag will be displayed at half-staff at the headquarters of the several military divisions and departments, and at all military posts, stations, forts, and buildings and vessels under the control of the department until the remains of the late Chief Magistrate are consigned to their final resting place at Canton, Ohio, on the afternoon of Thursday, the 19th instant, on which day all labor will be suspended at all military posts and stations and on all public works under the direction of the department, and at 12 o'clock meridian twenty-one minute guns will be fired from all military posts and stations.

The officers of the army of the United States will wear the usual badge of mourning on their swords and the colors of the various military organizations of the army will be draped in mourning for the period of one month.

4. The following officers of the army will, with a like number of officers of the navy selected for the purpose, compose the guard of honor, and accompany the remains of their late Commander-in-Chief from the National Capital to Canton, Ohio, and continue with them until they are consigned to their final resting place:

The Lieutenant-General of the Army.

Maj.-Gen. John R. Brooke.

Maj.-Gen. Elwell S. Otis.

Maj.-Gen. Arthur MacArthur.

Brig.-Gen. George L. Gillespie.

By command of Lieut.-Gen. Miles.

THOMAS WARD,
Acting Adjutant-General.

The following order then issued:

WAR DEPARTMENT,
Washington, Sept. 14.

The Secretary of War announces to the army that upon the death of William McKinley, President of the United States, Theodore Roosevelt, Vice-President, has succeeded to the office of President of the United States, by virtue of the Constitution.   ELIHU ROOT,
Secretary of War.

Secretary Root also gave directions to the officers of the department to make the necessary arrangements and issue orders for the participation of the army in the funeral ceremonies, following the Garfield precedent.

The following order was issued by the Secretary of the Treasury to the Revenue Cutter Service:

The department announces to the service the sad tidings of the death of the President. The flags of all vessels of the Revenue Cutter Service will be carried at half-mast until otherwise ordered.

MR. GAGE ANNOUNCES DEATH.

HEAD OF TREASURY PAYS TRIBUTE TO THE LATE PRESIDENT MCKINLEY.

Secretary Gage issued the following announcement of the death of President McKinley:

It has been thought proper to make sad but official announcement in this issue of Treasury Decisions of the tragic death of William McKinley, twenty-fifth President of the United States, and to give some expression of that tribute which his character and deeds compel.

It needed not the shadows of death to make the figure of the late President loom large in the estimate of mankind.

The republic he loved he lived to broaden and unify as no previous President had done. Under his prudent and far-seeing statesmanship it took exalted place in the community of nations.

From his place as private citizen, on through many and increasing honors to his final post as ruler of his people, he remained true to the highest ideals.

By the people of the nation at large and by the world he was known and will live in grateful annals as a gentleman of noble heart, an affectionate husband, a sturdy friend, and a faithful and illustrious President.

In a long public life, ever open to his fellows, nothing was ever found, even by intemperate partisan zeal, that would cast a shade upon his character.

The kindly and unselfish attributes which his colleagues knew and loved, the public felt, and now men of every faith and following join in reverent acknowledgment of those distinctive virtues and abilities that lift him among the truly great of all ages.

The passing of Presidents and Kings usually evokes tributes of praise, but in William McKinley's life there was an element that made him more than ruler, and which, in the hour of his death, is above the tribute of speech and tears.

The ordinary tributes paid to the memory of the great when they pass from earth utterly fail to satisfy the mind in an attempted application of them to our dead President.   L. J. GAGE,
Secretary.

Certificate of the Coroner.

Formal Record of McKinley's Death for Bureau of Vital Statistics.

The coroner of Erie County issued the following certificate of death of the late President:

CITY OF BUFFALO,
BUREAU OF VITAL STATISTICS,
COUNTY OF ERIE, STATE OF NEW YORK.

Certificate and record of death of William McKinley:

I hereby certify that he died on the 14th day of September, 1901, about 2:15 o'clock A. M., and that to the best of my knowledge and belief the cause of death was as hereunder written:

Cause, gangrene of both walls of stomach and pancreas following gunshot wound.

Witness my hand this 14th day of September, 1901.

H. R. GAYLORD, M. D.
H. Z. MATZINGER, M. D.
JAMES F. WILSON, *Coroner*

Date of death—September 14, 1901.
Age—58 years, 7 months, 15 days.
Color—White.
Single, married, etc.—Married.
Occupation—President of the United States.
Birthplace—Niles, Ohio.
How long in the United States, if foreign born—
Father's name—William McKinley.
Father's birthplace—Pennsylvania, U. S.
Mother's name—Nancy McKinley.
Mother's birthplace—Ohio, U. S.
Place of death—1168 Delaware avenue.
Last previous residence—Washington, D. C.
Direct cause of death—Gangrene of both walls of stomach and pancreas following gunshot wound.

Official Order of Observances.

Order of Arrangements for the Obsequies at Washington City of William McKinley, Late President of the United States.

The remains of the late President will arrive in Washington at 8:30 o'clock P. M. on Monday, the 16th of September, 1901, and will be escorted to the Executive Mansion by a squadron of United States Cavalry.

On Tuesday, the 17th instant, at 9 o'clock A. M., they will be borne to the Capitol, where they will lie in state in the rotunda from 10 o'clock P. M. until 6 P. M. that date.

The following morning there will be exercises at the Capitol at 10 o'clock. At 1 P. M. the remains will be borne to the depot of the Pennsylvania Railroad, and thence conveyed to their final resting place at Canton, Ohio.

FROM WHITE HOUSE TO CAPITOL.
ORDER OF PROCESSION FOR TUESDAY.

SECTION I.

Funeral Escort,
Under Command of
Maj.-Gen. John R. Brooke, U. S. A.
Artillery Band.
Squadron of Cavalry.
Company A, United States Engineers.
Two Batteries C Artillery.
Marine Band.
Battalion of Marines.
Battalion of United States Seamen.
Brigade of National Guard, District of Columbia.

SECTION II.

Under Command of Chief Marshal,
Gen. Henry V. Boynton.
Clergymen in Attendance.
Physicians who attended the late President.
Military Order of the Loyal Legion of the United States.
Grand Army of the Republic.
Guard of Honor.   Guard of Honor.
Hearse.
Bearers.   Bearers.

Officers of the army, Navy and Marine Corps in this city who are not on duty with the troops forming the escort will form, in full dress, right in front, on either side of the hearse—the army on the right and the Navy and Marine Corps on the left—and compose the guard of honor.

Family of the late President.
Relatives of the late President.
Ex-President of the United States.

SECTION III.

THE PRESIDENT.
The Cabinet Ministers.
The Diplomatic Corps.
The Chief Justice and Associate Justices of the Supreme
Court of the United States.
The Senators of the United States.
Members of the U. S. House of Representatives.
Governors of States and Territories.
Commissioners of the District of Columbia.
The Judges of the Court of Claims, the Judiciary of the District
of Columbia, and Judges of the United States Courts.

ROOSEVELT DAM

IRRIGATION

"June 17, 1902, Congress passed the reclamation law, which provided for the construction of irrigation works by the United States Government. The cost of the works is to be repaid by the settlers, who use the water, in ten annual installments, and when the payments have been made for a majority of the lands included in any project the management and operation of such project are to be turned over to the owners, to be maintained at their expense. The receipts from the sale of land and the use of water are to form a perpetual reclamation fund. Public lands included in reclamation projects may be acquired only under the terms of the homestead law, and the commutation clause of that law does not apply to such lands.

"Up to 1909 the Government had selected for reclamation more than two million acres at an estimated cost of nearly $90,000,000. Under the Carey act the States have selected for reclamation and had assigned to them up to July 1, 1908, 3,239,285 acres. Idaho and Wyoming, each having disposed of the 1,000,000 acres allowed them under the law, were granted an additional 1,000,000 acres for the same purpose."

Quoted from the article "Irrigation" in the Encyclopedic Index.

The upper panel shows a certain tract of desert land, absolutely worthless; the center panel shows a typical irrigation project, the Gunnison tunnel, by means of which water is guided to the parched soil; the third panel shows the same tract under cultivation, worth $500 an acre.

The Assistant Secretaries of State, Treasury, War, Navy,
Interior and Agricultural Departments.
The Assistant Postmasters General.
The Solicitor General and the Assistant Attorneys General.
Organized Societies.

The troops designated to form the escort will assemble on the north side of Pennsylvania avenue, facing the Executive Mansion, left resting on the eastern entrance to the grounds, and in inverse order, so that when the column is formed to the left, the organizations will be in the order above described. The formation will be completed at 9 A. M. on Tuesday, the 17th instant.

The civic procession will form in accordance with the directions to be given by the chief marshal.

The officers of the army and navy selected to compose the special guard of honor will be at the Capitol so as to receive the remains upon arrival there.

WEDNESDAY'S SOLEMN PAGEANT.

Order of procession for Wednesday:

The military guard will escort the remains from the Capitol to the railroad station.

The troops on that date will assemble on the east side of the Capitol and form line fronting the eastern portico of the Capitol precisely at 1 o'clock P. M.

The procession will move, upon the conclusion of the services at the Capitol (commencing at 1 o'clock P. M.), when minute guns will be fired at the navy yard, by the vessels of war which may be in port, and at Fort Myer, and by a battery of artillery stationed near the Capitol for that purpose.

At the same hour the bells of the several churches, fire engine-houses, and schoolhouses will be tolled, the firing of the minute-guns and the tolling of the bells to continue until the departure of the remains of the late Chief Magistrate for the railroad depot.

At 2:30 o'clock P. M. the officers of the army and navy selected to compose the special guard of honor will assemble at the Pennsylvania depot in time to receive the body of the late President, and deposit it in the car prepared for that purpose.

As the necessary limits of time do not permit personal communication with the public officers of the United States and of the several States enumerated in the foregoing order, they are respectfully requested to accept the invitation to take part in the exercises conveyed through the publication hereof, and to send notice of their intention to be present to the Secretary of War at the War Department in Washington.

211

Organizations and civic societies desiring to take part are requested to send similar notice at the earliest time practicable to the chief marshal of the civic procession, Gen. Henry V. Boynton, Wyatt Building, Washington, D. C.

JOHN HAY,
Secretary of State.

ELIHU ROOT,
Secretary of War.

JOHN D. LONG,
Secretary of the Navy.

HENRY B. F. MACFARLAND,
President of the Board of Commissioners of the District of Columbia.

ORDER OF PROCESSION.

The procession then started at slow march up Pennsylvania avenue toward the White House. It moved in the following order:

Four mounted police outriders.

Platoon of forty policemen on foot, Capt. Francis E. Cross, commanding.

Platoon of sixteen mounted policemen abreast, Sergt. Matthews, commanding.

Cavalry escort from Fort Myer, consisting of Troops I and L, under command of Maj. Walter L. Finlay. Staff, Maj. Thomas, Fifth Cavalry; Maj. George L. Davis, surgeon; Chaplain C. E. Pierce, Capt. S. H. Elliott, adjutant. Troop I, under command of Capt. C. E. Brooks and Second Lieut. A. S. Fuger, and Troop L, under command of Lieut. W. B. Scales.

Three veteran society representatives, Mr. John McElroy, national senior vice-commander of the Grand Army of the Republic; Israel W. Stone, commander of the Department of the Potomac of the Grand Army of the Republic, and Gen. R. G. Dyrenforth, national commander of the Union Veteran Union.

Platoon of representatives of veteran organizations, Col. J. T. Wilkinson, Spanish War Veterans; Col. J. Edwin Browne, Union Veteran Legion; Chaplain C. E. Stevens, Department of the Potomac, Grand Army of the Republic; A. M. Daniels, commander Post No. 6, Department of the Potomac; Past Commander George Y Davis, of Burnside Post; A. R. Greene, past department commander of Kansas Grand Commander John M. Meacham, Department of the Potomac, Union Veterans' Union; Arthur Hendricks, past commander Department of the Potomac, Grand Army of the Republic; L. K. Brown, of Burnside Post, Grand Army of the Republic.

Remains of the President.

ORDERS TO GUARD OF HONOR.

The following special order was issued on the 16th:

The special guard of honor, composed of general officers of the army and admirals of the navy, will not march in the procession contemplated for Tuesday. The special guard of honor—general officers of the army, active and retired; the admirals

of the navy, active and retired—not otherwise instructed will assemble in full dress
as follows:

Monday, September 16, 1901, at the White House at 8 P. M.

Tuesday, September 17, 1901, at the east front of the Capitol at 9:30 A. M.

Acting Secretary Hackett has issued the following order to govern
the navy in the funeral ceremonies:

[SPECIAL ORDER NO. 13.]

NAVY DEPARTMENT,
Washington, Sept. 16, 1901.

All officers on the active list of the navy and Marine Corps on duty in Washington will assemble in full dress uniform at 7:30 P. M. Monday evening, September 16,
at Pennsylvania Railroad station for the purpose of meeting the remains of the late
President of the United States. They will again assemble in the same uniform in
the grounds of the Executive Mansion and near the eastern gate at 9 A. M. on Tuesday, September 17, to march as guard of honor in the procession from the Executive
Mansion to the Capitol.

The following special guard of honor is hereby appointed:

The Admiral of the Navy, Rear Admiral A. S. Crowninshield, Rear Admiral
Charles O'Neil, Paymaster-General A. S. Kenny, Brig.-Gen. Charles Heywood,
U. S. M. C.

The special guard of honor will assemble in special full dress uniform at the Ex-
ecutive Mansion at 8 P. M. Monday, September 16, to receive the remains of the late
President, and will again assemble in the same uniform at the Capitol at 10 A. M.
Tuesday, September 17, and will thence accompany the remains of President Mc-
Kinley to their final resting place in Canton, Ohio.

All officers of flag rank will constitute an additional special guard of honor, and
will assemble at the places hereinbefore mentioned for the special guard of honor.
The additional special guard of honor will not, however, accompany the remains of
the late President to Canton.

F. W. HACKETT,
Acting Secretary.

The following official statement, making important changes in the
plans for the funeral services over the remains of President McKinley
in this city, was made public:

In compliance with the earnest wishes of Mrs. McKinley that the body of her
husband shall rest in her home at Canton Wednesday night, the following changes
in the obsequies of the late President will be made:

Funeral services in the rotunda of the Capitol will be held Tuesday morning on
the arrival of the escort which will accompany the remains from the White House.
The body of the late President will lie in state in the rotunda for the remainder of
Tuesday, and will be escorted to the railroad station Tuesday evening. The funeral
train will leave Washington at or about 8 o'clock Tuesday evening, and thus will
arrive at Canton during the day Wednesday.

JOHN HAY,
Secretary of State.

ELIHU ROOT,
Secretary of War.

JOHN D. LONG,
Secretary of the Navy.

H. B. F. MACFARLAND,
President Board of Commissioners of the District of Columbia

211*

HOUSE COMMITTEE NAMED.

LIST WIRED BY SPEAKER HENDERSON.

The following dispatch from Speaker Henderson named the House committee:

New York, Sept. 15, 1901.

Hon. Henry Casson, Sergeant-at-arms, House of Representatives, Washington, D. C.:

I have appointed the following committee for Presidential funeral and escort. Notify them at once, requesting answer. Give each date of funeral and hour of leaving Washington:

Grosvenor, Ohio; Burton, Ohio; Tayler, Ohio; Loud, California; Russell, Connecticut; Ball, Delaware; Cannon, Illinois; Hitt, Illinois; Hopkins, Illinois; Steele, Indiana; Hepburn, Iowa; Curtis, Kansas; Burleigh, Maine; Mudd, Maryland; Gillett, Massachusetts; Corliss, Michigan; Fletcher, Minnesota; Mercer, Nebraska; Sulloway, New Hampshire; Loudenslager, New Jersey; Payne, New York; Sherman, New York; Marshall, North Dakota; Tongue, Oregon; Bingham, Pennsylvania; Grow, Pennsylvania; Dalzell, Pennsylvania; Capron, Rhode Island; Burke, South Dakota; Foster, Vermont; Cushman, Washington; Dovener, West Virginia; Babcock, Wisconsin; Mondell, Wyoming; Richardson, Tennessee; Bankhead, Alabama; McRae, Arkansas; Bell, Colorado; Sparkman, Florida; Lester, Georgia; Glenn, Idaho; Smith, Kentucky; Robertson, Louisiana; Williams, Mississippi; De Armond, Missouri; Edwards, Montana; Newlands, Nevada; Cummings, New York; W. W. Kitchin, North Carolina; Norton, Ohio; Elliott, South Carolina; Lanham, Texas; Swanson, Virginia; Bodie, New Mexico; Flynn, Oklahoma; Smith, Arizona.

Acknowledge receipt of this telegram. I will be at funeral.

D. E. HENDERSON.

ACTION OF CONGRESS.

Upon the assembly of the Fifty-seventh Congress in its first session convened, President Roosevelt referred in touching terms to the assassination of the late President McKinley. (Page 6641.)

The Senate on December 3, 1901, adopted the following resolution:

Resolved, That a committee of eleven Senators be appointed on the part of the Senate, to join such committee as may be appointed on the part of the House, to consider and report on what token of respect and affection it may be proper for the Congress of the United States to express the deep sensibility of the nation to the tragic death of the late President, William McKinley, and that so much of the message of the President as relates to that deplorable event be referred to such committee.

The committee on the part of the Senate comprised the following named gentlemen: Mr. Foraker, Mr. Allison, Mr. Fairbanks, Mr. Kean, Mr. Aldrich, Mr. Nelson, Mr. Perkins, Mr. Jones of Arkansas, Mr. Morgan, Mr. Cockrell and Mr. McEnery.

The House of Representatives on December 3, passed the following resolution:

Resolved, That a committee of one member from each State represented in this House be appointed on the part of the House to join such committee as may be appointed on the part of the Senate, to consider and report by what token of respect and affection it may be proper for the Congress of the United States to express the deep sensibility of the nation to the tragic death of the late President, William McKinley, and that so much of the message of the President as relates to that deplorable event be referred to that committee.

The committee on the part of the House of Representatives comprised the following named gentlemen:

Ohio, Charles H. Grosvenor; California, Julius Kahn; Connecticut, E. Steven Henry; Delaware, L. Heister Ball; Illinois, Vespasian Warner; Indiana, James E. Watson; Iowa, Robert G. Cousins; Idaho, Thomas L. Glenn; Kansas, Justin D. Bowersock; Maine, Amos L. Allen; Maryland, George A. Pearre; Massachusetts, William C. Lovering; Michigan, William Alden Smith; Minnesota, Page Morris; Montana, Caldwell Edwards; Nebraska, Elmer J. Burkett; New Hampshire, Frank D. Currier; New Jersey, Richard Wayne Parker; New York, John H. Ketcham; North Dakota, Thomas F. Marshall; North Carolina, Spencer Blackburn; Oregon, Malcolm A. Moody; Pennsylvania, Marlin E. Olmsted; Rhode Island, Melville Bull; South Dakota, Eben W. Martin; Utah, George Sutherland; Vermont, Kittredge Haskins; Washington, Wesley L. Jones; West Virginia, Alston G. Dayton; Wisconsin, Herman B. Dahle; Wyoming, Frank W. Mondell; Alabama, Oscar W. Underwood; Arkansas, Hugh A. Dinsmore; Florida, Robert W. Davis; Georgia, William H. Fleming; Kentucky, James N. Kehoe; Louisiana, Adolph Meyer; Mississippi, Charles E. Hooker; Missouri, Champ Clark; South Carolina, W. Jasper Talbert; Tennessee, John A. Moon; Texas, John L. Sheppard; Virginia, James Hay; Colorado, John F. Shafroth; Nevada, Francis G. Newlands.

The following concurrent resolutions were adopted by both Houses of Congress on January 15th, 1902:

Whereas the melancholy event of the violent and tragic death of William McKinley, late President of the United States, having occurred during the recess of Congress, and the two Houses sharing in the general grief and desiring to manifest their sensibility upon the occasion of the public bereavement: Therefore,

Be it resolved by the House of Representatives (the Senate concurring), That the two Houses of Congress will assemble in the Hall of the House of Representatives on a day and hour fixed and announced by the joint committee, to wit, Thursday, February 27, 1902, and that, in the presence of the two Houses there assembled, an address on the life and character of William McKinley, late President of the United States, be pronounced by Hon. John Hay, and that the President of the Senate pro tempore and the Speaker of the House of Representatives be requested to invite the President and ex-President of the United States, ex-Vice-Presidents, the heads of the several Departments, the judges of the Supreme Court, the representatives of the foreign governments, the governors of the several States, the Lieutenant-General of the Army and the Admiral of the Navy, and such officers of the Army and Navy as have received the thanks of Congress who may then be at the seat of Government to be present on the occasion, and such others as may be suggested by the executive committee.

And be it further resolved, That the President of the United States be requested to transmit a copy of these resolutions to Mrs. Ida S. McKinley, and to assure her of the profound sympathy of the two Houses of Congress for her deep personal affliction, and of their sincere condolence for the late national bereavement.

QUESTIONS.

1. What notable public service was performed by the revenue cutter *Bear* in 1897-98?   Page 6350.

2. When and why was the executive head of a European nation presented by the United States with the first coin minted of a new issue?   Page 6428.

3. How many Admirals of the Navy have there been, and what was McKinley's recommendation as to the rank?   See Index under "Admiral" and page 6345.

4. How long did it take our fleet to demolish the Spanish squadron at Santiago?   Page 6317.

5. On what date was Pekin, China, entered by our troops and the legations saved?   Page 6422.

6. When were the Hawaiian Islands annexed to the United States?   Pages 6399, 6453.   (See also Hawaii, Encyclopedic Index.)

7. What part did America play in the Boxer Rebellion?   Page 6417.   (See also Boxers, Encyclopedic Index.)

8. When was Dewey appointed acting Rear-Admiral?   Page 6568.

9. What was the date of Vice-President Hobart's death?   Page 6356.

10. When was the Pan-American Exposition held, and what tragic event took place there?   Pages 6382, 6436, 6618. (See also Pan-American Exposition, Encyclopedic Index.)

SUGGESTIONS.

The Spanish-American War occupied much of McKinley's attention. Read his policy. Pages 6280, 6295, 6297, 6298, 6302, 6305, 6307, 6428. (See also Cuba and citations, Encyclopedic Index, for causes leading to the war. See also Spanish-American War and citations, Encyclopedic Index.)

The tariff question was also important; McKinley himself being a tariff expert, and the author of the McKinley Bill, which had been superseded by the Wilson Bill during Cleveland's second administration. The Dingley Tariff Bill became a law in 1897. Pages 6238, 6246.

Read McKinley's Foreign Policy. Pages 6241, 6248, 6280, 6295, 6307.

NOTE.

For further suggestions on McKinley's administration see McKinley, William, Encyclopedic Index.

By reading the Foreign Policy of each President, and by scanning the messages as to the state of the nation, a thorough knowledge of the history of the United States will be acquired from the most authentic sources; because, as has been said, "Each President reviews the past, depicts the present and forecasts the future of the nation."

Theodore Roosevelt

September 14, 1901, to March 4, 1909

Messages, Proclamations, and Executive Orders,

to March 4, 1909.

SEE ENCYCLOPEDIC INDEX.

The Encyclopedic Index is not only an index to the other volumes, not only a key that unlocks the treasures of the entire publication, but it is in itself an alphabetically arranged brief history or story of the great controlling events constituting the History of the United States.

Under its proper alphabetical classification the story is told of every great subject referred to by any of the Presidents in their official Messages, and at the end of each story the official utterances of the Presidents themselves are cited upon the subject, so that you may readily turn to the page in the body of the work itself for this original information.

Next to the possession of knowledge is the ability to turn at will to where knowledge is to be found.

THEODORE ROOSEVELT

With reproduction of official portrait by Sargent, from the White House Collection

"SAGAMORE HILL," HOME AT OYSTER BAY, NEW YORK, OF
THEODORE ROOSEVELT

With reproduction of official portrait, by Sargent, from the White House Collection

Theodore Roosevelt

ROOSEVELT

There are two kinds who seek a Presidency. One aims at eminence, the other hungers for fame. With one the White House is an object; with the other a method. The first, if made President, sits calmly down; he has had his victory and the White House is his. With him of the fame-hunger, it is the other way about. Given the White House his great work begins. He does not think to write his name with the immortals by simply signing himself "President." He can only achieve the purpose that has called him to the field, by labors of lasting good to the whole people. Of our entire line of Presidents no more than six were of the latter. Six there were who sought and found their wreaths. The others will live in history whenever and wherever Presidents are enumerated; not one by his record, however, bequeathed himself to fame.

It shone out as a best hope of the hour that Mr. Roosevelt was heart and soul a fame-hunter. The nobility of one's action is determined by the nobility of one's aspirations. Mr. Roosevelt did not rest content with being merely a President. He must go down the aisles of coming time a great President, or in his own conscience he would fail. To that end, he set before himself the examples of those mighty ones of time past. The Washingtons, the Jeffersons, the Jacksons, the Lincolns and the Grants were his exemplars. With such to be as guides to him—and because he was true and bold and wise, and no man owned him—it was not strange if he conquered entrance to Valhalla. Moreover, it is good for the public to know and say these things.

If there be any worth-while thing in mere experience, if reading and travel and the study of men be of good avail, Mr. Roosevelt had the making of a great President. Before he went to the White House he was taught how State laws were made as a member of the assembly at Albany, and subsequently took lessons in executing those laws as Governor. He was shown the inner workings of a great city as a Commissioner of Police. As Chief of Civil Service, Assistant Secretary of the Navy, Soldier in the field, and Vice-President it was given him to look into every nook and corner of national government. Even as a Deputy Sheriff in the utter West it may safely be assumed that he was learning. Also his travels had been wide, and he knew from practical touch and observation not only Europe, but every phase of American existence. He had wandered East and West and North and South, and ate and drank and talked and slept with the peoples of those regions. He knew what they felt and thought and desired; he could gauge their needs, anticipate their drift of sentiment.

6636-C

Mr. Roosevelt intended the Panama Canal to be the great work of his regime. With all the power in his hands—and no one has measured the power of a President—he pushed the Panama business to its conclusion. By this or that, he meant to split the Isthmus with that Canal. American ships should translate themselves from one ocean to the other without troubling Cape Horn; upon that marine miracle he stood resolved. And it was likewise current that, as demanded by a long-ago Secretary of State, now dead and under the grass-roots, he was determined that both banks of the Canal should be part of the coast line of this country. Such decision was native to and in keeping with the Roosevelt character, which is American; and its carrying out by no means inconsistent with Roosevelt tastes, which never fail to favor boldness.

The propriety of the Canal, no one American—save the trans-Continental railways—was ever heard to deny. But to the last crowned head of them, every European ruler, and even the elected one of France had been opposed. They believed with Sir Walter Raleigh that he who held the Isthmus of Darien held the keys to the world, and were solicitous that no such lockopener should hang at the girdle of America.

It was well for the world while Mr. Roosevelt abode in Washington. He was not duped abroad or deluded at home. The government was neither a plutocracy nor a mobocracy, but a democracy, while he prevailed. He was the friend of Capital, the friend of Labor, the fool and tool of neither. It was he who said that during his stay the door of the White House should yield as easily to the touch of Labor as to the touch of Capital, but no easier.

During those years of on-coming towards a Presidency, Mr. Roosevelt was not morally or mentally going backward or standing still. He ripened and rounded, and grew in wisdom as he grew in politics. With experience his prudence increased, while his courage was not diminished. Over all and beyond all, towered his indomitable honesty. He is a big man—big for the country, big for mankind. Whole peoples respect him, kings are jealous of his fame. To-day, to that Fate which waits ever at the elbow of time, the nation may say:

"Bring on the Hour; here stands the Man!"

Alfred Henry Lewis

EDITH KERMIT CAROW ROOSEVELT

Edith Kermit Carow, the playmate of her husband in childhood and "perfect comrade" since their marriage in 1886, transformed the White House into an ideal American home. She was a model housekeeper, and in spite of the exactions of time and duties, tuned her household in perfect accord amid the unusual stir of young life there. She was splendidly equipped for her arduous task by her delightful charm of manner, tact, and an unusual ability to connect names, faces and incidents. She is endowed with rare good sense, to which, combined with many winning attributes and accomplishments, she owes her remarkable social success. She has a charming ally in her step-daughter, Miss Alice Lee Roosevelt, later, Mrs. Nicholas Longworth, a typical "out-of-doors" American girl, who shares with Mrs. Roosevelt's five children a mother's full-hearted devotion.

THEODORE ROOSEVELT

THEODORE ROOSEVELT, the twenty-sixth President of the United States, was born in the city of New York, October 27, 1858. His ancestors on the paternal side were of an old Dutch family, and on the maternal side, of Scotch-Irish descent. His early education was received under private tuition. He was graduated from Harvard College in 1880, and spent the following year in study and travel. From 1882 to 1884 he was a member of the Assembly of the State of New York as an independent Republican, and gained a wide reputation for his work for political reform, particularly in the field of the civil service. In 1884 he was chairman of the New York delegation to the National Republican Convention, and two years later was an unsuccessful candidate as an independent Republican for the office of Mayor of New York. He was made a member of the National Civil Service Commission by President Harrison in 1889, and served as president of the board until May, 1895, when he resigned to become president of the board of Police Commissioners of the city of New York. In 1897 he was made Assistant Secretary of the Navy by President McKinley, but on the breaking out of the Spanish-American War, in 1898, he resigned and organized the First United States Volunteer Regiment of Cavalry, popularly known as the "Rough Riders," of which he was made lieutenant-colonel. He was attached to the army of General Shafter, for the invasion of Cuba, and participated in every engagement preceding the fall of Santiago. He won distinction at the Battle of San Juan Hill, on July 1, 1898, and was promoted to the rank of colonel on July 11, for conspicuous bravery in action. He received the nomination for governor of New York on the Republican ticket, September 27, 1898, and was elected by a large plurality. At the Republican National Convention held in Philadelphia, in June, 1900, he was nominated for Vice-President of the United States, William McKinley being the candidate for President, and was elected. The shooting of President McKinley on September 6, 1901, proved fatal on September 14 following, and the Vice-President took the oath of President before Judge John R. Hazel, at Buffalo, N. Y., on that day. He was nominated for President of the United States by the Republican National Convention which met at Chicago, June 21, 1904, and was elected. Some of the important achievements of President Roosevelt during his administrations were: the settlement by arbitration of the Anthracite Coal Strike, in 1902; the reorganization of the Army and the National Guard; the recognition of the Republic of Panama; the negotiation of a treaty with the Republic of Panama for the building of the Panama Canal; and the restoration of peace between Russia and Japan, consummated by the Treaty of Portsmouth. During his administrations President Roosevelt has made speaking tours which have included every State and Territory in the Union, and in his speeches he has been an earnest advocate of an adequate navy; the protection of the forests of the country; the extension of irrigation; and the enlargement of the powers of the Federal Government in controlling interstate commerce.

VICE-PRESIDENT ROOSEVELT'S INAUGURAL ADDRESS AS VICE-PRESIDENT.

THE history of free government is in large part the history of those representative legislative bodies in which, from the earliest times, free government has found its loftiest expression. They must ever hold a peculiar and exalted position in the record which tells how the great nations of the world have endeavored to achieve and preserve orderly freedom. No man can render to his fellows greater service than is rendered by him who, with fearlessness and honesty, with sanity and disinterestedness, does his life work as a member of such a body. Especially is this the case when the legislature in which the service is rendered is a vital part in the governmental machinery of one of those world powers to whose hands, in the course of the ages, is intrusted a leading part in shaping the destinies of mankind. For weal or for woe, for good or for evil, this is true of our own mighty nation. Great privileges and great powers are ours, and heavy are the responsibilities that go with these privileges and these powers. Accordingly as we do well or ill, so shall mankind in the future be raised or cast down. We belong to a young nation, already of giant strength, yet whose political strength is but a forecast of the power that is to come. We stand supreme in a continent, in a hemisphere. East and west we look across the two great oceans toward the larger world life in which, whether we will or not, we must take an ever-increasing share. And as, keen-eyed, we gaze into the coming years, duties, new and old, rise thick and fast to confront us from within and from without. There is every reason why we should face these duties with a sober appreciation alike of their importance and of their difficulty. But there is also every reason for facing them with high-hearted resolution and eager and confident faith in our capacity to do them aright. A great work lies already to the hand of this generation; it should count itself happy, indeed, that to it is given the privilege of doing such a work. A leading part therein must be taken by this the august and powerful legislative body over which I have been called upon to, preside. Most deeply do I appreciate the privilege of my position; for high, indeed, is the honor of presiding over the American Senate at the outset of the twentieth century.

MARCH 4, 1901.

PROCLAMATION

Announcing the assassination of President McKinley.

BY THE PRESIDENT OF THE UNITED STATES OF AMERICA.

A PROCLAMATION.

To the people of the United States:

A terrible bereavement has befallen our people. The President of the United States has been struck down; a crime not only against the Chief Magistrate, but against every law-abiding and liberty-loving citizen.

President McKinley crowned a life of largest love for his fellow men, of earnest endeavor for their welfare, by a death of Christian fortitude; and both the way in which he lived his life and the way in which, in the supreme hour of trial, he met his death will remain forever a precious heritage of our people.

It is meet that we as a nation express our abiding love and reverence for his life, our deep sorrow for his untimely death.

Now, therefore, I, THEODORE ROOSEVELT, President of the United States of America, do appoint Thursday next, September 19, the day in which the body of the dead President will be laid in its last earthly resting place, as a day of mourning and prayer throughout the United States. I earnestly recommend all the people to assemble on that day in their respective places of divine worship, there to bow down in submission to the will of Almighty God, and to pay out of full hearts the homage of love and reverence to the memory of the great and good President, whose death has so sorely smitten the nation.

In witness whereof I have hereunto set my hand and caused the seal of the United States to be affixed.

Done at the city of Washington, the fourteenth day of [SEAL.] September, A. D. 1901, and of the Independence of the United States the one hundred and twenty-sixth.

THEODORE ROOSEVELT.

By the President:
JOHN HAY,
    Secretary of State.

THANKSGIVING PROCLAMATION

By the President of the United States of America.

A PROCLAMATION.

The season is nigh when, according to the time-hallowed custom of our people, the President appoints a day as the especial occasion for praise and thanksgiving to God.

This Thanksgiving finds the people still bowed with sorrow for the death of a great and good President. We mourn President McKinley because we so loved and honored him; and the manner of his death should awaken in the breasts of our people a keen anxiety for the country, and at the same time a resolute purpose not to be driven by any calamity from the path of strong, orderly, popular liberty which as a nation we have thus far safely trod.

Yet in spite of this great disaster, it is nevertheless true that no people on earth have such abundant cause for thanksgiving as we have. The past year in particular has been one of peace and plenty. We have prospered in things material and have been able to work for our own uplifting in things intellectual and spiritual. Let us remember that, as much has been given us, much will be expected from us; and that true homage comes from the heart as well as from the lips and shows itself in deeds. We can best prove our thankfulness to the Almighty by the way in which on this earth and at this time each of us does his duty to his fellow men.

Now, therefore, I, Theodore Roosevelt, President of the United States, do hereby designate as a day of general thanksgiving Thursday, the 28th of this present November, and do recommend that throughout the land the people cease from their wonted occupations, and at their several homes and places of worship reverently thank the Giver of all good for the countless blessings of our national life

In witness whereof I have hereunto set my hand and caused the seal of the United States to be affixed.

Done at the city of Washington this second day of November, A. D. 1901, and of the Independence of the United States the one hundred and twenty-sixth.

[SEAL.]

THEODORE ROOSEVELT.

By the President:

John Hay,

Secretary of State.

The Federal courts should be given jurisdiction over any man who kills or attempts to kill the President or any man who by the Constitution or by law is in line of succession for the Presidency, while the punishment for an unsuccessful attempt should be proportioned to the enormity of the offence against our institutions.—*From Roosevelt's first message to Congress following the assassination of President McKinley.*

FIRST ANNUAL MESSAGE

WHITE HOUSE, *December 3, 1901.*

To the Senate and House of Representatives:

The Congress assembles this year under the shadow of a great calamity. On the sixth of September, President McKinley was shot by an anarchist while attending the Pan-American Exposition at Buffalo, and died in that city on the fourteenth of that month.

Of the last seven elected Presidents, he is the third who has been murdered, and the bare recital of this fact is sufficient to justify grave alarm among all loyal American citizens. Moreover, the circumstances of this, the third assassination of an American President, have a peculiarly sinister significance. Both President Lincoln and President Garfield were killed by assassins of types unfortunately not uncommon in history; President Lincoln falling a victim to the terrible passions aroused by four years of civil war, and President Garfield to the revengeful vanity of a disappointed office-seeker. President McKinley was killed by an utterly depraved criminal belonging to that body of criminals who object to all governments, good and bad alike, who are against any form of popular liberty if it is guaranteed by even the most just and liberal laws, and who are as hostile to the upright exponent of a free people's sober will as to the tyrannical and irresponsible despot.

It is not too much to say that at the time of President McKinley's death he was the most widely loved man in all the United States; while we have never had any public man of his position who has been so wholly free from the bitter animosities incident to public life. His political opponents were the first to bear the heartiest and most generous tribute to the broad kindliness of nature, the sweetness and gentleness of character which so endeared him to his close associates. To a standard of lofty integrity in public life he united the tender affections and home virtues which are all-important in the make-up of national character. A gallant soldier in the great war for the Union, he also shone as an example to all our people because of his conduct in the most sacred and intimate of home relations. There could be no personal hatred of him, for he never acted with aught but consideration for the welfare of others. No one could fail to respect him who knew him in public or private life. The defenders of those murderous criminals who seek to excuse their criminality by asserting that it is exercised for political ends, inveigh against wealth and irresponsible power. But for this assassination even this base apology cannot be urged.

President McKinley was a man of moderate means, a man whose stock sprang from the sturdy tillers of the soil, who had himself belonged among the wage-workers, who had entered the Army as a private soldier. Wealth was not struck at when the President was assassinated, but the honest toil which is content with moderate gains after a lifetime of unremitting labor, largely in the service of the public. Still less was power struck at in the sense that power is irresponsible or centered in the hands of any one individual. The blow was not aimed at tyranny or wealth. It was aimed at one of the strongest champions the wage-worker has ever had; at one of the most faithful representatives of the system of public rights and representative government who has ever risen to public office. President McKinley filled that political office for which the entire people vote, and no President — not even Lincoln himself — was ever more earnestly anxious to represent the well thought-out wishes of the people; his one anxiety in every crisis was to keep in closest touch with the people — to find out what they thought and to endeavor to give expression to their thought, after having endeavored to guide that thought aright. He had just been reelected to the Presidency because the majority of our citizens, the majority of our farmers and wage-workers, believed that he had faithfully upheld their interests for four years. They felt themselves in close and intimate touch with him. They felt that he represented so well and so honorably all their ideals and aspirations that they wished him to continue for another four years to represent them.

And this was the man at whom the assassin struck! That there might be nothing lacking to complete the Judas-like infamy of his act, he took advantage of an occasion when the President was meeting the people generally; and advancing as if to take the hand out-stretched to him in kindly and brotherly fellowship, he turned the noble and generous confidence of the victim into an opportunity to strike the fatal blow. There is no baser deed in all the annals of crime.

The shock, the grief of the country, are bitter in the minds of all who saw the dark days, while the President yet hovered between life and death. At last the light was stilled in the kindly eyes and the breath went from the lips that even in mortal agony uttered no words save of forgiveness to his murderer, of love for his friends, and of unfaltering trust in the will of the Most High. Such a death, crowning the glory of such a life, leaves us with infinite sorrow, but with such pride in what he had accomplished and in his own personal character, that we feel the blow not as struck at him, but as struck at the Nation

We mourn a good and great President who is dead; but while we mourn we are lifted up by the splendid achievements of his life and the grand heroism with which he met his death.

When we turn from the man to the Nation, the harm done is so great as to excite our gravest apprehensions and to demand our wisest and most resolute action. This criminal was a professed anarchist, inflamed by the teachings of professed anarchists, and probably also by the reckless utterances of those who, on the stump and in the public press, appeal to the dark and evil spirits of malice and greed, envy and sullen hatred. The wind is sowed by the men who preach such doctrines, and they cannot escape their share of responsibility for the whirlwind that is reaped. This applies alike to the deliberate demagogue, to the exploiter of sensationalism, and to the crude and foolish visionary who, for whatever reason, apologizes for crime or excites aimless discontent.

The blow was aimed not at this President, but at all Presidents; at every symbol of government. President McKinley was as emphatically the embodiment of the popular will of the Nation expressed through the forms of law as a New England town meeting is in similar fashion the embodiment of the law-abiding purpose and practice of the people of the town. On no conceivable theory could the murder of the President be accepted as due to protest against " inequalities in the social order," save as the murder of all the freemen engaged in a town meeting could be accepted as a protest against that social inequality which puts a malefactor in jail. Anarchy is no more an expression of " social discontent " than picking pockets or wife-beating.

The anarchist, and especially the anarchist in the United States, is merely one type of criminal, more dangerous than any other because he represents the same depravity in a greater degree. The man who advocates anarchy directly or indirectly, in any shape or fashion, or the man who apologizes for anarchists and their deeds, makes himself morally accessory to murder before the fact. The anarchist is a criminal whose perverted instincts lead him to prefer confusion and chaos to the most beneficent form of social order. His protest of concern for workingmen is outrageous in its impudent falsity; for if the political institutions of this country do not afford opportunity to every honest and intelligent son of toil, then the door of hope is forever closed against him. The anarchist is everywhere not merely the enemy of system and of progress, but the deadly foe of liberty. If ever anarchy is triumphant, its triumph will last for but one red moment, to be succeeded for ages by the gloomy night of despotism.

For the anarchist himself, whether he preaches or practices his doctrines, we need not have one particle more concern than for any ordinary murderer. He is not the victim of social or political injustice. There are no wrongs to remedy in his case. The cause of his criminality is to be found in his own evil passions and in the evil conduct of those who urge him on, not in any failure by others or by the State to do justice to him or his. He is a malefactor and nothing else. He is in no sense, in no shape or way, a " product of social conditions," save as a highwayman is " produced" by the fact than an unarmed man happens to have a purse. It is a travesty upon the great and holy names of liberty and freedom to permit them to be invoked in such a cause. No man or body of men preaching anarchistic doctrines should be allowed at large any more than if preaching the murder of some specified private individual. Anarchistic speeches, writings, and meetings are essentially seditious and treasonable.

I earnestly recommend to the Congress that in the exercise of its wise discretion it should take into consideration the coming to this country of anarchists or persons professing principles hostile to all government and justifying the murder of those placed in authority. Such individuals as those who not long ago gathered in open meeting to glorify the murder of King Humbert of Italy perpetrate a crime, and the law should ensure their rigorous punishment. They and those like them should be kept out of this country; and if found here they should be promptly deported to the country whence they came; and far-reaching provision should be made for the punishment of those who stay. No matter calls more urgently for the wisest thought of the Congress.

The Federal courts should be given jurisdiction over any man who kills or attempts to kill the President or any man who by the Constitution or by law is in line of succession for the Presidency, while the punishment for an unsuccessful attempt should be proportioned to the enormity of the offense against our institutions.

Anarchy is a crime against the whole human race; and all mankind should band against the anarchist. His crime should be made an offense against the law of nations, like piracy and that form of man-stealing known as the slave trade; for it is of far blacker infamy than either. It should be so declared by treaties among all civilized powers. Such treaties would give to the Federal Government the power of dealing with the crime.

A grim commentary upon the folly of the anarchist position was afforded by the attitude of the law toward this very criminal who had just taken the life of the President. The people would have torn him limb from limb if it had not been that the law he defied was at once invoked in his behalf. So far from his deed being committed on behalf of the people against the Government, the Government was obliged at once to exert its full police power to save him from instant death at the hands of the people. Moreover, his deed worked not the slightest dislocation in our governmental system, and the danger of a recurrence of such deeds, no matter how great it might grow, would work only in the direction of strengthening and giving harshness to the forces of order. No man will ever be restrained from becoming President by any fear as to his personal safety. If the risk to the President's life became great, it would mean that the office would more and more come to be filled by men of a spirit which would make them resolute and merciless in dealing with every friend of disorder. This great country will not fall into anarchy, and if anarchists should ever become a serious menace to its institutions, they would not merely be stamped out, but would involve in their own ruin every active or passive sympathizer with their doctrines. The American people are slow to wrath, but when their wrath is once kindled it burns like a consuming flame.

During the last five years business confidence has been restored, and the nation is to be congratulated because of its present abounding prosperity. Such prosperity can never be created by law alone, although it is easy enough to destroy it by mischievous laws. If the hand of the Lord is heavy upon any country, if flood or drought comes, human wisdom is powerless to avert the calamity. Moreover, no law can guard us against the consequences of our own folly. The men who are idle or credulous, the men who seek gains not by genuine work with head or hand but by gambling in any form, are always a source of menace not only to themselves but to others. If the business world loses its head, it loses what legislation cannot supply. Fundamentally the welfare of each citizen, and therefore the welfare of the aggregate of citizens which makes the nation, must rest upon individual thrift and energy, resolution, and intelligence. Nothing can take the place of this individual capacity; but wise legislation and honest and intelligent administration can give it the fullest scope, the largest opportunity to work to good effect.

The tremendous and highly complex industrial development which went on with ever accelerated rapidity during the latter half of the nineteenth century brings us face to face, at the beginning of the twentieth, with very serious social problems. The old laws, and the old customs which had almost the binding force of law, were once quite sufficient to regulate the accumulation and distribution of wealth. Since the industrial changes which have so enormously increased the productive power of mankind, they are no longer sufficient.

The growth of cities has gone on beyond comparison faster than the growth of the country, and the upbuilding of the great industrial centers has meant a startling increase, not merely in the aggregate of wealth, but in the number of very large individual, and especially of very large corporate, fortunes. The creation of these great corporate fortunes has not been due to the tariff nor to any other governmental action, but to natural causes in the business world, operating in other countries as they operate in our own.

The process has aroused much antagonism, a great part of which is wholly without warrant. It is not true that as the rich have grown richer the poor have grown poorer. On the contrary, never before has the average man, the wage-worker, the farmer, the small trader, been so well off as in this country and at the present time. There have been abuses connected with the accumulation of wealth; yet it remains true that a fortune accumulated in legitimate business can be accumulated by the person specially benefited only on condition of conferring immense incidental benefits upon others. Successful enterprise, of the type which benefits all mankind, can only exist if the conditions are such as to offer great prizes as the rewards of success.

The captains of industry who have driven the railway systems across this continent, who have built up our commerce, who have developed our manufactures, have on the whole done great good to our people. Without them the material development of which we are so justly proud could never have taken place. Moreover, we should recognize the immense importance of this material development of leaving as unhampered as is compatible with the public good the strong and forceful men upon whom the success of business operations inevitably rests. The slightest study of business conditions will satisfy anyone capable of forming a judgment that the personal equation is the most important factor in a business operation; that the business ability of the man at the head of any business concern, big or little, is usually the factor which fixes the gulf between striking success and hopeless failure.

An additional reason for caution in dealing with corporations is to be found in the international commercial conditions of to-day. The same business conditions which have produced the great aggregations of corporate and individual wealth have made them very potent factors in international commercial competition. Business concerns which have the largest means at their disposal and are managed by the ablest men are naturally those which take the lead in the strife for commercial supremacy among the nations of the world. America has only just begun to assume that commanding position in the international business world which we believe will more and more be hers. It is of the utmost importance that this position be not jeoparded, especially at a time when the overflowing abundance of our own natural resources and the skill, business energy, and mechanical aptitude of our people make foreign markets essential. Under such conditions it would be most unwise to cramp or to fetter the youthful strength of our Nation.

Moreover, it can not too often be pointed out that to strike with ignorant violence at the interests of one set of men almost inevitably endangers the interests of all. The fundamental rule in our national life — the rule which underlies all others — is that, on the whole, and in the long run, we shall go up or down together. There are exceptions; and in times of prosperity some will prosper far more, and in times of adversity, some will suffer far more, than others; but speaking generally, a period of good times means that all share more or less in them, and in a period of hard times all feel the stress to a greater or less degree. It surely ought not to be necessary to enter into any proof of this statement; the memory of the lean years which began in 1893 is still vivid, and we can contrast them with the conditions in this very year which is now closing. Disaster to great business enterprises can never have its effects limited to the men at the top. It spreads throughout, and while it is bad for everybody, it is worst for those farthest down. The capitalist may be shorn of his luxuries; but the wage-worker may be deprived of even bare necessities.

The mechanism of modern business is so delicate that extreme care must be taken not to interfere with it in a spirit of rashness or ignorance. Many of those who have made it their vocation to denounce the great industrial combinations which are popularly, although with technical inaccuracy, known as "trusts," appeal especially to hatred and fear. These are precisely the two emotions, particularly when combined with ignorance, which unfit men for the exercise of cool and steady judgment. In facing new industrial conditions, the whole history of the world shows that legislation will generally be both unwise and ineffective unless undertaken after calm inquiry and with sober self-restraint. Much of the legislation directed at the trusts would have been exceedingly mischievous had it not also been entirely ineffective. In accordance with a well-known sociological law, the ignorant or reckless agitator has been the really effective friend of the evils which he has been nominally opposing. In dealing with business interests, for the Government to undertake by crude and ill-considered legislation to do what may turn out to be bad, would be to incur the risk of such far-reaching national disaster that it would be preferable to undertake nothing at all. The men who demand the impossible or the undesirable serve as the allies of the forces with which they are nominally at war, for they hamper those who would endeavor to find out in rational fashion what the wrongs really are and to what extent and in what manner it is practicable to apply remedies.

All this is true; and yet it is also true that there are real and grave evils, one of the chief being over-capitalization because of its many baleful consequences; and a resolute and practical effort must be made to correct these evils.

There is a widespread conviction in the minds of the American people that the great corporations known as trusts are in certain of their features and tendencies hurtful to the general welfare. This springs from no spirit of envy or uncharitableness, nor lack of pride in the great industrial achievements that have placed this country at the head of the nations struggling for commercial supremacy. It does not rest upon a lack of intelligent appreciation of the necessity of meeting changing and changed conditions of trade with new methods, nor upon ignorance of the fact that combination of capital in the effort to accomplish great things is necessary when the world's progress demands that great things be done. It is based upon sincere conviction that combination and concentration should be, not prohibited, but supervised and within reasonable limits controlled; and in my judgment this conviction is right.

It is no limitation upon property rights or freedom of contract to require that when men receive from Government the privilege of doing business under corporate form, which frees them from individual responsibility, and enables them to call into their enterprises the capital of the public, they shall do so upon absolutely truthful representations as to the value of the property in which the capital is to be invested. Corporations engaged in interstate commerce should be regulated if they are found to exercise a license working to the public injury. It should be as much the aim of those who seek for social betterment to rid the business world of crimes of cunning as to rid the entire body politic of crimes of violence. Great corporations exist only because they are created and safeguarded by our institutions; and it is therefore our right and our duty to see that they work in harmony with these institutions.

The first essential in determining how to deal with the great industrial combinations is knowledge of the facts — publicity. In the interest of the public, the Government should have the right to inspect and examine the workings of the great corporations engaged in interstate business. Publicity is the only sure remedy which we can now invoke. What further remedies are needed in the way of governmental regulation, or taxation, can only be determined after publicity has been obtained, by process of law, and in the course of administration. The first requisite is knowledge, full and complete — knowledge which may be made public to the world.

Artificial bodies, such as corporations and joint stock or other associations, depending upon any statutory law for their existence or privileges, should be subject to proper governmental supervision, and full and accurate information as to their operations should be made public regularly at reasonable intervals.

The large corporations, commonly called trusts, though organized in one State, always do business in many States, often doing very little business in the State where they are incorporated. There is utter lack of uniformity in the State laws about them; and as no State has any exclusive interest in or power over their acts, it has in practice proved impossible to get adequate regulation through State action. Therefore, in the interest of the whole people, the Nation should, without interfering with the power of the States in the matter itself, also assume power of supervision and regulation over all corporations doing an interstate business. This is especially true where the corporation derives a portion of its wealth from the existence of some monopolistic element or tendency in its business. There would be no hardship in such supervision; banks are subject to it, and in their case it is now accepted as a simple matter of course. Indeed, it is probable that supervision of corporations by the National Government need not go so far as is now the case with the supervision exercised over them by so conservative a State as Massachusetts, in order to produce excellent results.

When the Constitution was adopted, at the end of the eighteenth century, no human wisdom could foretell the sweeping changes, alike in industrial and political conditions, which were to take place by the beginning of the twentieth century. At that time it was accepted as a matter of course that the several States were the proper authorities to regulate, so far as was then necessary, the comparatively insignificant and strictly localized corporate bodies of the day. The conditions are now wholly different and wholly different action is called for. I believe that a law can be framed which will enable the National Government to exercise control along the lines above indicated; profiting by the experience gained through the passage and administration of the Interstate-Commerce Act. If, however, the judgment of the Congress is that it lacks the constitutional power to pass such an act, then a constitutional amendment should be submitted to confer the power.

There should be created a Cabinet officer, to be known as Secretary of Commerce and Industries, as provided in the bill introduced at the last session of the Congress. It should be his province to deal with commerce in its broadest sense; including among many other things whatever concerns labor and all matters affecting the great business corporations and our merchant marine.

The course proposed is one phase of what should be a comprehensive and far-reaching scheme of constructive statesmanship for the purpose of broadening our markets, securing our business interests on a safe basis, and making firm our new position in the international industrial world; while scrupulously safeguarding the rights of wage-worker and capitalist, of investor and private citizen, so as to secure equity as between man and man in this Republic.

With the sole exception of the farming interest, no one matter is of such vital moment to our whole people as the welfare of the wage-workers. If the farmer and the wage-worker are well off, it is absolutely certain that all others will be well off too. It is therefore a matter for hearty congratulation that on the whole wages are higher to-day in the United States than ever before in our history, and far higher than in any other country. The standard of living is also higher than ever before. Every effort of legislator and administrator should be bent to secure the permanency of this condition of things and its improvement wherever possible. Not only must our labor be protected by the tariff, but it should also be protected so far as it is possible from the presence in this country of any laborers brought over by contract.

or of those who, coming freely, yet represent a standard of living so depressed that they can undersell our men in the labor market and drag them to a lower level. I regard it as necessary, with this end in view, to re-enact immediately the law excluding Chinese laborers and to strengthen it wherever necessary in order to make its enforcement entirely effective.

The National Government should demand the highest quality of service from its employees; and in return it should be a good employer. If possible legislation should be passed, in connection with the Interstate Commerce Law, which will render effective the efforts of different States to do away with the competition of convict contract labor in the open labor market. So far as practicable under the conditions of Government work, provision should be made to render the enforcement of the eight-hour law easy and certain. In all industries carried on directly or indirectly for the United States Government women and children should be protected from excessive hours of labor, from night work, and from work under unsanitary conditions. The Government should provide in its contracts that all work should be done under "fair" conditions, and in addition to setting a high standard should uphold it by proper inspection, extending if necessary to the subcontractors. The Government should forbid all night work for women and children, as well as excessive overtime. For the District of Columbia a good factory law should be passed; and, as a powerful indirect aid to such laws, provision should be made to turn the inhabited alleys, the existence of which is a reproach to our Capital city, into minor streets, where the inhabitants can live under conditions favorable to health and morals.

American wage-workers work with their heads as well as their hands. Moreover, they take a keen pride in what they are doing; so that, independent of the reward, they wish to turn out a perfect job. This is the great secret of our success in competition with the labor of foreign countries.

The most vital problem with which this country, and for that matter he whole civilized world, has to deal, is the problem which has for one side the betterment of social conditions, moral and physical, in large cities, and for another side the effort to deal with that tangle of far-reaching questions which we group together when we speak of "labor." The chief factor in the success of each man — wage-worker, farmer, and capitalist alike — must ever be the sum total of his own individual qualities and abilities. Second only to this comes the power of acting in combination or association with others. Very great good has been and will be accomplished by associations or unions of wage-workers, when managed with forethought, and when they combine insistence upon their own rights with law-abiding respect for the rights of others. The display of these qualities in such bodies is a duty to the nation no less than to the associations themselves. Finally, there must also in many cases be action by the Government in order to safeguard the rights and interests of all. Under our Constitution there is much more scope for such action by the State and the municipality than by the nation. But on points such as those touched on above the National Government can act.

When all is said and done, the rule of brotherhood remains as the indispensable prerequisite to success in the kind of national life for which we strive. Each man must work for himself, and unless he so works no outside help can avail him; but each man must remember also that he is indeed his brother's keeper, and that while no man who refuses to walk can be carried with advantage to himself or anyone else, yet that each at times stumbles or halts, that each at times needs to have the helping hand outstretched to him. To be permanently effective, aid must always take the form of helping a man to help himself; and we can all best help ourselves by joining together in the work that is of common interest to all.

Our present immigration laws are unsatisfactory. We need every honest and efficient immigrant fitted to become an American citizen, every immigrant who comes here to stay, who brings here a strong body, a stout heart, a good head, and a resolute purpose to do his duty well in every way and to bring up his children as law-abiding and God-fearing members of the community. But there should be a comprehensive law enacted with the object of working a threefold improvement over our present system. First, we should aim to exclude absolutely not only all persons who are known to be believers in anarchistic principles or members of anarchistic societies, but also all persons who are of a low moral tendency or of unsavory reputation. This means that we should require a more thorough system of inspection abroad and a more rigid system of examination at our immigration ports, the former being especially necessary.

The second object of a proper immigration law ought to be to secure by a careful and not merely perfunctory educational test some intelligent capacity to appreciate American institutions and act sanely as American citizens. This would not keep out all anarchists, for many of them belong to the intelligent criminal class. But it would do what is also in point, that is, tend to decrease the sum of ignorance, so potent in producing the envy, suspicion, malignant passion, and hatred of order, out of which anarchistic sentiment inevitably springs. Finally, all persons should be excluded who are below a certain standard of economic fitness to enter our industrial field as competitors with American labor. There should be proper proof of personal capacity to earn an American living and enough money to insure a decent start under American conditions. This would stop the influx of cheap labor, and the resulting competition which gives rise to so much of bitterness in

American industrial life; and it would dry up the springs of the pestilential social conditions in our great cities, where anarchistic organizations have their greatest possibility of growth.

Both the educational and economic tests in a wise immigration law should be designed to protect and elevate the general body politic and social. A very close supervision should be exercised over the steamship companies which mainly bring over the immigrants, and they should be held to a strict accountability for any infraction of the law.

There is general acquiescence in our present tariff system as a national policy. The first requisite to our prosperity is the continuity and stability of this economic policy. Nothing could be more unwise than to disturb the business interests of the country by any general tariff change at this time. Doubt, apprehension, uncertainty are exactly what we most wish to avoid in the interest of our commercial and material well-being. Our experience in the past has shown that sweeping revisions of the tariff are apt to produce conditions closely approaching panic in the business world. Yet it is not only possible, but eminently desirable, to combine with the stability of our economic system a supplementary system of reciprocal benefit and obligation with other nations. Such reciprocity is an incident and result of the firm establishment and preservation of our present economic policy. It was specially provided for in the present tariff law.

Reciprocity must be treated as the handmaiden of protection. Our first duty is to see that the protection granted by the tariff in every case where it is needed is maintained, and that reciprocity be sought for so far as it can safely be done without injury to our home industries. Just how far this is must be determined according to the individual case, remembering always that every application of our tariff policy to meet our shifting national needs must be conditioned upon the cardinal fact that the duties must never be reduced below the point that will cover the difference between the labor cost here and abroad. The well-being of the wage-worker is a prime consideration of our entire policy of economic legislation.

Subject to this proviso of the proper protection necessary to our industrial well-being at home, the principle of reciprocity must command our hearty support. The phenomenal growth of our export trade emphasizes the urgency of the need for wider markets and for a liberal policy in dealing with foreign nations. Whatever is merely petty and vexatious in the way of trade restrictions should be avoided. The customers to whom we dispose of our surplus products in the long run, directly or indirectly, purchase those surplus products by giving us something in return. Their ability to purchase our products should as far as possible be secured by so arranging our tariff as to enable us to take from them those products which we can use without harm to our own industries and labor, or the use of which will be of marked benefit to us.

It is most important that we should maintain the high level of our present prosperity. We have now reached the point in the development of our interests where we are not only able to supply our own markets but to produce a constantly growing surplus for which we must find markets abroad. To secure these markets we can utilize existing duties in any case where they are no longer needed for the purpose of protection, or in any case where the article is not produced here and the duty is no longer necessary for revenue, as giving us something to offer in exchange for what we ask. The cordial relations with other nations which are so desirable will naturally be promoted by the course thus required by our own interests.

The natural line of development for a policy of reciprocity will be in connection with those of our productions which no longer require all of the support once needed to establish them upon a sound basis, and with those others where either because of natural or of economic causes we are beyond the reach of successful competition.

I ask the attention of the Senate to the reciprocity treaties laid before it by my predecessor.

The condition of the American merchant marine is such as to call for immediate remedial action by the Congress. It is discreditable to us as a Nation that our merchant marine should be utterly insignificant in comparison to that of other nations which we overtop in other forms of business. We should not longer submit to conditions under which only a trifling portion of our great commerce is carried in our own ships. To remedy this state of things would not merely serve to build up our shipping interests, but it would also result in benefit to all who are interested in the permanent establishment of a wider market for American products, and would provide an auxiliary force for the Navy. Ships work for their own countries just as railroads work for their terminal points. Shipping lines, if established to the principal countries with which we have dealings, would be of political as well as commercial benefit. From every standpoint it is unwise for the United States to continue to rely upon the ships of competing nations for the distribution of our goods. It should be made advantageous to carry American goods in American-built ships.

At present American shipping is under certain great disadvantages when put in competition with the shipping of foreign countries. Many of the fast foreign steamships, at a speed of fourteen knots or above, are subsidized; and all our ships, sailing vessels and steamers alike, cargo carriers of slow speed and mail carriers of high speed, have to meet the fact that the original cost of building American ships is greater than is the case abroad; that the wages paid American officers and seamen are very much higher than those paid the officers and sea-men of foreign competing countries; and that the standard of living on our ships is far superior to the standard of living on the ships of our commercial rivals.

Our Government should take such action as will remedy these inequalities. The American merchant marine should be restored to the ocean.

The Act of March 14, 1900, intended unequivocally to establish gold as the standard money and to maintain at a parity therewith all forms of money medium in use with us, has been shown to be timely and judicious. The price of our Government bonds in the world's market, when compared with the price of similar obligations issued by other nations, is a flattering tribute to our public credit. This condition it is evidently desirable to maintain.

In many respects the National Banking Law furnishes sufficient liberty for the proper exercise of the banking function; but there seems to be need of better safeguards against the deranging influence of commercial crises and financial panics. Moreover, the currency of the country should be made responsive to the demands of our domestic trade and commerce.

The collections from duties on imports and internal taxes continue to exceed the ordinary expenditures of the Government, thanks mainly to the reduced army expenditures. The utmost care should be taken not to reduce the revenues so that there will be any possibility of a deficit; but, after providing against any such contingency, means should be adopted which will bring the revenues more nearly within the limit of our actual needs. In his report to the Congress the Secretary of the Treasury considers all these questions at length, and I ask your attention to the report and recommendations.

I call special attention to the need of strict economy in expenditures. The fact that our national needs forbid us to be niggardly in providing whatever is actually necessary to our well-being, should make us doubly careful to husband our national resources, as each of us husbands his private resources, by scrupulous avoidance of anything like wasteful or reckless expenditure. Only by avoidance of spending money on what is needless or unjustifiable can we legitimately keep our income to the point required to meet our needs that are genuine.

In 1887 a measure was enacted for the regulation of interstate railways, commonly known as the Interstate Commerce Act. The cardinal provisions of that act were that railway rates should be just and reasonable and that all shippers, localities, and commodities should be accorded equal treatment. A commission was created and endowed with what were supposed to be the necessary powers to execute the provisions of this act.

That law was largely an experiment. Experience has shown the wisdom of its purposes, but has also shown, possibly that some of its requirements are wrong, certainly that the means devised for the enforcement of its provisions are defective. Those who complain of the management of the railways allege that established rates are not maintained; that rebates and similar devices are habitually resorted to; that these preferences are usually in favor of the large shipper; that they drive out of business the smaller competitor; that while many rates are too low, many others are excessive; and that gross preferences are made, affecting both localities and commodities. Upon the other hand, the railways assert that the law by its very terms tends to produce many of these illegal practices by depriving carriers of that right of concerted action which they claim is necessary to establish and maintain non-discriminating rates.

The act should be amended. The railway is a public servant. Its rates should be just to and open to all shippers alike. The Government should see to it that within its jurisdiction this is so and should provide a speedy, inexpensive, and effective remedy to that end. At the same time it must not be forgotten that our railways are the arteries through which the commercial lifeblood of this Nation flows. Nothing could be more foolish than the enactment of legislation which would unnecessarily interfere with the development and operation of these commercial agencies. The subject is one of great importance and calls for the earnest attention of the Congress.

The Department of Agriculture during the past fifteen years has steadily broadened its work on economic lines, and has accomplished results of real value in upbuilding domestic and foreign trade. It has gone into new fields until it is now in touch with all sections of our country and with two of the island groups that have lately come under our jurisdiction, whose people must look to agriculture as a livelihood. It is searching the world for grains, grasses, fruits, and vegetables specially fitted for introduction into localities in the several States and Territories where they may add materially to our resources. By scientific attention to soil survey and possible new crops, to breeding of new varieties of plants, to experimental shipments, to animal industry and applied chemistry, very practical aid has been given our farming and stock-growing interests. The products of the farm have taken an unprecedented place in our export trade during the year that has just closed.

Public opinion throughout the United States has moved steadily toward a just appreciation of the value of forests, whether planted or of natural growth. The great part played by them in the creation and maintenance of the national wealth is now more fully realized than ever before.

Wise forest protection does not mean the withdrawal of forest re sources, whether of wood, water, or grass, from contributing their full share to the welfare of the people, but, on the contrary, gives the assurance of larger and more certain supplies. The fundamental idea of forestry is the perpetuation of forests by use. Forest protection is not an end of itself; it is a means to increase and sustain the resources of our country and the industries which depend upon them. The preservation of our forests is an imperative business necessity. We have come to see clearly that whatever destroys the forest, except to make way for agriculture, threatens our well being.

The practical usefulness of the national forest reserves to the mining, grazing, irrigation, and other interests of the regions in which the reserves lie has led to a widespread demand by the people of the West for their protection and extension. The forest reserves will inevitably be of still greater use in the future than in the past. Additions should be made to them whenever practicable, and their usefulness should be increased by a thoroughly business-like management.

At present the protection of the forest reserves rests with the General Land Office, the mapping and description of their timber with the United States Geological Survey, and the preparation of plans for their conservative use with the Bureau of Forestry, which is also charged with the general advancement of practical forestry in the United States. These various functions should be united in the Bureau of Forestry, to which they properly belong. The present diffusion of responsibility is bad from every standpoint. It prevents that effective co-operation between the Government and the men who utilize the resources of the reserves, without which the interests of both must suffer. The scientific bureaus generally should be put under the Department of Agriculture. The President should have by law the power of transferring lands for use as forest reserves to the Department of Agriculture. He already has such power in the case of lands needed by the Departments of War and the Navy.

The wise administration of the forest reserves will be not less helpful to the interests which depend on water than to those which depend on wood and grass. The water supply itself depends upon the forest. In the arid region it is water, not land, which measures production. The western half of the United States would sustain a population greater than that of our whole country to-day if the waters that now run to waste were saved and used for irrigation. The forest and water problems are perhaps the most vital internal questions of the United States.

Certain of the forest reserves should also be made preserves for the wild forest creatures. All of the reserves should be better protected from fires. Many of them need special protection because of the great injury done by live stock, above all by sheep. The increase in deer, elk, and other animals in the Yellowstone Park shows what may be expected when other mountain forests are properly protected by law and properly guarded. Some of these areas have been so denuded of surface vegetation by overgrazing that the ground breeding birds, including grouse and quail, and many mammals, including deer, have been exterminated or driven away. At the same time the water-storing capacity of the surface has been decreased or destroyed, thus promoting floods in times of rain and diminishing the flow of streams between rains.

In cases where natural conditions have been restored for a few years, vegetation has again carpeted the ground, birds and deer are coming back, and hundreds of persons, especially from the immediate neighborhood, come each summer to enjoy the privilege of camping. Some at least of the forest reserves should afford perpetual protection to the native fauna and flora, safe havens of refuge to our rapidly diminishing wild animals of the larger kinds, and free camping grounds for the ever-increasing numbers of men and women who have learned to find rest, health, and recreation in the splendid forests and flower-clad meadows of our mountains. The forest reserves should be set apart forever for the use and benefit of our people as a whole and not sacrificed to the shortsighted greed of a few.

The forests are natural reservoirs. By restraining the streams in flood and replenishing them in drought they make possible the use of waters otherwise wasted. They prevent the soil from washing, and so protect the storage reservoirs from filling up with silt. Forest conservation is therefore an essential condition of water conservation.

The forests alone cannot, however, fully regulate and conserve the waters of the arid region. Great storage works are necessary to equalize the flow of streams and to save the flood waters. Their construction has been conclusively shown to be an undertaking too vast for private effort. Nor can it be best accomplished by the individual States acting alone. Far-reaching interstate problems are involved; and the resources of single States would often be inadequate. It is properly a national function, at least in some of its features. It is as right for the National Government to make the streams and rivers of the arid region useful by engineering works for water storage as to make useful the rivers and harbors of the humid region by engineering works of another kind. The storing of the floods in reservoirs at the headwaters of our rivers is but an enlargement of our present policy of river control, under which levees are built on the lower reaches of the same streams.

The Government should construct and maintain these reservoirs as it does other public works. Where their purpose is to regulate the flow of streams, the water should be turned freely into the channels in the dry season to take the same course under the same laws as the natural flow.

The reclamation of the unsettled arid public lands presents a different problem. Here it is not enough to regulate the flow of streams. The object of the Government is to dispose of the land to settlers who will build homes upon it. To accomplish this object water must be brought within their reach.

The pioneer settlers on the arid public domain chose their homes along streams from which they could themselves divert the water to reclaim their holdings. Such opportunities are practically gone. There remain, however, vast areas of public land which can be made available for homestead settlement, but only by reservoirs and main-line canals impracticable for private enterprise. These irrigation works should be built by the National Government. The lands reclaimed by them should be reserved by the Government for actual settlers, and the cost of construction should so far as possible be repaid by the land reclaimed. The distribution of the water, the division of the streams among irrigators, should be left to the settlers themselves in conformity with State laws and without interference with those laws or with vested rights. The policy of the National Government should be to aid irrigation in the several States and Territories in such manner as will enable the people in the local communities to help themselves, and as will stimulate needed reforms in the State laws and regulations governing irrigation.

The reclamation and settlement of the arid lands will enrich every portion of our country, just as the settlement of the Ohio and Mississippi valleys brought prosperity to the Atlantic States. The increased demand for manufactured articles will stimulate industrial production, while wider home markets and the trade of Asia will consume the larger food supplies and effectually prevent Western competition with Eastern agriculture. Indeed, the products of irrigation will be consumed chiefly in upbuilding local centers of mining and other industries, which would otherwise not come into existence at all. Our people as a whole will profit, for successful home-making is but another name for the upbuilding of the nation.

The necessary foundation has already been laid for the inauguration of the policy just described. It would be unwise to begin by doing too much, for a great deal will doubtless be learned, both as to what can and what cannot be safely attempted, by the early efforts, which must of necessity be partly experimental in character. At the very beginning the Government should make clear, beyond shadow of doubt, its intention to pursue this policy on lines of the broadest public interest. No reservoir or canal should ever be built to satisfy selfish personal or local interests; but only in accordance with the advice of trained experts, after long investigation has shown the locality where all the conditions combine to make the work most needed and fraught with the greatest usefulness to the community as a whole. There should be no extravagance, and the believers in the need of irrigation will most benefit their cause by seeing to it that it is free from the least taint of excessive or reckless expenditure of the public moneys.

Whatever the nation does for the extension of irrigation should harmonize with, and tend to improve, the condition of those now living on irrigated land. We are not at the starting point of this development. Over two hundred millions of private capital has already been expended in the construction of irrigation works, and many million acres of arid land reclaimed. A high degree of enterprise and ability has been shown in the work itself; but as much cannot be said in reference to the laws relating thereto. The security and value of the homes created depend largely on the stability of titles to water; but the majority of these rest on the uncertain foundation of court decisions rendered in ordinary suits at law. With a few creditable exceptions, the arid States have failed to provide for the certain and just division of streams in times of scarcity. Lax and uncertain laws have made it possible to establish rights to water in excess of actual uses or necessities, and many streams have already passed into private ownership, or a control equivalent to ownership.

Whoever controls a stream practically controls the land it renders productive, and the doctrine of private ownership of water apart from land cannot prevail without causing enduring wrong. The recognition of such ownership, which has been permitted to grow up in the arid regions, should give way to a more enlightened and larger recognition of the rights of the public in the control and disposal of the public water supplies. Laws founded upon conditions obtaining in humid regions, where water is too abundant to justify hoarding it, have no proper application in a dry country.

In the arid States the only right to water which should be recognized is that of use. In irrigation this right should attach to the land reclaimed and be inseparable therefrom. Granting perpetual water rights to others than users, without compensation to the public, is open to all the objections which apply to giving away perpetual franchises to the public utilities of cities. A few of the Western States have already recognized this, and have incorporated in their constitutions the doctrine of perpetual State ownership of water.

The benefits which have followed the unaided development of the past justify the nation's aid and co-operation in the more difficult and important work yet to be accomplished. Laws so vitally affecting homes as those which control the water supply will only be effective when they have the sanction of the irrigators; reforms can only be final and satisfactory when they come through the enlightenment of the people most concerned. The larger development which national aid insures should, however, awaken in every arid State the determination to make its irrigation system equal in justice and effectiveness that of any country in the civilized world. Nothing could be more unwise than for isolated communities to continue to learn everything experimentally instead of profiting by what is already known elsewhere. We are dealing with a new and momentous question, in the pregnant years while institutions are forming, and what we do will affect not only the present but future generations.

Our aim should be not simply to reclaim the largest area of land and provide homes for the largest number of people, but to create for this new industry the best possible social and industrial conditions; and this requires that we not only understand the existing situation, but avail ourselves of the best experience of the time in the solution of its problems. A careful study should be made, both by the Nation and the States, of the irrigation laws and conditions here and abroad. Ultimately it will probably be necessary for the Nation to co-operate with the several arid States in proportion as these States by their legislation and administration show themselves fit to receive it.

In Hawaii our aim must be to develop the Territory on the traditional American lines. We do not wish a region of large estates tilled by cheap labor; we wish a healthy American community of men who themselves till the farms they own. All our legislation for the islands should be shaped with this end in view; the well-being of the average home-maker must afford the true test of the healthy development of the islands. The land policy should as nearly as possible be modeled on our homestead system.

It is a pleasure to say that it is hardly more necessary to report as to Puerto Rico than as to any State or Territory within our continental limits. The island is thriving as never before, and it is being administered efficiently and honestly. Its people are now enjoying liberty and order under the protection of the United States, and upon this fact we congratulate them and ourselves. Their material welfare must be as carefully and jealously considered as the welfare of any other portion of our country. We have given them the great gift of free access for their products to the markets of the United States. I ask the attention of the Congress to the need of legislation concerning the public lands of Puerto Rico.

In Cuba such progress has been made toward putting the independent government of the island upon a firm footing that before the present session of the Congress closes this will be an accomplished fact. Cuba will then start as her own mistress; and to the beautiful Queen of the Antilles, as she unfolds this new page of her destiny, we extend our heartiest greetings and good wishes. Elsewhere I have discussed the question of reciprocity. In the case of Cuba, however, there are weighty reasons of morality and of national interest why the policy should be held to have a peculiar application, and I most earnestly ask your attention to the wisdom, indeed to the vital need, of providing for a substantial reduction in the tariff duties on Cuban imports into the United States. Cuba has in her constitution affirmed what we desired, that she should stand, in international matters, in closer and more friendly relations with us than with any other power; and we are bound by every consideration of honor and expediency to pass commercial measures in the interest of her material well-being.

In the Philippines our problem is larger. They are very rich tropical islands, inhabited by many varying tribes, representing widely different stages of progress toward civilization. Our earnest effort is to help these people upward along the stony and difficult path that leads to self-government. We hope to make our administration of the islands honorable to our Nation by making it of the highest benefit to the Filipinos themselves; and as an earnest of what we intend to do, we point to what we have done. Already a greater measure of material prosperity and of governmental honesty and efficiency has been attained in the Philippines than ever before in their history.

It is no light task for a nation to achieve the temperamental qualities without which the institutions of free government are but an empty mockery. Our people are now successfully governing themselves, because for more than a thousand years they have been slowly fitting themselves, sometimes consciously, sometimes unconsciously, toward this end. What has taken us thirty generations to achieve, we cannot expect to see another race accomplish out of hand, especially when large portions of that race start very far behind the point which our ancestors had reached even thirty generations ago. In dealing with the Philippine people we must show both patience and strength, forbearance and steadfast resolution. Our aim is high. We do not desire to do for the islanders merely what has elsewhere been done for tropic peoples by even the best foreign governments. We hope to do for them what has never before been done for any people of the tropics — to make them fit for self-government after the fashion of the really free nations.

History may safely be challenged to show a single instance in which a masterful race such as ours, having been forced by the exigencies of war to take possession of an alien land, has behaved to its inhabitants with the disinterested zeal for their progress that our people have shown in the Philippines. To leave the islands at this time would mean that they would fall into a welter of murderous anarchy. Such desertion of duty on our part would be a crime against humanity. The character of Governor Taft and of his associates and subordinates is a proof, if such be needed, of the sincerity of our effort to give the islanders a constantly increasing measure of self-government, exactly as fast as they show themselves fit to exercise it. Since the civil government was established not an appointment has been made in the islands with any reference to considerations of political influence, or to aught else save the fitness of the man and the needs of the service.

In our anxiety for the welfare and progress of the Philippines, it may be that here and there we have gone too rapidly in giving them local self-government. It is on this side that our error, if any, has been committed. No competent observer, sincerely desirous of finding out the facts and influenced only by a desire for the welfare of the natives, can assert that we have not gone far enough. We have gone to the very verge of safety in hastening the process. To have taken a single step farther or faster in advance would have been folly and weakness, and might well have been crime. We are extremely anxious that the natives shall show the power of governing themselves. We are anxious, first for their sakes, and next, because it relieves us of a great burden. There need not be the slightest fear of our not continuing to give them all the liberty for which they are fit.

The only fear is lest in our overanxiety we give them a degree of independence for which they are unfit, thereby inviting reaction and disaster. As fast as there is any reasonable hope that in a given district the people can govern themselves, self-government has been given in that district. There is not a locality fitted for self-government which has not received it. But it may well be that in certain cases it will have to be withdrawn because the inhabitants show themselves unfit to exercise it; such instances have already occurred. In other words, there is not the slightest chance of our failing to show a sufficiently humanitarian spirit. The danger comes in the opposite direction.

There are still troubles ahead in the islands. The insurrection has become an affair of local banditti and marauders, who deserve no higher regard than the brigands of portions of the Old World. Encouragement, direct or indirect, to these insurrectors stands on the same footing as encouragement to hostile Indians in the days when we still had Indian wars. Exactly as our aim is to give to the Indian who remains peaceful the fullest and amplest consideration, but to have it understood that we will show no weakness if he goes on the warpath, so we must make it evident, unless we are false to our own traditions and to the demands of civilization and humanity, that while we will do everything in our power for the Filipino who is peaceful, we will take the sternest measures with the Filipino who follows the path of the insurrecto and the ladrone.

The heartiest praise is due to large numbers of the natives of the islands for their steadfast loyalty. The Macabebes have been conspicuous for their courage and devotion to the flag. I recommend that the Secretary of War be empowered to take some systematic action in the way of aiding those of these men who are crippled in the service and the families of those who are killed.

The time has come when there should be additional legislation for the Philippines. Nothing better can be done for the islands than to introduce industrial enterprises. Nothing would benefit them so much a throwing them open to industrial development. The connection between idleness and mischief is proverbial, and the opportunity to do remunerative work is one of the surest preventatives of war. Of course no business man will go into the Philippines unless it is to his interest to do so; and it is immensely to the interest of the islands that he should go in. It is therefore necessary that the Congress should pass laws by which the resources of the islands can be developed; so that franchises (for limited terms of years) can be granted to companies doing business in them, and every encouragement be given to the incoming of business men of every kind.

Not to permit this is to do a wrong to the Philippines. The franchises must be granted and the business permitted only under regulations which will guarantee the islands against any kind of improper exploitation. But the vast natural wealth of the islands must be developed, and the capital willing to develop it must be given the opportunity. The field must be thrown open to individual enterprise, which has been the real factor in the development of every region over which our flag has flown. It is urgently necessary to enact suitable laws dealing with general transportation, mining, banking, currency, homesteads, and the use and ownership of the lands and timber. These laws will give free play to industrial enterprise; and the commercial development which will surely follow will accord to the people of the islands the best proofs of the sincerity of our desire to aid them.

I call your attention most earnestly to the crying need of a cable to Hawaii and the Philippines, to be continued from the Philippines to points in Asia. We should not defer a day longer than necessary the construction of such a cable. It is demanded not merely for commercial but for political and military considerations.

Either the Congress should immediately provide for the construction of a Government cable, or else an arrangement should be made by which like advantages to those accruing from a Government cable may be secured to the Government by contract with a private cable company.

No single great material work which remains to be undertaken on this continent is of such consequence to the American people as the building of a canal across the Isthmus connecting North and South America. Its importance to the Nation is by no means limited merely to its material effects upon our business prosperity; and yet with view to these effects alone it would be to the last degree important for us immediately to begin it. While its beneficial effects would perhaps be most marked upon the Pacific Coast and the Gulf and South Atlantic States, it would also greatly benefit other sections. It is emphatically a work which it is for the interest of the entire country to begin and complete as soon as possible; it is one of those great works which only a great nation can undertake with prospects of success, and which when done are not only permanent assets in the nation's material interests, but standing monuments to its constructive ability.

I am glad to be able to announce to you that our negotiations on this subject with Great Britain, conducted on both sides in a spirit of friendliness and mutual good will and respect, have resulted in my being able to lay before the Senate a treaty which if ratified will enable us to begin preparations for an Isthmian canal at any time, and which guarantees to this Nation every right that it has ever asked in connection with the canal. In this treaty, the old Clayton-Bulwer treaty, so long recognized as inadequate to supply the base for the construction and maintenance of a necessarily American ship canal, is abrogated. It specifically provides that the United States alone shall do the work of building and assume the responsibility of safeguarding the canal and shall regulate its neutral use by all nations on terms of equality without the guaranty or interference of any outside nation from any quarter. The signed treaty will at once be laid before the Senate, and if approved the Congress can then proceed to give effect to the advantages it secures us by providing for the building of the canal.

The true end of every great and free people should be self-respecting peace; and this Nation most earnestly desires sincere and cordial friendship with all others. Over the entire world, of recent years, wars between the great civilized powers have become less and less frequent. Wars with barbarous or semi-barbarous peoples come in an entirely different category, being merely a most regrettable but necessary international police duty which must be performed for the sake of the welfare of mankind. Peace can only be kept with certainty where both sides wish to keep it; but more and more the civilized peoples are realizing the wicked folly of war and are attaining that condition of just and intelligent regard for the rights of others which will in the end, as we hope and believe, make world-wide peace possible. The peace conference at The Hague gave definite expression to this hope and belief and marked a stride toward their attainment.

This same peace conference acquiesced in our statement of the Monroe Doctrine as compatible with the purposes and aims of the conference.

The Monroe Doctrine should be the cardinal feature of the foreign policy of all the nations of the two Americas, as it is of the United States. Just seventy-eight years have passed since President Monroe in his Annual Message announced that "The American continents are henceforth not to be considered as subjects for future colonization by any European power." In other words, the Monroe Doctrine is a declaration that there must be no territorial aggrandizement by any non-American power at the expense of any American power on American soil. It is in no wise intended as hostile to any nation in the Old World. Still less is it intended to give cover to any aggression by one New World power at the expense of any other. It is simply a step, and a long step, toward assuring the universal peace of the world by securing the possibility of permanent peace on this hemisphere.

During the past century other influences have established the permanence and independence of the smaller states of Europe. Through the Monroe Doctrine we hope to be able to safeguard like independence and secure like permanence for the lesser among the New World nations.

This doctrine has nothing to do with the commercial relations of any American power, save that it in truth allows each of them to form such as it desires. In other words, it is really a guaranty of the commercial independence of the Americas. We do not ask under this doctrine for any exclusive commercial dealings with any other American state. We do not guarantee any state against punishment if it misconducts itself, provided that punishment does not take the form of the acquisition of territory by any non-American power.

Our attitude in Cuba is a sufficient guaranty of our own good faith. We have not the slightest desire to secure any territory at the expense of any of our neighbors. We wish to work with them hand in hand, so that all of us may be uplifted together, and we rejoice over the good fortune of any of them, we gladly hail their material prosperity and political stability, and are concerned and alarmed if any of them fall into industrial or political chaos. We do not wish to see any Old World military power grow up on this continent, or to be compelled to become a military power ourselves. The peoples of the Americas can prosper best if left to work out their own salvation in their own way.

The work of upbuilding the Navy must be steadily continued. No one point of our policy, foreign or domestic, is more important than this to the honor and material welfare, and above all to the peace, of our nation in the future. Whether we desire it or not, we must henceforth recognize that we have international duties no less than international rights. Even if our flag were hauled down in the Philippines and Puerto Rico, even if we decided not to build the Isthmian Canal, we should need a thoroughly trained Navy of adequate size, or else be prepared definitely and for all time to abandon the idea that our nation is among those whose sons go down to the sea in ships. Unless our commerce is always to be carried in foreign bottoms, we must have war craft to protect it.

Inasmuch, however, as the American people have no thought of abandoning the path upon which they have entered, and especially in view of the fact that the building of the Isthmian Canal is fast becoming one of the matters which the whole people are united in demanding, it is imperative that our Navy should be put and kept in the highest state of efficiency, and should be made to answer to our growing needs. So far from being in any way a provocation to war, an adequate and highly trained navy is the best guaranty against war, the cheapest and most effective peace insurance. The cost of building and maintaining such a navy represents the very lightest premium for insuring peace which this nation can possibly pay.

Probably no other great nation in the world is so anxious for peace as we are. There is not a single civilized power which has anything whatever to fear from aggressiveness on our part. All we want is peace; and toward this end we wish to be able to secure the same respect for our rights from others which we are eager and anxious to extend to their rights in return, to insure fair treatment to us commercially, and to guarantee the safety of the American people.

Our people intend to abide by the Monroe Doctrine and to insist upon it as the one sure means of securing the peace of the Western Hemisphere. The Navy offers us the only means of making our insistence upon the Monroe Doctrine anything but a subject of derision to whatever nation chooses to disregard it. We desire the peace which comes as of right to the just man armed; not the peace granted on terms of ignominy to the craven and the weakling.

It is not possible to improvise a navy after war breaks out. The ships must be built and the men trained long in advance. Some auxiliary vessels can be turned into makeshifts which will do in default of any better for the minor work, and a proportion of raw men can be mixed with the highly trained, their shortcomings being made good by the skill of their fellows; but the efficient fighting force of the Navy when pitted against an equal opponent will be found almost exclusively in the war ships that have been regularly built and in the officers and men who through years of faithful performance of sea duty have been trained to handle their formidable but complex and delicate weapons with the highest efficiency. In the late war with Spain the ships that dealt the decisive blows at Manila and Santiago had been launched from two to fourteen years, and they were able to do as they did because the men in the conning towers, the gun turrets, and the engine-rooms had through long years of practice at sea learned how to do their duty.

Our present Navy was begun in 1882. At that period our Navy consisted of a collection of antiquated wooden ships, already almost as out of place against modern war vessels as the galleys of Alcibiades and Hamilcar—certainly as the ships of Tromp and Blake. Nor at that time did we have men fit to handle a modern man-of-war. Under the wise legislation of the Congress and the successful administration of a succession of patriotic Secretaries of the Navy, belonging to both political parties, the work of upbuilding the Navy went on, and ships equal to any in the world of their kind were continually added; and what was even more important, these ships were exercised at sea singly and in squadrons until the men aboard them were able to get the best possible service out of them. The result was seen in the short war with Spain, which was decided with such rapidity because of the infinitely greater preparedness of our Navy than of the Spanish Navy.

While awarding the fullest honor to the men who actually commanded and manned the ships which destroyed the Spanish sea forces in the Philippines and in Cuba, we must not forget that an equal meed of praise belongs to those without whom neither blow could have been struck. The Congressmen who voted years in advance the money to lay down the ships, to build the guns, to buy the armor-plate; the Department officials and the business men and wage-workers who furnished what the Congress had authorized; the Secretaries of the Navy who asked for and expended the appropriations; and finally the officers who, in fair weather and foul, on actual sea service, trained and disciplined the crews of the ships when there was no war in sight — all are entitled to a full share in the glory of Manila and Santiago, and the respect accorded by every true American to those who wrought such signal triumph for our country. It was forethought and preparation which secured us the overwhelming triumph of 1898. If we fail to show forethought and preparation now, there may come a time when disaster will befall us instead of triumph; and should this time come, the fault will rest primarily, not upon those whom the accident of events puts in supreme command at the moment, but upon those who have failed to prepare in advance.

There should be no cessation in the work of completing our Navy. So far ingenuity has been wholly unable to devise a substitute for the great war craft whose hammering guns beat out the mastery of the high seas. It is unsafe and unwise not to provide this year for several additional battle ships and heavy armored cruisers, with auxiliary and lighter craft in proportion; for the exact numbers and character I refer you to the report of the Secretary of the Navy. But there is something we need even more than additional ships, and this is additional officers and men. To provide battle ships and cruisers and then lay them up, with the expectation of leaving them unmanned until they are needed in actual war, would be worse than folly; it would be a crime against the Nation.

To send any war ship against a competent enemy unless those aboard it have been trained by years of actual sea service, including incessant gunnery practice, would be to invite not merely disaster, but the bitterest shame and humiliation. Four thousand additional seamen and one thousand additional marines should be provided; and an increase in the officers should be provided by making a large addition to the classes at Annapolis. There is one small matter which should be mentioned in connection with Annapolis. The pretentious and unmeaning title of "naval cadet" should be abolished; the title of "midshipman," full of historic association, should be restored.

Even in time of peace a war ship should be used until it wears out, for only so can it be kept fit to respond to any emergency. The officers and men alike should be kept as much as possible on blue water, for it is there only they can learn their duties as they should be learned. The big vessels should be manœuvred in squadrons containing not merely battle ships, but the necessary proportion of cruisers and scouts. The torpedo boats should be handled by the younger officers in such manner as will best fit the latter to take responsibility and meet the emergencies of actual warfare.

Every detail ashore which can be performed by a civilian should be so performed, the officer being kept for his special duty in the sea service. Above all, gunnery practice should be unceasing. It is important to have our Navy of adequate size, but it is even more important that ship for ship it should equal in efficiency any navy in the world. This is possible only with highly drilled crews and officers, and this in turn imperatively demands continuous and progressive instruction in target practice, ship handling, squadron tactics, and general discipline. Our ships must be assembled in squadrons actively cruising away from harbors and never long at anchor. The resulting wear upon engines and hulls must be endured; a battle ship worn out in long training of officers and men is well paid for by the results, while, on the other hand, no matter in how excellent condition, it is useless if the crew be not expert.

We now have seventeen battle ships appropriated for, of which nine are completed and have been commissioned for actual service. The remaining eight will be ready in from two to four years, but it will take at least that time to recruit and train the men to fight them. It is of vast concern that we have trained crews ready for the vessels by the time they are commissioned. Good ships and good guns are simply good weapons, and the best weapons are useless save in the hands of men who know how to fight with them. The men must be trained and drilled under a thorough and well-planned system of progressive instruction, while the recruiting must be carried on with still greater vigor. Every effort must be made to exalt the main function of the officer — the command of men. The leading graduates of the Naval Academy should be assigned to the combatant branches, the line and marines.

Many of the essentials of success are already recognized by the General Board, which, as the central office of a growing staff, is moving steadily toward a proper war efficiency and a proper efficiency of the whole Navy, under the Secretary. This General Board, by fostering the creation of a general staff, is providing for the official and then the general recognition of our altered conditions as a Nation and of the true meaning of a great war fleet, which meaning is, first, the best men, and, second, the best ships.

The Naval Militia forces are State organizations, and are trained for coast service, and in event of war they will constitute the inner line of defense. They should receive hearty encouragement from the General Government.

But in addition we should at once provide for a National Naval Reserve, organized and trained under the direction of the Navy Department, and subject to the call of the Chief Executive whenever war becomes imminent. It should be a real auxiliary to the naval seagoing peace establishment, and offer material to be drawn on at once for manning our ships in time of war. It should be composed of graduates of the Naval Academy, graduates of the Naval Militia, officers and crews of coast-line steamers, longshore schooners, fishing vessels, and steam yachts, together with the coast population about such centers as life-saving stations and light-houses.

The American people must either build and maintain an adequate navy or else make up their minds definitely to accept a secondary position in international affairs, not merely in political, but in commercial, matters. It has been well said that there is no surer way of courting national disaster than to be " opulent, aggressive, and unarmed."

It is not necessary to increase our Army beyond its present size at this time. But it is necessary to keep it at the highest point of efficiency. The individual units who as officers and enlisted men compose this Army, are, we have good reason to believe, at least as efficient as those of any other army in the entire world. It is our duty to see that their training is of a kind to insure the highest possible expression of power to these units when acting in combination.

The conditions of modern war are such as to make an infinitely heavier demand than ever before upon the individual character and capacity of the officer and the enlisted man, and to make it far more difficult for men to act together with effect. At present the fighting must be done in extended order, which means that each man must act for himself and at the same time act in combination with others with whom he is no longer in the old-fashioned elbow-to-elbow touch. Under such conditions a few men of the highest excellence are worth more than many men without the special skill which is only found as the result of special training applied to men of exceptional physique and morale. But nowadays the most valuable fighting man and the most difficult to perfect is the rifleman who is also a skillful and daring rider.

The proportion of our cavalry regiments has wisely been increased. The American cavalryman, trained to manœuvre and fight with equal facility on foot and on horseback, is the best type of soldier for general purposes now to be found in the world. The ideal cavalryman of the present day is a man who can fight on foot as effectively as the best infantryman, and who is in addition unsurpassed in the care and management of his horse and in his ability to fight on horseback.

A general staff should be created. As for the present staff and supply departments, they should be filled by details from the line, the men so detailed returning after a while to their line duties. It is very undesirable to have the senior grades of the Army composed of men who have come to fill the positions by the mere fact of seniority. A system should be adopted by which there shall be an elimination grade by grade of those who seem unfit to render the best service in the next grade. Justice to the veterans of the Civil War who are still in the Army would seem to require that in the matter of retirements they be given by law the same privileges accorded to their comrades in the Navy.

The process of elimination of the least fit should be conducted in a manner that would render it practically impossible to apply political or social pressure on behalf of any candidate, so that each man may be judged purely on his own merits. Pressure for the promotion of civil officials for political reasons is bad enough, but it is tenfold worse where applied on behalf of officers of the Army or Navy. Every promotion and every detail under the War Department must be made solely with regard to the good of the service and to the capacity and merit of the man himself. No pressure, political, social, or personal, of any kind, will be permitted to exercise the least effect in any question of promotion or detail; and if there is reason to believe that such pressure is exercised at the instigation of the officer concerned, it will be held to militate against him. In our Army we cannot afford to have rewards or duties distributed save on the simple ground that those who by their own merits are entitled to the rewards get them, and that those who are peculiarly fit to do the duties are chosen to perform them

Every effort should be made to bring the Army to a constantly increasing state of efficiency. When on actual service no work save that directly in the line of such service should be required. The paper work in the Army, as in the Navy, should be greatly reduced. What is needed is proved power of command and capacity to work well in the field. Constant care is necessary to prevent dry rot in the transportation and commissary departments.

Our Army is so small and so much scattered that it is very difficult to give the higher officers (as well as the lower officers and the enlisted men) a chance to practice manœuvres in mass and on a comparatively large scale. In time of need no amount of individual excellence would avail against the paralysis which would follow inability to work as a coherent whole, under skillful and daring leadership. The Congress should provide means whereby it will be possible to have field exercises by at least a division of regulars, and if possible also a division of national guardsmen, once a year. These exercises might take the form of field manœuvres; or, if on the Gulf Coast or the Pacific or Atlantic Seaboard, or in the region of the Great Lakes, the army corps when assembled could be marched from some inland point to some point on the water, there embarked, disembarked after a couple of days' journey at some other point, and again marched inland. Only by actual handling and providing for men in masses while they are marching, camping, embarking, and disembarking, will it be possible to train the higher officers to perform their duties well and smoothly.

A great debt is owing from the public to the men of the Army and Navy. They should be so treated as to enable them to reach the highest point of efficiency, so that they may be able to respond instantly to any demand made upon them to sustain the interests of the Nation and the honor of the flag. The individual American enlisted man is probably on the whole a more formidable fighting man than the regular of any other army. Every consideration should be shown him, and in return the highest standard of usefulness should be exacted from him. It is well worth while for the Congress to consider whether the pay of enlisted men upon second and subsequent enlistments should not be increased to correspond with the increased value of the veteran soldier.

Much good has already come from the act reorganizing the Army, passed early in the present year. The three prime reforms, all of them of literally inestimable value, are, first, the substitution of four-year details from the line for permanent appointments in the so-called staff divisions; second, the establishment of a corps of artillery with a chief at the head; third, the establishment of a maximum and minimum limit for the Army. It would be difficult to overestimate the improvement in the efficiency of our Army which these three reforms are making, and have in part already effected.

The reorganization provided for by the act has been substantially accomplished. The improved conditions in the Philippines have enabled the War Department materially to reduce the military charge upon our revenue and to arrange the number of soldiers so as to bring this number much nearer to the minimum than to the maximum limit established by law. There is, however, need of supplementary legislation. Thorough military education must be provided, and in addition to the regulars the advantages of this education should be given to the officers of the National Guard and others in civil life who desire intelligently to fit themselves for possible military duty. The officers should be given the chance to perfect themselves by study in the higher branches of this art. At West Point the education should be of the kind most apt to turn out men who are good in actual field service; too much stress should not be laid on mathematics, nor should proficiency therein be held to establish the right of entry to a *corps d'élite*. The typical American officer of the best kind need not be a good mathematician; but he must be able to master himself, to control others, and to show boldness and fertility of resource in every emergency.

Action should be taken in reference to the militia and to the raising of volunteer forces. Our militia law is obsolete and worthless. The organization and armament of the National Guard of the several States, which are treated as militia in the appropriations by the Congress, should be made identical with those provided for the regular forces. The obligations and duties of the Guard in time of war should be carefully defined, and a system established by law under which the method of procedure of raising volunteer forces should be prescribed in advance. It is utterly impossible in the excitement and haste of impending war to do this satisfactorily if the arrangements have not been made long beforehand. Provision should be made for utilizing in the first volunteer organizations called out the training of those citizens who have already had experience under arms, and especially for the selection in advance of the officers of any force which may be raised; for careful selection of the kind necessary is impossible after the outbreak of war.

That the Army is not at all a mere instrument of destruction has been shown during the last three years. In the Philippines, Cuba, and Puerto Rico it has proved itself a great constructive force, a most potent implement for the upbuilding of a peaceful civilization.

No other citizens deserve so well of the Republic as the veterans, the survivors of those who saved the Union. They did the one deed which if left undone would have meant that all else in our history went for nothing. But for their steadfast prowess in the greatest crisis of our history, all our annals would be meaningless, and our great experiment in popular freedom and self-government a gloomy failure. Moreover, they not only left us a united Nation, but they left us also as a heritage the memory of the mighty deeds by which the Nation was kept united. We are now indeed one Nation, one in fact as well as in name; we are united in our devotion to the flag which is the symbol of national greatness and unity; and the very completeness of our union enables us all, in every part of the country, to glory in the valor shown alike by the sons of the North and the sons of the South in the times that tried men's souls.

The men who in the last three years have done so well in the East and the West Indies and on the mainland of Asia have shown that this remembrance is not lost. In any serious crisis the United States must rely for the great mass of its fighting men upon the volunteer soldiery who do not make a permanent profession of the military career; and whenever such a crisis arises the deathless memories of the Civil War will give to Americans the lift of lofty purpose which comes to those whose fathers have stood valiantly in the forefront of the battle.

The merit system of making appointments is in its essence as democratic and American as the common school system itself. It simply means that in clerical and other positions where the duties are entirely non-political, all applicants should have a fair field and no favor, each standing on his merits as he is able to show them by practical test. Written competitive examinations offer the only available means in many cases for applying this system. In other cases, as where laborers are employed, a system of registration undoubtedly can be widely extended. There are, of course, places where the written competitive examination cannot be applied, and others where it offers by no means an ideal solution, but where under existing political conditions it is, though an imperfect means, yet the best present means of getting satisfactory results.

Wherever the conditions have permitted the application of the merit system in its fullest and widest sense, the gain to the Government has been immense. The navy-yards and postal service illustrate, probably better than any other branches of the Government, the great gain in economy, efficiency, and honesty due to the enforcement of this principle.

I recommend the passage of a law which will extend the classified service to the District of Columbia, or will at least enable the President thus to extend it. In my judgment all laws providing for the temporary employment of clerks should hereafter contain a provision that they be selected under the Civil Service Law.

It is important to have this system obtain at home, but it is even more important to have it applied rigidly in our insular possessions. Not an office should be filled in the Philippines or Puerto Rico with any regard to the man's partisan affiliations or services, with any regard to the political, social, or personal influence which he may have at his command; in short, heed should be paid to absolutely nothing save the man's own character and capacity and the needs of the service.

The administration of these islands should be as wholly free from the suspicion of partisan politics as the administration of the Army and Navy. All that we ask from the public servant in the Philippines or Puerto Rico is that he reflect honor on his country by the way in which he makes that country's rule a benefit to the peoples who have come under it. This is all that we should ask, and we cannot afford to be content with less.

The merit system is simply one method of securing honest and efficient administration of the Government; and in the long run the sole justification of any type of government lies in its proving itself both honest and efficient.

The consular service is now organized under the provisions of a law passed in 1856, which is entirely inadequate to existing conditions. The interest shown by so many commerical bodies throughout the country in the reorganization of the service is heartily commended to your attention. Several bills providing for a new consular service have in recent years been submitted to the Congress. They are based upon the just principle that appointments to the service should be made only after a practical test of the applicant's fitness, that promotions should be governed by trustworthiness, adaptability, and zeal in the performance of duty, and that the tenure of office should be unaffected by partisan considerations.

The guardianship and fostering of our rapidly expanding foreign commerce, the protection of American citizens resorting to foreign countries in lawful pursuit of their affairs, and the maintenance of the dignity of the nation abroad, combine to make it essential that our consuls should be men of character, knowledge and enterprise. It is true that the service is now, in the main, efficient, but a standard of excellence cannot be permanently maintained until the principles set forth in the bills heretofore submitted to the Congress on this subject are enacted into law.

In my judgment the time has arrived when we should definitely make up our minds to recognize the Indian as an individual and not as a member of a tribe. The General Allotment Act is a mighty pulverizing engine to break up the tribal mass. It acts directly upon the family and the individual. Under its provisions some sixty thousand Indians have already become citizens of the United States. We should now break up the tribal funds, doing for them what allotment does for the tribal lands; that is, they should be divided into individual holdings. There will be a transition period during which the funds will in many cases have to be held in trust. This is the case also with the lands. A stop should be put upon the indiscriminate permission to Indians to lease their allotments. The effort should be steadily to make the Indian work like any other man on his own ground. The marriage laws of the Indians should be made the same as those of the whites.

In the schools the education should be elementary and largely industrial. The need of higher education among the Indians is very, very limited. On the reservations care should be taken to try to suit the teaching to the needs of the particular Indian. There is no use in attempting to induce agriculture in a country suited only for cattle raising, where the Indian should be made a stock grower. The ration system, which is merely the corral and the reservation system, is highly detrimental to the Indians. It promotes beggary, perpetuates pauperism, and stifles industry. It is an effectual barrier to progress. It must continue to a greater or less degree as long as tribes are herded on reservations and have everything in common. The Indian should be treated as an individual — like the white man. During the change of treatment inevitable hardships will occur; every effort should be made to minimize these hardships; but we should not because of them hesitate to make the change. There should be a continuous reduction in the number of agencies.

In dealing with the aboriginal races few things are more important than to preserve them from the terrible physical and moral degradation resulting from the liquor traffic. We are doing all we can to save our own Indian tribes from this evil. Wherever by international agreement this same end can be attained as regards races where we do not possess exclusive control, every effort should be made to bring it about.

I bespeak the most cordial support from the Congress and the people for the St. Louis Exposition to commemorate the One Hundredth Anniversary of the Louisiana Purchase. This purchase was the greatest instance of expansion in our history. It definitely decided that we were to become a great continental republic, by far the foremost power in the Western Hemisphere. It is one of three or four great landmarks in our history — the great turning points in our development. It is eminently fitting that all our people should join with heartiest good will in commemorating it, and the citizens of St. Louis, of Missouri, of all the adjacent region, are entitled to every aid in making the celebration a noteworthy event in our annals. We earnestly hope that foreign nations will appreciate the deep interest our country takes in this Exposition, and our view of its importance from every standpoint, and that they will participate in securing its success. The National Government should be represented by a full and complete set of exhibits.

The people of Charleston, with great energy and civic spirit, are carrying on an Exposition which will continue throughout most of the present session of the Congress. I heartily commend this Exposition to the good will of the people. It deserves all the encouragement that can be given it. The managers of the Charleston Exposition have requested the Cabinet officers to place thereat the Government exhibits which have been at Buffalo, promising to pay the necessary expenses. I have taken the responsibility of directing that this be done, for I feel that it is due to Charleston to help her in her praiseworthy effort. In my opinion the management should not be required to pay all these expenses. I earnestly recommend that the Congress appropriate at once the small sum necessary for this purpose.

The Pan-American Exposition at Buffalo has just closed. Both from the industrial and the artistic standpoint this Exposition has been in a high degree creditable and useful, not merely to Buffalo but to the United States. The terrible tragedy of the President's assassination interfered materially with its being a financial success. The Exposition was peculiarly in harmony with the trend of our public policy, because it represented an effort to bring into closer touch all the peoples of the

Western Hemisphere, and give them an increasing sense of unity. Such an effort was a genuine service to the entire American public.

The advancement of the highest interests of national science and learning and the custody of objects of art and of the valuable results of scientific expeditions conducted by the United States have been committed to the Smithsonian Institution. In furtherance of its declared purpose — for the "increase and diffusion of knowledge among men" — the Congress has from time to time given it other important functions. Such trusts have been executed by the Institution with notable fidelity. There should be no halt in the work of the Institution, in accordance with the plans which its Secretary has presented, for the preservation of the vanishing races of great North American animals in the National Zoological Park. The urgent needs of the National Museum are recommended to the favorable consideration of the Congress.

Perhaps the most characteristic educational movement of the past fifty years is that which has created the modern public library and developed it into broad and active service. There are now over five thousand public libraries in the United States, the product of this period. In addition to accumulating material, they are also striving by organization, by improvement in method, and by co-operation, to give greater efficiency to the material they hold, to make it more widely useful, and by avoidance of unnecessary duplication in process to reduce the cost of its administration.

In these efforts they naturally look for assistance to the Federal library, which, though still the Library of Congress, and so entitled, is the one national library of the United States. Already the largest single collection of books on the Western Hemisphere, and certain to increase more rapidly than any other through purchase, exchange, and the operation of the copyright law, this library has a unique opportunity to render to the libraries of this country — to American scholarship — service of the highest importance. It is housed in a building which is the largest and most magnificent yet erected for library uses. Resources are now being provided which will develop the collection properly, equip it with the apparatus and service necessary to its effective use, render its bibliographic work widely available, and enable it to become, not merely a center of research, but the chief factor in great co-operative efforts for the diffusion of knowledge and the advancement of learning.

For the sake of good administration, sound economy, and the advancement of science, the Census Office as now constituted should be made a permanent Government bureau. This would insure better, cheaper, and more satisfactory work, in the interest not only of our business but of statistic, economic, and social science.

The remarkable growth of the postal service is shown in the fact that its revenues have doubled and its expenditures have nearly doubled within twelve years. Its progressive development compels constantly increasing outlay, but in this period of business energy and prosperity its receipts grow so much faster than its expenses that the annual deficit has been steadily reduced from $11,411,779 in 1897 to $3,923,727 in 1901. Among recent postal advances the success of rural free delivery wherever established has been so marked, and actual experience has made its benefits so plain, that the demand for its extension is general and urgent.

It is just that the great agricultural population should share in the improvement of the service. The number of rural routes now in operation is 6,009, practically all established within three years, and there are 6,000 applications awaiting action. It is expected that the number in operation at the close of the current fiscal year will reach 8,600. The mail will then be daily carried to the doors of 5,700,000 of our people who have heretofore been dependent upon distant offices, and one-third of all that portion of the country which is adapted to it will be covered by this kind of service.

The full measure of postal progress which might be realized has long been hampered and obstructed by the heavy burden imposed on the Government through the intrenched and well-understood abuses which have grown up in connection with second-class mail matter. The extent of this burden appears when it is stated that while the second-class matter makes nearly three-fifths of the weight of all the mail, it paid for the last fiscal year only $4,294,445 of the aggregate postal revenue of $111,631,193. If the pound rate of postage, which produces the large loss thus entailed, and which was fixed by the Congress with the purpose of encouraging the dissemination of public information, were limited to the legitimate newspapers and periodicals actually contemplated by the law, no just exception could be taken. That expense would be the recognized and accepted cost of a liberal public policy deliberately adopted for a justifiable end. But much of the matter which enjoys the privileged rate is wholly outside of the intent of the law, and has secured admission only through an evasion of its requirements or through lax construction. The proportion of such wrongly included matter is estimated by postal experts to be one-half of the whole volume of second-class mail. If it be only one-third or one-quarter, the magnitude of the burden is apparent. The Post-Office Department has now undertaken to remove the abuses so far as is possible by a stricter application of the law; and it should be sustained in its effort.

Owing to the rapid growth of our power and our interests on the Pacific, whatever happens in China must be of the keenest national concern to us.

The general terms of the settlement of the questions growing out of the antiforeign uprisings in China of 1900, having been formulated in a joint note addressed to China by the representatives of the injured powers in December last, were promptly accepted by the Chinese Government. After protracted conferences the plenipotentiaries of the several powers were able to sign a final protocol with the Chinese plenipotentiaries on the 7th of last September, setting forth the measures taken by China in compliance with the demands of the joint note, and expressing their satisfaction therewith. It will be laid before the Congress, with a report of the plenipotentiary on behalf of the United States, Mr. William Woodville Rockhill, to whom high praise is due for the tact, good judgment, and energy he has displayed in performing an exceptionally difficult and delicate task.

The agreement reached disposes in a manner satisfactory to the powers of the various grounds of complaint, and will contribute materially to better future relations between China and the powers. Reparation has been made by China for the murder of foreigners during the uprising and punishment has been inflicted on the officials, however high in rank, recognized as responsible for or having participated in the outbreak. Official examinations have been forbidden for a period of five years in all cities in which foreigners have been murdered or cruelly treated, and edicts have been issued making all officials directly responsible for the future safety of foreigners and for the suppression of violence against them.

Provisions have been made for insuring the future safety of the foreign representatives in Peking by setting aside for their exclusive use a quarter of the city which the powers can make defensible and in which they can if necessary maintain permanent military guards; by dismantling the military works between the capital and the sea; and by allowing the temporary maintenance of foreign military posts along this line. An edict has been issued by the Emperor of China prohibiting for two years the importation of arms and ammunition into China. China has agreed to pay adequate indemnities to the states, societies, and individuals for the losses sustained by them and for the expenses of the military expeditions sent by the various powers to protect life and restore order.

Under the provisions of the joint note of December, 1900, China has agreed to revise the treaties of commerce and navigation and to take such other steps for the purpose of facilitating foreign trade as the foreign powers may decide to be needed.

The Chinese Government has agreed to participate financially in the work of bettering the water approaches to Shanghai and to Tientsin, the centers of foreign trade in central and northern China, and an international conservancy board, in which the Chinese Government is largely represented, has been provided for the improvement of the

Shanghai River and the control of its navigation. In the same line of commercial advantages a revision of the present tariff on imports has been assented to for the purpose of substituting specific for *ad valorem* duties, and an expert has been sent abroad on the part of the United States to assist in this work. A list of articles to remain free of duty, including flour, cereals, and rice, gold and silver coin and bullion, has also been agreed upon in the settlement.

During these troubles our Government has unswervingly advocated moderation, and has materially aided in bringing about an adjustment which tends to enhance the welfare of China and to lead to a more beneficial intercourse between the Empire and the modern world; while in the critical period of revolt and massacre we did our full share in safeguarding life and property, restoring order, and vindicating the national interest and honor. It behooves us to continue in these paths, doing what lies in our power to foster feelings of good will, and leaving no effort untried to work out the great policy of full and fair intercourse between China and the nations, on a footing of equal rights and advantages to all. We advocate the "open door" with all that it implies; not merely the procurement of enlarged commercial opportunities on the coasts, but access to the interior by the waterways with which China has been so extraordinarily favored. Only by bringing the people of China into peaceful and friendly community of trade with all the peoples of the earth can the work now auspiciously begun be carried to fruition. In the attainment of this purpose we necessarily claim parity of treatment, under the conventions, throughout the Empire for our trade and our citizens with those of all other powers.

We view with lively interest and keen hopes of beneficial results the proceedings of the Pan-American Congress, convoked at the invitation of Mexico, and now sitting at the Mexican capital. The delegates of the United States are under the most liberal instructions to co-operate with their colleagues in all matters promising advantage to the great family of American commonwealths, as well in their relations among themselves as in their domestic advancement and in their intercourse with the world at large.

My predecessor communicated to the Congress the fact that the Weil and La Abra awards against Mexico have been adjudged by the highest courts of our country to have been obtained through fraud and perjury on the part of the claimants, and that in accordance with the acts of the Congress the money remaining in the hands of the Secretary of State on these awards has been returned to Mexico. A considerable portion of the money received from Mexico on these awards had been paid by this Government to the claimants before the decision of the courts was rendered. My judgment is that the Congress should return to Mexico an amount equal to the sums thus already paid to the claimants.

The death of Queen Victoria caused the people of the United States deep and heartfelt sorrow, to which the Government gave full expres-sion. When President McKinley died, our Nation in turn received from every quarter of the British Empire expressions of grief and sym-pathy no less sincere. The death of the Empress Dowager Frederick of Germany also aroused the genuine sympathy of the American people; and this sympathy was cordially reciprocated by Germany when the President was assassinated. Indeed, from every quarter of the civilized world we received, at the time of the President's death, assurances of such grief and regard as to touch the hearts of our people. In the midst of our affliction we reverently thank the Almighty that we are at peace with the nations of mankind; and we firmly intend that our policy shall be such as to continue unbroken these international rela-tions of mutual respect and good will.

THEODORE ROOSEVELT.

SPECIAL MESSAGES

White House, *Washington, May 12, 1902.*

To the Senate and House of Representatives:

One of the greatest calamities in history has fallen upon our neigh-boring island of Martinique. The consul of the United States at Gua-deloupe has telegraphed from Fort de France, under date of yesterday, that the disaster is complete; that the city of St. Pierre has ceased to exist; and that the American consul and his family have perished. He is informed that 30,000 people have lost their lives and that 50,000 are homeless and hungry; that there is urgent need of all kinds of provi-sions, and that the visit of vessels for the work of supply and rescue is imperatively required.

The Government of France, while expressing their thanks for the marks of sympathy which have reached them from America, inform us that Fort de France and the entire island of Martinique are still threatened. They therefore request that, for the purpose of rescuing the people who are in such deadly peril and threatened with starvation, the Government of the United States may send, as soon as possible, the means of transporting them from the stricken island. The island of St. Vincent and, perhaps, others in that region are also seriously menaced by the calamity which has taken so appalling a form in Martinique.

I have directed the departments of the Treasury, of War, and of the Navy to take such measures for the relief of these stricken people as lies within the Executive discretion, and I earnestly commend this case of unexampled disaster to the generous consideration of the Con-gress. For this purpose I recommend that an appropriation of $500,000 be made, to be immediately available.

THEODORE ROOSEVELT.

WHITE HOUSE, *December 16, 1901.*

To the Senate and House of Representatives:

I transmit herewith a report from the Secretary of State, with accompanying papers, showing that a civil government for Puerto Rico has been organized in accordance with the provisions of the act of Congress approved April 12, 1900, entitled "An act to provide revenues and a civil Government for Puerto Rico, and for other purposes," and that the legislative assembly of Puerto Rico has enacted and put into operation a system of local taxation to meet the necessities of the government of Puerto Rico.   THEODORE ROOSEVELT.

WHITE HOUSE, *June 13, 1902.*

To the Senate and House of Representatives:

I transmit herewith a report from the Secretary of State covering a statement showing the receipts and disbursements of the Louisiana Purchase Exposition Company for the month of April, 1902, furnished by the Louisiana Purchase Exposition Commission, in pursuance of section 11 of the act to provide for celebrating the one hundredth anniversary of the purchase of the Louisiana territory," etc., approved March 3, 1901.   THEODORE ROOSEVELT.

[Similar messages were transmitted weekly to Congress while in session, and at the close of the exposition a complete report was submitted, showing in detail receipts and expenditures of the Commission.]

To the House of Representatives: WHITE HOUSE, *June 23, 1902.*

I transmit herewith a report from the Secretary of State in response to the resolution of the House of Representatives of June 9, 1902, requesting him, if not incompatible with the public interests, to furnish the House of Representatives with a complete list showing the names of all American citizens (and their residence) who are now detained by the British authorities as prisoners of war, together with information as to what investigation, if any, has been made by the State Department concerning the cause of their detention and what action has been taken to secure their release.   THEODORE ROOSEVELT.

To the Senate: WHITE HOUSE, *June 23, 1902.*

I transmit herewith a report from the Secretary of State, with accompanying papers, in further response to the Senate's resolution of May 15, 1900, requesting copies of all correspondence and papers in regard to claims of citizens of the United States against the Government of Colombia growing out of the withdrawal of the military forces and police from Colon by that Government and the firing of the city by insurgents in 1885.   THEODORE ROOSEVELT.

WHITE HOUSE, *June 13, 1902.*

To the Senate and House of Representatives:

I deem it important before the adjournment of the present session of Congress to call attention to the following expressions in the message which in the discharge of the duty imposed upon me by the Constitution I sent to Congress on the first Tuesday of December last:

> Elsewhere I have discussed the question of reciprocity. In the case of Cuba, however, there are weighty reasons of morality and of national interest why the policy should be held to have a peculiar application, and I most earnestly ask your attention to the wisdom, indeed to the vital need, of providing for a substantial reduction in the tariff duties on Cuban imports into the United States. Cuba has in her Constitution affirmed what we desired, that she should stand, in international matters, in closer and more friendly relations with us than with any other power; and we are bound by every consideration of honor and expediency to pass commercial measures in the interest of her material well being.

This recommendation was merely giving practical effect to President McKinley's words, when, in his messages of December 5, 1898, and December 5, 1899, he wrote:

> It is important that our relations with this people (of Cuba) shall be of the most friendly character and our commercial relations close and reciprocal. * * * We have accepted a trust, the fulfillment of which calls for the sternest integrity of purpose and the exercise of the highest wisdom. The new Cuba yet to arise from the ashes of the past must needs be bound to us by ties of singular intimacy and strength if its enduring welfare is to be assured. * * * The greatest blessing which can come to Cuba is the restoration of her agricultural and industrial prosperity.

Yesterday, June 12, I received, by cable from the American minister in Cuba, a most earnest appeal from President Palma for "legislative relief before it is too late and (his) country financially ruined."

The granting of reciprocity with Cuba is a proposition which stands entirely alone. The reasons for it far outweigh those for granting reciprocity with any other nation, and are entirely consistent with preserving intact the protective system under which this country has thriven so marvelously. The present tariff law was designed to promote the adoption of such a reciprocity treaty, and expressly provided for a reduction not to exceed 20 per cent upon goods coming from a particular country, leaving the tariff rates on the same articles unchanged as regards all other countries. Objection has been made to the granting of the reduction on the ground that the substantial benefit would not go to the agricultural producer of sugar, but would inure to the American sugar refiners. In my judgment provision can and should be made which will guarantee us against this possibility, without having recourse to a measure of doubtful policy, such as a bounty in the form of a rebate.

The question as to which if any of the different schedules of the tariff ought most properly to be revised does not enter into this matter in any way or shape. We are concerned with getting a friendly reciprocal arrangement with Cuba. This arrangement applies to all the articles that Cuba grows or produces. It is not in our power to determine what these articles shall be, and any discussion of the tariff as it affects special schedules or countries other than Cuba is wholly aside from the subject matter to which I call your attention.

Some of our citizens oppose the lowering of the tariff on Cuban products just as three years ago they opposed the admission of the Hawaiian Islands lest free trade with them might ruin certain of our interests here. In the actual event their fears proved baseless as regards Hawaii, and their apprehensions as to the damage to any industry of our own because of the proposed measure of reciprocity with Cuba seem to me equally baseless. In my judgment no American industry will be hurt, and many American industries will be benefited by the proposed action. It is to our advantage as a nation that the growing Cuban market should be controlled by American producers.

The events following the war with Spain, and the prospective building of the Isthmian Canal, render it certain that we must take in the future a far greater interest than hitherto in what happens throughout the West Indies, Central America, and the adjacent coasts and waters. We expect Cuba to treat us on an exceptional footing politically, and we should put her in the same exceptional position economically. The proposed action is in line with the course we have pursued as regards all the islands with which we have been brought into relations of varying intimacy by the Spanish war. Puerto Rico and Hawaii have been included within our tariff lines, to their great benefit as well as ours, and without any of the feared detriment to our own industries. The Philippines, which stand in a different relation, have been granted substantial tariff concessions.

Cuba is an independent republic, but a republic which has assumed certain special obligations as regards her international position in compliance with our request. I ask for her certain special economic concessions in return; these economic concessions to benefit us as well as her. There are few brighter pages in American history than the page which tells of our dealings with Cuba during the past four years. On her behalf we waged a war of which the mainspring was generous indignation against oppression; and we have kept faith absolutely. It is earnestly to be hoped that we will complete in the same spirit the record so well begun, and show in our dealings with Cuba that steady continuity of policy which it is essential for our nation to establish in foreign affairs if we desire to play well our part as a world power.

We are a wealthy and powerful nation; Cuba is a young republic, still weak, who owes to us her birth, whose whole future, whose very life, must depend on our attitude toward her. I ask that we help her as she struggles upward along the painful and difficult road of self-governing independence. I ask this aid for her, because she is weak, because she needs it, because we have already aided her. I ask that open-handed help, of a kind which a self-respecting people can accept, be given to Cuba, for the very reason that we have given her such help in the past. Our soldiers fought to give her freedom; and for three years our representatives, civil and military, have toiled unceasingly, facing disease of a peculiarly sinister and fatal type, with patient and uncomplaining fortitude, to teach her how to use aright her new freedom. Never in history has any alien country been thus administered, with such high integrity of purpose, such wise judgment, and such single-minded devotion to the country's interests. Now, I ask that the Cubans be given all possible chance to use to the best advantage the freedom of which Americans have such right to be proud, and for which so many American lives have been sacrificed.

THEODORE ROOSEVELT.

VETO MESSAGES

WHITE HOUSE, *March 11, 1902.*

To the Senate of the United States:

I return without approval Senate bill, No. 1258 entitled "An act to remove the charge of desertion from the naval record of John Glass."

There can be no graver crime than the crime of desertion from the Army or Navy, especially during war; it is then high treason to the nation, and is justly punishable by death. No man should be relieved from such a crime, especially when nearly forty years have passed since it occurred, save on the clearest possible proof of his real innocence. In this case the statement made by the affiant before the committee does not in all points agree with his statement made to the Secretary of the Navy. In any event it is incomprehensible to me that he should not have made effective effort to get back into the Navy.

He had served but little more than a month when he deserted, and the war lasted for over a year afterwards, yet he made no effort whatever to get back into the war. Under such circumstances it seems to me that to remove the charge of desertion from the Navy and give him an honorable discharge would be to falsify the records and do an injustice to his gallant and worthy comrades who fought the war to a finish. The names of the veterans who fought in the civil war make the honor list of the Republic, and I am not willing to put upon it the name of a man unworthy of the high position.

THEODORE ROOSEVELT.

WHITE HOUSE, *June 23, 1902.*

To the House of Representatives:

I return herewith, without approval, House bill No. 3309, entitled "An act to remove charge of desertion against Ephraim H. Gallio.

The bill authorizes and directs the Secretary of War to remove the charge of desertion standing against Ephraim H. Gallion, late of Company B, Eleventh Regiment of Tennessee Cavalry, as he was never mustered into the United States Service, which was not his fault or neglect, and was refused any pay for his service period.

The records of the War Department show that he was enrolled April 21, 1862, as a private of Company B, Sixth Tennessee Infantry Volunteers; that he was a prisoner of war from September 18 to October 11, 1862; that he was discharged from service on surgeon's certificate of disability February 13, 1863; that he again enlisted August 27, 1863, as a private in Company B, Eleventh Tennessee Cavalry, to serve three years; that he was again captured by the enemy and held as a prisoner of war from March 9 to March 21, 1864, when he was paroled. He subsequently rejoined his company and served with it until September 4, 1864, when he deserted. No later record of him has been found.

While the records of the Eleventh Tennessee Cavalry are incomplete, and it is impossible to ascertain from them whether Gallion was formally mustered into service as a member of it or not, they show conclusively that he was actually made a soldier in this regiment by being placed on duty in it, and by being clothed and paid by the United States as a soldier.

In an affidavit submitted by Gallion, it is declared that he never received any moneys during his service as a member of the Eleventh Tennessee Cavalry. A pay roll on file in the office of the Auditor for the War Department shows that on May 13, 1864, at Camp Chase, Ohio, Gallion received from a United States paymaster $105.73, being his pay, at the rate of $13 per month, for eight months and four days from the date of his enlistment.

In view of the facts above set forth I am constrained to withhold my approval.

THEODORE ROOSEVELT

The Man With the Muck-Rake—In Bunyan's "Pilgrim's Progress" you may recall the description of the man with the muck-rake, the man who could look no way but downward, with the muck-rake in his hand, who was offered a celestial crown for his muck-rake, but who would neither look up nor regard the crown he was offered, but continued to rake to himself the filth of the floor.—*From Roosevelt's Address at the Laying of the Corner-stone of the office building of the House of Representatives, April 14, 1906.*

PROCLAMATIONS
BY THE PRESIDENT OF THE UNITED STATES OF AMERICA.
A PROCLAMATION.

Whereas the President on August 20, 1901, issued his proclamation stating that he has been advised by the Louisiana Purchase Exposition Commission, pursuant to the provisions of section 9 of the act of Congress approved March 3, 1901, entitled "An act to provide for celebrating the one hundredth anniversary of the purchase of the Louisiana Territory by the United States by holding an international exhibition of arts, industries, manufactures, and the products of the soil, mine, forest, and sea in the city of St. Louis, in the State of Missouri," that provision had been made for grounds and buildings for the uses specified in the said mentioned act of Congress;

Whereas it was declared and proclaimed by the President in his aforesaid proclamation that such international exhibition would be opened in the city of St. Louis, in the State of Missouri, not later than the first day of May, 1903, and be closed not later than the first day of December thereafter;"

And whereas section 8 of the act of Congress approved June 28, 1902, entitled "An act making appropriations for sundry civil expenses of the government for the fiscal year ending June 30, 1903, and for other purposes," fixes a subsequent date for the holding of the said international exhibition and specifically states that "said commission shall provide for the dedication of the buildings of the Louisiana Purchase Exposition, in said city of St. Louis, not later than the thirtieth day of April, 1903, with appropriate ceremonies, and thereafter said exposition shall be opened to visitors at such time as may be designated by said company, subject to the approval of said commission, not later than the first day of May, 1904, and shall be closed at such time as the national commission may determine, subject to the approval of said company, but not later than the first day of December thereafter;"

Now, therefore, I, Theodore Roosevelt, President of the United States, do hereby declare and proclaim the aforesaid provision of law to the end that it may definitely and formally be known that such international exhibition will be opened in the city of St. Louis, in the State of Missouri, not later than May 1, 1904, and will be closed not later than December first of that year.

In testimony whereof I have hereunto set my hand and caused the seal of the United States to be affixed.

Done at the city of Washington, the first day of July, [SEAL.] A. D. 1902, and of the Independence of the United States the one hundred and twenty-sixth.

By the President: THEODORE ROOSEVELT.
DAVID J. HILL, *Acting Secretary of State.*

BY THE PRESIDENT OF THE UNITED STATES OF AMERICA.

A PROCLAMATION.

Whereas by an agreement between the Shoshone and Bannock Indians of the Fort Hall Reservation in Idaho, on the one part and certain commissioners of the United States on the other part, ratified by act of Congress approved June 6, 1900 (31 Stat., 672) the said Indians ceded, granted, and relinquished to the United States all right, title, and interest which they had to the following described land, the same being a part of the land obtained through the treaty of Fort Bridger on the third day of July, 1868, and ratified by the United States Senate on the sixteenth day of February, 1869:

All that portion of the said reservation embraced within and lying east and south of the following described lines:

Commencing at a point in the south boundary of the Fort Hall Indian Reservation, being the southwest corner of township nine (9) south, range thirty-four (34) east of the Boise meridian, thence running due north on the range line between townships 33 and 34 east to a point two (2) miles north of the township line between townships five (5) and six (6) south, thence due east to the range line between ranges 35 and 36 east, thence south on said range line four (4) miles, thence due east to the east boundary line of the reservation; from this point the east and south boundaries of the said reservation as it now exists to the point of beginning, namely, the southwest corner of township nine (9) south, range thirty-four (34) east, being the remainder of the description and metes and bounds of the said tract of land herein proposed to be ceded.

And whereas, in pursuance of said act of Congress ratifying said agreement, allotments of land have been regularly made to each Indian occupant who desired it, and a schedule has been made of the lands to be abandoned and the improvements thereon appraised, and such improvements will be offered for sale to the highest bidder at not less than the appraised price prior to the date fixed for the opening of the ceded lands to settlement, and the classification as to agricultural and grazing lands has been made;

And whereas, in the act of Congress ratifying said agreement it is provided:

That on the completion of the allotments and the preparation of the schedule provided for in the preceding section, and the classification of the lands as provided for herein, the residue of said ceded lands shall be opened to settlement by the proclamation of the President, and shall be subject to disposal under the homestead, townsite, stone and timber, and mining laws of the United States only, excepting as to price and excepting the sixteenth and thirty-sixth sections in each Congressional township, which shall be reserved for common school purposes and be subject to the laws of Idaho; *Provided*, That all purchasers of lands lying under the canal of the Idaho Canal Company, and which are susceptible of irrigation from the water from said canal, shall pay for the same at the rate of ten dollars per acre; all agricultural lands not under said canal shall be paid for at the rate of two dollars and fifty cents per acre, and grazing lands at the rate of one dollar and twenty-five cents per acre, one-fifth of the respective sums to be paid at time of original entry, and four-fifths thereof at the time of making final proof; but no purchaser shall be permitted in any manner to purchase more than one hundred and sixty acres of the land hereinbefore referred to; but the rights of honorably discharged Union soldiers and sailors, as defined and described in sections twenty-three hundred and four and twenty-three hundred and five of the Revised Statutes of the United States, shall not be abridged, except as to the sum to be paid as aforesaid.

     *   *   *   *   *   *   *

No lands in sections sixteen and thirty-six now occupied, as set forth in article three of the agreement herein ratified, shall be reserved for school purposes, but the State of Idaho shall be entitled to indemnity for any lands so occupied: *Provided*, That none of said lands shall be disposed of under the townsite laws for less than ten dollars per acre: *And provided further*, That all of said lands within five miles of the boundary line of the town of Pocatello shall be sold at public auction, payable as aforesaid, under the direction of the Secretary of the Interior for not less than ten dollars per acre: *And provided further*, That any mineral lands within said five mile limit shall be disposed of under the mineral land laws of the United States, excepting that the price of such mineral lands shall be fixed at ten dollars per acre, instead of the price fixed by the said mineral land laws.

And whereas, all the conditions required by law to be performed prior to the opening of said lands to settlement and entry have been, as I hereby declare, duly performed, except the sale of the improvements mentioned above, but as this is not considered a bar to the opening of the unallotted and unreserved lands to settlement and entry.

Now, therefore, I, Theodore Roosevelt, President of the United States of America, by virtue of the power vested in me by law, do hereby declare and make known that all of the lands so as aforesaid ceded by the Shoshone and Bannock Indians, saving and excepting all lands allotted to the Indians, and saving and excepting the lands on which the Indian improvements have been appraised, and saving and excepting the sixteenth and thirty-sixth sections in each Congressional township, and saving and excepting Lots 7 and 8, section 21, NW ¼ SW ¼ and Lots 9 and 10, section 22, T. 9 S., R. 38 E., B. M., known as " Lava Hot Springs," and saving and excepting all of the lands within five miles of the boundary line of the town of Pocatello, Idaho and saving and excepting the lands ceded under the act of September 1, 1888 (25 Stat., 452), for the purposes of a townsite, will on the 17th day of June, 1902, at and after the hour of 12 o'clock, noon (Mountain Standard time), be opened to settlement and entry under the terms of and subject to all the conditions, limitations, reservations, and restrictions contained in the statutes above specified, and the laws of the United States applicable thereto.

In view of the provision in said act " That all of said lands within five miles of the boundary line of the town of Pocatello shall be sold at public auction, payable as aforesaid, under the direction of the Secretary of the Interior for not less than ten dollars per acre," the lands ".within five miles of the boundary line of the town of Pocatello," saving and excepting all lands allotted to the Indians, and saving and excepting the sixteenth and thirty-sixth sections in each Congressional township, and saving and excepting the lands ceded under the act of September 1, 1888 (25 Stat., 452), for the purposes of a townsite, will on the 17th day of July, 1902, at and after the hour of 12 o'clock, noon (Mountain Standard time), be offered at public auction at not less than ten dollars per acre, under the terms and subject to all the conditions, limitations, reservations and restrictions, contained in the statutes above specified, and the laws of the United States applicable thereto.

Because of the provision in the act ratifying said agreement that " The purchaser of said improvements shall have thirty days after such purchase for preference right of entry, under the provisions of this act, of the lands upon which the improvements purchased by him are situated, not to exceed one hundred and sixty acres," the said lands upon which such Indian improvements purchased are situated outside of the lands within five miles of the town of Pocatello, shall for the period of thirty days after said opening be subject to homestead entry, townsite entry, stone and timber entry, and entry under the mineral laws only by those who may have purchased the improvements thereon, and who are accorded a preference right of entry for thirty days as aforesaid, such entries to be made in accordance with the terms and conditions of this act. Persons entitled to make entry under this preference right will be permitted to do so at any time during the said period of thirty days following the opening, and at the expiration of that period any of said lands not so entered will come under the general provisions of this proclamation.

The purchaser of the improvements on lands situated within five ,miles of the town of Pocatello will have no preference right of entry of the tract on which such improvements are situated, as the law provides that "all of said lands within five miles of the boundary line of the town of Pocatello shall be sold at public auction."

In witness whereof I have hereunto set my hand and caused the seal of the United States to be affixed.

Done at the city of Washington the seventh day of May,
[SEAL.] A. D. 1902, and of the Independence of the United States the one hundred and twenty-sixth.

THEODORE ROOSEVELT.

By the President:
John Hay,
Secretary of State.

BY THE PRESIDENT OF THE UNITED STATES OF AMERICA.

A PROCLAMATION.

Whereas, satisfactory proof has been given to me by the Government of Cuba that no discriminating duties of tonnage or imposts are imposed or levied in the ports of Cuba, upon vessels wholly belonging to citizens of the United States or upon the produce, manufactures, or merchandise imported in the same from the United States, or from any foreign country:

Now, therefore, I, Theodore Roosevelt, President of the United States of America, by virtue of the authority vested in me by section 4228 of the Revised Statutes of the United States, do hereby declare and proclaim that, from and after the date of this, my Proclamation, so long as vessels of the United States and their cargoes shall be exempt from discriminating duties as aforesaid, any such duties on Cuban vessels entering the ports of the United States, or on the produce, manufactures, or merchandise imported in such vessels, shall be suspended and discontinued, and no longer.

In testimony whereof, I have hereunto set my hand and caused the seal of the United States to be affixed.

Done at the city of Washington, the third day of July,
[SEAL.] A. D. 1902, and of the Independence of the United States the one hundred and twenty-sixth.

THEODORE ROOSEVELT.

By the President:
JOHN HAY,
Secretary of State.

BY THE PRESIDENT OF THE UNITED STATES OF AMERICA.

A PROCLAMATION.

Whereas many of the inhabitants of the Philippine archipelago were in insurrection against the authority and sovereignty of the kingdom of Spain at divers times from August, 1896, until the cession of the archipelago by that kingdom to the United States of America, and since such cession many of the persons so engaged in insurrection have until recently resisted the authority and sovereignty of the United States; and

Whereas the insurrection against the authority and sovereignty of the United States is now at an end, and peace has been established in all parts of the archipelago except in the country inhabited by the Moro tribes, to which this proclamation does not apply; and

Whereas during the course of the insurrection against the kingdom of Spain and against the government of the United States, persons engaged therein, or those in sympathy with and abetting them, committed many acts in violation of the laws of civilized warfare; but it is believed that such acts were generally committed in ignorance of these laws, and under orders issued by the civil or military insurrectionary leaders; and

Whereas it is deemed to be wise and humane, in accordance with the beneficent purposes of the government of the United States toward the Filipino people, and conducive to peace, order and loyalty among them, that the doers of such acts who have not already suffered punishment shall not be held criminally responsible, but shall be relieved from punishment for participation in these insurrections and for unlawful acts committed during the course thereof by a general amnesty and pardon;

Now, therefore, be it known that I, Theodore Roosevelt, President of the United States of America, by virtue of the power and authority vested by the Constitution, do hereby proclaim and declare, without reservation or condition, except as hereinafter provided, a full and complete pardon and amnesty to all persons in the Philippine archipelago who have participated in the insurrections aforesaid, or who have given aid and comfort to persons participating in said insurrections, for the offenses of treason or sedition, and for all offenses political in their character committed in the course of such insurrections pursuant to orders issued by the civil or military insurrectionary authorities, or which grow out of internal political feuds or dissensions between Filipinos and Spaniards, or the Spanish authorities, or which resulted from internal political feuds or dissensions among the Filipinos themselves during either of said insurrections.

Provided, however, that the pardon and amnesty hereby granted shall not include such persons committing crimes since May 1, 1902, in any province of the archipelago in which at the time civil government was established, nor shall it include such persons as have been heretofore finally convicted of the crimes of murder, rape, arson, or robbery, by any military or civil tribunal organized under the authority of Spain or of the United States of America, but special application may be made to the proper authority for pardon by any person belonging to the exempted classes and such clemency as is consistent with humanity and justice will be liberally extended; and, further

Provided, That this amnesty and pardon shall not affect the title or right of the Government of the United States or that of the Philippine Islands to any property or property rights heretofore used or appropriated by the military or civil authorities of the Government of the United States or that of the Philippine Islands organized under authority of the United States by way of confiscation or otherwise; and

Provided further, That every person who shall seek to avail himself of this proclamation shall take and subscribe the following oath before any authority in the Philippine archipelago authorized to administer oaths, namely: "I solemnly swear (or affirm) that I recognize and accept the supreme authority of the United States of America in the Philippine Islands and will maintain true faith and allegiance thereto; that I impose upon myself this obligation voluntarily without mental reservation or purpose of evasion so help me God."

Given under my hand at the city of Washington, this 4th day of July, A. D. 1902, and in the one hundred and twenty-seventh year of the Independence of the United States.

THEODORE ROOSEVELT.

By the President:

ELIHU ROOT,
Secretary of War.

Gen. Chaffee is relieved of his civil duties, and the Philippine Commission is made the superior authority in the following order:

The insurrection against the sovereign authority of the United States in the Philippine archipelago having ended, and provincial civil governments having been established throughout the entire territory of the archipelago not inhabited by Moro tribes, under the instructions of the President to the Philippine Commission, dated April 7, 1900, now ratified and confirmed by the act of Congress approved July 1, 1902, entitled "An act temporarily to provide for the administration of affairs of civil government in the Philippine Islands, and for other purposes," the general commanding the division of the Philippines is hereby relieved from the further performance of the duties of military governor, and the office of military governor in said archipelago is terminated. The general commanding the Division of the Philippines and all military officers in authority therein will continue to observe the direction contained in the aforesaid instructions of the President that the military forces in the division of the Philippines shall be at all times subject, under the orders of the military commander, to the call of the civil authorities for the maintenance of law and order, and the enforcement of their authority.

Finally the President, through Secretary Root, pronounces the following eulogy upon the United States Army:

HEADQUARTERS OF THE ARMY, }
ADJUTANT-GENERAL'S OFFICE, }
Washington, July 4, 1902. }

General Order, No. 66.

The following has been received from the War Department:

THE INAUGURATION OF THEODORE ROOSEVELT

FORECAST OF ROOSEVELT'S ADMINISTRATION

There are two kinds who seek a Presidency. One aims at eminence, the other hungers for fame. With one the White House is an object; with the other a method. The first, if made President, sits calmly down; he has had his victory and the White House is his. With him of the fame-hunger, it is the other way about. Given the White House his great work begins. He does not think to write his name with the immortals by simply signing himself "President." He can only achieve the purpose that has called him to the field by labors of lasting good to the whole people.

It shines out as a best hope of the hour that Mr. Roosevelt is heart and soul a fame-hunter. He must go down the aisles of coming time a great President, or in his own conscience he will have failed. To that end, he sets before himself the examples of those mighty ones of time past. The Washingtons, the Jeffersons, the Jacksons, the Lincolns and the Grants are his exemplars. With such to be as guides to him—and because he is true and bold and wise, and no man owns him—it will not be strange should he conquer entrance to Valhalla.

Mr. Roosevelt intends the Panama Canal to be the great work of his régime. With all the power in his hands—and no one has measured the power of a President—he will push the Panama business to its conclusion.

The propriety of the Canal, no one American—save the trans-Continental railways—was ever heard to deny. But, to the last crowned head of them, every European ruler, and even the elected one of France, has been and is opposed. They believe with Sir Walter Raleigh that he who holds the Isthmus of Darien holds the key to the world, and are solicitous that no such lock-opener shall hang at the girdle of America.

It will be well for the world while Mr. Roosevelt abides in Washington. He will not be duped abroad or deluded at home. The Government will be neither a plutocracy nor a mobocracy, but a democracy, while he prevails. He will be the friend of Capital, the friend of Labor, the fool and tool of neither. It was he who said during his stay the door of the White House should yield as easily to the touch of Labor as to the touch of Capital, but no easier.

ALFRED HENRY LEWIS

See the article "Roosevelt, Theodore," in the Encyclopedic Index, for a brief record of Roosevelt's work. The article, "Panama Canal," should also be read in the record.

WAR DEPARTMENT,
Washington, July 4, 1902.

To the Army of the United States:

The President, upon this anniversary of national independence, wishes to express to the officers and enlisted men of the United States Army his deep appreciation of the service they have rendered to the country in the great and difficult undertakings which they have brought to a successful conclusion during the past year.

He thanks the officers and the enlisted men who have been maintaining order and carrying on the military government in Cuba, because they have faithfully given effect to the humane purposes of the American people. They have with sincere kindness helped the Cuban people to take all the successive steps necessary to the establishment of their own constitutional government. During the time required for that process they have governed Cuba wisely, regarding justice and respecting individual liberty; have honestly collected and expended for the best interests of the Cuban people the revenues, amounting to over $60,000,000; have carried out practical and thorough sanitary measures, greatly improving the health and lowering the death rate of the island. By patient, scientific research they have ascertained the causes of yellow fever, and by good administration have put an end to that most dreadful disease which has long destroyed the lives and hindered the commercial prosperity of the Cubans. They have expedited justice and secured protection for the rights of the innocent, while they have cleansed the prisons and established sound discipline and healthful conditions for the punishment of the guilty.

They have re-established and renovated and put upon a substantial basis adequate hospitals and asylums for the care of the unfortunate. They have established a general system of free common schools throughout the island, in which over two hundred thousand children are in actual attendance. They have constructed great and necessary public works. They have gradually trained the Cubans themselves in all branches of administration, so that the new government upon assuming power has begun its work with an experienced force of Cuban civil service employees competent to execute its orders. They have borne themselves with dignity and self-control, so that nearly four years of military government have passed unmarred by injury or insult to man or woman. They have transferred the government of Cuba to the Cuban people amid universal expressions of friendship and good will, and have left a record of ordered justice and liberty of rapid improvement in material and moral conditions and progress in the art of government which reflects great credit upon the people of the United States.

The President thanks the officers and enlisted men of the army in

213

the Philippines, both regulars and volunteers, for the courage and fortitude, the indomitable spirit and loyal devotion with which they have put down and ended the great insurrection which has raged throughout the archipelago against the lawful sovereignty and just authority of the United States. The task was peculiarly difficult and trying. They were required at first to overcome organized resistance of superior numbers, well equipped with modern arms of precision, intrenched in an unknown country of mountain defiles, jungles, and swamps, apparently capable of interminable defense. When this resistance had been overcome they were required to crush out a general system of guerrilla warfare conducted among a people speaking unknown tongues, from whom it was almost impossible to obtain the information necessary for successful pursuit or to guard against surprise and ambush.

The enemies by whom they were surrounded were regardless of all obligations of good faith and of all the limitations which humanity has imposed upon civilized warfare. Bound themselves by the laws of war, our soldiers were called upon to meet every device of unscrupulous treachery and to contemplate without reprisal the infliction of barbarous cruelties upon their comrades and friendly natives. They were instructed, while punishing armed resistance, to conciliate the friendship of the peaceful, yet had to do with a population among whom it was impossible to distinguish friend from foe, and who in countless instances used a false appearance of friendship for ambush and assassination. They were obliged to deal with problems of communication and transportation in a country without roads and frequently made impassable by torrential rains. They were weakened by tropical heat and tropical disease. Widely scattered over a great archipelago, extending a thousand miles from north to south, the gravest responsibilities, involving the life or death of their comrades, frequently devolved upon young and inexperienced officers beyond the reach of specific orders or advice.

Under all these adverse circumstances the army of the Philippines has accomplished its task rapidly and completely. In more than two thousand combats, great and small, within three years, it has exhibited unvarying courage and resolution. Utilizing the lessons of the Indian wars it has relentlessly followed the guerrilla bands to their fastness in mountain and jungle, and crushed them. It has put an end to the vast system of intimidation and secret assassination, by which the peaceful natives were prevented from taking a genuine part in government under American authority. It has captured or forced to surrender substantially all the leaders of the insurrection. It has submitted to no discouragement and halted at no obstacle. Its officers have shown high qualities of command, and its men have shown devotion and discipline. Its splendid virile energy has been accompanied by self-control, patience, and magnanimity.

With surprisingly few individual exceptions its course has been characterized by humanity and kindness to the prisoner and the noncombatant. With admirable good temper, sympathy, and loyalty to American ideals its commanding generals have joined with the civilian agents of the government in healing the wounds of war and assuring to the people of the Philippines the blessings of peace and prosperity. Individual liberty, protection of personal rights, civil order, public instruction and religious freedom have followed its footsteps. It has added honor to the flag, which it defended, and has justified increased confidence in the future of the American people, whose soldiers do not shrink from labor or death, yet love liberty and peace. The President feels that he expresses the sentiments of all the loyal people of the United States in doing honor to the whole army which has joined in the performance and shares in the credit of these honorable services.

This general order will be read aloud at parade in every military post on the 4th day of July, 1902, or on the first day after it shall have been received. ELIHU ROOT,

H. C. CORBIN, *Secretary of War.*
Adjutant-General, Major-General, U. S. A.

BY THE PRESIDENT OF THE UNITED STATES OF AMERICA.

A PROCLAMATION.

Whereas, in the opening of the Kiowa, Comanche, Apache, and Wichita Indian lands in the Territory of Oklahoma, by proclamation dated July 4, 1901, pursuant to section six of the act of Congress approved June 6, 1900 (31 Stat., 672, 676), the southwest quarter of the northwest quarter of section nineteen in township two north, of range eleven west of the Indian principal meridian, containing forty acres, was reserved for the use of the Fort Sill Indian sub-agency;

Now, therefore, I, THEODORE ROOSEVELT, President of the United States, by virtue of the power in me vested by section six of said act of Congress of June 6, 1900, do hereby declare and make known that said land is hereby restored to the public domain, to be disposed of to said city for cemetery purposes under said act of Congress.

In witness whereof, I have hereunto set my hand and caused the seal of the United States to be affixed.

DONE at the City of Washington this 4th day of September, in the year of our Lord one thousand nine hundred and two, [SEAL.] and of the Independence of the United States the one hundred and twenty-seventh. THEODORE ROOSEVELT.

By the President:

ALVEY A. ADEE, *Acting Secretary of State.*

BY THE PRESIDENT OF THE UNITED STATES OF AMERICA.

A PROCLAMATION.

Whereas the act of Congress entitled "An Act to ratify and confirm a supplemental agreement with the Creek tribe of Indians, and for other purposes," approved on the thirtieth day of June, nineteen hundred and two, contains a provision as follows:

That the following supplemental agreement, submitted by certain commissioners of the Creek tribe of Indians, as herein amended, is hereby ratified and confirmed on the part of the United States, and the same shall be of full force and effect if ratified by the Creek tribal council on or before the first day of September, nineteen hundred and two, * * *

And whereas the principal chief of the said tribe has transmitted to me an act of the Creek national council entitled "An Act to ratify and confirm a supplemental agreement with the United States" approved the twenty-sixth day of July, nineteen hundred and two, which contains a provision as follows:

That the following supplemental agreement by and between the United States and the Muskogee (or Creek) Tribe of Indians, in Indian Territory, ratified and confirmed on the part of the United States by Act of Congress approved June 30, 1902 (Public—No. 200.), is hereby confirmed on the part of the Muskogee (or Creek) Nation, * * *

And whereas paragraph twenty-two provides as follows:

The principal chief, as soon as practicable after the ratification of this agreement by Congress, shall call an extra session of the Creek Nation council and submit this agreement, as ratified by Congress, to such council for its consideration, and if the agreement be ratified by the National council, as provided in the constitution of the tribe, the principal chief shall transmit to the President of the United States a certified copy of the act of the council ratifying the agreement, and thereupon the President shall issue his proclamation making public announcement of such ratification, thenceforward all the provisions of this agreement shall have the force and effect of law.

Now, therefore, I, THEODORE ROOSEVELT, President of the United States, do hereby declare said agreement duly ratified and that all the provisions thereof became law according to the terms thereof upon the twenty-sixth day of July, nineteen hundred and two.

In witness whereof, I have hereunto set my hand and caused the seal of the United States to be affixed.

[SEAL.] DONE at the City of Washington this 8th day of August, in the year of our Lord one thousand nine hundred and two and of the Independence of the United States the one hundred and twenty-sixth.

THEODORE ROOSEVELT.

By the President:
ALVEY A. ADEE,
Acting Secretary of State.

By the President of the United States of America.

A PROCLAMATION.

Whereas, it is provided by section twenty-four of the Act of Congress, approved March third, eighteen hundred and ninety-one, entitled, "An act to repeal timber-culture laws, and for other purposes", "That the President of the United States may, from time to time, set apart and reserve, in any State or Territory having public land bearing forests, in any part of the public lands wholly or in part covered with timber or undergrowth, whether of commercial value or not, as public reservations, and the President shall, by public proclamation, declare the establishment of such reservations and the limits thereof";

And whereas, the following described public lands in the Territory of Alaska are in part covered with timber, and it appears that the public good would be promoted by setting apart and reserving said lands as a public reservation;

Now, therefore, I, Theodore Roosevelt, President of the United States, by virtue of the power in me vested by section twenty-four of the aforesaid Act of Congress, do hereby make known and proclaim that there are hereby reserved from settlement, entry or sale, and set apart as a Public Reservation, Chichagof Island and the adjacent islands to the seaward thereof, Kupreanof Island, Kuiu Island, Zarembo Island, and Prince of Wales Island and the adjacent islands to the seaward thereof, in Alaska: *Provided*, that this proclamation shall not be so construed as to deprive any person of any valid right possessed under the Treaty for the cession of the Russian possessions in North America to the United States, concluded at Washington on the thirtieth day of March, eighteen hundred and sixty-seven, or acquired under any act of Congress relating to the Territory of Alaska.

Warning is hereby expressly given to all persons not to unlawfully enter upon or occupy any of the lands reserved by this proclamation.

The reservation hereby established shall be known as The Alexander Archipelago Forest Reserve.

In witness whereof, I have hereunto set my hand and caused the seal of the United States to be affixed.

Done at the City of Washington this 20th day of August, [SEAL.] in the year of our Lord one thousand nine hundred and two, and of the Independenc of the United States the one hundred and twenty-sevent!

THEODORE ROOSEVELT.

By the President:
Alvey A. Adee, *Acting Secretary of State.*

THANKSGIVING PROCLAMATION

By the President of the United States of America

A PROCLAMATION.

According to the yearly custom of our people, it falls upon the President at this season to appoint a day of festival and thanksgiving to God.

Over a century and a quarter has passed since this country took its place among the nations of the earth, and during that time we have had on the whole more to be thankful for than has fallen to the lot of any other people. Generation after generation has grown to manhood and passed away. Each has had to bear its peculiar burdens, each to face its special crises, and each has known years of grim trial, when the country was menaced by malice domestic or foreign levy, when the hand of the Lord was heavy upon it in drouth or flood or pestilence, when in bodily distress and anguish of soul it paid the penalty of folly and a froward heart. Nevertheless, decade by decade, we have struggled onward and upward; we now abundantly enjoy material well-being, and under the favor of the Most High we are striving earnestly to achieve moral and spiritual uplifting. The year that has just closed has been one of peace and of overflowing plenty. Rarely has any people enjoyed greater prosperity than we are now enjoying. For this we render heartfelt and solemn thanks to the Giver of Good; and we seek to praise Him not by words only but by deeds, by the way in which we do our duty to ourselves and to our fellow men.

Now, therefore, I, Theodore Roosevelt, President of the United States, do hereby designate as a day of general thanksgiving Thursday, the twenty-seventh of the coming November, and do recommend that throughout the land the people cease from their ordinary occupations, and in their several homes and places of worship render thanks unto Almighty God for the manifold blessings of the past year.

In witness whereof, I have hereunto set my hand and caused the seal of the United States to be affixed.

[SEAL.] Done at the City of Washington this 29th day of October, in the year of our Lord one thousand nine hundred and two and of the independence of the United States the one hundred and twenty-seventh.

THEODORE ROOSEVELT.

By the President:
John Hay,
Secretary of State.

ADDRESS

[At a Banquet of Spanish War Veterans at Detroit, Mich.,
Sept. 22, 1902.]

Mr. Mayor, and you, my Comrades, and all of you, my Fellow-Americans, Men and Women of Detroit:

While the war with Spain was easy enough, the tasks left behind, though glorious, have been hard. You, the men of the Spanish War, and your comrades in arms who fought in Cuba and Porto Rico and in the Philippines, won renown for the country, added to its moral grandeur and to its material prosperity; but you also left duties to be done by those who came after you. In Porto Rico the duty has been merely administrative, and it has been so well done that very little need be said about it.

I speak in the presence not only of the men who fought in the Spanish War and in the Philippine War, which was its aftermath, but in the presence of those who fought in the great Civil War; and more than that, I speak here in a typical city of the old Northwest, what is now the Middle West, in a typical State of our Union. You men of Michigan have been mighty in war and mighty in peace. I preach the gospel of hope to you men of the West who in thought and life embody this gospel of hope, this gospel of resolute and confident belief in your own powers and in the destiny of this mighty Republic. I believe in the future—not in a spirit which will sit down and look for the future to work itself out—but with a determination to do its part in making the future what it can and shall be made. We are optimists. We spurn the teachings of despair and distrust. We have an abiding faith in the growing strength, the growing future of the mighty young nation, still in the flush of its youth, and yet with the might of a giant, which stands on a continent and grasps an ocean with either hand.

Succeed? Of course we shall succeed! How can success fail to come to a race of masterful energy and resoluteness, which has a continent for the base of its domain, and which feels within its veins the thrill that comes to generous souls when their strength stirs in them, and they know that the future is theirs? No great destiny ever yet came to a people walking with their eyes on the ground and their faces shrouded in gloom. No great destiny ever yet came to a people who feared the future, who feared failure more than they hoped for success. Stout of heart, we see across the dangers the great future that lies beyond, and we rejoice as a giant refreshed, as a strong man girt for the race; and we go down into the arena where the nations strive for mastery, our hearts lifted with the faith that to us and to our children and our children's children it shall be given to make this Republic the mightiest among the peoples of mankind.

EXECUTIVE ORDERS.

EXECUTIVE MANSION, *September 23, 1901.*

In accordance with the provisions of the act of Congress approved June 4, 1897 (30 Stat., 34-36), and by virtue of the authority thereby given, and on the recommendation of the Secretary of the Interior, it is hereby ordered that sections 23, 24 of township seven south, range 93 west, 6th principal meridian, Colorado, within the limits of the Black Mesa Forest Reserve be restored to the public domain after sixty days' notice hereof by publication, as required by law; these tracts having been found upon personal and official inspection to be better adapted to agricultural than forest purposes.

THEODORE ROOSEVELT.

To all to whom these present shall come, greeting:

Know ye that reposing special trust and confidence in the integrity, prudence, and ability of Thaddeus S. Sharretts, United States General Appraiser, I have invested him with full and all manner of authority for and in the name of the United States of America, to meet and confer with any person or persons duly authorized by the government of China or by any government or governments having treaties with China being invested with like power and authority, and with him or them to agree on a plan for the conversion into specific duties, as far as possible, and as soon as may be, of all *ad valorem* duties on imports into China in conformity with the provisions in this regard contained in the final protocol signed by the diplomatic representatives of China and the Powers at Peking on September 7, 1901, the same to be submitted to the President of the United States for approval.

In testimony whereof I have caused the seal of the United States to be hereunto affixed.

Given under my hand at the City of Washington, this first [SEAL] day of October, A. D. 1901, and of the Independence of the United States the one hundred and twenty-sixth.

THEODORE ROOSEVELT.

WHITE HOUSE, *October 15, 1901.*

On and after January 1, 1902, the following ratings and pay per month are established for the petty officers and other enlisted men of the Commissary Branch of the United States Navy:

RATING.	MONTHLY PAY.
Chief Commissary Steward	$70
Commissary Steward	60
Ship's Cook, 1st class	55

RATING.	MONTHLY PAY.
Ship's Cook, 2d class	$40
Ship's Cook, 3d class	30
Ship's Cook, 4th class	25
Baker, 1st class	45
Baker, 2d class	35

Landsmen detailed as crew messmen shall while so acting except when appointed as reliefs during temporary absence of the regular crew messmen receive extra compensation at the rate of $5 per month.

THEODORE ROOSEVELT.

WHITE HOUSE, *October 30, 1901.*

It is hereby ordered that Harbor Island, and three islets southeast thereof in Sitka Harbor, District of Alaska, be and they are hereby reserved for the use of the Revenue Cutter Service subject to any legal existing rights.

THEODORE ROOSEVELT.

WHITE HOUSE, *November 9, 1901.*

It is hereby ordered that all tracts and parcels of land belonging to the United States situate in the provinces of Zambales and Bataan, in the Island of Luzon, Philippine Islands to the southward and westward of a line beginning at the mouth of the Rio Pamatuan, near Capones Islands, and following the imaginary course of the Pamatuan to the headwaters of the easternmost branch of said river; from thence east, true, to meet a line running north, true, from Santa Rita Peak; from this intersection to Santa Rita itself; thence to Santa Rosa Peak, and thence in a straight line in a southerly direction to the sea at the town of Bagac, and including said town as well as all adjacent islands, bays, harbors, estuaries, and streams within its limits, be and the same are hereby reserved for naval purposes, and said reservations and all lands included within said boundaries are hereby placed under the governance and control of the Navy Department.

THEODORE ROOSEVELT.

WHITE HOUSE, *November 11, 1901.*

It is hereby ordered that the southwest quarter, section twenty-nine, and the southeast quarter, section thirty, township one south, range eighteen west, San Bernardino base and meridian, California, be and they are hereby reserved for lighthouse purposes, subject to any legal existing rights.

THEODORE ROOSEVELT.

WHITE HOUSE, *November 14, 1901.*

It is hereby ordered that the following described tract of country in Arizona, viz., commencing at a point where the south line of the Navaho Indian Reservation (addition of January 8, 1900) intersects the Little Colorado River; thence due south to the fifth standard parallel north; thence east on said standard to the middle of the south line of township 21 north, range 15 east; thence north on the line bisecting townships 21, 22, 23, 24, said range 15 east, to the south line of the Moqui Reservation; thence due west to the place of beginning, be, and the same is hereby, withdrawn from sale and settlement until such time as the Indians residing thereon shall have been settled permanently under the provisions of the homestead laws or the general allotment act approved February 8, 1887 (24 Stats., 388), and the act amendatory thereof, approved February 28, 1891 (26 Stats., 794).

THEODORE ROOSEVELT.

WHITE HOUSE, *November 15, 1901.*

It is hereby ordered that San Nicolas Island, California, be and it is hereby reserved for lighthouse purposes.

THEODORE ROOSEVELT.

November 26, 1901.

From and after January 1, 1901, all enlisted men of the Navy will be allowed seventy-five cents per month in addition to the pay of their ratings for each good conduct medal, pin. or bar, issued for service, terminating after December 31, 1901.

THEODORE ROOSEVELT.

WHITE HOUSE, *December 3, 1901.*

From and after January 1, 1902, each enlisted man of the Navy who holds a certificate as a credit from the Petty Officers' School of Instruction, Navy Training Station, Newport, R. I., shall receive two dollars per month in addition to the pay of his rating.

THEODORE ROOSEVELT.

WHITE HOUSE, *December 9, 1901.*

From and after January 1, 1902, the classification and monthly pay of Mess Attendants in the United States Navy shall be as follows:

Mess Attendants, 1st class........................... $24
Mess Attendants, 2d class............................. 20
Mess Attendants, 3d class............................. 16

THEODORE ROOSEVELT.

WHITE HOUSE, *December 19, 1901.*

Such public lands as may exist on Culebra Island between the parallels of 18°15′ and 18°23′ north latitude, and between the meridians of 65° 10′ and 65° 25′ west longitude, are hereby placed under the jurisdiction of the Navy Department.

THEODORE ROOSEVELT.

WHITE HOUSE, *January 17, 1902.*

The attention of the Departments is hereby called to the provisions of the laws giving preference to veterans in appointment and retention.

The President desires that wherever the needs of the service will justify it and the law will permit preference shall be given alike in appointment and retention to honorably discharged veterans of the Civil War, who are fit and well qualified to perform the duties of the places which they seek or are filling.

THEODORE ROOSEVELT.

WHITE HOUSE, *January 31, 1902.*

All officers and employees of the United States of every description serving in or under any of the Executive Departments and whether so serving in or out of Washington are hereby forbidden either direct or indirect, individually or through associations, to solicit an increase of pay, or to influence or to attempt to influence in their own interest any legislation whatever, either before Congress or its Committees, or in any way save through the heads of the Departments in or under which they serve, on penalty of dismissal from the government service.

THEODORE ROOSEVELT.

WHITE HOUSE, *February 5, 1902.*

As it is desirable in view of the expected visit of his Royal Highness, Prince Henry of Prussia, ˆ the United States that suitable arrangements should be made for his reception and entertainment during his sojourn in the United States, I hereby designate the following named persons to serve as delegates for this purpose, and do hereby authorize and empower them to make such engagements, incur such expenses, and to draw upon the Secretary of State for such moneys as may be necessary with which to pay the expenses thus incurred, to an amount to be determined by the Secretary of State.

The Assistant Secretary of State, David J. Hill, reperesenting the Department of State.

Mayor-General Henry C. Corbin, Adjutant-General, U. S. A., representing the War Department.

Rear-Admiral Robley D. Evans, U. S. N., representing the Navy Department, and to be Honorary A. D. C. to his Royal Highness.

The following officers are detailed to assist the delegates:

Colonel T. A. Bingham, U. S. A., Military Aide to the President; Commander W. S. Cowles, U. S. N., Navy Aide to the President.

THEODORE ROOSEVELT.

WHITE HOUSE, *February 15, 1902.*

In accordance with the provisions of Section 2212 of the Revised Statutes and by virtue of the authority thereby given, it is hereby ordered that the office of Surveyor-General in the surveying district of the Territory of Arizona, be and it is hereby located at Phœnix, Arizona, and the office of Surveyor-General at Tucson, Arizona, is hereby discontinued, and the records and business thereof are hereby transferred to the office of Surveyor-General at Tucson, Arizona.

THEODORE ROOSEVELT.

WHITE HOUSE, *March 24, 1902.*

Paragraph 451 of the Consular Regulations of 1896 is hereby amended by the addition of the following:

No consular officer shall accept an appointment to office from any foreign state as administrator, guardian or any other fiduciary capacity for the settlement or conservation of the estate of deceased persons, or of their heirs or of other persons under legal disabilities, without having been previously authorized by the Secretary of State to do so.

THEODORE ROOSEVELT.

WHITE HOUSE, *March 26, 1902.*

It is hereby ordered that the building known as the "office" and a tract of land 200 feet square, the center of which shall be identical with that of the building, and the sides of which shall be parallel with those of the building in the limits of the Fort Yuma Abandoned Military

Reservation, Arizona, be and they are hereby reserved and set apart for the use of the Weather Bureau.

THEODORE ROOSEVELT.

WHITE HOUSE, *March 27, 1902.*

To the heads of the Executive Departments:

As a mark of respect to the memory of the Right Honorable Lord Pauncefote, of Preston, Late Ambassador Extraordinary and Plenipotentiary of Great Britain to the United States, the President directs that the National flag be displayed at half-mast upon the White House and other federal buildings in the city of Washington on Wednesday, March 28, 1902, the day of the funeral.

GEORGE B. CORTELYOU,
Secretary to the President.

WHITE HOUSE, *April 29, 1902.*

To the heads of the Executive Departments:

As a mark of respect to the memory of J. Sterling Morton, formerly Secretary of Agriculture, the President directs that the National flag be displayed at half-mast upon the White House and other federal buildings in the city of Washington on Wednesday, April 30, 1902, the day of the funeral.

GEORGE B. CORTELYOU,
Secretary to the President.

WHITE HOUSE, *April 29, 1902.*

It is hereby ordered that the building known as the "Residence" and the tract of land bounded on the north, east, and south by the rights of way grant to the Yuma Pumping Irrigation Company by the act of Congress approved January 20, 1893 (27 Stat., 420), and on the west by the east line of the tract reserved by Executive Order of March 26, 1902, for the Weather Bureau and the extension thereof to intersections with the rights of way herein mentioned in the limits of the Fort Yuma Abandoned Military Reservation, Arizona, be and they are hereby reserved and set apart for the Customs Service.

THEODORE ROOSEVELT.

WHITE HOUSE, *April 30, 1902.*

It is hereby ordered that the northwest quarter of the northwest quarter and lot 4 of section 32, township one south, range 18 west, San

Bernardino base and meridian, California, be and they are hereby reserved for light-house purposes, subject to any legal existing rights.

THEODORE ROOSEVELT.

WHITE HOUSE, *May 12, 1902.*

It is hereby ordered that such employees of the Executive Departments, the Government Printing Office, and the Navy Yard and Station at Washington, D. C., as served in the Military or Navy service
of the United States in the late Civil War shall be excused from duty
on Saturday, the 17th instant, to enable them to attend the ceremonies
incident to the reburial of the late Major-General W. S. Rosecrans.

THEODORE ROOSEVELT.

WHITE HOUSE, *May 12, 1902.*

It is hereby ordered that upon Wednesday, the 21st instant, such
employees of the Executive Departments, the Government Printing
Office, and the Navy Yard and Station at Washington, D. C., as served
in the military or naval service of the United States in the Spanish-
American War, or the insurrection in the Philippine Islands, shall be
excused from duty at 12 o'clock noon for the remainder of that day, to
enable them to participate in the ceremonies incident to the dedication
of a statue erected to the memory of the Spanish War dead at Arlington.

THEODORE ROOSEVELT.

WHITE HOUSE, *June 13, 1902.*

It is hereby ordered that the southwest quarter section thirty-four,
township twenty-three north, range one east, Willamette Meridian,
Washington, be and it is hereby reserved and set apart for the use of
the Navy Department for the purpose of a target range.

THEODORE ROOSEVELT.

WHITE HOUSE, *June 13, 1902.*

In accordance with the provisions of section 2253 Revised Statutes
of the United States, and by virtue of the authority thereby given, it is
hereby ordered that the existing boundaries of the Wakeeney land district and of the Colby land district, in the State of Kansas, be, and

they are hereby, changed and re-established by the transfer from the Wakeeney land district to the Colby land district of that portion of the State of Kansas included in township 10, ranges 26 to 42 inclusive.

THEODORE ROOSEVELT.

WHITE HOUSE, *July 3, 1902.*

In the exercise of power vested in the President by the Constitution and of the authority given to him by the seventeen hundred and fifty-third section of the Revised Statutes, it is hereby ordered that appointments of all unclassified laborers in and under the several Executive Departments and independent offices shall be made in accordance with regulations to be approved and promulgated by the heads of the several Departments and offices and the Civil Service Commission; such regulations to be in full force and effect on and after the date of their promulgation.

THEODORE ROOSEVELT.

WHITE HOUSE, *July 10, 1902.*

No enlisted person in the Navy service of the United States shall be discharged therefrom prior to the completion of his term of enlistment, except for one of the following causes: Undesirability, inaptitude, physical or mental disability, or unfitness.

In every case, the recommendation for such discharge must be made by the commanding officer of the vessel on which the man may be serving.

Applications for discharges which reach the department except through the commanding officers of vessels shall be without exception disregarded.

THEODORE ROOSEVELT.

OYSTER BAY, *July 19, 1902.*

The act of Congress approved June 14, 1902, having amended the Revised Statutes of the United States so as to permit of the issuance of passports to persons owing allegiance to the United States, whether citizens of the United States or not, and under such rules as the President shall designate and prescribe on behalf of the United States, the instructions to the diplomatic officers of the United States and the United States Consular regulations are hereby so modified and amended as to permit diplomatic and consular officers of the United States having authority to issue passports to issue them to residents of the Insular Possessions of the United States who make satisfactory application. Each applicant under this provision must state in addition to the information now required in the application of a citizen of the United States that he owes allegiance to the United States and that he does not acknowledge allegiance to any other government and must submit an affidavit from at least two credible witnesses having good means of the knowledge in substantiation of his statements of birth and residence and loyalty. The same fee shall be collected by diplomatic and consular officers of the United States for issuing passports to residents of the Insular Possessions as is now required for issuing passports to citizens of the United States.

THEODORE ROOSEVELT.

WHITE HOUSE, *Washington, July 22, 1902.*

By virtue of the authority vested in me by the act of Congress approved July 1, 1902, entitled "An act authorizing the President to reserve public lands and buildings in the Island of Puerto Rico for public uses, and granting other public lands and buildings to the government of Puerto Rico and for other purposes," Miraflores Island in the Harbor of San Juan, Puerto Rico, is hereby reserved for use as a quarantine station or a site for a marine hospital or for both said purposes under the control of the Public Health and Marine Hospital service of the United States.

THEODORE ROOSEVELT.

WHITE HOUSE, *July 25, 1902.*

It is hereby ordered under the provisions of section 4 of the act of Congress approved April 12, 1902, "To promote the efficiency of the Revenue Cutter Service," that the Secretary of the Treasury shall "by direction of the President" when officers of the Revenue Cutter Service reach the age limit of 64 years, retire them from active service.

THEODORE ROOSEVELT.

WHITE HOUSE, *August 1, 1902.*

From and after July 1, 1902, each enlisted man that has been rated Seaman Gunner prior to April 1, 1902, or that holds certificate of graduation from the Petty Officers' Schools, Seaman Gunner Class, shall receive $2.00 per month in addition to the pay of his rating during current and subsequent enlistments.

THEODORE ROOSEVELT.

WHITE HOUSE, *August 9, 1902.*

It is hereby ordered that the south half of the southeast quarter and the southwest quarter of section 3, township 22 north, range 26 west, 6th principal meridian, Nebraska, be, and they are hereby, reserved and set apart for the use of the Department of Agriculture for purposes in connection with experimental tree planting.

THEODORE ROOSEVELT.

SECOND ANNUAL MESSAGE.

WHITE HOUSE, *December 2, 1902.*

To the Senate and House of Representatives:

We still continue in a period of unbounded prosperity. This prosperity is not the creature of law, but undoubtedly the laws under which we work have been instrumental in creating the conditions which made it possible, and by unwise legislation it would be easy enough to destroy it. There will undoubtedly be periods of depression. The wave will recede; but the tide will advance. This Nation is seated on a continent flanked by two great oceans. It is composed of men the descendants of pioneers, or, in a sense, pioneers themselves; of men winnowed out from among the nations of the Old World by the energy, boldness, and love of adventure found in their own eager hearts. Such a Nation, so placed, will surely wrest success from fortune.

As a people we have played a large part in the world, and we are bent upon making our future even larger than the past. In particular, the events of the last four years have definitely decided that, for woe or for weal, our place must be great among the nations. We may either fail greatly or succeed greatly; but we can not avoid the endeavor from which either great failure or great success must come. Even if we would, we can not play a small part. If we should try, all that would follow would be that we should play a large part ignobly and shamefully.

But our people, the sons of the men of the Civil War, the sons of the men who had iron in their blood, rejoice in the present and face the future high of heart and resolute of will. Ours is not the creed of the weakling and the coward; ours is the gospel of hope and of triumphant endeavor. We do not shrink from the struggle before us. There are many problems for us to face at the outset of the twentieth century—grave problems abroad and still graver at home; but we know that we can solve them and solve them well, provided only that we bring to the solution the qualities of head and heart which were shown by the men who, in the days of Washington, founded this Government, and, in the days of Lincoln, preserved it.

No country has ever occupied a higher plane of material well-being than ours at the present moment. This well-being is due to no sudden or accidental causes, but to the play of the economic forces in this country for over a century; to our laws, our sustained and continuous policies; above all, to the high individual average of our citizenship. Great fortunes have been won by those who have taken the lead in this phenomenal industrial development, and most of these fortunes have been won not by doing evil, but as an incident to action which has benefited the community as a whole. Never before has material well-being been so widely diffused among our people. Great fortunes have been accumulated, and yet in the aggregate these fortunes are small indeed when compared to the wealth of the people as a whole. The plain people are better off than they have ever been before. The insurance companies, which are practically mutual benefit societies—especially helpful to men of moderate means—represent accumulations of capital which are among the largest in this country. There are more deposits in the savings banks, more owners of farms, more well-paid wage-workers in this country now than ever before in our history. Of course, when the conditions have favored the growth of so much that was good, they have also favored somewhat the growth of what was evil. It is eminently necessary that we should endeavor to cut out this evil, but let us keep a due sense of proportion; let us not in fixing our gaze upon the lesser evil forget the greater good. The evils are real and some of them are menacing, but they are the outgrowth, not of misery or decadence, but of prosperity—of the progress of our gigantic industrial development. This industrial development must not be checked, but side by side with it should go such progressive regulation as will diminish the evils. We should fail in our duty if we did not try to remedy the evils, but we shall succeed only if we proceed patiently, with practical common sense as well as resolution, separating the good from the bad and holding on to the former while endeavoring to get rid of the latter.

In my Message to the present Congress at its first session I discussed at length the question of the regulation of those big corporations commonly doing an interstate business, often with some tendency to monopoly, which are popularly known as trusts. The experience of the past year has emphasized, in my opinion, the desirability of the steps I then proposed. A fundamental requisite of social efficiency is a high standard of individual energy and excellence; but this is in no wise inconsistent with power to act in combination for aims which can not so well be achieved by the individual acting alone. A fundamental base of civilization is the inviolability of property; but this is in no wise inconsistent with the right of society to regulate the exercise of the artificial powers which it confers upon the owners of property, under the name of corporate franchises, in such a way as to prevent the misuse of these powers. Corporations, and especially combinations of corporations, should be managed under public regulation. Experience has shown that under our system of government the necessary supervision can not be obtained by State action. It must therefore be achieved by national action. Our aim is not to do away with corporations; on the contrary, these big aggregations are an inevitable development of modern industrialism, and the effort to destroy them would be futile unless accomplished in ways that would work the utmost mischief to the entire body politic. We can do nothing of good in the way of regulating and supervising these corporations until we fix clearly in our minds that we are not attacking the corporations, but endeavoring to do away with any evil in them. We are not hostile to them; we are merely determined that they shall be so handled as to subserve the public good. We draw the line against misconduct, not against wealth. The capitalist who, alone or in conjunction with his fellows, performs some great industrial feat by which he wins money is a welldoer, not a wrongdoer, provided only he works in proper and legitimate lines. We wish to favor such a man when he does well. We wish to supervise and control his actions only to prevent him from doing ill. Publicity can do no harm to the honest corporation; and we need not be over tender about sparing the dishonest corporation.

In curbing and regulating the combinations of capital which are, or may become, injurious to the public we must be careful not to stop the great enterprises which have legitimately reduced the cost of production, not to abandon the place which our country has won in the leadership of the international industrial world, not to strike down wealth with the result of closing factories and mines, of turning the wageworker idle in the streets and leaving the farmer without a market for what he grows. Insistence upon the impossible means delay in achieving the possible, exactly as, on the other hand, the stubborn defense alike of what is good and what is bad in the existing system, the resolute effort to obstruct any attempt at betterment, betrays blindness to the historic truth that wise evolution is the sure safeguard against revolution.

No more important subject can come before the Congress than this of the regulation of interstate business. This country can not afford to sit supine on the plea that under our peculiar system of government we are helpless in the presence of the new conditions, and unable to grapple with them or to cut out whatever of evil has arisen in connection with them. The power of the Congress to regulate interstate commerce is an absolute and unqualified grant, and without limitations other than those prescribed by the Constitution. The Congress has constitutional authority to make all laws necessary and proper for executing this power, and I am satisfied that this power has not been exhausted by any legislation now on the statute books. It is evident, therefore, that evils restrictive of commercial freedom and entailing restraint upon national commerce fall within the regulative power of the Congress, and that a wise and reasonable law would be a necessary and proper exercise of Congressional authority to the end that such evils should be eradicated.

I believe that monopolies, unjust discriminations, which prevent or cripple competition, fraudulent overcapitalization, and other evils in trust organizations and practices which injuriously affect interstate trade can be prevented under the power of the Congress to "regulate commerce with foreign nations and among the several States" through regulations and requirements operating directly upon such commerce, the instrumentalities thereof, and those engaged therein.

I earnestly recommend this subject to the consideration of the Congress with a view to the passage of a law reasonable in its provisions and effective in its operations, upon which the questions can be finally adjudicated that now raise doubts as to the necessity of constitutional amendment. If it prove impossible to accomplish the purposes above set forth by such a law, then, assuredly, we should not shrink from amending the Constitution so as to secure beyond peradventure the power sought.

The Congress has not heretofore made any appropriation for the better enforcement of the antitrust law as it now stands. Very much has been done by the Department of Justice in securing the enforcement of this law, but much more could be done if the Congress would make a special appropriation for this purpose, to be expended under the direction of the Attorney-General.

One proposition advocated has been the reduction of the tariff as a means of reaching the evils of the trusts which fall within the category I have described. Not merely would this be wholly ineffective, but the diversion of our efforts in such a direction would mean the abandonment of all intelligent attempt to do away with these evils. Many of the largest corporations, many of those which should certainly be included in any proper scheme of regulation, would not be affected in the slightest degree by a change in the tariff, save as such change interfered with the general prosperity of the country. The only relation of the tariff to big corporations as a whole is that the tariff makes manufactures profitable, and the tariff remedy proposed would be in effect simply to make manufactures unprofitable. To remove the tariff as a punitive measure directed against trusts would inevitably result in ruin to the weaker competitors who are struggling against them. Our aim should be not by unwise tariff changes to give foreign products the advantage over domestic products, but by proper regulation to give domestic competition a fair chance; and this end can not be reached by any tariff changes which would affect unfavorably all domestic competitors, good and bad alike. The question of regulation of the trusts stands apart from the question of tariff revision.

Stability of economic policy must always be the prime economic need of this country. This stability should not be fossilization. The country has acquiesced in the wisdom of the protective-tariff principle. It is exceedingly undesirable that this system should be destroyed or that there should be violent and radical changes therein. Our past experience shows that great prosperity in this country has always come under a protective tariff; and that the country can not prosper under fitful tariff changes at short intervals. Moreover, if the tariff laws as a whole work well, and if business has prospered under them and is prospering, it is better to endure for a time slight inconveniences and inequalities in some schedules than to upset business by too quick and too radical changes. It is most earnestly to be wished that we could treat the tariff from the standpoint solely of our business needs. It is, perhaps, too much to hope that partisanship may be entirely excluded from consideration of the subject, but at least it can be made secondary to the business interests of the country—that is, to the interests of our people as a whole. Unquestionably these business interests will best be served if together with fixity of principle as regards the tariff we combine a system which will permit us from time to time to make the necessary reapplication of the principle to the shifting national needs. We must take scrupulous care that the reapplication shall be made in such a way that it will not amount to a dislocation of our system, the mere threat of which (not to speak of the performance) would produce paralysis in the business energies of the community. The first consideration in making these changes would, of course, be to preserve the principle which underlies our whole tariff system— that is, the principle of putting American business interests at least on a full equality with interests abroad, and of always allowing a sufficient rate of duty to more than cover the difference between the labor cost here and abroad. The well-being of the wage-worker, like the well-being of the tiller of the soil, should be treated as an essential in shaping our whole economic policy. There must never be any change which will jeopardize the standard of comfort, the standard of wages of the American wage-worker.

One way in which the readjustment sought can be reached is by reciprocity treaties. It is greatly to be desired that such treaties may be adopted. They can be used to widen our markets and to give a greater field for the activities of our producers on the one hand, and on the other hand to secure in practical shape the lowering of duties when they are no longer needed for protection among our own people, or when the minimum of damage done may be disregarded for the sake of the maximum of good accomplished. If it prove impossible to ratify the pending treaties, and if there seem to be no warrant for the endeavor to execute others, or to amend the pending treaties so that they can be ratified, then the same end—to secure reciprocity— should be met by direct legislation.

Wherever the tariff conditions are such that a needed change can not with advantage be made by the application of the reciprocity idea, then it can be made outright by a lowering of duties on a given product. If possible, such change should be made only after the fullest consideration by practical experts, who should approach the subject from a business standpoint, having in view both the particular interests affected and the commercial well-being of the people as a whole. The machinery for providing such careful investigation can readily be supplied. The executive department has already at its disposal methods of collecting facts and figures; and if the Congress desires additional consideration to that which will be given the subject by its own committees, then a commission of business experts can be appointed whose duty it should be to recommend action by the Congress after a deliberate and scientific examination of the various schedules as they are affected by the changed and changing conditions. The unhurried and unbiased report of this commission would show what changes should be made in the various schedules, and how far these changes could go without also changing the great prosperity which this country is now enjoying, or upsetting its fixed economic policy.

The cases in which the tariff can produce a monopoly are so few as to constitute an inconsiderable factor in the question; but of course if in any case it be found that a given rate of duty does promote a monopoly which works ill, no protectionist would object to such reduction of the duty as would equalize competition.

In my judgment, the tariff on anthracite coal should be removed, and anthracite put actually, where it now is nominally, on the free list. This would have no effect at all save in crises; but in crises it might be of service to the people.

Interest rates are a potent factor in business activity, and in order that these rates may be equalized to meet the varying needs of the seasons and of widely separated communities, and to prevent the recurrence of financial stringencies which injuriously affect legitimate business, it is necessary that there should be an element of elasticity in our monetary system. Banks are the natural servants of commerce, and upon them should be placed, as far as practicable, the burden of furnishing and maintaining a circulation adequate to supply the needs of our diversified industries and of our domestic and foreign commerce; and the issue of this should be so regulated that a sufficient supply should be always available for the business interests of the country.

It would be both unwise and unnecessary at this time to attempt to reconstruct our financial system, which has been the growth of a century; but some additional legislation is, I think, desirable. The mere outline of any plan sufficiently comprehensive to meet these requirements would transgress the appropriate limits of this communication. It is suggested, however, that all future legislation on the subject should be with the view of encouraging the use of such instrumentalities as will automatically supply every legitimate demand of productive industries and of commerce, not only in the amount, but in the character of circulation; and of making all kinds of money interchangeable, and, at the will of the holder, convertible into the established gold standard.

I again call your attention to the need of passing a proper immigration law, covering the points outlined in my Message to you at the first session of the present Congress; substantially such a bill has already passed the House.

How to secure fair treatment alike for labor and for capital, how to hold in check the unscrupulous man, whether employer or employee, without weakening individual initiative, without hampering and cramping the industrial development of the country, is a problem fraught with great difficulties and one which it is of the highest importance to solve on lines of sanity and far-sighted common sense as well as of devotion to the right. This is an era of federation and combination. Exactly as business men find they must often work through corporations, and as it is a constant tendency of these corporations to grow larger, so it is often necessary for laboring men to work in federations, and these have become important factors of modern industrial life. Both kinds of federation, capitalistic and labor, can do much good, and as a necessary corollary they can both do evil. Opposition to each kind of organization should take the form of opposition to whatever is bad in the conduct of any given corporation or union—not of attacks upon corporations as such nor upon unions as such; for some of the most far-reaching beneficent work for our people has been accomplished through both corporations and unions. Each must refrain from arbitrary or tyrannous interference with the rights of others. Organized capital and organized labor alike should remember that in the long run the interest of each must be brought into harmony with the interest of the general public; and the conduct of each must conform to the fundamental rules of obedience to the law, of individual freedom, and of justice and fair dealing toward all. Each should remember that in addition to power it must strive after the realization of healthy, lofty, and generous ideals. Every employer, every wage-worker, must be guaranteed his liberty and his right to do as he likes with his property or his labor so long as he does not infringe upon the rights of others. It is of the highest importance that employer and employee alike should endeavor to appreciate each the viewpoint of the other and the sure disaster that will come upon both in the long run if either grows to take as habitual an attitude of sour hostility and distrust toward the other. Few people deserve better of the country than those representatives both of capital and labor—and there are many such— who work continually to bring about a good understanding of this kind, based upon wisdom and upon broad and kindly sympathy between employers and employed. Above all, we need to remember that any kind of class animosity in the political world is, if possible, even more wicked, even more destructive to national welfare, than sectional, race, or religious animosity. We can get good government only upon condition that we keep true to the principles upon which this Nation was founded, and judge each man not as a part of a class, but upon his individual merits. All that we have a right to ask of any man, rich or poor, whatever his creed, his occupation, his birthplace, or his residence, is that he shall act well and honorably by his neighbor and by his country. We are neither for the rich man as such nor for the poor man as such; we are for the upright man, rich or poor. So far as the constitutional powers of the National Government touch these matters of general and vital moment to the Nation, they should be exercised in conformity with the principles above set forth.

It is earnestly hoped that a secretary of commerce may be created, with a seat in the Cabinet. The rapid multiplication of questions affecting labor and capital, the growth and complexity of the organizations through which both labor and capital now find expression, the steady tendency toward the employment of capital in huge corporations, and the wonderful strides of this country toward leadership in the international business world justify an urgent demand for the creation of such a position. Substantially all the leading commercial bodies in this country have united in requesting its creation. It is desirable that some such measure as that which has already passed the Senate be enacted into law. The creation of such a department would in itself be an advance toward dealing with and exercising supervision over the whole subject of the great corporations doing an interstate business; and with this end in view, the Congress should endow the department with large powers, which could be increased as experience might show the need.

I hope soon to submit to the Senate a reciprocity treaty with Cuba. On May 20 last the United States kept its promise to the island by formally vacating Cuban soil and turning Cuba over to those whom her own people had chosen as the first officials of the new Republic.

Cuba lies at our doors, and whatever affects her for good or for ill affects us also. So much have our people felt this that in the Platt amendment we definitely took the ground that Cuba must hereafter have closer political relations with us than with any other power. Thus in a sense Cuba has become a part of our international political system. This makes it necessary that in return she should be given some of the benefits of becoming part of our economic system. It is, from our own standpoint, a short-sighted and mischievous policy to fail to recognize this need. Moreover, it is unworthy of a mighty and generous nation, itself the greatest and most successful republic in history, to refuse to stretch out a helping hand to a young and weak sister republic just entering upon its career of independence. We should always fearlessly insist upon our rights in the face of the strong, and we should with ungrudging hand do our generous duty by the weak. I urge the adoption of reciprocity with Cuba not only because it is eminently for our own interests to control the Cuban market and by every means to foster our supremacy in the tropical lands and waters south of us, but also because we, of of the giant republic of the north, should make all our sister nations of the American Continent feel that whenever they will permit it we desire to show ourselves disinterestedly and effectively their friend.

A convention with Great Britain has been concluded, which will be at once laid before the Senate for ratification, providing for reciprocal trade arrangements between the United States and Newfoundland on substantially the lines of the convention formerly negotiated by the Secretary of State, Mr. Blaine. I believe reciprocal trade relations will be greatly to the advantage of both countries.

As civilization grows warfare becomes less and less the normal condition of foreign relations. The last century has seen a marked diminution of wars between civilized powers; wars with uncivilized powers are largely mere matters of international police duty, essential for the welfare of the world. Wherever possible, arbitration or some similar method should be employed in lieu of war to settle difficulties between civilized nations, although as yet the world has not progressed sufficiently to render it possible, or necessarily desirable, to invoke arbitration in every case. The formation of the international tribunal which sits at The Hague is an event of good omen from which great consequences for the welfare of all mankind may flow. It is far better, where possible, to invoke such a permanent tribunal than to create special arbitrators for a given purpose.

It is a matter of sincere congratulation to our country that the United States and Mexico should have been the first to use the good offices of The Hague Court. This was done last summer with most satisfactory results in the case of a claim at issue between us and our sister Republic. It is earnestly to be hoped that this first case will serve as a precedent for others, in which not only the United States but foreign nations may take advantage of the machinery already in existence at The Hague.

I commend to the favorable consideration of the Congress the Hawaiian fire claims, which were the subject of careful investigation during the last session.

The Congress has wisely provided that we shall build at once an isthmian canal, if possible at Panama. The Attorney-General reports that we can undoubtedly acquire good title from the French Panama Canal Company. Negotiations are now pending with Colombia to secure her assent to our building the canal. This canal will be one of the greatest engineering feats of the twentieth century; a greater engineering feat than has yet been accomplished during the history of mankind. The work should be carried out as a continuing policy without regard to change of Administration; and it should be begun under circumstances which will make it a matter of pride for all Administrations to continue the policy.

The canal will be of great benefit to America, and of importance to all the world. It will be of advantage to us industrially and also as improving our military position. It will be of advantage to the countries of tropical America. It is earnestly to be hoped that all of these countries will do as some of them have already done with signal success, and will invite to their shores commerce and improve their material conditions by recognizing that stability and order are the prerequisites of successful development. No independent nation in America need have the slightest fear of aggression from the United States. It behoves each one to maintain order within its own borders and to discharge its just obligations to foreigners. When this is done, they can rest assured that, be they strong or weak, they have nothing to dread from outside interference. More and more the increasing interdependence and complexity of international political and economic relations render it incumbent on all civilized and orderly powers to insist on the proper policing of the world.

During the fall of 1901 a communication was addressed to the Secretary of State, asking whether permission would be granted by the President to a corporation to lay a cable from a point on the California coast to the Philippine Islands by way of Hawaii. A statement of conditions or terms upon which such corporation would undertake to lay and operate a cable was volunteered.

Inasmuch as the Congress was shortly to convene, and Pacific-cable legislation had been the subject of consideration by the Congress for several years, it seemed to me wise to defer action upon the application until the Congress had first an opportunity to act. The Congress adjourned without taking any action, leaving the matter in exactly the same condition in which it stood when the Congress convened.

Meanwhile it appears that the Commercial Pacific Cable Company had promptly proceeded with preparations for laying its cable. It also made application to the President for access to and use of soundings taken by the U. S. S. *Nero,* for the purpose of discovering a practicable route for a trans-Pacific cable, the company urging that with access to these soundings it could complete its cable much sooner than if it were required to take soundings upon its own account. Pending consideration of this subject, it appeared important and desirable to attach certain conditions to the permission to examine and use the soundings, if it should be granted.

In consequence of this solicitation of the cable company, certain conditions were formulated, upon which the President was willing to allow access to these soundings and to consent to the landing and laying of the cable, subject to any alterations or additions thereto imposed by the Congress. This was deemed proper, especially as it was clear that a cable connection of some kind with China, a foreign country, was a part of the company's plan. This course was, moreover, in accordance with a line of precedents, including President Grant's action in the case of the first French cable, explained to the Congress in his Annual Message of December, 1875, and the instance occurring in 1879 of the second French cable from Brest to St. Pierre, with a branch to Cape Cod.

These conditions prescribed, among other things, a maximum rate for commercial messages and that the company should construct a line from the Philippine Islands to China, there being at present, as is well known, a British line from Manila to Hongkong.

The representatives of the cable company kept these conditions long under consideration, continuing, in the meantime, to prepare for laying the cable. They have, however, at length acceded to them, and an all-American line between our Pacific coast and the Chinese Empire, by way of Honolulu and the Philippine Islands, is thus provided for, and is expected within a few months to be ready for business.

Among the conditions is one reserving the power of the Congress to modify or repeal any or all of them. A copy of the conditions is herewith transmitted.

Of Porto Rico it is only necessary to say that the prosperity of the island and the wisdom with which it has been governed have been such as to make it serve as an example of all that is best in insular administration.

On July 4 last, on the one hundred and twenty-sixth anniversary of the declaration of our independence, peace and amnesty were promulgated in the Philippine Islands. Some trouble has since from time to time threatened with the Mohammedan Moros, but with the late insurrectionary Filipinos the war has entirely ceased. Civil government has now been introduced. Not only does each Filipino enjoy such rights to life, liberty, and the pursuit of happiness as he has never before known during the recorded history of the islands, but the people taken as a whole now enjoy a measure of self-government greater than that granted to any other Orientals by any foreign power and greater than that enjoyed by any other Orientals under their own governments, save the Japanese alone. We have not gone too far in granting these rights of liberty and self-government; but we have certainly gone to the limit that in the interests of the Philippine people themselves it was wise or just to go. To hurry matters, to go faster than we are now going, would entail calamity on the people of the islands. No policy ever entered into by the American people has vindicated itself in more signal manner than the policy of holding the Philippines. The triumph of our arms, above all the triumph of our laws and principles, has come sooner than we had any right to expect. Too much praise can not be given to the Army for what it has done in the Philippines both in warfare and from an administrative standpoint in preparing the way for civil government; and similar credit belongs to the civil authorities for the way in which they have planted the seeds of self-government in the ground thus made ready for them. The courage, the unflinching endurance, the high soldierly efficiency, and the general kind-heartedness and humanity of our troops have been strikingly manifested. There now remain only some fifteen thousand troops in the islands. All told, over one hundred thousand have been sent there. Of course, there have been individual instances of wrongdoing among them. They warred under fearful difficulties of climate and surroundings; and under the strain of the terrible provocations which they continually received from their foes, occasional instances of cruel retaliation occurred. Every effort has been made to prevent such cruelties, and finally these efforts have been completely successful. Every effort has also been made to detect and punish the wrongdoers. After making all allowance for these misdeeds, it remains true that few indeed have been the instances in which war has been waged by a civilized power against semicivilized or barbarous forces where there has been so little wrongdoing by the victors as in the Philippine Islands. On the other hand, the amount of difficult, important, and beneficent work which has been done is well-nigh incalculable.

Taking the work of the Army and the civil authorities together, it may be questioned whether anywhere else in modern times the world has seen a better example of real constructive statesmanship than our people have given in the Philippine Islands. High praise should also be given those Filipinos, in the aggregate very numerous, who have accepted the new conditions and joined with our representatives to work with hearty good will for the welfare of the islands.

The Army has been reduced to the minimum allowed by law. It is very small for the size of the Nation, and most certainly should be kept at the highest point of efficiency. The senior officers are given scant chance under ordinary conditions to exercise commands commensurate with their rank, under circumstances which would fit them to do their duty in time of actual war. A system of maneuvering our Army in bodies of some little size has been begun and should be steadily continued. Without such maneuvers it is folly to expect that in the event of hostilities with any serious foe even a small army corps could be handled to advantage. Both our officers and enlisted men are such that we can take hearty pride in them. No better material can be found. But they must be thoroughly trained, both as individuals and in the mass. The marksmanship of the men must receive special attention. In the circumstances of modern warfare the man must act far more on his own individual responsibility than ever before, and the high individual efficiency of the unit is of the utmost importance. Formerly this unit was the regiment; it is now not the regiment, not even the troop or company; it is the individual soldier. Every effort must be made to develop every workmanlike and soldierly quality in both the officer and the enlisted man.

I urgently call your attention to the need of passing a bill providing for a general staff and for the reorganization of the supply departments on the lines of the bill proposed by the Secretary of War last year. When the young officers enter the Army from West Point they probably stand above their compeers in any other military service. Every effort should be made, by training, by reward of merit, by scrutiny into their careers and capacity, to keep them of the same high relative excellence throughout their careers.

The measure providing for the reorganization of the militia system and for securing the highest efficiency in the National Guard, which has already passed the House, should receive prompt attention and action. It is of great importance that the relation of the National Guard to the militia and volunteer forces of the United States should be defined, and that in place of our present obsolete laws a practical and efficient system should be adopted.

Provision should be made to enable the Secretary of War to keep cavalry and artillery horses, worn-out in long performance of duty. Such horses fetch but a trifle when sold; and rather than turn them out to the misery awaiting them when thus disposed of, it would be better to employ them at light work around the posts, and when necessary to put them painlessly to death.

For the first time in our history naval maneuvers on a large scale are being held under the immediate command of the Admiral of the Navy. Constantly increasing attention is being paid to the gunnery of the Navy, but it is yet far from what it should be. I earnestly urge that the increase asked for by the Secretary of the Navy in the appropriation for improving the markmanship be granted. In battle the only shots that count are the shots that hit. It is necessary to provide ample funds for practice with the great guns in time of peace. These funds must provide not only for the purchase of projectiles, but for allowances for prizes to encourage the gun crews, and especially the gun pointers, and for perfecting an intelligent system under which alone it is possible to get good practice.

There should be no halt in the work of building up the Navy, providing every year additional fighting craft. We are a very rich country, vast in extent of territory and great in population; a country, moreover, which has an Army diminutive indeed when compared with that of any other first-class power. We have deliberately made our own certain foreign policies which demand the possession of a first-class navy. The isthmian canal will greatly increase the efficiency of our Navy if the Navy is of sufficient size; but if we have an inadequate navy, then the building of the canal would be merely giving a hostage to any power of superior strength. The Monroe Doctrine should be treated as the cardinal feature of American foreign policy; but it would be worse than idle to assert it unless we intended to back it up, and it can be backed up only by a thoroughly good navy. A good navy is not a provocative of war. It is the surest guaranty of peace.

Each individual unit of our Navy should be the most efficient of its kind as regards both material and personnel that is to be found in the world. I call your special attention to the need of providing for the manning of the ships. Serious trouble threatens us if we can not do better than we are now doing as regards securing the services of a sufficient number of the highest type of sailormen, of sea mechanics. The veteran seamen of our war ships are of as high a type as can be found in any navy which rides the waters of the world; they are unsurpassed in daring, in resolution, in readiness, in thorough knowledge of their profession. They deserve every consideration that can be shown them. But there are not enough of them. It is no more possible to improvise a crew than it is possible to improvise a war ship. To build the finest ship, with the deadliest battery, and to send it afloat with a raw crew, no matter how brave they were individually, would be to insure disaster if a foe of average capacity were encountered. Neither ships nor men can be improvised when war has begun.

We need a thousand additional officers in order to properly man the ships now provided for and under construction. The classes at the Naval School at Annapolis should be greatly enlarged. At the same time that we thus add the officers where we need them, we should facilitate the retirement of those at the head of the list whose usefulness has become impaired. Promotion must be fostered if the service is to be kept efficient.

The lamentable scarcity of officers, and the large number of recruits and of unskilled men necessarily put aboard the new vessels as they have been commissioned, has thrown upon our officers, and especially on the lieutenants and junior grades, unusual labor and fatigue and has gravely strained their powers of endurance. Nor is there sign of any immediate let-up in this strain. It must continue for some time longer, until more officers are graduated from Annapolis, and until the recruits become trained and skillful in their duties. In these difficulties incident upon the development of our war fleet the conduct of all our officers has been creditable to the service, and the lieutenants and junior grades in particular have displayed an ability and a steadfast cheerfulness which entitles them to the ungrudging thanks of all who realize the disheartening trials and fatigues to which they are of necessity subjected.

There is not a cloud on the horizon at present. There seems not the slightest chance of trouble with a foreign power. We most earnestly hope that this state of things may continue; and the way to insure its continuance is to provide for a thoroughly efficient navy. The refusal to maintain such a navy would invite trouble, and if trouble came would insure disaster. Fatuous self-complacency or vanity, or short-sightedness in refusing to prepare for danger, is both foolish and wicked in such a nation as ours; and past experience has shown that such fatuity in refusing to recognize or prepare for any crisis in advance is usually succeeded by a mad panic of hysterical fear once the crisis has actually arrived.

The striking increase in the revenues of the Post-Office Department shows clearly the prosperity of our people and the increasing activity of the business of the country.

The receipts of the Post-Office Department for the fiscal year ending June 30 last amounted to $121,848,047.26, an increase of $10,-216,853.87 over the preceding year, the largest increase known in the history of the postal service. The magnitude of this increase will best appear from the fact that the entire postal receipts for the year 1860 amounted to but $8,518,067.

Rural free-delivery service is no longer in the experimental stage; it has become a fixed policy. The results following its introduction have fully justified the Congress in the large appropriations made for its establishment and extension. The average yearly increase in post-office receipts in the rural districts of the country is about two per cent. We are now able, by actual results, to show that where rural free-delivery service has been established to such an extent as to enable us to make comparisons the yearly increase has been upward of ten per cent.

On November 1, 1902, 11,650 rural free-delivery routes had been established and were in operation, covering about one-third of the territory of the United States available for rural free-delivery service. There are now awaiting the action of the Department petitions and applications for the establishment of 10,748 additional routes. This shows conclusively the want which the establishment of the service has met and the need of further extending it as rapidly as possible. It is justified both by the financial results and by the practical benefits to our rural population; it brings the men who live on the soil into close relations with the active business world; it keeps the farmer in daily touch with the markets; it is a potential educational force; it enhances the value of farm property, makes farm life far pleasanter and less isolated, and will do much to check the undesirable current from country to city.

It is to be hoped that the Congress will make liberal appropriations for the continuance of the service already established and for its further extension.

Few subjects of more importance have been taken up by the Congress in recent years than the inauguration of the system of nationally-aided irrigation for the arid regions of the far West. A good beginning therein has been made. Now that this policy of national irrigation has been adopted, the need of thorough and scientific forest protection will grow more rapidly than ever throughout the public-land States.

Legislation should be provided for the protection of the game, and the wild creatures generally, on the forest reserves. The senseless slaughter of game, which can by judicious protection be permanently

RUSSIAN BATTLESHIPS SUNK BY JAPANESE

RUSSIAN BATTLESHIPS SUNK IN THE RUSSO-JAPANESE WAR.

Of the ships shown in the preceding illustration, the "Korietz" was attacked on February 7, 1904, two days after war was declared, in the harbor of Chemulpo, Korea, by the battleships of Admiral Uriu, which had been conveying transports carrying Japanese troops to Korea. The "Korietz" was supported by the "Variag," but both ships were so badly damaged by the fire of the Japanese that they sank in Chemulpo harbor.

The "Retvisan" and the "Czarevitch" were attacked outside the harbor of Port Arthur by light battleships of Togo's fleet three days after war was declared, and each was disabled. The "Czarevitch," however, was repaired, and with other Russian battleships attempted a sortie from the harbor on August 10, only to be so heavily battered by the Japanese that she repaired to Tsien-tao harbor, where she was promptly interned. (See article Russo-Japanese War in Encyclopedic Index.)

preserved on our national reserves for the people as a whole, should be stopped at once. It is, for instance, a serious count against our national good sense to permit the present practice of butchering off such a stately and beautiful creature as the elk for its antlers or tusks.

So far as they are available for agriculture, and to whatever extent they may be reclaimed under the national irrigation law, the remaining public lands should be held rigidly for the home builder, the settler who lives on his land, and for no one else. In their actual use the desert-land law, the timber and stone law, and the commutation clause of the homestead law have been so perverted from the intention with which they were enacted as to permit the acquisition of large areas of the public domain for other than actual settlers and the consequent prevention of settlement. Moreover, the approaching exhaustion of the public ranges has of late led to much discussion as to the best manner of using these public lands in the West which are suitable chiefly or only for grazing. The sound and steady development of the West depends upon the building up of homes therein. Much of our prosperity as a nation has been due to the operation of the homestead law. On the other hand, we should recognize the fact that in the grazing region the man who corresponds to the homesteader may be unable to settle permanently if only allowed to use the same amount of pasture land that his brother, the homesteader, is allowed to use of arable land. One hundred and sixty acres of fairly rich and well-watered soil, or a much smaller amount of irrigated land, may keep a family in plenty, whereas no one could get a living from one hundred and sixty acres of dry pasture land capable of supporting at the outside only one head of cattle to every ten acres. In the past great tracts of the public domain have been fenced in by persons having no title thereto, in direct defiance of the law forbidding the maintenance or construction of any such unlawful inclosure of public land. For various reasons there has been little interference with such inclosures in the past, but ample notice has now been given the trespassers, and all the resources at the command of the Government will hereafter be used to put a stop to such trespassing.

In view of the capital importance of these matters, I commend them to the earnest consideration of the Congress, and if the Congress finds difficulty in dealing with them from lack of thorough knowledge of the subject, I recommend that provision be made for a commission of experts specially to investigate and report upon the complicated questions involved.

I especially urge upon the Congress the need of wise legislation for Alaska. It is not to our credit as a nation that Alaska, which has been ours for thirty-five years, should still have as poor a system of laws as is the case. No country has a more valuable possession—

in mineral wealth, in fisheries, furs, forests, and also in land avail-able for certain kinds of farming and stockgrowing. It is a territory of great size and varied resources, well fitted to support a large perma-nent population. Alaska needs a good land law and such provisions for homesteads and pre-emptions as will encourage permanent settle-ment. We should shape legislation with a view not to the exploiting and abandoning of the territory, but to the building up of homes therein. The land laws should be liberal in type, so as to hold out inducements to the actual settler whom we most desire to see take possession of the country. The forests of Alaska should be protected, and, as a secondary but still important matter, the game also, and at the same time it is imperative that the settlers should be allowed to cut timber, under proper regulations, for their own use. Laws should be enacted to protect the Alaskan salmon fisheries against the greed which would destroy them. They should be preserved as a permanent industry and food supply. Their management and control should be turned over to the Commission of Fish and Fisheries. Alaska should have a Delegate in the Congress. It would be well if a Congressional committee could visit Alaska and investigate its needs on the ground.

In dealing with the Indians our aim should be their ultimate absorp-tion into the body of our people. But in many cases this absorption must and should be very slow. In portions of the Indian Territory the mixture of blood has gone on at the same time with progress in wealth and education, so that there are plenty of men with varying degrees of purity of Indian blood who are absolutely indistinguishable in point of social, political, and economic ability from their white associates. There are other tribes which have as yet made no per-ceptible advance toward such equality. To try to force such tribes too fast is to prevent their going forward at all. Moreover, the tribes live under widely different conditions. Where a tribe has made con-siderable advance and lives on fertile farming soil it is possible to allot the members lands in severalty much as is the case with white settlers. There are other tribes where such a course is not desirable. On the arid prairie lands the effort should be to induce the Indians to lead pastoral rather than agricultural lives, and to permit them to settle in villages rather than to force them into isolation.

The large Indian schools situated remote from any Indian reserva-tion do a special and peculiar work of great importance. But, excellent though these are, an immense amount of additional work must be done on the reservations themselves among the old, and above all among the young, Indians.

The first and most important step toward the absorption of the Indian is to teach him to earn his living; yet it is not necessarily to be assumed that in each community all Indians must become either tillers of the soil or stock raisers. Their industries may properly be diversified, and those who show special desire or adaptability for industrial or even commercial pursuits should be encouraged so far as practicable to follow out each his own bent.

Every effort should be made to develop the Indian along the lines of natural aptitude, and to encourage the existing native industries peculiar to certain tribes, such as the various kinds of basket weaving, canoe building, smith work, and blanket work. Above all, the Indian boys and girls should be given confident command of colloquial English, and should ordinarily be prepared for a vigorous struggle with the conditions under which their people live, rather than for immediate absorption into some more highly developed community.

The officials who represent the Government in dealing with the Indians work under hard conditions, and also under conditions which render it easy to do wrong and very difficult to detect wrong. Consequently they should be amply paid on the one hand, and on the other hand a particularly high standard of conduct should be demanded from them, and where misconduct can be proved the punishment should be exemplary.

In no department of governmental work in recent years has there been greater success than in that of giving scientific aid to the farming population, thereby showing them how most efficiently to help themselves. There is no need of insisting upon its importance, for the welfare of the farmer is fundamentally necessary to the welfare of the Republic as a whole. In addition to such work as quarantine against animal and vegetable plagues, and warring against them when here introduced, much efficient help has been rendered to the farmer by the introduction of new plants specially fitted for cultivation under the peculiar conditions existing in different portions of the country. New cereals have been established in the semi-arid West. For instance, the practicability of producing the best types of macaroni wheats in regions of an annual rainfall of only ten inches or thereabouts has been conclusively demonstrated. Through the introduction of new rices in Louisiana and Texas the production of rice in this country has been made to about equal the home demand. In the Southwest the possibility of regrassing overstocked range lands has been demonstrated; in the North many new forage crops have been introduced, while in the East it has been shown that some of our choicest fruits can be stored and shipped in such a way as to find a profitable market abroad.

I again recommend to the favorable consideration of the Congress the plans of the Smithsonian Institution for making the Museum under its charge worthy of the Nation, and for preserving at the National Capital not only records of the vanishing races of men but of the animals of this continent which, like the buffalo, will soon become extinct unless specimens from which their representatives may be renewed are sought in their native regions and maintained there in safety.

The District of Columbia is the only part of our territory in which the National Government exercises local or municipal functions, and where in consequence the Government has a free hand in reference to certain types of social and economic legislation which must be essentially local or municipal in their character. The Government should see to it, for instance, that the hygienic and sanitary legislation affecting Washington is of a high character. The evils of slum dwellings, whether in the shape of crowded and congested tenement-house districts or of the back-alley type, should never be permitted to grow up in Washington. The city should be a model in every respect for all the cities of the country. The charitable and correctional systems of the District should receive consideration at the hands of the Congress to the end that they may embody the results of the most advanced thought in these fields. Moreover, while Washington is not a great industrial city, there is some industrialism here, and our labor legislation, while it would not be important in itself, might be made a model for the rest of the Nation. We should pass, for instance, a wise employer's-liability act for the District of Columbia, and we need such an act in our navy-yards. Railroad companies in the District ought to be required by law to block their frogs.

The safety-appliance law, for the better protection of the lives and limbs of railway employees, which was passed in 1893, went into full effect on August 1, 1901. It has resulted in averting thousands of casualties. Experience shows, however, the necessity of additional legislation to perfect this law. A bill to provide for this passed the Senate at the last session. It is to be hoped that some such measure may now be enacted into law.

There is a growing tendency to provide for the publication of masses of documents for which there is no public demand and for the printing of which there is no real necessity. Large numbers of volumes are turned out by the Government printing presses for which there is no justification. Nothing should be printed by any of the Departments unless it contains something of permanent value, and the Congress could with advantage cut down very materially on all the printing which it has now become customary to provide. The excessive cost of Government printing is a strong argument against the position of those who are inclined on abstract grounds to advocate the Government's doing any work which can with propriety be left in private hands.

Gratifying progress has been made during the year in the extension of the merit system of making appointments in the Government service. It should be extended by law to the District of Columbia. It is much to be desired that our consular system be established by law on a basis providing for appointment and promotion only in consequence of proved fitness.

Through a wise provision of the Congress at its last session the White House, which had become disfigured by incongruous additions and changes, has now been restored to what it was planned to be by Washington. In making the restorations the utmost care has been exercised to come as near as possible to the early plans and to supplement these plans by a careful study of such buildings as that of the University of Virginia, which was built by Jefferson. The White House is the property of the Nation, and so far as is compatible with living therein it should be kept as it originally was, for the same reasons that we keep Mount Vernon as it originally was. The stately simplicity of its architecture is an expression of the character of the period in which it was built, and is in accord with the purposes it was designed to serve. It is a good thing to preserve such buildings as historic monuments which keep alive our sense of continuity with the Nation's past.

The reports of the several Executive Departments are submitted to the Congress with this communication.

THEODORE ROOSEVELT.

SPECIAL MESSAGES.

WHITE HOUSE, *December 8, 1902.*

To the Senate and House of Representatives:

I transmit herewith a report from the Secretary of State covering a statement showing the receipts and disbursements of the Louisiana Purchase Exposition Company for the months of May, June, July, August, September, and October, 1902, furnished by the Louisiana Purchase Exposition Commission, in pursuance of section 11 of the "Act to provide for celebrating the one hundredth anniversary of the purchase of the Louisiana Territory," etc., approved March 3, 1901.

THEODORE ROOSEVELT.

WHITE HOUSE, *December 8, 1902.*

To the Senate and House of Representatives:

Referring to section 32 of the act approved April 12, 1900, entitled "An act temporarily to provide revenues and a civil government for

Porto Rico, and for other purposes," I transmit herewith an ordinance approved by me on October 27, 1902, granting the consent of the executive council of Porto Rico to the assignment by the Compañia de los Ferrocarriles de Puerto Rico to Henry De Ford, his heirs, executors, and assigns, and to a proposed corporation to be designated and known as "The American Railroad Company of Porto Rico, Central Aguirre Operator," of the right to construct, operate, and maintain the railroad line from Ponce to Guayama, authorized by the executive council of Porto Rico on October 28, 1901, and to construct and operate a branch line from Ponce to the Ponce Playa and a branch line from Guayama to Arroyo.

THEODORE ROOSEVELT.

WHITE HOUSE, *Washington, December 8, 1902.*

To the Senate:

I transmit herewith a report from the Acting Secretary of State, with accompanying papers, in response to the Senate's resolution of June 30, 1902, requesting the Secretary of State "to send to the Senate a statement of the expenditures of the Isthmian Canal Commission, under the act approved March 3, 1899, 'making appropriations for the construction, repair, and preservation of certain public works on rivers and harbors, and for other purposes,' as the same are accounted for by said Isthmian Canal Commission, and also whether there is any deficit in the appropriation which is to be or has been provided for by further appropriations."

THEODORE ROOSEVELT.

WHITE HOUSE, *Washington, December 9, 1902.*

To the Senate and House of Representatives:

I transmit herewith a communication from the Secretary of State accompanying the second annual report of the governor of Porto Rico, and indorse the suggestion that the interest attaching to it may warrant its being printed for the use of Congress.

THEODORE ROOSEVELT.

WHITE HOUSE, *Washington, December 9, 1902.*

To the Senate and House of Representatives:

I transmit herewith, for the determination of Congress as to whether relief should not be afforded to the owners of the British schooner *Lillie,* a report of the Secretary of State, with accompanying papers, showing that the vessel sustained damages by a fire which broke out within her while she was being disinfected with sulphur and while she was in charge of the United States quarantine officer at Ship Island. near Biloxi, Miss.

THEODORE ROOSEVELT.

WHITE HOUSE, *Washington, December 9, 1902.*

To the Senate:

In response to the Senate resolution of the 4th instant, I transmit herewith a report from the Secretary of State forwarding the report of the agent of the United States in the case of the United States *v.* Mexico before the Permanent Court of Arbitration under the Hague Convention.

THEODORE ROOSEVELT.

WHITE HOUSE, *December 10, 1902.*

To the Senate and House of Representatives:

I transmit herewith a report from the Secretary of State, with accompanying papers, relative to the proceedings of the International Congress for the Study of the Production and Consumption of Coffee, which, in pursuance of a resolution adopted by the Second International Conference of American States, was in session at the city of New York from October 1 to October 31, 1902, investigating the causes which are producing the crisis through which that industry is passing.

THEODORE ROOSEVELT.

WHITE HOUSE, *December 15, 1902.*

To the Congress:

I transmit herewith a report from the Secretary of State in regard to the killing, on July 11, 1901, by an armed mob, at Erwin, Miss., of Giovanni and Vincenzo Serio, and the wounding by the same mob of Salvatore Liberto, all subjects of the King of Italy, and recommend that, as an act of grace and without reference to the question of the liability of the United States, Congress make suitable provision for the heirs of the two Italian subjects killed and for the survivor, Salvatore Liberto, who was injured, the proceeds to be distributed by the Italian Government in such manner as it may deem proper.

THEODORE ROOSEVELT.

WHITE HOUSE, *January 6, 1903.*

To the Senate and House of Representatives:

Referring to section 32 of the act approved April 12, 1900, entitled "An act temporarily to provide revenues and a civil government for Porto Rico, and for other purposes," I transmit herewith an ordinance enacted by the executive council of Porto Rico on December 3, 1902, granting to Benjamin J. Horton the right to construct, operate, and maintain a system of long-distance telephone lines extending through the islands of Porto Rico and connecting various cities and towns thereof, together with local telephone exchanges in such cities and towns.

This ordinance was approved by the President of the United States on December 31, 1902.

THEODORE ROOSEVELT.

WHITE HOUSE, *January 6, 1903.*

To the Senate and House of Representatives:

I transmit herewith a report from the Secretary of State covering a statement showing the receipts and disbursements of the Louisiana Purchase Exposition Company for the month of November, 1902, furnished by the Louisiana Purchase Exposition Commission in pursuance of section 11 of the "Act to provide for celebrating the one hundredth anniversary of the purchase of the Louisiana Territory," etc., approved March 3, 1901.

THEODORE ROOSEVELT.

WHITE HOUSE, *January 7, 1903.*

To the Senate and House of Representatives:

I herewith send a letter from the Secretary of War, transmitting the third annual report of the Philippine Commission, covering the year ending October 1, 1902, and the laws passed by the Commission between July 1, 1902, and October 27, 1902.

I call your special attention to the recommendations contained in this letter of the Secretary of War. I most earnestly feel that the enactment of the measures already pending in your body for the betterment of the Philippine Islands is imperatively demanded by the situation in those islands, and serious calamity may come from failure to enact them. Furthermore, I with equal earnestness ask your attention to the recommendation of the Secretary of War in the accompanying letter and urge its adoption, so that the sum of money therein specified may be appropriated for the uses and in the manner likewise specified, in order that the present distress in the islands may be remedied.

THEODORE ROOSEVELT.

WHITE HOUSE, *January 12, 1903.*

To the Senate:

In compliance with a resolution of the Senate of the 8th instant (the House of Representatives concurring), I return herewith Senate bill No. 3316, entitled "An act to amend an act entitled 'An act to create a new division in the western judicial district of the State of Missouri,' approved January 24, 1901."

THEODORE ROOSEVELT.

WHITE HOUSE, *January 19, 1903.*

To the Senate and House of Representatives:

I transmit herewith the annual report of the Office of Experiment Stations, prepared under the direction of the Secretary of Agriculture, which includes a report on the work and expenditures of the agricultural experiment stations in the United States for the fiscal year ended June 30, 1902, in accordance with the act making appropriations for the Department of Agriculture for the said fiscal year.

The attention of Congress is called to the request of the Secretary of Agriculture that 5,000 copies of the report be printed for the use of the Department of Agriculture, and that provision be made to print such a report annually.

THEODORE ROOSEVELT.

WHITE HOUSE, *January 19, 1903.*

To the Senate and House of Representatives:

Referring to section 32 of the act approved April 12, 1900, entitled "An act temporarily to provide revenues and a civil government for Porto Rico, and for other purposes," I transmit herewith an ordinance enacted by the executive council of Porto Rico on December 3, 1902, with the approval of the governor thereof, granting to J. H. D. Luce, his heirs, executors, administrators, and assigns, the right to construct and operate a landing pier or wharf on the east side of the harbor of Ponce and on the shores thereof, and for other purposes.

This ordinance was approved by the President of the United States on January 8, 1903.

THEODORE ROOSEVELT.

WHITE HOUSE, *Washington, January 19, 1903.*

To the Senate and House of Representatives:

I transmit herewith a report from the Acting Secretary of State, with accompanying papers, relating to the claim of Messrs. Sivewright, Bacon & Co., of Manchester, England, British subjects, for compensation for damages sustained by their vessel, the British steamship *Eastry,* in consequence of collisions in June, 1901, at Manila, with certain coal hulks belonging to the United States Government.

I recommend that as an act of equity and comity provision be made by the Congress for reimbursement to the firm of the money expended by it in making the repairs to the ship which the collisions rendered necessary.

THEODORE ROOSEVELT.

WHITE HOUSE, *Washington, January 19, 1903.*

To the Senate and House of Representatives:

I transmit herewith a communication from the Secretary of State, accompanying the Commercial Relations of the United States for the year 1902, being the annual and other reports of consular and diplomatic officers upon the industries and commerce of foreign countries. In view of the importance of these reports to our business interests, I approve the recommendation of the Secretary of State that Congress authorize the printing of an edition of 10,000 copies of the summary entitled "Review of the World's Commerce," and of 5,000 copies of Commercial Relations (including this summary), to be distributed by the Department of State.

THEODORE ROOSEVELT

WHITE HOUSE, *January 19, 1903.*

To the Senate and House of Representatives:

I transmit herewith a report, by the Secretary of Agriculture, of the operations of the Bureau of Animal Industry of that Department for the fiscal year ended June 30, 1902, in compliance with the requirements of section 11 of the act approved May 29, 1884, for the establishment of that Bureau.

THEODORE ROOSEVELT.

WHITE HOUSE, *January 24, 1903.*

To the Senate:

In response to the resolution of January 15, I transmit the attached letter from the Acting Secretary of the Navy, with inclosures, which contain fully and specifically the information asked for.

In reference to the case of Mabini, especial attention is drawn to the communications of the Secretary of War, notably his communication to the Department of the Navy of July 18, 1902; the special dispatch of July 18 from the War Department to General Chaffee, commanding the Division of the Philippines, and to the communication of the Acting Secretary of the Navy of July 26 to the governor of Guam inclosing said letter from the Secretary of War and directing that action in accordance therewith be taken.

By these letters the governor of Guam is explicitly directed to release from detention all prisoners, and it is presumed that he has acted accordingly; but to provide against the slightest chance of misapprehension he has been specifically directed that all persons found in the island under the direction of the War Department shall be released in accordance with the terms of the Secretary of War's letter of July 18. In other words, the inhabitant of the Philippine Islands named Mabini, concerning whom a special inquiry is made in the resolution of the Senate, is at liberty to go on a Government transport anywhere outside of the Philippine Islands where such transports touch without taking any oath of allegiance whatsoever, and is allowed to go to any part of the world save the Philippine Islands without taking the oath of allegiance, and he will be allowed to go on any private vessel to the Philippine Islands, but he can not land there save on condition of complying with the act of the Philippine Commission demanding that he take the oath of allegiance. This is also a condition of the proclamation of peace and amnesty.

THEODORE ROOSEVELT.

WHITE HOUSE, *January 29, 1903.*
To the Senate:

Referring to Senate Document No. 264, Fifty-seventh Congress, first session, I transmit herewith a report by the Secretary of State, with accompanying papers, in the claim of Messrs. George A. Tarler & Co. against the Government of Colombia, which were inadvertently omitted from the papers sent to the Senate on March 20, 1902, in response to the Senate's resolution of March 15, 1900.

THEODORE ROOSEVELT.

WHITE HOUSE, *January 29, 1903.*
To the Senate and House of Representatives:

I transmit herewith a report from the Secretary of State, with accompanying notes from the Mexican ambassador and the Chinese chargé d'affaires ad interim, which seek the co-operation of the Government of the United States in such measures as will tend to restore and maintain a fixed relationship between the moneys of the gold-standard countries and the silver-using countries.

I recommend that the Executive be given sufficient powers to lend the support of the United States in such manner and to such degree as he may deem expedient to the purposes of the two Governments.

THEODORE ROOSEVELT.

WHITE HOUSE, *February 4, 1903.*

To the Senate:

In compliance with a resolution of the Senate of the 3d instant (the House of Representatives concurring), I return herewith Senate bill No. 1115, entitled "An act for the relief of Francis S. Davidson, late first lieutenant, Ninth United States Cavalry."

THEODORE ROOOSEVELT.

WHITE HOUSE, *February 9, 1903.*

To the Senate and House of Representatives:

I transmit herewith a report from the Secretary of State, covering a statement showing the receipts and disbursements of the Louisiana Purchase Exposition Company for the month of December, 1902, furnished by the Louisiana Purchase Exposition Commission, in pursuance of section 11 of the "Act to provide for celebrating the one hundredth anniversary of the purchase of the Louisiana Territory," etc., approved March 3, 1901.

THEODORE ROOSEVELT.

WHITE HOUSE, *February 13, 1903.*

To the Senate and House of Representatives:

I transmit herewith a report by the Secretary of State with an accompanying draft of an act making an appropriation to carry out on the part of the United States the provisions of the convention between the United States and Great Britain, concluded January 24, 1903.

In order that there may be no delay in the appointment and assembling of the tribunal provided for in the convention, I ask for the matter the favorable consideration of the present Congress.

THEODORE ROOSEVELT.

WHITE HOUSE, *February 14, 1903.*

To the Senate:

I transmit herewith a report from the Secretary of State, with accompanying papers, in regard to the equitable distribution of the waters of the Rio Grande, called for by the Senate resolution of June 6, 1902.

THEODORE ROOSEVELT.

WHITE HOUSE, *February 21, 1903.*

To the Senate and House of Representatives:

I transmit herewith a communication from the Anthracite Coal Strike Commission, with an accompanying draft of a joint resolution providing for the printing of the report of said Commission, and approve of the suggestion therein contained.

THEODORE ROOSEVELT.

WHITE HOUSE, *February 23, 1903.*

To the Senate and House of Representatives:

I transmit herewith a report by the Secretary of State, with accompanying papers, concerning the transactions of the First International Sanitary Convention of the American Republics, held at Washington in December, 1902.

THEODORE ROOSEVELT.

WHITE HOUSE, *February 25, 1903.*

To the Senate and House of Representatives:

I transmit herewith a report by the Secretary of State, with accompanying papers, relative to the proceedings of the First Customs Congress of the American Republics, held at New York in January, 1903.

THEODORE ROOSEVELT.

WHITE HOUSE, *February 27, 1903.*

To the Senate:

I have just received a cable from Governor Taft which runs as follows:

"Necessity for passage House tariff bill most urgent. The conditions of productive industry and business considerably worse than in November, the date of last report, and growing worse each month.

Some revival in sugar, tobacco prices due to expectation of tariff law. The interest of Filipinos in sugar and tobacco extensive, and failure of bill will be blow in face of those interests. Number of tobacco factories will have to close, and many sugar haciendas will be put up for sale at a sacrifice, if the bill will not pass. Customs receipts have fallen off this month one-third, showing decrease of purchasing power of islands. General business stagnant. All political parties, including labor unions, most strenuous in petition for tariff bill. Effect of its failure very discouraging."

Vice-Governor Luke Wright indorses in the strongest manner all that Governor Taft has said, and states that he has the gravest apprehension as to the damage that may come to the islands if there is not a substantial reduction in the tariff levied against Philippine goods coming into the United States. I very earnestly ask that this matter receive the immediate attention of Congress and that the relief prayed for be granted.

As Congress knows, a series of calamities have befallen the Philippine people. Just as they were emerging from nearly six years of devastating warfare, with the accompanying destruction of property and the breaking up of the bonds of social order and the habits of peaceful industry, there occurred an epidemic of rinderpest, which destroyed 90 per cent of the carabaos, the Filipino cattle, leaving the people without draft animals to till the land or to aid in the ordinary work of farm and village life. The extent of the disaster can be seen from the fact that the surviving carabaos have increased over tenfold in value. At the same time a peculiar oriental horse disease became epidemic, further crippling transportation. The rice crop, already reduced by various causes to but a fourth of its ordinary size, has been damaged by locusts, so that the price of rice has nearly doubled.

Under these circumstances there is imminent danger of famine in the islands. Congress is in course of generously appropriating $3,000,000 to meet the immediate needs; but the indispensable and preeminent need is the resurrection of productive industry from the prostration into which it has been thrown by the causes above enumerated. I ask action in the tariff matter, not merely from the standpoint of wise governmental policy, but as a measure of humanity in response to an appeal to which this great people should not close its ears. We have assumed responsibilities toward the Philippine Islands which we are in honor bound to fulfill. We have the specific duty of taking every measure in our power to see to their prosperity. The first and most important step in this direction has been accomplished by the joint action of the military and civil authorities in securing peace and civil government. The wisdom of Congress at the present session has provided for them a stable currency, and its spirit of humane liberality and justice toward them will be shown in the appropriation now substantially agreed upon of $3,000,000 to meet the pressing, immediate necessities; but there remains a vital need that one thing further shall be done. The calamities which have befallen them as above enumerated could have been averted by no human wisdom. They can not be completely repaired; but the suffering can be greatly alleviated and a permanent basis of future prosperity assured if the economic relations of the islands with the United States are put upon a satisfactory basis.

THEODORE ROOSEVELT.

WHITE HOUSE, *February 28, 1903.*

To the Senate and House of Representatives:

I transmit herewith for the information of the Congress a report by the architects, with accompanying pictures, regarding the work of repairing and refurnishing the White House and the erection of the executive office building.

THEODORE ROOSEVELT.

WHITE HOUSE, *February 28, 1903.*

To the Senate:

In response to the resolution of the Senate of February 16, 1903, requesting the President "if, in his judgment, the same be not incompatible with the public interests, to inform the Senate as to the present status of the Isle of Pines, and what Government is exercising authority and control in said island, what instructions, if any, regarding said island were given at the time when the military occupation of Cuba by the United States was terminated; and what action, if any, has been taken for the protection of the interests of citizens of the United States who have purchased property and settled in the Isle of Pines," I transmit herewith a report from the Secretary of War.

THEODORE ROOSEVELT.

WHITE HOUSE, *February 28, 1903.*

To the Senate and House of Representatives:

I transmit herewith reports by the Secretary of State, Secretary of the Treasury, Secretary of War, Attorney-General, Postmaster-General, Secretary of the Navy, Secretary of the Interior, Secretary of Agriculture, and the Commissioner of Fish and Fisheries, in compliance with the following provision of the sundry civil bill approved June 28, 1902:

"The President is hereby requested to cause to be prepared and submitted to Congress at the commencement of its next session a statement showing what lots or parcels of land, other than public lands held for settlement under the public land laws, are owned by the United States and held by the several Executive Departments or other branches of the public service, the area of each, the purposes for which each is held or occupied, in what State, Territory, or country, and in or near what town or city each is located."

THEODORE ROOSEVELT.

WHITE HOUSE, *March 3, 1903.*

To the Senate and House of Representatives:

I transmit herewith a report from the Secretary of State, covering a statement showing the receipts and disbursements of the Louisiana Purchase Exposition Company for the month of January, 1903, furnished by the Louisiana Purchase Exposition Commission in pursuance of section 11 of the "Act to provide for celebrating the one hundredth anniversary of the purchase of the Louisiana Territory," etc., approved March 3, 1901.

THEODORE ROOSEVELT.

WHITE HOUSE, *March 3, 1903.*

To the Senate and House of Representatives:

In compliance with the provision of the act making appropriation for the support of the Army, approved June 30, 1902, I transmit herewith a report from the Secretary of War showing expenditures made from the appropriation for "Barracks and quarters, Philippine Islands, 1903."

THEODORE ROOSEVELT.

WHITE HOUSE, *March 5, 1903.*

To the Senate:

I have called the Senate in extraordinary session to consider the treaties concerning which it proved impossible to take action during the session of Congress just ended. I ask your special attention to the treaty with the Republic of Colombia, securing to the United States the right to build an isthmian canal, and to the treaty with the Republic of Cuba, for securing a measure of commercial reciprocity between the two countries.

The great and far-reaching importance of these two treaties to the welfare of the United States and the urgent need for their adoption require me to impose upon you the inconvenience of meeting at this time.

THEODORE ROOSEVELT.

WHITE HOUSE, *March 19, 1903.*

To the Senate:

In compliance with the resolution of the Senate of February 13, 1903, requesting the President, "if not incompatible with the public interests, to send to the Senate copies of all reports and of all correspondence in the Navy Department with naval or other officers of the United States on duty in the bays of Panama and Colon since April, 1902, which relate to the military occupation of said bays and the regions between them and the cities of Colon and Panama by the forces of the United States; or that relate to the operation of military or police forces of Colombia or of any insurgents that were in arms against the Government of Colombia in that region of country since April, 1902; or that relate to any measures of any officers of the United States to bring about the pacification of that region or any intervention by such officers to that end; or that relate to the terms and conditions of the surrender of insurgent forces in that quarter to the forces or authorities of the Republic of Colombia," I transmit herewith a report by the Secretary of the Navy, with accompanying papers.

THEODORE ROOSEVELT.

SPECIAL SESSION MESSAGE.

WHITE HOUSE, *November 10, 1903.*

To the Senate and House of Representatives:

I have convened the Congress that it may consider the legislation necessary to put into operation the commercial treaty with Cuba, which was ratified by the Senate at its last session, and subsequently by the Cuban Government. I deem such legislation demanded not only by our interest, but by our honor. We can not with propriety abandon the course upon which we have so wisely embarked. When the acceptance of the Platt amendment was required from Cuba by the action of the Congress of the United States, this Government thereby definitely committed itself to the policy of treating Cuba as occupying a unique position as regards this country. It was provided that when the island became a free and independent republic she should stand in such close relations with us as in certain respects to come within our system of international policy; and it necessarily followed that she must also to a certain degree become included within the lines of our economic policy. Situated as Cuba is, it would not be possible for this country to permit the strategic abuse of the island by any foreign military power. It is for this reason that certain limitations have been imposed upon her financial policy, and that naval stations have been conceded by her to the United States. The negotiations as to the details of these naval stations are on the eve of completion. They are so situated as to prevent any idea that there is the intention ever to use them against Cuba, or otherwise than for the protection of Cuba from the assaults of foreign foes, and for the better safeguarding of American interests in the waters south of us.

These interests have been largely increased by the consequences of the war with Spain, and will be still further increased by the building of the isthmian canal. They are both military and economic. The granting to us by Cuba of the naval stations above alluded to is of the utmost importance from a military standpoint, and is proof of the good faith with which Cuba is treating us. Cuba has made great progress since her independence was established. She has advanced steadily in every way. She already stands high among her sister republics of the New World. She is loyally observing her obligations to us; and she is entitled to like treatment by us.

The treaty submitted to you for approval secures to the United States economic advantages as great as those given to Cuba. Not an American interest is sacrificed. By the treaty a large Cuban market is secured to our producers. It is a market which lies at our doors, which is already large, which is capable of great expansion, and which is especially important to the development of our export trade. It would be indeed shortsighted for us to refuse to take advantage of such an opportunity, and to force Cuba into making arrangements with other countries to our disadvantage.

This reciprocity treaty stands by itself. It is demanded on considerations of broad national policy as well as by our economic interest. It will do harm to no industry. It will benefit many industries. It is in the interest of our people as a whole, both because of its importance from the broad standpoint of international policy, and because economically it intimately concerns us to develop and secure the rich Cuban market for our farmers, artisans, merchants, and manufacturers. Finally, it is desirable as a guaranty of the good faith of our Nation towards her young sister Republic to the south, whose welfare must ever be closely bound with ours. We gave her liberty. We are knit to her by the memories of the blood and the courage of our soldiers who fought for her in war; by the memories of the wisdom and integrity of our administrators who served her in peace and who started her so well on the difficult path of self-government. We must help her onward and upward; and in helping her we shall help ourselves.

The foregoing considerations caused the negotiation of the treaty with Cuba and its ratification by the Senate. They now with equal force support the legislation by the Congress which by the terms of the treaty is necessary to render it operative. A failure to enact such legislation would come perilously near a repudiation of the pledged faith of the Nation.

I transmit herewith the treaty, as amended by the Senate and ratified by the Cuban Government.

THEODORE ROOSEVELT.

SPECIAL MESSAGES.

WHITE HOUSE, *November 10, 1903.*

To the Senate and House of Representatives:

It being required by the resolution of the Senate of March 19, 1903, that the approval of Congress shall be given to the Reciprocal Commercial Convention between the United States and Cuba, signed December 11, 1902, before the same shall take effect, I transmit herewith the text of the said Convention as amended by the Senate.

THEODORE ROOSEVELT.

The President of the United States of America and the President of the Republic of Cuba, animated by the desire to strengthen the bonds of friendship between the two countries, and to facilitate their commercial intercourse by improving the conditions of trade between them, have resolved to enter into a convention for that purpose, and have appointed their respective Plenipotentiaries, to wit:

The President of the United States of America, the Honorable General Tasker H. Bliss;

The President of the Republic of Cuba, the Honorable Carlos de Zaldo y Beurmann, Secretary of State and Justice, and the Honorable José M. Garcia y Montes, Secretary of the Treasury;

who, after an exchange of their full powers found to be in good and due form, have, in consideration of and in compensation for the respective concessions and engagements made by each to the other as hereinafter recited, agreed and do hereby agree upon the following Articles for the regulation and government of their reciprocal trade, namely:

ARTICLE I.

During the term of this convention, all articles of merchandise being the product of the soil or industry of the United States which are now imported into the Republic of Cuba free of duty and all articles of merchandise being the product of the soil or industry of the Republic of Cuba which are now imported into the United States free of duty, shall continue to be so admitted by the respective countries free of duty.

ARTICLE II.

During the term of this convention, all articles of merchandise not included in the foregoing Article I and being the product of the soil or industry of the Republic of Cuba imported into the United States shall be admitted at a reduction of twenty per centum of the rates of duty thereon as provided by the Tariff Act of the United States approved July 24, 1897, or as may be provided by any tariff law of the United States subsequently enacted.

ARTICLE III.

During the term of this convention, all articles of merchandise not included in the foregoing Article I and not hereinafter enumerated, being the product of the soil or industry of the United States, imported into the Republic of Cuba shall be admitted at a reduction of twenty per centum of the rates of duty thereon as now provided or as may hereafter be provided in the Customs Tariff of said Republic of Cuba.

ARTICLE IV.

During the term of this convention, the following articles of merchandise as enumerated and described in the existing Customs Tariff of the Republic of Cuba, being the product of the soil or industry of the United States imported into Cuba shall be admitted at the following respective reductions of the rates of duty thereon as now provided or as may hereafter be provided in the Customs Tariff of the Republic of Cuba:

Schedule A.

To be admitted at a reduction of twenty-five (25) per centum:
Machinery and apparatus of copper or its alloys or machines and apparatus in which copper or its alloys enter as the component of chief value; cast iron, wrought iron and steel, and manufactures thereof; articles of crystal and glass, except window glass; ships and water borne vessels of all kinds, of iron or steel; whiskies and brandies; fish, salted, pickled, smoke or marinated; fish or shell-fish, preserved in oil or otherwise in tins; articles of pottery or earthenware now classified under Paragraphs 21 and 22 of the Customs Tariff of the Republic of Cuba.

Schedule B.

To be admitted at a reduction of thirty (30) per centum:
Butter; flour of wheat; corn; flour of corn or corn meal; chemical and pharmaceutical products and simple drugs; malt liquors in bottles; non-alcoholic beverages; cider; mineral waters; colors and dyes; window glass; complete or partly made up articles of hemp, flax, pita, jute, henequen, ramie, and other vegetable fibers now classified under the paragraphs of Group 2, Class V, of the Customs Tariff of the Republic of Cuba; musical instruments; writing and print-

ing paper, except for newspapers; cotton and manufactures thereof, except knitted goods (see Schedule C); all articles of cutlery; boots, shoes and slippers, now classified under Paragraphs 197 and 198 of the Customs Tariff of the Republic of Cuba; gold and silver plated ware; drawings, photographs, engravings, lithographs, chromolithographs, oleographs, etc., printed from stone, zinc, aluminium, or other material, used as labels, flaps, bands and wrappers for tobacco or other purposes, and all the other papers (except paper for cigarettes, and excepting maps and charts), pasteboard and manufactures thereof, now classified under Paragraphs 157 to 164 inclusive of the Customs Tariff of the Republic of Cuba; common or ordinary soaps, now classified under Paragraph 105, letters "A" and "B", of the Customs Tariff of the Republic of Cuba; vegetables, pickled or preserved in any manner; all wines, except those now classified under Paragraph 279 (a) of the Customs Tariff of the Republic of Cuba.

Schedule C.

To be admitted at a reduction of forty (40) per centum:

Manufactures of cotton, knitted, and all manufactures of cotton not included in the preceding schedules; cheese; fruits, preserved; paper pulp; perfumery and essences; articles of pottery and earthenware now classified under Paragraph 20 of the Customs Tariff of the Republic of Cuba; porcelain; soaps, other than common, now classified under Paragraph 105 of the Customs Tariff of the Republic of Cuba; umbrellas and parasols; dextrine and glucose; watches; wool and manufactures thereof; silk and manufactures thereof; rice; cattle.

ARTICLE V.

It is understood and agreed that the laws and regulations adopted, or that may be adopted, by the United States and by the Republic of Cuba, to protect their revenues and prevent fraud in the declarations and proofs that the articles of merchandise to which this convention may apply are the product or manufacture of the United States and the Republic of Cuba, respectively, shall not impose any additional charge or fees therefor on the articles imported, excepting the consular fees established, or which may be established, by either of the two countries for issuing shipping documents, which fees shall not be higher than those charged on the shipments of similar merchandise from any other nation whatsoever.

ARTICLE VI.

It is agreed that the tobacco, in any form, of the United States or of any of its insular possessions, shall not enjoy the benefit of any concession or rebate of duty when imported into the Republic of Cuba.

ARTICLE VII.

It is agreed that similar articles of both countries shall receive equal treatment on their importation into the ports of the United States and of the Republic of Cuba, respectively.

ARTICLE VIII.

The rates of duty herein granted by the United States to the Republic of Cuba are and shall continue during the term of this convention preferential in respect to all like imports from other countries, and, in return for said preferential rates of duty granted to the Republic of Cuba by the United States, it is agreed that the concession herein granted on the part of the said Republic of Cuba to the products of the United States shall likewise be, and shall continue, during the term of this convention, preferential in respect to all like imports from other countries: Provided, That while this convention is in force, no sugar imported from the Republic of Cuba, and being the product of the soil or industry of the Republic of Cuba, shall be admitted into the United States at a reduction of duty greater than twenty per centum of the rates of duty thereon as provided by the tariff act of the United States approved July 24, 1897, and no sugar, the product of any other foreign country, shall be admitted by treaty or convention into the United States, while this convention is in force, at a lower rate of duty than that provided by the tariff act of the United States approved July 24, 1897.

ARTICLE IX.

In order to maintain the mutual advantages granted in the present convention by the United States to the Republic of Cuba and by the Republic of Cuba to the United States, it is understood and agreed that any tax or charge that may be imposed by the national or local authorities of either of the two countries upon the articles of merchandise embraced in the provisions of this convention, subsequent to importation and prior to their entering into consumption in the respective countries, shall be imposed and collected without discrimination upon like articles whensoever imported.

ARTICLE X.

It is hereby understood and agreed that in case of changes in the tariff of either country which deprive the other of the advantage which is represented by the percentages herein agreed upon, on the actual rates of the tariffs now in force, the country so deprived of this protection reserves the right to terminate its obligations under this convention after six months' notice to the other of its intention to arrest the operations thereof.

And it is further understood and agreed that if, at any time during the term of this convention, after the expiration of the first year, the protection herein granted to the products and manufactures of the United States on the basis of the actual rates of the tariff of the Republic of Cuba now in force, should appear to the government of the said Republic to be excessive in view of a new tariff law that may be adopted by it after this convention becomes operative, then the said Republic of Cuba may reopen negotiations with a view to securing such modifications as may appear proper to both contracting parties.

ARTICLE XI.

The present convention shall be ratified by the appropriate authorities of the respective countries, and the ratifications shall be exchanged at Washington, District of Columbia, United States of America, as soon as may be before the thirty-first day of January, 1903, and the convention shall go into effect on the tenth day after the exchange of ratifications, and shall continue in force for the term of five (5) years from the date of going into effect, and from year to year thereafter until the expiration of one year from the day when either of the contracting parties shall give notice to the other of its intention to terminate the same.

This convention shall not take effect until the same shall have been approved by the Congress.

In witness whereof we, the respective Plenipotentiaries, have signed the same in duplicate, in English and Spanish, and have affixed our respective seals, at Havana, Cuba, this eleventh day of December, in the year one thousand nine hundred and two.

TASKER H. BLISS. [SEAL.]
CARLOS DE ZALDO. [SEAL.]
JOSÉ M. GARCIA MONTES. [SEAL.]

WHITE HOUSE, *Washington, November 16, 1903.*

To the House of Representatives:

In response to a resolution of the House of Representatives of November 9, 1903, requesting the President "to communicate to the House if not, in his judgment, incompatible with the interests of the public service, all correspondence and other official documents relating to the recent revolution on the Isthmus of Panama," I transmit herewith copies of the papers called for.

THEODORE ROOSEVELT.

DEPARTMENT OF STATE,
Washington, November 13, 1903.

The PRESIDENT:

The Secretary of State, to whom was referred a copy of the resolution of the House of Representatives of November 9, 1903, requesting copies of all correspondence and other official documents relating to the recent revolution on the Isthmus of Panama, has the honor to lay before the President copies of the correspondence from and to the Department of State on the subject.

Respectfully submitted. JOHN HAY.

CORRESPONDENCE BETWEEN THE DEPARTMENT OF STATE AND THE UNITED STATES CONSULATE-GENERAL AT PANAMA.

A press bulletin having announced an outbreak on the Isthmus, the following cablegram was sent both to the consulate-general at Panama and the consulate at Colon:

DEPARTMENT OF STATE,
Washington, November 3, 1903.

(Sent 3:40 p. m.)

Uprising on Isthmus reported. Keep Department promptly and fully informed. LOOMIS, *Acting.*

Mr. Ehrman to Mr. Hay.

PANAMA, *November 3, 1903.*

(Received 8:15 p. m.)

No uprising yet. Reported will be in the night. Situation is critical.   EHRMAN.

Mr. Ehrman to Mr. Hay.

[TELEGRAM.]

PANAMA, *November 3, 1903.*

(Received 9:50 p. m.)

Uprising occurred to-night, 6; no bloodshed. Army and Navy officials taken prisoners. Government will be organized to-night, consisting three consuls, also cabinet. Soldiers changed. Supposed some movement will be effected in Colon. Order prevails so far. Situation serious. Four hundred soldiers landed Colon to-day Barranquilla.   EHRMAN.

Mr. Loomis to Mr. Ehrman.

[TELEGRAM.]

DEPARTMENT OF STATE,
Washington, November 3, 1903.

(Sent 11:18 p. m.)

Message sent to *Nashville* to Colon may not have been delivered. Accordingly see that following message is sent to *Nashville* immediately.

NASHVILLE, *Colon:*
  In the interests of peace make every effort to prevent Government troops at Colon from proceeding to Panama. The transit of the Isthmus must be kept open and order maintained. Acknowledge. (Signed) DARLING, *Acting.*

Secure special train, if necessary. Act promptly.

LOOMIS, *Acting.*

Mr. Loomis to Mr. Ehrman.

[TELEGRAM.]

DEPARTMENT OF STATE,
Washington, November 4, 1903.

(Sent 12:02 p. m.)

Communicate with commander of gunboat *Bogota* and state plainly that this Government being responsible for maintaining peace and keeping transit open across Isthmus desires him to refrain from wantonly shelling the city. We shall have a naval force at Panama in two days, and are now ordering men from the *Nashville* to Panama in the interests of peace. Loomis, *Acting.*

Mr. Ehrman to Mr. Hay.

[TELEGRAM.]

PANAMA, *November 4, 1903.*

(Received 7:10 p. m.)

Mass meeting held. Independence publicly declared. Three consuls approved organize government, composed Federico Boyd, José Augustin Arango, Tomas Arias. *Bogota* in sight. EHRMAN.

Mr. Ehrman to Mr. Hay.

[TELEGRAM.]

PANAMA *November 4, 1903.*

(Received 9:50 a. m.)

Cables *Nashville* received. *Nashville* notified. Troops will not be moved. Last night gunboat *Bogota* fired several shells on city; one Chinaman killed. *Bogota* threatens bombard city to-day.

EHRMAN.

Mr. Ehrman to Mr. Hay.

[TELEGRAM.]

PANAMA, *November 5, 1903.*

(Received 12:50 p. m.)

Received an official circular letter from the committee of the provisional government saying that on 4th political move occurred, and the Department of Panama withdraws from the Republic of the United States of Colombia and formed the Republic of Panama.

Requested to acknowledge the receipt of circular letter.

EHRMAN.

Mr. Loomis to Mr. Ehrman.

[TELEGRAM.]

DEPARTMENT OF STATE,

Washington, November 5, 1903.

(Sent 3:15 p. m.)

Acknowledge the receipt of circular letter and await instructions before taking any further action in this line. Loomis, *Acting.*

Mr. Loomis to Mr. Ehrman.

[TELEGRAM.]

DEPARTMENT OF STATE,
Washington, November 5, 1903.

(Sent 5.09 p. m.)

Keep Department informed as to situation.

LOOMIS, *Acting.*

Mr. Ehrman to Mr. Hay.

[TELEGRAM.]

PANAMA, *November 5, 1903.*

(Received 9:42 p. m.)

Colombian troops re-embarked per Royal Mail for Cartagena *Bogota* supposed at Buenaventura. Quiet prevails.   EHRMAN.

Mr. Ehrman to Mr. Hay.

[TELEGRAM.]

PANAMA, *November 6, 1903.*

(Received 11:55 a. m.)

The situation is peaceful. Isthmian movement has obtained so far success. Colon and interior provinces have enthusiastically joined independence. Not any Colombian soldiers known on isthmian soil at present. *Padilla* equipped to pursue *Bogota*. Bunau Varilla has been appointed officially confidential agent of the Republic of Panama at Washington.   EHRMAN.

Mr. Hay to Mr. Ehrman.

[TELEGRAM.]

DEPARTMENT OF STATE,
Washington, November 6, 1903.

(Sent 12.51 p. m.)

The people of Panama have, by an apparently unanimous movement, dissolved their political connection with the Republic of Colombia and resumed their independence. When you are satisfied that a de facto government, republican in form, and without substantial opposition from its own people, has been established in the State of Panama, you will enter into relations with it as the responsible government of the territory and look to it for all due action to protect the persons and property of citizens of the United States and to keep open the isthmian transit in accordance with the obligations of existing treaties governing the relation of the United States to that territory.

Communicate above to Malmros, who will be governed by these instructions in entering into relations with the local authorities.

HAY.

Mr. Hay to Mr. Ehrman.

[TELEGRAM.]

DEPARTMENT OF STATE,
Washington, November 6, 1903.

(Sent 2:45 p. m.)

I send, for your information and guidance in the execution of the instructions cabled to you to-day, the text of a telegram dispatched this day to the United States minister at Bogota:

The people of Panama having by an apparently unanimous movement dissolved their political connection with the Republic of Colombia and resumed their independence, and having adopted a government of their own, republican in form, with which the Government of the United States of America has entered into relations, the President of the United States, in accordance with the ties of friendship which have so long and so happily existed between the respective nations, most earnestly commends to the Governments of Colombia and of Panama the peaceful and equitable settlement of all questions at issue between them. He holds that he is bound, not merely by treaty obligations, but by the interests of civilization, to see that the peaceable traffic of the world across the Isthmus of Panama shall not longer be disturbed by a constant succession of unnecessary and wasteful civil wars.

HAY.

Mr. Ehrman to Mr. Hay.

[TELEGRAM.]

PANAMA, *November 6, 1903.*

(Received 7:23 p. m.)

Filippe Bunau Varilla has been appointed envoy extraordinary and minister plenipotentiary to the United States of America. Perfect quiet.

EHRMAN.

Mr. Ehrman to Mr. Hay.

[TELEGRAM.]

PANAMA, *November 7, 1903.*

(Received 12:20 p. m.)

I have communicated to Panama Government that they will be held responsible for the protection of the persons and property of citizens of the United States, as well as to keep the isthmian transit free in accordance with obligations of existing treaties relative to the isthmian territory.

EHRMAN.

Mr. Ehrman to Mr. Hay.

[TELEGRAM.]

PANAMA, *November 8, 1903.*

(Received 11 :23 p. m.)

It is reported that Colombian authorities have detained English steamers *Manavi* and *Quito* at Buenaventura. Supposed to be to bring troops to the Isthmus.   EHRMAN.

Mr. Ehrman to Mr. Hay.

[TELEGRAM.]

PANAMA, *November 10, 1903.*

(Received 1 :35 p. ₁)

Federico Boyd, a member of the Committee of the Government, Amador Guerrero, both delegates, on the way to Washington to arrange in satisfactory manner to the United States the canal treaty and other matters. Pablo Arosemena, attorney, proceeds next steamer. English steamers were not held at Buenaventura. Gunboat *Bogota* has left Buenaventura.   EHRMAN.

Mr. Loomis to Mr. Ehrman.

[TELEGRAM.]

DEPARTMENT OF STATE,

Washington, November 10, 1903.

(Sent 3 :42 p. m.)

Keep in touch with commander of United States naval forces at Panama, advising him concerning news bearing on military situation.

LOOMIS, *Acting.*

Mr. Ehrman to Mr. Hay.

[TELEGRAM.]

PANAMA, *November 11, 1903.*

(Received 5 :32 p. m.)

I am officially informed that Bunau Varilla is the authorized party to make treaties. Boyd and Amador have other missions and to assist their minister.   EHRMAN.

CORRESPONDENCE BETWEEN THE DEPARTMENT OF STATE AND THE UNITED STATES CONSULATE AT COLON.

Mr. Malmros to Mr. Hay.

[TELEGRAM.]

COLON, *November 3, 1903.*

(Received 2 :35 p. m.)

Revolution imminent. Government force on the Isthmus about

500 men. Their official promised support revolution. Fire department Panama, 441, are well organized and favor revolution. Government vessel, *Cartagena,* with about 400 men, arrived early to-day with new commander in chief, Tobar. Was not expected until November 10. Tobar's arrival is not probable to stop revolution.

MALMROS

Mr. Loomis to Mr. Malmros.

[TELEGRAM.]

DEPARTMENT OF STATE,
Washington, November 3, 1903.
(Sent 4 p. m.)

Are troops from the vessel *Cartagena* disembarking or preparing to land? LOOMIS.

Mr. Loomis to Mr. Malmros.

[TELEGRAM.]

DEPARTMENT OF STATE,
Washington, November 3, 1903.
(Sent 4:28 p. m.)

Did you receive and deliver to *Nashville* last night or early this morning a message? LOOMIS, *Acting.*

Mr. Malmros to Mr. Hay.

[TELEGRAM.]

COLON, *November 3, 1903.*
(Received 8:20 p. m.)

Troops from vessel *Cartagena* have disembarked; are encamping on Pacific dock awaiting orders to proceed to Panama from commander in chief, who went there this morning. No message for *Nashville* received. MALMROS.

Mr. Loomis to Mr. Malmros.

[TELEGRAM.]

DEPARTMENT OF STATE,
Washington, November 3, 1903.
(Sent 8:45 p. m.)

The troops which landed from the *Cartagena* should not proceed to Panama. LOOMIS, *Acting.*

Mr. Loomis to Mr. Malmros.

[TELEGRAM.]

DEPARTMENT OF STATE,
Washington, November 3, 1903.

(Sent 10:10 p. m.)

An important message was sent at 6 Monday night in your care for the *Nashville*. Make all possible effort to get it.   LOOMIS.

Mr. Hay to Mr. Malmros.

[TELEGRAM.]

DEPARTMENT OF STATE,
Washington, November 3, 1903.

(Sent 10:30 p. m.)

If dispatch to *Nashville* has not been delivered inform her captain immediately that she must prevent Government troops departing for Panama or taking any action which would lead to bloodshed, and must use every endeavor to preserve order on Isthmus.   HAY.

Mr. Malmros to Mr. Hay.

[TELEGRAM.]

COLON, *November 4, 1903.*

(Received 3:35 p. m.)

Met captain of *Nashville* at 6 p. m. yesterday. Heard that message had been delivered to captain boat alongside of wharf instead of to me. No rebels or invading force near Panama or Colon or line of transit. Panama intended revolutionary movement known here to few persons only, up to 8 a. m. to-day. Revolutionary committee of six in Panama at 6 p. m. took charge of revolutionary movement. General Tobar and five officers taken prisoners. Panama in possession of committee with consent of entire population. This fact appears not known as yet to conservatives in Colon. Panama committee expect to have 1,500 men armed by this time. State of affairs at Panama not known by Colombian force at Colon as yet. Official in command of disembarked force applied for transportation this morning. Captain meanwhile communicated to committee about 10 p. m. last night his refusal to allow train with force to be sent to Panama and the committee assented. This leaves Colon in the possession of the Government.   MALMROS.

Mr. Malmros to Mr. Hay.

[TELEGRAM.]

COLON, *November 5, 1903.*

(Received 11:50 a. m.)

On arrival yesterday morning's train Panama revolution and Tobar's imprisonment became generally known; 12:30 commander Colombian troops threatens to kill every American unless Tobar released by 2 p. m. Provisional Government informed these facts. *Nashville* landed 50 men; stationed in and near railroad office where Americans, armed, met. Negotiations Colombian commander and Panama Government commenced and progressing. Hostilities suspended. Colombians occupy Colon and Monkey Hill.   MALMROS.

Mr. Loomis to Mr. Malmros.

[TELEGRAM.]

DEPARTMENT OF STATE,

Washington, November 5, 1903.

(Sent 5:10 p. m.)

What is the situation this evening?

LOOMIS, *Acting.*

Mr. Malmros to Mr. Hay.

[TELEGRAM.]

COLON, *November 5, 1903.*

(Received 9:34 p. m.)

All Colombian soldiers at Colon now, 7 p. m., going on board Royal Mail steamer returning to Cartagena. Vessel, supposed to be *Dixie*, in sight.   MALMROS.

Mr. Malmros to Mr. Hay.

[TELEGRAM.]

COLON, *November 6, 1903.*

(Received 4:50 p. m.)

Tranquillity absolute in Colon. Porfirio Melendez appointed governor of this province. Proclaimed Republic of Panama at Colon prefectura at 10 o'clock a. m. English and French consuls present. I arrived after proclamation, and upon my suggestion I told governor that presence of consuls must not be looked upon recognition of revolutionary state by their respective governments. Melendez sent steam launch to Bocas del Toro to proclaim independence.

· MALMROS.

COMMUNICATIONS FROM THE PANAMA GOVERNMENT.

[TELEGRAM.—TRANSLATION.]

PANAMA, *November 4, 1903.*
(Received 8:45 p. m.)

SECRETARY OF STATE, *Washington:*

We take the liberty of bringing to the knowledge of your Government that on yesterday afternoon, in consequence of a popular and spontaneous movement of the people of this city, the independence of the Isthmus was proclaimed and, the Republic of Panama being instituted, its provisional government organizes an (executive) board consisting of ourselves, who are assured of the military strength necessary to carry out our determination.

JOSÉ A. ARANGO.
FEDERICO BOYD.
TOMAS ARIAS.

———

[TELEGRAM.—TRANSLATION.]

PANAMA, *November 4, 1903.*
(Received 10:30 p. m.)

A. SU EXCELENCIA PRESIDENTE DE LOS ESTADOS UNIDOS, *Washington:*

The municipality of Panama is now (10 p. m.) holding a solemn session, and joins in the movement of separation of the Isthmus of Panama from the rest of Colombia. It hopes for recognition of our cause by your Government.   DEMETRO S. BRIDA.

———

[TELEGRAM.—TRANSLATION.]

PANAMA, *November 5, 1903.*
(Received 8:48 p. m.)

SECRETARY OF STATE, *Washington:*

We notify you that we have appointed Señor Philippe Bunau Varilla confidential agent of the Republic of Panama near your Government and Dr. Francisco V. de la Espriella minister of foreign affairs.

ARANGO.
BOYD.
ARIAS.

———

[TELEGRAM.—TRANSLATION.]

PANAMA, *November 6, 1903.*
(Received 10:40 a. m.)

SECRETARY OF STATE, *Washington:*

Colon and all the towns of the Isthmus have adhered to the

PANAMA CANAL: GATUN UPPER LOCKS

THE PANAMA CANAL.

The commencement of the task of constructing the Panama Canal was the most important event of Roosevelt's Administration. The history of the undertaking is written by Roosevelt himself on pages 6662, 6758, 6881, 6901, 7401, 7480, 7611, 7648, 7667, 7685 and 7728. The message commencing on page 7685 describes his visit of inspection to the canal zone. President Taft continued the narrative, pages 7750, 7754, 7803, 7863 and 7898. The reader who desires a brief recital of the facts should refer to the article entitled "Panama Canal" in the Encyclopedic Index. The index references following this article will enable the reader to glean a complete and authentic knowledge of the subject from the messages of the Presidents, from Jackson to Taft, who have discussed the project.

There are three tiers of Gatun locks, which raise the level of the water in the Panama Canal from sea level to 85 feet above sea level. The three sets of locks together represent a length of .78 mile, and are located about 6 miles from the Atlantic entrance of the Canal. The view in the preceding picture shows the upper or highest of the three pairs of locks.

declaration of independence proclaimed in this city. The authority of the Republic of Panama is obeyed throughout its territory.

ARANGO.
ARIAS.
BOYD.

[TELEGRAM.—TRANSLATION.]

PANAMA, *November 6, 1903.*

SECRETARY OF STATE, *Washington:*

The board of provisional government of the Republic of Panama has appointed Señor Philippe Bunau Varilla envoy extraordinary and minister plenipotentiary near your Government with full powers to conduct diplomatic and financial negotiations. Deign to receive and heed him.

J. M. ARANGO,
TOMAS ARIAS,
FEDERICO BOYD,
Foreign Relations.

[TELEGRAM.—TRANSLATION.]

NEW YORK, *November 7, 1903.*
(Received 1 :40 p. m.)

His Excellency, JOHN HAY, *Secretary of State:*

I have the privilege and the honor of notifying you that the Government of the Republic of Panama has been pleased to designate me as its envoy extraordinary and minister plenipotentiary near the Government of the United States. In selecting for its first representative at Washington a veteran servant and champion of the Panama Canal, my Government has evidently sought to show that it considers a loyal and earnest devotion to the success of that most heroic conception of human genius as both a solemn duty and the essential purpose of its existence. I congratulate myself, sir, that my first official duty should be to respectfully request you to convey to His Excellency the President of the United States on behalf of the people of Panama an expression of the grateful sense of their obligation to his Government. In extending her generous hand so spontaneously to her latest born, the Mother of the American Nations is prosecuting her noble mission as the liberator and the educator of the peoples. In spreading her protecting wings over the territory of our Republic the American Eagle has sanctified it. It has rescued it from the barbarism of unnecessary and wasteful civil wars to consecrate it to the destiny assigned to it by Providence, the service of humanity and the progress of civilization.
PHILIPPE BUNAU VARILLA.

215

CORRESPONDENCE BETWEEN THE DEPARTMENT OF STATE AND THE UNITED STATES LEGATION AT BOGOTA.

Mr. Beaupré to Mr. Hay.

[TELEGRAM.]

BOGOTA, *November 4, 1903.*

(Received November 6, 1903, 5 p. m.)

Fourth, 5 p. m. Confidential. I have been shown telegram from reliable source in Panama to the effect that Isthmus is preparing for secession and that proclamation of independence may be expected soon. The particulars carefully guarded. Reliable information hard to obtain. This Government is evidently alarmed and troops are being sent to Isthmus. Repeat telegrams of importance from United States consul-general. His telegrams to me may be interfered with.

BEAUPRÉ.

———

Mr. Hay to Mr. Beaupré.

DEPARTMENT OF STATE,

Washington, November 6, 1903.

The people of Panama having by an apparently unanimous movement dissolved their political connection with the Republic of Colombia and resumed their independence, and having adopted a government of their own—republican in form—with which the Government of the United States of America has entered into relations, the President of the United States, in accordance with the ties of friendship which have so long and so happily existed between the respective nations, most earnestly commends to the Governments of Colombia and of Panama the peaceful and equitable settlement of all questions at issue between them. He holds that he is bound not merely by treaty obligations but by the interests of civilization, to see that the peaceful traffic of the world across the Isthmus of Panama shall not longer be disturbed by a constant succession of unnecessary and wasteful civil wars.   HAY.

———

Mr. Beaupré to Mr. Hay.

[TELEGRAM.]

BOGOTA, *November 6, 1903.*

(Received November 8, 11.05 p. m.)

November 6, 6 p. m. Knowing that the revolution has already commenced in Panama, ——— ——— says that if the Government of the United States will land troops to preserve Colombian sovereignty, and the transit, if requested by the Colombian chargé d'affaires, this Government will declare martial law, and by virtue of vested constitutional authority, when public order is disturbed, will approve by decree the ratification of the canal treaty as signed; or, if the Government of the United States prefers, will call extra session of Congress with new and friendly members next May to approve the treaty. General Reyes has the perfect confidence of Vice-President, he says, and if it becomes necessary will go to the Isthmus or send representatives there to adjust matters along above lines to the satisfaction of the people there. If he goes he would like to act in harmony with the commander of the United States forces. This is the personal opinion of Reyes, and he will advise this Government to act accordingly. There is a great reaction of public opinion in favor of the treaty, and it is considered certain that the treaty was not legally rejected by Congress. To-morrow martial law will be declared; 1,000 troops will be sent from the Pacific side; about the same number from the Atlantic side. Please answer by telegraph.

BEAUPRÉ.

Mr. Beaupré to Mr. Hay.
[TELEGRAM.]
BOGOTA, *November 7, 1903.*
(Received November 10, 7:30 p. m.)

November 7, 2 p. m. General Reyes leaves next Monday for Panama, invested with full powers. He has telegraphed chiefs of the insurrection that his mission is to the interests of Isthmus. He wishes answer from you, before leaving, to the inquiry in my telegram of yesterday and wishes to know if the American commander will be ordered to co-operate with him and with new Panama Government to arrange peace and the approval of canal treaty, which will be accepted on condition that the integrity of Colombia be preserved. He has telegraphed President of Mexico to ask the Government of the United States and all the countries represented at the Pan-American conference to aid Colombia to preserve her integrity. The question of the approval of the treaty mentioned in my telegram of yesterday will be arranged in Panama. He asks that before taking definite action you will await his arrival there, and that the Government of the United States in the meantime preserve the neutrality and transit of the Isthmus and do not recognize the new Government. Great excitement here. Martial law has been declared in the Cauca and Panama. Answer. BEAUPRÉ.

Mr. Beaupré to Mr. Hay.
[TELEGRAM.]
BOGOTA, *November 7, 1903.*
(Received November 10, 7:55 p. m.)
November 7, 6 p. m. As the Government of the United States

has war vessels at Panama and Colon, minister for foreign affairs has requested me to ask, Will you allow Colombian Government to land troops at those ports to fight there and on the line of railway? Also if the Government of the United States will take action to maintain Colombian right and sovereignty on the Isthmus in accordance with article 35, the treaty of 1846, in case the Colombian Government is entirely unable to suppress the secession movement there?

I am entirely unable to elicit from minister for foreign affairs confirmation of the promises made by ———— ————.   BEAUPRÉ.

Mr. Beaupré to Mr. Hay.

[TELEGRAM.]

BOGOTA, *November* 9, 1903.

(Received November 11, 12:30 a. m.).

November 9, 9 a. m. I am desired to inform you by General Reyes that Gen. Bedronel Ospina and Lucas Cabellero, prominent party leaders, accompany him on his mission.

Very great excitement here. Large crowds paraded streets yesterday, crying "Down with Marroquin." Mass meeting denounced him; called for a change of government. Hundreds gathered at the palace, and their orator, a prominent national general, addressed the President, calling for his resignation. Troops dispersed gathering, wounding several. Martial law is declared here, and the city is being guarded by soldiers. Legation of the United States under strong guard, but apparently no indications of hostile demonstration.

The residence of Lorenzo Marroquin attacked with stones.

Referring to the questions presented by minister for foreign affairs in my telegram of 7th, I have preserved silence, but bear in mind page 578, Foreign Relations, part 3, 1866, and instructions 134 to minister to the United States of Colombia, 1865.   BEAUPRÉ.

Mr. Hay to Mr. Beaupré.

[TELEGRAM.]

DEPARTMENT OF STATE,
Washington, November 11, 1903.

(Sent 12:12 p. m.)

Earnestly desiring an amicable solution of matters at issue between Colombia and Panama, we have instructed our consul-general at Panama to use good offices to secure for General Reyes a courteous reception and considerate hearing. It is not thought desirable to permit landing of Colombian troops on Isthmus, as such a course would precipitate civil war and disturb for an indefinite period the free transit which we are pledged to protect. I telegraphed you on November 6 that we had entered into relations with the provisional government. HAY.

CORRESPONDENCE BETWEEN THE SECRETARY OF STATE AND THE CHARGÉ D'AFFAIRES OF COLOMBIA.

Mr. Hay to Doctor Herran.

DEPARTMENT OF STATE,
Washington, November 6, 1903.

DEAR DOCTOR HERRAN: I inclose copy of a dispatch which has to-day been sent to our minister at Bogota.

Very sincerely, yours, JOHN HAY.

[INCLOSURE.]

Mr. Hay to Mr. Beaupré.
[TELEGRAM.]

NOVEMBER 6, 1903.

BEAUPRÉ, *Bogota:*

The people of Panama having by an apparently unanimous movement dissolved their political connection with the Republic of Colombia and resumed their independence, and having adopted a government of their own, republican in form, with which the Government of the United States of America has entered into relations, the President of the United States, in accordance with the ties of friendship which have so long and so happily existed between the respective nations, most earnestly commends to the governments of Colombia and Panama the peaceful and equitable settlement of all questions at issue between them. He holds that he is bound not merely by treaty obligations, but by the interests of civilization, to see that the peaceable traffic of the world across the Isthmus of Panama shall not longer be disturbed by a constant succession of unnecessary and wasteful civil wars.

HAY.

Dr. Herran to Mr. Hay.
[TRANSLATION.]

LEGATION OF COLOMBIA,
Washington, D. C., November 6, 1903.

EXCELLENCY: I acknowledge the reception of your excellency's note of the 6th instant, inclosing a copy of the telegram sent on the same day to the legation of the United States at Bogota by the Department of State.

In that telegram your excellency refers to the relations already

entered into by the Government of the United States of America
with the Colombian rebels who on the evening of the 3rd usurped
the power in the capital of the Colombian Department of Panama and
imprisoned the lawful civil and military authorities.

Your excellency will undoubtedly receive the reply of the Colombian Government through the same channel that was used to forward
the notice of which your excellency was pleased to send me a copy,
but, in the meanwhile, I am discharging a duty by lodging in advance
with your excellency, in the name of my Government, a solemn protest
against the attitude assumed in the Department of Panama, by the
Government of the United States to the injury of Colombia's rights
and in disaccord with the stipulations of article 35 of the still existing treaty of 1846-1848 between Colombia and the United States of
America.

I reiterate, etc.   THOMAS HERRAN.

Mr. Hay to Dr. Herran.

No. 22.]   DEPARTMENT OF STATE,
                                  Washington, November 11, 1903.

SIR: I have the honor to acknowledge the receipt of your note of
the 7th instant, in which, acknowledging my communication of the
6th instant, you are pleased, of your own motion and in the absence
of instruction from your Government, to lodge a protest against the
attitude assumed by the Government of the United States in respect
to the situation on the Isthmus of Panama.

Accept, sir, etc.   JOHN HAY.

Mr. Tower to Mr. Hay.
[TELEGRAM.]
EMBASSASY OF THE UNITED STATES,
Berlin, November 10, 1903.

(Received 5:40 p. m.)

In regard to the report telegraphed from New York that the
Colombian consul-general there had declared that Colombian citizens
had petitioned the Colombian Government to send a deputation to
thank the German Government for its offered protection and to make
concessions of land to Germany therefor, I have just received the
assurance of the German minister for foreign affairs that there is no
truth whatever in this report. He added that Germany has no interest in the Panama matter, and that the question of an interference
on the part of Germany does not exist.   TOWER.

Mr. Porter to Mr. Hay.

[TELEGRAM.]

EMBASSY OF THE UNITED STATES,
Paris, November 11, 1903.

(Received 3:50 p. m.)

The French generally are much pleased with events in Panama and our attitude there. In conversation with minister for foreign affairs he expressed himself in very sympathetic manner. Has authorized French consul at Panama to enter into relations with de facto government. Recognition will no doubt follow in time, and it seems to be disposition of European powers to await formal recognition by the United States before acting.   PORTER.

RECEPTION OF MINISTERS OF PANAMA.

Mr. Varilla to Mr. Hay.

[TRANSLATION.]

LEGATION OF THE REPUBLIC OF PANAMA,
Washington, November 11, 1903.

MR. SECRETARY OF STATE:

I have the very great honor to bring to your knowledge the fact that the Republic of Panama has designated me to fill, near the Government of the United States of America, the post of envoy extraordinary and minister plenipotentiary with full powers to negotiate.

While begging you, Mr. Secretary of State, to transmit to His Excellency the President of the Republic of the United States the substance of the present communication, I venture to ask you to solicit from his kindness the appointment of a date on which he will authorize me to present to him my letters of credence.

I have, etc.   P. BUNAU VARILLA.

Mr. Loomis to Mr. Varilla.

No. 1.]   DEPARTMENT OF STATE,
Washington, November 12, 1903.

SIR: I have the honor to acknowledge the receipt of your note of the 11th instant, in which you advise me that the Republic of Panama has appointed you to fill, near this Government, the post of envoy extraordinary and minister plenipotentiary, with full powers to negotiate.

You further ask that this information may be communicated to the President and that he will kindly fix a date at which you may present your letters of credence.

In reply I have the honor to say that the President will be pleased to receive you for the purpose mentioned to-morrow, Friday, at 9:30 a. m.

If you will be good enough to call at this Department shortly before the hour mentioned, the Secretary of State will be pleased to accompany you to the White House.

Accept, etc.   FRANCIS B. LOOMIS.
                              Acting Secretary.

REMARKS MADE BY THE MINISTER OF PANAMA.

MR. PRESIDENT: In according to the minister plenipotentiary of the Republic of Panama the honor of presenting to you his letters of credence you admit into the family of nations the weakest and the last born of the republics of the New World.

It owes its existence to the outburst of the indignant grief which stirred the hearts of the citizens of the Isthmus on beholding the despotic action which sought to forbid their country from fulfilling the destinies vouchsafed to it by Providence.

In consecrating its right to exist, Mr. President, you put an end to what appeared to be the interminable controversy as to the rival waterways, and you definitely inaugurate the era of the achievement of the Panama Canal.

From this time forth the determination of the fate of the canal depends upon two elements alone, now brought face to face, singularly unlike as regards their authority and power, but wholly equal in their common and ardent desire to see at last the accomplishment of the heroic enterprise for piercing the mountain barrier of the Andes.

The highway from Europe to Asia, following the pathway of the sun, is now to be realized.

The early attempts to find such a way unexpectedly resulted in the greatest of all historic achievements, the discovery of America. Centuries have since rolled by, but the pathway sought has hitherto remained in the realm of dreams. To-day, Mr. President, in response to your summons, it becomes a reality.

THE PRESIDENT'S REPLY TO THE REMARKS MADE BY SEÑOR BUNAU VARILLA ON THE OCCASION OF THE PRESENTATION OF HIS LETTERS OF CREDENCE.

MR. MINISTER: I am much gratified to receive the letters whereby you are accredited to the Government of the United States in the capacity of envoy extraordinary and minister plenipotentiary of the Republic of Panama.

In accordance with its long-established rule, this Government has taken cognizance of the act of the ancient territory of Panama in reasserting the right of self-control and, seeing in the recent events on the Isthmus an unopposed expression of the will of the people of Panama and the confirmation of their declared independence by the institution of a de facto government, republican in form and spirit, and alike able and resolved to discharge the obligations pertaining to sovereignty, we have entered into relations with the new Republic. It is fitting that we should do so now, as we did nearly a century ago when the Latin peoples of America proclaimed the right of popular government, and it is equally fitting that the United States should, now as then, be the first to stretch out the hand of fellowship and to observe toward the new-born State the rules of equal intercourse that regulate the relations of sovereignties toward one another.

I feel that I express the wish of my countrymen in assuring you, and through you the people of the Republic of Panama, of our earnest hope and desire that stability and prosperity shall attend the new State, and that, in harmony with the United States, it may be the providential instrument of untold benefit to the civilized world through the opening of a highway of universal commerce across its exceptionally favored territory.

For yourself, Mr. Minister, I wish success in the discharge of the important mission to which you have been called.

NAVY DEPARTMENT,
Washington, November 12, 1903.

SIR: In accordance with the resolution of the House of Representatives of the 9th instant, calling for all correspondence and other official documents relating to the recent revolution on the Isthmus of Panama, I have the honor to transmit herewith all such matter on file in the Navy Department.

Very Respectfully,   WILLIAM H. MOODY,
Secretary.

The PRESIDENT.

NAVY DEPARTMENT,
Washington, D. C., November 2, 1903.
[TRANSLATION.]

NASHVILLE, *care American Consul, Colon* :*

Maintain free and uninterrupted transit. If interruption threatened by armed force, occupy the line of railroad. Prevent landing of

*Same order to commander of *Dixie*, at Kingston, Jamaica.

any armed force with hostile intent, either Government or insurgent, either at Colon, Porto Bello, or other point. Send copy of instructions to the senior officer present at Panama upon arrival of *Boston*. Have sent copy of instructions and have telegraphed *Dixie* to proceed with all possible dispatch from Kingston to Colon. Government force reported approaching the Isthmus in vessels. Prevent their landing if in your judgment this would precipitate a conflict. Acknowledgment is required.   DARLING, *Acting*.

NAVY DEPARTMENT,
Washington, D. C., November 2, 1903.

GLASS, *Marblehead, Acapulco:**

Proceed with all possible dispatch to Panama. Telegraph in cipher your departure. Maintain free and uninterrupted transit. If interruption is threatened by armed force occupy the line of railroad. Prevent landing of any armed force, either Government or insurgent, with hostile intent at any point within 50 miles of Panama. If doubtful as to the intention of any armed force, occupy Ancon Hill strongly with artillery. If the *Wyoming* would delay *Concord* and *Marblehead* her disposition must be left to your discretion. Government force reported approaching the Isthmus in vessels Prevent their landing if in your judgment landing would precipitate a conflict.   DARLING, *Acting*.

NAVY DEPARTMENT,
Washington, D. C., November 3, 1903.

CRUISER ATLANTA, *Kingston, Jamaica*:

Proceed with all possible dispatch to Colon. Acknowledge immediately. When will you sail?   DARLING, *Acting*.

NAVY DEPARTMENT,
Washington, D. C., November 3, 1903.

NASHVILLE, *Colon:*

In the interest of peace make every effort to prevent Government troops at Colon from proceeding to Panama. The transit of the Isthmus must be kept open and order maintained. Acknowledge.
                        DARLING, *Acting*.

---

*Same to commander of *Boston*, at San Juan del Sur, Nicaragua.

Navy Department,
Washington, D. C., November 3, 1903.

American Consul, *Panama:*

Message sent *Nashville* to Colon may not have been delivered. Accordingly see that the following message is sent to *Nashville* immediately:

Nashville, *Colon:*

In the interest of peace make every effort to prevent Government troops at Colon from proceeding to Panama. The transit of the Isthmus must be kept open and order maintained. Acknowledge.   Darling, *Acting.*

Secure special trains if necessary. Act promptly.
Loomis, *Acting.*

———

[TRANSLATION.]

Navy Department,
Washington, D. C., November 4, 1903

Nashville, *Colon:*

Gunboat of Colombia shelling Panama. Send immediately battery 3-inch field gun and 6-pounder with a force of men to Panama to compel cessation bombardment. Railroad must furnish transportation immediately.   Darling, *Acting.*

———

[TRANSLATION.]

Washington, D. C., November 5, 1903.

Boston, *care of American consul, Panama:*

Prevent recurrence bombardment of Panama. Acknowledge.
Moody.

———

Navy Department,
Washington, D. C., November 5, 1903.

Nashville, *Colon:*

Prevent any armed force of either side from landing at Colon, Porto Bello, or vicinity.   Moody.

———

[TRANSLATION.]

Washington, D. C., November 6, 1903.

Maine, *Woods Hole, Mass.:*

Proceed at once to Colon, coaling wherever necessary to expedite your arrival. Acknowledge.   Moody.

[TRANSLATION.]

Washington, D. C., November 9, 1903.

DIEHL, *Boston:*

Upon the arrival of the *Marblehead* sufficient force must be sent to watch movements closely of the British steamers seized at Buenaventura and to prevent the landing of men with hostile intent within limits of the State of Panama. Protect the British steamers if necessary.   MOODY.

[TRANSLATION.]

Washington, D. C., November 10, 1903.

GLASS, *Marblehead, Panama:*

Reported that the British steamers at Buenaventura were not detained. Did they leave with Colombian troops aboard?   MOODY.

[TRANSLATION.]

Colon, October 15, 1903.

SECRETARY OF THE NAVY, *Washington, D. C.:*

Report is current to the effect that a revolution has broken out in the State of Cauca. Everything is quiet on the Isthmus unless a change takes place. On this account there is no necessity to remain here. Do not think it necessary to visit St. Andrews Island.

HUBBARD,
Commanding Officer U. S. S. Nashville.

[TRANSLATION.]

Colon, November 3, 1903.

SECRETARY OF THE NAVY, *Washington, D. C.:*

Receipt of your telegram of November 2 is acknowledged. Prior to receipt this morning about 400 men were landed here by the Government of Colombia from Cartagena. No revolution has been declared on the Isthmus and no disturbances. Railway company have declined to transport these troops except by request of the governor of Panama. Request has not been made. It is possible that movement may be made to-night at Panama to declare independence, in which event I will . . . (message mutilated here) here. Situation is most critical if revolutionary leaders act.   HUBBARD.

[TRANSLATION.]

Colon, November 4, 1903.

SECRETARY OF THE NAVY, *Washington, D. C.:*

Provisional government was established at Panama Tuesday evening; no organized opposition. Governor of Panama, General Tobar, General Amaya, Colonel Morales, and three others of the Colombian Government troops who arrived Tuesday morning taken prisoner at Panama. I have prohibited transit of troops now here across the Isthmus. HUBBARD.

Colon, November 4, 1903.

SECRETARY OF THE NAVY, *Washington, D. C.:*

Government troops yet in Colon. Have prohibited transportation of troops either direction. No interruption of transit as yet. Will make every effort to preserve peace and order. HUBBARD.

Colon, November 4, 1903.

SECRETARY OF THE NAVY, *Washington, D. C.:*

I have landed force to protect the lives and property of American citizens here against threats of Colombian soldiery. I am protecting water front with ship. I can not possibly send to Panama until affairs are settled at Colon. HUBBARD.

Acapulco, Mexico, November 4, 1903.

SECRETARY OF THE NAVY, *Washington, D. C.:*

Marblehead and *Concord* to Panama to-day 4 p. m.; *Wyoming* will follow to-morrow afternoon. If *Boston* is to go with squadron, I would suggest Department will order her to rendezvous off Cape Mala, Colombia, about 6 p. m., on November 9. I have ordered *Nero* to Acapulco. I will leave sealed orders for her to proceed without delay to Panama unless otherwise directed. GLASS.

Colon, November 5, 1903—9.41 a. m.

SECRETARY OF THE NAVY, *Washington, D. C.:*

British man-of-war *Amphion* is protecting American interests at Panama. Reported bombardment much exaggerated. HUBBARD.

Colon, November 5, 1903—9.45 a. m.

SECRETARY OF THE NAVY, *Washington, D. C.:*

Have withdrawn force landed Wednesday afternoon. No bloodshed. I do not apprehend difficulty of any serious nature.

HUBBARD.

Colon, November 5, 1905.

SECRETARY OF THE NAVY, *Washington, D. C.:*

Situation here this morning again acute. Have deemed advisable to reland force.   HUBBARD.

[TRANSLATION.]

Colon, November 5, 1903.

SECRETARY OF THE NAVY, *Washington, D. C.:*

Atlas Line's steamer, with large body of troops, reported sailing from Cartagena, Colombia.   HUBBARD.

Colon, November 6, 1903.

SECRETARY OF THE NAVY, *Washington, D. C.:*

All quiet. Independents declare Government established as Republic of Panama. Have withdrawn marines.   DELANO.

Colon, November 6, 1903—9.15 a. m

SECRETARY OF THE NAVY, *Washington, D. C.:*

Arrived Thursday evening; landed force. Following conditions prevailing: Just before landing all the troops of Colombia have left for R. M. S. P. Company's steamer *Orinoco* for Cartagena. Independent party in possession of Colon, Panama, and railroad line. *Nashville* withdrawn force.   DELANO.

[TRANSLATION.]

Panama, November 7, 1903—7.40 p. m.

SECRETARY OF THE NAVY, *Washington, D. C.:*

All quiet; traffic undisturbed; message to prevent received.

DIEHL.

Colon, November 8, 1903—7.05 p. m.

SECRETARY OF THE NAVY, *Washington, D. C.:*

Atlanta left yesterday for Bocas del Toro.   DELANO.

Panama, November 9, 1903.

SECRETARY OF THE NAVY, *Washington, D. C.:*

The British consul and the minister of war of the provisional government fear seizure of two British steamers at Buenaventura to transport troops convoyed by gunboat. Prevailed upon minister to dispatch gunboat, fearing possible destruction British steamers. The landing of troops in the territory within the limit under my control will cause prolonged campaign. Instructions from the Department are requested.

DIEHL.

Panama, November 10, 1903.

SECRETARY OF THE NAVY, *Washington, D. C.:*

Your telegram of the 9th of November to the *Boston* acknowledged. No interference British vessels yet. Report seems to be well founded that the steamship *Bogota* sailed from Buenaventura yesterday afternoon with 1,000 for Rio Dulce. Have sent *Concord* to patrol in that vicinity in order to prevent landing. Everything is quiet at Panama.

GLASS.

SPECIAL MESSAGES.

WHITE HOUSE, *Washington, November 20, 1903.*

To the Senate and House of Representatives:

I transmit herewith a statement showing the receipts and disbursements of the Louisiana Purchase Exposition Company from date of incorporation to September 30, 1903, furnished by the Louisiana Purchase Exposition Commission in pursuance of section 11 of the "Act to provide for celebrating the one hundredth anniversary of the purchase of the Louisiana Territory," etc., approved March 3, 1901, together with a report submitted by the Exposition Company, showing progress made by the various departments of the exposition.

THEODORE ROOSEVELT

WHITE HOUSE, *Washington, November 27, 1903.*

To the House of Representatives:

In response to a resolution of the House of Representatives of November 9, 1903, requesting the President "to communicate to the House, if not, in his judgment, incompatible with the interests of the public service, all correspondence and other official documents relating to the revolution on the Isthmus of Panama," I transmit herewith copies of additional papers on the subject, which have been received subsequent to the resolution referred to.

THEODORE ROOSEVELT.

WHITE HOUSE, *December 4, 1903.*

To the Senate and House of Representatives:

I transmit herewith for the information of the Congress the third annual report of the governor of Porto Rico, covering the period from July 1, 1902, to June 30, 1903, with appendices.

THEODORE ROOSEVELT.

VETO MESSAGES.

WHITE HOUSE, *February 5, 1903.*

To the House of Representatives:

I return herewith, without approval, Senate bill 1115, entitled "An act providing for additional terms of court in the western judicial district of the State of South Carolina."

The Attorney-General reports that the establishment of the two additional places for holding court in the western judicial district of South Carolina at Spartanburg and Rockhill would be accompanied by considerable expense, which would be hardly justifiable, as the necessity is at least very doubtful.

In response to requests for their views on the subject, the judges of the circuit and district courts in this district also report that there is no necessity for and that the public business does not require such additional terms.

In view of these statements, I am constrained to withhold my approval of the bill.

THEODORE ROOSEVELT.

WHITE HOUSE, *February 11, 1903.*

To the Senate:

I return herewith Senate bill No. 4308, entitled "An act for the relief of Katie A. Nolan."

Executive approval of this bill is withheld for the reason that it appears to be a duplication of legislation. The deficiency act of July 1, 1902, contained the following provision:

"To enable the Postmaster-General to pay Katie A. Nolan balance of salary due her as stamp clerk in the post-office at San Antonio, Tex., from July 1, 1889, to July 1, 1893, $800."

Under this provision of said act Katie A. Nolan, the beneficiary named in this bill, was paid $800 by the postmaster at San Antonio, Tex., by direction of the Postmaster-General, as shown by the records of the Post-Office Department.

THEODORE ROOSEVELT.

WHITE HOUSE, *February 21, 1903.*

To the Senate:

I return herewith, without approval, Senate bill 1115, entitled "An act for the relief of Francis S. Davidson, late first lieutenant, Ninth United States Cavalry."

The beneficiary of this bill was in the service for about nine years ending in December, 1875. He has not been in the service for the past twenty-seven years.

When in the service he appears to have been an insubordinate and unprofitable officer. He was at one time a cadet at the West Point Academy, and was discharged January 31, 1865, by reason of deficiency in study and conduct. The Academic board remarked of him at that time:

"This is the second deficiency of Cadet Davidson in conduct, and he having shown himself regardless of the leniency heretofore extended to him, the board recommends that he be discharged."

From June 9 to October 31, 1865, after the end of active hostilities of the civil war, he was a lieutenant of volunteers. He was appointed second lieutenant in the Regular Army March 7, 1867; promoted to be first lieutenant July 31, 1867.

On the 20th of June, 1868, he was tried by court-martial for "Neglect of duty, disobedience of orders, and conduct prejudicial to good order and military discipline," and acquitted. The finding of acquittal was disapproved by the reviewing authority, with the remark that the conduct of the accused "was not only irregular, but insubordinate and disrespectful to his commanding officer."

On the 4th of January, 1872, he was again tried by court-martial and found guilty of disobedience of orders and violation of the sixth article of war, and was suspended from rank and pay for one month and reprimanded in general orders.

On November 15, 1875, he was again tried by court-martial and found guilty of "conduct unbecoming an officer and a gentleman," consisting of breach of arrest and gambling with enlisted men. Upon this he was dismissed the service, from which he has remained separated for now more than twenty-seven years.

No act of special gallantry or conspicuous service marked the short period during which he was an officer of the Army. He is 56 years of age. This bill proposes to put him upon the retired list, where he would be supported for the remainder of his life at public expense without rendering any return. It does not appear that he is subject to any physical disability incurred in the line of duty or otherwise. The treatment thus proposed is denied by law to all the officers whose service has been continuous and faithful, for they are not entitled to the benefits of the retired list until after forty years' service, or reaching the age of 64, or being physically disabled.

That an officer with this record should be rewarded is wholly without justification, and if that should be done it would involve a confusion between the treatment accorded to loyal and faithful service and that accorded to insubordination and unfaithful service, which could not fail to be most prejudicial to the morale and efficiency of the Army.

THEODORE ROOSEVELT.

WHITE HOUSE, *February 25, 1903.*

To the House of Representatives:

I return herewith, without approval, House bill No. 10095, entitled "An act for the relief of Levi L. Reed."

The beneficiary of this bill was enlisted July 24, 1861, at Reading, Pa., and was discharged from Battery H, Fifth United States Artillery, July 24, 1864, at Nashville, Tenn., by expiration of service, a sergeant. He re-enlisted July 26, 1864, for three years, in Troop H., Fifth United States Cavalry, deserted therefrom July 31, 1865, while a corporal, at Cumberland, Md., and never returned to his command. Through his attorney he was furnished a "deserter's release" on June 2, 1892, in view of the act of Congress, approved April 11, 1890, amending the one hundred and third article of war, so as to prescribe a limitation as to prosecution of the offense of desertion.

This action is regarded as releasing the soldier from service as well as protecting him from liability to apprehension and trial, so that, being no longer in the service, he can not be discharged therefrom. Finally, as he deserted from the military service while holding the rank of corporal, I do not regard him as deserving an honorable discharge.

THEODORE ROOSEVELT.

WHITE HOUSE, *March 3, 1903.*

To the House of Representatives:

I return without approval House bill No. 9632, entitled "An act for the allowance of claims of certain citizens of Virginia for damages to their property incident to the encampment at Manassas and march from Camp Alger to Thoroughfare Gap, Virginia, as recommended by a board of officers appointed for the consideration of claims for damages to property by volunteer soldiers during the war with Spain," with a view to having it reconsidered and amended.

Attention is invited to the accompanying letter and statement of the Quartermaster-General of the Army.

THEODORE ROOSEVELT.

WHITE HOUSE, *Washington, D. C., March 3, 1903.*

To the Senate:

I return herewith without approval Senate bill No. 1168, entitled "An act to authorize the appointment of Edward L. Bailey as captain of infantry, United States Army, and to place him on the retired list."

The beneficiary of this bill was undoubtedly a gallant officer in the volunteer forces during the civil war, and the sentiments of gratitude awakened by the consideration of his services as a volunteer officer have created a strong desire on my part to concur in the action of the Senate and the House expressed in the bill for his restoration to the Army.

An examination of Captain Bailey's military record while in the Regular Army, however, makes it plain that this natural desire can not be gratified by the officers who are charged with the administration of military justice consistently with their duty to enforce the law in such a way as to maintain discipline and a high standard of morals and honorable conduct among the officers of the Army.

While a volunteer officer Captain Bailey was twice tried by court-martial for disobedience of orders. Upon the first trial, in January, 1863, he was acquitted. Upon the second trial, in February, 1863, he was convicted and sentenced to forfeit two months' pay and emoluments and be reprimanded in General Orders.

On the 7th of March, 1867, he was appointed a second lieutenant of infantry, and he remained an officer of the Regular Army until the 15th of October, 1893. During that time he was five times tried by court-martial.

In September, 1871, he was tried and convicted of embezzlement and misappropriation of public moneys coming into his hands officially. The conviction was confirmed by the department commander who convened the court, but was disapproved by the President upon the ground that the money that was in his possession was lost by robbery, and his only wrongdoing was his failure to report the fact immediately.

In January, 1873, he was tried and convicted of neglect of duty in failing to attend at guard mounting when officer of the day, and at roll call on numerous occasions, not being prevented by sickness or other evident necessity, and was sentenced to be reprimanded.

In July, 1874, he was tried for neglect of duty, for conduct unbecoming an officer and a gentleman in borrowing money from enlisted men and failing to repay it, notwithstanding their repeated and persistent efforts to secure payment, and for purchasing supplies from various persons for the officers' mess, of which he was caterer, collecting the money from his fellow-officers to pay for the supplies, and appropriating the money to his own use, leaving the debts for the supplies unpaid; and he was sentenced to be dismissed the service. This sentence was approved by the department commander, but was mitigated by the President to suspension from rank and command for six months.

In April, 1890, he was tried for obtaining money on worthless checks drawn on banking firm with whom he had no credit, and acquitted. The department commander reviewing the action of the court disapproved the acquittal.

In September, 1893, he was tried and convicted of conduct unbecoming an officer and a gentleman in borrowing money from a fellow-officer and not repaying it, although repeatedly promising to do so; in entering a private house, in uniform, without permission, in the absence of the owner, beckoning to the owner's wife with his hand; refusing to leave the house when requested so to do by her; and in going to a public saloon in Boise City, Idaho, and chasing a prostitute about the saloon, and going to a corner of the saloon, holding a conversation with her while in uniform of a commissioned officer.

It appears that pending his trial upon these charges, he being under arrest, he was authorized by his commanding officer to visit Boise City for four hours, exclusive of meal time, beginning at 11.30 a. m., for the purpose of attending to personal business; that in disregard of his arrest he went to Boise City in the night of April 15-16, and there visited a saloon and drank with citizens at the bar between 11.30 p. m. and 1 a. m., and also visited a house of prostitution and behaved in a boisterous and disorderly manner in company with the same prostitute whom he was charged with chasing about the saloon, being at the time in the uniform of a commissioned officer.

Upon these acts additional charges were made of conduct to the prejudice of good order and military discipline and conduct unbecoming an officer and a gentleman, and he was convicted upon these charges also. He was sentenced to be dismissed the service, and the sentence was approved and confirmed by the President.

The proceedings upon this last trial show that the sentence was not approved without a very careful review and examination both by General Schofield and by the President. Were I now empowered to review the proceedings again, I should be compelled to reach the same conclusion.

Captain Bailey has produced before the committees of the respective Houses a number of affidavits, some of which tend to impeach one of the principal witnesses for the prosecution, and in some of which other witnesses to some degree modify the testimony given by them ten years before. Giving full effect, however, to these ex parte affidavits, the conviction still remains sustained by the evidence.

It is plain that, when the President disapproved the conviction of embezzlement in 1871, when the conviction of the neglect of duty in 1873 was punished only by a reprimand, and when the conviction "unbecoming an officer and a gentleman," involving the misappropriation of public moneys in 1874, was followed by the President's mitigation of the sentence of dismissal to suspension for six months, the captain had the full benefit of his record as a volunteer officer in the civil war.

I do not think that further clemency can be extended on this ground consistently with the due administration of the law. I should not regard it as a proper exercise of the appointing power vested in me by the Constitution to appoint as an officer in the Army a man with the record of Captain Bailey, and with the sentence standing against him of dismissal from the Army, based upon sufficient grounds, after a fair trial, and after approval by my predecessor in the performance of his official duty.

THEODORE ROOSEVELT.

WHITE HOUSE, *March 3, 1903.*

To the House of Representatives:

I return without approval House bill 14051, entitled "An act granting the consent of Congress to N. F. Thompson and associates to erect a dam and construct a power station at Muscle Shoals, Alabama."

The recent development of the application of water power to the production of electricity available for use at considerable distances has revealed an element of substantial value in streams which the Government is or is liable to be called upon to improve for purposes of navigation, and this value, in my judgment, should be properly utilized to defray the cost of the improvement. Wherever the Government constructs a dam and lock for the purpose of navigation there is a waterfall of great value. It does not seem right or just that this element of local value should be given away to private individuals of the vicinage, and at the same time the people of the whole country should be taxed for the local improvement.

It seems clear that justice to the taxpayers of the country demands that when the Government is or may be called upon to improve a stream the improvement should be made to pay for itself, so far as practicable. I am advised that at another point on the same river to which this bill refers there is an authorized project for improvement by the Government at a cost of over $800,000, and that an offer has been made by a responsible citizen to do the entire work without expense to the Government provided he can be authorized to use the water power. I think it is desirable that the entire subject of granting privileges of the kind referred to in this bill should be considered in a comprehensive way and that a general policy appropriate to the new conditions caused by the advance in electrical science should be adopted under which these valuable rights will not be practically given away, but will be disposed of after full competition in such a way as shall best conserve the public interests.

THEODORE ROOSEVELT.

PROCLAMATIONS.

By the President of the United States of America.

A PROCLAMATION.

Whereas, it is provided by section one of the Act of Congress, approved July first, nineteen hundred and two, entitled, "An Act Authorizing the President to reserve public lands and buildings in the island of Porto Rico for public uses, and granting other public lands and buildings to the government of Porto Rico, and for other purposes", "That the President be, and he is hereby, authorized to make within one year after the approval of this Act, such reservation of public lands and buildings belonging to the United States in the island of Porto Rico, for military, naval, light-house, marine-hospital, post-offices, custom-houses, United States courts, and other public purposes, as he may deem necessary";

And whereas, the public lands in the island of Porto Rico, within the limits hereinafter described, are in part covered with timber, and it appears that the public good would be promoted by setting apart and reserving said lands as a public reservation;

Now, therefore, I, Theodore Roosevelt, President of the United States, by virtue of the power in me vested by section one of the aforesaid Act of Congress, do hereby make known and proclaim that there are hereby reserved and set apart as a Public Forest Reservation all those certain tracts, pieces or parcels of public lands, not heretofore appropriated or reserved, lying and being situate in the island of Porto Rico, and within the boundaries particularly described as follows, to wit:

Beginning at the point where the parallel of eighteen (18) degrees and twenty-two (22) minutes, north latitude, intersects the meridian of sixty-five (65) degrees and fifty-five (55) minutes, west longitude; thence due east along said parallel to its intersection with the meridian of sixty-five (65) degrees and forty-five (45) minutes, west longitude; thence due south along said meridian to its intersection with the parallel of eighteen (18) degrees and fourteen (14) minutes, north latitude; thence due west along said parallel to its intersection with the meridian of sixty-five (65) degrees and fifty-five (55) minutes, west longitude; thence due north along said meridian to its intersection with the parallel of eighteen (18) degrees and twenty-two (22) minutes, north latitude, the place of beginning.

Warning is hereby expressly given to all persons not to occupy or use the lands reserved by this proclamation.

The reservation hereby established shall be known as The Luquillo Forest Reserve.

In witness whereof, I have hereunto set my hand and caused the seal of the United States to be affixed.

[SEAL.] DONE at the City of Washington this 17th day of January, in the year of our Lord one thousand, nine hundred and three, and of the Independence of the United States the one hundred and twenty-seventh.

THEODORE ROOSEVELT.

By the President:
JOHN HAY,
Secretary of State.

BY THE PRESIDENT OF THE UNITED STATES OF AMERICA.

A PROCLAMATION.

Whereas, public interests require that the Senate should convene in extraordinary session:

Now, therefore, I, THEODORE ROOSEVELT, President of the United States of America, do hereby proclaim and declare that an extraordinary occasion requires the Senate of the United States to convene at the Capitol, in the city of Washington, on the 5th day of March next, at 12 o'clock noon, of which all persons who shall at that time be entitled to act as members of that body are hereby required to take notice.

Given under my hand and the seal of the United States at Washington, the 2d day of March, in the year of our Lord one thousand nine hundred and three, and of the Independence of the United States the one hundred and twenty-seventh.

[SEAL.]

THEODORE ROOSEVELT.

By the President:
JOHN HAY,
Secretary of State.

BY THE PRESIDENT OF THE UNITED STATES OF AMERICA

A PROCLAMATION.

Whereas, by the resolution of the Senate of March 19, 1903, the approval by Congress of the reciprocal Commercial Convention between the United States and the Republic of Cuba, signed at Havana on December 11, 1902, is necessary before the said Convention shall take effect;

And Whereas, it is important to the public interests of the United States that the said Convention shall become operative as early as may be;

Now, therefore, I, THEODORE ROOSEVELT, President of the United States of America, by virtue of the power vested in me by the Constitution, do hereby proclaim and declare that an extraordinary occasion requires the convening of both Houses of the Congress of the United States at their respective Chambers in the city of Washington on the 9th day of November next, at 12 o'clock noon, to the end that they may consider and determine whether the approval of the Congress shall be given to the said Convention.

All persons entitled to act as members of the 58th Congress are required to take notice of this proclamation.

[SEAL.]   GIVEN under my hand and the Seal of the United States at Washington the 20th day of October in the year of our Lord one thousand nine hundred and three and of the Independence of the United States the one hundred and twenty-eighth.

THEODORE ROOSEVELT.

By the President:

JOHN HAY,
            Secretary of State.

EXECUTIVE ORDER

It is deemed desirable that the regulations governing appointments and employments of mere laborers and workmen in the Departments at Washington shall be extended, as rapidly as may be found practicable, to offices in the executive civil service outside of Washington.

The United States Civil Service Commission is therefore directed to render such assistance as may be practicable to the heads of the Executive Departments for the establishment and maintenance of a system of registration to test the relative fitness of applicants for appointment or employment as mere laborers and workmen.

THEODORE ROOSEVELT.

WHITE HOUSE, *March 26, 1903.*

PROCLAMATIONS

BY THE PRESIDENT OF THE UNITED STATES OF AMERICA.

A PROCLAMATION.

Whereas, it is provided by section 13 of the act of Congress of March 3, 1891, entitled, "An act to amend title sixty, chapter three, of the Revised Statutes of the United States, relating to copyrights", that said act "shall only apply to a citizen or subject of a foreign state or nation when such foreign state or nation permits to citizens of the United States of America the benefit of copyright on substantially the same basi: as its own citizens; or when such foreign state or nation .s a party to an international agreement which provides for reciprocity in the granting of copyright, by the terms of which agreement the United States of America may, at its pleasure, become a party to such agreement";

And whereas, it is also provided by said section that "the existence of either of the conditions aforesaid shall be determined by the President of the United States by proclamation made from time to time as the purposes of this act may require";

And whereas, satisfactory official assurances have been given that in Cuba the law permits to citizens of the United States the benefit of copyright on substantially the same basis as to the citizens of Cuba:

Now, therefore, I, THEODORE ROOSEVELT, President of the United States of America, do declare and proclaim that the first of the conditions specified in section 13 of the act of March 3, 1891, now exists and is fulfilled in respect to the citizens of Cuba.

In testimony whereof, I have hereunto set my hand and caused the seal of the United States to be affixed.

[SEAL.] DONE at the City of Washington this 17th day of November, one thousand nine hundred and three, and of the independence of the United States the one hundred and twenty-eighth.

THEODORE ROOSEVELT.

By the President:
JOHN HAY,
    Secretary of State.

Distrust as a demigogue the man who talks only of the wrong done by the men of wealth. Distrust as a demagogue the man who measures iniquity by the purse.—*Roosevelt at Oyster Bay, July 4, 1906.*

THANKSGIVING PROCLAMATION

BY THE PRESIDENT OF THE UNITED STATES OF AMERICA.

A PROCLAMATION.

The season is at hand when according to the custom of our people it falls upon the President to appoint a day of praise and thanksgiving to God.

During the last year the Lord has dealt bountifully with us, giving us peace at home and abroad and the chance for our citizens to work for their welfare unhindered by war, famine or plague. It behoves us not only to rejoice greatly because of what has been given us, but to accept it with a solemn sense of responsibility, realizing that under Heaven it rests with us ourselves to show that we are worthy to use aright what has thus been entrusted to our care. In no other place and at no other time has the experiment of government of the people, by the people, for the people, been tried on so vast a scale as here in our own country in the opening years of the 20th Century. Failure would not only be a dreadful thing for us, but a dreadful thing for all mankind, because it would mean loss of hope for all who believe in the power and the righteousness of liberty. Therefore, in thanking God for the mercies extended to us in the past, we beeseech Him that He may not withhold them in the future, and that our hearts may be roused to war steadfastly for good and against all the forces of evil, public and private. We pray for strength, and light, so that in the coming years we may with cleanliness, fearlessness, and wisdom, do our allotted work on the earth in such manner as to show that we are not altogether unworthy of the blessings we have received.

unless the entryman, settler or claimant continues to comply with the law under which the entry, filing or settlement was made.

Warning is hereby expressly given to all persons not to make settlement upon the lands reserved by this proclamation.

The reservation hereby established shall be known as The Aquarius Forest Reserve.

In witness whereof, I have hereunto set my hand and caused the seal of the United States to be affixed.

DONE at the City of Washington this 24th day of October, [SEAL.] in the year of our Lord one thousand nine hundred and three and of the Independence of the United States the one hundred and twenty-eighth.

By the President: THEODORE ROOSEVELT.
JOHN HAY,
  Secretary of State.

ATTITUDE TOWARD UNION LABOR
Bookbinders in the Government Printing Office.

On May 18, 1903, William A. Miller was removed by the Public Printer from his position of Assistant Foreman at the Government Printing Office. Mr. Miller filed a complaint with the Civil Service Commission alleging that his removal had been made in violation of the civil service law and rules. After an investigation of the complaint, and upon July 6th, the Civil Service Commission advised the Public Printer of its decision as follows:

"Section 2 of Civil Service Rule XII, governing removals, provides that no person shall be removed from a competitive position except for such cause as will promote the efficiency of the public service. The Commission does not consider expulsion from a labor union, being the action of a body is no way connected with the public service nor having authority over public employees, to be such a cause as will promote the efficiency of the public service.

"As the only reason given by you for your removal of Mr. Miller is that he was expelled from Local Union No. 4, International Brotherhood of Bookbinders, you are advised that the Commission can not recognize his removal and must request that he be reassigned to duty in his position."

Mr. Miller's complaint had also been filed with the President, under whose direction it was being investigated by the Secretary of Commerce and Labor simultaneously with the investigation by the Civil Service Commission. As a result of such investigations, the following letters, under dates of July 13th and 14th, 1903, were written by the President:

My Dear Secretary Cortelyou: OYSTER BAY, N. Y., *July 13, 1903.*
In accordance with the letter of the Civil Service Commission of July 6th, the Public Printer will reinstate Mr. W. A. Miller in his position. Meanwhile I will withhold my final decision of the whole case until I have received the report of the investigation on Miller's second communication, which you notify me has been begun today, July 13th.

On the face of the papers presented, Miller would appear to have been removed in violation of law. There is no objection to the employees of the Government Printing Office constituting themselves into a union if they so desire; but no rules or resolutions of that union can be permitted to over-ride the laws of the United States, which it is my sworn duty to enforce.

Please communicate a copy of this letter to the Public Printer for his information and that of his subordinates.   Very truly yours,
THEODORE ROOSEVELT.
HON. GEORGE B. CORTELYOU, *Secretary of Commerce and Labor.*

Settlement of the Anthracite Coal-Miners' Strike

My Dear Mr. Cortelyou: OYSTER BAY, N. Y., *July 14, 1903.*
In connection with my letter of yesterday I call attention to this judgment and award by the Anthracite Coal Strike Commission in its report to me of March 18th last:
It is adjudged and awarded that no person shall be refused employment or in any way discriminated against on account of membership or non-membership in any labor organization, and that there shall be no discrimination against or interference with any employee who is not a member of any labor organization by members of such organization.
I heartily approve of this award and judgment by the commission appointed by me, which itself included a member of a labor union. This commission was

dealing with labor organizations working for private employers. It is of course mere elementary decency to require that all the Government departments shall be handled in accordance with the principle thus clearly and fearlessly enunciated.

Please furnish a copy of this letter both to Mr. Palmer and to the Civil Service Commission for their guidance.   Sincerely yours,

THEODORE ROOSEVELT.

HON. GEO. B. CORTELYOU, *Secretary of Commerce and Labor.*

THIRD ANNUAL MESSAGE.

WHITE HOUSE, *December 7, 1903.*

To the Senate and House of Representatives:

The country is to be congratulated on the amount of substantial achievement which has marked the past year both as regards our foreign and as regards our domestic policy.

With a nation as with a man the most important things are those of the household, and therefore the country is especially to be congratulated on what has been accomplished in the direction of providing for the exercise of supervision over the great corporations and combinations of corporations engaged in interstate commerce. The Congress has created the Department of Commerce and Labor, including the Bureau of Corporations, with for the first time authority to secure proper publicity of such proceedings of these great corporations as the public has the right to know. It has provided for the expediting of suits for the enforcement of the Federal anti-trust law; and by another law it has secured equal treatment to all producers in the transportation of their goods, thus taking a long stride forward in making effective the work of the Interstate Commerce Commission.

The establishment of the Department of Commerce and Labor, with the Bureau of Corporations thereunder, marks a real advance in the direction of doing all that is possible for the solution of the questions vitally affecting capitalists and wage-workers. The act creating the Department was approved on February 14, 1903, and two days later the head of the Department was nominated and confirmed by the Senate. Since then the work of organization has been pushed as rapidly as the initial appropriations permitted, and with due regard to thoroughness and the broad purposes which the Department is designed to serve. After the transfer of the various bureaus and branches to the Department at the beginning of the current fiscal year, as provided for in the act, the personnel comprised 1,289 employees in Washington and 8,836 in the country at large. The scope of the Department's duty and authority embraces the commercial and industrial interests of the Nation. It is not designed to restrict or control the fullest liberty of legitimate business action, but to secure exact and authentic information which will aid the Executive in enforcing existing laws, and which will enable the Congress to enact additional legislation, if any should be found necessary, in order to prevent the few from obtaining privileges at the expense of diminished opportunities for the many.

The preliminary work of the Bureau of Corporations in the Department has shown the wisdom of its creation. Publicity in corporate affairs will tend to do away with ignorance, and will afford facts upon which intelligent action may be taken. Systematic, intelligent investigation is already developing facts the knowledge of which is essential to a right understanding of the needs and duties of the business world. The corporation which is honestly and fairly organized, whose managers in the conduct of its business recognize their obligation to deal squarely with their stockholders, their competitors, and the public, has nothing to fear from such supervision. The purpose of this Bureau is not to embarrass or assail legitimate business, but to aid in bringing about a better industrial condition—a condition under which there shall be obedience to law and recognition of public obligation by all corporations, great or small. The Department of Commerce and Labor will be not only the clearing house for information regarding the business transactions of the Nation, but the executive arm of the Government to aid in strengthening our domestic and foreign markets, in perfecting our transportation facilities, in building up our merchant marine, in preventing the entrance of undesirable immigrants, in improving commercial and industrial conditions, and in bringing together on common ground those necessary partners in industrial progress—capital and labor. Commerce between the nations is steadily growing in volume, and the tendency of the times is toward closer trade relations. Constant watchfulness is needed to secure to Americans the chance to participate to the best advantage in foreign trade; and we may confidently expect that the new Department will justify the expectation of its creators by the exercise of this watchfulness, as well as by the businesslike administration of such laws relating to our internal affairs as are intrusted to its care.

In enacting the laws above enumerated the Congress proceeded on sane and conservative lines. Nothing revolutionary was attempted; but a common-sense and successful effort was made in the direction of seeing that corporations are so handled as to subserve the public good. The legislation was moderate. It was characterized throughout by the idea that we were not attacking corporations, but endeavoring to provide for doing away with any evil in them; that we drew the line against misconduct, not against wealth; gladly recognizing the great good done by the capitalist who alone, or in conjunction with his fellows, does his work along proper and legitimate lines. The purpose of the legislation, which purpose will undoubtedly be fulfilled, was to favor such a man when he does well, and to supervise his action only to prevent him from doing ill. Publicity can do no harm to the honest corporation. The only corporation that has cause to dread it is the corporation which shrinks from the light, and about the welfare of such corporations we need not be oversensitive. The work of the Department of Commerce and Labor has been conditioned upon this theory, of securing fair treatment alike for labor and for capital.

The consistent policy of the National Government, so far as it has the power, is to hold in check the unscrupulous man, whether employer or employee; but to refuse to weaken individual initiative or to hamper or cramp the industrial development of the country. We recognize that this is an era of federation and combination, in which great capitalistic corporations and labor unions have become factors of tremendous importance in all industrial centers. Hearty recognition is given the far-reaching, beneficent work which has been accomplished through both corporations and unions, and the line as between different corporations, as between different unions, is drawn as it is between different individuals; that is, it is drawn on conduct, the effort being to treat both organized capital and organized labor alike; asking nothing save that the interest of each shall be brought into harmony with the interest of the general public, and that the conduct of each shall conform to the fundamental rules of obedience to law, of individual freedom, and of justice and fair dealing towards all. Whenever either corporation, labor union, or individual disregards the law or acts in a spirit of arbitrary and tyrannous interference with the rights of others, whether corporations or individuals, then where the Federal Government has jurisdiction, it will see to it that the misconduct is stopped, paying not the slightest heed to the position or power of the corporation, the union or the individual, but only to one vital fact—that is, the question whether or not the conduct of the individual or aggregate of individuals is in accordance with the law of the land. Every man must be guaranteed his liberty and his right to do as he likes with his property or his labor, so long as he does not infringe the rights of others. No man is above the law and no man is below it; nor do we ask any man's permission when we require him to obey it. Obedience to the law is demanded as a right; not asked as a favor.

We have cause as a nation to be thankful for the steps that have been so successfully taken to put these principles into effect. The progress has been by evolution, not by revolution. Nothing radical has been done; the action has been both moderate and resolute. Therefore the work will stand. There shall be no backward step. If in the working of the laws it proves desirable that they shall at any point be expanded or amplified, the amendment can be made as its desirability is shown. Meanwhile they are being administered with judgment, but with insistence upon obedience to them, and their need has been emphasized in signal fashion by the events of the past year.

From all sources, exclusive of the postal service, the receipts of the Government for the last fiscal year aggregated $560,396,674. The expenditures for the same period were $506,099,007, the surplus for the fiscal year being $54,297,667. The indications are that the surplus for the present fiscal year will be very small, if indeed there be any surplus. From July to November the receipts from customs were, approximately, nine million dollars less than the receipts from the same source for a corresponding portion of last year. Should this decrease continue at the same ratio throughout the fiscal year, the surplus would be reduced by, approximately, thirty million dollars. Should the revenue from customs suffer much further decrease during the fiscal year, the surplus would vanish. A large surplus is certainly undesirable. Two years ago the war taxes were taken off with the express intention of equalizing the governmental receipts and expenditures, and though the first year thereafter still showed a surplus, it now seems likely that a substantial equality of revenue and expenditure will be attained. Such being the case it is of great moment both to exercise care and economy in appropriations, and to scan sharply any change in our fiscal revenue system which may reduce our income. The need of strict economy in our expenditures is emphasized by the fact that we can not afford to be parsimonious in providing for what is essential to our national well-being. Careful economy wherever possible will alone prevent our income from falling below the point required in order to meet our genuine needs.

The integrity of our currency is beyond question, and under present conditions it would be unwise and unnecessary to attempt a reconstruction of our entire monetary system. The same liberty should be granted the Secretary of the Treasury to deposit customs receipts as is granted him in the deposit of receipts from other sources. In my Message of December 2, 1902, I called attention to certain needs of the financial situation, and I again ask the consideration of the Congress for these questions.

During the last session of the Congress at the suggestion of a joint note from the Republic of Mexico and the Imperial Government of China, and in harmony with an act of the Congress appropriating $25,000 to pay the expenses thereof, a commission was appointed to confer with the principal European countries in the hope that some plan might be devised whereby a fixed rate of exchange could be assured between the gold-standard countries and the silver-standard countries. This commission has filed its preliminary report, which has been made public. I deem it important that the commission be continued, and that a sum of money be appropriated sufficient to pay the expenses of its further labors.

A majority of our people desire that steps be taken in the interests of American shipping, so that we may once more resume our former position in the ocean carrying trade. But hitherto the differences of opinion as to the proper method of reaching this end have been so wide that it has proved impossible to secure the adoption of any particular scheme. Having in view these facts, I recommend that the Congress direct the Secretary of the Navy, the Postmaster-General, and the Secretary of Commerce and Labor, associated with such a representation from the Senate and House of Representatives as the Congress in its wisdom may designate, to serve as a commission for the purpose of investigating and reporting to the Congress at its next session what legislation is desirable or necessary for the development of the American merchant marine and American commerce, and incidentally of a national ocean mail service of adequate auxiliary naval crusiers and naval reserves. While such a measure is desirable in any event, it is especially desirable at this time, in view of the fact that our present governmental contract for ocean mail with the American Line will expire in 1905. Our ocean mail act was passed in 1891. In 1895 our 20-knot transatlantic mail line was equal to any foreign line. Since then the Germans have put on 23-knot steamers, and the British have contracted for 24-knot steamers. Our service should equal the best. If it does not, the commercial public will abandon it. If we are to stay in the business it ought to be with a full understanding of the advantages to the country on one hand, and on the other with exact knowledge of the cost and proper methods of carrying it on. Moreover, lines of cargo ships are of even more importance than fast mail lines; save so far as the latter can be depended upon to furnish swift auxiliary cruisers in time of war. The establishment of new lines of cargo ships to South America, to Asia, and elsewhere would be much in the interest of our commercial expansion.

We can not have too much immigration of the right kind, and we should have none at all of the wrong kind. The need is to devise some system by which undesirable immigrants shall be kept out entirely, while desirable immigrants are properly distributed throughout the country. At present some districts which need immigrants have none; and in others, where the population is already congested, immigrants come in such numbers as to depress the conditions of life for those already there. During the last two years the immigration service at New York has been greatly improved, and the corruption and inefficiency which formerly obtained there have been eradicated. This service has just been investigated by a committee of New York citizens of high standing, Messrs. Arthur V. Briesen, Lee K. Frankel, Eugene A. Philbin, Thomas W. Hynes, and Ralph Trautman. Their

THE LAST PHOTOGRAPH OF GROVER CLEVELAND

LAST PHOTOGRAPH OF GROVER CLEVELAND

No testimony to the value of the life that Grover Cleveland devoted to his country is more sincere than this paragraph from Roosevelt's proclamation of June 24, 1908 (found on page 7339):

"Grover Cleveland, President of the United States from 1885 to 1889 and again from 1893 to 1897, died at 8:40 o'clock this morning at his home in Princeton, N. J. In his death the Nation has been deprived of one of its greatest citizens. By profession a lawyer, his chief services to his country were rendered during his long, varied and honorable career in public life. As Mayor of his city, as Governor of his State, and twice as President, he showed signal power as an administrator, coupled with entire devotion to the country's good and the courage that quailed before no hostility when once he was convinced where his duty lay. Since his retirement from the Presidency he has continued well and faithfully to serve his countrymen by the simplicity, dignity and uprightness of his private life."

The story of Cleveland's Administrations is briefly told in the article entitled "Cleveland, Grover," in the Encyclopedic Index.

report deals with the whole situation at length, and concludes with certain recommendations for administrative and legislative action. It is now receiving the attention of the Secretary of Commerce and Labor.

The special investigation of the subject of naturalization under the direction of the Attorney-General, and the consequent prosecutions reveal a condition of affairs calling for the immediate attention of the Congress. Forgeries and perjuries of shameless and flagrant character have been perpetrated, not only in the dense centers of population, but throughout the country; and it is established beyond doubt that very many so-called citizens of the United States have no title whatever to that right, and are asserting and enjoying the benefits of the same through the grossest frauds. It is never to be forgotten that citizenship is, to quote the words recently used by the Supreme Court of the United States, an "inestimable heritage," whether it proceeds from birth within the country or is obtained by naturalization; and we poison the sources of our national character and strength at the fountain, if the privilege is claimed and exercised without right, and by means of fraud and corruption. The body politic can not be sound and healthy if many of its constituent members claim their standing through the prostitution of the high right and calling of citizenship. It should mean something to become a citizen of the United States; and in the process no loophole whatever should be left open to fraud.

The methods by which these frauds—now under full investigation with a view to meting out punishment and providing adequate remedies—are perpetrated, include many variations of procedure by which false certificates of citizenship are forged in their entirety; or genuine certificates fraudulently or collusively obtained in blank are filled in by the criminal conspirators; or certificates are obtained on fraudulent statements as to the time of arrival and residence in this country; or imposition and substitution of another party for the real petitioner occur in court; or certificates are made the subject of barter and sale and transferred from the rightful holder to those not entitled to them; or certificates are forged by erasure of the original names and the insertion of the names of other persons not entitled to the same.

It is not necessary for me to refer here at large to the causes leading to this state of affairs. The desire for naturalization is heartily to be commended where it springs from a sincere and permanent intention to become citizens, and a real appreciation of the privilege. But it is a source of untold evil and trouble where it is traceable to selfish and dishonest motives, such as the effort by artificial and improper means, in wholesale fashion to create voters who are ready-made tools of corrupt politicians, or the desire to evade certain labor laws creating discriminations against alien labor. All good citizens, whether naturalized or native born, are equally interested in protecting our citizenship against fraud in any form, and, on the other hand, in affording every facility for naturalization to those who in good faith desire to share alike our privileges and our responsibilities.

The Federal grand jury lately in session in New York City dealt with this subject and made a presentment which states the situation briefly and forcibly and contains important suggestions for the consideration of the Congress. This presentment is included as an appendix to the report of the Attorney-General.

In my last annual Message, in connection with the subject of the due regulation of combinations of capital which are or may become injurious to the public, I recommend a special appropriation for the better enforcement of the antitrust law as it now stands, to be extended under the direction of the Attorney-General. Accordingly (by the legislative, executive, and judicial appropriation act of February 25, 1903, 32 Stat., 854, 904), the Congress appropriated, for the purpose of enforcing the various Federal trust and interstate-commerce laws, the sum of five hundred thousand dollars, to be expended under the direction of the Attorney-General in the employment of special counsel and agents in the Department of Justice to conduct proceedings and prosecutions under said laws in the courts of the United States. I now recommend, as a matter of the utmost importance and urgency, the extension of the purposes of this appropriation, so that it may be available, under the direction of the Attorney-General, and until used, for the due enforcement of the laws of the United States in general and especially of the civil and criminal laws relating to public lands and the laws relating to postal crimes and offenses and the subject of naturalization. Recent investigations have shown a deplorable state of affairs in these three matters of vital concern. By various frauds and by forgeries and perjuries, thousands of acres of the public domain, embracing lands of different character and extending through various sections of the country, have been dishonestly acquired. It is hardly necessary to urge the importance of recovering these dishonest acquisitions, stolen from the people, and of promptly and duly punishing the offenders. I speak in another part of this Message of the widespread crimes by which the sacred right of citizenship is falsely asserted and that "inestimable heritage" perverted to base ends. By similar means—that is, through frauds, forgeries, and perjuries, and by shameless briberies—the law relating to the proper conduct of the public service in general and to the due administration of the Post-Office Department have been notoriously violated, and many indictments have been found, and the consequent prosecutions are in course of hearing or on the eve thereof.

For the reasons thus indicated, and so that the Government may be prepared to enforce promptly and with the greatest effect the due penalties for such violations of law, and to this end may be furnished with sufficient instrumentalities and competent legal assistance for the investigations and trials which will be necessary at many different points of the country, I urge upon the Congress the necessity of making the said appropriation available for immediate use for all such purposes, to be expended under the direction of the Attorney-General.

Steps have been taken by the State Department looking to the making of bribery an extraditable offense with foreign powers. The need of more effective treaties covering this crime is manifest. The exposures and prosecutions of official corruption in St. Louis, Mo., and other cities and States have resulted in a number of givers and takers of bribes becoming fugitives in foreign lands. Bribery has not been included in extradition treaties heretofore, as the necessity for it has not arisen. While there may have been as much official corruption in former years, there has been more developed and brought to light in the immediate past than in the preceding century of our country's history. It should be the policy of the United States to leave no place on earth where a corrupt man fleeing from this country can rest in peace. There is no reason why bribery should not be included in all treaties as extraditable. The recent amended treaty with Mexico, whereby this crime was put in the list of extraditable offenses, has established a salutary precedent in this regard. Under this treaty the State Department has asked, and Mexico has granted, the extradition of one of the St. Louis bribe givers.

There can be no crime more serious than bribery. Other offenses violate one law while corruption strikes at the foundation of all law. Under our form of Government all authority is vested in the people and by them delegated to those who represent them in official capacity. There can be no offense heavier than that of him in whom such a sacred trust has been reposed, who sells it for his own gain and enrichment; and no less heavy is the offense of the bribe giver. He is worse than the thief, for the thief robs the individual, while the corrupt official plunders an entire city or State. He is as wicked as the murderer, for the murderer may only take one life against the law, while the corrupt official and the man who corrupts the official alike aim at the assassination of the commonwealth itself. Government of the people, by the people, for the people will perish from the face of the earth if bribery is tolerated. The givers and takers of bribes stand on an evil pre-eminence of infamy. The exposure and punishment of public corruption is an honor to a nation, not a disgrace. The shame lies in toleration, not in correction. No city or State, still less the Nation, can be injured by the enforcement of law. As long as public plunderers when detected can find a haven of refuge in any foreign land and avoid punishment, just so long encouragement is given them to continue their practices. If we fail to do all that in us lies to stamp out corruption we can not escape our share of responsibility for the guilt. The first requisite of successful self-government is unflinching enforcement of the law and the cutting out of corruption.

For several years past the rapid development of Alaska and the establishment of growing American interests in regions theretofore unsurveyed and imperfectly known brought into prominence the urgent necessity of a practical demarcation of the boundaries between the jurisdictions of the United States and Great Britain. Although the treaty of 1825 between Great Britain and Russia, the provisions of which were copied in the treaty of 1867, whereby Russia conveyed Alaska to the United States, was positive as to the control, first by Russia and later by the United States, of a strip of territory along the continental mainland from the western shore of Portland Canal to Mount St. Elias, following and surrounding the indentations of the coast and including the islands to the westward, its description of the landward margin of the strip was indefinite, resting on the supposed existence of a continuous ridge or range of mountains skirting the coast, as figured in the charts of the early navigators. It had at no time been possible for either party in interest to lay down, under the authority of the treaty, a line so obviously exact according to its provisions as to command the assent of the other. For nearly three-fourths of a century the absence of tangible local interests demanding the exercise of positive jurisdiction on either side of the border left the question dormant. In 1878 questions of revenue administration on the Stikine River led to the establishment of a provisional demarcation, crossing the channel between two high peaks on either side about twenty-four miles above the river mouth. In 1899 similar questions growing out of the extraordinary development of mining interests in the region about the head of Lynn Canal brought about a temporary *modus vivendi*, by which a convenient separation was made at the watershed divides of the White and Chilkoot passes and to the north of Klukwan, on the Klehini River. These partial and tentative adjustments could not, in the very nature of things, be satisfactory or lasting. A permanent disposition of the matter became imperative.

After unavailing attempts to reach an understanding through a Joint High Commission, followed by prolonged negotiations, conducted in an amicable spirit, a convention between the United States and Great Britain was signed, January 24, 1903, providing for an examination of the subject by a mixed tribunal of six members, three on a side, with a view to its final disposition Ratifications were exchanged on March 3 last, whereupon the two Governments appointed their respective members. Those on behalf of the United States were Elihu Root, Secretary of War, Henry Cabot Lodge, a Senator of the United States, and George Turner, an ex-Senator of the United States, while Great Britain named the Right Honourable Lord Alverstone, Lord Chief Justice of England, Sir Louis Amable Jetté, K. C. M. G., retired judge of the Supreme Court of Quebec, and A. B. Aylesworth, K. C., of Toronto. This Tribunal met in London on September 3, under the Presidency of Lord Alverstone. The proceedings were expeditious, and marked by a friendly and conscientious spirit. The respective cases, counter cases, and arguments presented the issues clearly and fully. On the 20th of October a majority of the Tribunal reached and signed an agreement on all the questions submitted by the terms of the Convention. By this award the right of the United States to the control of a continuous strip or border of the mainland shore, skirting all the tide-water inlets and sinuosities of the coast, is confirmed; the entrance to Portland Canal (concerning which legitimate doubt appeared) is defined as passing by Tongass Inlet and to the northwestward of Wales and Pearse islands; a line is drawn from the head of Portland Canal to the fifty-sixth degree of north latitude; and the interior border line of the strip is fixed by lines connecting certain mountain summits lying between Portland Canal and Mount St. Elias, and running along the crest of the divide separating the coast slope from the inland watershed at the only part of the frontier where the drainage ridge approaches the coast within the distance of ten marine leagues stipulated by the treaty as the extreme width of the strip around the heads of Lynn Canal and its branches.

While the line so traced follows the provisional demarcation of 1878 at the crossing of the Stikine River, and that of 1899 at the summits of the White and Chilkoot passes, it runs much farther inland from the Klehini than the temporary line of the later *modus vivendi*, and leaves the entire mining district of the Porcupine River and Glacier Creek within the jurisdiction of the United States.

The result is satisfactory in every way. It is of great material advantage to our people in the Far Northwest. It has removed from the field of discussion and possible danger a question liable to become more acutely accentuated with each passing year. Finally, it has furnished a signal proof of the fairness and good will with which two friendly nations can approach and determine issues involving national sovereignty and by their nature incapable of submission to a third power for adjudication.

The award is self-executing on the vital points. To make it effective as regards the others it only remains for the two Governments to appoint, each on its own behalf, one or more scientific experts, who shall, with all convenient speed, proceed together to lay down the boundary line in accordance with the decision of the majority of the Tribunal. I recommend that the Congress make adequate provision for the appointment, compensation, and expenses of the members to serve on this joint boundary commission on the part of the United States.

It will be remembered that during the second session of the last Congress Great Britain, Germany, and Italy formed an alliance for the purpose of blockading the ports of Venezuela and using such other means of pressure as would secure a settlement of claims due, as they alleged, to certain of their subjects. Their employment of force for the collection of these claims was terminated by an agreement brought about through the offices of the diplomatic representatives of the United States at Caracas and the Government at Washington, thereby ending a situation which was bound to cause increasing friction, and which jeoparded the peace of the continent. Under this agreement Venezuela agreed to set apart a certain percentage of the customs receipts of two of her ports to be applied to the payment of whatever obligations might be ascertained by mixed commissions appointed for that purpose to be due from her, not only to the three powers already mention·d, whose proceedings against her had resulted in a state of war, ut also to the United States, France, Spain, Belgium, the Netherland . Sweden and Norway, and Mexico, who had not employed force for the collection of the claims alleged to be due to certain of their citizens.

A demand was then made by the so-called blockading powers that the sums ascertained to be due to their citizens by such mixed commissions should be accorded payment in full before anything was paid upon the claims of any of the so-called peace powers. Venezuela, on the other hand, insisted that all her creditors should be paid upon a basis of exact equality. During the efforts to adjust this dispute it was suggested by the powers in interest that it should be referred to me for decision, but I was clearly of the opinion that a far wiser course would be to submit the question to the Permanent Court of Arbitration at The Hague. It seemed to me to offer an admirable opportunity to advance the practice of the peaceful settlement of disputes between nations and to secure for the Hague Tribunal a memorable increase of its practical importance. The nations interested in the controversy were so numerous and in many instances so powerful as to make it evident that beneficent results would follow from their appearance at the same time before the bar of that august tribunal of peace.

Our hopes in that regard have been realized. Russia and Austria are represented in the persons of the learned and distinguished iurists who compose the Tribunal, while Great Britain, Germany, France, Spain, Italy, Belgium, the Netherlands, Sweden and Norway, Mexico, the United States, and Venezuela are represented by their respective agents and counsel. Such an imposing concourse of nations presenting their arguments to and invoking the decision of that high court of international justice and international peace can hardly fail to secure a like submission of many future controversies. The nations now appearing there will find it far easier to appear there a second time, while no nation can imagine its just pride will be lessened by following the example now presented. This triumph of the principle of international arbitration is a subject of warm congratulation and offers a happy augury for the peace of the world.

There seems good ground for the belief that there has been a real growth among the civilized nations of a sentiment which will permit a gradual substitution of other methods than the method of war in the settlement of disputes. It is not pretended that as yet we are near a position in which it will be possible wholly to prevent war, or that a just regard for national interest and honor will in all cases permit of the settlement of international disputes by arbitration; but by a mixture of prudence and firmness with wisdom we think it is possible to do away with much of the provocation and excuse for war, and at least in many cases to substitute some other and more rational method for the settlement of disputes. The Hague Court offers so good an example of what can be done in the direction of such settlement that it should be encouraged in every way.

Further steps should be taken. In President McKinley's annual Message of December 5, 1898, he made the following recommendation:

"The experiences of the last year bring forcibly home to us a sense of the burdens and the waste of war. We desire in common with most civilized nations, to reduce to the lowest possible point the damage sustained in time of war by peaceable trade and commerce. It is true we may suffer in such cases less than other communities, but all nations are damaged more or less by the state of uneasiness and apprehension into which an outbreak of hostilities throws the entire commercial world. It should be our object, therefore, to minimize, so far as practicable, this inevitable loss and disturbance. This purpose can probably best be accomplished by an international agreement to regard all private property at sea as exempt from capture or destruction by the forces of belligerent powers. The United States Government has for many years advocated this humane and beneficent principle, and is now in a position to recommend it to other powers without the imputation of selfish motives. I therefore suggest for your consideration that the Executive be authorized to correspond with the governments of the principal maritime powers with a view of incorporating into the permanent law of civilized nations the principle of the exemption of all private property at sea, not contraband of war, from capture or destruction by belligerent powers."

I cordially renew this recommendation.

The Supreme Court, speaking on December 11. 1899, through Peckham, J., said:

"It is, we think, historically accurate to say that this Government has always been, in its views, among the most advanced of the governments of the world in favor of mitigating, as to all non-combatants, the hardships and horrors of war. To accomplish that object it has always advocated those rules which would in most cases do away with the right to capture the private property of an enemy on the high seas."

I advocate this as a matter of humanity and morals. It is anachronistic when private property is respected on land that it should not be respected at sea. Moreover, it should be borne in mind that shipping represents, internationally speaking, a much more generalized species of private property than is the case with ordinary property on land—that is, property found at sea is much less apt than is the case with property found on land really to belong to any one nation. Under the modern system of corporate ownership the flag of a vessel often differs from the flag which would mark the nationality of the real ownership and money control of the vessel; and the cargo may belong to individuals of yet a different nationality. Much American capital is now invested in foreign ships; and among foreign nations it often happens that the capital of one is largely invested in the shipping of another. Furthermore, as a practical matter, it may be mentioned that while commerce destroying may cause serious loss and great annoyance, it can never be more than a subsidiary factor in bringing to terms a resolute foe. This is now well recognized by all of our naval experts. The fighting ship, not the commerce destroyer, is the vessel whose feats add renown to a nation's history, and establish her place among the great powers of the world.

Last year the Interparliamentary Union for International Arbitration met at Vienna, six hundred members of the different legislatures of civilized countries attending. It was provided that the next meeting should be in 1904 at St. Louis, subject to our Congress extending an invitation. Like the Hague Tribunal, this Interparliamentary Union is one of the forces tending towards peace among the nations of the earth, and it is entitled to our support. I trust the invitation can be extended.

Early in July, having received intelligence, which happily turned out to be erroneous, of the assassination of our vice-consul at Beirut, I dispatched a small squadron to that port for such service as might be found necessary on arrival. Although the attempt on the life of our vice-consul had not been successful, yet the outrage was symptomatic of a state of excitement and disorder which demanded immediate attention. The arrival of the vessels had the happiest result. A feeling of security at once took the place of the former alarm and disquiet; our officers were cordially welcomed by the consular body and the leading merchants, and ordinary business resumed its acitivity. The Government of the Sultan gave a considerate hearing to the representations of our minister; the official who was regarded as responsible for the disturbed condition of affairs was removed. Our relations with the Turkish Government remain friendly; our claims founded on inequitable treatment of some of our schools and missions appear to be in process of amicable adjustment.

The signing of a new commercial treaty with China, which took place at Shanghai on the 8th of October, is a cause for satisfaction. This act, the result of long discussion and negotiation, places our commercial relations with the great Oriental Empire on a more satisfactory footing than they have ever heretofore enjoyed. It provides not only for the ordinary rights and privileges of diplomatic and consular officers, but also for an important extension of our commerce by increased facility of access to Chinese ports, and for the relief of trade by the removal of some of the obstacles which have embarrassed it in the past. The Chinese Government engages, on fair and equitable conditions, which will probably be accepted by the principal commercial nations, to abandon the levy of "liken" and other transit dues throughout the Empire, and to introduce other desirable administrative reforms. Larger facilities are to be given to our citizens who desire to carry on mining enterprises in China. We have secured for our missionaries a valuable privilege, the recognition of their right to rent and lease in perpetuity such property as their religious societies may need in all parts of the Empire. And, what was an indispensable condition for the advance and development of our commerce in Manchuria, China, by treaty with us, has opened to foreign commerce the cities of Mukden, the capital of the province of Manchuria, and Antung, an important port on the Yalu River, on the road to Korea. The full measure of development which our commerce may rightfully expect can hardly be looked for until the settlement of the present abnormal state of things in the Empire; but the foundation for such development has at last been laid.

I call your attention to the reduced cost in maintaining the consular service for the fiscal year ending June 30, 1903, as shown in the annual report of the Auditor for the State and other Departments, as compared with the year previous. For the year under consideration the excess of expenditures over receipts on account of the consular service amounted to $26,125.12, as against $96,972.50 for the year ending June 30, 1902, and $147,040.16 for the year ending June 30, 1901. This is the best showing in this respect for the consular service for the past fourteen years, and the reduction in the cost of the service to the Government has been made in spite of the fact that the expenditures for the year in question were more than $20,000 greater than for the previous year.

The rural free-delivery service has been steadily extended. The attention of the Congress is asked to the question of the compensation of the letter carriers and clerks engaged in the postal service, especially on the new rural free-delivery routes. More routes have been installed since the first of July last than in any like period in the Department's history. While a due regard to economy must be kept in mind in the establishment of new routes, yet the extension of the rural free-delivery system must be continued, for reasons of sound public policy. No governmental movement of recent years has resulted in greater immediate benefit to the people of the country districts. Rural free delivery, taken in connection with the telephone, the bicycle, and the trolley, accomplishes much toward lessening the isolation of farm life and making it brighter and more attractive. In the immediate past the lack of just such facilities as these has driven many of the more active and restless young men and women from the farms to the cities; for they rebelled at loneliness and lack of mental companionship. It is unhealthy and undesirable for the cities to grow at the expense of the country; and rural free delivery is not only a good thing in itself, but is good because it is one of the causes which check this unwholesome tendency towards the urban concentration of our population at the expense of the country districts. It is for the same reason that we sympathize with and approve of the policy of building good roads. The movement for good roads is one fraught with the greatest benefit to the country districts.

I trust that the Congress will continue to favor in all proper ways the Louisiana Purchase Exposition. This Exposition commemorates the Louisiana purchase, which was the first great step in the expansion which made us a continental nation. The expedition of Lewis and Clark across the continent followed thereon, and marked the beginning of the process of exploration and colonization which thrust our national boundaries to the Pacific. The acquisition of the Oregon country, including the present States of Oregon and Washington, was a fact of immense importance in our history; first giving us our place on the Pacific seaboard, and making ready the way for our ascendency in the commerce of the greatest of the oceans. The centennial of our establishment upon the western coast by the expedition of Lewis and Clark is to be celebrated at Portland, Oregon, by an exposition in the summer of 1905, and this event should receive recognition and support from the National Government.

I call your special attention to the Territory of Alaska. The country is developing rapidly, and it has an assured future. The mineral wealth is great and has as yet hardly been tapped. The fisheries, if wisely handled and kept under national control, will be a business as permanent as any other, and of the utmost importance to the people. The forests if properly guarded will form another great source of wealth. Portions of Alaska are fitted for farming and stock raising, although the methods must be adapted to the peculiar conditions of the country. Alaska is situated in the far north; but so are Norway and Sweden and Finland; and Alaska can prosper and play its part in the New World just as those nations have prospered and played their parts in the Old World. Proper land laws should be enacted; and the survey of the public lands immediately begun. Coal-land laws should be provided whereby the coal-land entryman may make his location and secure patent under methods kindred to those now prescribed for homestead and mineral entrymen. 'Salmon hatcheries, exclusively under Government control, should be established. The cable should be extended from Sitka westward. Wagon roads and trails should be built, and the building of railroads promoted in all legitimate ways. Light-houses should be built along the coast. Attention should be paid to the needs of the Alaska Indians; provision should be made for an officer, with deputies, to study their needs, relieve their immediate wants, and help them adapt themselves to the new conditions.

The commission appointed to investigate, during the season of 1903, the condition and needs of the Alaskan salmon fisheries, has finished its work in the field, and is preparing a detailed report thereon. A preliminary report reciting the measures immediately required for the protection and preservation of the salmon industry has already been submitted to the Secretary of Commerce and Labor for his attention and for the needed action.

I recommend that an appropriation be made for building light-houses in Hawaii, and taking possession of those already built. The Territory should be reimbursed for whatever amounts it has already expended for light-houses. The governor should be empowered to suspend or remove any official appointed by him, without submitting the matter to the legislature.

Of our insular possessions the Philippines and Porto Rico it is gratifying to say that their steady progress has been such as to make it unnecessary to spend much time in discussing them. Yet the Congress should ever keep in mind that a peculiar obligation rests upon us to further in every way the welfare of these communities. The Philippines should be knit closer to us by tariff arrangements. It would, of course, be impossible suddenly to raise the people of the islands to the high pitch of industrial prosperity and of governmental efficiency to which they will in the end by degrees attain; and the caution and moderation shown in developing them have been among the main reasons why this development has hitherto gone on so smoothly. Scrupulous care has been taken in the choice of governmental agents, and the entire elimination of partisan politics from the public service. The condition of the islanders is in material things far better than ever before, while their governmental, intellectual, and moral advance has kept pace with their material advance. No one people ever benefited another people more than we have benefited the Filipinos by taking possession of the islands.

The cash receipts of the General Land Office for the last fiscal year were $11,024,743.65, an increase of $4,762,816.47 over the preceding year. Of this sum, approximately, $8,461,493 will go to the credit of the fund for the reclamation of arid land, making the total of this fund, up to the 30th of June, 1903, approximately, $16,191,836.

A gratifying disposition has been evinced by those having unlawful inclosures of public land to remove their fences. Nearly two million acres so inclosed have been thrown open on demand. In but comparatively few cases has it been necessary to go into court to accomplish this purpose. This work will be vigorously prosecuted until all unlawful inclosures have been removed.

Experience has shown that in the western States themselves, as well as in the rest of the country, there is widespread conviction that certain of the public-land laws and the resulting administrative practice no longer meet the present needs. The character and uses of the remaining public lands differ widely from those of the public lands which Congress had especially in view when these laws were passed. The rapidly increasing rate of disposal of the public lands is not followed by a corresponding increase in home building. There is a tendency to mass in large holdings public lands, especially timber and grazing lands, and thereby to retard settlement. I renew and emphasize my recommendation of last year that so far as they are available for agriculture in its broadest sense, and to whatever extent they may be reclaimed under the national irrigation law, the remaining public lands should be held rigidly for the home builder. The attention of the Congress is especially directed to the timber and stone law, the desert-land law, and the commutation clause of the homestead law, which in their operation have in many respects conflicted with wise public-land policy. The discussions in the Congress and elsewhere have made it evident that there is a wide divergence of opinions between those holding opposite views on these subjects; and that the opposing sides have strong and convinced representatives of weight both within and without the Congress; the differences being not only as to matters of opinion but as to matters of fact. In order that definite information may be available for the use of the Congress, I have appointed a commission composed of W. A. Richards, Commissioner of the General Land Office; Gifford Pinchot, Chief of the Bureau of Forestry of the Department of Agriculture, and F. H. Newell, Chief Hydrographer of the Geological Survey, to report at the earliest practicable moment upon the condition, operation, and effect of the present land laws and on the use, condition, disposal, and settlement of the public lands. The commission will report especially what changes in organization, laws, regulations, and practice affecting the public lands are needed to effect the largest practicable disposition of the public lands to actual settlers who will build permanent homes upon them, and to secure in permanence the fullest and most effective use of the resources of the public lands; and it will make such other reports and recommendations as its study of these questions may suggest. The commission is to report immediately upon those points concerning which its judgment is clear; on any point upon which it has doubt it will take the time necessary to make investigation and reach a final judgment.

The work of reclamation of the arid lands of the West is progressing steadily and satisfactorily under the terms of the law setting aside the proceeds from the disposal of public lands. The corps of engineers known as the Reclamation Service, which is conducting the surveys and examinations, has been thoroughly organized, especial pains being taken to secure under the civil-service rules a body of skilled, experienced, and efficient men. Surveys and examinations are progressing throughout the arid States and Territories, plans for reclaiming works being prepared and passed upon by boards of engineers before approval by the Secretary of the Interior. In Arizona and Nevada, in localities where such work is pre-eminently needed, construction has already been begun. In other parts of the arid West various projects are well advanced towards the drawing up of contracts, these being delayed in part by necessities of reaching agreements or understanding as regards rights of way or acquisition of real estate. Most of the works contemplated for construction are of national importance, involving interstate questions or the securing of stable, self-supporting communities in the midst of vast tracts of vacant land. The Nation as a whole is of course the gainer by the creation of these homes, adding as they do to the wealth and stability of the country, and furnishing a home market for the products of the East and South. The reclamation law, while perhaps not ideal, appears at present to answer the larger needs for which it is designed. Further legislation is not recommended until the necessities of change are more apparent.

The study of the opportunities of reclamation of the vast extent of arid land shows that whether this reclamation is done by individuals, corporations, or the State, the sources of water supply must be effectively protected and the reservoirs guarded by the preservation of the forests at the headwaters of the streams. The engineers making the preliminary examinations continually emphasize this need and urge that the remaining public lands at the headwaters of the important streams of the West be reserved to insure permanency of water supply for irrigation. Much progress in forestry has been made during the past year. The necessity for perpetuating our forest resources, whether in public or private hands, is recognized now as never before. The demand for forest reserves has become insistent in the West, because the West must use the water, wood, and summer range which only such reserves can supply. Progressive lumbermen are striving, through forestry, to give their business permanence. Other great business interests are awakening to the need of forest preservation as a business matter. The Government's forest work should receive from the Congress hearty support, and especially support adequate for the protection of the forest reserves against fire. The forest-reserve policy of the Government has passed beyond the experimental stage and has reached a condition where scientific methods are essential to its successful prosecution. The administrative features of forest reserves are at present unsatisfactory, being divided between three Bureaus of two Departments. It is therefore recommended that all matters pertaining to forest reserves, except those involving or pertaining to land titles, be consolidated in the Bureau of Forestry of the Department of Agriculture.

The cotton-growing States have recently been invaded by a weevil that has done much damage and threatens the entire cotton industry. I suggest to the Congress the prompt enactment of such remedial legislation as its judgment may approve.

In granting patents to foreigners the proper course for this country to follow is to give the same advantages to foreigners here that the countries in which these foreigners dwell extend in return to our citizens; that is, to extend the benefits of our patent laws on inventions and the like where in return the articles would be patentable in the foreign countries concerned—where an American could get a corresponding patent in such countries.

The Indian agents should not be dependent for their appointment or tenure of office upon considerations of partisan politics; the practice of appointing, when possible, ex-army officers or bonded superintendents to the vacancies that occur is working well. Attention is invited to the widespread illiteracy due to lack of public schools in the Indian Territory. Prompt heed should be paid to the need of education for the children in this Territory.

In my last annual Message the attention of the Congress was called to the necessity of enlarging the safety-appliance law, and it is gratifying to note that this law was amended in important respects. With the increasing railway mileage of the country, the greater number of men employed, and the use of larger and heavier equipment, the urgency for renewed effort to prevent the loss of life and limb upon the railroads of the country, particularly to employees, is apparent. For the inspection of water craft and the Life-Saving Service upon the water the Congress has built up an elaborate body of protective legislation and a thorough method of inspection and is annually spending large sums of money. It is encouraging to observe that the Congress is alive to the interests of those who are employed upon our wonderful arteries of commerce—the railroads—who so safely transport millions of passengers and billions of tons of freight. The Federal inspection of safety appliances, for which the Congress is now making appropriations, is a service analogous to that which the Government has upheld for generations in regard to vessels, and it is believed will prove of great practical benefit, both to railroad employees and the traveling public. As the greater part of commerce is interstate and exclusively under the control of the Congress the needed safety and uniformity must be secured by national legislation.

No other class of our citizens deserves so well of the Nation as those to whom the Nation owes its very being, the veterans of the civil war. Special attention is asked to the excellent work of the Pension Bureau in expediting and disposing of pension claims. During the fiscal year ending July 1, 1903, the Bureau settled 251,982 claims, an average of 825 claims for each working day of the year. The number of settlements since July 1, 1903, has been in excess of last year's average, approaching 1,000 claims for each working day, and it is believed that the work of the Bureau will be current at the close of the present fiscal year.

During the year ended June 30 last 25,566 persons were appointed through competitive examinations under the civil-service rules. This was 12,672 more than during the preceding year, and 40 per cent of those who passed the examinations. This abnormal growth was largely occasioned by the extension of classification to the rural free-delivery service and the appointment last year of over 9,000 rural carriers. A revision of the civil-service rules took effect on April 15 last, which has greatly improved their operation. The completion of the reform of the civil service is recognized by good citizens everywhere as a matter of the highest public importance, and the success of the merit system largely depends upon the effectiveness of the rules and the machinery provided for their enforcement. A very gratifying spirit of friendly co-operation exists in all the Departments of the

Government in the enforcement and uniform observance of both the letter and spirit of the civil-service act. Executive orders of July 3, 1902; March 26, 1903, and July 8, 1903, require that appointments of all unclassified laborers, both in the Departments at Washington and in the field service, shall be made with the assistance of the United States Civil Service Commission, under a system of registration to test the relative fitness of applicants for appointment or employment. This system is competitive, and is open to all citizens of the United States qualified in respect to age, physical ability, moral character, industry, and adaptability for manual labor; except that in case of veterans of the Civil War the element of age is omitted. This system of appointment is distinct from the classified service and does not classify positions of mere laborer under the civil-service act and rules. Regulations in aid thereof have been put in operation in several of the Departments and are being gradually extended in other parts of the service. The results have been very satisfactory, as extravagance has been checked by decreasing the number of unnecessary positions and by increasing the efficiency of the employees remaining.

The Congress, as the result of a thorough investigation of the charities and reformatory institutions in the District of Columbia, by a joint select committee of the two Houses which made its report in March, 1898, created in the act approved June 6, 1900, a board of charities for the District of Columbia, to consist of five residents of the District, appointed by the President of the United States, by and with the advice and consent of the Senate, each for a term of three years, to serve without compensation. President McKinley appointed five men who had been active and prominent in the public charities in Washington, all of whom upon taking office July 1, 1900, resigned from the different charities with which they had been connected. The members of the board have been reappointed in successive years. The board serves under the Commissioners of the District of Columbia. The board gave its first year to a careful and impartial study of the special problems before it, and has continued that study every year in the light of the best practice in public charities elsewhere. Its recommendations in its annual reports to the Congress through the Commissioners of the District of Columbia "for the economical and efficient administration of the charities and reformatories of the District of Columbia," as required by the act creating it, have been based upon the principles commended by the joint select committee of the Congress in its report of March, 1898, and approved by the best administrators of public charities, and make for the desired systematization and improvement of the affairs under its supervision. They are worthy of favorable consideration by the Congress.

The effect of the laws providing a General Staff for the Army and for the more effective use of the National Guard has been excellent. Great improvement has been made in the efficiency of our Army in recent years. Such schools as those erected at Fort Leavenworth and Fort Riley and the institution of fall maneuver work accomplish satisfactory results. The good effect of these maneuvers upon the National Guard is marked, and ample appropriation should be made to enable the guardsmen of the several States to share in the benefit. The Government should as soon as possible secure suitable permanent camp sites for military maneuvers in the various sections of the country. The service thereby rendered not only to the Regular Army, but to the National Guard of the several States, will be so great as to repay many times over the relatively small expense. We should not rest satisfied with what has been done, however. The only people who are contented with a system of promotion by mere seniority are those who are contented with the triumph of mediocrity over excellence. On the other hand, a system which encouraged the exercise of social or political favoritism in promotions would be even worse. But it would surely be easy to devise a method of promotion from grade to grade in which the opinion of the higher officers of the service upon the candidates should be decisive upon the standing and promotion of the latter. Just such a system now obtains at West Point. The quality of each year's work determines the standing of that year's class, the man being dropped or graduated into the next class in the relative position which his military superiors decide to be warranted by his merit. In other words, ability, energy, fidelity, and all other similar qualities determine the rank of a man year after year in West Point, and his standing in the Army when he graduates from West Point; but from that time on, all effort to find which man is best or worst, and reward or punish him accordingly, is abandoned; no brilliancy, no amount of hard work, no eagerness in the performance of duty, can advance him, and no slackness or indifference that falls short of a court-martial offense can retard him. Until this system is changed we can not hope that our officers will be of as high grade as we have a right to expect, considering the material upon which we draw. Moreover, when a man renders such service as Captain Pershing rendered last spring in the Moro campaign, it ought to be possible to reward him without at once jumping him to the grade of brigadier-general.

Shortly after the enunciation of that famous principle of American foreign policy now known as the "Monroe Doctrine," President Monroe, in a special Message to Congress on January 30, 1824, spoke as follows: "The Navy is the arm from which our Government will always derive most aid in support of our * * * rights. Every power engaged in war will know the strength of our naval power, the number of our ships of each class, their condition, and the promptitude with which we may bring them into service, and will pay due consideration to that argument."

I heartily congratulate the Congress upon the steady progress in building up the American Navy. We can not afford a let-up in this great work. To stand still means to go back. There should be no cessation in adding to the effective units of the fighting strength of the fleet. Meanwhile the Navy Department and the officers of the Navy are doing well their part by providing constant service at sea under conditions akin to those of actual warfare. Our officers and enlisted men are learning to handle the battleships, cruisers, and torpedo boats with high efficiency in fleet and squadron formations, and the standard of marksmanship is being steadily raised. The best work ashore is indispensable, but the highest duty of a naval officer is to exercise command at sea.

The establishment of a naval base in the Philippines ought not to be longer postponed. Such a base is desirable in time of peace; in time of war it would be indispensable, and its lack would be ruinous. Without it our fleet would be helpless. Our naval experts are agreed that Subig Bay is the proper place for the purpose. The national interests require that the work of fortification and development of a naval station at Subig Bay be begun at an early date; for under the best conditions it is a work which will consume much time.

It is eminently desirable, however, that there should be provided a naval general staff on lines similar to those of the General Staff lately created for the Army. Within the Navy Department itself the needs of the service have brought about a system under which the duties of a general staff are partially performed; for the Bureau of Navigation has under its direction the War College, the Office of Naval Intelligence, and the Board of Inspection, and has been in close touch with the General Board of the Navy. But though under the excellent officers at their head, these boards and bureaus do good work, they have not the authority of a general staff, and have not sufficient scope to insure a proper readiness for emergencies. We need the establishment by law of a body of trained officers, who shall exercise a systematic control of the military affairs of the Navy, and be authorized advisers of the Secretary concerning it.

By the act of June 28, 1902, the Congress authorized the President to enter into treaty with Colombia for the building of the canal across the Isthmus of Panama; it being provided that in the event of failure to secure such treaty after the lapse of a reasonable time, recourse should be had to building a canal through Nicaragua. It has not been necessary to consider this alternative, as I am enabled to lay before the Senate a treaty providing for the building of the canal across the Isthmus of Panama. This was the route which commended itself to the deliberate judgment of the Congress, and we can now acquire by treaty the right to construct the canal over this route. The question now, therefore, is not by which route the isthmian canal shall be built, for that question has been definitely and irrevocably decided. The question is simply whether or not we shall have an isthmian canal.

When the Congress directed that we should take the Panama route under treaty with Colombia, the essence of the condition, of course, referred not to the Government which controlled that route, but to the route itself; to the territory across which the route lay, not to the name which for the moment the territory bore on the map. The purpose of the law was to authorize the President to make a treaty with the power in actual control of the Isthmus of Panama. This purpose has been fulfilled.

In the year 1846 this Government entered into a treaty with New Granada, the predecessor upon the Isthmus of the Republic of Colombia and of the present Republic of Panama, by which treaty it was provided that the Government and citizens of the United States should always have free and open right of way or transit across the Isthmus of Panama by any modes of communication that might be constructed, while in turn our Government guaranteed the perfect neutrality of the above-mentioned Isthmus with the view that the free transit from the one to the other sea might not be interrupted or embarrassed. The treaty vested in the United States a substantial property right carved out of the rights of sovereignty and property which New Granada then had and possessed over the said territory. The name of New Granada has passed away and its territory has been divided. Its successor, the Government of Colombia, has ceased to own any property in the Isthmus. A new Republic, that of Panama, which was at one time a sovereign state, and at another time a mere department of the successive confederations known as New Granada and Columbia, has now succeeded to the rights which first one and then the other formerly exercised over the Isthmus. But as long as the Isthmus endures, the mere geographical fact of its existence, and the peculiar interest therein which is required by our position, perpetuate the solemn contract which binds the holders of the territory to respect our right to freedom of transit across it, and binds us in return to safeguard for the Isthmus and the world the exercise of that inestimable privilege. The true interpretation of the obligations upon which the United States entered in this treaty of 1846 has been given repeatedly in the utterances of Presidents and Secretaries of State. Secretary Cass in 1858 officially stated the position of this Government as follows:

"The progress of events has rendered the interoceanic route across the narrow portion of Central America vastly important to the commercial world, and especially to the United States, whose possessions extend along the Atlantic and Pacific coasts, and demand the speediest and easiest modes of communication. While the rights of sovereignty of the states occupying this region should always be respected, we shall expect that these rights be exercised in a spirit befitting the occasion and the wants and circumstances that have arisen. Sovereignty has its duties as well as its rights, and none of these local governments, even if administered with more regard to the just demands of other nations than they have been, would be permitted, in a spirit of Eastern isolation, to close the gates of intercourse on the great highways of the world, and justify the act by the pretension that these avenues of trade and travel belong to them and that they choose to shut them, or, what is almost equivalent, to encumber them with such unjust relations as would prevent their general use."

Seven years later, in 1865, Mr. Seward in different commuications took the following position:

"The United States have taken and will take no interest in any question of internal revolution in the State of Panama, or any State of the United States of Colombia, but will maintain a perfect neutrality in connection with such domestic altercations. The United States will, nevertheless, hold themselves ready to protect the transit trade across the Isthmus against invasion of either domestic or foreign disturbers of the peace of the State of Panama. * * * Neither the text nor the spirit of the stipulation in that article by which the United States engages to preserve the neutrality of the Isthmus of Panama, imposes an obligation on this Government to comply with the requisition [of the President of the United States of Colombia for a force to protect the Isthmus of Panama from a body of insurgents of that country]. The purpose of the stipulation was to guarantee the Isthmus against seizure or invasion by a foreign power only."

Attorney-General Speed, under date of November 7, 1865, advised Secretary Seward as follows:

"From this treaty it can not be supposed that New Granada invited the United States to become a party to the intestine troubles of that Government, nor did the United States become bound to take sides in the domestic broils of New Granada. The United States did guarantee New Granada in the sovereignty and property over the territory. This was as against other and foreign governments."

For four hundred years, ever since shortly after the discovery of this hemisphere, the canal across the Isthmus has been planned. For two score years it has been worked at. When made it is to last for the ages. It is to alter the geography of a continent and the trade routes of the world. We have shown by every treaty we have negotiated or attempted to negotiate with the peoples in control of the Isthmus and with foreign nations in reference thereto our consistent good faith in observing our obligations; on the one hand to the peoples of the Isthmus, and on the other hand to the civilized world whose commercial rights we are safeguarding and guaranteeing by our action. We have done our duty to others in letter and in spirit, and we have shown the utmost forbearance in exacting our own rights.

Last spring, under the act above referred to, a treaty concluded between the representatives of the Republic of Colombia and of our Government was ratified by the Senate. This treaty was entered into at the urgent solicitation of the people of Colombia and after a body of experts appointed by our Government especially to go into the matter of the routes across the Isthmus had pronounced unanimously in favor of the Panama route. In drawing up this treaty every concession was made to the people and to the Government of Colombia. We were more than just in dealing with them. Our generosity was such as to make it a serious question whether we had not gone too far in their interest at the expense of our own; for in our scrupulous desire to pay all possible heed, not merely to the real but even to the fancied rights of our weaker neighbor, who already owed so much to our protection and forbearance, we yielded in all possible ways to her desires in drawing up the treaty. Nevertheless the Government of Colombia not merely repudiated the treaty, but repudiated it in such manner as to make it evident by the time the Colombian Congress adjourned that not the scantiest hope remained of ever getting a satisfactory treaty from them. The Government of Colombia made the treaty, and yet when the Colombian Congress was called to ratify it the vote against ratification was unanimous. It does not appear that the Government made any real effort to secure ratification.

Immediately after the adjournment of the Congress a revolution broke out in Panama. The people of Panama had long been discontented with the Republic of Colombia, and they had been kept quiet only by the prospect of the conclusion of the treaty, which was to them a matter of vital concern. When it became evident that the treaty was hopelessly lost, the people of Panama rose literally as one man. Not a shot was fired by a single man on the Isthmus in the interest of the Colombian Government. Not a life was lost in the accomplishment of the revolution. The Colombian troops stationed on the Isthmus, who had long been unpaid, made common cause with the people of Panama, and with astonishing unanimity the new Republic was started. The duty of the United States in the premises was clear. In strict accordance with the principles laid down by Secretaries Cass and Seward in the official documents above quoted, the United States gave notice that it would permit the landing of no expeditionary force, the arrival of which would mean chaos and destruction along the line of the railroad and of the proposed canal, and an interruption of transit as an inevitable consequence. The de facto Government of Panama was recognized in the following telegram to Mr. Ehrman:

"The people of Panama have, by apparently unanimous movement, dissolved their political connection with the Republic of Colombia and resumed their independence. When you are satisfied that a de facto government, republican in form and without substantial opposition from its own people, has been established in the State of Panama, you will enter into relations with it as the responsible government of the territory and look to it for all due action to protect the persons and property of citizens of the United States and to keep open the isthmian transit, in accordance with the obligations of existing treaties governing the relations of the United States to that Territory."

The Government of Colombia was notified of our action by the following telegram to Mr. Beaupre:

"The people of Panama having, by an apparently unanimous movement, dissolved their political connection with the Republic of Colombia and resumed their independence, and having adopted a Government of their own, republican in form, with which the Government of the United States of America has entered into relations, the President of the United States, in accordance with the ties of friendship which have so long and so happily existed between the respective nations, most earnestly commends to the Governments of Colombia and of Panama the peaceful and equitable settlement of all questions at issue between them. He holds that he is bound not merely by treaty obligations, but by the interests of civilization, to see that the peaceful traffic of the world across the Isthmus of Panama shall not longer be disturbed by a constant succession of unnecessary and wasteful civil wars."

When these events happened, fifty-seven years had elapsed since the United States had entered into its treaty with New Granada. During that time the Governments of New Granada and of its successor, Colombia, have been in a constant state of flux. The following is a partial list of the disturbances on the Isthmus of Panama during the period in question as reported to us by our consuls. It is not possible to give a complete list, and some of the reports that speak of "revolutions" must mean unsuccessful revolutions.

May 22, 1850.—Outbreak; two Americans killed. War vessel demanded to quell outbreak.

October, 1850.—Revolutionary plot to bring about independence of the Isthmus.

July 22, 1851.—Revolution in four southern provinces.

November 14, 1851.—Outbreak at Chagres. Man-of-war requested for Chagres.

June 27, 1853.—Insurrection at Bogota, and consequent disturbance on Isthmus. War vessel demanded.

May 23, 1854.—Political disturbances; war vessel requested.

June 28, 1854.—Attempted revolution.

October 24, 1854.—Independence of Isthmus demanded by provincial legislature.

April, 1856.—Riot, and massacre of Americans.

May 4, 1856.—Riot.

May 18, 1856.—Riot.

June 3, 1856.—Riot.

October 2, 1856.—Conflict between two native parties. United States forces landed.

December 18, 1858.—Attempted secession of Panama.

April, 1859.—Riots.

September, 1860.—Outbreak.

October 4, 1860.—Landing of United States forces in consequence.

May 23, 1861.—Intervention of the United States forces required by intendente.

October 2, 1861.—Insurrection and civil war.

April 4, 1862.—Measures to prevent rebels crossing Isthmus

June 13, 1862.—Mosquera's troops refused admittance to Panama.

March, 1865.—Revolution, and United States troops landed.

August, 1865.—Riots; unsuccessful attempt to invade Panama.

March, 1866.—Unsuccessful revolution.

April, 1867.—Attempt to overthrow Government.

August, 1867.—Attempt at revolution.

July 5, 1868.—Revolution; provisional government inaugurated.

August 29, 1868.—Revolution; provisional government overthrown.

April, 1871.—Revolution; followed apparently by counter revolution.

April, 1873.—Revolution and civil war which lasted to October, 1875.

August, 1876.—Civil war which lasted until April, 1877.

July, 1878.—Rebellion.

December, 1878.—Revolt.

April, 1879.—Revolution.

June, 1879.—Revolution.

March, 1883.—Riot.

May, 1883.—Riot.

June, 1884.—Revolutionary attempt.

December, 1884.—Revolutionary attempt.

January, 1885.—Revolutionary disturbances.

March, 1885.—Revolution.

April, 1887.—Disturbance on Panama Railroad.

November, 1887.—Disturbance on line of canal.
January, 1889.—Riot.
January, 1895.—Revolution which lasted until April.
March, 1895.—Incendiary attempt.
October, 1899.—Revolution.
February, 1900, to July, 1900.—Revolution.
January, 1901.—Revolution.
July, 1901.—Revolutionary disturbances.
September, 1901.—City of Colon taken by rebels.
March, 1902.—Revolutionary disturbances.
July, 1902.—Revolution.

The above is only a partial list of the revolutions, rebellions, insurrections, riots, and other outbreaks that have occurred during the period in question; yet they number 53 for the 57 years. It will be noted that one of them lasted for nearly three years before it was quelled; another for nearly a year. In short, the experience of over half a century has shown Colombia to be utterly incapable of keeping order on the Isthmus. Only the active interference of the United States has enabled her to preserve so much as a semblance of sovereignty. Had it not been for the exercise by the United States of the police power in her interest, her connection with the Isthmus would have been sundered long ago. In 1856, in 1860, in 1873, in 1885, in 1901, and again in 1902, sailors and marines from United States war ships were forced to land in order to patrol the Isthmus, to protect life and property, and to see that the transit across the Isthmus was kept open. In 1861, in 1862, in 1885, and in 1900, the Colombian Government asked that the United States Government would land troops to protect its interests and maintain order on the Isthmus. Perhaps the most extraordinary request is that which has just been received and which runs as follows:

"Knowing that revolution has already commenced in Panama [an eminent Colombian] says that if the Government of the United States will land troops to preserve Colombian sovereignty, and the transit, if requested by Colombian chargé d'affaires, this Government will declare martial law; and, by virtue of vested constitutional authority, when public order is disturbed, will approve by decree ratification of the canal treaty as signed; or, if the Government of the United States prefers, will call extra session of the Congress—with new and friendly members—next May to approve the treaty. [An eminent Colombian] has the perfect confidence of vice-president, he says, and if it became necessary will go to the Isthmus or send representatives there to adjust matters along above lines to the satisfaction of the people there."

This dispatch is noteworthy from two standpoints. Its offer of immediately guaranteeing the treaty to us is in sharp contrast with the positive and contemptuous refusal of the Congress which has just closed its sessions to consider favorably such a treaty; it shows that the Government which made the treaty really had absolute control over the situation, but did not choose to exercise this control. The dispatch further calls on us to restore order and secure Colombian supremacy in the Isthmus from which the Colombian Government has just by its action decided to bar us by preventing the construction of the canal.

The control, in the interest of the commerce and traffic of the whole civilized world, of the means of undisturbed transit across the Isthmus of Panama has become of transcendent importance to the United States. We have repeatedly exercised this control by intervening in the course of domestic dissension, and by protecting the territory from foreign invasion. In 1853 Mr. Everett assured the Peruvian minister that we should not hesitate to maintain the neutrality of the Isthmus in the case of war between Peru and Colombia. In 1864 Colombia, which has always been vigilant to avail itself of its privileges conferred by the treaty, expressed its expectation that in the event of war between Peru and Spain the United States would carry into effect the guaranty of neutrality. There have been few administrations of the State Department in which this treaty has not, either by the one side or the other, been used as a basis of more or less important demands. It was said by Mr. Fish in 1871 that the Department of State had reason to believe that an attack upon Colombian sovereignty on the Isthmus had, on several occasions, been averted by warning from this Government. In 1886, when Colombia was under the menace of hostilities from Italy in the Cerruti case, Mr. Bayard expressed the serious concern that the United States could not but feel, that a European power should resort to force against a sister republic of this hemisphere, as to the sovereign and uninterrupted use of a part of whose territory we are guarantors under the solemn faith of a treaty.

The above recital of facts establishes beyond question: First, that the United States has for over half a century patiently and in good faith carried out its obligations under the treaty of 1846; second, that when for the first time it became possible for Colombia to do anything in requital of the services thus repeatedly rendered to it for fifty-seven years by the United States, the Colombian Government peremptorily and offensively refused thus to do its part, even though to do so would have been to its advantage and immeasurably to the advantage of the State of Panama, at that time under its jurisdiction; third, that throughout this period revolutions, riots, and factional disturbances of every kind have occurred one after the other in almost uninterrupted succession, some of them lasting for months and even for years, while the central government was unable to put them down or to make peace with the rebels; fourth, that these disturbances instead of show-ing any sign of abating have tended to grow more numerous and more serious in the immediate past; fifth, that the control of Colombia over the Isthmus of Panama could not be maintained without the armed intervention and assistance of the United States. In other words, the Government of Colombia, though wholly unable to main-tain order on the Isthmus, has nevertheless declined to ratify a treaty the conclusion of which opened the only chance to secure its own stability and to guarantee permanent peace on, and the construction of a canal across, the Isthmus.

Under such circumstances the Government of the United States would have been guilty of folly and weakness, amounting in their sum to a crime against the Nation, had it acted otherwise than it did when the revolution of November 3 last took place in Panama. This great enterprise of building the interoceanic canal can not be held up to gratify the whims, or out of respect to the governmental impotence, or to the even more sinister and evil political peculiarities, of people who, though they dwell afar off, yet, against the wish of the actual dwellers on the Isthmus, assert an unreal supremacy over the territory. The possession of a territory fraught with such peculiar capacities as the Isthmus in question carries with it obligations to mankind. The course of events has shown that this canal can not be built by private enterprise, or by any other nation than our own; there-fore it must be built by the United States.

Every effort has been made by the Government of the United States to persuade Colombia to follow a course which was essentially not only to our interests and to the interests of the world, but to the inter-ests of Colombia itself. These efforts have failed; and Colombia, by her persistence in repulsing the advances that have been made, has forced us, for the sake of our own honor, and of the interest and well-being, not merely of our own people, but of the people of the Isthmus of Panama and the people of the civilized countries of the world, to take decisive steps to bring to an end a condition of affairs which had become intolerable. The new Republic of Panama immediately offered to negotiate a treaty with us. This treaty I herewith submit. By it our interests are better safeguarded than in the treaty with Colombia which was ratified by the Senate at its last session. It is better in its terms than the treaties offered to us by the Republics of Nicaragua and Costa Rica. At last the right to begin this great undertaking is made available. Panama has done her part. All that remains is for the American Congress to do its part, and forthwith this Republic will enter upon the execution of a project colossal in its size and of well-nigh incalculable possibilities for the good of this country and the nations of mankind.

By the provisions of the treaty the United States guarantees and will maintain the independence of the Republic of Panama. There is granted to the United States in perpetuity the use, occupation, and control of a strip ten miles wide and extending three nautical miles into the sea at either terminal, with all lands lying outside of the zone necessary for the construction of the canal or for its auxiliary works, and with the islands in the Bay of Panama. The cities of Panama and Colon are not embraced in the canal zone, but the United States assumes their sanitation and, in case of need, the maintenance of order therein; the United States enjoys within the granted limits all the rights, power, and authority which it would possess were it the sovereign of the territory to the exclusion of the exercise of sovereign rights by the Republic. All railway and canal property rights belonging to Panama and needed for the canal pass to the United States, including any property of the respective companies in the cities of Panama and Colon; the works, property, and personnel of the canal and railways are exempted from taxation as well in the cities of Panama and Colon as in the canal zone and its dependencies. Free immigration of the personnel and importation of supplies for the construction and operation of the canal are granted. Provision is made for the use of military force and the building of fortifications by the United States for the protection of the transit. In other details, particularly as to the acquisition of the interests of the New Panama Canal Company and the Panama Railway by the United States and the condemnation of private property for the uses of the canal, the stipulations of the Hay-Herran treaty are closely followed, while the compensation to be given for these enlarged grants remains the same, being ten millions of dollars payable on exchange of ratifications; and, beginning nine years from that date, an annual payment of $250,000 during the life of the convention.

THEODORE ROOSEVELT.

SPECIAL MESSAGES.

WHITE HOUSE, *December 7, 1903.*

To the Senate and House of Representatives:

I submit herewith, with my approval thereof, rules and regulations for the lease, sale, or other disposition of the public lands, other than timber or mineral lands, in the Philippine Islands, made by the government of said islands, pursuant to the provisions of section 13 of the act entitled "An act temporarily to provide for the administration of the affairs of civil government in the Philippine Islands, and for other purposes," approved July 1, 1902.

I also transmit therewith a letter from the Secretary of War, dated December 5, 1903, with inclosures.

THEODORE ROOSEVELT.

WHITE HOUSE, *December 7, 1903.*

To the Senate:

I transmit for the advice and consent of the Senate to its ratification a convention between the United States of America and the Republic of Panama for the construction of a ship canal, etc., to connect the waters of the Atlantic and Pacific oceans, signed on November 18, 1903.

I also inclose a report from the Secretary of State submitting the convention for my consideration.

THEODORE ROOSEVELT.

DEPARTMENT OF STATE,
Washington, November 19, 1903.

THE PRESIDENT:

The undersigned, Secretary of State, has the honor to lay before the President for his consideration, and, if his judgment approve thereof, for submission to the Senate, with a view to receiving the advice and consent of that body to its ratification, a convention between the United States of America and the Republic of Panama for the construction of a ship canal, etc., to connect the waters of the Atlantic and Pacific oceans, signed by the respective plenipotentiaries of the two countries on November 18, 1903.

Respectfully submitted, JOHN HAY.

ISTHMIAN CANAL CONVENTION.

The United States of America and the Republic of Panama being desirous to insure the construction of a ship canal across the Isthmus of Panama to connect the Atlantic and Pacific oceans, and the Congress of the United States of America having passed an act approved June 28, 1902, in furtherance of that object, by which the President of the United States is authorized to acquire within a reasonable time the control of the necessary territory of the Republic of Colombia, and the sovereignty of such territory being actually vested in the Republic of Panama, the high contracting parties have resolved for that purpose to conclude a convention, and have accordingly appointed as their plenipotentiaries—

The President of the United States of America, John Hay, Secretary of State, and

The Government of the Republic of Panama, Philippe Bunau-Varilla, envoy extraordinary and minister plenipotentiary of the Republic of Panama, thereunto specially empowered by said Government, who, after communicating with each other their respective full powers, found to be in good and due form, have agreed upon and concluded the following articles:

ARTICLE I.

The United States guarantees and will maintain the independence of the Republic of Panama.

ARTICLE II.

The Republic of Panama grants to the United States in perpetuity the use, occupation and control of a zone of land and land under water for the construction, maintenance, operation, sanitation, and protection of said canal of the width of 10 miles, extending to the distance of 5 miles on each side of the center line of the route of the canal to be constructed, the said zone beginning in the Caribbean Sea 3 marine miles from mean low-water mark and extending to and across the Isthmus of Panama into the Pacific Ocean to a distance of 3 marine miles from mean low-water mark, with the proviso that the cities of Panama and Colon and the harbors adjacent to said cities, which are included within the boundaries of the zone above described, shall not be included within this grant.

The Republic of Panama further grants to the United States in perpetuity the use, occupation, and control of any other lands and waters outside of the zone above described which may be necessary and convenient for the construction, maintenance, operation, sanitation, and protection of the said canal or of any auxiliary canals or other works necessary and convenient for the construction, maintenance, operation, sanitation, and protection of the said enterprise.

The Republic of Panama further grants in like manner to the United States in perpetuity all islands within the limits of the zone above described and in addition thereto the group of small islands in the Bay of Panama, named Perico, Naos, Culebra, and Flamenco.

ARTICLE III.

The Republic of Panama grants to the United States all the rights, power, and authority within the zone mentioned and described in Article II of this agreement and within the limits of all auxiliary lands and waters mentioned and described in said Article II which the United States would possess and exercise if it were the sovereign of the territory within which said lands and waters are located to the entire exclusion of the exercise by the Republic of Panama of any sovereign rights, power, or authority.

ARTICLE IV.

As rights subsidiary to the above grants the Republic of Panama grants in perpetuity to the United States the right to use the rivers, streams, lakes, and other bodies of water within its limits for navigation, the supply of water or water power, or other purposes, so far as the use of said rivers, streams, lakes, and bodies of water and the waters thereof may be necessary and convenient for the construction, maintenance, operation, sanitation, and protection of the said canal.

ARTICLE V.

The Republic of Panama grants to the United States in perpetuity a monopoly for the construction, maintenance, and operation of any system of communication by means of canal or railroad across its territory between the Caribbean Sea and the Pacific Ocean.

ARTICLE VI.

The grants herein contained shall in no manner invalidate the titles or rights of private land holders or owners of private property in the said zone or in or to any of the lands or waters granted to the United States by the provisions of any article of this treaty, nor shall they interfere with the rights of way over the public roads passing through the said zone or over any of the said lands or waters unless said rights of way or private rights shall conflict with rights herein granted to the United States, in which case the rights of the United States shall be superior.

All damages caused to the owners of private lands or private property of any kind by reason of the grants contained in this treaty or by reason of the operations of the United States, its agents or employees, or by reason of the construction, maintenance, operation, sanitation, and protection of the said canal or of the works of sanitation and protection herein provided for, shall be appraised and settled by a joint commission appointed by the Governments of the United States and of the Republic of Panama, whose decisions as to such damages shall be final, and whose awards as to such damages shall be paid solely by the United States. No part of the work on said canal or the Panama Railroad or on any auxiliary works relating thereto and authorized by the terms of this treaty shall be prevented, delayed, or impeded by or pending such proceedings to ascertain such damages. The appraisal of said private lands and private property and the assessment of damages to them shall be based upon their value before the date of this convention.

ARTICLE VII.

The Republic of Panama grants to the United States within the limits of the cities of Panama and Colon and their adjacent harbors and within the territory adjacent thereto the right to acquire, by purchase or by the exercise of the right of eminent domain, any lands, buildings, water rights, or other properties necessary and convenient for the construction, maintenance, operation, and protection of the canal and of any works of sanitation, such as the collection and disposition of sewage and the distribution of water in the said cities of Panama and Colon, which, in the discretion of the United States, may be necessary and convenient for the construction, maintenance, operation, sanitation, and protection of the said canal and railroad.

All such works of sanitation, collection, and disposition of sewage and distribution of water in the cities of Panama and Colon shall be made at the expense of the United States, and the Government of the United States, its agents or nominees, shall be authorized to impose and collect water rates and sewerage rates which shall be sufficient to provide for the payment of interest and the amortization of the principal of the cost of said works within a period of fifty years, and upon the expiration of said term of fifty years the system of sewers and waterworks shall revert to and become the properties of the cities of Panama and Colon, respectively, and the use of the water shall be free to the inhabitants of Panama and Colon, except to the extent that water rates may be necessary for the operation and maintenance of said system of sewers and waters.

The Republic of Panama agrees that the cities of Panama and Colon shall comply in perpetuity with the sanitary ordinances, whether of a preventive or curative character, prescribed by the United States, and in case the Government of Panama is unable or fails in its duty to enforce this compliance by the cities of Panama and Colon with the sanitary ordinances of the United States the Republic of Panama grants to the United States the right and authority to enforce the same.

The same right and authority are granted to the United States for the maintenance of public order in the cities of Panama and Colon and the territories and harbors adjacent thereto in case the Republic of Panama should not be, in the judgment of the United States, able to maintain such order.

ARTICLE VIII.

The Republic of Panama grants to the United States all rights which it now has or hereafter may acquire to the property of the New Panama Canal Company and the Panama Railroad Company as a result of the transfer of sovereignty from the Republic of Colombia to the Republic of Panama over the Isthmus of Panama and authorizes the New Panama Canal Company to sell and transfer to the United States its rights, privileges, properties, and concessions, as well as the Panama Railroad, and all the shares, or part of the shares of that company; but the public lands situated outside of the zone described in Article II of this treaty, now included in the concessions to both said enterprises and not required in the construction or operation of the canal, shall revert to the Republic of Panama, except any property now owned by or in the possession of said companies within Panama or Colon or the ports or terminals thereof.

ARTICLE IX.

The United States agrees that the ports at either entrance of the canal and the waters thereof and the Republic of Panama agrees that the towns of Panama and Colon shall be free for all time, so that there shall not be imposed or collected custom-house tolls, tonnage, anchorage, light-house, wharf, pilot, or quarantine dues, or any other charges or taxes of any kind upon any vessel using or passing through the canal or belonging to or employed by the United States, directly or indirectly, in connection with the construction, maintenance, operation, sanitation, and protection of the main canal, or auxiliary works, or upon the cargo, officers, crew, or passengers of any such vessels, except such tolls and charges as may be imposed by the United States for the use of the canal and other works, and except tolls and charges imposed by the Republic of Panama upon merchandise destined to be introduced for the consumption of the rest of the Republic of Panama, and upon vessels touching at the ports of Colon and Panama and which do not cross the canal.

The Government of the Republic of Panama shall have the right to establish in such ports and in the towns of Panama and Colon such houses and guards as it may be necessary to collect duties on importations destined to other portions of Panama and to prevent contraband trade. The United States shall have the right to make use of the towns and harbors of Panama and Colon as places of anchorage, and for making repairs, for loading, unloading, depositing, or transshipping cargoes either in transit or destined for the service of the canal and for other works pertaining to the canal.

Article X.

The Republic of Panama agrees that there shall not be imposed any taxes, national, municipal, departmental, or of any other class, upon the canal, the railways and auxiliary works, tugs and other vessels employed in the service of the canal, storehouses, workshops, offices, quarters for laborers, factories of all kinds, warehouses, wharves, machinery and other works, property, and effects appertaining to the canal or railroad and auxiliary works, or their officers or employees, situated within the cities of Panama and Colon, and that there shall not be imposed contributions or charges of a personal character of any kind upon officers, employees, laborers, and other individuals in the service of the canal and railroad and auxiliary works.

Article XI.

The United States agrees that the official dispatches of the Government of the Republic of Panama shall be transmitted over any telegraph and telephone lines established for canal purposes and used for public and private business at rates not higher than those required from officials in the service of the United States.

Article XII.

The Government of the Republic of Panama shall permit the immigration and free access to the lands and workshops of the canal and its auxiliary works of all employees and workmen of whatever nationality under contract to work upon or seeking employment upon or in any wise connected with the said canal and its auxiliary works, with their respective families, and all such persons shall be free and exempt from the military service of the Republic of Panama.

Article XIII.

The United States may import at any time into the said zone and auxiliary lands, free of custom duties, imposts, taxes, or other charges, and without any restrictions, any and all vessels, dredges, engines, cars, machinery, tools, explosives, materials, supplies, and other articles necessary and convenient in the construction, maintenance, operation, sanitation, and protection of the canal and auxiliary works, and all provisions, medicines, clothing, supplies, and other things necessary and convenient for the officers, employees, workmen, and laborers in the service and employ of the United States and for their families. If any such articles are disposed of for use outside of the zone and auxiliary lands granted to the United States, and within the territory of the Republic, they shall be subject to the same import or other duties as like articles imported under the laws of the Republic of Panama.

Article XIV.

As the price or compensation for the rights, powers, and privileges granted in this convention by the Republic of Panama to the United States, the Government of the United States agrees to pay to the Republic of Panama the sum of $10,000,000 in gold coin of the United States on the exchange of the ratification of this convention, and also an annual payment during the life of this convention of $250,000 in like gold coin, beginning nine years after the date aforesaid.

The provisions of this article shall be in addition to all other benefits assured to the Republic of Panama under this convention.

But no delay or difference of opinion under this article or any other provisions of this treaty shall affect or interrupt the full operation and effect of this convention in all other respects.

Article XV.

The joint commission referred to in Article VI shall be established as follows:

The President of the United States shall nominate two persons and the President of the Republic of Panama shall nominate two persons and they shall proceed to a decision; but in case of disagreement of the commission (by reason of their being equally divided in conclusion) an umpire shall be appointed by the two Governments, who shall render the decision. In the event of the death, absence, or incapacity of a commissioner or umpire, or of his omitting, declining, or ceasing to act, his place shall be filled by the appointment of another person in the manner above indicated. All decisions by a majority of the commission or by the umpire shall be final.

Article XVI.

The two Governments shall make adequate provision by future agreement for the pursuit, capture, imprisonment, detention, and delivery within said zone and auxiliary lands to the authorities of the Republic of Panama of persons charged with the commitment of crimes, felonies, or misdemeanors without said zone, and for the pursuit, capture, imprisonment, detention, and delivery without said zone to the authorities of the United States of persons charged with the commitment of crimes, felonies, and misdemeanors within said zone and auxiliary lands.

Article XVII.

The Republic of Panama grants to the United States the use of all the ports of the Republic open to commerce as places of refuge for any vessels employed in the canal enterprise, and for all vessels passing or bound to pass through the canal which may be in distress and be driven to seek refuge in said ports. Such vessels shall be exempt from anchorage and tonnage dues on the part of the Republic of Panama.

Article XVIII.

The canal, when constructed, and the entrances thereto shall be neutral in perpetuity, and shall be opened upon the terms provided for by Section 1 of Article III of, and in conformity with all the stipulations of, the treaty entered into by the Governments of the United States and Great Britain on November 18, 1901.

Article XIX.

The Government of the Republic of Panama shall have the right to transport over the canal its vessels and its troops and munitions of war in such vessels at all times without paying charges of any kind. The exemption is to be extended to the auxiliary railway for the transportation of persons in the service of the Republic of Panama, or of the police force charged with the preservation of public order outside of said zone, as well as to their baggage, munitions of war, and supplies.

217

ARTICLE XX.

If by virtue of any existing treaty in relation to the territory of the Isthmus of Panama, whereof the obligations shall descend or be assumed by the Republic of Panama, there may be any privilege or concession in favor of the Government or the citizens and subjects of a third power relative to an interoceanic means of communication which in any of its terms may be incompatible with the terms of the present convention, the Republic of Panama agrees to cancel or modify such treaty in due form, for which purpose it shall give to the said third power the requisite notification within the term of four months from the date of the present convention, and in case the existing treaty contains no clause permitting its modification or annulment, the Republic of Panama agrees to procure its modification or annulment in such form that there shall not exist any conflict with the stipulations of the present convention.

ARTICLE XXI.

The rights and privileges granted by the Republic of Panama to the United States in the preceding articles are understood to be free of all anterior debts, liens, trusts, or liabilities, or concessions or privileges to other governments, corporations, syndicates, or individuals, and consequently, if there should arise any claims on account of the present concessions and privileges or otherwise, the claimants shall resort to the Government of the Republic of Panama and not to the United States for any indemnity or compromise which may be required.

ARTICLE XXII.

The Republic of Panama renounces and grants to the United States the participation to which it might be entitled in the future earnings of the canal under Article XV of the concessionary contract with Lucien N. B. Wyse now owned by the New Panama Canal Company and any and all other rights or claims of a pecuniary nature arising under or relating to said concession, or arising under or relating to the concessions to the Panama Railroad Company or any extension or modification thereof; and it likewise renounces, confirms, and grants to the United States, now and hereafter, all the rights and property reserved in the said concessions which otherwise would belong to Panama at or before the expiration of the terms of ninety-nine years of the concessions granted to or held by the above-mentioned party and companies, and all right, title and interest which it now has or may hereafter have, in and to the lands, canal, works, property, and rights held by the said companies under said concessions or otherwise, and acquired or to be acquired by the United States from or through the New Panama Canal Company, including any property and rights which might or may in the future, either by lapse of time, forfeiture, or otherwise, revert to the Republic of Panama under any contracts or concessions, with said Wyse, the Universal Panama Canal Company, the Panama Railroad Company, and the New Panama Canal Company.

The aforesaid rights and property shall be and are free and released from any present or revisionary interest in or claims of Panama, and the title of the United States thereto, upon consummation of the contemplated purchase by the United States from the New Panama Canal Company, shall be absolute, so far as concerns the Republic of Panama, excepting always the rights of the Republic specifically secured under this treaty.

ARTICLE XXIII.

If it should become necessary at any time to employ armed forces for the safety or protection of the canal, or of the ships that make use of the same, or the railways and auxiliary works, the United States shall have the right, at all times and in its discretion, to use its police and its land and naval forces or to establish fortifications for these purposes.

ARTICLE XXIV.

No change either in the Government or in the laws and treaties of the Republic of Panama shall, without the consent of the United States, affect any right of the United States under the present convention or under any treaty stipulation between the two countries that now exists or may hereafter exist touching the subject-matter of this convention.

If the Republic of Panama shall hereafter enter as a constituent into any other government or into any union or confederation of states, so as to merge her sovereignty or independence in such government, union, or confederation, the rights of the United States under this convention shall not be in any respect lessened or impaired.

ARTICLE XXV.

For the better performance of the engagements of this convention and to the end of the efficient protection of the canal and the preservation of its neutrality, the Government of the Republic of Panama will sell or lease to the United States lands adequate and necessary for naval or coaling stations on the Pacific coast and on the western Caribbean coast of the Republic at certain points to be agreed upon with the President of the United States.

ARTICLE XXVI.

This convention when signed by the plenipotentiaries of the contracting parties shall be ratified by the respective Governments, and the ratifications shall be exchanged at Washington at the earliest date possible.

In faith whereof the respective plenipotentiaries have signed the present convention in duplicate and have hereunto affixed their respective seals.

Done at the city of Washington, the 18th day of November, in the year of our Lord, 1903.

JOHN HAY. [SEAL.]
P. BUNAU-VARILLA. [SEAL.]

WHITE HOUSE, *December 9, 1903.*

To the Senate and House of Representatives:

I transmit herewith the first annual report of the Secretary of Commerce and Labor.

THEODORE ROOSEVELT.

WHITE HOUSE, *December 11, 1903.*

To the Senate and House of Representatives:

I transmit herewith a report from the Secretary of State relating to the International Sanitary Bureau created by the First International

Sanitary Conference of the American Republics, in pursuance of a resolution of the Pan-American Conference during the winter of 1901-2, and asking for an appropriation to meet the annual share of the United States in the expenses of the Bureau.

In view of the importance of this Bureau, I recommend that the appropriation asked for be granted.

THEODORE ROOSEVELT.

WHITE HOUSE, *December 11, 1903.*

To the Senate and House of Representatives:

I transmit herewith for the consideration of the Congress a report by the Secretary of State, with accompanying papers, in the claim of the British schooner *Lillie.*

THEODORE ROOSEVELT.

WHITE HOUSE, *December 11, 1903.*

To the Senate and House of Representatives:

I transmit herewith a report from the Secretary of State looking to the payment of this Government's quota of a fund to be contributed by the governments forming the International Union of American Republics for the erection of a building in the city of Washington for the use of the Bureau of the American Republics.

I approve the recommendations made by the Secretary of State, and strongly recommend the matter to the favorable consideration of Congress.

THEODORE ROOSEVELT.

WHITE HOUSE, *December 11, 1903.*

To the Senate and House of Representatives:

I transmit herewith for the consideration of Congress a report by the Secretary of State, with accompanying papers, relative to the claims of the Eastern Extension, Australasia and China Telegraph Company, the Cuba Submarine Telegraph Company, and La Compagnie Française des Cables Télégraphiques, for damages done to their cables and property by United States naval and military authorities during the Spanish-American war.

THEODORE ROOSEVELT.

WHITE HOUSE, *December 15, 1903.*

To the Senate and House of Representatives:

I transmit herewith a supplemental report by the Secretary of War, submitting additional data regarding land owned by the United States and under control of the War Department, in further compliance with an item contained in the sundry civil appropriation act approved June 28, 1902.

THEODORE ROOSEVELT.

WHITE HOUSE, *December 15, 1903.*

To the Senate and House of Representatives:

Referring to section 32 of the act approved April 12, 1900, entitled "An act temporarily to provide revenues and a civil government for Porto Rico, and for other purposes," I transmit herewith an ordinance enacted by the executive council of Porto Rico on March 2, 1903, granting to the Vandegrift Construction Company the right to build and operate a line of railway between the municipality of Ponce and the playa of Ponce in the island of Porto Rico, and to develop energy by water or other power for distribution and sale for railway, lighting, and industrial purposes.

This ordinance was approved by the President of the United States on March 21, 1903.

THEODORE ROOSEVELT.

WHITE HOUSE, *December 15, 1903.*

To the Senate and House of Representatives:

I transmit herewith the report of the Commission on International Exchange constituted under authority of the act of March 3, 1903, in compliance with the request of the Governments of Mexico and China, for the co-operation of the United States in an effort to bring about a fixed relationship between the moneys of the gold-standard countries and the present silver-using countries.

The attention of Congress is invited to the accompanying report of the Secretary of State, whose request for an appropriation of $100,000 for the completion of the work of the Commission in China, and other expenditures incidental to the work of the Commission, I heartily indorse.

THEODORE ROOSEVELT.

WHITE HOUSE, *December 15, 1903.*

To the Senate and House of Representatives:

I transmit herewith a report from the Secretary of State, covering a statement showing the receipts and disbursements of the Louisiana Purchase Exposition Company for the month of October, 1903, furnished by the Louisiana Purchase Exposition Commission in pursuance of section 2 of the "Act to provide for celebrating the one hundredth anniversary of the purchase of the Louisiana Territory," etc., approved March 3, 1901.

THEODORE ROOSEVELT.

WHITE HOUSE, *December 15, 1903.*

To the Senate and House of Representatives:

I transmit herewith a report from the Secretary of State, with accompanying papers, concerning the claim of Lieut. Col. L. K. Scott, a British subject, on account of the adoption by the Ordnance Department of the United States Army of a system of sighting of which he is the inventor.

THEODORE ROOSEVELT.

WHITE HOUSE, *December 15, 1903.*

To the Congress of the United States:

I transmit herewith, as a case not acted upon by the Fifty-seventh Congress, a report from the Secretary of State, and accompanying papers, relating to the appeal for indemnity addressed to the equitable consideration of the Government of the United States by the owners of the Norwegian steamer *Nicaragua.*

THEODORE ROOSEVELT.

WHITE HOUSE, *December 18, 1903.*

To the Senate and House of Representatives:

I transmit herewith a communication from the Acting Secretary of State covering the report of the agent of the United States before the Alaskan boundary tribunal, with appendices.

The attention of Congress is invited to the request of the Acting Secretary of State that 500 copies of the report and appendices be printed for the use of the Department of State.

THEODORE ROOSEVELT.

WHITE HOUSE, *December 18, 1903.*

To the Senate and House of Representatives:

I transmit for the information of the Congress, in connection with the correspondence already transmitted relating to the recent revolution on the Isthmus of Panama, and contained in House Document No. 8, Fifty-eighth Congress, first session, parts 1 and 2, a report from the Secretary of State, with accompanying papers, concerning the convention between the United States and Colombia for the construction of an interoceanic canal across the Isthmus of Panama.

THEODORE ROOSEVELT.

WHITE HOUSE, *January 4, 1904.*

To the Senate and House of Representatives:

I lay before the Congress for its information a statement of my action up to this time in executing the act entitled "An act to provide for the construction of a canal connecting the waters of the Atlantic and Pacific oceans," approved June 28, 1902.

By the said act the President was authorized to secure for the United States the property of the Panama Canal Company and the perpetual control of a strip 6 miles wide across the Isthmus of Panama. It was further provided that "should the President be unable to obtain for the United States a satisfactory title to the property of the New Panama Canal Company and the control of the necessary territory of the Republic of Colombia * * * within a reasonable time and upon reasonable terms, then the President" should endeavor to provide for a canal by the Nicaragua route. The language quoted defines with exactness and precision what was to be done, and what as a matter of fact has been done. The President was authorized to go to the Nicaragua route only if within a reasonable time he could not obtain "control of the necessary territory of the Republic of Colombia." This control has now been obtained; the provision of the act has been complied with; it is no longer possible under existing legislation to go to the Nicaragua route as an alternative.

This act marked the climax of the effort on the part of the United States to secure, so far as legislation was concerned, an interoceanic canal across the Isthmus. The effort to secure a treaty for this purpose with one of the Central American republics did not stand on the same footing with the effort to secure a treaty under any ordinary conditions. The proper position for the United States to assume in reference to this canal, and therefore to the governments of the Isthmus, had been clearly set forth by Secretary Cass in 1858. In my annual message I have already quoted what Secretary Cass said; but I repeat the quotation here, because the principle it states is fundamental:

"While the rights of sovereignty of the states occupying this region (Central America) should always be respected, we shall expect that these rights be exercised in a spirit befitting the occasion and the wants and circumstances that have arisen. Sovereignty has its duties as well as its rights, and none of these local governments, even if administered with more regard to the just demands of other nations than they have been, would be permitted in a spirit of Eastern isolation to close the gates of intercourse on the great highways of the world and justify the act by the pretension that these avenues of trade and travel belong to them and that they choose to shut them, or, what is almost equivalent, to encumber them with such unjust relations as would prevent their general use."

The principle thus enunciated by Secretary Cass was sound then and it is sound now. The United States has taken the position that no other government is to build the canal. In 1889, when France proposed to come to the aid of the French Panama Company by guaranteeing their bonds, the Senate of the United States in executive session, with only some three votes dissenting, passed a resolution as follows:

"That the Government of the United States will look with serious concern and disapproval upon any connection of any European government with the construction or control of any ship canal across the Isthmus of Darien or across Central America, and must regard any such connection or control as injurious to the just rights and interests of the United States and as a menace to their welfare."

Under the Hay-Pauncefote treaty it was explicitly provided that the United States should control, police, and protect the canal which was to be built, keeping it open for the vessels of all nations on equal terms. The United States thus assumed the position of guarantor of the canal and of its peaceful use by all the world. The guarantee included as a matter of course the building of the canal. The enterprise was recognized as responding to an international need; and it would be the veriest travesty on right and justice to treat the governments in possession of the Isthmus as having the right, in the language of Mr. Cass, "to close the gates of intercourse on the great highways of the world, and justify the act by the pretension that these avenues of trade and travel belong to them and that they choose to shut them."

When this Government submitted to Colombia the Hay-Herran treaty three things were, therefore, already settled.

One was that the canal should be built. The time for delay, the time for permitting the attempt to be made by private enterprise, the time for permitting any government of anti-social spirit and of imperfect development to bar the work, was past. The United States had assumed in connection with the canal certain responsibilities not only to its own people, but to the civilized world, which imperatively demanded that there should no longer be delay in beginning the work.

Second. While it was settled that the canal should be built without unnecessary or improper delay, it was no less clearly shown to be our purpose to deal not merely in a spirit of justice, but in a spirit of generosity with the people through whose land we might build it. The Hay-Herran treaty, if it erred at all, erred in the direction of an over-generosity towards the Colombian Government. In our anxiety to be fair we had gone to the very verge in yielding to a weak nation's demands what that nation was helplessly unable to enforce from us against our will. The only criticisms made upon the Administration for the terms of the Hay-Herran treaty were for having granted too much to Colombia, not for failure to grant enough. Neither in the Congress nor in the public press, at the time that this treaty was formulated, was there complaint that it did not in the fullest and amplest manner guarantee to Colombia everything that she could by any color of title demand.

Nor is the fact to be lost sight of that the rejected treaty, while generously responding to the pecuniary demands of Colombia, in other respects merely provided for the construction of the canal in conformity with the express requirements of the act of the Congress of June 28, 1902. By that act, as heretofore quoted, the President was authorized to acquire from Colombia, for the purposes of the canal, "perpetual control" of a certain strip of land; and it was expressly required that the "control" thus to be obtained should include "jurisdiction" to make police and sanitary regulations and to establish such judicial tribunals as might be agreed on for their enforcement. These were conditions precedent prescribed by the Congress; and for their fulfillment suitable stipulations were embodied in the treaty. It has been stated in public prints that Colombia objected to these stipulations, on the ground that they involved a relinquishment of her "sovereignty;" but in the light of what has taken place, this alleged objection must be considered as an afterthought. In reality, the treaty, instead of requiring a cession of Colombia's sovereignty over the canal strip, expressly acknowledged, confirmed, and preserved her sovereignty over it. The treaty in this respect simply proceeded on the lines on which all the negotiations leading up to the present situation have been conducted. In those negotiations the exercise by the United States, subject to the paramount rights of the local sovereign, of a substantial control over the canal and the immediately adjacent territory, has been treated as a fundamental part of any arrangement that might be made. It has formed an essential feature of all our plans, and its necessity is fully recognized in the Hay-Pauncefote treaty. The Congress, in providing that such control should be secured, adopted no new principle, but only incorporated in its legislation a condition the importance and propriety of which were universally recognized. During all the years of negotiation and discussion that preceded the conclusion of the Hay-Herran treaty, Colombia never intimated that the requirement by the United States of control over the canal strip would render unattainable the construction of a canal by way of the Isthmus of Panama; nor were we advised, during the months when legislation of 1902 was pending before the Congress, that the terms which i embodied would render negotiations with Colombia impracticable. It is plain that no nation could construct and guarantee the neutrality of the canal with a less degree of control than was stipulated for in the Hay-Herran treaty. A refusal to grant such degree of control was necessarily a refusal to make any practicable treaty at all. Such refusal therefore squarely raised the question whether Colombia was entitled to bar the transit of the world's traffic across the Isthmus.

That the canal itself was eagerly demanded by the people of the locality through which it was to pass, and that the people of this locality no less eagerly longed for its construction under American control, are shown by the unanimity of action in the new Panama Republic. Furthermore, Colombia, after having rejected the treaty in spite of our protests and warnings when it was in her power to accept it, has since shown the utmost eagerness to accept the same treaty if only the status quo could be restored. One of the men standing highest in the official circles of Colombia, on November 6, addressed the American minister at Bogota, saying that if the Government of the United States would land troops to preserve Colombian sovereignty and the transit, the Colombian Government would "declare martial law; and, by virtue of vested constitutional authority, when public order is disturbed, [would] approve by decree the ratification of the canal treaty as signed; or, if the Government of the United States prefers [would] call extra session of the Congress—with new and friendly members—next May to approve the treaty." Having these facts in view, there is no shadow of question that the Government of the United States proposed a treaty which was not merely just, but generous to Colombia, which our people regarded as erring, if at all, on the side of overgenerosity; which was hailed with delight by the people of the immediate locality through which the canal was to pass, who were most concerned as to the new order of things, and which the Colombian authorities now recognize as being so good that they are willing to promise its unconditional ratification if only we will desert those who have shown themselves our friends and restore to those who have shown themselves unfriendly the power to undo what they did. I pass by the question as to what assurance we have that they would now keep their pledge and not again refuse to ratify the treaty if they had the power; for, of course, I will not for one moment discuss the possibility of the United States committing an act of such baseness as to abandon the new Republic of Panama.

Third. Finally the Congress definitely settled where the canal was to be built. It was provided that a treaty should be made for building the canal across the Isthmus of Panama; and if, after reasonable time, it proved impossible to secure such treaty, that then we should go to Nicaragua. The treaty has been made; for it needs no argument to show that the intent of the Congress was to insure a canal across Panama, and that whether the Republic granting the title was called New Granada, Colombia, or Panama mattered not one whit. As events turned out, the question of "reasonable time" did not enter into the matter at all. Although, as the months went by, it became increasingly improbable that the Colombian Congress would ratify the treaty or take steps which would be equivalent thereto, yet all chance for such action on their part did not vanish until the Congress closed at the end of October; and within three days thereafter the revolution in Panama had broken out. Panama became an independent State, and the control of the territory necessary for building the canal then became obtainable. The condition under which alone we could have gone to Nicaragua thereby became impossible of fulfillment. If the pending treaty with Panama should not be ratified by the Senate this would not alter the fact that we could not go to Nicaragua. The Congress has decided the route and there is no alternative under existing legislation.

When in August it began to appear probable that the Colombian Legislature would not ratify the treaty, it became incumbent upon me to consider well what the situation was and to be ready to advise the Congress as to what were the various alternatives of action open to us. There were several possibilities. One was that Colombia would at the last moment see the unwisdom of her position. That there might be nothing omitted, Secretary Hay, through the minister at Bogota, repeatedly warned Colombia that grave consequences might follow from her rejection of the treaty. Although it was a constantly diminishing chance, yet the possibility of ratification did not wholly pass away until the close of the session of the Colombian Congress.

A second alternative was that by the close of the session on the last day of October, without the ratification of the treaty by Colombia and without any steps taken by Panama, the American Congress on assembling early in November would be confronted with a situation in which there had been a failure to come to terms as to building the canal along the Panama route, and yet there had not been a lapse of a reasonable time—using the word reasonable in any proper sense—such as would justify the Administration going to the Nicaragua route. This situation seemed on the whole the most likely, and as a matter of fact I had made the original draft of my Message to the Congress with a view to its existence.

It was the opinion of eminent international jurists that in view of the fact that the great design of our guarantee under the treaty of 1846 was to dedicate the Isthmus to the purposes of interoceanic transit, and above all to secure the construction of an interoceanic canal, Colombia could not under existing conditions refuse to enter into a proper arrangement with the United States to that end, without violating the spirit and substantially repudiating the obligations of a treaty the full benefits of which she had enjoyed for over fifty years. My intention was to consult the Congress as to whether under such circumstances it would not be proper to announce that the canal was to be dug forthwith; that we would give the terms that we had offered and no others; and that if such terms were not agreed to we would enter into an arrangement with Panama direct, or take what other steps were needful in order to begin the enterprise.

A third possibility was that the people of the Isthmus, who had formerly constituted an independent state, and who until recently were united to Colombia only by a loose tie of federal relationship, might take the protection of their own vital interests into their own hands, reassert their former rights, declare their independence upon just grounds, and establish a government competent and willing to do its share in this great work for civilization. This third possibility is what actually occurred. Everyone knew that it was a possibility, but it was not until towards the end of October that it appeared to be an imminent probability. Although the Administration, of course, had special means of knowledge, no such means were necessary in order to appreciate the possibility, and toward the end the likelihood, of such a revolutionary outbreak and of its success. It was a matter of common notoriety. Quotations from the daily papers could be indefinitely multiplied to show this state of affairs; a very few will suffice. From Costa Rica on August 31 a special was sent to the Washington Post, running as follows:

"SAN JOSÉ, COSTA RICA, *August 31.*

"Travelers from Panama report the Isthmus alive with fires of a new revolution. It is inspired, it is believed, by men who, in Panama and Colon, have systematically engendered the pro-American feeling to secure the building of the Isthmian canal by the United States.

"The Indians have risen, and the late followers of Gen. Benjamin Herrera are mustering in the mountain villages, preparatory to joining in an organized revolt, caused by the rejection of the canal treaty.

"Hundreds of stacks of arms, confiscated by the Colombian Government at the close of the late revolution, have reappeared from some mysterious source, and thousands of rifles that look suspiciously like the Mausers the United States captured in Cuba are issuing to the gathering forces from central points of distribution. With the arms goes ammunition, fresh from factories, showing the movement is not spasmodic, but is carefully planned.

*　　*　　*　　*　　*　　*　　*　　*　　*　　*　　*

"The Government forces in Panama and Colon, numbering less than 1,500 men, are reported to be a little more than friendly to the revolutionary spirit. They have been ill paid since the revolution closed and their only hope of prompt payment is another war.

"General Huertes, commander of the forces, who is ostensibly loyal to the Bogota Government, is said to be secretly friendly to the proposed revolution. At least, all his personal friends are open in denunciation of the Bogota Government and the failure of the Colombian Congress to ratify the canal treaty.

"The consensus of opinion gathered from late arrivals from the Isthmus is that the revolution is coming, and that it will succeed."

A special dispatch to the Washington Post, under date of New York, September 1, ran as follows:

"B. G. Duque, editor and proprietor of the Panama Star and Herald, a resident of the Isthmus during the past twenty-seven years, who arrived to-day in New York, declared that if the canal treaty fell through a revolution would be likely to follow.

"'There is a very strong feeling in Panama,' said Mr. Duque, 'that Colombia, in negotiating the sale of a canal concession in Panama, is looking for profits that might just as well go to Panama herself.

"'The Colombian Government, only the other day, suppressed a newspaper that dared to speak of independence for Panama. A while ago there was a secret plan afoot to cut loose from Colombia and seek the protection of the United States.'"

In the New York Herald of September 10 the following statement appeared:

"Representatives of strong interests on the Isthmus of Panama who make their headquarters in this city are considering a plan of action to be undertaken in co-operation with men of similar views of Panama and Colon to bring about a revolution and form an independent government in Panama opposed to that in Bogota.

"There is much indignation on the Isthmus on account of the failure of the canal treaty, which is ascribed to the authorities at Bogota. This opinion is believed to be shared by a majority of the Isthmians of all shades of political belief, and they think it is to their best interest for a new republic to be formed on the Isthmus, which may negotiate directly with the United States a new treaty which will permit the digging of the Panama canal under favorable conditions."

In the New York Times, under date of September 13, there appeared from Bogota the following statement:

"A proposal made by Señor Prez y Sotos to ask the Executive to appoint an anti-secessionist governor in Panama has been approved by the Senate. Speakers in the Senate said that Señor Obaldia, who was recently appointed governor of Panama, and who is favorable to a canal treaty, was a menace to the national integrity. Senator Marroquin protested against the action of the Senate.

"President Marroquin succeeded later in calming the Congressmen. It appears that he was able to give them satisfactory reasons for Governor Obaldia's appointment. He appears to realize the imminent peril of the Isthmus of Panama declaring its independence.

"Señor Deroux, representative for a Panama constituency, recently delivered a sensational speech in the House. Among other things he said:

" 'In Panama the bishops, governors, magistrates, military chiefs, and their subordinates have been and are foreign to the department. It seems that the Government, with surprising tenacity, wishes to exclude the Isthmus from all participation in public affairs. As regards international dangers in the Isthmus, all I can say is that if these dangers exist they are due to the conduct of the national government which is in the direction of reaction.

" 'If the Colombian Government will not take action with a view to preventing disaster, the responsibility will rest with it alone.' "

In the New York Herald of October 26 it was reported that a revolutionary expedition of about 70 men had actually landed on the Isthmus. In the Washington Post of October 29 it was reported from Panama that in view of the impending trouble on the Isthmus the Bogota Government had gathered troops in sufficient numbers to at once put down an attempt at secession. In the New York Herald of October 30 it was announced from Panama that Bogota was hurrying troops to the Isthmus to put down the projected revolt. In the New York Herald of November 2 it was announced that in Bogota the Congress had indorsed the energetic measures taken to meet the situation on the Isthmus and that 6,000 men were about to be sent thither.

Quotations like the above could be multiplied indefinitely. Suffice it to say that it was notorious that revolutionary trouble of a serious nature was impending upon the Isthmus. But it was not necessary to rely exclusively upon such general means of information. On October 15 Commander Hubbard, of the Navy, notified the Navy Department that, though things were quiet on the Isthmus, a revolution had broken out in the State of Cauca. On October 16, at the request of Lieutenant-General Young, I saw Capt. C. B. Humphrey and Lieut. Grayson Mallet-Prevost Murphy, who had just returned from a four months' tour through the northern portions of Venezuela and Colombia. They stopped in Panama on their return in the latter part of September. At the time they were sent down there had been no thought of their going to Panama, and their visit to the Isthmus was but an unpremeditated incident of their return journey; nor had they been spoken to by anyone at Washington regarding the possibility of a revolt. Until they landed at Colon they had no knowledge that a revolution was impending, save what they had gained from the newspapers. What they saw in Panama so impressed them that they reported thereon to Lieutenant-General Young, according to his memorandum—"that while on the Isthmus they became satisfied beyond question that, owing largely to the dissatisfaction because of the failure of Colombia to ratify the Hay-Herran treaty, a revolutionary party was in course of organization having for its object the separation of the State of Panama from Colombia, the leader being Dr. Richard Arango, a former governor of Panama; that when they were on the Isthmus arms and ammunition were being smuggled into the city of Colon in piano boxes, merchandise crates, etc., the small arms received being principally the Gras French rifle, the Remington, and the Mauser; that nearly every citizen in Panama had some sort of rifle or gun in his possession, with ammunition therefor; that in the city of Panama there had been organized a fire brigade which was really intended for a revolutionary military organization; that there were representatives of the revolutionary organization at all important points on the Isthmus; that in Panama, Colon, and the other principal places of the Isthmus police forces had been organized which were in reality revolutionary forces; that the people on the Isthmus seemed to be unanimous in their sentiment against the Bogota Government, and their disgust over the failure of that Government to ratify the treaty providing for the construction of the canal, and that a revolution might be expected immediately upon the adjournment of the Colombian Congress without ratification of the treaty."

Lieutenant-General Young regarded their report as of such importance as to make it advisable that I should personally see these officers. They told me what they had already reported to the Lieutenant-General, adding that on the Isthmus the excitement was seething, and that the Colombian troops were reported to be disaffected. In response to a question of mine, they informed me that it was the general belief that the revolution might break out at any moment, and if it did not happen before, would doubtless take place immediately after the closing of the Colombian Congress (at the end of October) if the canal treaty were not ratified. They were certain that the revolution would occur, and before leaving the Isthmus had made their own reckoning as to the time, which they had set down as being probably from three to four weeks after their leaving. The reason they set this as the probable inside limit of time was that they reckoned that it would be at least three or four weeks—say not until October 20— before a sufficient quantity of arms and munitions would have been landed.

In view of all these facts, I directed the Navy Department to issue instructions such as would insure our having ships within easy reach of the Isthmus in the event of need arising. Orders were given on October 19 to the *Boston* to proceed to San Juan del Sur, Nicaragua; to the *Dixie* to prepare to sail from League Island; and to the *Atlanta* to proceed to Guantanamo. On October 30 the *Nashville* was ordered to proceed to Colon. On November 2 when, the Colombian Congress having adjourned, it was evident that the outbreak was imminent, and when it was announced that both sides were making ready forces whose meeting would mean bloodshed and disorder, the Colombian troops having been embarked on vessels, the following instructions were sent to the commanders of the *Boston, Nashville,* and *Dixie:*

"Maintain free and uninterrupted transit. If interruption is threatened by armed force, occupy the line of railroad. Prevent landing of any armed force with hostile intent, either Government or insurgent, at any point within 50 miles of Panama. Government force reported approaching the Isthmus in vessels. Prevent their landing if, in your judgment, the landing would precipitate a conflict."

These orders were delivered in pursuance of the policy on which our Government had repeatedly acted. This policy was exhibited in the following orders, given under somewhat similar circumstances last year, and the year before, and the year before that. The first two telegrams are from the Department of State to the consul at Panama:

"JULY 25, 1900.

"You are directed to protest against any act of hostility which may involve or imperil the safe and peaceful transit of persons or property across the Isthmus of Panama. The bombardment of Panama would have this effect, and the United States must insist upon the neutrality of the Isthmus as guaranteed by the treaty."

"NOVEMBER 20, 1901.

"Notify all parties molesting or interfering with free transit across the Isthmus that such interference must cease and that the United States will prevent the interruption of traffic upon the railroad. Consult with the captain of the *Iowa,* who will be instructed to land marines, if necessary, for the protection of the railroad, in accordance with the treaty rights and obligations of the United States. Desirable to avoid bloodshed, if possible."

The next three telegrams are from and to the Secretary of the Navy:

"SEPTEMBER 12, 1902.
"RANGER, *Panama:*

"United States guarantees perfect neutrality of Isthmus and that a free transit from sea to sea be not interrupted or embarrassed. * * * Any transportation of troops which might contravene these provisions of treaty should not be sanctioned by you nor should use of road be permitted which might convert the line of transit into theater of hostility.

"MOODY."

"COLON, *September 20, 1902.*

"SECRETARY NAVY, *Washington:*

"Everything is conceded. The United States guards and guarantees traffic and the line of transit. To-day I permitted the exchange of Colombian troops from Panama to Colon, about 1,000 men each way, the troops without arms in train guarded by American naval force in the same manner as other passengers; arms and ammunition in separate train, guarded also by naval force in the same manner as other freight.

"McLEAN."

"PANAMA, *October 3, 1902.*

"SECRETARY NAVY,

   "*Washington, D. C.:*

"Have sent this communication to the American consul at Panama:

   "'Inform governor while trains running under United States protection I must decline transportation any combatants, ammunition, arms, which might cause interruption traffic or convert line of transit into theater hostilities.'

"CASEY."

On November 3 Commander Hubbard responded to the above-quoted telegram of November 2, 1903, saying that before the telegram had been received 400 Colombian troops from Cartagena had landed at Colon; that there had been no revolution on the Isthmus, but that the situation was most critical if the revolutionary leaders should act. On this same date the Associated Press in Washington received a bulletin stating that a revolutionary outbreak had occurred. When this was brought to the attention of the Assistant Secretary of State, Mr. Loomis, he prepared the following cablegram to the consul-general at Panama and the consul at Colon:

"Uprising on Isthmus reported. Keep Department promptly and fully informed."

Before this telegram was sent, however, one was received from Consul Malmros at Colon, running as follows:

"Revolution imminent. Government force on the Isthmus about 500 men. Their official promised support revolution. Fire department, Panama, 441, are well organized and favor revolution. Government vessel, *Cartagena,* with about 400 men, arrived early to-day with new commander in chief, Tobar. Was not expected until November 10. Tobar's arrival is not probable to stop revolution."

This cablegram was received at 2:35 p. m., and at 3:40 p. m. Mr. Loomis sent the telegram which he had already prepared to both

Panama and Colon. Apparently, however, the consul general at Panama had not received the information embodied in the Associated Press bulletin, upon which the Assistant Secretary of State based his dispatch: for his answer was that there was no uprising, although the situation was critical, this answer being received at 8:15 p. m. Immediately afterwards he sent another dispatch, which was received at 9:50 p. m., saying that the uprising had occurred, and had been successful, with no bloodshed. The Colombian gunboat *Bogota* next day began to shell the city of Panama, with the result of killing one Chinaman. The consul-general was directed to notify her to stop firing. Meanwhile, on November 4, Commander Hubbard notified the Department that he had landed a force to protect the lives and property of American citizens against the threats of the Colombian soldiery.

Before any step whatever had been taken by the United States troops to restore order, the commander of the newly landed Colombian troops had indulged in wanton and violent threats against American citizens, which created serious apprehension. As Commander Hubbard reported in his letter of November 5, this officer and his troops practically began war against the United States, and only the forbearance and coolness of our officers and men prevented bloodshed. The letter of Commander Hubbard is of such interest that it deserves quotation in full, and runs as follows:

"U. S. S. NASHVILLE, THIRD RATE,
"*Colon, U. S. Colombia, November 5, 1903.*

"SIR: Pending a complete report of the occurrences of the last three days in Colon, Colombia, I most respectfully invite the Department's attention to those of the date of Wednesday, November 4, which amounted to practically the making of war against the United States by the officer in command of the Colombian troops in Colon. At 1 o'clock p. m. on that date I was summoned on shore by a preconcerted signal, and on landing met the United States consul, vice-consul, and Colonel Shaler, the general superintendent of the Panama Railroad. The consul informed me that he had received notice from the officer commanding the Colombian troops, Colonel Torres, through the prefect of Colon, to the effect that if the Colombian officers, Generals Tobal and Amaya, who had been seized in Panama on the evening of the 3d of November by the Independents and held as prisoners, were not released by 2 o'clock p. m., he, Torres, would open fire on the town of Colon and kill every United States citizen in the place, and my advice and action were requested. I advised that all the United States citizens should take refuge in the shed of the Panama Railroad Company, a stone building susceptible of being put into good state for defense, and that I would immediately land such body of men, with extra arms for arming the citizens, as the complement of the ship would permit. This was agreed to and I immediately returned on board, arriving at 1:15 p. m. The order for landing was immediately given, and at 1:30 p. m. the boats left the ship with a party of 42 men under the command of Lieut. Commander H. M. Witzel, with Midshipman J. P. Jackson as second in command. Time being pressing I gave verbal orders to Mr. Witzel to take the building above referred to, to put it into the best state of defense possible, and protect the lives of the citizens assembled there—not firing unless fired upon. The women and children took refuge on the German steamer *Marcomania* and Panama Railroad steamer *City of Washington*, both ready to haul out from dock if necessary. The *Nashville* I got under way and patrolled with her along the water front close in and ready to use either small-arm or shrapnel fire. The Colombians surrounded the building of the railroad company almost immediately after we had taken possession, and for about one and a half hours their attitude was most threatening, it being seemingly their purpose to provoke an attack. Happily our men were cool and steady, and while the tension was very great no shot was fired. At about 3:15 p. m. Colonel Torres came into the building for an interview and expressed himself as most friendly to Americans, claiming that the whole affair was a misapprehension and that he would like to send the alcalde of Colon to Panama to see General Tobal and have him direct the discontinuance of the show of force. A special train was furnished and safe conduct guaranteed. At about 5:30 p. m. Colonel Torres made the proposition of withdrawing his troops to Monkey Hill, if I would withdraw the *Nashville's* force and leave the town in possession of the police until the return of the alcalde on the morning of the 5th. After an interview with the United States consul and Colonel Shaler as to the probability of good faith in the matter, I decided to accept the proposition and brought my men on board, the disparity in numbers between my force and that of the Colombians, nearly ten to one, making me desirous of avoiding a conflict so long as the object in view, the protection of American citizens, was not imperiled.

"I am positive that the determined attitude of our men, their coolness and evident intention of standing their ground, had a most salutary and decisive effect on the immediate situation and was the initial step in the ultimate abandoning of Colon by these troops and their return to Cartagena the following day. Lieutenant-Commander Witzel is entitled to much praise for his admirable work in command on the spot.

"I feel that I can not sufficiently strongly represent to the Department the grossness of this outrage and the insult to our dignity, even apart from the savagery of the threat.

"Very respectfully,

"JOHN HUBBARD,

"*Commander, U. S. Navy, Commanding.*

"THE SECRETARY OF THE NAVY,

"*Navy Department, Washington, D. C.*"

In his letter of November 8 Commander Hubbard sets forth the facts more in detail:

"U. S. S. NASHVILLE, THIRD RATE,

"*Porto Bello, U. S. Colombia, November 8, 1903.*

"SIR: I. I have the honor to make the following report of the occurrences which took place at Colon and Panama in the interval between the arrival of the *Nashville* at Colon on the evening of November 2, 1903, and the evening of November 5, 1903, when by the arrival of the U. S. S. *Dixie* at Colon I was relieved as senior officer by Commander F. H. Delano, U. S. Navy.

"2. At the time of the arrival of the *Nashville* at Colon at 5:30 p. m. on November 2 everything on the Isthmus was quiet. There was talk of proclaiming the independence of Panama, but no definite action had been taken and there had been no disturbance of peace and order. At daylight on the morning of November 3 it was found that a vessel which had come in during the night was the Colombian gunboat *Cartagena* carrying betwen 400 and 500 troops. I had her boarded and learned that these troops were for the garrison at Panama. Inasmuch as the Independent party had not acted and the Government of Colombia was at the time in undisputed control of the Province of Panama, I did not feel, in the absence of any instructions, that I was justified in preventing the landing of these troops, and at 8:30 o'clock they were disembarked. The commanding officers, Generals Amaya and Tobal, with four others, immediately went over to Panama to make arrangements for receiving and quartering their troops, leaving the command in charge of an officer whom I later learned to be Colonel Torres. The Department's message addressed to the care of the United States consul I received at 10:30 a. m.; it was delivered to one of the ship's boats while I was at the consul's and not to the consul as addressed. The message was said to have been received at the cable office at 9:30 a. m. Immediately on deciphering the message I went on shore to see what arrangements the railroad company had made for the transportation of these troops to Panama, and learned that the company would not transport them except on request of the governor of Panama, and that the prefect at Colon and the officer left in command of the troops had been so notified by the general superintendent of the Panama Railroad Company. I remained at the company's office until it was sure that no action on my part would be needed to prevent the transportation of the troops that afternoon, when I returned on board and cabled the Department the situation of affairs. At about 5:30 p. m. I again went on shore, and received notice from the general superintendent of the railroad that he had received the request for the transportation of the troops and that they would leave on the 8 a. m. train on the following day. I immediately went to see the general superintendent, and learned that it had just been announced that a provisional government had been established at Panama—that Generals Amaya and Tobal, the governor of Panama, and four officers, who had gone to Panama in the morning, had been seized and were held as prisoners; that they had an organized force of 1,500 troops and wished the Government troops in Colon to be sent over. This I declined to permit, and verbally prohibited the general superintendent from giving transportation to the troops of either party.

"It being then late in the evening, I sent early in the morning of November 4 written notification to the general superintendent of the Panama Railroad, to the prefect of Colon, and to the officer left in command of the Colombian troops, later ascertained to be Colonel Torres, that I had prohibited the transportation of troops in either direction, in order to preserve the free and uninterrupted transit of the Isthmus. Copies of these letters are hereto appended; also copy of my notification to the consul. Except to a few people, nothing was known in Colon of the proceedings in Panama until the arrival of the train at 10:45 on the morning of the 4th. Some propositions were, I was later told, made to Colonel Torres by the representatives of the new Government at Colon, with a view to inducing him to re-embark in the *Cartagena* and return to the port of Cartagena, and it was in answer to this proposition that Colonel Torres made the threat and took the action reported in my letter No. 96, of November 5, 1903. The *Cartagena* left the port just after the threat was made and I did not deem it expedient to attempt to detain her, as such action would certainly, in the then state of affairs, have precipitated a conflict on shore which I was not prepared to meet. It is my understanding that she returned to Cartagena. After the withdrawal of the Colombian troops on the evening of November 4, and the return of the *Nashville's* force on board, as reported in my letter No. 96, there was no disturbance on shore, and the night passed quietly. On the morning of the 5th I discovered that the commander of the Colombian troops had not withdrawn so far from the town as he had agreed, but was occupying buildings near the outskirts of the town. I immediately inquired into the matter and learned that he had some trivial excuse for not carrying out his agreement, and also that it was his intention to occupy Colon again on the arrival of the alcalde due at 10:45 a. m., unless General Tobal sent word by the alcalde that he, Colonel Torres, should withdraw. That General Tobal had declined to give any instructions I was cognizant of, and the situation at once became quite as serious as on the day previous. I immediately landed an armed force, reoccupied the same building; also landed two 1-pounders and mounted them on platform cars behind protection of cotton bales, and then in company with the United States consul had an interview with Colonel Torres, in the course of which I informed him that I had relanded my men because he had not kept his agreement; that I had no interest in the affairs of either party; that my attitude was strictly neutral; that the troops of neither side should be transported; that my sole purpose in landing was to protect the lives and property of American citizens if threatened, as they had been threatened, and to maintain the free and uninterrupted transit of the Isthmus, and that purpose I should maintain by force if necessary. I also strongly advised that in the interests of peace, and to prevent the possibility of a conflict that could not but be regrettable, he should carry out his agreement of the previous evening and withdraw to Monkey Hill.

"Colonel Torres's only reply was that it was unhealthy at Monkey Hill, a reiteration of his love of Americans, and persistence in his intention to occupy Colon, should General Tobal not give him directions to the contrary.

"On the return of the alcalde at about 11 a. m. the Colombian troops marched into Colon, but did not assume the threatening demeanor of the previous day. The American women and children again went on board the *Marcomania* and *City of Washington,* and through the British vice-consul I offered protection to British subjects as directed in the Department's cablegram. A copy of the British vice-consul's acknowledgment is hereto appended. The *Nashville* I got under way as on the previous day and moved close in to protect the water front. During the afternoon several propositions were made to Colonel Torres by the representatives of the new Government, and he was finally persuaded by them to embark on the Royal Mail steamer *Orinoco* with all his troops and return to Cartagena. The *Orinoco* left her dock with the troops—474 all told—at 7:35 p. m. The *Dixie* arrived and anchored at 7:05 p. m., when I went on board and acquainted the commanding officer with the situation. A portion of the marine battalion was landed and the *Nashville's* force withdrawn.

"3. On the evening of November 4 Maj. William M. Black and Lieut. Mark Brooke, Corps of Engineers, U. S. Army, came to Colon from Culebra and volunteered their services, which were accepted, and they rendered very efficient help on the following day.

"4. I beg to assure the Department that I had no part whatever in the negotiations that were carried on between Colonel Torres and the representatives of the provisional government; that I landed an armed force only when the lives of American citizens were threatened and withdrew this force as soon as there seemed to be no grounds for further apprehension of injury to American lives or property; that I relanded an armed force because of the failure of Colonel Torres to carry out his agreement to withdraw and announced intention of returning, and that my attitude throughout was strictly neutral as between the two parties, my only purpose being to protect the lives and property of American citizens and to preserve the free and uninterrupted transit of the Isthmus.

"Very respectfully,

"JOHN HUBBARD,
"*Commander, U. S. Navy, Commanding.*

"The SECRETARY OF THE NAVY,
"*Bureau of Navigation, Navy Department,*
"*Washington, D. C.*"

This plain official account of the occurrences of November 4 shows that, instead of there having been too much provision by the American Government for the maintenance of order and the protection of life and property on the Isthmus, the orders for the movement of the American war ships had been too long delayed; so long, in fact, that there were but forty-two marines and sailors available to land and protect the lives of American men and women. It was only the coolness and gallantry with which this little band of men wearing the American uniform faced ten times their number of armed foes, bent on carrying out the atrocious threat of the Colombian commander, that prevented a murderous catastrophe. At Panama, when the revolution broke out, there was no American man-of-war and no American troops of sailors. At Colon, Commander Hubbard acted with entire impartiality towards both sides, preventing any movement, whether by the Colombians or the Panamans, which would tend to produce bloodshed. On November 9 he prevented a body of the revolutionists from landing at Colon. Throughout he behaved in the most creditable manner. In the New York Evening Post, under date of Panama, December 8, there is an article from a special correspondent, which sets forth in detail the unbearable oppression of the Colombian Government in Panama. In this article is an interesting interview with a native Panaman, which runs in part as follows:

"* * * We looked upon the building of the canal as a matter of life or death to us. We wanted that because it meant, with the United States in control of it, peace and prosperity for us. President

Marroquin appointed an Isthmian to be governor of Panama; and we looked upon that as of happy augury. Soon we heard that the canal treaty was not likely to be approved at Bogota; next we heard that our Isthmian governor, Obaldía, who had scarcely assumed power, was to be superseded by a soldier from Bogota. * * *

"Notwithstanding all that Colombia has drained us of in the way of revenues, she did not bridge for us a single river, nor make a single roadway, nor erect a single college where our children could be educated, nor do anything at all to advance our industries. * * * Well, when the new generals came we seized them, arrested them, and the town of Panama was in joy. Not a protest was made, except the shots fired from the Colombian gunboat *Bogota*, which killed one Chinese lying in his bed. We were willing to encounter the Colombian troops at Colon and fight it out; but the commander of the United States cruiser *Nashville* forbade Superintendent Shaler to allow the railroad to transport troops for either party. That is our story."

I call special attention to the concluding portion of this interview which states the willingness of the Panama people to fight the Colombian troops and the refusal of Commander Hubbard to permit them to use the railroad and therefore to get into a position where the fight could take place. It thus clearly appears that the fact that there was no bloodshed on the Isthmus was directly due—and only due—to the prompt and firm enforcement by the United States of its traditional policy. During the past forty years revolutions and attempts at revolution have succeeded one another with monotonous regularity on the Isthmus, and again and again United States sailors and marines have been landed as they were landed in this instance and under similar instructions to protect the transit. One of these revolutions resulted in three years of warfare; and the aggregate of bloodshed and misery caused by them has been incalculable. The fact that in this last revolution not a life was lost, save that of the man killed by the shells of the Colombian gunboat, and no property destroyed, was due to the action which I have described. We, in effect, policed the Isthmus in the interest of its inhabitants and of our own national needs, and for the good of the entire civilized world. Failure to act as the Administration acted would have meant great waste of life, great suffering, great destruction of property; all of which was avoided by the firmness and prudence with which Commander Hubbard carried out his orders and prevented either party from attacking the other. Our action was for the peace both of Colombia and of Panama. It is earnestly to be hoped that there will be no unwise conduct on our part which may encourage Colombia to embark on a war which can not result in her regaining control of the Isthmus, but which may cause much bloodshed and suffering.

I hesitate to refer to the injurious insinuations which have been made of complicity by this Government in the revolutionary movement in Panama. They are as destitute of foundation as of propriety. The only excuse for my mentioning them is the fear lest unthinking persons might mistake for acquiescence the silence of mere self-respect. I think proper to say, therefore, that no one connected with this Government had any part in preparing, inciting, or encouraging the late revolution on the Isthmus of Panama, and that save from the reports of our military and naval officers, given above, no one connected with this Government had any previous knowledge of the revolution except such as was accessible to any person of ordinary intelligence who read the newspapers and kept up a current acquaintance with public affairs.

By the unanimous action of its people, without the firing of a shot— with a unanimity hardly before recorded in any similar case—the people of Panama declared themselves an independent Republic. Their recognition by this Government was based upon a state of facts in no way dependent for its justification upon our action in ordinary cases. I have not denied, nor do I wish to deny, either the validity or the propriety of the general rule that a new state should not be recognized as independent till it has shown its ability to maintain its independence. This rule is derived from the principle of nonintervention, and as a corollary of that principle has generally been observed by the United States. But, like the principle from which it is deduced, the rule is subject to exceptions; and there are in my opinion clear and imperative reasons why a departure from it was justified and even required in the present instance. These reasons embrace, first, our treaty rights; second, our national interests and safety; and, third, the interests of collective civilization.

I have already adverted to the treaty of 1846, by the thirty-fifth article of which the United States secured the right to a free and open transit across the Isthmus of Panama, and to that end agreed to guarantee to New Granada her rights of sovereignty and property over that territory. This article is sometimes discussed as if the latter guarantee constituted its sole object and bound the United Sates to protect the sovereignty of New Granada against domestic revolution. Nothing, however, could be more erroneous than this supposition. That our wise and patriotic ancestors, with all their dread of entangling alliances, would have entered into a treaty with New Granada solely or even primarily for the purpose of enabling that remnant of the original Republic of Colombia, then resolved into the State of New Granada, Venezuela, and Ecuador, to continue from Bogota to rule over the Isthmus of Panama, is a conception that would in itself be incredible, even if the contrary did not clearly appear. It is true that since the treaty was made the United States has again and again been obliged forcibly to intervene for the preservation of order and the maintenance of an open transit, and that this intervention has usually operated to the advantage of the titular Government of Colombia, but it is equally true that the United States in intervening, with or without Colombia's consent, for the protection of the transit, has disclaimed any duty to defend the Colombian Government against domestic insurrection or against the erection of an independent government on the Isthmus of Panama. The attacks against which the United States engaged to protect New Granadian sovereignty were those of foreign powers; but this engagement was only a means to the accomplishment of a yet more important end. The great design of the article was to assure the dedication of the Isthmus to the purposes of free and unobstructed interoceanic transit, the consummation of which would be found in an interoceanic canal. To the accomplishment of this object the Government of the United States had for years directed its diplomacy. It occupied a place in the instructions to our delegates to the Panama Congress during the Administration of John Quincy Adams. It formed the subject of a resolution of the Senate in 1835, and of the House of Representatives in 1839. In 1846 its importance had become still more apparent by reason of the Mexican war. If the treaty of 1846 did not in terms bind New Granada to grant reasonable concessions for the construction of means of interoceanic communication, it was only because it was not imagined that such concessions would ever be withheld. As it was expressly agreed that the United States, in consideration of its onerous guarantee of New Granadian sovereignty, should possess the right of free and open transit on any modes of communication that might be constructed, the obvious intent of the treaty rendered it unnecessary, if not superfluous, in terms to stipulate that permission for the construction of such modes of communication should not be denied.

Long before the conclusion of the Hay-Herran treaty the course of events had shown that a canal to connect the Atlantic and Pacific oceans must be built by the United States or not at all. Experience had demonstrated that private enterprise was utterly inadequate for the purpose; and a fixed policy, declared by the United States on many memorable occasions, and supported by the practically unanimous voice of American opinion, had rendered it morally impossible that the work should be undertaken by European powers, either single or in combination. Such were the universally recognized conditions on which the legislation of the Congress was based, and on which the late negotiations with Colombia were begun and concluded. Nevertheless, when the well-considered agreement was rejected by Colombia and the revolution on the Isthmus ensued, one of Colombia's first acts was to invoke the intervention of the United States; nor does her invitation appear to have been confined to this Government alone. By a telegram from Mr. Beaupré, our minister at Bogota, of the 7th of November last, we were informed that General Reyes would soon leave Panama invested with full powers; that he had telegraphed the President of Mexico to ask the Government of the United States and all countries represented at the Pan-American Conference "to aid Colombia to preserve her integrity;" and that he had requested that the Government of the United States should meanwhile "preserve the neutrality and transit of the Isthmus" and should "not recognize the new Government." In another telegram from Mr. Beaupré, which was sent later in the day, this Government was asked whether it would take action "to maintain Colombian right and sovereignty on the Isthmus in accordance with article 35 [of] the treaty of 1846" in case the Colombian Government should be "entirely unable to suppress the secession movement there." Here was a direct solicitation to the United States to intervene for the purpose of suppressing, contrary to the treaty of 1846 as this Government has uniformly construed it, a new revolt against Colombia's authority brought about by her own refusal to permit the fulfillment of the great design for which that treaty was made. It was under these circumstances that the United States, instead of using its forces to destroy those who sought to make the engagement of the treaty a reality, recognized them as the proper custodians of the sovereignty of the Isthmus.

This recognition was, in the second place, further justified by the highest considerations of our national interests and safety. In all the range of our international relations, I do not hesitate to affirm that there is nothing of greater or more pressing importance than the construction of an interoceanic canal. Long acknowledged to be essential to our commercial development, it has become, as the result of the recent extension of our territorial dominion, more than ever essential to our national self-defense. In transmitting to the Senate the treaty of 1846, President Polk pointed out as the principal reason for its ratification that the passage of the Isthmus, which it was designed to secure, "would relieve us from a long and dangerous navigation of more than 9,000 miles around Cape Horn, and render our communication with our own possessions on the northwest coast of America comparatively easy and speedy." The events of the past five years have given to this consideration an importance immeasurably greater than it possessed in 1846. In the light of our present situation, the establishment of easy and speedy communication by sea between the Atlantic and the Pacific presents itself not simply as something to be desired, but as an object to be positively and promptly attained. Reasons of convenience have been superseded by reasons of vital necessity, which do not admit of indefinite delays.

To such delays the rejection by Colombia of the Hay-Herran treaty directly exposed us. As proof of this fact I need only refer to the programme outlined in the report of the majority of the Panama canal committee, read in the Colombian Senate on the 14th of October last. In this report, which recommended that the discussion of a law to authorize the Government to enter upon new negotiations should be indefinitely postponed, it is proposed that the consideration of the subject should be deferred till October 31, 1904, when the next Colombian Congress should have met in ordinary session. By that time, as the report goes on to say, the extension of time granted to the New Panama Canal Company by treaty in 1893 would have expired, and the new Congress would be in a position to take up the question whether the company had not, in spite of further extensions that had been granted by legislative acts, forfeited all its property and rights. "When that time arrives," the report significantly declares, "the Republic, without any impediment, will be able to contract, and will be in more clear, more definite, and more advantageous possession, both legally and materially." The naked meaning of this report is that Colombia proposed to wait until, by the enforcement of a forfeiture repugnant to the ideas of justice which obtain in every civilized nation, the property and rights of the New Panama Canal Company could be confiscated.

Such is the scheme to which it was proposed that the United States should be invited to become a party. The construction of the canal was to be relegated to the indefinite future, while Colombia was, by reason of her own delay, to be placed in the "more advantageous" position of claiming not merely the compensation to be paid by the United States for the privilege of completing the canal, but also the forty millions authorized by the act of 1902 to be paid for the property of the New Panama Canal Company. That the attempt to carry out this scheme would have brought Colombia into conflict with the Government of France can not be doubted; nor could the United States have counted upon immunity from the consequences of the attempt, even apart from the indefinite delays to which the construction of the canal was to be subjected. On the first appearance of danger to Colombia, this Government would have been summoned to interpose, in order to give effect to the guarantees of the treaty of 1846; and all this in support of a plan which, while characterized in its first stage by the wanton disregard of our own highest interests, was fitly to end in further injury to the citizens of a friendly nation, whose enormous losses in their generous efforts to pierce the Isthmus have become a matter of history.

In the third place, I confidently maintain that the recognition of the Republic of Panama was an act justified by the interests of collective civilization. If ever a government could be said to have received a mandate from civilization to effect an object the accomplishment of which was demanded in the interest of mankind, the United State holds that position with regard to the interoceanic canal. Since our purpose to build the canal was definitely announced there have come from all quarters assurances of approval and encouragement, in which even Colombia herself at one time participated; and to general assurances were added specific acts and declarations. In order that no obstacle might stand in our way, Great Britain renounced important rights under the Clayton-Bulwer treaty and agreed to its abrogation, receiving in return nothing but our honorable pledge to build the canal and protect it as an open highway. It was in view of this pledge, and of the proposed enactment by the Congress of the United States of legislation to give it immediate effect, that the second Pan-American Conference, at the City of Mexico, on January 22, 1902, adopted the following resolution:

"The Republics assembled at the International Conference of Mexico applaud the purpose of the United States Government to construct an interoceanic canal, and acknowledge that this work will not only be worthy of the greatness of the American people, but also in the highest sense a work of civilization, and to the greatest degree beneficial to the development of commerce between the American States and the other countries of the world."

Among those who signed this resolution on behalf of their respective governments was General Reyes, the delegate of Colombia. Little could it have been foreseen that two years later the Colombian Government, led astray by false allurements of selfish advantage, and forgetful alike of its international obligations and of the duties and responsibilities of sovereignty, would thwart the efforts of the United States to enter upon and complete a work which the nations of America, re-echoing the sentiment of the nations of Europe, had pronounced to be not only "worthy of the greatness of the American people," but also "in the highest sense a work of civilization."

That our position as the mandatary of civilization has been by no means misconceived is shown by the promptitude with which the powers have, one after another, followed our lead in recognizing Panama as an independent State. Our action in recognizing the new Republic has been followed by like recognition on the part of France, Germany, Denmark, Russia, Sweden and Norway, Nicaragua, Peru, China, Cuba, Great Britain, Italy, Costa Rica, Japan, and Austria-Hungary.

In view of the manifold considerations of treaty right and obligation, of national interest and safety, and of collective civilization, by which our Government was constrained to act, I am at a loss to comprehend the attitude of those who can discern in the recognition of the Republic of Panama only a general approval of the principle of "revolution" by which a given government is overturned or one portion of a country separated from another. Only the amplest justification can warrant a revolutionary movement of either kind. But there is no fixed rule which can be applied to all such movements. Each case must be judged on its own merits. There have been many revolutionary movements, many movements for the dismemberment of countries, which were evil, tried by any standard. But in my opinion no disinterested and fair-minded observer acquainted with the circumstances can fail to feel that Panama had the amplest justification for separation from Colombia under the conditions existing, and, moreover, that its action was in the highest degree beneficial to the interests of the entire civilized world by securing the immediate opportunity for the building of the interoceanic canal. It would be well for those who are pessimistic as to our action in peacefully recognizing the Republic of Panama, while we lawfully protected the transit from invasion and disturbances, to recall what has been done in Cuba, where we intervened even by force on general grounds of national interest and duty. When we interfered it was freely prophesied that we intended to keep Cuba and administer it for our own interests. The result has demonstrated in singularly conclusive fashion the falsity of these prophecies. Cuba is now an independent Republic. We governed it in its own interests for a few years, till it was able to stand alone, and then started it upon its career of self-government and independence, granting it all necessary aid. We have received from Cuba a grant of two naval stations, so situated that they in no possible way menace the liberty of the island, and yet serve as important defenses for the Cuban people, as well as for our own people, against possible foreign attack. The people of Cuba have been immeasurably benefited by our interference in their behalf, and our own gain has been great. So it will be with Panama. The people of the Isthmus, and as I firmly believe of the adjacent parts of Central and South America, will be greatly benefited by the building of the canal and the guarantee of peace and order along its line; and hand in hand with the benefit to them will go the benefit to us and to mankind. By our prompt and decisive action, not only have our interests and those of the world at large been conserved, but we have forestalled complications which were likely to be fruitful in loss to ourselves and in bloodshed and suffering to the people of the Isthmus.

Instead of using our forces, as we were invited by Colombia to do, for the twofold purpose of defeating our own rights and interests and the interests of the civilized world, and of compelling the submission of the people of the Isthmus to those whom they regarded as oppressors, we shall, as in duty bound, keep the transit open and prevent its invasion. Meanwhile, the only question now before us is that of the ratification of the treaty. For it is to be remembered that a failure to ratify the treaty will not undo what has been done, will not restore Panama to Colombia, and will not alter our obligation to keep the transit open across the Isthmus, and to prevent any outside power from menacing this transit.

It seems to have been assumed in certain quarters that the proposition that the obligations of article 35 of the treaty of 1846 are to be considered as adhering to and following the sovereignty of the Isthmus, so long as that sovereignty is not absorbed by the United States, rests upon some novel theory. No assumption could be further from the fact. It is by no means true that a state in declaring its independence rids itself of all the treaty obligations entered into by the parent government. It is a mere coincidence that this question was once raised in a case involving the obligations of Colombia as an independent state under a treaty which Spain had made with the United States many years before Spanish-American independence. In that case Mr. John Quincy Adams, Secretary of State, in an instruction to Mr. Anderson, our minister to Colombia, of May 27, 1823, said:

"By a treaty between the United States and Spain concluded at the time when Colombia was a part of the Spanish dominions * * * the principle that free ships make free goods was expressly recognized and established. It is asserted that by her declaration of independence Colombia has been entirely released from all the obligations by which, as a part of the Spanish nation, she was bound to other nations. This principle is not tenable. To all the engagements of Spain with other nations, affecting their rights and interests, Colombia, so far as she was affected by them, remains bound in honor and in justice. The stipulation now referred to is of that character."

The principle thus asserted by Mr. Adams was afterwards sustained by an international commission in respect to the precise stipulation to which he referred; and a similar position was taken by the United States with regard to the binding obligation upon the independent State of Texas of commercial stipulations embodied in prior treaties between the United States and Mexico when Texas formed a part of the latter country. But in the present case it is unnecessary to go so far. Even if it be admitted that prior treaties of a political and commercial complexion generally do not bind a new state formed by separation, it is undeniable that stipulations having a local application to the territory embraced in the new state continue in force and are binding upon the new sovereign. Thus it is on all hands conceded that treaties relating to boundaries and to rights of navigation continue in force without regard to changes in government or in sovereignty. This principle obviously applies to that part of the treaty of 1846 which relates to the Isthmus of Panama.

In conclusion let me repeat that the question actually before this Government is not that of the recognition of Panama as an independent republic. That is already an accomplished fact. The question, and the only question, is whether or not we shall build an isthmian canal.

I transmit herewith copies of the latest notes from the minister of the Republic of Panama to this Government, and of certain notes which have passed between the special envoy of the Republic of Colombia and this Government.

THEODORE ROOSEVELT.

DEPARTMENT OF STATE,
Washington, January 4, 1904.

The PRESIDENT:

The undersigned, Acting Secretary of State, has the honor to lay before the President copies of the notes exchanged between General Reyes and the Secretary of State concerning this Government's attitude in case Colombian troops should be sent to the Republic of Panama; also copies of two notes addressed to this Department by the minister of the Republic of Panama at this capital, the first stating that it is the purpose of the Government of that Republic, as soon as its independence shall have been recognized by the Government of the Republic of Colombia, to assume a portion of the exterior debt of Colombia proportionate to the relative populations of the two Republics; the second in regard to the method of payment of the $10,000,000, the payment of which by the United States to Panama is stipulated by the convention concluded between them on November 18, 1903.

Respectfully submitted,   FRANCIS B. LOOMIS,
                                           Acting Secretary.

[TRANSLATION.]
LEGATION OF COLOMBIA ON SPECIAL MISSION,

ARLINGTON HOTEL,
Washington, D. C., December 8, 1903.

Mr. SECRETARY: I have the honor to address your excellency for the purpose of stating respectfully that I have received from my Government instructions to inquire what attitude would be assumed by the Government of the United States in the event which may take place of

Colombian troops or forces under the Colombian flag making their appearance on the isthmus, or attempting a landing on that territory, for the defense of the sovereignty and integrity of Colombia, and respecting the railroad line and the terminal points in accordance with the stipulation of the treaty of 1846, which my country is ever ready to observe.

I salute your excellency with my distinguished consideration.

RAFAEL REYES.

Hon. JOHN HAY,
    Secretary of State of the United States,
        Department of State.

No. 1.]
                              DEPARTMENT OF STATE,
                        Washington, December 11, 1903.

SIR: I beg leave to acknowledge your communication of December 8, in which you state that you have been directed by your Government to ask "what attitude would be assumed by the Government of the United States in the event, which may take place, of Colombian troops or forces under the Colombian flag making their appearance on the Isthmus, or attempting a landing in that territory for the defense of the sovereignty and integrity of Colombia, and respecting the railroad line and the terminal points, in accordance with the stipulation of the treaty of 1846, which my country is ever ready to observe."

I have quoted your question textually, and in reference to it I am instructed by the President to bring to the attention of your excellency the following facts: That the Republic of Panama proclaimed its independence on the 3d of last month; that in consequence of this movement the independence of Panama has been recognized by this Government and by many others; that a treaty has been signed between the United States and Panama, which has been ratified by the latter State and is now waiting ratification by the American Senate; that by the provisions of the said treaty the United States agrees to maintain the independence of the Republic of Panama; that although the treaty has not yet become law by the action of the Senate, there are already inchoate rights and duties created by it which place the responsibility of preserving peace and order on the isthmus in the hands of the Government of the United States and of Panama, even if such responsibilities were not imposed by the historical events of the last fifty years.

In view of these facts I am instructed to say to your excellency that the Government of the United States would regard with the gravest concern any invasion of the territory of Panama by Colombian troops. for the reason that bloodshed and disorder would inev-

218

itably result throughout the whole extent of the Isthmus, and for the broader reason that, in the opinion of the President, the time has come, in the interest of universal commerce and civilization, to close the chapter of sanguinary and ruinous civil war in Panama.

I have the honor to be, sir, your obedient servant,

Gen. RAFAEL REYES, *Etc.* JOHN HAY.

DEPARTMENT OF STATE,
Washington, December 30, 1903.

DEAR MR. MINISTER: I have received the letter which you have done me the honor to address me under date of yesterday, in which, obeying the instructions of your Government, you ask me to say whether the invasion of the territory of the Republic of Panama by Colombian soldiers will be considered by the United States as a declaration of war.

I beg to remind your excellency that when, on the 8th of December, you addressed a similar question to this Department I replied on the 11th, reciting the following facts:

"That the Republic of Panama proclaimed its independence on the 3d of last month; that, in consequence of this movement, the independence of Panama has been recognized by this Government and by many others; that a treaty has been signed between the United States and Panama which has been ratified by the latter State and is now awaiting ratification by the American Senate; that by the provisions of the said treaty the United States agrees to maintain the independence of the Republic of Panama; that although the treaty has not yet become a law by the action of the Senate, there are already inchoate rights and duties created by it which place the responsibility of preserving peace and order on the Isthmus in the hands of the Government of the United States and of Panama, even if such responsibility were not imposed by the historical events of the last fifty years."

I then had the honor to inform you that—

"The Government of the United States would regard with the gravest concern any invasion of the territory of Panama by Colombian troops, for the reason that bloodshed and disorder would inevitably result throughout the whole extent of the Isthmus, and for the broader reason that, in the opinion of the President, the time has come, in the interest of universal commerce and civilization, to close the chapter of sanguinary and ruinous civil war in Panama."

In reply to your question received yesterday, I can only reiterate what I had the honor to say on the 11th of this month, and to add that the time which has elapsed since then has only tended to deepen the painful impression which would be created in this country by the armed invasion of Panaman territory by Colombian troops, and the sense of the responsibility which would thereby be imposed on the Government of the United States; but that the formal action we should take upon such a cintingency must be determined by the circumstances of the case. I am instructed further to inform you that this Government has only the friendliest intentions toward Colombia, and will not lightly be provoked into assuming a hostile attitude toward that Republic.

I have, etc.,   JOHN HAY.

Gen. RAFAEL REYES, *Etc.*

The Minister of Panama to the Secretary of State.

THE LEGATION OF THE REPUBLIC OF PANAMA,
Washington, D. C., December 31, 1903.

DEAR SIR: The treaty of the 18th of November, 1903, provides for the payment to the Republic of Panama of the sum of $10,000,000 after the exchange of ratifications.

The Government of the Republic of Panama has always been anxious to insure a proper and useful employment of said sum. The delegates of the government, Doctor Amador and Señor Don Frederico Boyd have repeatedly told me that the principle which the government intended to carry out for the employment of said sum was, not to invest any part of the capital in anything but consistent works which would permanently represent the counter value of the expenses incurred.

According to this principle the Government expressed the desire to take only $2,000,000 out of the $10,000,000 from the United States Treasury after exchange of ratifications, leaving the remaining $8,000,000 in the United States Treasury to be later on employed according to the necessities of the future and to the principle which I explained above.

At the same time the Government desired that this sum should be productive of interest in order to help to obtain the equilibrium of the budget.

According to the recommendations that were made to me by the Government of the Republic, I was requested to ask the Government of the United States if it would accept to pay an interest of 3 per cent on the sum remaining in its hands out of the total sum of $10,000,000 provided for in the treaty of the 18th of November.

The interest to be paid on the $8,000,000 that the Government intends now to leave in the American Treasury would be $240,000.

The expression of this desire of my Government came by mail after the signature of the treaty, and I did not feel justified at that moment to call your attention to this point on account of the more important matters which required your attention, but now that the situation has progressed and that the Treasury Department may be considering the measures to be taken in the event of a prompt ratification of the treaty, I feel justified in submitting the case to your excellency so that if the United States Government thinks the intentions of the Republic of Panama in harmony with its own, a special convention may be drafted to settle this particular point.

I am, sir, with great respect, your very obedient servant,

P. BUNAU VARILLA.

His Excellency JOHN HAY,
Secretary of State, Washington, D. C.

The Minister of Panama to the Secretary of State.

LEGATION OF THE REPUBLIC OF
PANAMA AT WASHINGTON,
Washington, D. C., December 31, 1903.

DEAR SIR: I have the honor of bringing to your knowledge that by a telegram received during the night of the 21st of December, I have been authorized by my Government to declare that the Republic of Panama, as soon as its independence shall be recognized by the Republic of Colombia, intends to assume a part of Colombia's exterior debt of which the principal was settled at £2,000,000 by special convention, and which is now accrued by the unpaid interest. The Republic of Panama has determined that the proportion of that debt it is ready to assume will be equal to the proportion between its population and the population of Colombia, a proportion which is not very far from 1 to 15.

I beg, sir, to call your attention to the fact that the Government of the Republic of Panama, in making such declaration, is actuated by the desire of showing its good faith and its liberality toward the citizens of foreign countries who may think they have a just claim against it rather than by the sentiment that by right they owe any part of the Colombian debt.

The distribution, according to the number of inhabitants of the two Republics, would be just only if it could be established, which is generally the case, that the money has been employed for the common utility of all the parts of the Republic and that Panama has enjoyed its share of it. On the contrary, this distribution is not just and ought not to be made in strict right if, as is the case, no part of the loans were ever employed for the benefit of the State of Panama, now the Republic of Panama. Since its union to greater Colombia, for the liberation of which said loans were made, the State of Panama has never received any money from the mother country, but, on the contrary, it has sent to it very important sums, and one can say, as a rule, that the funds never went from Bogota to Panama, but always from Panama to Bogota. It will be easy to establish that the Department of Panama is the creditor of Colombia and not its debtor and that, therefore, it does not owe to Colombia anything either for its external debt or from any other cause.

This would have been a substantial and legal ground for non-assumption of any part of the Colombian debt, but, as I had the honor of stating to you, the Government of the Republic has felt itself bound to justify, not by arguments, but by facts, the testimony of confidence, esteem, and good will which have come from all the governments of the greatest nations of earth since the recent date of its birth.

I am, sir, with great respect, your very obedient servant,

P. BUNAU VARILLA.

His Excellency JOHN HAY,
    Secretary of State, Washington, D. C.

WHITE HOUSE, *January 7, 1904.*
To the Senate and House of Representatives:

I transmit herewith a report from the Acting Secretary of State covering a statement showing the receipts and disbursements of the Louisiana Purchase Exposition Company for the month of November, 1903, together with a summary of the receipts and disbursements of the company from its incorporation to November 30, 1903, furnished by the Louisiana Purchase Exposition Commission in pursuance of section 11 of the "Act to provide for celebrating the one hundredth anniversary of the purchase of the Louisiana territory," etc., approved March 3, 1901.

THEODORE ROOSEVELT.

WHITE HOUSE, *January 11, 1904.*
To the Senate and House of Representatives:

I transmit herewith a report by the Secretary of Agriculture of the operations of the Bureau of Animal Industry of that Department for the fiscal year ended June 30, 1903, in compliance with the requirements of section 11 of the act approved May 29, 1884, for the establishment of that Bureau.

THEODORE ROOSEVELT.

WHITE HOUSE, *January 12, 1904.*
To the Senate and House of Representatives:

I transmit a report by the Acting Secretary of State, with accompanying papers, in regard to the application of the British Embassy in behalf of Messrs. Gordon, Ironsides & Fares Company (Limited), of Canada, for reimbursement of $7,626.08, which they allege the

United States customs authorities improperly exacted of them in November, 1902, as duties on certain sheep and cattle.

In view of the facts as recited by the Acting Secretary of State and shown in the correspondence, I recommend that provision be made for the company's reimbursement.

THEODORE ROOSEVELT.

WHITE HOUSE, *January 12, 1904.*

To the Senate:

In response to the resolution of the Senate of December 19, 1903, requesting the President, "if not incompatible with the public interests, to transmit to the Senate a list of any claims now pending in the Department of State by British subjects against the United States, or of citizens of the United States against Great Britain," I transmit herewith a report from the Acting Secretary of State covering the list called for.

THEODORE ROOSEVELT

WHITE HOUSE, *January 12, 1904.*

To the Senate and House of Representatives:

I transmit herewith a report from the Acting Secretary of State, with inclosure from the ambassador of the French Republic, relative to the desire of certain French citizens to present to this Government a reproduction of the bust of Washington by David d'Angers, which the donors wish to be placed in the Capitol.

I recommend that Congress accept this gift by joint resolution and that suitable provisions be made for its ceremonial installation.

THEODORE ROOSEVELT.

JOINT RESOLUTION OF BOTH HOUSES.

Whereas Count de Rochambeau, Marquis de Lafayette, Marquis de Grasse, Mr. Henry Jouin, and other citizens of France have tendered to the Government of the United States a reproduction of the bust of Washington by David d'Angers, which was destroyed in the fire at the Capitol in 1851, to be placed in the Capitol of the United States: Therefore,

Resolved, etc., That said gift is hereby accepted in the name of the people of the United States, and the thanks of Congress are tendered to the donors therefor.

SEC. 2. That the Joint Committee on the Library are hereby instructed to make arrangements for the formal presentation of said gift to Congress on a day to be hereafter fixed by said committee, and that said committee shall cause said bust to be placed in an appropriate and conspicuous place in the Capitol building.

SEC. 3. That the Secretary of State be directed to transmit a copy of this joint resolution to the donors, through the Government of the French Republic.

WHITE HOUSE, *January 15, 1904.*

To the Senate and House of Representatives:

I transmit herewith a petition to the President of the United States to aid in preserving the Calaveras groves of big trees, submitted by the Calaveras Big Tree Committee and the citizens of California and elsewhere.

I cordially recommend it to the favorable consideration of the Congress. The Calaveras Big Tree Grove is not only a Californian, but a national inheritance, and all that can be done by the Government to insure its preservation should be done.

THEODORE ROOSEVELT.

WHITE HOUSE, *January 18, 1904.*

To the Senate and House of Representatives:

I transmit herewith for the information of the Congress a report from the Secretary of State covering copies of additional papers bearing upon the relations of the United States with Colombia and the Republic of Panama.

THEODORE ROOSEVELT.

WHITE HOUSE, *January 20, 1904.*

To the Senate and House of Representatives:

I transmit herewith a report from the Secretary of State, with accompanying papers, relating to the claim of Messrs. Sivewright, Bacon & Co., of Manchester, England, British subjects, for compensation for damages sustained by their vessel, the British steamship *Eastry,* in consequence of collisions, in June, 1901, at Manila, with certain coal hulks belonging to the United States Government.

I recommend that, as an act of equity and comity, provision be made by the Congress for reimbursement to the firm of the money expended by it in making the repairs to the ship which the collisions rendered necessary.

THEODORE ROOSEVELT.

WHITE HOUSE, *January 27, 1904*

To the Senate and House of Representatives:

I transmit herewith a communication from the Secretary of Commerce and Labor submitting a preliminary report of the Alaska Salmon Commission, appointed in accordance with the instructions in my letter of November 8, 1902.

THEODORE ROOSEVELT.

WHITE HOUSE, *January 27, 1904.*

To the Senate:

In response to the resolution of the Senate of January 18, 1904, requesting the President, "if not in his opinion incompatible with the public interest, to inform the Senate whether any report has been made to the Treasury Department by L. Cullom, special agent of the Treasury, with respect to the conduct of A. R. Cruzen, collector of customs in Porto Rico, and if so, to transmit the same to the Senate with a statement of what action, if any, has been taken thereon," I send herewith the accompanying letter from the Secretary of the Treasury. For the reasons therein given I deem it incompatible with the public interest to forward the report by the special agent of the Treasury in question.

THEODORE ROOSEVELT.

WHITE HOUSE, *January 28, 1904.*

To the Senate and House of Representatives:

I herewith lay before the Congress a letter from the Polish organizations of the United States, and the report thereon from Col. Thomas W. Symons, Superintendent of Public Buildings and Grounds. In view of the recommendation of Colonel Symons I advise that the very patriotic offer of the Polish organizations be accepted, and that instead of the statue of Pulaski (which, in the judgment of his Polish compatriots should be an equestrian statue, and which it is now proposed to place in reservation 33, on the north side of Pennsylvania avenue, between Thirteenth and Fourteenth streets), there be a pedestrian statue of Kosciusko accepted by the Government, to be placed on one of the four corners of Lafayette Square. These four corners would thus ultimately be occupied by statues of Lafayette, Rochambeau, Von Steuben, and Kosciusko, all of whom in the stormy days which saw the birth of the Republic rendered service which can never be forgotten by our people.

THEODORE ROOSEVELT.

WHITE HOUSE, *February 1, 1904.*

To the Senate and House of Representatives:

I transmit herewith, for the information of the Congress, a letter from the Secretary of War, dated January 28, 1904, accompanied by the annual report of the Philippine Commission, dated December 23, 1903, and the appendixes thereto, submitted in compliance with the provisions of the act of Congress entitled "An act temporarily to provide for the administration of the affairs of civil government in the Philippines, and for other purposes," approved July 1, 1902, and the act entitled "An act making appropriation for sundry civil expenses of the Government for the fiscal year ending June 30, 1904, and for other purposes," approved March 3, 1903.

THEODORE ROOSEVELT.

WHITE HOUSE, *February 3, 1904.*

To the Senate:

In response to the resolution of the Senate of January 22, 1904, I transmit herewith reports from the Acting Secretary of State and the Secretary of the Navy, with accompanying papers.

The correspondence since November 16, 1902, referred to in the letter of the Secretary of the Navy, which has not already been transmitted to the Senate, has no reference to the matters covered by the resolution and deals with military movements, and it is for that reason deemed incompatible with the public interest to make it public at this time.

THEODORE ROOSEVELT.

WHITE HOUSE, *February 5, 1904.*

To the Senate and House of Representatives:

I transmit herewith the annual report of the Office of Experiment Stations, prepared under the direction of the Secretary of Agriculture, which includes a report on the work and expenditures of the agricultural experiment stations in the United States for the fiscal year ended June 30, 1903, in accordance with the act making appropriations for the Department of Agriculture for the said fiscal year.

The attention of the Congress is called to the request of the Secretary of Agriculture that 5,000 copies of the report be printed for the use of the Department of Agriculture, and that provision be made to print such a report annually.

THEODORE ROOSEVELT

WHITE HOUSE, *February 9, 1904.*

To the House of Representatives:

I transmit herewith the response of the Secretary of State to the resolution adopted by the House of Representatives on January 25, 1904, calling for information in regard to carriages, horses, etc., maintained at Government expense by the Department of State.

THEODORE ROOSEVELT.

WHITE HOUSE, *February 11, 1904.*

To the Senate and House of Representatives:

I transmit herewith a report from the Secretary of State covering a statement showing the receipts and disbursements of the Louisiana Purchase Exposition Company for the month of December, 1903, furnished by the Louisiana Purchase Exposition Commission in pursuance of section 11 of the "Act to provide for celebrating the one hundredth anniversary of the purchase of the Louisiana territory," etc., approved March 3, 1901.

THEODORE ROOSEVELT.

WHITE HOUSE, *February 24, 1904.*

To the Senate:

In response to the resolution of the Senate of February 18, 1904, as follows:

"*Resolved,* That the President is requested, if not incompatible with the public interests, to send to the Senate such information as is in possession of the Government of the United States as to the present state of organization of the Government of the Republic of Panama.

"And a copy of the constitution of said Republic, or such information as to the provisions thereof as may have been received by him.

"And that he will inform the Senate as to any ordinance, or other proceeding of the constitutional convention recently in session at Panama, relating to the Hay-Varilla treaty now pending in the Senate."

I transmit herewith a report from the Secretary of State on the subject.

THEODORE ROOSEVELT.

WHITE HOUSE, *February 29, 1904.*

To the Senate:

In compliance with the resolution of the Senate of the 26th instant (the House of Representatives concurring), I return herewith Senate bill No. 167, entitled "An act granting an increase of pension to J. Hudson Kibbe."

THEODORE ROOSEVELT.

WHITE HOUSE, *March 2, 1904.*

To the Senate:

I transmit herewith a report by the Secretary of State furnishing the information concerning the Red Cross Society in foreign countries requested by the Senate resolution of January 19, 1904.

THEODORE ROOSEVELT.

WHITE HOUSE, *March 2, 1904.*

To the Senate:

In compliance with the resolution of the Senate of the 1st instant (the House of Representatives concurring), I return herewith Senate bill No. 2323, entitled "An act relating to ceded lands on the Fort Hall Indian Reservation."

THEODORE ROOSEVELT.

WHITE HOUSE, *March 7, 1904.*

To the Senate and House of Representatives:

I submit herewith the preliminary report of the Public Lands Commission appointed by me October 22, 1903, to report upon the condition, operation, and effect of the present land laws, and to recommend such changes as are needed to effect the largest practicable disposition of the public lands to actual settlers who will build permanent homes upon them, and to secure in permanence the fullest and most effective use of the resources of the public lands. The subject is one of such great importance and great intricacy that it is impossible for the Commission to report in full thereon at this time. It is now ready, however, to suggest certain changes in the law as set forth in the accompanying report. I commend these suggestions to the favorable consideration of the Congress.

THEODORE ROOSEVELT.

WHITE HOUSE, *March 7, 1904.*

To the Senate and House of Representatives:

I transmit herewith a letter from the Secretary of the Interior, with accompanying report of Charles J. Bonaparte and Clinton Rogers Woodruff, special inspectors, in the matter of alleged abuses and irregularities in the public service of the Indian Territory, and I call special attention to the condition of affairs in the Indian Territory as there set forth. In accordance with the recommendation of Messrs. Bonaparte and Woodruff, the members of the Commission to the Five Civilized Tribes have been informed that if they are to continue in the service they must at once cease all connection with business operations of any kind in the Territory where it is possible that their official positions could be of any effect upon their private business, even though no such effect be in fact shown.

What further action, if any, is to be taken in regard to the Commission or any of its members by the Executive will be determined upon after full consultation with the Secretary of the Interior and careful consideration of all the facts in the case. It will be noticed that the Secretary of the Interior does not believe that it would be possible, in accordance with the suggestions of Messrs. Bonaparte and Woodruff, to close up the work of the Commission this year and discontinue it accordingly. If it should be found to be possible, I would regard this as desirable, and invite the attention of the Congress to the matter.

I also inclose a memorandum of work of the Commission to the Five Civilized Tribes.

THEODORE ROOSEVELT.

WHITE HOUSE, *Washington, March 12, 1904.*

To the Senate:

I inclose herewith a report by the Secretary of State forwarding the correspondence and papers called for by the Senate resolution of December 8, 1903, in regard to the claims against Colombia known as the Colon "fire claims."

THEODORE ROOSEVELT.

WHITE HOUSE, *March 15, 1904.*

To the House of Representatives:

In compliance with the resolution of the House of Representatives of the 12th instant (the Senate concurring), I return herewith House bill No. 9791, entitled "An act granting a pension to Abram Claypool."

THEODORE ROOSEVELT

WHITE HOUSE, *Washington, March 15, 1904.*

To the Senate and House of Representatives:

I transmit herewith, for the information of Congress, a letter from the Secretary of State submitting a copy of the report of the commissioner appointed to carry out the resolution with respect to the Pan-

American Railway, adopted by the second international conference of American States, held in the City of Mexico during the winter of 1901-2.

THEODORE ROOSEVELT.

WHITE HOUSE, *March 15, 1904.*

To the Senate and House of Representatives:

I transmit herewith a report from the Secretary of State covering a statement showing the receipts and disbursements of the Louisiana Purchase Exposition Company for the month of January, 1904, furnished by the Louisiana Purchase Exposition Commission in pursuance of section 11 of the "act to provide for celebrating the one hundredth anniversary of the purchase of the Louisiana territory," etc., approved March 3, 1901.

THEODORE ROOSEVELT.

WHITE HOUSE, *March 16, 1904.*

To the Senate:

I transmit herewith a report from the Secretary of State, with accompanying papers, in further response to the Senate resolution of February 18, 1904, requesting information concerning the organization of the Government of the Republic of Panama.

THEODORE ROOSEVELT.

WHITE HOUSE, *March 17, 1904.*

To the Senate:

In compliance with a resolution of the Senate of the 15th instant (the House of Representatives concurring), I return herewith Senate bill No. 2323, entitled "An act relating to ceded lands on the Fort Hall Indian Reservation."

THEODORE ROOSEVELT.

WHITE HOUSE, *April 1, 1904.*

To the Senate and House of Representatives:

I transmit herewith for the information of the Congress a report on the progress of the beet-sugar industry in the United States during the year 1903, together with a letter from the Secretary of Agriculture relating to the same.

Your attention is invited to the recommendation of the Secretary that 10,000 copies of the report be printed for the use of the Department of Agriculture in addition to such number as may be desired for the use of the Senate and House of Representatives.

THEODORE ROOSEVELT.

WHITE HOUSE, *April 5, 1904.*

To the Senate and House of Representatives:

In further compliance with a provision of the act of Congress approved June 30, 1902, entitled "An act making appropriation for the support of the Army," I transmit herewith a supplementary statement showing additional expenditures for building materials in the United States to March 15, 1904, and for rents, repairs, and construction in the Philippine Islands to February 29, 1904.

THEODORE ROOSEVELT.

WHITE HOUSE, *April 7, 1904.*

To the Senate and House of Representatives:

I transmit herewith a report from the Secretary of State covering a statement showing the receipts and disbursements of the Louisiana Purchase Exposition Company for the month of February, 1904, furnished by the Louisiana Purchase Exposition Commission in pursuance of section 11 of the act to provide for celebrating the one hundredth anniversary of the purchase of the Louisiana territory, etc., approved March 3, 1901.

THEODORE ROOSEVELT.

WHITE HOUSE, *April 14, 1904.*

To the Senate and House of Representatives:

I transmit herewith a report from the Secretary of State, with accompanying papers, relating to the claim of William Radcliffe, a British subject, for compensation for the destruction of his fish hatchery and other property at the hands of a mob in Delta County, Colo., in the summer of 1901.

I recommend that, as an act of equity and comity, provision be made by the Congress for the payment of the sum of $25,000 to Mr. Radcliffe in full settlement of this claim.

THEODORE ROOSEVELT.

WHITE HOUSE, *April 22, 1904.*

To the Senate and House of Representatives:

I transmit herewith a communication from the Secretary of Commerce and Labor, accompanying the Commercial Relations of the United States for the year 1903, being the annual and other reports of consular and diplomatic officers upon the industries and commerce of foreign countries.

In view of the importance of these reports to our business interests, I approve the recommendation of the Secretary of Commerce and

Labor that Congress authorize the printing of an edition of 10,000 copies of the summary entitled "Review of the World's Commerce," and of 5,000 copies of Commercial Relations, including the summary, to be distributed by the Department of Commerce and Labor.

THEODORE ROOSEVELT.

PROCLAMATIONS

By the President of the United States of America.

A PROCLAMATION.

Whereas, the maintenance of light-houses and other aids to navigation in the Territory of Hawaii is necessary for the safe navigation of the waters thereof by the vessels of the Navy and of the merchant marine of the United States, and for the promotion of its commercial interests;

Now, therefore, I, Theodore Roosevelt, President of the United States, by virtue of the authority in me vested, and pursuant to Section 91 of the Act of April 30, 1900, entitled An Act to provide a government for the Territory of Hawaii, do hereby declare and proclaim that all the public property of the former government of the Republic of Hawaii ceded heretofore to the United States, consisting of light-houses and the public lands adjacent thereto and used in connection therewith, to the extent of five acres, or thereabout, adjacent to each light-house, when practicable to obtain so much, the exact location of said land and its metes and bounds to be hereafter determined and defined by the Light-House Board, light-vessels, light-house tenders, beacons, buoys, sea-marks and their appendages, and all apparatus, supplies and materials of all kinds provided therefor, and all the archives, books, documents, drawings, models, returns, and all other things appertaining to any light-house establishment maintained by the said government of the former Republic of Hawaii, be and hereby are taken for the uses and purposes of the United States, and the Department of Commerce and Labor, through the Light-House Board, is hereby charged with all administrative duties relating to the said light-house establishment.

In witness whereof, I have hereunto set my hand and caused the seal of the United States to be affixed.

Done at the City of Washington, this twenty-eighth day of December, in the year of our Lord one thousand nine hundred and three, and of the Independence of the United States the one hundred and twenty-eighth.

[SEAL.]

By the President: THEODORE ROOSEVELT.

Francis B. Loomis, *Acting Secretary of State.*

By the President of the United States of America.

A PROCLAMATION.

Whereas a state of war unhappily exists between Japan, on the one side, and Russia, on the other side;

And Whereas the United States are on terms of friendship and amity with both the contending powers, and with the persons inhabiting their several dominions;

And Whereas there are citizens of the United States residing within the territories or dominions of each of the said belligerents and carrying on commerce, trade, or other business or pursuits therein, protected by the faith of treaties;

And Whereas there are subjects of each of the said belligerents residing within the territory or jurisdiction of the United States, and carrying on commerce, trade, or other business or pursuits therein;

And Whereas the laws of the United States, without interfering with the free expression of opinion and sympathy, or with the open manufacture or sale of arms or munitions of war, nevertheless impose upon all persons who may be within their territory and jurisdiction the duty of an impartial neutrality during the existence of the contest;

And Whereas it is the duty of a neutral government not to permit or suffer the making of its waters subservient to the purposes of war;

Now, therefore, I, Theodore Roosevelt, President of the United States of America, in order to preserve the neutrality of the United States and of their citizens and of persons within their territory and jurisdiction, and to enforce their laws, and in order that all persons, being warned of the general tenor of the laws and treaties of the United States in this behalf, and of the law of nations, may thus be prevented from an unintentional violation of the same, do hereby declare and proclaim that by the act passed on the 20th day of April, A. D. 1818, commonly known as the "neutrality law", the following acts are forbidden to be done, under severe penalties, within the territory and jurisdiction of the United States, to wit:

1. Accepting and exercising a commission to serve either of the said belligerents by land or by sea against the other belligerent.

2. Enlisting or entering into the service of either of the said belligerents as a soldier, or as a marine, or seaman on board of any vessel of war, letter of marque, or privateer.

3. Hiring or retaining another person to enlist or enter himself in the service of either of the said belligerents as a soldier, or as a marine, or seaman on board of any vessel of war, letter of marque, or privateer.

4. Hiring another person to go beyond the limits or jurisdiction of the United States with intent to be enlisted as aforesaid.

5. Hiring another person to go beyond the limits of the United States with intent to be entered into service as aforesaid.

6. Retaining another person to go beyond the limits of the United States with intent to be enlisted as aforesaid.

7. Retaining another person to go beyond the limits of the United States with intent to be entered into service as aforesaid. (But the said act is not to be construed to extend to a citizen or subject of either belligerent who, being transiently within the United States, shall, on board of any vessel of war, which, at the time of its arrival within the United States, was fitted and equipped as such vessel of war, enlist or enter himself or hire or retain another subject or citizen of the same belligerent, who is transiently within the United States, to enlist or enter himself to serve such belligerent on board such vessel of war, if the United States shall then be at peace with such belligerent.)

8. Fitting out and arming, or attempting to fit out and arm, or procuring to be fitted out and armed, or knowingly being concerned in the furnishing, fitting out, or arming of any ship

or vessel with intent that such ship or vessel shall be employed in the service of either of the said belligerents.

9.   Issuing or delivering a commission within the territory or jurisdiction of the United States for any ship or vessel to the intent that she may be employed as aforesaid.

10.   Increasing or augmenting, or procuring to be increased or augmented, or knowingly being concerned in increasing or augmenting, the force of any ship of war, cruiser, or other armed vessel, which at the time of her arrival within the United States was a ship of war, cruiser, or armed vessel in the service of either of the said belligerents, or belonging to the subjects of either, by adding to the number of guns of such vessels, or by changing those on board of her for guns of a larger calibre, or by the addition thereto of any equipment solely applicable to war.

11.   Beginning or setting on foot or providing or preparing the means for any military expedition or enterprise to be carried on from the territory or jurisdiction of the United States against the territories or dominions of either of the said belligerents.

And I do hereby further declare and proclaim that any frequenting and use of the waters within the territorial jurisdiction of the United States by the armed vessels of either belligerent, whether public ships or privateers, for the purpose of preparing for hostile operations, or as posts of observations upon the ships of war or privateers or merchant vessels of the other belligerent lying within or being about to enter the jurisdiction of the United States, must be regarded as unfriendly and offensive, and in violation of that neutrality which it is the determination of this government to observe; and to the end that the hazard and inconvenience of such apprehended practices may be avoided, I further proclaim and declare that from and after the fifteenth day of February instant, and during the continuance of the present hostilities between Japan and Russia, no ship of war or privateer of either belligerent shall be permitted to make use of any port, harbor, roadstead, or waters subject to the jurisdiction of the United States from which a vessel of the other belligerent (whether the same shall be a ship of war, a privateer, or a merchant ship) shall have previously departed, until after the expiration of at least twenty-four hours from the departure of such last-mentioned vessel beyond the jurisdiction of the United States. If any ship of war or privateer of either belligerent shall, after the time this notification takes effect, enter any port, harbor, roadstead, or waters of the United States, such vessel shall be required to depart and to put to sea within twenty-four hours after her entrance into such port, harbor, roadstead, or waters, except in case of stress of weather or of her requiring provisions or things necessary for the subsistence of her crew, or for repairs; in either of which cases the authorities of the port or of the nearest port (as the case may be) shall require her to put to sea as soon as possible after the expiration of such period of twenty-four hours, without permitting her to take in supplies beyond what may be necessary for her immediate use; and no such vessel which may have been permitted to remain within the waters of the United States for the purpose of repair shall continue within such port, harbor, roadstead, or waters for a longer period than twenty-four hours after her necessary repairs shall have been completed, unless within such twenty-four hours a vessel, whether ship of war, privateer, or merchant ship of the other belligerent, shall have departed therefrom, in which case the time limited for the departure of such ship of war or privateer shall be extended so far as may be necessary to secure an interval of not less than twenty-four hours between such departure and that of any ship of war, privateer, or merchant ship of the other belligerent which may have previously quit the same port, harbor, roadstead, or waters. No ship of war or privateer of either belligerent shall be detained in any port, harbor, roadstead, or waters of the United States more than twenty-four hours, by reason of the successive departures from such port, harbor, roadstead, or waters of more than one vessel of the other belligerent. But if there be several vessels of each or either of the two belligerents in the same port, harbor, roadstead, or waters, the order of their departure therefrom shall be so arranged as to afford the opportunity of leaving alternately to the vessels of the respective belligerents, and to cause the least detention consistent with the objects of this proclamation. No ship of war or privateer of either belligerent shall be permitted, while in any port, harbor, roadstead, or waters within the jurisdiction of the United States, to take in any supplies except provisions and such other things as may be requisite for the subsistence of her crew, and except so much coal only as may be sufficient to carry such vessel, if without any sail power, to the nearest port of her own country; or in case the vessel is rigged to go under sail, and may also be propelled by steam power, then with half the quantity of coal which she would be entitled to receive, if dependent upon steam alone, and no coal shall be again supplied to any such ship of war or privateer in the same or any other port, harbor, roadstead, or waters of the United States, without special permission, until after the expiration of three months from the time when such coal may have been last supplied to her within the waters of the United States, unless such ship of war or privateer shall, since last thus supplied, have entered a port of the government to which she belongs.

And I further declare and proclaim that by the first article of the Convention as to rights of neutrals at sea, which was concluded between the United States of America and His Majesty the Emperor of all the Russias on the 22nd day of July A. D. 1854, the following principles were recognized as permanent and immutable, to wit:

"1. That free ships make free goods, that is to say, that the effects or goods belonging to subjects or citizens of a Power or State at war are free from capture and confiscation when found on board of neutral vessels, with the exception of articles contraband of war.

"2. That the property of neutrals on board an enemy's vessel is not subject to confiscation, unless the same be contraband of war."

And I do further declare and proclaim that the statutes of the

Theodore Roosevelt 6871

United States and the law of nations alike require that no person, within the territory and jurisdiction of the United States, shall take part, directly or indirectly, in the said war, but shall remain at peace with each of the said belligerents, and shall maintain a strict and impartial neutrality, and that whatever privileges shall be accorded to one belligerent within the ports of the United States, shall be, in like manner, accorded to the other.

And I do hereby enjoin all the good citizens of the United States, and all persons residing or being within the territory or jurisdiction of the United States, to observe the laws thereof, and to commit no act contrary to the provisions of the said statutes, or in violation of the law of nations in that behalf.

And I do hereby warn all citizens of the United States, and all persons residing or being within their territory or jurisdiction that, while the free and full expression of sympathies in public and private is not restricted by the laws of the United States, military forces in aid of either belligerent cannot lawfully be originated or organized within their jurisdiction; and that while all persons may lawfully, and without restriction by reason of the aforesaid state of war, manufacture and sell within the United States arms and munitions of war, and other articles ordinarily known as "contraband of war", yet they cannot carry such articles upon the high seas for the use or service of either belligerent, nor can they transport soldiers and officers of either, or attempt to break any blockade which may be lawfully established and maintained during the war, without incurring the risk of hostile capture, and the penalties denounced by the law of nations in that behalf.

And I do hereby give notice that all citizens of the United States and others who may claim the protection of this government, who may misconduct themselves in the premises, will do so at their peril, and that they can in no wise obtain any protection from the government of the United States against the consequences of their misconduct.

In witness whereof, I have hereunto set my hand and caused the seal of the United States to be affixed.

[SEAL.] Done at the City of Washington this 11th **day of February**, in the year of our Lord one thousand nine hundred and four, and of the Independence of the United States the one hundred and twenty-eighth.

By the President: THEODORE ROOSEVELT.
    JOHN HAY,
       Secretary of State.

BY THE PRESIDENT OF THE UNITED STATES OF AMERICA.

A PROCLAMATION.

Whereas, it is provided in the Act of Congress approved March 3, 1893, entitled "An Act making appropriations for sundry civil expenses of the Government for the fiscal year ending June thirtieth, eighteen hundred and ninety-four, and for other purposes", "That the President is hereby authorized by proclamation to withold from sale and grant for public use to the municipal corporation in which the same is situated all or any portion of any abandoned military reservation not exceeding twenty acres in one place";

And Whereas, the Fort Marcy Military reservation at Santa Fe, New Mexico, containing seventeen and three-quarters acres more or less, as described in Executive Order of August 28, 1868, creating same, was by Executive Order of June 15, 1895, placed under the custody of the Interior Department for disposal under the Act of July 5, 1884, being "An Act to provide for the disposal of abandoned and useless military reservations";

And Whereas, the Legislative Assembly of the Territory of New Mexico has petitioned that the said reservation be granted to the municipal corporation of Santa Fe, New Mexico;

And Whereas, it appears that on the fourteenth day of August, 1902, the city of Santa Fe, New Mexico, entered into an agreement with the Board of Education of the said city of Santa Fe, whereby it was agreed on the part of said city that in case the President of the United States should grant, under the provisions of said Act of March 3, 1893, said reservation to the city of Santa Fe for public purposes, the said city would, by its municipal authorities, turn over and deliver to the said Board of Education and its successors, the said reservation to be held by said Board forever, to aid and assist in the support of the public schools of the city of Santa Fe; and that, by the same agreement, the said Board of Education, on its part, agreed and undertook that it would accept the said reservation, for the purposes so designated by the city of Santa Fe, and keep and use the same and the proceeds thereof, for the use, benefit and maintenance of the public schools and turn over said property or such parts of it as might be in its possession, to its successors;

Now, Therefore, I, THEODORE ROOSEVELT, by virtue of the power in me vested by the Act of Congress aforesaid, do hereby withdraw from sale, entry or other disposition, the lands embraced within the former Fort Marcy Military reservation, as the same are described in Executive Order approved August 28, 1868, and do hereby grant for public use, the said described land to the incorporated city of Santa Fe, New Mexico.

In witness whereof, I have hereunto set my hand and caused the seal of the United States to be affixed.

DONE at the City of Washington, this 10th day of March, [SEAL.] in the year of our Lord, one thousand nine hundred and four, and of the Independence of the United States the one hundred and twenty-eighth.

THEODORE ROOSEVELT.

By the President:

JOHN HAY,
Secretary of State

BY THE PRESIDENT OF THE UNITED STATES OF AMERICA.

A PROCLAMATION.

Whereas, a proclamation was issued February 10, 1890, by the President, making known and proclaiming the acceptance of the Sioux Act approved March 2, 1889 (25 Stats., 888) by the different bands of the Sioux Nation of Indians, and the consent thereto by them as required by the said Act:

And Whereas, the proclamation contains the following clause:

That there is also reserved as aforesaid the following tract within which the Cheyenne River Agency, school and certain other buildings are located, to wit: Commencing at a point in the center of the main channel in the Missouri River opposite Deep Creek, about three miles south of the Cheyenne River; thence due west five and one half miles; thence due north to the Cheyenne River; thence down said river to the center of the main channel thereof to a point in the center of the Missouri River due east or opposite the mouth of said Cheyenne River; thence down the center of the main channel of the Missouri River to the place of beginning:

And Whereas, a proclamation was issued February 7, 1903, by the President, declaring said lands subject to disposal under the provisions of the said Act, except 160 acres of land reserved and set apart for the use of St. John's Mission School;

And Whereas, due notice has been received that the Domestic and Foreign Missionary Society no longer desires the use of the lands set apart for the St. John's Mission School by the Secretary of the Interior, and excepted from disposal in the proclamation of February 7, 1903, as aforesaid, said lands being described as follows:

Beginning at the north-west corner of Section 29, Township 9 N., Range 29 E., at a stake and four witness holes, and running east 40 chains to a stake and stones, near the west bank of the Missouri River; thence south along said river to the center of said section, 40 chains; thence west 40 chains to a stake and two witness holes; thence north

40 chains to the place of beginning, and containing 160 acres, more or less;

Now, Therefore, I, Theodore Roosevelt, President of the United States, by virtue of the power in me vested, do declare the said tract of land subject to disposal under the provisions of said Act.

In witness whereof, I have hereunto set my hand and caused the seal of the United States to be affixed.

[SEAL.]   Done at the City of Washington, this 30th day of March, in the year of our Lord, one thousand nine hundred and four, and of the Independence of the United States the one hundred and twenty-eighth.

THEODORE ROOSEVELT

By the President:

John Hay,
    Secretary of State.

By the President of the United States of America.

A PROCLAMATION.

Whereas, under the provisions of the Reclamation Act approved June 17, 1902—31 Stat., 388—the Secretary of the Interior, by Departmental order dated November 17, 1902, withdrew from entry, except under the homestead law, the following described tracts of land, among others, in the Hailey land district, Idaho:

In township nine south, range twenty-four east, Boise Meridian.

The south-east quarter, the south half of north-east quarter, the east half of south-west quarter, and the south-east quarter of north-west quarter, all in section one;

The south half of south-east quarter, of section twenty; and

The north-east quarter, the east half of north-west quarter, of section twenty-nine.

In township ten south, range twenty-three east, B. M.

The north-east quarter, the north-west quarter, the south-west quarter, and the west half of south-east quarter, of section fifteen;

The south-east quarter of north-east quarter, and lots six and seven, of section sixteen, and

Lots three and four, of section twenty-two;

And whereas, by Departmental order dated April 26, 1904, the said order of withdrawal of said lands was vacated, and they were at once temporarily withdrawn from all entry whatever for the purpose of securing their subsequent reservation for townsite purposes under sections 2380 and 2381 of the Revised Statutes of the United States;

And whereas the Director of the United States Geological Survey, by letter dated April 15, 1904, has represented that said lands have been found suitable for townsite purposes along the line of a proposed railroad which may be extended through large tracts of land to be irrigated under the operation of said Reclamation Act, and will thereby become centers of population and necessary to the proper development of the project;

And whereas, the Secretary of the Interior, under date of April 30, 1904, has requested that said lands be reserved for townsites to be created under existing statute;

Now, therefore, I, THEODORE ROOSEVELT, President of the United States, by virtue of the power in me vested by sections 2380 and 2381 of the Revised Statutes of the United States, do hereby declare and make known that said lands are hereby reserved for occupation as townsites, to be disposed of by the United States under the terms of the statutes applicable thereto.

In witness whereof, I have hereunto set my hand and caused the seal of the United States to be affixed.

DONE at the City of Washington this 2nd day of May in [SEAL.] the year of our Lord one thousand nine hundred and four, and of the Independence of the United States the one hundred and twenty-eighth.   THEODORE ROOSEVELT.

By the President: FRANCIS B. LOOMIS, *Acting Secretary of State.*

BY THE PRESIDENT OF THE UNITED STATES OF AMERICA.

A PROCLAMATION.

Whereas, by an agreement between the Sioux tribe of Indians on the Rosebud Reservation, in the State of South Dakota, on the one part, and James McLaughlin, a United States Indian Inspector, on the other part, amended and ratified by act of Congress approved April 23, 1904 (Public—No. 148), the said Indian tribe ceded, conveyed, transferred, relinquished, and surrendered, forever and absolutely, without any reservation whatsoever, expressed or implied, unto the United States of America, all their claim, title, and interest of every kind and character in and to the unallotted lands embraced in the following described tract of country now in the State of South Dakota, to wit:

Commencing in the middle of the main channel of the Missouri River at the intersection of the south line of Brule County; thence down said middle of the main channel of said river to the intersection of the ninety-ninth degree of west longitude from Greenwich; thence due south to the forty-third parallel of latitude; thence west along said parallel of latitude to its intersection with the tenth guide meridian; thence north along said guide meridian to its intersection with the township line between townships one hundred and one hundred and one north; thence east along said township line to the point of beginning.

The unallotted and unreserved land to be disposed of hereunder approximates three hundred and eighty-two thousand (382,000) acres, lying and being within the boundaries of Gregory County, South Dakota, as said county is at present defined and organized.

And whereas, in pursuance of said act of Congress ratifying the agreement named, the lands necessary for sub-issue station, Indian day school, Catholic and Congregational missions are by this proclamation, as hereinafter appears, reserved for such purposes, respectively: And whereas, in the act of Congress ratifying the said agreement, it is provided:

SEC. 2. That the lands ceded to the United States under said agreement, excepting such tracts as may be reserved by the President, not exceeding three hundred and ninety-eight and sixty-seven one-hundredths acres in all, for sub-issue station, Indian day school, one Catholic mission, and two Congregational missions, shall be disposed of under the general provisions of the homestead and townsite laws of the United States, and shall be opened to settlement and entry by proclamation of the President, which proclamation shall prescribe the manner in which these lands may be settled upon, occupied, and entered by persons entitled to make entry thereof; and no person shall be permitted to settle upon, occupy, or enter any of said lands, except as prescribed in such proclamation, until after the expiration of sixty days from the time when the same are opened to settlement and entry: *Provided,* That the rights of honorably discharged Union soldiers and sailors of the late civil and the Spanish war or Philippine insurrection, as defined and described in sections twenty-three hundred and four and twenty-three hundred and five of the Revised Statutes, as amended by the Act of March first, nineteen hundred and one, shall not be abridged; *And provided further,* That the price of said lands entered as homesteads under the provisions of this Act shall be as follows: Upon all lands entered or filed upon within three months after the same shall be opened for settlement and entry, four dollars per acre, to be paid as follows: One dollar per acre when entry is made; seventy-five cents per acre within two years after entry; seventy-five cents per acre within three years after entry; seventy-five cents per acre within four years after entry, and seventy-five cents per acre within six months after the expiration of five years after entry. And upon all land entered or filed upon after the expiration of three months and within six months after the same shall be opened for settlement and entry, three dollars per acre, to be paid as follows: One dollar per acre when entry is made; fifty cents per acre within two years after entry; fifty cents per acre within three years after entry; fifty cents per acre within four years after entry, and fifty cents per acre within six months after the expiration of five years after entry. After the expiration of six months after the same shall be opened for settlement and entry the price shall be two dollars and fifty cents per acre, to be paid as follows: Seventy-five cents when entry is made; fifty cents per acre within two years after entry; fifty cents per acre within three years after entry; fifty cents per acre within four years after entry, and twenty-five cents per acre within six months after the expiration of five years after entry: *Provided,* That in case any entryman fails to make such payment or any of them within the time stated all rights in and to the land covered by his or her entry shall at once cease, and any payments theretofore made shall be forfeited, and the entry shall be forfeited and held for cancellation and the same shall be canceled: *And provided,* That nothing in this Act shall prevent homestead settlers from commuting their entries under section twenty-three hundred and one, Revised Statutes, by paying for the land entered the price fixed herein, receiving credit for payments previously made. In addition to the price to be paid for the land, the entryman shall pay the same fees and commissions at the time of commutation or final entry, as now provided by law, where the price of the land is one dollar and twenty-five cents per acre; *And provided further,* That all lands herein ceded and opened to settlement under this Act, remaining undisposed of at the expiration of four years from the taking effect of this act, shall be sold and disposed of for cash, under rules and regulations to be prescribed by the Secretary of the Interior, not more than six hundred and forty acres to any one purchaser.

SEC. 4. That sections sixteen and thirty-six of the lands hereby acquired in each township shall not be subject to entry, but shall be reserved for the use of the common schools and paid for by the United States at two dollars and fifty cents per acre, and the same are hereby granted to the State of South Dakota for such purpose; and in case any of said sections, or parts thereof, of the land in said county of Gregory are lost to said State of South Dakota by reason of allotments thereof to any Indian or Indians, now holding the same, or otherwise, the governor of said state, with the approval of the Secretary of the Interior, is hereby authorized, in the tract herein ceded, to locate other lands not occupied not exceeding two sections in any one township, which shall be paid for by the United States as herein provided in quantity equal to the loss, and such selections shall be made prior to the opening of such lands to settlement.

And whereas, all of the conditions required by law to be performed prior to the opening of said tracts of land to settlement and entry have been, as I hereby declare, duly performed:

Now, therefore, I, THEODORE ROOSEVELT, President of the United States of America, by virtue of the power vested in me by law, do hereby declare and make known that all of the lands so as aforesaid ceded by the Sioux tribe of Indians of the Rosebud Reservation, saving and excepting sections sixteen and thirty-six in each township, and all lands located or selected by the State of South Dakota as indemnity school or educational lands, and saving and excepting the W½ of the NE¼ and the E½ of the NW¼ of Sec. 25, T. 96 N., R. 72 W., of the 5th P. M., which is hereby reserved for use as a sub-issue station; and the NE¼ of the SW¼ of Sec. 23, T. 96 N., R. 72 W., of the 5th P. M., which is hereby reserved for use as an Indian day school; and saving and excepting the N½ of the NE¼ of Sec. 25, T. 95 N., R. 71 W., of the 5th P. M., and the NW¼ of the NW¼ of Sec. 20, T. 95 N., R. 70 W., of the 5th P. M., both of which tracts are hereby reserved for use of the American Missionary Society for mission purposes; and the N½ of the NW¼ of Sec. 7, T. 96 N., R. 71 W., of the 5th P. M., which is hereby reserved for the Roman Catholic Church for use for mission purposes, will, on the eighth day of August, 1904, at 9 o'clock a. m., in the manner herein prescribed and not otherwise, be opened to entry and settlement and to disposition under the general provisions of the homestead and townsite laws of the United States.

Commencing at 9 o'clock a. m., Tuesday, July 5, 1904, and ending at 6 o'clock p. m., Saturday, July 23, 1904, a registration will be had at Chamberlain, Yankton, Bonesteel, and Fairfax, State of South Dakota, for the purpose of ascertaining what persons desire to enter, settle upon, and acquire title to any of said lands under the homestead law, and of ascertaining their qualifications so to do. To obtain registration each applicant will be required to show himself duly qualified, by written application to be made only on a blank form provided by the Commissioner of the General Land Office, to make homestead entry of these lands under existing laws and to give the registering officer such appropriate matters of description and identity as will protect the applicant and the government against any attempted impersonation. Registration can not be effected through the use of the mails or the employment of an agent, excepting that honorably discharged soldiers and sailors entitled to the benefits of section twenty-three hundred and four of the Revised Statutes of the United States, as amended by the act of Congress approved March 1, 1901, (31 Stat., 847) may present their applications for registration and due proofs of their qualifications through an agent of their own selection, having a duly executed power of attorney, but no person will be permitted to act as agent for more than one such soldier or sailor. No person will be permitted to register more than once or in any other than his true name. Each applicant who shows himself duly qualified will be registered and given a non-transferable certificate to that effect, which will entitle him to go upon and examine the lands to be opened hereunder; but the only purpose for which he can go upon and examine said lands is that of enabling him later on, as herein provided, to understandingly select the lands for which he will make entry. No one will be permitted to make settlement upon any of said lands in advance of the opening herein provided for, and during the first sixty days following said opening no one but registered applicants will be permitted to make homestead settlement upon any of said lands, and then only in pursuance of a homestead entry duly allowed by the local land officers, or of a soldier's declaratory statement duly accepted by such officers.

The order in which, during the first sixty days following the opening, the registered applicants will be permitted to make homestead entry of the lands opened hereunder, will be determined by a drawing for the district publicly held at Chamberlain, South Dakota, commencing at 9 o'clock a. m., Thursday, July 28, 1904, and continuing for such period as may be necessary to complete the same. The drawing will be had under the supervision and immediate observance of a committee of three persons whose integrity is such as to make their control of the drawing a guaranty of its fairness. The members of this committee will be appointed by the Secretary of the Interior, who will prescribe suitable compensation for their services. Preparatory to this drawing the registration officers will, at the time of registering each applicant who shows himself duly qualified, make out a card, which must be signed by the applicant, and giving such a description of the applicant as will enable the local land officers to thereafter identify him. This card will be subsequently sealed in a separate envelope which will bear no other distinguishing label or mark than such as may be necessary to show that it is to go into the drawing. These envelopes will be carefully preserved and remain sealed until opened in the course of the drawing herein provided. When the registration is completed, all of these sealed envelopes will be brought together at the place of drawing and turned over to the committee in charge of the drawing, who, in such manner as in their judgment will be attended with entire fairness and equality of opportunity, shall proceed to draw out and open the separate envelopes and to give to each enclosed card a number in the order in which the envelope containing the same is drawn. The result of the drawing will be certified by the committee to the officers of the district and will determine the order in which the applicants may make homestead entry of said lands and settlement thereon.

Notice of the drawings, stating the name of each applicant and number assigned to him by the drawing, will be posted each day at the place of drawing, and each applicant will be notified of his number and of the day upon which he must make his entry, by a postal card mailed to him at the address given by him at the time of registration. The result of each day's drawing will also be given to the press to be published as a matter of news. Applications for homestead entry of said lands during the first sixty days following the opening can be made only by registered applicants and in the order established by the drawing. The land officers for the district will receive applications for entries at Bonesteel, South Dakota, in their district, beginning August 8, 1904, and until and including September 10, 1904, and thereafter at Chamberlain. Commencing Monday, August 8, 1904, at 9 o'clock a. m., the applications of those drawing numbers 1 to 100, inclusive, must be presented and will be considered in their numerical order during the first day, and the applications of those drawing numbers 101 to 200, inclusive, must be presented and will be considered in their numerical order during the second day, and so on at that rate until all of said lands subject to entry under the homestead law, and desired thereunder have been entered. If any applicant fails to appear and present his application for entry when the number assigned to him by the drawing is reached, his right to enter will be passed until after the other applications assigned for that day have been disposed of, when he will be given another opportunity to make entry, failing in which he will be deemed to have abandoned his right to make entry under such drawing. To obtain the allowance of a homestead entry, each applicant must personally present the certificate of registration theretofore issued to him, together with a regular homestead application and the necessary accompanying proofs, and make the first payment of one dollar per acre for the land embraced in his application, together with the regular land office fees, but an honorably discharged soldier or sailor may file his declaratory statement through his agent, who can represent but one soldier or sailor as in the matter of registration. The production of the certificate of registration will be dispensed with only upon satisfactory proof of its loss or destruction. If at the time of considering his regular application for entry it appear that an applicant is disqualified from making homestead entry of these lands his application will be rejected, notwithstanding his prior registration. If any applicant shall register more than once hereunder, or in any other than his true name, or shall transfer his registration certificate, he will thereby lose all the benefits of the registration and drawing herein provided for, and will be precluded from entering or settling upon any of said lands during the first sixty days following said opening.

Any person or persons desiring to found, or to suggest establishing, a townsite upon any of said ceded lands, at any point, may, at any time before the opening herein provided for, file in the land office a written application to that effect, describing by legal subdivisions the lands intended to be affected, and stating fully and under oath the necessity or propriety of founding or establishing a town at that place. The local officers will forthwith transmit said petition to the Commissioner of the General Land Office with their recommendation in the premises. Such Commissioner, if he believes the public interests will be subserved thereby, will, if the Secretary of the Interior approve thereof, issue an order withdrawing the lands described in such petition, or any portion thereof, from homestead entry and settlement and directing that the same be held for the time being for townsite settlement, entry, and disposition only. In such event, the lands so withheld from homestead entry and settlement will, at the time of said opening and not before, become subject to settlement, entry, and disposition under the general townsite laws of the United States. None of said ceded lands will be subject to settlement, entry, or disposition under such general townsite laws except in the manner herein prescribed until after the expiration of sixty days from the time of said opening.

All persons are especially admonished that under the said act of Congress approved April 23, 1904, it is provided that no person shall be permitted to settle upon, occupy, or enter any of said ceded lands except in the manner prescribed in this proclamation until after the expiration of sixty days from the time when the same are opened to settlement and entry. After the expiration of the said period of sixty days, but not before, and until the expiration of three months after the same shall have been opened for settlement and entry, as hereinbefore prescribed, any of said lands remaining undisposed of may be settled upon, occupied, and entered under the general provisions of the homestead and townsite laws of the United States in like manner as if the manner of effecting such settlement, occupancy, and entry had not been prescribed herein in obedience to law, subject, however, to the payment of four dollars per acre for the land entered, in the manner and at the time required by the said act of Congress above mentioned. After the expiration of three months, and not before, and until the expiration of six months after the same shall have been opened for settlement and entry, as aforesaid, any of said lands remaining undisposed of may also be settled upon, occupied, and entered under the general provisions of the same laws and in the same manner, subject, however, to the payment of three dollars per acre for the land entered in the manner and at the times required by the same act of Congress. After the expiration of six months, and not before, after the same shall have been opened for settlement and entry, as aforesaid, any of said lands remaining undisposed of may also be settled upon, occupied, and entered under the general provisions of the same laws and in the same manner, subject, however, to the payment of two dollars and fifty cents per acre for the land entered, in the manner and at the times required by the same act of Congress. And after the expiration of four years from the taking effect of this act, and not before, any of said lands remaining undisposed of shall be sold and disposed of for cash, under rules and regulations to be prescribed by the Secretary of the Interior, not more than six hundred and forty acres to any one purchaser.

The Secretary of the Interior shall prescribe all needful rules and regulations necessary to carry into effect the opening herein provided for.

In witness whereof, I have hereunto set my hand and caused the seal of the United State to be affixed.

Done at the City of Washington this 13th day of May, in [SEAL.] the year of our Lord one thousand nine hundred and four, and of the Independence of the United States the one hundred and twenty-eighth.

THEODORE ROOSEVELT.

By the President: FRANCIS B. LOOMIS, *Acting Secretary of State.*

BY THE PRESIDENT OF THE UNITED STATES OF AMERICA.

A PROCLAMATION.

Whereas, by an agreement between the Sisseton, Wahpeton, and Cut-Head bands of the Sioux tribe of Indians on the Devils Lake Reservation, in the State of North Dakota, on the one part, and James McLaughlin, a United States Indian Inspector, on the other part, amended and ratified by act of Congress approved April 27, 1904 (Public No. 179), the said bands of the said Indian tribes ceded, conveyed, transferred, relinquished, and surrendered, forever and absolutely, without any reservation whatsover, expressed or implied, unto the United States of America, all their claim, title, and interest of every kind and character in and to the unallotted lands embraced in the following-described tract of country now in the State of North Dakota, to wit:

All that part of the Devils Lake Indian Reservation now remaining unallotted, including the tract of land at present known as the Fort Totten Military Reserve, situated within the boundaries of the said Devils Lake Indian Reservation, and being a part thereof; except six thousand one hundred and sixty acres required for allotments to sixty-one Indians of said reservation entitled to allotments.

The unallotted and unreserved land to the disposed of hereunder approximates 88,000 acres.

And whereas, in pursuance of said act of Congress ratifying the agreement named, the lands necessary for church, mission, and agency purposes, and for the Fort Totten Indian school, and for a public park, are by this proclamation, as hereinafter appears, reserved for such purposes, respectively:

And whereas, in the act of Congress ratifying the said agreement, it is provided:

SEC. 4. That the lands ceded to the United States under said agreement, including the Fort Totten abandoned military reservation, which are exclusive of six thousand one hundred and sixty acres which are required for allotments, excepting sections sixteen and thirty-six or an equivalent of two sections in each township, and such tracts as may be reserved by the President as hereinafter provided, shall be disposed of under the general provisions of the homestead and townsite laws of the United States, and shall be opened to settlement and entry by proclamation of the President, which proclamation shall prescribe the manner in which these lands may be settled upon, occupied, and entered by persons entitled to make entry thereof, and no person shall be permitted to settle upon, occupy, or enter any of said lands, except as prescribed in such proclamation, until after the expiration of sixty days from the time when the same are opened to settlement and entry; *Provided,* That the rights of honorably discharged Union soldiers and sailors of the late civil and the Spanish war, as defined and described in sections twenty-three hundred and four and twenty-three hundred and five of the Revised Statutes, as amended by the Act of March first, nineteen hundred and one, shall not be abridged: *And provided further,*

That the price of said lands entered under the provisions of this Act shall be four dollars and fifty cents per acre, payable as follows: One dollar and fifty cents when the entry is made, and the remainder in annual installments of fifty cents per acre until paid for: *Provided further,* That in case any entryman fails to make such payments, or any of them, within the time stated, all rights in and to the land covered by his or her entry shall at once cease, and any payments theretofore made shall be forfeited and the entry shall be canceled: *And provided further,* That the lands embraced within such canceled entry shall, after the cancellation of such entry, be subject to entry under the provisions of the homestead law at four dollars and fifty cents per acre up to and until provision may be made for the disposition of said land by proclamation of the President as hereinafter provided: *And provided further,* That nothing in this Act shall prevent homestead settlers from commuting their entries under section twenty-three hundred and one, Revised Statutes, by paying for the land entered the price fixed herein, receiving credit for payments previously made. In addition to the price to be paid for the land, the entryman shall pay the same fees and commissions at the time of commutation or final entry, as now provided by law, where the price of the land is one dollar and twenty-five cents per acre: *And provided further,* That aliens who have declared their intention to become citizens of the United States may become purchasers under this Act, but before proving up and acquiring title must take out their full naturalization papers: *And provided further,* That when, in the judgment of the President, no more of the land herein ceded can be disposed of at said price, he may by proclamation, to be repeated in his discretion, sell from time to time the remaining lands subject to the provisions of the homestead law or otherwise as he may deem most advantageous, at such price or prices, in such manner, upon such conditions, with such restrictions, and upon such terms as he may deem best for all interests concerned: *And provided further,* That the President is hereby authorized to reserve, in his proclamation for the opening of the said lands, so much of the tracts heretofore reserved for church, mission, and agency purposes, as he may deem necessary, not to exceed nine hundred acres, and also not exceeding two and one-half sections for the Fort Totten Indian school, and the United States stipulates and agrees to pay for said reserved lands at the rate of three dollars and twenty-five cents per acre. The President is also authorized to reserve a tract embracing Sullys Hill, in the northeastern portion of the abandoned military reservation, about nine hundred and sixty acres, as a public park.

SEC. 5. That sections sixteen and thirty-six of the lands hereby acquired in each township shall not be subject to entry, but shall be reserved for the use of the common schools and paid for by the United States at three dollars and twenty-five cents per acre, and the same are hereby granted to the State of North Dakota for such purpose; and in case any of said sections, or parts thereof, of the land in the said Devils Lake Indian Reservation or Fort Totten abandoned military reservation should be lost to said State of North Dakota by reason of allotments thereof to any Indian or Indians now holding the same, or otherwise, the governor of said State, with the approval of the Secretary of the Interior, is hereby authorized to locate other lands not occupied, in the townships where said lands are lost, provided sufficient lands are to be had in the said townships, otherwise the selections to be made elsewhere within the ceded tract, which shall be paid for by the United States, as provided in article two of the treaty as herein amended, in quantity equal to the loss, and such selections shall be made prior to the opening of such lands to settlement.

And whereas, all of the conditions required by law to be performed prior to the opening of said tracts of land to settlement and entry have been, as I hereby declare, duly performed;

Now, therefore, I, THEODORE ROOSEVELT, President of the United States of America, by virtue of the power vested in me by law, do hereby declare and make known that all of the lands so as aforesaid ceded by the Sisseton, Wahpeton, and Cut-Head bands of the Sioux tribe of Indians belonging to the Devils Lake Reservation, saving and excepting sections 16 and 36 in each township, and all lands located or selected by the State of North Dakota as indemnity school or educational lands, and saving and excepting the N ½ of the NW ¼ and the SW ¼ of the NW ¼ of Sec. 14, and the SE ¼ of the NE ¼ of Sec. 15, T. 152 N., R. 66 W., of the fifth principal meridian, which are hereby reserved for the use of the Raven Hill Presbyterian Church; and saving and excepting the N ½ of the NW ¼ of Sec. 14, the NE ¼ of the NE¼ of Sec. 15, the SE ¼ of the SW¼ of Sec. 11, and the S ½ of the SE ¼ of the SE ¼ of the SE ¼ of Sec. 10, T. 151 N., R. 64 W., of the fifth principal meridian, which are hereby reserved for the use of the Wood Lake Presbyterian Church; and saving and excepting the SE ¼ of the SW ¼ and Lot 8 of Sec. 8, the NE ¼ of the NW¼, the NW¼ of the NE¼ and a tract of 4.43 acres in the southwest corner of Lot 1, Sec. 17, T. 152 N., R. 65 W., of the fifth principal meridian, which are hereby reserved for the use of the Mission of Sisters of Charity from Montreal; and saving and excepting the N ½ of the SE¼, the NE¼ of the SW ¼, Lot 5, and a tract of 1.60 acres in Lot 6, Sec. 17, T. 152 N., R. 64 W., of the fifth principal meridian, which are hereby reserved for the use of St. Michiel's Church, Bureau of Catholic Indian Missions; and saving and excepting the W ½ of the NW ¼ of Sec. 15, T. 152 N., R. 66 W., of the fifth principal meridian, which is hereby reserved for the use of St. Jerome's Church, Bureau of Catholic Indian Missions; and saving and excepting the W ½ of Sec. 21, the W ½ of the NE ¼ of Sec. 21, the E ½ of Sec. 20, the NW ¼ of Sec. 20, and Lots 6, 7, and 8 and the SE ¼ of the SW ¼ of Sec. 16 (excepting 7 acres thereof, which are hereby reserved for the use of the Protestant Episcopal Church), and Lots 6, 7, 8, and 9 of Sec. 17, T. 152 N., R. 65 W., of the fifth principal meridian, which are hereby reserved for the use of the Fort Totten School; and saving and excepting the SE ¼ of the NE ¼ and Lot 1 (excepting 4.43 acres of said Lot 1, reserved for the use of the Mission of Sisters of Charity from Montreal), Sec. 17, and Lot 1 of Sec. 16, T. 152 N., R. 65 W., of the fifth principal meridian, which are hereby reserved for the use of the Fort Totten School, Grey Nuns Department; and saving and excepting the NW ¼ of the NW ¼ of Sec. 8, the E ½ of the NE ¼, the SW¼ of the NE¼ and the SE¼ of Sec. 7, T. 151 N., R. 65 W.,

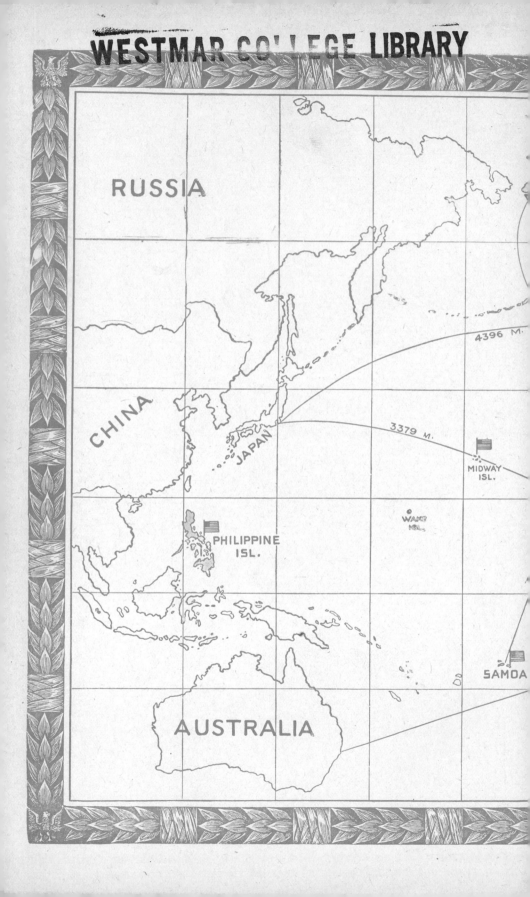